INVENTING THE BUSINESS OF OPERA

INVENTING THE BUSINESS OF OPERA.

The Impresario and His World
in Seventeenth-Century Venice

Beth L. Glixon, B.L.
Jonathan E. Glixon

OXFORD
UNIVERSITY PRESS
2006

OXFORD
UNIVERSITY PRESS

Oxford University Press, Inc., publishes works that further
Oxford University's objective of excellence
in research, scholarship, and education.

Oxford New York
Auckland   Cape Town   Dar es Salaam   Hong Kong   Karachi
Kuala Lumpur   Madrid   Melbourne   Mexico City   Nairobi
New Delhi   Shanghai   Taipei   Toronto

With offices in
Argentina   Austria   Brazil   Chile   Czech Republic   France   Greece
Guatemala   Hungary   Italy   Japan   Poland   Portugal   Singapore
South Korea   Switzerland   Thailand   Turkey   Ukraine   Vietnam

Published by Oxford University Press, Inc.
198 Madison Avenue, New York, New York 10016

www.oup.com

Oxford is a registered trademark of Oxford University Press

Library of Congress Cataloging-in-Publication Data
Glixon, Beth Lise, 1952–
Inventing the business of opera : the impresario
and his world in seventeenth-century Venice /
Beth L. Glixon, Jonathan E. Glixon.
p. cm.—(AMS studies in music)
Includes bibliographical references and index.
ISBN-13 978-0-19-515416-0
ISBN 0-19-515416-9
1. Opera—Production and direction—Italy—Venice—
History—17th century. I. Glixon, Jonathan Emmanuel.
II. Title. III. Series.
ML1733.8.V4G65 2005
792.502′3′09453109032—dc22   2005021570

2 4 6 8 9 7 5 3 1
Printed in the United States of America
on acid-free paper

To our parents

David Glixon
Helen Glixon (1913–2003)
Selma Jacowitz
Seymour Jacowitz (1927–2003)

PREFACE

"Opera in seventeenth-century Venice": the phrase brings to mind a number of
pathbreaking studies published during the last century; not only Ellen
Rosand's comprehensive look at the genre and the history behind it, but also
Simon Towneley Worsthorne's earlier volume and a number of significant articles,
including seminal works by Nino Pirrotta, Giovanni Morelli, Lorenzo Bianconi,
Thomas Walker, and Rosand, as well as other studies by Hermann Kretzschmar,
Henry Prunières, Helmut Christian Wolff, and Wolfgang Osthoff. Books and
articles on Venetian theaters by Remo Giazotto, Nicola Mangini, and Franco
Mancini, Maria Teresa Muraro, and Elena Povoledo have also done much to further our understanding of the systems that operated in Venice (see the relevant
entries in the Bibliography). In the last three decades scholarship in the field
of Baroque opera has flourished, with a good part of it dedicated to opera in
seventeenth-century Venice, where the genre first emerged from courts and private
homes to become a vibrant form of public entertainment.

Most published research has concentrated on the surviving music itself, on the
associated poetic texts, and on societal and cultural issues reflected in them. Recently, Mauro Calcagno has, among other things, explored new areas regarding
text–music relationships, and has investigated both aesthetic and political ramifica-
tions of seventeenth-century librettos and musical scores; Tim Carter has investigated many aspects of Monteverdi's operas, including issues of production; Wendy
Heller has looked at the portrayal of women on the Venetian stage, describing the
many classical and contemporary views of women that found their way into opera
librettos, and showing how composers brought these famous and infamous women
to life; Jennifer Williams Brown has charted the impact of Venetian productions in
opera revivals outside the city, and has also studied Antonio Cesti's operas and
documented how their scores changed when they reached Venice; and Irene Alm
demonstrated for the first time the importance of dance to staged operas.

A number of studies have drawn on the well-known papers of the Venetian impresario Marco Faustini; many of those documents received a thorough synthesis
in Rosand's *Opera in Seventeenth-Century Venice* and Bruno Brunelli's "L'impresario
in angustie," while Lorenzo Bianconi and Thomas Walker's "Opera Production and

Consumption" looked in depth at one account book found among the papers. During the 1970s smaller collections of documentary material concerning two Venetian theaters, S. Cassiano and the Novissimo, were introduced by Bianconi, Giovanni Morelli, and Walker. Several years earlier Remo Giazotto's "La guerra dei palchi," with its sampling of notarial documents regarding opera production and opera boxes, showed the importance that archival research might play in reaching a new understanding and appreciation of opera in Venice. These studies have established a basis for understanding opera production in Venice, especially regarding both Faustini's companies at S. Cassiano and S. Aponal, and the dynamics of re-cruiting as revealed by singers' letters to the impresario.

Our book offers a new look at Venetian opera production through a much wider examination of archival sources. It differs in its scope from all of the studies mentioned above, drawing on documents spanning roughly four decades, from 1636 to the late 1670s (but with special emphasis on the period of Marco Faustini's activity, 1650 to 1668); these are the years that saw the operas of Claudio Monteverdi, Francesco Cavalli, Pietro Andrea Ziani, Giovanni Antonio Boretti, and Carlo Pallavicino, among others. We examine the business of opera from four separate but often complementary angles: the financial underpinnings, the musical production (including libretto, composers, singers, dancers, and instrumentalists), the scenery and costumes, and, finally, the audience. We look not at the texts and the music—those artistic elements that remain with us to this day—but at the genesis and development of the systems that fostered and sustained the production of opera in mid-seventeenth-century Venice, and provided the foundation for commercial opera. In examining the efforts to transform court spectacle into public entertainment, we witness nothing less than the invention of a new enterprise, the opera business.

The project originated with Jonathan's serendipitous discovery of new materials regarding the opera companies of the impresario Marco Faustini, found in conjunction with his ongoing research on the musical activities of the Venetian *scuole grandi*. These archival gems—three new account books for Faustini's productions, as well as the receipt book where his singers and artisans signed for their wages—encouraged Beth to embark on her own search for new materials. She began with the Faustini papers, moved on to notarial volumes, and eventually branched out into various Venetian governmental and church records as well as private family and ambassadorial papers housed in Venice, Florence, Ferrara, Turin, and Parma. As this list of archives suggests, much of the data concerning opera in Venice survive only in scattered records, or in the assorted tidbits that accompany correspondence surrounding the Duke of Brunswick and three families, the Medici (Tuscany), Bentivoglios (Ferrara), and Michiels (Venice).

A large part of our study derives from thousands of volumes of various types in Venice's Archivio di Stato and the Archivio Storico del Patriarcato di Venezia (the diocesan archive): notarial acts, court, criminal, and birth and death records, diplomatic reports, and other sorts of testimonies. The fact that very few of these volumes contain any references to opera or other forms of music makes the researcher's task more daunting and, perhaps, more tedious, but also more fruitful, for the pages provide a broad panorama of the daily activities and concerns of the inhabitants of mid-seventeenth-century Venice. In reading these volumes one begins to get a sense of the various populations living and working in Venice; for the first time we can begin to look at the people who supported opera as more than mere names in an incorporation document or in an opera libretto. Men and women from all walks of life appear; some of them come briefly into focus only to fade away quickly, while others are present more frequently. Marco Faustini's impresarial activities certainly emerge more fully, but we also begin to see him as a son, a brother, and a vibrant member of one of Venice's most important confraternities; the breadth of his legal activities becomes apparent, and we can observe his personal interactions with nobles and other Venetians, as well as with some of the most famous singers of the time. The worlds of Faustini's noble partners, Marc'Antonio Correr and Alvise Duodo, also emerge more clearly, providing a greater understanding of the networks that helped to sustain opera production, and of the people willing to spend and lose money to put opera on stage. Indeed, these archives help to "humanize" nearly all of the figures who appear in the book, and reinforce one finding of so many other investigations into early modern European history: the overriding importance of local and family connections.

Through learning more about the men who helped to finance Venice's opera productions, we gain a much richer appreciation of the extent of the efforts necessary to sustain the city's most influential carnival entertainment, for the volumes yield ample evidence of the financial struggles that nearly every opera company faced. The utility of the documents extends beyond the furthering of our understanding of the opera companies, however; they also provide priceless information regarding that wider base of support, Venice's boxholders, at the same time supplying details about the careers of the musicians and other artists who brought opera to the stage. The archives, then, furnish important data regarding every sector of the opera business. The collection and interpretation of these data also allow us to put into better perspective the story of seventeenth-century opera told by the chronicler and librettist Cristoforo Ivanovich, whose descriptions have informed many of the studies of the past few decades.

A number of the areas covered in our book, perforce, build on the work of Worsthorne, Giazotto, Bianconi, Morelli, Walker, and Rosand (as well as that of their predecessors such as Bartolomeo Cecchetti and Bruno Brunelli, who had begun to examine the Faustini papers), but we present both an expanded range of topics, and a greater wealth of detail within them.

The book begins with four chapters addressing the business side of opera. Chapter 1 looks at the tradition of public theaters in Venice, and at the families who owned and sometimes ran them. The phrase "Venetian nobleman" goes only a small way toward situating such a person within the social hierarchy, as members of the nobility ranged from the enormously wealthy to those whose lives were quite humble. Here we examine how various nobles, both rich and poor, might have benefited monetarily from the production of opera. The remainder of the chapter considers how opera companies were financed, and the sources of income the impresarios found: these included investors within the company, loans and advances from outside, income from the performances and, finally, the reliance on guarantors.

Chapter 2 concerns the boxes, one of the major sources of income for the theaters; here we focus on the box as a financial instrument that assumed greater importance as opera became more fully established in Venice. The archives reveal information of different kinds. The distribution of the large and nearly guaranteed income from boxes among owner and tenant was a key element of theater rental contracts, and could be crucial in determining the success of an opera company. Collecting the box fees, however, was often difficult for owners and tenants, and their efforts left a substantial trail in notarial acts; on the other hand, individual boxholders might pursue this same avenue when complaining about deficiencies or changes in their boxes. We examine how the theater owners and tenants at times catered to the audience (also with an eye to their prospective profits) either by decreasing or increasing the number of boxes in the theater. Finally, we explore the box's transformation from a privilege rented for a season into a piece of property that could be passed down to future generations, but that could also be used as security in financial transactions.

Chapter 3 focuses on the companies of Marco Faustini, who might legitimately be called the first professional impresario. Faustini's association with four partners (the noblemen Marc'Antonio Correr and Alvise Duodo, mentioned earlier, but also the citizens Bortolo Pasinetto and Polifilo Zancarli) demonstrates the variety of social classes that might join to form an opera company (at one point, Faustini even sublet the theater to a company the majority of whose members were craftsmen). Faustini's continuing activity during this period of operatic growth in Venice is remarkable, and speaks both to his competence in the field and to his willingness to devote his time to an area that was secondary to his long-standing career as a lawyer. The chapter opens with a new examination of Faustini's professional life, pointing up how his success as a lawyer enabled his brother Giovanni to pursue a career as a librettist. Faustini's journey from the small Teatro S. Aponal, which his brother had originally rented, to the much grander Teatro SS. Giovanni e Paolo shows how Marco's skills as an impresario came to be valued by the most influential theater owner in Venice, Giovanni Grimani. New documentation enables us to see how both Faustini's relationship with his partners and his approaches to management changed over the years, and also reveals a wider circle of associates than has previously been known.

Chapter 4 concludes the section on the business of opera with case studies of four theaters with very different histories: S. Cassiano, the Novissimo, S. Aponal, and S. Luca. Here we explore three different types of theaters: two owned by nobles, one by members of the professional class (*cittadini*), and one constructed as a temporary structure on the property of a monastery. Our studies build on the information outlined in chapters 1 and 3, and provide a more detailed look at the different types of nobles and cittadini who provided their resources, both finanical and managerial, to the growing opera trade in Venice. The instability of the typical opera company is one of the striking (if predictable) findings in our book. The theater owners at S. Cassiano were unable to sustain any particular company for more than a few years, the Novissimo was doomed to a short existence, and one of S. Aponal's owners failed to encourage the long-term operation of his own theater. S. Luca provides us the rare opportunity of seeing the birth of an opera theater that would eventually find stability in the marketplace despite a shaky financial beginning. We shall also see how the personalities and histories of the men and women behind the scenes contributed to the development of the theaters.

The remainder of the book follows the tasks and procedures of the seventeenth-century Venetian opera impresario, from the recruitment of the creative personnel and drafting of contracts, through the preparations for opening night and the performances themselves. In each of the chapters, insofar as possible, we provide a look at the people who brought opera to the stage. Many of the librettists, composers, singers, and dancers, whether they resided in Venice temporarily or permanently, left behind evidence that helps us to situate them within society and within the opera business.

Chapter 5 (on the libretto) looks first at the social class of the poets and at their varied professions outside of the theater (lawyers, government secretaries and officials of various ranks, men of the church, and a doctor). The rest of the chapter focuses primarily on the libretto itself: its production, financing, the cost to the buyer, and the profit to the librettist; here again we offer insights into the possible earnings and risks inherent in libretto production, and new documents allow us to go beyond the often-quoted descriptions on the topic by Cristoforo Ivanovich. Multiple printings and the changing of characters and scenes in the librettos themselves also furnish many clues about opera production; here we build on the work of Rosand, who has written extensively on the stages of libretto printing, and of the development of the practice of providing the members of the audience with a text that incorporated a librettist's "preferred" text along with changes to it. This chapter provides ample proof of the Venetians' desire for novelty: reuse of a text, whether with an old or new score, was rare, and most often indicated troubles experienced along the way.

Chapter 6 (on the composer and the procuring of scores) begins with a discussion of the relationship between the impresario and the composer, and also examines how the growth of opera changed the lives of composers in Venice. Impresarios paid a considerable sum in order to gain a new score, so that a composer's income might well be multiplied several times over through this new type of work. We look in particular at three composers, Francesco Lucio, Pietro Andrea Ziani, and Francesco Cavalli, to see how opera composition fit into their lives. Given the extraordinary amount of time required on the composers' part, they naturally sought adequate remuneration as a reward. Cavalli's position as the predominant opera composer in Venice is borne out by a series of surviving contracts between him and a number of impresarios. A close reading of those, along with two unsuccessful sets of negotiations—especially when considered along with new data concerning the fees of his contemporaries—illuminates in new ways what it meant to succeed financially in the world of Venetian opera. The chapter concludes with the consideration of issues that move beyond the financial aspects to the actual production of the score and the composer's collaboration with the librettist.

In the most basic terms, the search for singers (chap. 7) echoed the impresario's search for a composer: the process involved recruitment, a contract, and payment. The task was much more complicated, however, because each opera required a number of singers, and the singers' careers were often more changeable and fleeting than those of the composers. Impresarios developed networks of contacts to facilitate recruitment of singers from outside of Venice, both for locating promising performers, and negotiating with their employers or patrons. Details concerning a number of singers active in Venetian opera have already been known from certain of the Faustini papers, and from a small number of opera librettos, but our research opens up new avenues of investigation. Notarial documents help to place singers in Venice on specific dates, and show how a number of women singers took up residence in Venice following their initial debuts there. Perhaps most importantly, Faustini's account and receipt books supply the names and payments for singers over a fifteen-year period, allowing a better understanding both of personnel and of the inflation of singers' fees. Court records document one of the negative sides of the business, the failure to pay singers, and also add to our knowledge of other issues, such as living expenses while in Venice. The chapter concludes with a case study of the recruiting of the diva Giulia Masotti; new documentation, especially letters in the Medici archives in Florence and the Bentivoglio archives in Ferrara, demonstrate how assiduously a singer could be recruited, and how burdensome the demands of performing could become. We also see the fascination that Masotti exerted upon the impresarios of Venice, who were apparently determined to hire her at any cost.

The section on musical production concludes with a brief look at dance, extras, and the orchestra (chap. 8). Dance, a vibrant element of Venetian opera, was little studied before the contributions of Irene Alm. Our archival work supplements Alm's work in several ways. First and foremost, we can now name and situate several dance masters, none of whom were known to earlier researchers, and can document their fees. We also examine briefly the employment of extras. While the orchestra members remain for the most part nameless, Faustini's account books provide us with the numbers of string and continuo players he paid, documenting the small size of the orchestra at this time.

The next section of the book concerns the two major visual elements of opera production: scenery and costumes. The chapter on scenery (chap. 9) draws together a wide range of data illuminating both the production and the mechanical operation of scenery in seventeenth-century Venice. We discuss the scheduling of manufacture and costs of a number of operas, and show that, contrary to modern conceptions, mid-seventeenth-century impresarios felt obliged to seek novelty in this area as well, rather than relying on older materials stored in a warehouse. In addition, a close reading of contemporary descriptions, theater inventories, and theatrical drawings enables us to arrive at a new understanding of the systems that resulted in scenography capable of achieving multiple levels of perspective.

Costumes (chap. 10) were an important part of the visual spectacle of opera, and the Venetians were known for their skill in that aspect of production. Faustini's account books supply unique data concerning the cost of the manufacturing process. They reveal the different suppliers, and make clear the disparity that existed between the more pedestrian costumes and those made of the richest materials, designed to produce a spectacular effect and to enhance the images of the leading singers. We also discuss costumes in their function as a type of capital, for they were the quintessential movable property that could be shared among partners, turned over to creditors, or reused by the theater's tailors, functioning as merchandise in an economy that valued second-hand goods.

Chapter 11 surveys the operatic audience from several points of view: opera boxes and their occupants, attendance figures and ticket receipts, and the activities of the audience in the theater, which were not limited to watching the opera. We also discuss the issue of patronage, examining the intended audience for operatic productions and the underlying nature of the financial support: in the end—quite predictably—a successful company required a series of financial backers and guarantors, a willing group of boxholders, and frequent attendees. We conclude by addressing the question of whether opera in seventeenth-century Venice was, as some have claimed, merely another form of "court opera," or whether it can legitimately be considered the first "public opera."

Our research illuminates discrete moments in opera history. If at times we can see trends develop over several decades as companies sought to find the right path in this emerging business, at others the activities seem more sui generis, one impresario's solution to a particular problem. During the mid-seventeenth-century the craft of opera production was a learning process, if not an apprenticeship program; with the exception of Faustini in his later years, few if any participants had experience to fall back on. While it is true that in some ways opera production represented merely one more category of business venture in a city filled with them, the complexities and mutabilities of the business, not to mention the egos of a collection of artists, made it more difficult to manage than a more traditional undertaking such as a printing press or a cloth shop. The likelihood of profit was also considerably smaller.

In order to appreciate particular strategies, or the subtle differences between one contract and another, we describe a number of negotiations and events in some detail. Many of these are presented as case studies, where we focus on a theater, a singer, a pay sheet, or an inventory. As mentioned earlier, we have also chosen to supply a number of biographical details regarding the "cast of characters" in our book. With the exception of Marco Faustini and several composers, librettists, and singers, none of these figures appear in secondary sources of any kind; in most cases we have also been able to flesh out the lives and careers even of those already known to scholars. Other particulars, such as the cast lists for Faustini's operas, appear in appendices.

Our study of Venetian opera brings home what every opera company recognizes even today: because of its multifaceted nature, opera is expensive to produce and sustain. Each year any impresario must make countless decisions regarding the quality of the company's productions. Risks must be taken concerning the hiring of singers whose demands for high fees must be weighed against their powers to draw in large audiences. Recent stars such as Renee Fleming, Cecilia Bartoli, Luciano Pavarotti, and Placido Domingo had their forebears on the Venetian stage in singers such as Antonia Coresi, Giulia Masotti, and Giovanni Antonio Cavagna. Costumes and scenery were also expensive, and the Venetian desire for novelty exacerbated this cost. Figuring into all of this is the competition among theaters; in contrast to today, where opera must contend with many other forms of entertainment, in seventeenth-century Venice different companies largely competed against each other (at the same time as commedia dell'arte played in other theaters). Throughout our period, there were always at least two opera theaters active, and sometimes as many as four (the offerings of five different theaters active between 1650 and 1668 are highlighted in app. 1). Companies often strove to outdo each other by hiring the best composers, singers, dancers, set designers, and costumers, in some cases driving up the costs; even an impresario could be persuaded (or forced) to switch theaters. We shall see how certain singers such as "Vincenzino" and Giulia Masotti were pursued by several theaters over a number of years, and how company members attempted to hire them partly to uphold their reputations. The different companies were also in competition for prospective audience members. While wealthy Venetians rented boxes for the entire season—often at several theaters simultaneously—they still had to buy tickets in order to attend each performance, as did audience members in the parterre (unlike modern season-ticket holders who prepay everything in advance). It was thus vital to the impresario that his operas supply enough excitement to keep the spectators coming back for the entire season, especially at the end of Carnival, when all theaters staged performances every night. We shall see (in chap. 11) how in 1667 one night a spectator heard different acts in the two competing theaters; this may have been a common occurrence in order to catch a favorite aria or scenic device.

In examining public opera in its infancy we see reflections of opera production as it exists in our own day. While much has remained the same over the past four centuries, the differences are also clear. Today's opera companies, while certainly having to struggle to remain viable, can count on certain basic underlying systems for raising capital, selling tickets, and hiring artists that remain essentially the same from year to year. They do not have to try every year or so to invent a new procedure to manage a problem never before encountered, as did the impresarios of seventeenth-century Venice. It was the extraordinarily creative efforts of these men, impresarios and investors, from several segments of Venetian society, that made it possible for opera to take hold as public entertainment, and to survive to this day.

As mentioned above, our project began with Jonathan's serendipitous discovery in June 1989 of two of Marco Faustini's account books in the archives of the Scuola Grande di S. Marco; the research began more earnestly in September 1990 when several other Faustini materials surfaced, and Beth then began her archival work. We had originally hoped to complete our book by 1995, and then by 2000; by now ours has become one of those works often described as "long-awaited." A book's delay, however, brings its own rewards; the passage of so many years past our original deadline has meant the incorporation of data from many more months of archival research, and has also resulted in significant refinements in our conclusions. The work accomplished during the 1997/98 academic year was especially crucial to our understanding of opera production; documents retrieved during the summers of 2001, 2002, and 2003 added even more depth to our arguments; and Jonathan's study of the history of scenography transpired only over the last three years. These delays also enabled us to incorporate some of the findings of younger scholars such as Wendy Heller and Mauro Calcagno.

A project such as ours, happily, requires some expanse of time spent in Venice searching the archives. We thank the Gladys Krieble Delmas Foundation, the National Endowment of the Humanities, and the Research and Teaching Enhancement Grants of the University of Kentucky Honors Program, which generously funded portions of our work. We have used many archives and libraries in Italy over the past fourteen years. We thank the staffs of the Archivi di Stato at Bologna, Florence, Mantua, Modena, Parma, Padua, Turin, and Vicenza for their assistance. The archivists at the Archivio di Stato of Ferrara were particularly helpful in allowing us to make the most of our time there when we made the commute from Venice; our consultation of the incomparable Bentivoglio archive, undertaken before the publication of Sergio Monaldini's indispensible book, was consistently exhilarating. We also thank the staff of the archive of the Basilica of S. Antonio in Padua for their help.

The bulk of the primary research took place in Venice. The Microfilm Library of the Institute for the History of the Venetian State and Society at the Fondazione Cini, with its films of dispatches from Venice housed throughout Europe, made our tasks much easier; we thank Paola De Piante for her assistance. The staff of the Archivio Storico del Patriarcato di Venezia, led by Manuela Barausse, has always served us with kindness, and our work there with the Examinum Matrimoniorum and the parish records enriched our study in many ways. This archive's staff also facilitated our visits to some of the Venetian parish archives, and the parish priests graciously let us consult their records in search of data on our opera personnel. The staff of the Biblioteca Correr assisted us with our perusal of the invaluable Dandolo/Michiel correspondence. Librettos were consulted in the Biblioteca Nazionale Marciana and the Casa Goldoni, where the Archivio Vendramin also supplied crucial data. Libraries at the Fondazione Cini, the Fondazione Levi, and the Querini Stampaglia made available some essential reference materials. The bulk of the research was undertaken at the Archivio di Stato. The initial work with the Faustini papers was facilitated through the assistance of Francesca Cavazzana Romanelli, who provided us with a general outline for the Faustini *buste* in the scuola papers. Other archivists, including Edoardo Giufridda, Claudia Salmini, Sandra Sambo, and Alessandra Schiavon, have provided friendly guidance, and Michela Dal Borgo has gone above and beyond her duties to aid us in numerous ways. The staff members who retrieve the documents have always helped us with the utmost courtesy, and have contributed greatly to making our work at the archive such a wonderful experience.

Franki Hand of the Special Collections Library at the University of Michigan, Susan Snyder of the Bancroft Library at the University of California, Berkeley, and Laurie Klein of the Beinecke Library at Yale provided invaluable assistance in our search for and acquisition of illustrations.

For their permission to reproduce materials from their collections, we gratefully thank the following institutions: the Bancroft Library of the University of California, Berkeley, for figure 9.1, and the Special Collections Library, University of Michigan, for figures 9.2–9.8. Figure 2.1 is reproduced by courtesy of the Trustees of Sir John Soane's Museum, London. The photographs for figures 3.1, 3.2, 7.1, 8.1, and 9.9–9.12 were made by the Sezione di fotoriproduzione dell'Archivio di Stato in Venezia, and they are published with the permission of the Ministero per i Beni e le Attività Culturali (Atto di concessione n. 24/2003, prot. 3007 V.12).

Our work could not have been completed without the cooperative staff of the University of Kentucky Libraries. We thank in particular Paula Hickner of the Fine Arts Library and the staff of the Interlibrary Loan Department. We are also grateful to the faculty of the School of Music at the University of Kentucky, especially our fellow musicologists Lance Brunner, Diana Hallman, and Ron Pen, and our colleagues David Sogin, Cecilia Wang, and Ben Arnold. Many of our students, both musicologists and performers, have also shown their support in a number of ways; we thank especially Sherri Phelps, Jennifer Sgroe, Kimberly Venhuizen, and Kay Sherwood White. We also thank the wonderful people at Ohavay Zion Synagogue, who have welcomed us into their family and encouraged us during the final stages of the production of this book.

Musicologists specializing in the seventeenth century are, of course, among the most fortunate in the profession, for we are blessed with the Society for Seventeenth-Century Music, and its much-anticipated annual meetings. We have many friends among the society who have encouraged us over the years; some of them have offered generous help of various kinds. Mauro Calcagno, Giulio Ongaro, and Colleen Reardon (with her husband Nello Barbieri) have aided us with a number of tricky translations. Mauro Calcagno and Ellen Rosand supplied materials unavailable to us in Kentucky; they, as well as Wendy Heller, Roger Freitas, Louise Stein, and Margaret Murata always answered our e-mail queries cheerfully. Mary Frandsen shared details regarding some of our musicians who travelled between Italy and Dresden. We also thank Mauro Calcagno, Roger Freitas, Jean Lionnet, John Whenham, and the late Irene Alm, who shared their work with us in advance of its publication.

We also owe a debt of gratitude to the community of scholars who work in Venice. The Archivio di Stato in particular has been a congenial place where people from all parts of the world gather; casual conversations and coffee breaks with scholars across the disciplines almost inevitably lead to a greater understanding of one's "fondi." We thank in particular Patricia Fortini Brown, Monica Chojnacka, Stanley Chojnacki, Paula Clarke, Tracy Cooper, Julia DeLancey, James Grubb, Holly Hurlburt, Marion Kuntz, Patricia Labalme, Guido Ruggiero, and Micky White. Vittorio Mandelli has enthusiastically shared references at the archive to all things musical. E. J. Johnson has offered assistance with theater architecture, and Benjamin Ravid with the Jewish community of seventeenth-century Venice.

Our stays in Venice have also been brightened through the warm friendship and hospitality of a number of people. We recall in particular the many kindnesses of Jane and Felix Blunt, Sally and Franco Nogara, Maria-Grazia Cecchini, and Michela Dal Borgo and Sandro Bosato.

We offer our thanks to Larry Bernstein, who encouraged us to submit our manuscript for consideration for the A. M. S. Studies in Music series. His successor, Mary Hunter, has been an insightful and enthusiastic editor. Her initial evaluation showed us how we could finish the book in a timely manner, and her suggestions have improved every page of the manuscript. Ellen Rosand also read the manuscript; we thank her for careful reading, as well for her continuing generous support over the years. Finally, we would like to express our gratitude to those who have helped bring this project to its conclusion: Eve Bachrach, Kim Robinson, Norman Hirschy, and Bob Milks of Oxford University Press USA, and Bonnie Blackburn, whose careful copyediting improved the manuscript in many ways.

Our families have tolerated the length of this project with understanding and good humor. We have fond memories of visits to Beth's family in Pennsylvania, and treasure the enthusiasm for our work shown by their circle of friends and neighbors. We remember in particular the support of Carole Horn and Elvira Waldman, who died before the book's completion. We thank our aunts and uncles and our sisters Amy, Connie, and Judith, and their families, for their sympathetic ears over the years. Our parents, David and Helen Glixon and Seymour and Selma Jacowitz, offered their support and showed their interest throughout the many decades of our academic studies, and we dedicate the book to them. They all taught us that a job worth doing was worth doing well. Through their lessons of patience and striving for excellence, we have grown together as scholars and people. It was our hope, unfortunately not realized, that all of them would have the joy of holding this book in their hands and sharing it with their friends and relatives. We remember fondly those no longer with us, and offer our heartfelt thanks to those still here.

CONTENTS

A NOTE ON THE TRANSCRIPTIONS

In the transcriptions of original documents, abbreviations, except for those of monetary units, have been expanded silently, and punctuation and capitalization have been modified for clarity. Spelling has been left unaltered, but accents have been added as needed. In the text of the book, we have treated proper names as follows: (1) for individuals who appear in modern reference books, we use the forms employed there; (2) for authors of librettos, we have used the form that appears most often in the original editions (therefore Giovanni Faustini rather than the Venetian form Zuane, and Giacomo Badoaro rather than the Venetian form Badoer); (3) when there are extant documents preserving an individual's signature (unless the first two conditions apply), we use his or her preferred form; (4) if none of the above apply, we use Venetian forms for Venetians (thus Alvise Duodo, not Luigi) and Italian forms for non-Venetians; (5) because of the great variety of spellings we have standardized the Venetian and Italian versions of the English names Catherine as Caterina and Jerome as Girolamo.

A NOTE ON THE VENETIAN
MONETARY SYSTEM

For most usages, the basic Venetian monetary units were the ducato (or ducat; abbreviated D.), the lira (£), and the soldo (s.). In the standard arrangement (employing what was called the lira di piccolo), used in nearly all the documents cited in this study, the relationships were as follows:

1 lira = 20 soldi

1 ducat = 6 lire and 4 soldi

These denominations, however, were primarily for accounting purposes. Cash payments were made using various coins whose values varied. Those that appear most often in the operatic documents are the following:

1 reale = 7 lire 10 soldi

1 ducatone = about 8 lire 4 soldi

1 scudo d'argento = $\frac{1}{2}$ ducats = 9 lire and 6 soldi

1 ongaro = 15 lire 10 soldi

1 zecchino (or cecchino) = 17 lire

1 doppia = 28 lire (sometimes 27)

The value of this currency is very difficult to express in modern terms, and for that reason the amounts discussed should be considered primarily in comparative terms. Inflation does not seem to have been an issue within the span of years covered in this study. For a recent brief discussion of the prices of basic commodities in Venice between 1534 and 1769, see Sperling, *Convents and the Body Politic*, 242–43.

ABBREVIATIONS

ASF	Archivio di Stato di Firenze
—, MP	Mediceo del principato
ASFe, AB	Archivio di Stato di Ferrara, Archivio Bentivoglio, Lettere sciolte
ASMa, AG	Archivio di Stato di Mantova, Archivio Gonzaga
ASMo, CAV	Archivio di Stato di Modena, Archivio Segreto Estense, Cancelleria, Sezione estero, Carteggio ambasciatori, Venezia
ASPV	Archivio storico del patriarcato di Venezia
—, EM	Curia patriarcale, sezione antica, Examinum Matrimoniorum
AST, LMV	Archivio di Stato di Torino, Sezione corte, Lettere ministre, Venezia
ASV	Archivio di Stato di Venezia
—, AN	Archivio notarile
—, CD	Consiglio dei dieci
—, DS	Dieci savi sopra le decime in Rialto
—, GE	Giudici dell'esaminador
—, GM	Giudici del mobile
—, GP	Giudici di petizion
—, SGSM	Scuola Grande di S. Marco
b.	busta
D.	ducats
DBI	*Dizionario biografico degli italiani* (Rome: Istituto della enciclopedia italiana, 1960–)
HVsa, AK	Hannover, Niedersächsisches Haupstaatsarchiv, Aktes-Korrespondenzen italienischer Kardinäle und anderer Personen, besonders Italiener an Herzog Johann Friedrich
£	lire
m.v.	more veneto ("the Venetian way," according to which the year begins on 1 March)
NG II	*New Grove Dictionary of Music and Musicians*, 2d ed., ed. Stanley Sadie (New York: Grove's Dictionaries, 2000)

NGO	*New Grove Dictionary of Opera*, ed. Stanley Sadie (New York: Grove's Dictionaries of Music, 1992)
reg.	registro
s.	soldi
VAP	Venice, Archivio parrocchiale (followed by the name of the parish)
Vcg	Venice, Biblioteca della Casa Goldoni
Vmc	Venice, Biblioteca del Museo Civico Correr
Vnm	Venice, Biblioteca Nazionale Marciana

PART I

THE BUSINESS OF OPERA

INTRODUCTION TO THE BUSINESS OF OPERA IN SEVENTEENTH-CENTURY VENICE: PEOPLE AND FINANCES

Venice has long been famous as the city that nurtured the first public opera theaters. With its famous Carnival, which attracted revelers from all over Europe,[1] and a thriving theatrical tradition, it already had two of the most important ingredients to create this new genre: an audience and theaters. It was also the commercial city par excellence, with many people willing to invest capital in new ventures, and others possessing the legal and financial skills needed to run a complex business in a competitive market. Venetians discovered that producing opera required different procedures than those in place for spoken comedy, and, as we shall see, companies tried various strategies in their efforts to compete successfully in this new entertainment market.

THE CAST OF CHARACTERS

In the chapters that follow we will meet a series of men (and a few women) who came from all walks of life: nobles, citizens (cittadini, i.e., the civil servant and professional class), tradesmen, and artisans (see app. 2 on the social classes of Venice). The roles they filled—sometimes more than one at a time, and all vital for the success of the theatrical enterprise—are introduced briefly here:

> *Theater owner.* An absolute necessity, of course, was a place to perform. This might be a purpose-built theater, or even a converted warehouse owned by someone who might, or might not, have an interest in the theater. As we shall see, however, this was the one person almost guaranteed to make a profit on the venture, as long as he succeeded in finding someone to produce plays or operas, and did not suffer the misfortune of a

---

1 Carnival is usually described as running from 26 Dec. through the day before Lent, but the opera season often began earlier (see app. 1). During this period certain Venetian laws were relaxed, notably those regarding the wearing of masks in public and those limiting public entertainment. On the role of carnival in Venetian society see Muir, *Civic Ritual*, 156–81. See also Heller, *Emblems of Eloquence*, 6–9. The issue of the scheduling of opera performances in Venice will be addressed in detail in Selfridge-Field, *Calendar of Venetian Opera*. See also Whenham, "Perspectives."

3

government-ordered closure of the theaters. His income came in the form of a fixed rent on the building or from the rental of boxes.

Theater renter (tenant). Most of the time, the theater owner chose not to produce comedy or operas himself, but rented the theater to a person or company who took on that responsibility.

Investor. We use this term, in its most general sense, to describe anyone who provides capital for the production. An investor might form part of a company that produced operas, participating to a greater or lesser degree in the management, or might be an outsider. Some investors, particularly those in a company, participated both in any profits and, more often, in the losses from the production. Others, most often external investors, expected to be repaid; that is, their "investment" was actually a sort of loan, although usually without interest.

Guarantor (pieggio). Given the shaky financial status of most theatrical companies, as we shall show, loans and other contracts were often guaranteed by someone outside the production company, a person known in the Venetian business world as a *pieggio*.

Cashier (cassier). Within any production company, one person, the cashier, managed the cash, both receipts and payments.

Impresario. While this term has been defined in many different ways, we use it here to designate the person in charge of the production, who selected the creative team and the performers (unless they were already members of the company), and made the business and artistic decisions (sometimes with the assistance or interference of one or more of the other characters listed above). This person often played simultaneously many of the roles previously described, especially theater renter, investor, and cashier, but could also be a hired professional.[2]

Protector. Often, a powerful nobleman, without necessarily any legal or financial obligations to the theater or company (although he might be the owner of the theater, when he had rented it out to someone else), would lend his name and prestige to the enterprise. He might write letters on behalf of the impresario, affix his name to legal documents, or otherwise act in situations where a cittadino or commoner might be less effective.

Opera production was from its outset a difficult and expensive proposition, with demands and complications that exceeded those of more ordinary business ventures; yet, despite all the inherent drawbacks, a series of new partners and investors—some of them perhaps naive, or at least overly optimistic—presented

2 On the idea of the impresario in eighteenth-century Venice, see Talbot, "Venetian Operatic Contract," esp. 22–23. Talbot's analysis of a 1714 contract for Teatro S. Angelo touches on many of the same issues that will be addressed in this and the following chapters. On an eighteenth-century Florentine impresario, see Holmes, *Opera Observed*. On the role of the impresario in Italian opera in the eighteenth and nineteenth centuries, see Rosselli, *Opera Industry*.

themselves throughout the mid-seventeenth century, willing to lend a hand in order to promote one of Venice's most attractive and exciting forms of entertainment. As we shall see, owners and renters often developed different solutions to operational problems, even year to year.

VENETIAN THEATERS AND THEIR NOBLE BUILDERS

In Venice most theaters, which were usually known by the name of their parish or a nearby church, were built and owned by a noble family (see table 1.1A). This seems quite logical from our modern viewpoint, given the social makeup of the city, yet many non-noble Venetian businessmen had funds more than adequate to build and operate a theater; they did not, however, possess that certain mystique that came with Venetian nobility. These theaters were strongly identified with their

TABLE 1.1.   Ownership of Seventeenth-Century Venetian Theaters

Theater	Date built (or rebuilt)	Owning family
A. Built and owned by patrician families		
S. Cassiano	1580 (1607)	Tron
S. Moisè	1620	Giustinian
		(Zane from 1628 to 1715)
S. Luca	1622	Vendramin
SS. Giovanni e Paolo	1630s (1639)	Grimani
S. Samuele	1656[a]	Grimani
S. Angelo	1677	Marcello and Cappello[b]
S. Giovanni Grisostomo	1678	Grimani
B. Built and owned by cittadini		
S. Aponal	before 1635	Zanetta Diamante and Francesco Ceroni
C. Others		
Novissimo	1641	Monastery of SS. Giovanni e Paolo
SS. Apostoli	1649	unknown

For more details, see Mangini, *Teatri di Venezia* and Mancini, Muraro, and Povoledo, *Teatri di Venezia*.
[a] The date for the building of S. Samuele has traditionally been given as 1655, the year cited in Ivanovich's history. In a document of April 1656 (ASV, AN, Atti, b. 6059, f. 29), however, Giovanni Grimani referred to the theater as not yet built.
[b] Built by impresario Francesco Santurini on property owned by these two families; after the expiration of the seven-year contract, control would revert to the patricians.

proprietors; indeed, they were often referred to by names such as "Teatro Grimani" and "Teatro Vendramin" after the families that owned them: they represented more than a building housed in a certain parish, for they helped to focus attention on the patricians of Venice, and on their contributions to the city.[3]

The importance of these noble owners to the functioning of the most success-ful theaters becomes more evident when we look at other theaters (whether for comedy or opera) that operated more sporadically and had origins that are now less clear. Indeed, it is probably no coincidence that the more ephemeral theaters such as I Saloni and SS. Apostoli had no strong connection to noble families (see table 1.1C). As we shall see below, in one of a series of case studies of opera theaters (chap. 4), even an artistically successful theater such as the Novissimo (1640–45), with support from a variety of noblemen, suffered from the lack of a single noble family's backing. Another case study will center on a theater owned by two citta-dini, Francesco Ceroni and Zanetta Diamante (see table 1.1B), whose commit-ment to foster theatrical activity was not sufficient to ensure its long-term success. In Venice, noble ownership and continued success in theatrical ventures often went hand in hand.

One might ask what the noble theater owners stood to gain from their prop-erty other than a sense of civic pride or glorification of their family name. Cer-tainly, when they rented their theaters to outside parties, they would have received a specified rental payment for the theater, and, moreover, they would have been in-sulated from any losses suffered by the impresario.[4] The census (decima) of 1661—a city-wide reporting of income from properties and investments—reveals that most of the noble theater owners were among the wealthy, if not the wealthiest of Venice.[5] Andrea Vendramin and the brothers Marin and Domenico Zane had nearly equal income from property and leases, just over 5,000 ducats, while Gio-vanni Grimani declared 2,881 ducats. One thousand ducats of Vendramin's income came from his theater, while Grimani's income from his two theaters amounted only to 450 ducats, at least according to his own estimation.[6] Carlo Andrea Tron's taxable income, on the other hand—not including the theater—was listed as only 242 ducats.[7]

---

3 On theaters in Venice, see also Zorzi, Il teatro e la città.

4 See Bianconi and Walker, "Production, Consumption."

5 Since Venetian patricians were not permitted to work, and very few of them in the seventeenth century owned businesses, their income was primarily derived from land and some investments. The Republic assessed a tax amounting to 10 percent of the annual income from these sources, based on a declaration made to the Dieci savi sopra le decime in Rialto. Of the approximately 6,000 declarations by Venetians of all classes made for the 1661 decima (new, city-wide declarations were usually made only once a century, with modifications submitted as necessary), barely more than 100, nearly all of them pa-tricians, recorded incomes over 2,000 ducats. Of these, only fifty were over 5,000, including six over 10,000 (the highest was Lodovico Vidman, at 13,957 ducats). ASV, DS, bb. 212–28.

6 For Andrea Vendramin, see ASV, DS, b. 220, no. 750; for Marin and Lunardo Zane b. 223, nos. 317, 319; for Giovanni Grimani b. 218, no. 1036.

7 For the Tron family, see ASV, DS, b. 218, no. 793. The Tron family had originally built Teatro S. Cassiano in order to gain a profit; see Johnson, "Short, Lascivious Lives," 952–54.

RENTERS AND MANAGERS OF COMEDY
THEATERS: NOBLES AND OTHERS

Public opera did not erupt spontaneously in 1637. Its growth was facilitated by the presence of a number of theaters that presented spoken comedy (commedia dell'arte), each with boxes already in place.[8] Our study of Venetian opera, then, begins with a brief look at the city's comedy theaters and their systems of finance and management. Studies of opera in seventeenth-century Venice have asserted that the system featured theaters owned by the noble or patrician class, but rented, and often administered, either by cittadini or artisans, that is, lower layers of society.[9] This view is, on the whole, accurate, as we shall see (this will be explored further in the case studies in chap. 4). If we look at the two comedy theaters, however, both at the time of the introduction of opera in Venice as well as in the successive decades, we often find patricians—but not necessarily the owners—at the helm.

The Teatro S. Luca, owned by the Vendramin family, was rented by a series of noblemen from the 1630s through the 1660s. As early as 1638 Ettor Tron, proprietor of the Teatro S. Cassiano, rented the theater (Almorò Zane, the proprietor of the Teatro S. Moisè, was joint renter with him, although from an unspecified date); Cristoforo Boldù, who was also associated with the theater at times with Zane and Tron, would formally rent the theater with Zane in 1651.[10] During the early 1650s Boldù remained at the theater, with Zane's place eventually taken by his widow, Caterina, who appears to have been the only Venetian woman of her time to take an active role in the business.[11] Tron and Zane first rented S. Luca when their own theaters had taken up the presentation of opera; they must have brought with them knowledge gleaned from their familiarity with the theater business. The other comedy theater, S. Moisè, also had its share of noble renters during the 1650s and 1660s, that is, after Almorò Zane's death: first Lunardo Battagia, and then Polo Boldù.[12] Such nobles inevitably had assistants (*fattori*) to help with the renting of the palchi and other duties; these tasks, predictably, usually fell to members of the working or artisan class.[13]

8 On the early history of theaters in Venice, see Mangini, *Teatri di Venezia* and Mancini, Muraro, and Povoledo, *Teatri di Venezia*. For the early history of S. Cassiano, see Johnson, "Short, Lascivious Lives."

9 See Morelli and Walker, "Tre controversie," 103.

10 The initial rental contract has not yet surfaced. The earliest documentation that mentions Ettor Tron dates from 1638, the earliest with Zane from 1639 (ASV, AN, Atti, b. 647, f. 478ᵛ, 16 Sept. 1638 and b. 649, f. 19ʳ, 13 Sept. 1639). Boldù's name first surfaces in a document of 7 Aug. 1645 (ASV, AN, Atti, b. 661, f. 142ᵛ).

11 Caterina Zane was not a noblewoman by birth; rather, she married Almorò Zane in 1647, after having lived with him for several years "as his woman" (ASPV, EM, b. 43, 15 April 1647, f. 53ʳ⁻ᵛ). Women did on occasion act as impresarios in other cities, notably Giulia de Caro in Naples (see Maione, "Giulia de Caro") and Anna Francesca Costa in Bologna (see Megale, "Il principe," and id., "Altre novità").

12 With Almorò Zane's death in March of 1652, the theater passed to his nephews, Marin and Lunardo Zane. Battagia rented the theater several months later, on 13 May 1652 (ASV, AN, Atti, b. 12042, f. 110ᵛ). After Battagia's death, the rental passed to Polo Boldù (ASV, AN, Atti, b. 12045, f. 122, 14 May 1655).

13 During the 1640s and 1650s the fattori at S. Luca were Iseppo Fassetta, Pietro Fassetta, and Giovanni Lorenzo Santa Chiara; at S. Moisè the post was held by Iseppo Fassetta and Paulo Morandi. Santa

In seeking to understand why some of these noblemen became involved in the theater business, and what their expectations might have been, we must look at that class with a more critical eye. Some opera scholars have tended to lump the noble class together, ignoring distinctions of political standing and economic status, assuming a certain level of homogeneity. The patricians, however, ranged widely in matters of prestige, wealth, and annual income, and some could have benefited substantially from running a successful comedy theater. Nobility in Venice, as elsewhere, was an inherited state; financial holdings, on the other hand, could fluctuate according to many factors. Indeed, Venice was a city where a successful notary, lawyer, doctor, artisan, or businessman could easily surpass in wealth the meager income of a poor nobleman. A noble family's wealth could be depleted through bad investments, the payment of too many large dowries, or excessive spending; the funding of new domestic construction, the restoration of old properties, the commission of artwork, or expenses incurred through taxes or other service to the Venetian government all affected a family's property and standing. Still other nobles had pretensions of great wealth but were cash-poor. Unlike the (mostly) rich theater owners discussed above, those nobles such as Polo Boldù and Caterina Zane who rented theaters tended to be considerably lower on the scale of wealth, and stood to earn several hundred ducats per year through the operation of a successful comedy theater.[14]

THE BUSINESS OF SPOKEN THEATER

In order to appreciate what the change from comedy to opera production meant for both the owners and the managers, we must first consider the demands of the comedy theater. Certainly the production of comedy entailed far fewer complications than opera, with issues of repertory, commissions, costumes, intricate scenery, and librettos largely absent. The impresario or the theater owner hired a company of *comici*, most often those of the Dukes of Parma, Mantua, or Modena.[15] Presumably these actors and actresses supplied their own costumes, and they largely controlled their own repertory and their own personnel. Thus, the impresario's main responsibility would have been to locate a comedy troupe, to keep the theater in good repair and guard it from fire (and perhaps construct a basic set, if the comedians did not provide one themselves), and to rent the boxes. According to Cristoforo Ivanovich the division of profits was also straightforward: the box rentals went to the owner or renter, and all other income went to the comedians.[16] In practice, the nature of the rewards to the comedy troupes changed over the years; certain

---

Chiara, unlike the other men, was not Venetian, but rather Neapolitan, and had previously been a *comico*. In Venice he earned his living, instead, as a businessman, selling acquavita (ASPV, EM, b. 57, ff. 448–51, 18 Oct. 1654).

14 Polo Boldù's property income, for example, was a mere 78 ducats (ASV, DS, b. 219, no. 233).

15 On the commedia dell'arte in seventeenth-century Italy, see (among others) Tessari, *Commedia dell'arte*; Richards and Richards, *Commedia dell'arte*; and Taviani and Marotti, *Commedia dell'arte*.

16 Ivanovich, *Memorie teatrali*, 410. Traditionally, the *padrone* of the theater also paid the comedians a *regalo* (gift), often poultry at Christmas.

incomes and benefits were negotiable.[17] The company might be paid a set fee, in which case they would not have been entitled to the ticket income, for example.[18] Whatever the negotiations, however, the convenience of dealing with a company rather than with separate singers constituted a major difference between comedy and opera production as it came to be practiced in Venice beginning in the 1640s. While the limited tasks that comprised the responsibilities of running a theater for comedy could at times be fraught with problems,[19] the presentation of comedy may well have proved to be a relatively carefree operation.

THE BUSINESS OF OPERA:
IMPRESARIOS AND COMPANIES

The production of opera mirrored that of comedy in its broadest outlines: performers were hired, boxes and seats were rented, nightly tickets were collected, and the theater was physically maintained and kept safe from fire. The demands of the genre on the management, however, were exponentially greater than for comedy, both in the material sense (costumes and scenery) and regarding personnel (librettist, composer, musicians, dancers, and extras), for self-contained companies were the exception rather than the rule. Moreover, a successful company had to develop and foster a pool of well-placed individuals (often noblemen, both in and outside of Venice) willing to facilitate the various contracts and agreements, principally, but not exclusively, those of the singers and, perhaps, the composer.

This added complexity led to a somewhat different cast of characters than for the production of comedy, and most especially gave rise to the impresario as a key figure. Many of the earliest operas in Venice were produced by nearly self-contained companies, somewhat in the manner of a comedy troupe. However, while the company of comedians usually included all the performers, the operatic company was usually formed of just a core group of the larger number of people required for performances (both onstage and off); the remainder would be hired as needed. Also, while a troupe of comedians was usually hired by an individual who had rented the theater (and would manage the finances), the early opera compa-

---

17 A contract of 2 Apr. 1622 for S. Luca specified that the comici would keep the income from the tickets and seats, and would receive 300 ducats at Christmas. The comici, for their part, had to maintain the lighting throughout the theater (Vcg, Archivio Goldoni, 42 F 16/4, f. 10; published in Mancini, Muraro, and Povoledo, *Teatri di Venezia*, 1:261).

18 For the arrangements for a late seventeenth-century company of comedians, see Monaldini, *Orto dell'Esperidi*, 607. The contract (10 Feb. 1684) between the comedian Angelo Costantini and the fattor for S. Cassiano, Iseppo Zerbato, specifies a payment of 850 ducats for the fall and carnival seasons, with the comici getting 3 soldi per seat (*cariega*).

19 Several letters of Claudio Monteverdi detail the difficulties that could arise in booking a company, in part due to the personalities of the leading actors of the day. In 1622 the composer helped the Venetian nobleman Lorenzo Giustinian, owner of the Teatro S. Moisè, recruit comedians by enlisting the help of Alessandro Striggio, his frequent correspondent in Mantua (see Monteverdi, *Letters*, ed. Stevens, 253–55). As far back as 1581 the Trons' theatrical venture faced ruin because the Duke of Modena wanted one of the star performers, "Pedrolino," to abandon his performances and return to Modena; see Mangini, *Teatri di Venezia*, 24–25.

nies typically rented the theater themselves, directly from the owner, as did the company that produced *Andromeda* in 1637 at S. Cassiano (see chap. 4). More common as time went on was the decision by a single member of the creative team, often the librettist (who might be a cittadino, such as Giovanni Faustini; see chaps. 3 and 4), to become an impresario in order to produce his own works; he would rent the theater, raise the capital, hire the other creators and the performers, and operate the business. Sometimes, the impresario would form a partnership, either with one or more members of the team, with a wealthy outsider, or with a businessman; the librettist Giacomo Dall'Angelo[20] followed this strategy in 1665, when he teamed up with the businessmen Cristoforo Raimondi and Camillo Coveglia to present operas at S. Moisè for the 1665/66 season.

Yet another model was the impresario who was not part of the artistic company, but rather a businessman (with or without financial or familial ties to operatic circles) or a member of the professional class with a desire to become part of this world (why is often not clear), or even an opera-loving patrician. Notable examples are Girolamo Lappoli, a Tuscan businessman who was impresario at the Teatro Novissimo (see chap. 4); Marco Faustini, a lawyer who entered the business through the activities of his brother Giovanni (treated at length in chap. 3); and the nobleman Vettor Grimani Calergi, a cousin of the theater owner Giovanni Grimani and a passionate lover of opera (see chaps. 4 and 7).[21]

The remainder of this chapter will focus on the first task of the opera impresario or management company (of whatever kind): finding capital for production. We will provide an overview of the types of financing available to an impresario, as well as the sources of income (excepting the boxes, which will be discussed in chap. 2) that would serve, under favorable circumstances, to balance all the expenses.

FINANCING OPERA, I: SOURCES OF CAPITAL

Like any business, opera production required capital in advance of sales—in this case before the beginning of the season—to pay for a variety of items: theater maintenance, scenery and costumes, and travel expenses for the "foreign" singers. This capital could be raised within the company or from outsiders. In some cases,

---

20 Dall'Angelo is more commonly referred to in Venetian documents as Giacomo Angeli.

21 S. Luca seems to have been rented by patricians more often than most other theaters (as we saw above, this was always the case when it was a comedy theater). The first renter of the theater when it was converted to opera in 1660 was the nobleman Antonio Boldù (Cristoforo's nephew), but after one year he sublet the theater to Girolamo Barbieri, a pharmacist, and in subsequent seasons it was run by companies of non-nobles including Barbieri and the librettists Nicolò Minato and Aurelio Aureli (this is discussed in more detail in chap. 4). By the 1670s, however, another Venetian nobleman, Francesco Bembo, would figure prominently in the management of S. Luca as an opera theater. On Bembo, see Mancini, Muraro, and Povoledo, *Teatri di Venezia*, 1:214. See also chapter 2, below. The noblewoman Zanetta Vendramin participated actively in the operation of S. Luca starting in the 1670s, that is, before the death of her husband, Andrea, owner of the theater. On Grimani Calergi, see *DBI*, s.v. "Grimani Calergi, Vettor," by Gino Benzoni. Grimani Calergi's connections with opera will be discussed in a forthcoming article.

those who provided this funding did so with the express condition that they be repaid, while in others the reimbursement would only be in proportion to the financial success of the season; these latter investors probably expected to lose money
(although they hoped not to lose too much), and were willing to do so either for
the love of opera or in order to be seen as artistic patrons.

Investors

Some companies apparently aimed for self-sufficiency; in Marco Faustini's company of 1657, for example (see chap. 3), the production costs were borne largely by
the impresario and his three partners, with no other known sponsors or benefactors. This model seems to have been often in play during the mid-seventeenth century, but as the costs of opera increased—largely because of the rising fees of the
lead singers—it became less practical; indeed, in nearly all of the case studies that
follow we shall see signs of its inadequacies. Later opera companies—and we see
evidence of this practice as early as 1678—obtained a more secure financial base
through the sale of *carati* (shares; literally carats), spreading the expenses of opera
over a much larger base.[22] A common form of financing in Venetian business, a
carato normally represented a 1/24 share in a company or financial arrangement, although the actual fraction varied in practice; the investors were referred to as
caratadori. In 1691, for example, a company formed at the Teatro S. Luca contributed 1,000 ducats toward the production, with a limit of 100 ducats per investor, rather than the twenty-four divisions evident in a balance sheet for S. Giovanni Grisostomo in 1729/30 (any profits would be divided in like manner).[23] This
system, then, allowed the "investors" to put in a reasonable sum with the possibility
of a profit, but also with protection from significant losses, and it became a staple in
cities throughout Italy.

Occasionally, the owner of the theater himself might become an investor in the
production, making up some of the losses of the company (although, of course,
also reducing his income from the rental of the theater). Giovanni Grimani's tax
declaration of 1661 suggests he supported the theater in a number of ways: "In
Calle della Testa a theater built by me in these last years to present operas in music.
. . . And so that this [theater] will bring me some income, I spend a significant
amount of money, with large fees to singers, whom I bring from foreign places, as
is well known to Your Excellencies. And on occasion I have shouldered consider-

---

22 On the *caratadori*, see Talbot, *Tomaso Albinoni*, 195–96. See also Talbot, "Venetian Operatic Contract," 19–22, 40–41.

23 A document of 9 Dec. 1678 mentions caratadori at S. Luca (ASV, AN, Atti, b. 1183, f. 173ᵛ), as
does one of 29 Jan. 1681 m.v. (ASV, AN, Atti, b. 3901). For caratadori at SS. Giovanni e Paolo, see ASV,
AN, Atti, b. 6112, f. 132, 5 Apr. 1682. For S. Luca, see Benedetti, "Teatro musicale," 216–18. A document
concerning the company of Barbieri, Morandi, and Castrovillari at S. Luca in 1664 makes use of the
term "carato," but in this case it seems to refer to "inside" investors rather than a more generalized
capitalization scheme involving a larger group of investors not involved more personally in the running
of the theater (ASV, AN, Atti, b. 703, f. 155ᵛ, 12 Jan. 1663 m.v.). The term is used similarly in following
years at S. Luca, with the company including Nicolò Minato (ASV, AN, Atti, b. 708, f. 254ᵛ, 18 Mar.
1665).

able loss."[24] He claimed to have garnered only a 200-ducat profit from the theater, a rather small figure when compared to the fee that might be had for renting a large opera or comedy theater. Still, for Grimani, the prestige and civic pride he enjoyed apparently made even a modest profit worthwhile.[25]

Loans

When a management team (the impresario and his partners) was unable to raise sufficient capital on its own, it was forced to look elsewhere for funds, and the typical solution during the mid-century was to take out loans, not from a bank, but from private citizens. The company at S. Cassiano in 1637, for its first season, borrowed 100 ducats from one of its members,[26] but a more typical source of funds was a nobleman or a businessman. During the 1640s, for example, the noble proprietors at S. Cassiano borrowed from the nobleman Massimo Contarini money that was only slowly repaid after a number of years (see chap. 4). At the same theater later in the decade (the agreement was signed on 27 November 1648), the impresarios Bortolo Castoreo and Rocco Maestri found financial support from another nobleman, Pietro Corner. They promised to supply the reimbursements in a typical manner: 100 ducats the morning after the first performance, and the other 150 immediately after the subsequent performances.[27] They fully expected, then, to reap sufficient income from the performances to cover the loan. By the time the premiere was at hand, however—nearly two months later—they needed still more cash, and returned to Corner for an additional 160 ducats on 18 January, shortly before *Giasone* opened on the twenty-fourth of that month.[28] As was so often the case, however, the management did not reimburse Corner in a timely manner, and he eventually went to court in search of his funds.[29] This circumstance would be repeated all too frequently throughout the period.

Corner's gesture of generosity went unacknowledged publicly, as *Giasone* was dedicated by the author, Giacinto Andrea Cicognini, to another nobleman, Vettor Grimani Calergi. Two years later, however, at a different theater, the scenographer

24 ASV, DS, b. 218, no. 1036, tax declaration of Giovanni Grimani fu di Ser Vettor: "In Calle della Testa un theatro fabricato da me questi ultimi anni per farmi recitar opere in musica . . . et perché questo mi renda qualche utile, convengo impiegarmi rilevante summa di dannaro con distributione di grossi donativi a cantanti, che faccio venir da lochi forestieri, come è ben noto a Vostre Eccellenze, et alle volte son restato con considerabile discapito."

25 It is unclear whether Faustini literally rented the theater in 1660, i.e. paid a sum directly to Grimani, for he did not do so in 1665; in the 1640s, however, the theater had rented for as much as 1,000 or 1,200 ducats (ASV, AN, Atti, b. 6047, f. 238, 14 Dec. 1644). In that same *condizione* of 1661, Grimani claimed a 250-ducat income from his other theater, S. Samuele.

26 ASV, AN, Atti, b. 5973, f. 221ᵛ, 22 Dec. 1636. For more on this company, see chapter 4.

27 ASV, AN, Atti, b. 2950, f. 428, 27 Nov. 1648.

28 ASV, AN, Atti, b. 2950, f. 429. On the performances of *Giasone* see Morelli and Walker, "Tre controversie."

29 ASV, Giudice del mobile, Sentenze a legge, reg. 330, f. 18, 27 July 1649. In April 1649 the company approached a different nobleman, Girolamo Zane, for a loan in preparation for an Ascension performance of *Giasone* (ASV, AN, Atti, b. 2951, f. 83ᵛ, 22 Apr. 1649). See also chapter 4.

and impresario Giovanni Burnacini dedicated Cicognini's posthumous *Gl'amori di Alessandro magno, e di Rossane* (SS. Apostoli, 1650/51) to Guglielmo Van Kessel, a businessman from Antwerp who had resided in Venice for a number of years.[30] It is evident from the wording of Burnacini's dedication that Van Kessel played some financial role in its production.[31] In this case, several documents allow us to see beyond the flowery words of the dedication; most importantly, a notarial act of 17 June 1653 supplies us with concrete numbers, revealing the generous nature of Van Kessel's support.[32] A series of entries shows that Van Kessel had loaned Burnacini a sum amounting to just over 800 ducats, a figure much higher than Corner's assistance at S. Cassiano two years earlier. Van Kessel took a much more active role than many others who loaned funds to impresarios, for he paid a number of merchants and musicians, and was even responsible for arranging for the printing of the libretto. Burnacini made disbursements to his benefactor from the ticket receipts as the performances progressed throughout the season, but the two later came to disagree over the nature of their financial transactions, and whether each man had met his financial responsibilities, and legal action ensued regarding their respective obligations.[33]

The gilder Francesco Piva, the impresario at SS. Giovanni e Paolo during the late 1650s, also entered into a dispute with one of his associates, Iseppo Zolio. While Piva insisted that Zolio had agreed to take on much of the responsibility of the production for Lucio's *Medoro* in 1658/59, Zolio said that he had never promised to lend financial support, but had only handled the nightly funds so as to maintain credibility between the management and the musicians.[34] Both Burnacini's and Piva's situations point to the difficulties that might emerge with informal agreements, especially oral ones, lacking even the weight of a *scrittura privata* (a contract signed by all parties but not registered with a notary). Without a written agreement to fall back on, these parties seem to have been destined to end up in the courts in order to resolve their problems. In one other case, the loan of cash—combined with the company's inability to repay it—was solved in an entirely different manner: it led to an investor's entry into the company itself. As we shall see

30 Van Kessel's name often appears in Venetian documents as "Vanchessel," "Vanchesel," or "Vankesel."

31 Cicognini, *Gl'amori di Alessandro Magno, e di Rossane*, 5. For a more complete discussion of the production of this opera, see B. Glixon, "Music for the Gods?" Van Kessel died sometime before May 1660, when his brothers claimed their inheritance (ASV, Giudici del proprio, Parentelle, b. 43, 8 May 1660).

32 ASV, AN, Atti, b. 1124, ff. 86v–88.

33 ASV, GP, Dimande, b. 33, filza 55, 1647–50, no. 565 and ASV, GP, Scritture e risposte, b. 180, no. 55 (1651).

34 ASV, GP, Dimande, b. 42, fasc. 79. The incidents regarding Van Kessel and Zolio will be explored in a future article. As Zolio was the dedicatee of Francesco Lucio's *Arie a voce sola* (1655), he may have become involved with the production of *Medoro* through the composer. Zolio maintained a connection with opera and the Grimanis long after the production of *Medoro*, however; he witnessed the agreement between Faustini and the Grimanis when Faustini left their theater in 1667, but he also was involved with recruiting singers for the theater during the 1670s. Letters from him survive in the Dandolo/Michiel collection: Vmc, PDC 1060, nos. 194, 242, 412 (all 1674) and PDC 1061, no. 212 (1675).

in chapter 4, in the 1660s Marco Mozzoni went from acting as a lender to owning one-third of the shares at S. Luca.

Advances from Printers and the Rental of Seats

While impresarios may have relied on traditional loans on a fairly regular basis, always with the intention of paying them back at the beginning of the opera season (or at the latest by the end of carnival), they also found other ways of obtaining capital before opening night, particularly by arranging for businessmen who stood to gain from the production to provide money up front, to be repaid as the season got underway. In 1657 the printer Salvadori provided 200 ducats—representing the librettist's share of the expected sales income—to Marco Faustini's company before the onset of the season (see chaps. 3 and 5); presumably this option was available to Faustini only because the author of *L'incostanza trionfante* would not be receiving the receipts, as he had left town before finishing the text (see chap. 5).

Another opportunity presented itself to the impresario in the form of one of the physical properties of the theater, the bench seats in the parterre, or scagni, which were rented on a nightly basis to those who purchased tickets but had not rented boxes. The impresario engaged someone to provide and rent these seats (and sometimes, in addition, to distribute and count the entrance tickets); a certain portion of the fee for the rentals would go to the impresario each evening, and the rest would remain with the rental agent, to cover his costs and provide some profit. At SS. Giovanni e Paolo, at least in his last term, Faustini used this system as a source of income in the form of a loan at a time of the season when capital was crucial.[35] That is, in two consecutive years Faustini signed contracts, first in 1665 with Andrea Bevilaqua (most likely the nephew of Pietro Andrea Ziani[36]), and then in 1666 with Gasparo Mauro, the scenographer at the theater, to provide and oversee the scagni. Each agreed to give Faustini 500 ducats at the signing of the contract, which would be paid back during the opera season out of the nightly income from rentals. Faustini set the price for the nightly rental for each scagno at no more than 32 soldi, all of which would go to Bevilaqua or Mauro until the 500 ducats had been repaid, after which Faustini would get 26 soldi, leaving a return of 6 soldi per scagno for Bevilaqua or Mauro. Mauro was also responsible for having someone sleep in the theater to guard against fire and theft (during the earlier seasons for which account books survive, the nightly expenses had included 1 lira for such a service). Neither contract specifies that Mauro or Bevilaqua had the further responsibility of distributing and counting the tickets.[37]

35 ASV, SGSM, b. 194, f. 123, 1 Apr. 1666.

36 Pietro Bevilaqua had married Maddalena Ziani by 1631. The couple had at least two sons, Bernardo and Andrea. See, among others, ASV, Giudici del proprio, Parentelle, b. 44, f. 96ᵛ , 21 May 1664, and ASV, AN, Atti, b. 11011, f. 28, 24 Mar. 1638.

37 If this system had been in effect at the Teatro S. Cassiano in 1657/58, for example (a year for which we have nightly attendance figures), Faustini would have paid off the loan on the fifth night; over the course of the season his income from this source would have been about 1,000 ducats, and the scagno supplier would have earned a little more than 300.

FINANCING OPERA, 2: INCOME FROM
THE PERFORMANCE

Once an opera (or comedy) had reached the stage, the most consistent income (aside from the season box rentals; see chap. 2) came from the sale of *bollettini* (entrance tickets), required of nearly all those who entered the theater (with the exception of proprietors and select others); from the rental of scagni, the seats in the parterre; and from the nightly rental of those boxes, usually in the highest, least desirable, row, not rented out for the season (see chap. 2). Receipts from bollettini almost always belonged to the impresario and his company, as did the profit from rental of scagni (see above), while that from the nightly box rental might come either to the company or to the impresario individually, as renter of the theater. This substantial income (see also chaps. 3 and 11), which usually went into a strongbox, first served to cover the nightly expenses (the orchestra members and other workers needed for each performance), and then the singers and other artisans and suppliers; some of the theater rental might also be paid in this manner.[38] At S. Luca during the 1662/63 season, for example, Vettor Grimani Calergi, who had stepped in to direct the preparations that year, made specific arrangements with Girolamo Barbieri (the impresario of record) to assure his reimbursement from the nightly expenses, and had them registered in the acts of a notary:

> Gerolemo Barberi . . . obligates and guarantees . . . to the Most Illustrious and Reverend Signor Abbot Vettor Grimani the rent from all of the palchi of that theater [S. Luca], and all of the money from the collection box that will be received every night at the door, and this until the said Most Illustrious and Reverend Signor Grimani will be completely reimbursed for that which might be necessary to spend in payment of the musicians, dancers, and instrumentalists, and for the operas that they are obliged to present this year. All of this money from the palchi and from the entrance fees must be placed in deposit in a collection box that will remain in care of Signor Carlo Morandi [one of Barbieri's partners, the *cassier* of the company], with two keys, one of which will be held by the said Most Illustrious and Reverend Signor Abbot, and the other by the said Signor Gerolimo. Once the said expenses of the singers, dancers, and instrumentalists have been satisfied for all of the time during which they shall perform, the remainder will belong to the said Signor Gerolimo.[39]

38 Irene Alm found papers (presented in her "Singer Goes to Court") concerning the expenses for a production at S. Moisè during the 1666/67 season. A number of singers were not paid, and one witness claimed that the noble protector, Andrea Mocenigo, took the strongbox home with him, and used the money to finance his son's trip to Brescia.

39 "Signor Gerolemo Barberi . . . obliga, et hippotheca . . . all'Illustrissimo et Reverendissimo Signor Abbate Vettor Grimani l'affitto di tutti li palchi d'esso teatro et tutti li dinari della cassetta che cadauna sera si riscuoterà alla porta, et ciò sino a tanto che detto Illustrissimo et Reverendissimo Signor Grimani sarà integralmente rimborsato di quanto egli occoresse spender in pagamento di musici, balarini, e sonatori, et per l'opere che doverano recitarsi il presente anno, dovendo tutti essi denari di palchi et della porta esser posto in deposito in una cassetta che doverà restar appresso il Signor Carlo Morandi con doi chiavi, una de' quali doverà esser tenuta dal detto Illustrissimo et Reverendissimo Signor Abbatte, et l'altra dal detto Signor Gerolemo, con quali dinari sodisfati prima le dette spese de musici, ballarini, et sonatori per tutto il tempo che si reciterano esse opere, il sopra più resterà poi per conto proprio di detto Signor Gerolemo." ASV, AN, Atti, b. 2989, ff. 828ᵛ–829, 2 Jan. 1662 m.v.

On the other hand, if, as mentioned above, loans had been obtained with the stipulation that the money had to be returned by the start of the season, the nightly income had to serve that purpose as well. A number of the loans mentioned above were secured in this fashion.

Other income was to be had from the selling of refreshments (the *scaleter*, who sold a sort of doughnut, and the *caneva*, for the sale of wine), although no documentation is extant on the amounts involved. For example, the incorporation agreement for S. Cassiano in 1657 specified that the income "that one extracts from the bollettini and the scagni will belong to the company; that of the palchi, the drinks, and the pastry seller will belong to Signor Faustini, as *padrone* of the theater."[40] While such income typically went to the renter of the theater, on at least one occasion, the 1663 rental of S. Luca to Barbieri, it remained with the owner, Andrea Vendramin.[41]

GUARANTEEING LOANS AND CONTRACTS:
THE PIEGGIO

As we will demonstrate below (see chap. 3), opera companies usually spent more money than they took in, so that, as with many speculative businesses, some sort of security was needed before people would lend money or sign contracts. A standard feature of many business contracts was the pieggio or guarantor, who agreed to step in in the event of nonpayment; the world of opera, not surprisingly, took advantage of this system. Impresarios often named guarantors in theater rental contracts, but they appeared in other sectors of the opera industry as well, for example in helping to secure the hiring of a top-rated singer, anxious for some assurance of payment beyond the word of the impresario. We shall see evidence of pieggi particularly in the case of the Teatro Novissimo, where Giovanni Penachin guaranteed the initial theater rental, and Josef Camis did so for the high salary of the diva, Anna Renzi, in 1643/44. Faustini himself acted as pieggio for the salary of the singer Amato Riminuzzi while S. Aponal was sublet in 1653/54 to Annibale Basso and Bortolo Castoreo, and Abbot Giuseppe Zanchi guaranteed Angelica Felice Curti's salary at the same theater in the successive season.[42] The practice was most probably more widespread in the opera industry than has so far been revealed in the extant documents; guarantors undoubtedly provided the underpinning of much of the security necessary to sustain the opera business, and in the case of insufficient capital, they helped to spread opera debts among the community, thus fostering the continuing development of the genre.

40 "che si caverà de' bollettini et scagni essere della compagnia; quello de' palchi, caneva et scaletaro di detto Signor Faustini, come padrone del theatro." ASV, SGSM, b. 194, f. 24ᵛ. When Francesco Tron rented S. Cassiano to Rocco Maestri and Bortolo Castoreo in 1648, however, the income from the drinks belonged to the theater owner.

41 ASV, AN, Atti, b. 2991, 11 Sept. 1663.

42 For Riminuzzi, see ASV, SGSM, b. 118, receipt book, f. 4ᵛ. For Curti, see ASV, SGSM, b. 113, account book 1654/55, ff. 43ᵛ–44. Several men acted as pieggio for the salary (1,500 ducats) of the prima donna Caterina Porri at S. Luca for the 1666/67 season (ASV, AN, Atti, b. 1166, f. 277, 4 Jan. 1666 m.v. and ASV, GP, b. 48, reg. 91, f. 97, 7 Jan. 1666 m.v.).

CHAPTER TWO

THE BOXES: A MAJOR SOURCE

OF INCOME

The box system made attending the opera attractive to a wealthy and aristo-cratic audience, offering not only choice seats at a popular entertainment, but also a chance to interact socially, both with other Venetians and with eminent for-eigners. Documents concerning opera boxes (palchi) in the papers of the impresa-rio Marco Faustini and, even more importantly, in notary archives, provide us with a multifaceted view of theatrical life of the city. They relay data not only about the audience, but also about the finances of the theater business, and about the role opera played in the social and financial world of seventeenth-century Venice (the social aspect of the box system will be covered in more detail in chap. 11). The sup-port of this segment of Venetian society, through an evolving system of rentals and purchases, made possible not only the functioning of opera companies on a day-by-day or season-by-season basis, but also the renovation and even construction of opera theaters.[1]

THE NATURE OF THE OPERA BOX
IN SEVENTEENTH-CENTURY VENICE

Neither ancient theaters nor Renaissance court theaters contained boxes; rather, they featured open seating, as the social structure of the audience was more or less uniform.[2] In Venice, however, theater construction with boxes opposite the stage (see figure 2.1, a diagram of the Teatro SS. Giovanni e Paolo from the 1690s) was the norm: open seating was not suitable for a public theater in the highly structured class system of Venice, where the nobility would have demanded an arrangement that al-

---

1 Opera boxes have attracted scholarly attention for some time. Remo Giazotto's documentary study of Venetian opera, "Guerra dei palchi," while examining the history of Venice's theaters in gen-eral, addressed the question of box rentals in particular, especially for the latter part of the seventeenth century. Giazotto published a number of notarial documents concerning palchi in his article; our study continues his efforts in that direction, drawing on a wider sample. Bianconi and Walker, in their "Pro-duction, Consumption," with reference to Ivanovich's *Memorie teatrali*, pointed to the box system as the Venetians' key to success in building theaters (222–23).

2 See *NGO*, s.v. "Seating," by Edward A. Langhans.

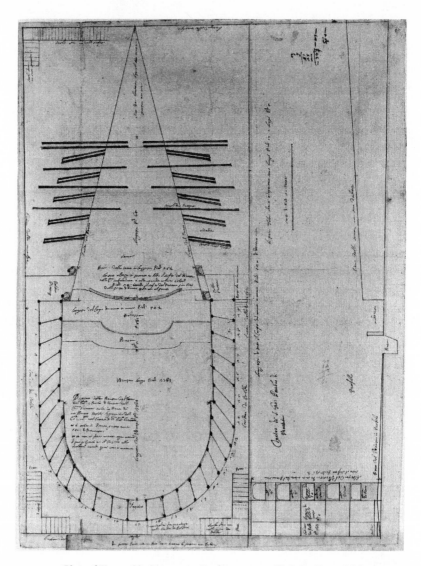

FIGURE 2.1.   Plan of Teatro SS. Giovanni e Paolo, ca. 1690 (Sir John Soane's Museum, London)

lowed for the option of separation from the more ordinary public. Boxes came into existence in the late sixteenth century, perhaps—as Eugene Johnson has suggested—in imitation of the balconies in the palace courtyards or public squares that had served as places to observe civic and private ceremonies and celebrations.[3] Sixteenth-century sources attest to palchi in the Teatro S. Cassiano (and the fact that

3 Johnson, "Jacopo Sansovino, Giacomo Torelli," 447, and Johnson, "Short, Lascivious Lives," 945–46.

nobles were renting them), as do documents regarding the Teatro S. Luca during the 1620s.[4] All of the theaters presenting the earliest operas in Venice, as well as the Teatro Novissimo, Venice's first newly-built opera theater, featured palchi.[5]

Private boxes offered those who could obtain them not only a guaranteed seat, one physically separate from and above the general crowd, but also a different sort of social evening than that afforded to those who sat in the parterre. The entertainment on stage was only one of several reasons for attending the opera: part of the theatrical experience centered on seeing and being seen by other members of the audience, activities facilitated by the shape and structure of theaters and boxes. Indeed, one might view each box as a sort of miniature stage on a small scale (after all, the shape of each box, viewed from outside, mirrored that of the proscenium), placing the distinguished occupants on view to at least part of the audience. Despite this visibility, however, guests could still be entertained, and conversations conducted with a degree of privacy.[6]

The construction of seventeenth-century opera theaters facilitated all of these goals. The basic shape was not the classical semicircle of ancient theaters (recreated more recently by Palladio in the Teatro Olimpico in Vicenza), but rather a "U."[7] The slightly raked parterre section, with temporary seats all facing the stage, was surrounded on three sides (the fourth being the stage) by superimposed balconies divided into separate compartments that could be accessed through corridors along the outside walls. The particular shape of the theater, and its rows of boxes, served several functions. The boxes opposite the stage, if somewhat distant from the proscenium in a large theater (about 55 feet to the front of the stage at the Teatro SS. Giovanni e Paolo[8]), provided the best views of the scenery. The remainder of

4 On palchi at the Teatro Michiel and Teatro Tron, both at S. Cassiano, in the late sixteenth century, see Mancini, Muraro, and Povoledo, *Teatri di Venezia*, 1:93–95 and 166–67, and Johnson, "Short, Lascivious Lives." For palchi at Teatro S. Luca in the 1620s, see Mancini, Muraro, and Povoledo, *Teatri di Venezia*, 1:222 and 261–62.

5 Some scholars have argued that Venetian theaters did not have boxes in their early years. See, for example, Pirrotta, "Theater, Sets," 262–65, especially regarding S. Moisè. A document of 1642, however, refers to palchi in that theater (ASV, AN, Atti, b. 8504, f. 8, 27 March 1642). Mangini (*Teatri di Venezia*, 63, n. 4) wrote that the Novissimo, unlike other Venetian theaters, lacked boxes, although surviving documentation, for example the October 1640 rental agreement, speaks to their presence, as recognized by Benedetti ("Teatro musicale a Venezia," 201) and Mancini, Muraro, Povoledo (*Teatri di Venezia*, 1:329). Di Luca's suggestion ("Tra 'sperimentazione' e 'professionismo'," 280–81) that the temporary structure built in Padua in 1639 by Alfonso Rivarola, il Chenda, was one of the first theaters to employ boxes, cannot be sustained in light of the Venetian documentation.

6 On opera seating in general, see *NGO*, s.v. "Sociology of Opera," by John Rosselli, and "Seating," by Edward A. Langhans. On masking at the theater, see chapter 11.

7 This is the early form of the "teatro all'italiana"; only at the end of the century did the more famous and longer-lasting form emerge, employing the horseshoe shape with the sides converging as they approached the stage, so that the facades of many of the boxes actually faced slightly away from the stage.

8 These and the following measurements, and those of the palchi below, are derived from the plan of the Teatro SS. Giovanni e Paolo in Sir John Soane's Museum in London (figure 2.1). The measurements given here are the modern equivalents of the old Venetian ones. The comparable distance at the late eighteenth-century Teatro La Fenice is about 70 feet (Mancini, Muraro, and Povoledo, *Teatri di Venezia*, 2:185), and at the Metropolitan Opera in New York, about 110 feet (Mayer, *The Met*, 300).

the boxes had poorer sightlines, especially those closest to the proscenium. Much of the illusion of the scenery, designed in perspective through consecutively spaced flats, was probably lost to occupants of those lateral boxes (and they could probably see directly backstage into the side wings), the compensation being, of course, close proximity to the singers. On the other hand, most of the patrons could see one another well: the sightlines to the other boxes were quite good, with many of them facing each other directly from a relatively close distance (at SS. Giovanni e Paolo, reputedly one of the largest theaters, the width was just over 40 feet). Those seated closest to the stage were the most visible of all.[9]

The individual palchi varied in size and shape depending not only on the theater, but on the location within the theater, so that precise measurements are hard to come by. The plan of SS. Giovanni e Paolo (figure 2.1) shows boxes about $4\frac{1}{2}$ feet wide at the front, narrowing in some parts of the "U" to 4 feet at the rear of the box. They varied in depth from less than 6 feet for the center box, to over 10 where the curved section meets the straight arms. The rows of boxes were separated vertically by 8 feet, leaving an interior height of probably about 7 feet. The palco rented at S. Luca in 1681 by the nobleman Pietro Zenobio was about the same size: approximately 5 feet wide, in both front and back, 11 feet long, and 7 feet high.[10] As the size of the boxes varied, so did their capacity, although once again, anecdotal evidence is rare. In 1652, the French ambassador complained loudly to the Doge when his box underwent changes after the rebuilding of the Teatro S. Luca following a fire: "the previous year . . . four people could sit in the front, and another four in back, that is, eight in all. Now it has been reduced by half, whereby only four people can fit in."[11] Those two figures, four and eight, probably represent the extremes.[12]

In most cases the boxes were provided unfurnished, and the renters would supply seats and decorations to their own taste. The Duke of Brunswick's agent made this clear in 1673 when writing about his employer's palco in S. Luca: "Because it would be too visible—and misunderstood—to leave such a conspicuous palco without tasteful decorative panels as well as all the accessories and appurtenances, I will fix it up from top to bottom, just like the one opposite [occupied by] the Most Excellent Bembo, unless you command me otherwise."[13] Legal documents

---

9 Much later, at the end of the eighteenth century, the position of the box determined its cost. When the Teatro La Fenice was contructed, the stage boxes and the center box in the pepian and first order were the most expensive, followed by the equivalent ones in the second order. Next in price were the remaining boxes in the pepian, first, and second orders, and then those in the third and fourth. See Bauman, "Society of La Fenice," 334–36.

10 ASV, AN, Atti, b. 1186, f. 186ᵛ, 2 Aug. 1681.

11 "l'anno passato . . . vi capivano quattro persone di prima fronte, et altre quattro doppo di quelle, in tutte otto; al presente mi è stato restretto per la metà, onde non ne capisse più di quattro in tutto." ASV, Collegio, Esposizioni principi, reg. 63, f. 36, 21 Dec. 1653.

12 Talbot ("Venetian Opera Contract," 40–41), reasoning from the way ownership of individual palchi in Teatro S. Angelo in the early eighteenth century was often divided among several patrons, arrives at a standard capacity of six.

13 "Perché, però, sarebbe troppo osservabile, e mal inteso, il lasciar palco così cospicuo senz'esser foderato di polite tavole, con tutte le sue abentie e pertinentie, io glielo farò agiustare di tutto punto,

concerning palchi almost never refer to decorations or furnishings,[14] with the exception of a few special cases in the 1680s, in which they were to be furnished to the acquirer "covered with panelling, with a door, and its seats, all done in good and praiseworthy fashion."[15]

The rows of boxes (known as *ordini*) varied in number from theater to theater (see table 2.1). The first numbered order began just above the level of the orchestra seats, but some theaters had an additional order, the *pepian* (Venetian for ground floor), just beneath it. The top row might also go unnumbered, called, instead, the *soffitto*, or attic. At mid-century S. Aponal, the smallest theater, had three orders, S. Moisè four or five, and both S. Luca and SS. Giovanni e Paolo featured a pepian and five numbered orders.[16] Within each order, the palchi were numbered (the numbers probably appeared on the lockable doors leading to each box from the corridors that encircled the theater at each level, providing access for the patrons, who held the keys), usually beginning on the left (facing the stage) and proceeding counterclockwise. Later in the century, theater reconstruction sometimes resulted in new palchi that were assigned letters (and on even rarer occasions, names) rather than numbers, so that the preexisting boxes (or at least boxes in approximately the same positions in the order) would keep their original numbers. This probably kept long-standing boxholders happy, since they would be less likely to feel displaced if the number remained the same; for the theater owners and

---

come appunto è quello dirimpetto dell'Eccellentissimo Bembo, se però non comandasse in contrario." HVsa, AK, Cal. Br. 22, vol. 2, no. 625, f. 456ᵛ, letter of Pietro Dolfin to Johann Friedrich, Duke of Brunswick, 1673. Other parts of the letter are transcribed in Rosand, *Opera*, App. III, n. 20, p. 444. We are grateful to Ellen Rosand for sharing her films of this valuable collection of letters with us.

14 While eighteenth-century decrees of the Provveditori sopra le pompe, the Venetian magistracy concerned with enforcing sumptuary laws, indicate that boxes could not be elaborately decorated (specifically outlawed were ornamental carpets, elaborate lamps, and fancy cushions; see Bistort, *Magistrato alle pompe*, 233), such restrictions do not seem to have been enacted in the mid-seventeenth century. A 1711 decree on this subject refers to one of 1661 (see Becker, *Quellentexte*, 73), but the magistracy's own records include nothing from that date; the reference may be to a more general regulation on sumptuary issues from 1661, to which rules about palchi were later added.

15 "fodrato di taole pianate, con porta e sue banche, il tutto aggiustato in buona e laudabil forma." ASV, AN, Atti, b. 8873, f. 107ᵛ, 22 July 1684.

16 A document of 1642 regarding palchi in S. Moisè lists four above ground level ("in soler") (ASV, AN, Atti, b. 8504, f. 9, 27 Mar. 1642), as does one of 1655 (ASV, AN, Atti, b. 12045, f. 123ᵛ). Documents from 1665 and 1666 refer also to a "piè pian" (ASV, AN, Atti, b. 8475, f. 175ᵛ, 24 Sept. 1665). Philip Skippon (*Journey*, 506) referred to SS. Giovanni e Paolo as having seven levels, and modern scholars have accepted his description at face value. Faustini's records, however, contain a sheet written by him that lists the boxes of the uppermost order of an unspecified theater, in our view SS. Giovanni e Paolo, labeled simply "quint'ordine" (ASV, SGSM, b. 194, f. 18). Rosand (after Giazotto, and Bianconi and Walker) identified the sheet as referring to the boxes of S. Cassiano (*Opera*, 80, n. 39). However, the box assigned to "Franceschi" (Gabriel Angelo Franceschi, the Grimani agent) and the two labeled "per la casa" provide specific links to the Faustini's contract with the Grimanis (see chap. 3). The assignment of two other boxes to Aureli (the librettist) and to Giovanni Maria Savioni (the man Pietro Andrea Ziani authorized to handle his business affairs during his sojourn in Vienna) point to Faustini's theatrical affairs in the 1660s, rather than the 1650s. The accounting of those boxes in the fifth order suggests that S. Luca and SS. Giovanni e Paolo had the same number of orders (the fifth order presumably referred to the fifth level above the pepian). For more on seating at SS. Giovanni e Paolo, see chapter 11.

TABLE 2.1.   The Number of Palchi in Venetian Theaters

Theater	Ordini	Palchi in each ordine	Total palchi
S. Aponal (1650s)[a]	1, 2, 3	16	48
S. Cassiano (before 1657)	Pepian	29	153
	1, 2, 3, 4	31	
SS. Giovanni e Paolo (1660s)	Pepian, 1, 2, 3, 4	29	ca. 145
SS. Giovanni e Paolo (ca. 1690)[b]	Pepian	30	154
	1, 2, 3, 4	31	
SS. Giovanni Grisostomo (1680s)	Pepian	ca. 32	ca. 198
	1, 2, 3, 4	ca. 34	
S. Luca (1653)[c]	Pepian	21	166
	1, 2, 3, 4, soffitto	29	
S. Luca (1687)[d]	Pepian	ca. 29	ca. 194
	1, 2, 3, 4, soffitto	ca. 33	
S. Moisè	Pepian, 1, 2, 3	ca. 27	ca. 106
S. Samuele (1688)	Pepian, 1, 2, 3	ca. 36	ca. 140

This table does not attempt to include all of the alterations in the number and arrangement of boxes in these theaters, but only a representative sample. When a single document provides the count, it is indicated here. In other cases, the estimate is based on a variety of pieces of evidence. For other attempts to calculate the number of boxes see Alm, "Theatrical Dance," 280, and Mancini, Muraro, and Povoledo, *Teatri di Venezia*.
[a] ASV, SGSM, b. 194.
[b] See figure 2.1.
[c] ASV, AN, Atti, b. 1083, f. 148[V].
[d] ASV, AN, Atti, b. 8878, f. 113.

renters, the practice simplified the tracking of debts (and, later, matters regarding ownership).

Several scholars have furnished palco counts for Venetian theaters during the seventeenth century,[17] but arriving at a precise figure presents a problem, as various waves of theater reconstruction often changed the number and size of boxes (as referred to above). One of the most exact lists survives in Faustini's papers from S. Aponal: each order contained sixteen palchi (numbered from 0 to 15), amounting to forty-eight boxes in all.[18] By 1665 the number had apparently risen to fifty-seven, still, however, a small number in comparison with the other theaters.[19] An-

17 The most recent attempt at enumerating boxes can be found in Mancini, Muraro, and Povoledo, *Teatri di Venezia*; for the theaters under consideration here: S. Cassian, 1:97; S. Moisè, 1:155; S. Luca, 1:209; SS. Giovanni e Paolo, 1:294; S. Aponal, 1:362; S. Samuele, 1:379; S. Angelo, 2:3; and S. Giovanni Grisostomo, 2:63. See also Rosand, *Opera*, 80 and 392, and Alm, "Theatrical Dance," 280.

18 Faustini's records of the boxes at S. Aponal are found in ASV, SGSM, b. 194, ff. 92–102. On the individuals who rented these boxes, see chapter 11.

19 ASV, Monastero di SS. Giovanni e Paolo, b. XXV. This document is discussed in Glixon and Glixon, "Oil and Opera." There may well have been sixty boxes in all, with three reserved for the owner or impresario, and therefore not income-producing.

other precise count of a theater's boxes comes from S. Luca around the time of Carnival 1654, when the joint renters, Cristoforo Boldù and Caterina Zane, specified twenty-nine for each of the four orders and the soffitto, with only twenty-one for the pepian.[20] These numbers point to a total of 166 boxes, or more than three times the number in S. Aponal. As table 2.1 shows, SS. Giovanni e Paolo was similar in size to S. Luca, with S. Cassiano and S. Samuele a bit smaller. When S. Giovanni Grisostomo opened for the 1677/78 season, it set a new standard for capacity, with nearly two hundred boxes, a size then matched at S. Luca after two expansions in the 1680s.

REBUILDING AND REARRANGING PALCHI
AT S. LUCA: A CASE STUDY

The rebuilding and rearranging of palchi often served one of two opposing goals: either an increase in number to allow for additional income, or, conversely, a reduction that permitted a few more commodious boxes; in both cases the overall number of spectators able to view the performances would have remained more or less the same. Alternatively, boxes might be removed to allow for an enlargement of the stage. The process is best documented for the Teatro S. Luca. Around 1662, the theater's tenants made some sort of alteration, the nature of which is unclear, which was then reversed by order of Andrea Vendramin, the owner.[21] In 1674, another tenant, the nobleman Francesco Bembo, agreed to "to alter the theater to make it suitable for opera, removing two boxes on each side [in each order], and thus rebuilding in a noble manner the proscenium, pit, stage, and everything necessary so that the wings, ceiling flats, and backdrops can move easily."[22]

Bembo's changes reduced the number of boxes in the theater by twenty-four, but much more was to follow in the 1680s. Gasparo Torelli, who rented the theater in March of 1681, had immediate plans for construction. The contract between him and Zanetta Vendramin states that he wished to "raise the [ceilings of the] palchi at the floor level as well as those at the top."[23] He also added new boxes over the stage, between the columns at the proscenium.[24] One of the new stage boxes on the pepian, occupied by Count Zenobio, was then enlarged in 1683, when the nobleman asked that the Vendramins remove an access stair to the

---

20 ASV, AN, Atti, b. 1083, f. 150, 29 Jan. 1653 m.v. The smaller number of boxes in the pepian allowed for entrances to the parterre seating. Mancini, Muraro, and Povoledo, *Teatri di Venezia*, 1:209, lists twenty-eight palchi in the pepian for 1653 and before, rather than the twenty-one specified by Zane and Boldù (and by Mangini, *Teatri di Venezia*, 51).

21 ASV, AN, Atti, b. 2987, f. 1158, 11 Jan. 1661 m.v.

22 "Che detto Eccellentissimo Bembo sia obligato ridurre il teatro a commodo uso d'opera, facendo levare due mani di palchetti per parte rifacendo nobilmente il prosennio, orchestra, pavimento, e tutto quello che occore per far ben caminar le sene, cieli, e prospetti." ASV, AN, Atti, b. 6796, f. 115ᵛ, 17 May 1674.

23 "alzare li palchi a pepiano, et alzare l'ordine della soffitta" (Vcg, Archivio Vendramin, 42 F 16/1, ff. 14–16); document transcribed in Mancini, Muraro, and Povoledo, *Teatri di Venezia*, 1:266.

24 ASV, AN, Atti, b. 1186, f. 185, 31 May 1681, refers to a newly built proscenium box numbered "one"; f. 266, 19 Aug. 1681, refers to a similar one numbered "thirty-two."

stage.[25] Torelli's improvements continued. In 1684, in a new rental agreement with the Vendramin family, he declared that he wanted to "rebuild the palchi with gilded stucchi" and, in the process, "add two palchi per order, one on each side, from the pepian to the soffitto."[26] This time, the new palchi were not added at the stage, but were created by remaking the entire row of boxes (probably excepting the proscenium boxes), decreasing the size of each one slightly.[27] In effect, with the reconstructions of 1681 and 1684, Torelli replaced the boxes that Bembo had removed (that is two on each side in each order), raising the number in the upper orders to thirty-five, for a total of about two hundred.

The discretionary power of the impresario or theater renter to reconstruct and change the size of the boxes could provoke anger and frustration from the box-holders. The documented controversies all involve distinguished foreigners; perhaps disputes with locals were resolved more amicably or through private channels. We saw earlier how the French ambassador complained when the size of his box was reduced. Owing to the changes mentioned above, Johann Friedrich, Duke of Brunswick, ran into problems with his palco at S. Luca at least twice, in part because he preferred to be close to the singers: the stage boxes were among those most likely to be affected by changes because they were so easily altered, not being hemmed in by others. The Duke's agent wrote to him in 1674 with news of Bembo's changes: "it seems certain that Your Serene Highness's palco will be demolished, as well as the neighboring one, because in order to perform [the] operas it is necessary to enlarge the stage. I have informed Signor Pietro Dolfino that Your Serene Highness should either be reimbursed for the 50 doble you have paid, or you should be given another similar palco in the first order."[28] The Duke, who had two boxes, seems to have been successful in retaining the box closest to the stage, but protested personally in 1681 when Torelli initiated his reconstruction. The

25 The box had been measured in 1681 as 4'10" wide and 10'4" long, and was now 4 feet longer and widened to 6 feet at the back. ASV, AN, Atti, b. 1186, f. 186^v, 2 Aug. 1681.

26 "refabricare li palchi, farli con stucchi dorati, . . . aneter due palchi per ordine, uno per parte, principiando dal pepian sino alla soffitta."Vcg, Archivio Vendramin, 42 F 16/1 (document transcribed in Mancini, Muraro, and Povoledo, *Teatri di Venezia*, 1:267).

27 To avoid renumbering the palchi and thus confusing the issue of which box belonged to whom, the new ones were considered to have been inserted adjacent to box 8 on one side, and box 23 on the other. Since these new boxes were outside the regular numbering scheme, those who first aquired one were, unusually, given the right to "place on it whatever number, inscription, or sign that seems most suitable" (di ponervi qual numero, inscription, ò segno, che più li parerà). ASV, AN, Atti, b. 8873, f. 107^v, 22 July 1684. Most were assigned letters at the end of the alphabet, but Chiara Grimani, the occupant of the one adjacent to number 23 in the first order, chose to mark hers with an eagle (ibid., f. 89^v, 28 June 1684). The possession of a palco by a woman, while in earlier decades quite rare, was by the 1680s no longer unusual. Since palchi were now treated much like property, widows often inherited them from their deceased husbands.

28 "Quanto al Theatro di San Salvador, certo è che si deve guastare il palco di Vostra Altezza Serenissima et il contiguo al medemo, per che per far opere bisogna allargare il proscenio. Ho motivato al Signor Pietro Dolfino, che Vostra Altezza Serenissima deve, ò esser rimborsata delle dobole 50 ò pure, che le sia dato un altro simil palco in prim'ordine, conforme alla promissione della scrittura; starò a vedere che cosa risolveranno di fare." HVsa, AK, Cal. Br. 22, vol. 4, no. 627, f. 563^v, 6 Apr. 1674.

Duke's complaints were specific: his box near the stage was no longer the closest to the performers, but was now the second in the row, while another valued for its size (and therefore its ability to accommodate greater numbers of guests) had been made smaller. He threatened legal action if his rights (and his palchi) were not preserved "in their original state."[29]

One of the motivating forces behind modifications to the box structure went beyond the simple question of income from the boxes themselves; rather, the evolution of the boxes within one theater may have sparked changes in another. In 1663 Elena Gonzaga, the sister-in-law of Giovanni Grimani, moved forward with renovations to SS. Giovanni e Paolo that the late theater owner had set in motion as early as 1659. Changes to the structure of the building and its surrounding areas required the permission of Francesco Morosini, whose property adjoined that of the theater. Among other things (in part also because Morosini's old palco was no longer available), Gonzaga promised Morosini that she would construct two proscenium boxes "similar to those that have been made in the Teatro S. Luca," one of which Morosini would choose as his own.[30] Morosini, then, found himself in an unusual moment of power: the Grimanis' renovations hinged on changes to property that only he could approve, and as a result he gained immediate access to a new, desirable palco in Venice's premier theater. The growing culture of opera attendance, then, served as a constant stimulant or catalyst, as various nobles vied for desirable boxes, and the theater owners and managers sought to cater to and anticipate demand.

THE DESTINATION OF THE BOX INCOME: OWNER OR IMPRESARIO?

The boxes provided either the theater owner or the impresario with a large amount of capital. Ivanovich spoke of them as the theater's most secure form of income: "The most certain profit for each theater consists of the box rents. These number at least one hundred, divided in several orders, plus the attics. They do not all have the same price, depending on the order and the number, which improves the site of the same."[31] The recipient of the box rental income varied from theater to theater, and from contract to contract. Generally, if the theater owner rented the building to a company or impresario, nearly all of the box rentals would go to the tenant (with a small number of palchi reserved for the owner's use), for the

29 The Duke's letter, dated Hannover, 12 Sept. 1681, was presented to the notary Francesco Simbeni in December, along with a complaint by the Duke's agent, Giovanni Druyvesteyn (ASV, AN, Atti, b. 12145, 17 Dec. 1681).

30 "et s'obliga detta gentildona di far formar nell'proscenio a guisa, e similitudine di quelli sono fabricati nell'Theatro in San Luca due palchi, uno de' quali a elettione di detto N.H. Morosini sij, et s'intendi di ragione sua senz'alcuna contraditione." ASV, AN, Atti, b. 3500, 29 May 1663, f. 284.

31 "Il più certo utile, che ha ogni Teatro, consiste negli affitti de' Palchetti. Questi sono almeno in numero di cento, oltre le soffitte compartite in più ordini, e non tutti anno lo stesso prezzo, mentre questo si considera dall'ordine, e dal numero, che migliora il sito de' medemi." Ivanovich, *Memorie teatrali*, 401–2.

proprietor usually received a large sum, often as much as 1,000 ducats, in rent.[32] Faustini's rental of S. Cassiano in 1657 represents a typical arrangement between proprietor and tenant: Faustini paid a rent of 840 ducats, balanced by the income from all of the boxes save the six belonging to the owners.[33] At S. Aponal, as well, Faustini took control of the palchi (and maintained copies of the records); in other words, the theater owners ceded their control of that part of the business to the impresario.

Before drawing up a contract, the theater owner and impresario would have determined a sort of formula, balancing the possible incomes either from the rental of the theater itself, or from the rental of the boxes; sometimes the result differed significantly from the model described above. At S. Cassiano in 1648 the owner, Francesco Tron, was to receive the rents from all of the palchi except for five assigned to the impresarios Rocco Maestri and Bortolamio Castoreo (see chap. 4, S. Cassiano). In compensation for the loss of the box income, Maestri and Castoreo paid a reduced rental fee, with a set amount disbursed on each night of the performance. A variation on this theme obtained at the Grimani theater during the mid-1660s: Faustini's contract of 1665 reveals no responsibilities for rent; the Grimani brothers paid a set fee to the impresario, and kept all of the palco monies except for the top level, which went to Faustini.[34] The opera boxes apparently remained under the domain of the Grimanis, and eighteenth-century inventories of the family's holdings list palchi registers among the theatrical items.[35] Undoubtedly other strategies were practiced at the various theaters throughout the years.

The size of the income available either to the owner or tenant necessarily hinged on the cost of each box, and on the eventual payment of the fees. Ivanovich mentioned the variety of prices for the boxes: those in the pepian and the soffitto—the highest and lowest regions—usually cost less than those in the more prized locations. During Faustini's period of activity the rate for a standard palco was typically 20 or 25 ducats (later in the century, with the opening of the luxurious S. Giovanni Grisostomo, the fees would increase substantially, to as high as 50 ducats). A clause in the rental contract for S. Luca in November 1660 makes it clear that the price of a palco was inherently flexible and subject to change: "All the palchi and their rents should be, and are intended to be, the property of the Most Illustrious Boldù, the renter; he may rent them, or 'unrent' them to whom he wishes, increasing or decreasing the price as he pleases, without the interference

---

32 For comedy theaters it would seem essential that the tenant receive the bulk of the box rentals, as the nightly income was traditionally the property of the actors, not the impresario. See Ivanovich, *Memorie teatrali*, 410. Ivanovich's statement is confirmed by the extant documentation. For example, the 1622 contract for the Accesi to perform the following carnival at S. Luca makes this arrangement clear (Vcg, Archivio Vendramin, 42 F 16/4; document transcribed in Mancini, Muraro, and Povoledo, *Teatri di Venezia*, 1:261), and it is implied in the 1625 arrangement for a company to perform at S. Moisè (Venice, Archivio Giustinian Recanati, Misc. IV n.1; document transcribed in Mancini, Muraro, and Povoledo, *Teatri di Venezia* 1:185).

33 In Faustini's company the box rental fees went to him alone, rather than to the company as a whole. See chapter 3 and Bianconi and Walker, "Production, Consumption," 222–23.

34 ASV, SGSM, b. 194, f. 134, 23 Feb. 1664 m.v. See chapter 3.

35 ASV, GP, Inventari, b. 411.

of the Most Illustrious Vendramin."[36] This practice is confirmed by Ivanovich: "an annual rent is agreed upon, and this happens every year in which the theater presents performances, and not otherwise, and this payment is based [on the one hand] on the expenses budgeted by the theater, [and on the other] on the value [of the particular box] to the renter."[37] Boldù may have had the right to set his own rates, but when he eventually raised the annual fee to 30 ducats he met with opposition from the boxholders: one of them responded that he had no intention of paying such high fees, and later notices bore the more typical amount of 25 ducats.[38] The nobles, then, willingly supported the opera trade through the rental of the boxes, but they could at times balk when they viewed the charges as excessive.

BOX INCOME AS FUNDING FOR BUILDING AND RENOVATION

The box fees on occasion served the theater owner or tenant in a far different manner: they funded construction costs. In the 1650s two projects demonstrate this process.

The Teatro S. Luca was destroyed by a fire in November 1652,[39] and the following summer the owner was well on his way to ensuring its return to operation. On 28 June 1653 Andrea Vendramin drew up a new contract with Cristoforo Boldù and Caterina Zane, who had previously rented the theater jointly. According to the agreement, the responsibility for rebuilding the theater fell on their shoulders, not Vendramin's, although half of the usual rent (500 ducats) would be credited towards their expenses.[40] Some six months later, Boldù approached "his" box holders (that is, half of those available to the two tenants); in order to speed the reconstruction of the theater, he increased the fees by 5 ducats, to 25 ducats per year, and asked that the boxholders pay two years' rent in advance.[41] Compliance with this request certainly would have accumulated a large amount of capital: even ten positive responses would have surpassed the 500-ducat "credit" allowed by Vendramin for the reconstruction of the theater. The notice stated that the boxholders had three days to re-

36 "Tutti li palchi, et affitti loro siano, et s'intendano di propria ragione dell'Illustrissimo Boldù conduttore, per poter quelli affittarli e desaffittarli a chi più a lui piacerà, con accrescere et sminuire il prezzo come li piace, senz'alcuna ingerenza dell'Illustrissimo Vendramin." ASV, AN, Atti, b. 2983, f. 1113, 13 Nov. 1660 (published in Mancini, Muraro, and Povoledo, *Teatri di Venezia*, 1:263–64).

37 "Si conviene in un affitto annuale, e si passa ogni volta, che in quell'anno fa recitar il Teatro, non altrimenti venendo fatto questo pagamento in riguardo della spesa, che impiega il Teatro, e del comodo, che riceve chi lo tiene ad affitto." Ivanovich, *Memorie teatrali*, 402.

38 ASV, AN, Atti, b. 700, f. 406, 11 Apr. 1661. Boldù had undoubtedly raised the rate to help recoup the losses resulting from the disastrous first opera season at S. Luca. See chapter 4, S. Luca. For Boldù's notice, see ASV, AN, Atti, b. 2892, f. 7, 7 Apr. 1661.

39 An investigation by the Council of Ten did not reach a definitive conclusion as to whether the fire at S. Luca occurred through accident or through arson (ASV, CD, Criminal, filza 84, 17 Dec. 1652).

40 ASV, AN, Atti, b. 679, f. 256, 28 June 1653.

41 The notice was sent by Boldù and by another nobleman, Lunardo Bernardo, who may have been an investor (ASV, AN, Atti, b. 5484, f. 96, 12 Dec. 1653). It is likely that Zane did the same for her half of the palchi.

spond; otherwise, the boxes would be rented to others. The theater was, indeed, rebuilt, presumably with the help of these extra payments.[42]

For the reconstruction of S. Cassiano in 1657 (see chaps. 3 and 4), Faustini had a different strategy: he requested that the boxholders pay their fees six months in advance.[43] The practice of a "double fee" (or in Faustini's case, an advance payment) serving as an investment toward the construction of a theater may well have been standard, but it had its drawbacks. An advance payment was just that: having already been used for the construction or renovation of a theater, those funds would not available for the following season's operating budget, practically guaranteeing a substantial loss to the company.

THE EMERGENCE OF THE *REGALO* OR *DONATIVO*: THE BOXES AS PROPERTY

After describing the palchi, Ivanovich spoke of the special advantage the boxes held for one who wanted to build a theater: "Whoever wishes to build a theater, starts out by making use of two sources of income: the first, a "gift" [regallo] in money for each box, and this serves in large part for the expense of the construction. This is the principal reason that so many theaters have been built with such ease and rapidity."[44] The regalo (or donativo) was a fee paid to guarantee possession of a box in a particular theater; in practice, the regalo came to be used in already existing theaters as well as those in the construction phase. Ivanovich's statement, published during the 1680s, certainly reflects the procedures of the late 1670s, but not necessarily those of earlier decades; the chronology of this economic change regarding the palchi has largely been ignored in general descriptions of theatrical enterprise in Venice. Certainly, its origins are obscure: no specific law or ruling signalling the beginnings of the regalo has yet been located. Most likely this type of gift had existed for some time as a casual practice. Indeed, the rental contract between Andrea Vendramin and Antonio Boldù in 1660 alludes to the "regalo ò donativo," and to the fact that Boldù could not expect to receive one for an additional palco that Vendramin planned to rent.[45] Perhaps, at this time, such payments were asked or offered as a courtesy, and to ease the way when a desirable palco became available.

Several notarial documents from 1673 make reference to the regalo, and after that year even more occurrences can be found. The gift—which varied in its

---

42 Several years later Giovanni Grimani allowed for the use of a similar system when he drew up the rental contract for his new comedy theater, which had yet to be built (ASV, AN, Atti, b. 6059, ff. 29ᵛ–30, 4 Apr. 1656).

43 For example, ASV, AN, Atti, b. 10864, f. 122, 4 Jan. 1657 m.v., cited in Bianconi and Walker, "Production, Consumption," 223.

44 "Sogliono dal principio, che si vuol fabricare un Teatro, praticarsi due capi d'utilità, il primo un regallo in denaro per cadaun Palchetto, e questo serve in gran parte alla spesa della fabrica, e quella è stata la causa principale, che si siano fabricati piu Teatri con tanta facilità, e prestezza." Ivanovich, *Memorie teatrali*, 402.

45 For the contract, see Mancini, Muraro, and Povoledo, *Teatri di Venezia*, 1:264.

amount—endowed the boxholder with a right of ownership, and already in the mid-1670s opera boxes took on the attributes of nearly every other form of property (see below).[46] (The regalo, however, did not exempt the boxholder from the annual rental fee, which was paid in perpetuity in years when the theater presented operas or plays.) One of the earliest references is imprecise regarding the date of original purchase, implying only a transaction occurring around the carnival of 1673,[47] but clearer indication of the new system appears in the records of the Venier family compiled late in the eighteenth century.[48] A series of entries traces the family's ownership of boxes in two of the city's theaters to around that same date: they took possession of one at the comedy theater, S. Samuele, on 2 March 1673 and another at S. Luca on 30 July, each with a regalo of 150 ducats. Also telling is a document of 7 July 1673, in which Francesco Bembo authorized Giacomo Perini, the fattor, or general agent at S. Luca, to rent the boxes for the duration, fees, and donativo that he thought appropriate.[49]

Despite this conjunction of documents, the year 1673 does not stand out in any particular way in the theatrical history of Venice. Certainly, no new theaters were built that year, yet, with the codification of this new system the theaters, both comedy and opera, must have experienced a new injection of capital; most likely the practice began slowly, as certain boxes became available for rental. The institutionalization of the regalo probably stemmed from the increasing demand for boxes: it served to make box ownership even more exclusive, owing to the increase in the "start-up" costs from those of a pure rental to rental plus a significant surcharge. Just a few years later the system served a different purpose, making possible the construction—precisely in the manner described by Ivanovich—of two new opera theaters, S. Angelo (1676) and S. Giovanni Grisostomo (1677).

With the institution of the regalo, the practice of families sharing boxes became even more common, with each party responsible for only half of the regalo, and half of the annual rent. Along with this division came the problem of who would enjoy the right to attend the premiere of an opera; this issue was often addressed officially, forming one part of a notarial document or *scrittura privata* celebrating the transfer of the palco.

While the regalo and the annual rental fees represented the chief financial benefits of the palchi to the theater owner or tenant, the boxes could serve a dif-

---

46 See the discussions of palchi in Mancini, Muraro, and Povoledo, *Teatri di Venezia*, 2:ix–xii, and Giazotto, "Guerra dei palchi." The focus in both of these is more on the late seventeenth and early eighteenth centuries, when the practice of the regalo was universal.

47 The transfer of a palco on 10 Dec. 1673 from Ottavian Malipiero to Marquis Guido Rangoni mentions Malipiero's purchase (rather than rental) of the box from the Grimanis "last year" (l'anno passato), probably during Jan. or Feb. 1673, that is, near the end of the previous carnival season (ASV, AN, Atti, b. 736, 3 Aug. 1674).

48 Vmc, Codice P. D. Venier 124, Tomo 1, ff. 379ᵛ–386.

49 ASV, AN, Atti, b. 3542, f. 237, 7 July 1673. This type of authorization—to set duration and cost of a rental—was quite common, but the appearance here of the "donativo" is novel. Since the term "duration" seems to conflict with the idea of a donativo granting rights in perpetuity, the phrase may be evidence of novelty of the situation.

ferent financial purpose: as security for a loan. In these cases, the palco, usually fully furnished (unlike the normal situation), was ceded for a specific period for a set fee, such as 1,000 ducats. That fee served as a loan to be paid back at the end of the period. During that time the "purchaser" could either make use of the palco, sub-let it, or transfer it to someone else, with whatever use or income he gained serving in place of interest on his loan.[50]

THE COLLECTING OF BOX FEES: THE AGENT

As mentioned above, most boxes were rented for the entire season or year, with the annual rent usually due by the end of carnival; indeed, the right to keep a box from season to season hinged, hypothetically, on the timely payment of the fees. A number of renters, however, no matter how wealthy, often failed to pay on time. Each theater employed an agent, the fattor, who assumed the responsibility of collecting the box fees (among other duties regarding the theater).

Working under the authority of either the owner or the impresario, the fattor enjoyed the right to pursue legal actions when the fees were not forthcoming. These men came from a variety of backgrounds, and in some cases already had some connection with the theater before taking on this responsibility. The wood-workers Iseppo Fassetta and Paulo Morandi became fattori for theaters such as S. Moisè, S. Cassiano, and S. Luca: their entrée into the job may have come as suppliers of the scagni, or benches, for the theater.[51] S. Luca's fattori in the 1650s and 1660s included Iseppo's relative Pietro Fassetta, also a woodworker, and Iseppo de Mio, a tailor; they too may have worked at the theater originally as artisans.[52] Camillo di Piccoli, the fattor at S. Moisè in the 1660s, was listed in a later document as a maker or dealer in false pearls, often used in costuming.[53] Regarding their earnings, one source suggests that the fattor benefited from gratuities from the boxholders rather than from the owner or impresario: the Duke of Brunswick's agent, Francesco Maria Massi, who oversaw the Duke's numerous palchi, mentioned, after paying the rental for two of them, that a tip of one ongaro (about 15 lire) was customary.[54] At S. Samuele in 1656, on the other hand, the rental contract

---

50 The Grimanis rented out a number of palchi in this manner in the 1670s and 1680s (for example, ASV, AN, Atti, b. 6110, f. 116ᵛ, 16 Feb. 1677 m.v. and b. 6111, f. 84, 21 Aug. 1679). The identical procedure can be seen during the next century with the purchase of several palchi by the singer Anna Girò in the 1740s; see Vio, "Anna Girò."

51 Both Fassetta and Morandi became involved in theatrical life in other ways, although this must not have been true of all who held the post. On Morandi, see chapters 3 and 10. See also chapter 1, n. 13.

52 Girolamo Carara, Cristoforo Castelli, and Cristoforo Tegassi performed the service for Marco Faustini, the first at S. Aponal, the second two at S. Cassiano; their professions are unknown, and their theatrical connections probably of short duration.

53 ASV, AN, Atti, b.1330, f. 357ᵛ, 23 June 1674. "Dalle perle false" may refer to glass beads more generally.

54 HVsa, AK, Cal. Br. 22, vol. 4, no. 389, 28 Jan. 1670. Even if one assumes that the duke was more generous than most, a tip of even 1 ducat for each of 150 palchi would have brought the fattor a substantial income.

specified that the fattor would be paid directly from the theater's income.[55] In a number of cases the fattor had the additional responsibility of acting as guarantor for the theater rent, presumably because he had direct access to the box income, the theater's "most certain profit," in Ivanovich's words.

While many fattori may have held the position for only a few years, one man, Vicenzo dei Devoti, worked for over two decades at the task in the employ of the Grimani family. He acted as fattor for SS. Giovanni e Paolo and S. Samuele, and lived in the house adjacent to the opera theater.[56] Devoti had already occupied that position by 1644 (and possibly earlier), and his connection with the Grimani theaters lasted, apparently, until near the time of his death on 29 May 1666, at the age of 85.[57] Given his advanced age at the time of his demise, Devoti had undoubtedly taken on these duties after pursuing one or more other professions previously; indeed, in 1652 he was referred to as "formerly a weaver of silk cloth."[58] Devoti's association with opera boxes became such that in one document, albeit one that concerned money from the theater, he was referred to simply as "Vicenzo dei palchi."[59]

Devoti's association with the Grimanis points up a basic contrast between SS. Giovanni e Paolo and the other theaters that is related to the situation we discussed earlier concerning the distribution of box monies. The Grimanis supported Vicenzo, providing him with housing near the theater; both parties benefited, as the Grimanis had an employee always near the theater should any problems arise. Devoti worked for the Grimanis, not for the impresario, whoever that might have been at any particular time, allowing him to remain associated with the theater for decades rather than for a limited number of years.

The Timing of Box-rental Payments

As mentioned earlier, Faustini's accounting of the boxes for four years at S. Aponal (1654–57) provides us with the most comprehensive figures regarding palchi and

55 ASV, AN, Atti, b. 6059, ff. 29ᵛ–30, 4 Apr. 1656. At S. Moisè in 1655, Paulo Morandi was to receive 10 ducats for his services, beyond which he supplied the scagni (for which he took in additional income).

56 ASV, DS, b. 218, no. 1036, 22 Aug. 1661.

57 ASPV, Parrocchia di S. Marina, Libro de' morti, 7, 1656–69, f. 92. Extant receipts for box monies from the Grimani theaters in 1664 bear Devoti's signature (ASV, Archivio Tiepolo, prima consegna, b. 116, no. 245).

58 "Vicenzo quondam Bernardo di Devotti olim testor da pani de seda al presente attende per custode nel teatro dell'Illustrissimo Grimani sopra le fondamente nove." ASV, AN, Atti, b. 8461, f. 29ᵛ, 16 Apr. 1652.

59 ASV, AN, Atti, b. 3500, f. 288 (transcription of a receipt regarding a transfer of funds from Devoti to Francesco Morosini dated 31 July 1664). Through Devoti and his long connection with the Grimanis, other members of his family eventually entered the orbit of the Grimani theater. Devoti's niece, Maddalena Melli, married the scene painter at SS. Giovanni e Paolo, Hippolito Mazzarini, in 1664 (ASPV, EM, b. 79, f. 58, testimony taken on 22 July 1664). Francesco Melli, Maddalena's brother, worked with Mazzarini as a scene painter at SS. Giovanni e Paolo, while Rocco Melli took on his uncle's previous job in the 1680s, collecting the box rents. Francesco Melli and Hippolito Mazzarini acted as witnesses for the will of pre Antonio Mazzuchelo. Melli styled himself as "pitor San Gioan e Paullo" (ASV, AN, Testamenti, b. 1004, no. 22). For Rocco Melli, see ASV, AN, Atti, b. 6113, f. 46ᵛ, 14 Aug. 1683.

their renters for this period;[60] while many of Faustini's entries do not specify a date of payment, those that do give us some idea of when the funds were likely to be received. Many boxholders made their payments during the carnival season itself, that is during January and February; a significant number, however, met their responsibilities only after the season had been completed: twenty-two in March over the four-year period, five in April, and three in December. These late dates may represent a common trend: several documents from the 1670s and 1680s specify that a particular boxholder's rent was due at the end of the carnival season.[61] The data suggest, then, that much of the palco money would have been received during the season or at its completion, and thus was unavailable to the impresario for timely payment for costumes, scenery, and the like.

Collecting from Recalcitrant Boxholders

The agent's job called for him to attempt to collect the rent from those boxholders unwilling to pay as required. The efforts apparently began with "courteous reminders";[62] when these failed, an "urbane" non-judicial notice[63] (submitted in the name of the impresario or one of the theater owners for added weight), served to the delinquent renter by a public official, was registered in the acts of a notary. In the case of the Teatro S. Angelo, the noble proprietors of the land on which the theater was built, the Capellos and Marcellos, offered to "lend" their names to the impresario for purposes of the dunning notices.[64] The notice typically bore an ultimatum: if the rent was not received in a specified period of time, usually three or eight days, the box would be made available to another renter; the sender of the ultimatum also usually indicated that he reserved the right to take official legal action through the courts. In his letter to the Duke of Brunswick, referred to above, Massi remarked on his own punctuality, adding that "he who does not pay on time always runs into some kind of lawsuit and some difficulty."[65] In some cases, payment was extraordinarily late, as much as a year or more.[66] During the 1670s, the Grimani brothers had particular difficulty collecting box rents, and consequently sent out a stream of notices in attempts to collect the fees.[67] Certainly, obtaining the monies from the box rentals could prove a troublesome burden to the theater owner, the impresario, and his agent.

---

60 ASV, SGSM, b. 194, ff. 92–102. Many papers regarding palchi, especially for the eighteenth century, are preserved in the Archivio Vendramin of the Casa Goldoni in Venice.

61 For example, ASV, AN, Atti, b. 6102, f. 249, 23 Feb. 1669 m.v.

62 "instantie cortesi"; ASV, AN, Atti, b. 732, f. 383ᵛ, 17 June 1672, in a note from Polo Boldù to boxholders of S. Cassiano.

63 In the note from Boldù cited in n. 62, the phrase is "questa urbana scrittura estragiudicial," but numerous variants occur.

64 See Giazotto, "Guerra dei palchi," 477, and Mangini, *Teatri di Venezia*, 73.

65 "chi non paga pontualmente trova sempre qualche lite, e qualche disgratia." HVsa, AK, Cal. Br. 22, vol. 4, no. 389, 28 Jan. 1670 [m.v.].

66 In 1655 at S. Moisè as many as thirty-one palchi (about one-third of the boxes) had not been paid in full from the previous two seasons (ASV, AN, Atti, b. 12045, f. 123ᵛ).

67 See Giazotto, "Guerra dei palchi," 494–98.

Danger and Violence Regarding Boxholders and
the Agents

The job of agent was not without risk; indeed, two incidents that occurred in 1662 point up, on the one hand, the dangers of carnival season, and on the other, the fierce possessiveness that might exist regarding an opera box. In January 1662, Abbot Vettor Grimani Calergi, attending the opera at SS. Giovanni e Paolo with the Duke of Mantua, sought a box for the evening. These two prominent men were told that only one was at that time unoccupied, and the superintendent (the fattor) gave the two entry to the box (it is unclear why Grimani Calergi had none available to him; perhaps the one he normally used had been lent to friends for the night). When the owner of the palco showed up, he unwillingly joined the Duke and Grimani Calergi. The account states that after the opera he reprimanded the superintendant for allowing Grimani and the Duke entry to the box, and, finally, stabbed him several times.[68] Another incident took place at S. Luca on nearly the same date, when Stefano Galinazza, who had been authorized to take charge of the boxes only earlier that January, was also stabbed.[69] The events at the two theaters evidently led the Capi of the Council of Ten to suspend the performances for several days.[70]

––––––––––

We will return to the boxes and their inhabitants at the end of our study, in chapter 11, looking in more detail at the social classes that populated them, as well as at attendance figures for the opera in general. We now, however, direct our attention to Marco Faustini's management of opera companies at three different theaters.

68 ASF, MP, filza 3029, f. 1556, 28 Jan. 1662. The superintendant's identity is not specified, so that we do not know if Devoti or one of his assistants was attacked; the attack does not seem to have been fatal.

69 ASV, CD, Criminal, filza 94, 1661. Some weeks later the unfortunate Galinazza was killed near his home by several men *in maschera*.

70 ASF, MP, filza 3029, f. 1556, 28 Jan. 1662.

CHAPTER THREE

MARCO FAUSTINI AND
HIS COMPANIES

During the first four decades of public opera in Venice, many individuals accepted the obligations and stresses of producing musical dramas. Most of these impresarios, however, remained active for only a few years, and their careers are little documented. One figure, however, stands out for both his longevity and the extensive records he left behind: Marco Faustini. Over nearly two decades, Faustini served as impresario at three theaters in succession, producing twenty operas in thirteen seasons. Fortunately for scholars, he also preserved many of his papers, which passed to two stable institutions (the Scuola Grande di S. Marco, and then the Archivio di Stato), and enough have survived for us to trace in some detail his career and the various strategies he used to become a successful impresario. As with most Venetian impresarios, Faustini worked as a member of a company, with a circle of partners and investors, rather than on his own. In general, we know little of the day-to-day relations among the members of operatic companies except when business concerns flared up into problems that found their way into a notary's records or into the courts. The company of Faustini, Alvise Duodo, and Marc'Antonio Correr, which lasted for nearly eighteen years—albeit with several interruptions—is much less remote to us. The various papers left by Faustini give us a more personal sense of the company, and of the dynamics within the group; they also make reference to other more peripheral characters who figured in the affairs of the opera business to a greater or lesser degree.

THE EARLY LIVES OF MARCO
AND GIOVANNI FAUSTINI

Marco Faustini was born on 17 May 1606,[1] the eldest child of Angelo Faustini, a Venetian cittadino,[2] and Isabetta Vecellio, a daughter of the painter and author Cesare Vecellio (and a cousin of Titian).[3] Their fourth and last child, following two

1 The documents for Faustini's early biography are found in ASV, SGSM, b. 117. We will be publishing a more detailed biography of Marco and Giovanni Faustini at a later time.

2 See appendix 2 for a discussion of the Venetian social classes.

3 Angelo Faustini, too, was descended from an artist, Paris Bordone, although more distantly. See ASV, Monastero Santa Maria delle Vergini, b. 2 bis, fasc. B, f. 23.

daughters, one of whom died in infancy, was Giovanni (known as Zuane), born on 19 May 1615.[4] While Angelo acted in several capacities in the civil service of the Venetian republic, Marco trained instead as a lawyer, and in 1627 began an association that would provide him work and, eventually, a steady and significant income: he served as an attorney for the important and prestigious Magistrato del Sal, which administered Venice's huge salt monopoly. Around the same time, Marco began another activity that would remain a significant part of his life: in March 1628, at the age of 21, he joined the Scuola Grande di S. Marco,[5] one of the six great lay confraternities of the city. When the plague arrived in Venice in 1630, the Faustini family was hit hard—within less than two years Angelo, Isabetta, and their daughter Daria had died.

In September 1631, Marco and Giovanni (now 26 and 17 years old, respectively) moved to the parish of S. Vidal. There they rented a house from the parish priest near the church, where they would live for the remainder of their lives. The choice of S. Vidal would prove fortunate in several ways. Marco Faustini had probably selected it because of its relative vicinity to the Piazza S. Marco and the Rialto (both areas important for business and legal activity), and many other lawyers lived nearby. In addition, however, the composer Francesco Cavalli was a neighbor, as were several other men who would figure in the operatic careers of the two brothers.[6]

The next few years passed with little incident, and Marco's legal career blossomed: he continued to serve the Magistrato del Sal, but also began to branch out, handling more general legal matters unconnected with the Salt Office. Much less is known of Giovanni Faustini's activities during this period. He frequented the offices of some of his fellow cittadini, appearing regularly as a witness to notarial documents; he undoubtedly continued his education, but whether this included any professional training comparable to Marco's legal apprenticeship is unknown. Marco continued as a member of the Scuola Grande di S. Marco, and his brother joined him in 1633. While Marco's service as an officer at the scuola stagnated during the 1640s, his legal career flourished. By 1645 he had accumulated annual retainers amounting to somewhat more than 300 ducats; he had, in other words, carved out a successful career for himself. Marco was not only a financial success, but was on familiar terms with members of some of the wealthiest and most powerful families in Venice; this ease of communication with patricians would serve him well during his years in the theater.

ENTRANCE INTO THE OPERATIC WORLD:
GIOVANNI FAUSTINI'S IMPRESARIAL CAREER

Giovanni Faustini chose quite a different path from that followed by his older brother. He never embarked on any of the careers traditionally open to cittadini. Beginning in 1641, however, at the age of 26, he made his impact on the city of

---

4 ASV, SGSM, b. 117.

5 ASV, SGSM, b. 6 bis.

6 Cavalli later moved to the parish of S. Pantalon. See Glover, *Cavalli* and Vio, "Francesco Cavalli." See appendix 2 on the importance of the parish in Venetian society.

Venice in a different way, as an opera librettist. It may have been Marco's very success that enabled his brother to enter the new and exciting world of opera, which had burst upon the Venetian scene just five years earlier. It is even possible that Giovanni's entry into that world was encouraged, or even inspired, by his neighbor in S.Vidal, Francesco Cavalli, who was on his way to becoming the most important composer in the genre. Faustini's first opus, *La virtù de' strali d'Amore*, was set to music by Cavalli and performed by the composer's company at the Teatro S. Cassiano for the 1641/42 season. Cavalli had worked there initially with Oratio Persiani, another member of the company; Persiani's transfer to the Teatro SS. Giovanni e Paolo opened the way for a new librettist, and after an initial collaboration with Giovanni Francesco Busenello, Cavalli chose the neophyte Faustini. The partnership of Faustini and Cavalli continued for several years at S. Cassiano even after the 1644 season, when Cavalli relinquished his role as impresario at the theater.[7] In fact, the team appears to have produced two new operas for the 1645 season: *Doriclea*, dedicated to Faustini's friend, the physician Mauritio Tirelli, and *Titone*, dedicated to the young Alvise Duodo, the nobleman who would later become his partner (and subsequently Marco's) in the management of the Teatro S.Aponal.

The Venetian theaters were partially closed for the 1645/46 and 1646/47 carnival seasons as a result of the Venetian participation in the war against the Turks at Crete.[8] By the time more normal operation resumed at the end of 1647, Giovanni deepened his involvement in the business of opera, becoming an impresario at the small Teatro S. Moisè, where Cavalli had held an interest earlier in the decade (see table 3.1A for the operas produced by Giovanni Faustini at S. Moisè).[9] On 26 Sep-

TABLE 3.1.   Operas for Which Giovanni Faustini Was Impresario and Librettist

Season	Opera	Composer
A. Operas produced at Teatro S. Moisè		
1647/48	Ersilla	various (including Cavalli?)
1648/49	Euripo	Cavalli
B. Operas produced at Teatro S. Aponal		
1650/51	Oristeo	Cavalli
	Rosinda	Cavalli
1651/52[a]	Calisto	Cavalli

[a] Giovanni Faustini died during the run of *Calisto*, and was succeeded by his brother Marco; see table 3.2, A.

7 See Morelli and Walker, "Tre controversie," 97–120.

8 Bianconi and Walker, "Dalla *Finta pazza* alla *Veremonda*," 379–454. For a different view, see Whenham, "Perspectives."

9 See Pirrotta, "Lame Horse," 325–34.

tember 1647 he had signed a three-year contract with the owner, Almorò Zane, to mount operas there.[10] Faustini's first production was his opus 6, *Ersilla*, with music, according to the chronicler Cristoforo Ivanovich, by several composers, perhaps including Cavalli.[11] For the second year, 1649, the team of Faustini and Cavalli was reunited for *Euripo*.

Giovanni Faustini had begun to prepare for his third season at S. Moisè, in which he planned to present two operas, *Oristeo* and *Rosinda*, when Zane informed him that he wished, instead, to present spoken comedies at his theater. Although Faustini had already hired and begun to pay singers, he agreed to the termination of his contract with Zane, putting a temporary end to his career as an impresario.[12] The notice sent to the theater owner was penned not by Giovanni, but, instead, by Marco Faustini, who, as a lawyer, had greater experience regarding contractual matters. Marco may have been consistently involved in Giovanni's impresarial ventures as a legal and financial advisor, given his expertise in those areas.

A little more than seven months later, Giovanni's brief retirement came to an end: on 19 May 1650, his thirty-fifth birthday, he rented the Teatro S. Aponal (see table 3.1B for operas he produced at S. Aponal). As he explained in the dedication to the first opera he produced at the new theater, *Oristeo*, he had decided to reenter the operatic world for two reasons. First of all, he was bored: he took a new theater "to cut short the boredom of my established life of leisure."[13] Secondly, he was in debt: he implies that he had been stuck in the small and inadequate Teatro S. Moisè, and that he had written *Oristeo* and its successor *Rosinda* to try to regain financial stability.[14] He wrote, however, that S. Aponal was not much of an improvement: "It is true that the stage I have built is not dissimilar to the theater in which *Ersilla* and *Euripo* appeared, and where afterwards these twins should have been shown."[15] The theater was in poor condition, but the owners, Francesco Ceroni and Zanetta Diamante, agreed to make the repairs.[16] It did, however, hold one distinct advantage over other Venetian theaters: its rent was substantially lower, a mere 60 ducats compared to a more usual 600 to 1,000. Despite the state of the theater, Faustini made an auspicious beginning in his new undertaking. He was able, once again, to persuade Cavalli to compose operas for his new enterprise. Moreover, he chose—just as he had planned for his aborted final season at S. Moisè—to mount an ambitious two operas per season, rather than one, which had by now become more typical of theaters in Venice. The librettos were dedicated to Alvise Duodo, previously honored in *Titone*.

10 ASV, AN, Atti, b. 6075, 5 Oct. 1649.

11 Ivanovich, *Memorie teatrali*, 435.

12 ASV, AN, Atti, b. 6075, 5 Oct. 1649.

13 "per decapitare l'otio della institutione del mio viver libero." Faustini, *Oristeo*, 4.

14 Faustini, *Oristeo*, 3.

15 "E vero, che non dissimile dal'Orchestra sudetta, nella quale comparsero Ersilla, et Euripo, e dove di poi dovevano farsi vedere questi gemelli, è il Palco da me eretto." Faustini, *Oristeo*, 3–4.

16 ASV, SGSM, b. 194, ff. 179–83.

THE BEGINNING OF MARCO'S IMPRESARIAL
CAREER: S. APONAL, 1651/52

No specific evidence points to Marco Faustini's participation in the first season of his younger brother's enterprise at S. Aponal; indeed, no documentation of any kind has surfaced for that season except for that regarding the rental of the theater. Several items do survive for the second season, however, and they reveal that Marco must have been deeply involved in the management of the theater. Perhaps Giovanni had tired of the practical side of the business, or perhaps he had deferred to Marco's greater experience with financial matters and contracts. Marco, not Giovanni, kept the account book for the 1651/52 opera season[17] (it is entirely in his hand), and he also drew up the contract for the singer Caterina Giani on 18 September 1651, although Giovanni was still officially in charge. The librettist dedicated the first of the new operas for the 1651/52 season, *Calisto*, to Marc'Antonio Correr, the nobleman who, along with Alvise Duodo, would be a partner in Marco Faustini's operatic companies.

By late November 1651, the libretto of *Calisto* had been issued, and performances had commenced. Then, with almost no warning, tragedy struck, as explained in the dedication to the second opera, *Eritrea*: "While the feigned death of Eritrea will sweetly delight Your Lordship's ear, the unfortunately real one of Signor Giovanni Faustini will sadly move your soul. That celebrated author died a few days ago, and, after the weaving of eleven works, left his dear *Eritrea* while it was still being printed."[18] Upon Giovanni's death on 19 December 1651, the Teatro S. Aponal passed to his brother: Faustini's rental contract had borne the typical phrase "per se, heredi, et successori suoi" (for him, his heirs and successors), and Marco, his only surviving relative, inherited his brother's interest in the theater, both literally and figuratively (see table 3.2A for operas produced by Marco Faustini at S. Aponal).[19] As we shall see, Marco's commitment to Giovanni's theatrical dreams and goals lasted throughout his career as an impresario, until 1668.

17 ASV, SGSM, b. 112.

18 "Mentre una finta morte d'Eritrea lusingherà a V.S. Illustrissima dolcemente l'orecchio, la pur troppo vera del Sig. Giovanni Faustini le commoverà dolorosamente l'anima. Morì pochi giorni sono questo celebre Litterato, et doppò la tessitura di undeci Opere, ha lasciato sotto il Torchio quella della sua cara Eritrea." Faustini, *Eritrea*, 3.

19 Giovanni's death record reads: "1651, on the day 19 December, Signor Zuane Faustini son of the late Signor Anzolo, 36 years old, of malignant fever [which he suffered] for three days, [visited by] the doctors Tirelli and Squadron, [in the parish of] San Vidal." ("1651 adì 19 decembre il signor Zuane Faustini del quondam signor Anzolo d'anni 36 da mal maligno giorni 3 medico Tireli e Squadron – San Vidal.") ASV, Provveditori alla Sanità, Necrologio, b. 877. Marco's personal monument to his brother can be found in the former church of S. Vidal in Venice (at present a concert hall), located centrally in front of the high altar. The inscription reads: JOANNES FAUSTINUS / GENERE / CIVIS VENETUS / GENIO / MUSARUM ALUMNUS / FATO / INFAUSTAE DEVOTUS URNAE PRAE PROPERE / AN. AET. XXXII / SAL. HUM. MDCLI. DIE XIX DECEMBRIS / QUAM / MARCUS FAUSTINUS / FRATRI AMANTISS.O / SUPERSTES LUCTU / P. (Giovanni Faustini: by state, citizen of Venice; by talent, child of the muses; by fate, surrendered prematurely to the luckless urn in his 32nd year, in the year 1651, 19 December, [placed] by Marco Faustini, his beloved brother and grieving survivor.) We are grateful to Jennifer Tunberg of the University of Kentucky for her assistance with the translation. Marco Faustini here, and in the preface to *Alciade* (1667), listed Giovanni's age as 32 rather than 36.

TABLE 3.2.   Operas Produced by Marco Faustini

Season	Opera	Librettist	Composer
A. At Teatro S. Aponal			
1651/52[a]	Calisto	Giovanni Faustini	Francesco Cavalli
	Eritrea	Giovanni Faustini	Francesco Cavalli
1654/55	Eupatra	Giovanni Faustini	Pietro Andrea Ziani
1655/56	Erismena	Aurelio Aureli	Francesco Cavalli
1656/57	Le fortune di Rodope e Damira	Aurelio Aureli	Pietro Andrea Ziani
B. At Teatro S. Cassiano			
1657/58	L'incostanza trionfante	Francesco Piccoli (and others)	Pietro Andrea Ziani
1658/59	Antioco	Nicolò Minato	Francesco Cavalli
1659/60	Elena	Nicolò Minato	Francesco Cavalli
C. At Teatro SS. Giovanni e Paolo			
1660/61	Gl'amori infrutuosi	Aurelio Aureli	Antonio Sartorio
	Annibale in Capua	Nicola Beregan	Pietro Andrea Ziani
1661/62	Gli scherzi di fortuna	Aurelio Aureli	Pietro Andrea Ziani
	Le fatiche d'Ercole per Deianira	Aurelio Aureli	Pietro Andrea Ziani
1662/63	Amor guerriero	Cristoforo Ivanovich	Pietro Andrea Ziani
	Gl'amori d'Apollo, e di Leucotoe	Aurelio Aureli	Giovanni Battista Volpe
1665/66	Orontea	Giacinto Andrea Cicognini	Antonio Cesti
	Tito	Nicola Beregan	Antonio Cesti
1666/67	Alciade	Giovanni Faustini	Pietro Andrea Ziani
	Dori	Apollonio Apolloni	Antonio Cesti
1667/68	Il tiranno humiliato d'Amore overo Meraspe	Giovanni Faustini	Carlo Pallavicino
	Eliogabalo	Aurelio Aureli	Giovanni Antonio Boretti

[a]Marco assumed control of the company when his brother Giovanni died during the run of Calisto.

Faustini's First Partners

The connections Giovanni had established with two noblemen, Alvise Duodo and Marc'Antonio Correr, formed the basis for the company that, with Marco at its head, would produce operas for many years (see table 3.3 for a list of Faustini's partners during his impresarial career). These two noble partners came from important families with a history of significant government service as well as an interest in the arts: both Correr and Duodo enjoyed many family and social connections that they could call upon when necessary in aid of their operatic interests. The family of Alvise Duodo (1624–74) resided in S. Maria del Giglio (S. Maria Zobenigo), quite near to Faustini's parish of S. Vidal. One of his relatives, Francesco Duodo, had commanded the victorious Venetian fleet at Lepanto in 1571, while his great uncle Pietro, after serving as Venetian ambassador to England, Savoy, and Rome, took a post late in his life in Padua, where he founded the Accademia Delia, and became a friend of Galileo Galilei during the scientist's years in that city.[20] Duodo's uncle Francesco Duodo was a patron of music, and the dedicatee of a book of songs by Alessandro Grandi.[21] Alvise Duodo's first publicly acknowledged connection with opera came in 1645, when, as mentioned above, Giovanni Faustini dedicated his *Titone* to the 21-year-old patrician. It is certainly possible that Alvise had developed a taste for the fostering of opera production through another uncle, Girolamo Lando, who was one of the supporters of the Teatro Novissimo several years earlier (see chap. 4).

TABLE 3.3.   Marco Faustini's Partners

Season	Partners and their shares
Teatro S. Aponal	
1651/52	Probably Alvise Duodo and Marc'Antonio Correr; shares unknown
1654/55	Bortolo Pasinetto (70%), Faustini (30%); Nicolò Personé also involved
1655/56	Simon Guglielmi (25%), Paulo Morandi (25%), Pasinetto (35%), Faustini (15%)
1656/57	Unknown
Teatro S. Cassiano	
1657/58	Correr (33%), Duodo (33%), Faustini (33%), and Polifilo Zancarli (limited partner with investment of 200 ducats)
1658/59	Correr (33%), Duodo (33%), Faustini (33%)
1659/60	Unknown (not Correr and Duodo)

20 *DBI*, s.v. "Duodo, Pietro," by Gino Benzoni, and "Duodo, Francesco," by Giuseppe Gullino.

21 Francesco Duodo (1592–1650) was the dedicatee of a book of poetry for music (Remegio Romano, *Prima raccolta di bellissime canzonette*, Venice, 1618) as well as Alessandro Grandi's *Cantade et arie* (Venice, 1626). See Miller, "Composers of San Marco," 181–82.

Duodo's letters to Marco Faustini (nineteen of them survive in the Faustini papers), written from Venice, from his villa in Monselice, and from Bergamo, chart his gradual maturation and rise in stature.[22] They date from all three of the company's business ventures; many of them are quite familiar in tone, going beyond the stilted, stiff language found in so much of the correspondence of the time. The letters of the 1650s often find Duodo—like many other nobles—short of cash, and thus unable to meet his responsibilities toward the company. He was quick to plead with Faustini, a cittadino with little property to his name, for loans and other favors, and he sometimes vented his frustration when the impresario was slow to honor his requests. In one letter, having already sought help from his father and other family members, he approached Faustini for money (which the impresario duly provided) to purchase a new set of underclothes ("sott'habiti");[23] in another he asked for an advance while he waited for income from sources such as the sale of grain.[24] He also left pieces of silverplate with Faustini as security for his debts.[25] Duodo's letters demonstrate the ease of communication that might exist between members of the nobility and the cittadini, and also show that the bond between these two men extended well beyond the formal necessities of business affairs.

Duodo's fortunes changed rather abruptly in 1660 when his father and brother died within two months of each other and he came into possession of his family's fortune.[26] Taking advantage of his inherited wealth, he purchased, for 25,000 ducats, a procuratorship of S. Marco, one of the highest positions in the Venetian governmental hierarchy.[27] This sudden rise in status did not change his involvement in opera production, however: he maintained that interest while carrying out his new responsibilities. In 1662, for example, he wrote a number of letters concerning the upcoming season to Faustini from Bergamo, where he was undertaking business for the procurators.[28] Duodo's new position must have augmented the prestige of the company, and it added weight to the company's requests for singers employed in foreign territories (see chap. 7).

22 Duodo's letters can be found in ASV, SGSM, b. 188, ff. 2 (18 Oct. 1662), 3 (27 Sept. 1662), 4 (20 Aug. 1652), 5 (undated), 6 (undated), 7 (undated), 8 (undated), 9 (undated), 11 (undated; around Aug. 1656), 12 (undated; ca. 1651–52), 13 (undated), 18 (undated), 19 (5 Nov. 1658), 21 (21 Oct. 1662), 372 (8 Aug. 1665), and 386 (undated, 1665); ASV, SGSM, b. 194, ff. 148 (7 Nov. 1665) and 150 (undated; 1665); and ASV, SGSM, b. 101, unnumbered (1 Nov. 1662). Some of the nine undated letters can be assigned to specific years according to their content.

23 ASV, SGSM, b. 188, f. 11.

24 Ibid., f. 18.

25 Ibid., f. 6.

26 ASPV, Parrocchia di S. Maria del Giglio, Morti, 1643–80. Girolamo Duodo died on 23 Mar. 1660 and Pietro Duodo on 4 May 1660.

27 On the procurators of S. Marco, see the discussion in Talbot, *Benedetto Vinaccesi*, 91. The most prestigious of procurators were those elected on their own merit ("per merito") by the Great Council to the nine statutory posts; the sale of positions beyond those nine during the seventeenth century, like the sale of nobility, brought much-needed cash to the Venetian government to help pay for the wars against the Turks. All procurators, elected or not, served for life.

28 Letters written from Bergamo are: ASV, SGSM, b. 188, ff. 2, 3, and 21; and ASV, SGSM, b. 101, unnumbered, dated 1 Nov. 1662. On his service in Bergamo, see ASV, Procuratia di S. Marco de supra, reg. 146, f. 101ᵛ, 12 Sept. 1662.

Faustini's other noble partner, Marc'Antonio Correr (1617–69), of the parish of S. Angelo (adjoining that of S. Vidal), may also have come to be involved in opera production through the interests of an uncle, Angelo Correr. The elder Correr (d. 1642), who left much of his estate to Marc'Antonio, was the dedicatee of Benedetto Ferrari's *Il pastor regio* (1640), and Ferrari authorized him in late February 1641 to settle theatrical debts in the composer's absence.[29] Angelo's estate included several musical instruments as well as a number of unidentified music manuscripts.[30] Marc'Antonio's connection with secular music of the day is further demonstrated by the three texts he wrote for musical setting that appear in one of the publications of the composer Barbara Strozzi.[31] During his travels outside of Venice he had occasion to witness singers performing in other venues, allowing him to offer advice on possible cast members.[32]

We may well wonder how these two particular noblemen came together in aid of Giovanni Faustini and the Teatro S. Aponal in 1650, and whether they had already formed a partnership or alliance that served them in other areas.[33] The extent of the friendship and social interaction between Correr and Duodo is uncertain, but both men had strong ties with another family, the Barbarigos of Duodo's parish of S. Maria del Giglio. Angelo and Giovanni Francesco Barbarigo figure prominently in Correr's will of 1652 (neither Duodo nor Faustini are mentioned), and a third brother, Antonio, had repaid a loan of Duodo's in 1648.[34] Duodo was drawn even closer into the affairs of the Barbarigo family when his sister Chiara married Giovanni Francesco Barbarigo's son, Antonio, in 1653;[35] indeed, he often found the financial help he needed to support the opera company in loans from the Barbarigos.

---

29 ASV, AN, Atti, b. 2918, f. 263, 28 Feb. 1640 m.v.

30 The instruments included a spinet, two theorbos, and a guitar (ASV, AN, Atti, b. 12445, ff. 48–51, 6 Aug. 1642). It should be noted that while instruments figure commonly in inventories of the seventeenth century, manuscripts or printed books of music rarely do.

31 Correr's texts are "Così non la voglio, no," "Pensaci ben, mio core," and "Sete pur fastidioso," all in Strozzi's *Diporti di Euterpe* (Venice, 1659).

32 Correr had heard Raffaele Caccialupi sing in Bologna, and consequently recruited him—successfully—for S. Aponal for the 1656/57 season (ASFe, Archivio Bentivoglio, Lettere sciolte, b. 324, f. 93, 16 Sept. 1656). In 1665 he would offer a critique of Anna Venturi, Carlo Righenzi, and a young singer from Mantua (ASV, SGSM, b. 188, f. 207, 6 Nov. 1665).

33 There is some indication that the two noblemen enjoyed some social interaction outside of their operatic activities. On 5 Nov. 1658 Duodo wrote to Faustini that Correr had spent several days at his villa in Monselice (ASV, SGSM, b. 188, f. 19).

34 In 1648 Antonio Barbarigo paid to Duodo's father-in-law, Francesco Viaro, 300 ducats that Duodo had borrowed in 1645 (Vmc, PDC 2469/vii). Marc'Antonio Correr also conducted business with a number of the Barbarigo brothers. In his will, he called Giovanni Francesco Barbarigo his "interessato congionto" (joint partner). In 1654 he sold a good part of the Correr palace in S. Angelo to Antonio Barbarigo. See Gios, *Itinerario biografico*, 96. For Correr's will, see ASV, AN, Testamenti, b. 1270, f. 119, no. 63.

35 The two families also had strong connections during the 1640s, when Alvise Duodo's brother Pietro, and the young Gregorio Barbarigo (later Saint Gregorio Barbarigo), one of the sons of Giovanni Francesco Barbarigo, spent several years together in Germany assisting Alvise Contarini, who acted as the Venetian minister for the negotiations at Münster for the settling of the Thirty Years War. See *DBI*, s.v. "Contarini, Alvise," by Gino Benzoni.

Marc'Antonio Correr also had relatives who helped the company in various ways. His brother-in-law Marc'Antonio Priuli was the patron of Bonifacio Ceretti, the Cappella di S. Marco contralto who lived in his house, and it was Priuli who facilitated Ceretti's contract to sing for the company in 1651.[36] Correr's family connections proved especially useful to the company when his cousin, Angelo Correr, served as ambassador to Pope Alexander VII. Various payments for several singers resident in that city were sent directly to him, and his influence must have extended to other areas as well. Duodo's close relative by marriage, Gregorio Barbarigo, in Rome simultaneously with Correr, socialized with the ambassador, so that Faustini's two noble partners, during the late 1650s, had easy access to channels in the Holy City.[37]

Unlike Alvise Duodo, Marc'Antonio Correr may have written very few letters to Faustini. Only two survive in the Faustini papers, but one of them suggests the social ties that must have existed among the partners and their friends. Correr began his letter of November 1658 by voicing his disappointment that an illness would prevent Faustini from visiting him at Piove di Sacco:

> Having arrived this evening in Piove, I was comforted with the hope given to me by my brother-in-law Signor Marc'Antonio that Your Excellency would be here on the feast of St. Martin. My contentment was very brief, saddened by another letter from Your Excellency written to Signor Marc'Antonio informing him that you do not feel in perfect health, and are deferring your arrival. Thus have I discovered that in this world hopes are fleeting.[38]

Correr refers in this letter to his brother-in-law Marc'Antonio Priuli (mentioned above), with whom Faustini would remain friends until his death.[39] Correr goes on to speak of the preparations for the opera: "In the meantime, Most Excellent Signor Marco, I live full of desire to see the opera of our lame one [Cavalli]. . . . Please advise me at the same time what the musicians from Rome have resolved, and in what manner they have [been hired]."[40] Correr closes his letter with his

36 Correr's wife was Bianca Priuli. In an entry in his account book for the 1651/52 season, Faustini noted that Ceretti had been hired with Priuli's help.

37 Gregorio Barbarigo related to his brother how the ambassador, Angelo Correr, had been called upon to "audition" a singer in Rome, and to facilitate her path to Venice. (Gios, *Itinerario biografico*, 400). See also chapter 7.

38 "Giunto questa sera in Piove, sono restato consolato dalla speranza datami dal Signor Marc'Antonio mio cognato, che Vostra Signoria Eccellentissima doveva ritrovarsi qui il giorno di San Martino. Brevissima è stata la dimora del mio contento, mentre viene ammareggiata con altra lettera di Vostra Signoria Eccellentissima al Signor Marc'Antonio che lo avvisa non sentirsi ella perfettamente bene, et sospenda la sua venuta. Così ho provato, che in questo mondo le speranze sono fallaci." ASV, SGSM, b. 188, f. 1, Nov. 1658.

39 As the Priuli family owned a villa in Piove di Sacco, Correr must have written his letter while staying there, where Faustini had made plans to visit both his friends. Correr's association with the Faustinis may have come about through Marc'Antonio Priuli, although we are unsure of when that friendship began. A number of letters to Faustini from Priuli survive in ASV, SGSM, bb. 101 and 188, largely from 1674 and 1675, and all of them written from Padua. We are grateful to Franco Nogara and to Luigi Ballan, who furnished us with information about the Palazzo Priuli in Piove di Sacco.

40 "In tanto Eccellentissimo Signor Marco, io vivo pien di brama di veder l'opera del nostro zoppo. . . . Pregola avvisarmi [insieme] quello hanno risolto di musici di Roma, et in che modo hanno scritto." ASV, SGSM, b. 188, f. 1, Nov. 1658.

condolences on the death of Faustini's servant, Anna Francese: "I send greetings to Signor Antonio Leffio, and certainly I felt sorrow upon hearing of the death of Madonna Anna, both because of her valor and for those beautiful curtsies that she made to me when I visited your house, and because of the grief I know that Your Excellency will have felt."[41] We see Faustini, then, interacting with his partners in the theater, in his home, and in mainland villas.

FAUSTINI'S COMPANY, 1651-1657: CONTINUITY AND CHANGE

The circumstances that led Marco Faustini to participate in the production of opera in Venice were familial; it is unlikely that he would have been drawn to it without this personal connection (although in the case of other impresarios not specifically connected to opera through a profession or avocation, it is generally impossible to provide a specific motivation). As Faustini was not a wealthy man, it was imperative that he build a strong financial foundation for his opera companies. He must have entered into some form of agreement—continuing the practice of his brother—with the noblemen Alvise Duodo and Marc'Antonio Correr, but the early stages of this partnership remain obscure (see table 3.3). The survival of the incorporation agreement of 1657—where Faustini, Duodo, Correr, and the cittadino Polifilo Zancarli each were to contribute 200 ducats, and Faustini, Duodo, and Correr would share the rest of the expenses (see below)—has led to the tacit assumption that this arrangement obtained throughout the whole of their association, that is, from 1650 to 1668, but this was not the case. We know that Correr and Duodo continued their association with Faustini, but on occasion their participation seems to have been more advisory and administrative rather than financial.

As mentioned above, documentation from the first two seasons at S. Aponal is scant: nothing survives for the first year, and for the second we have only the account book. While providing essential details regarding personnel, costuming, and scenery, the book offers little insight into the financial responsibilities of the company. We find Correr and Duodo paying for various expenses, and Correr also maintaining a presence in the hiring and contracting of singers; the data do not reveal, however, whether the three men shared expenses equally. In the end, as was almost always the case, the season was a financial failure: according to Faustini's accounting, the expenditures for the season amounted to 5,220 ducats, while the income from nightly ticket sales and seat rentals came to only 3,434 ducats, for a net loss of 1,786 ducats.[42]

When Faustini returned to the theater in 1654 after a two-year hiatus (during

---

41 "Saluto il Signor Antonio Leffio, et certo ho sentito dolore della morte di Madonna Anna come per il suo valore, come per il dolore, che so Vostra Signoria Eccelentissima haverà sentito, come per quelle belle riverenze, che mi faceva quando venivo alla sua casa." ASV, SGSM, b. 188, f. 1. Faustini's servant died on 1 Nov. 1658 (ASV, Provveditori alla sanità, Necrologia, b. 879). On Leffio, see below.

42 ASV, SGSM, b. 112, account book 1651/52, f. 42ᵛ. As discussed in chapter 2, the annual rental fees for boxes did not belong to the company, but to Faustini personally.

which time he sublet the theater to Bortolo Castoreo, Annibale Basso, and Paulo Morandi, a civil servant, an embroiderer, and a woodworker turned costume supplier), the company underwent a fundamental change, but the catalyst for the transformation has not come to light. We know of the noblemen's continuing participation in the company through libretto dedications and letters written for the recruitment of singers. Moreover, it was Duodo who unsuccessfully negotiated the return of Cavalli to the company (see chap. 6). The data from the 1654 account book, however, show that Faustini's financial partner for the production of Pietro Andrea Ziani's *Eupatra* was neither Duodo nor Correr, but one Bortolo Pasinetto. Indeed, the book shows that Pasinetto was the major investor, putting in 70 percent of the capital to Faustini's 30 percent.

Pasinetto reflects the variety of Venetians who were willing to invest capital in the opera industry.[43] Born in 1630, he was, among other things, a *cartoler* (manufacturer of playing cards, as were his father and grandfather before him), but he found vocations outside of the family business. His educational aspirations took him to the University of Padua, where, in September 1650, he earned his doctorate in law.[44] During the late 1650s he served as a notary at one of the Venetian courts, the Giudici di petizion.[45] Pasinetto's father died in October 1653,[46] and just seven months later this young man of 24 became the major sponsor of the opera at S. Aponal, at least for the 1654/55 season. We are unaware of previous connections between him and Faustini or his partners, but Pasinetto had an affinity for music, or at least for musical instruments, for he owned a sizable collection; at the time of his death in 1667 he left a spinet, a harpsichord, a viola, and fourteen plucked string instruments, including one of ivory.[47] Pasinetto's involvement at S. Aponal may have stemmed from his connections with the extended family of the composer Pietro Andrea Ziani—substantiated, at least, by February 1654—rather than from any prompting by Faustini or his noble partners.[48]

With Pasinetto's financial help, Faustini put on *Eupatra* (1654/55, with a libretto

43 On theatrical investing in the late sixteenth century see Johnson, "Short Lascivious Lives," 952–54.

44 Padua, Università degli studi di Padova, Archivio Antico, b. 152, f. 38. This feat represented a considerable achievement, one neither attempted nor attained by Marco Faustini (many of the lawyers active in Venice had never received such a degree). Pasinetto never practiced law, however.

45 A number of notarial documents allude to Pasinetto's post at the Petizion, and his hand and his signature can be seen in many inventories that survive in that *fondo* in the Archivio di Stato.

46 ASPV, Parrocchia di S. Moisè, Morti, 1633–58, f. 138, 25 Oct. 1653.

47 A number of these instruments could have been the work of Matteo Sellas, a string-instrument maker who, in 1659, was renting a house and a workshop from Pasinetto in S. Moisè; see ASV, AN, Atti, b. 8467, f. 8. Pasinetto committed suicide in Mar. 1667 by jumping out of a window. One of the apprentices in Pasinetto's shop, Antonio Albinoni, eventually inherited the business; Albinoni was the father of the composer Tomaso, born in 1671. On the business connections between the Pasinettos and Albinonis, see Vio, "Tomaso Albinoni," 111–22, and Talbot, *Tomaso Albinoni*, 26.

48 As Pasinetto—along with Nicolò Personé (see below)—formed part of a group of men who financed the release from the Turks of Ziani's brother, Iseppo, in Feb. 1654 (see ASV, AN, Atti, b. 8515, f. 104ᵛ, 26 Feb. 1653 m.v.), it is likely that his involvement with the opera company grew from an association either with the composer or, more likely, with his brother-in-law; Personé and Pasinetto had other joint financial dealings dating from later in 1654.

by his late brother). Beginning on 14 May 1654, Pasinetto made frequent deposits to the company, sometimes more than once a month, in sums ranging from 70 to 110 ducats; the final installment for that season came on 1 January 1655. His payments equaled nearly 1,153 ducats (compared to Faustini's deposits of 500), a considerable investment for a young man. Pasinetto's contribution went unacknowledged publicly, however, as the dedication of that year's libretto honored Alvise Duodo. On 15 August 1655 Pasinetto declared himself satisfied with Faustini's management of the production, and stated that he had reimbursed the cloth merchant Nicolò Personé for "materials from his shop, for musicians, and for Padre Ziani."[49] He also admitted to owing the company 81 ducats.

As we can see from Pasinetto's statement, Nicolò Personé's involvement with the company went beyond that of furnishing fabric and other items relating to costumes; rather, his actions in many ways resembled those of a partner. Personé most likely had been drawn to S. Aponal either through Ziani's participation as the composer of *Eupatra,* or even *La guerriera spartana,* presented the previous season, for the merchant had married Ziani's sister Desideria in 1652 (Personé and Desideria were the parents of the composer Marc'Antonio Ziani, born on 25 May 1654).[50] As an expert in the cloth trade, Personé could have served the company well, perhaps facilitating the acquisition of supplies, but his activities exceeded those of his occupation: he, along with Ziani (who had recruited a number of musicians), paid some of the singers who were members of the Cappella di S. Marco, sometimes merely delivering an installment turned over to them by Faustini.[51] By contrast, for the 1650/51 season four of the singers had been recruited with the help of Correr, and had been paid by Correr, Duodo, or by the cittadino Polifilo Zancarli. This suggests, then, a withdrawal, at least in some areas, by Faustini's original associates. Personé's involvement in the enterprise is further suggested by the manner in which he supplied 400 ducats' worth of materials from his shop (including cos-

49 "per roba tolta alla sua bottegha, come per musici e Padre Ziani." ASV, SGSM, b. 118, f. 11, 15 Aug. 1655.

50 The couple's marriage was solemnized in the home of the bride on 26 Dec. 1651, and the marriage was formalized at the church of S. Giacomo alla Zuecca on 7 Oct. 1652 (VAP, S. Salvatore, Matrimoni, 1647–99, f. 22. For the birth and baptism of Marc'Antonio Personé (who later adopted the family name of his uncle and teacher), see ibid., Battesimi, 1647–84, f. 49; we are most grateful to Don Natalino Bonazza, who permitted us consult the parish records. The Ziani family, including the early career of Marc'Antonio, will be the subject of a future study.

51 Evidence of Ziani's and Personé's payments can be found in the receipt book (ASV, SGSM, b. 118) and the account book (ASV, SGSM, b. 113). On 22 and 29 Dec. Faustini gave to Personé one-half of the salaries of "Lodovico" and Filippo and his brother (probably Filippo and Bortolo Melani), to be paid to these singers. Similarly, on 5 Jan. Faustini gave Ziani monies to be turned over to Francesco Simi and Giovanni Sigonfredi. Personé must have paid Lodovico and the Melanis the rest of their salaries, partly with his own funds, partly with funds given to him by Bortolo Pasinetto, with the understanding that both men would be reimbursed by Faustini at a later time. While it must have been common for composers to recommend various singers, and to help arrange for their employment, they would not necessarily have followed the process through to the end by paying them. Cavalli, however, on occasion took charge of paying his protégé, Zanetto Caliari, with funds turned over to him by Faustini or one of his associates.

tumes, apparently): Faustini did not fully reimburse him for these costs until the next autumn, a situation that most likely would not have obtained had he been simply a merchant "uninterested" in the affairs of the company.[52]

In part because of the financial participation of Personé, that is, someone other than the investors of record, the bottom line for the season is somewhat confused. Faustini lists, in his account book, expenses totaling 5,333 ducats and income amounting to 3,058 ducats, for a substantial loss to the company of 2,275 ducats. As of the start of the season, Faustini and Pasinetto had contributed capital in the amount of 1,601 ducats, still leaving a gap of 674 ducats, much of which is accounted for by the 400 ducats' worth of materials supplied by Personé but not yet paid for and the 81 ducats Pasinetto still owed the company. It is likely that, in the end, Pasinetto and Faustini covered the final 674-ducat loss in the same 70/30 portion as the original investment (as was done by the partners after the 1657/58 season; see below).

For the 1655/56 season (Cavalli's *Erismena*, with libretto by Aurelio Aureli), Faustini was forced to find new solutions to keep the theater operating; the makeup of the company changed once again, augmented by two men who had contributed to the productions for a number of years: the painter Simon Guglielmi and the woodturner Paulo Morandi (on Morandi, see chaps. 4 and 10). Guglielmi and Morandi each contributed 25 percent, with the remaining 50 percent split by Faustini and, once again, Pasinetto, according to the previous year's formula (30/70).[53] By means of this arrangement Faustini succeeded in operating the theater while bearing a much smaller percentage of the expenses (only 15 percent) than in many other years. Attracting investors must have been easier at the small S. Aponal than it would have been at a larger theater: given the low rental fees, an investor's chances to make a profit (or at least limit his losses) may have been relatively good. Unfortunately, the accounts for the season are too fragmentary to allow any realistic calculation of total expenses and income.

The formation of Faustini's company for the last year at S. Aponal is uncertain. The libretto of *Le fortune di Rodope e Damira* was dedicated to Correr and Duodo, but the author's words of praise do little to clarify the nature of the noblemen's assistance to the company. Pasinetto may by that time have withdrawn from the operatic world; he had certainly done so by the end of carnival, March 1657, when he had personal debts of 6,000 ducats, and his mother took stricter control of the family's finances.[54]

52 ASV, SGSM, b. 118, f. 11ᵛ, 2 Sept. 1655. Personé also supplied merchandise to the company for the 1656/57 season, when another opera by Ziani was presented. This time he was paid for materials by 22 Jan. 1656 m.v. (ASV, SGSM, b. 118, receipt book, f. 23).

53 This division of expenses is made clear by two entries in the receipt book, 18 Mar. and 1 Apr. 1656 (ASV, SGSM, b. 118, ff. 19ᵛ, 20).

54 ASV, AN, Atti, b. 8465, f. 18, 27 Mar. 1657. Pasinetto's days of investing were not finished, however, as he entered into a partnership with a goldsmith in Sept. 1658; his mother must have viewed that endeavor as a safer financial opportunity (ASV, AN, Atti, b. 8478, f. 90, 24 Sept. 1667).

THE MOVE TO A BIGGER THEATER:
FAUSTINI AT S. CASSIANO, 1657–1660

Faustini encountered increasing problems at S. Aponal with Francesco Ceroni, the co-owner of the theater, so that in 1657 he decided to leave for the considerably larger S. Cassiano (for more on the histories of both theaters, see chap. 4; for the operas produced by Faustini at S. Cassiano, see table 3.2B). Faustini would also have had other more personal reasons to move to a different theater, however. His brother had thought of S. Aponal as merely a launching point,[55] and a number of librettos refer to its restrictive space, with the consequent repercussions for the mounting of opera. Furthermore, it held only forty-eight boxes. A larger theater would accommodate greater spectacle on stage, as well as more boxes (S. Cassiano held over 100[56]), thus generating greater income. Faustini's rental contract for the new theater (for five years, renewable for another five; see chap. 4) was drawn up on 5 May 1657,[57] and a month and a half later he made formal arrangements to rent out S. Aponal (still under contract to him[58]) to one of Venice's academies, the Imperturbabili.[59]

A New Company

We have seen how Faustini's activities were sustained by a variety of men at S. Aponal following the death of Giovanni Faustini. When Faustini left S. Aponal to move to the larger S. Cassiano, he arrived at a new agreement, in the form of a private contract bearing the same date as the rental (see chap. 4), with Correr, Duodo, and a third man, Polifilo Zancarli, a cittadino who held a civic post, and who had occasionally helped out at S. Aponal.[60] Like Duodo and Correr, Zancarli had an

---

55 Faustini, *Oristeo*, 4.

56 ASV, AN, Atti, b. 10864, f. 122ᵛ. See chapter 2.

57 ASV, SGSM, b. 194, f. 69.

58 Despite his agreement with Ceroni on 16 Mar. 1657 to leave the theater (ASV, SGSM, b. 194, f. 169), Faustini continued to pay rent to Zanetta Diamante until 1662 (ASV, SGSM, b. 118, f. 61, 7 Mar. 1662).

59 Little is known about the Imperturbabili apart from the two published librettos produced during its use of S. Aponal: *Tolomeo* (Venice, 1658) and Domenico Gisberti's *La pazzia in trono overo Caligola delirante* (1660; published in a collection of Gisberti's works by Jecklino in Munich, 1675). See Glixon and Glixon, "Oil and Opera." Since tickets for these performances were not sold to the public, the arrangement did not violate the provisions of Faustini's agreement with Correr, Duodo, and Zancarli, which stated that Faustini could not produce operas with paid admission at S. Aponal, which he still controlled. We will be publishing an article on the Imperturbabili in the future.

60 ASV, SGSM, b. 194, ff. 24–25. See Bianconi and Walker, "Production, Consumption," 221–22. Zancarli held the post of comptroller (*scontro*) at the Rason nove (ASV, Avogaria di comun, b. 2173/123, 26 May 1655). The appearance of Zancarli's name in some records and accounts from S. Aponal suggests his participation in the company beyond that securely documented at S. Cassiano. In addition, Duodo mentioned him in a letter of 1652 regarding a credit of 20 ducats that Polifilo had held with Giovanni Faustini. The letter (ASV, SGSM, b. 188, f. 12) is undated, but internal evidence (the payment to "Nina" of 40 ducats, confirmed in the 1651/52 account book) places it in 1652. During that same season, on 22 Dec. 1651, Polifilo had delivered 25 ducats to a singer referred only as "la putella" (ASV, SGSM, b. 112, account book 1651/52, f. 31). His name is also mentioned several years later, in a receipt of Paulo Morandi signed 30 Jan. 1655 m.v. (ASV, SGSM, b. 118, f. 15ᵛ).

entrée into the world of opera through an uncle, in his case Tasio Zancarli, who had created the scenery for *La finta pazza* (1641), and for Giovanni Faustini and Cavalli's first collaboration, *La virtù de' strali d'Amore* (1642).[61] Polifilo's acquaintance with the Faustinis most likely extended back several decades, as various members of the Zancarli family lived in the parish of S. Vidal during the 1630s and 1640s, along with the Faustinis; during the 1660s, and possibly earlier, however, Polifilo resided in Marc'Antonio Correr's parish of S. Angelo.[62] The private contract between Correr, Duodo, Faustini, and Zancarli defined only the financial responsibilities of the members: other duties such as help with the recruiting of singers, or the supervision of other activities, went unmentioned.

Faustini's Incorporation Agreement of 1657

The 1657 agreement must have been drafted with Faustini's financial needs and security in mind, for it required Correr's and Duodo's commitment for five years, that is, for the length of the first term of the rental of the theater; indeed, the document states that Faustini had only come to rent the theater on the basis of that commitment.[63] Zancarli, on the other hand, was free to make contributions for as long as he wished, but the contract specified that he could leave the company after one year, giving notice by the first week of Lent so that another contributor could be found for the next season.

In this new venture each partner was to supply 200 ducats by 1 July 1657. The contract acknowledged, however, the inevitability of further expenditures:

> and there being necessary other payments, they should always be made in proportion to their investment in the company, and should be made in actual cash, until the opera reaches the stage. Excluded from this, however, will be Signor Polifilo, who will only have to expend 200 ducats; if a greater sum will be necessary, the other partners must meet that need. If there should be profits, Polifilo can receive no sum greater than 200 ducats; should there be a loss, he can lose no more than the said 200 ducats.[64]

Zancarli's initial outlay, therefore, would equal that of the other partners, but he alone would be insulated from further losses or expenses; he had found a way to participate in opera production, in a more limited, protected capacity. He was, in the end, generous in his support of the company: despite the reduced obligations implied in the contract, he paid for a number of materials, as well as portions of the

---

61 Tasio and Polifilo Zancarli are cited as uncle and nephew in a notary document of 14 Dec. 1655 (ASV, AN, Atti, b. 12666, f. 100ᵛ). On Tasio Zancarli and the Teatro S. Cassiano, see chapter 6.

62 Tasio Zancarli's wife died in the parish of S. Vidal on 22 Mar. 1642 (ASPV, Parrocchia di S. Vidal, Morti, Libro VII, 1627–65, f. 95).

63 ASV, SGSM, b. 194, ff. 24–25.

64 "et occorendo altri esborsi, doverano sempre esser fati a portione in dinaro effetivo; sino che si anderà in scena, eccetuado però detto Signor Polifilo, che non haverà da esborsar che soli ducati doicento, ma se occorerà maggior somma, gl'altri compagni doverano supplire, non potendo però egli ricever utile, mentre vi fosse guadagno, che per la suma di ducati doicento, et in occasione di perdita, non possendo perdere più, che 'l suo capitale di detti ducati doicento." ASV, SGSM, b. 194, ff. 24–25.

salaries of three singers, for which he was reimbursed at the end of the season.[65] Duodo, on the other hand, had trouble honoring his initial commitment; unable to meet the July deadline for the 200 ducats, he arranged for Antonio Barbarigo, mentioned above, to satisfy the commitment in a series of installments.[66] Both Duodo and Correr, however, paid for various expenses as the season progressed. Most of Correr's disbursements concerned payments to singers (something he had done in the past), while Duodo's covered a much wider range, including cloth merchants and a mask maker.[67]

Faustini placed himself at the head of this enterprise, taking charge of the financial aspects, an area that lay well within his expertise, by acting as *cassier*: through him would pass all the purchases, and he alone would control the cash from the sale of tickets and from the rental of the scagni; the others were expressly prohibited from doing so.[68] The monies from the tickets and bench seats belonged to the company as a whole, while those from the palchi and the food concessions went to Faustini alone, as renter of the theater. Any profits would be divided equally, as would the value of the costumes (for costumes as commodities, see chap. 10), but not improvements to the stage and mechanical systems: those, too, would belong to Faustini. The agreement made provisions for virtually any contingency, including the death of Faustini. In that case, his heirs would contribute his share of the necessary funds for the season then in production, after which the rental contract with the Trons would be considered null and void.

The benefit to the company of the noblemen Correr and Duodo went beyond their injection of needed capital: as had been the case at S. Aponal, they also provided that special aura possessed by the nobility. This served Faustini well when recruiting singers, but also when applying pressure to other nobles to pay promptly their opera box fees. A clear example of the utility of the noblemen's perceived influence can be seen in one such notice sent to an offending Venetian patrician, and subsequently registered in the acts of a notary: it reads as if it had been penned by Alvise Duodo, but the original copy included by the notary in the back of the volume is in Faustini's hand, and certainly had been drafted by him.[69] As impresario, Faustini would have wanted to maintain control over the letters and documents concerning "his" theater. Regarding the need for noble participation at the theater, we may well look to the example of S. Moisè in the 1660s for an example of what might happen when it was lacking. For the 1665/66 season that theater had been rented by the lawyer and occasional librettist Giacomo Dall'Angelo and two busi-

---

65 The singers were the prima donnas Ginevra Senardi and Silvia Manni, and the terza donna Caterina Perini.

66 ASV, SGSM, b. 194, f. 6, 12 July 1657. The Barbarigo in question was Giovanni Francesco's brother, rather than Duodo's brother-in-law.

67 According to the balance sheet (see table 3.4), Duodo had paid, among others, a cloth merchant, linen maker, cord seller, mask maker, and a barber (*marzer, tellarol, cordarol, mascherer, barbier*). ASV, SGSM, b. 101, unnumbered.

68 ASV, SGSM, b. 194, ff. 24–25.

69 ASV, AN, Atti, b. 691, f. 478v, 17 Jan. 1657 m.v. A comparison of the notary's transcription and of Faustini's original shows that even the impresario's contemporaries had trouble deciphering his difficult handwriting.

nessmen, Cristoforo Raimondi and Camillo Coveglia. Despite the participation of Dall'Angelo, the son of one of the most prominent lawyers in Venice, the company came to be perceived as run by "mere merchants," with a loss of prestige, and with problems thrown in their way.[70] Faustini steered clear of such potential pitfalls by maintaining his partnership with Correr and Duodo.

While Faustini obtained nearly all of the financing for the company from his partners, on some occasions he located other sources in advance of the opening of the production. We show elsewhere how earlier impresarios at S. Cassiano, Maestri and Castoreo, borrowed money from several noblemen (see chaps. 1 and 4). As we saw in chapter 1, the register of those supplying capital for Faustini's initial season at S. Cassiano includes, on 11 November 1657, a rudimentary contract with a different sort of investor, a printer named Salvadori.[71] Salvadori was obligated to contribute 200 ducats to the company in anticipation of sales of the libretto, to print the libretto at his own expense with an engraved frontispiece, and to provide one hundred bound copies. These 200 ducats must have represented Faustini's portion of the future profits of the sale of the libretto. Presumably, any other profits would have gone to the printer himself, as well as, perhaps, the fee paid by the dedicatee of the libretto (alternatively, this agreement could have represented a combination of Faustini's future profits with money already owed to the impresario from some unknown arrangement). Although Faustini's agreement with Salvadori suggests that he would have been responsible for the printing and sale of the libretto, L'incostanza trionfante was, instead, issued by Andrea Zulian, who must have made some arrangement with Salvadori.

Case Study: The Balance Sheet
for the 1657/58 Season

Among Faustini's papers survives a balance sheet for the 1657/58 season (see table 3.4 and figures 3.1 and 3.2).[72] Based on the figures entered in the account book for the same year,[73] it breaks down the final amounts owed by each of the part-

70 Giuseppe Ghini referred to the partners at S. Moisè as "questi signori tre furbi interessati" (these three partner-thieves) (ASF, MP, filza 5574, no. 80, 15 Apr. 1666). Earlier he wrote: "We others at S. Moisè are, after all, at a theater new to opera (and hated because it is merchants who are running it); at any rate, we cope with it, and the cognoscenti applaud us" ("Noi altri signori Moiseisti con tutto siamo d'un teatro nuovo per musica et invidiati per esser mercanti che la fa fare, ad'ogni modo facciamo fronte, e li huomini intendenti ci aplaudano") (ASF, MP, filza 5574, f. 83, 30 Jan. 1666).

71 ASV, SGSM, b. 112, section "C." Salvadori may have been a relative of Angelo Salvadori, a printer and bookseller who died on 7 Feb. 1642 at the age of 50 (ASPV, Parrocchia di S. Moisè, Morti, 1633–58, f. 44ᵛ). Angelo Salvadori was the printer of several editions of the anthologies of canzonette of Remigio Romano, as well as a number of dramatic works by, among others, Nicolò Crasso, Malatesta Leonelli, and the singer/playwright Paulo Veraldo. On the various editions of the Romano anthologies, see Miller, "Composers of San Marco," chapter 4.

72 ASV, SGSM, b. 101, unnumbered. The balance sheet is in the hand either of Alvise Duodo or his secretary (i.e., Duodo's letters reveal the same hand), and Duodo's payments are ticked off; no other copy of the balance sheet survives.

73 On the account book, see Glixon and Glixon, "Marco Faustini."

TABLE 3.4.   The Balance Sheet for the 1657/58 Season at Teatro S. Cassiano

Part A: Summary of income and expenses

Spent by Signor Faustini as in his accounts			£44865:10
From which are deducted the following [duplicate] amounts:			
Amount included in other accounts of Illustrissimo Duodo		£140	
Amount that should be credited to [illegible]		£17	
Amount in the accounts of Zancarli paid to Merope [Caterina Perini]		£310	
Amount in the said account paid to Santurini		£28	
Additional amount to be credited to Illustrissimo Correr		£1857:17	
Additional amount to be credited to Illustrissimo Duodo		£536:17	
		£2989:14	£2989:14
[Actual expenditure by Faustini]			£41875:16
Spent by Illustrissimo Duodo			£5280:14
Spent by Illustrissimo Correr			£5861:6
Still owed by the company			£6123:–
Cost of the entire opera			£59140:15
			÷3
Portion of [the costs assigned to] each member of the company			£19713:12
Income from tickets and *scagni*		£32161	
Paid [to the company] by Zancarli		£1240	
Paid [to the company] by the printer		£1240	
[Total income]		£34641	
		÷3	
Portion of the income [assigned to] each member of the company		£11537	

Part B: Accounting of each member of the company

Illustrissimo Duodo is responsible for his portion of the expenses	£19713:12		
[Credits and expenditures]	£16817:13		
Amount still owed	£2895:19		
Credit for his portion of the income:			£11537:–
Expenditures, as listed below:			
In cash to Signor Faustini		£536:17	
To the cloth merchant		£1019:3	
To the linen merchant		£395:17	
To the rope merchant		£661:15	
To the mask maker		£295:10	
To the nuns of S. Alvise		£364:17	
To the barber		£110:–	
Spent as in the list		£1896:14	
		£5280:13	£5280:13
[Credits and expenditures]			£16817:13

(continued)

TABLE 3.4.   The Balance Sheet for the 1657/58 Season at Teatro S. Cassiano (continued)

Illustrissimo Correr is responsible for his portion			
of the expenses	£19713:12		
[Credits and expenditures]	£17398:6		
Amount still owed	£2315:6		
Credit for his portion of the income:			£11537:–
Expenditures:			
In cash to Signor Faustini		£1957:17	
To Carlino [Rotari]		£1064:–	
[For his] travel		£139:10	
To Ginevra		£1625:14	
[For her] travel		£248:–	
To Caterina [Perini]		£307:15	
For the voyage of Giovanni Agostino [Poncelli]		£139:10	
To Cavagnino		£224:–	
Remainder of the room and board for Ginevra		£155:–	
		£5861:6	£5861:6
[Credits and expenditures]			£17398:6
Faustini is responsible for his portion of the expenses	£19713:12		
[Credits and expenditures]	£18771:16		
[Amount still owed]	£941:16		
Credit for his portion of the income:			£11537:–
Also for expenditures			£7234:16
			£18771:16
Part C: Remaining debts of the company			
Creditors			
Zancarli	£2515:3		
Petronio	£1344:17		
Oratio	£506:13		
Silvia Manni	£1019:5		
Blacksmith	£737:2		
	£6123:–		

Source: ASV, SGSM, b. 101.

ners, and specifies debts still outstanding. The costs were especially high that season, as the theater had to be converted once again for the production of opera after a six-year hiatus: the stage as well as the boxes underwent significant changes.

The final reckoning of the season begins with a summary of income and expenses (part A), to determine the responsibilities of the three partners. From the total expenses listed in his account book (£44,865 s.10), Faustini subtracts amounts (totaling £2,989 s.14) actually paid by other members of the company, but posted in the account book, in order to arrive at his actual expenditure; he then adds the expenditures made by Duodo and Correr along with the outstanding debts, coming up with a grand total of expenses for the season of £59,140 s.15 (or about 9,539 ducats), resulting in an obligation for each of the three associates of £19,713. He also calculates the overall income, adding the 400 ducats contributed by

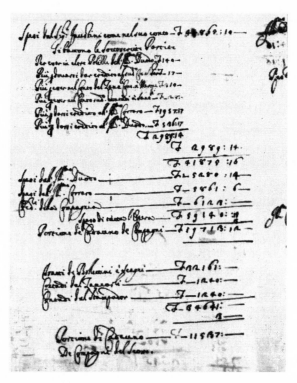

FIGURE 3.1.   Balance sheet for 1657/58 Season at S. Cassiano, pt. 1 (ASV, SGSM, b. 101)

Polifilo Zancarli and the printer Salvadori to the ticket and scagni receipts, for a total income of £34,641; this figure is likewise divided by three to arrive at a credit of £11,537 to be apportioned to the accounts of the partners. The net obligation of each of the three men, therefore, would be £8,176 s.12, or 1,319 ducats, more than 1,100 ducats above their initial contribution of 200 ducats in capital.

The second section of the balance sheet (part B) calculates the actual payments made by the three partners and the amount still owed. Duodo had spent just over £5,280, comprising cash payments to Faustini, payments to several merchants and suppliers, a tantalizing but unexplained payment of about 60 ducats to the nuns of S. Alvise, and a substantial number of miscellaneous expenditures enumerated on a separate (and unpreserved) account.[74] Of Correr's expenditures of £5,861 s.6, one third had been in cash to Faustini, and the remainder paid directly to singers, for wages, travel, and room and board. Faustini had spent £7,234 s.16 of his own funds, that is, the difference between the total expenditures in the account book and the total income. The company still owed over £6,000 at this point (Part C), comprising the reimbursement of Zancarli's expenses on behalf of the company,

74 The balance sheet specifies "spesi come in pol[izz]a," which would have been a separate sheet supplied to Faustini listing expenses paid by Duodo.

portions of the fees of the soprano Silvia Manni and the costume designer Horatio Franchi, and outstanding payments for wood (Petronio is probably the wood merchant Francesco Petroni) and metalwork. Calculating from what they had already spent, this left the three partners with substantial debts still to their names: over 460 ducats for Duodo, 370 for Correr, and 150 for Faustini. These stark figures point up the difference between Correr and Duodo's participation as compared to that of Girolamo Lando at the Novissimo, and of Antonio Boldù at S. Luca (to be discussed in chap. 4): Correr and Duodo had promised to pay the company's debts, not merely to supply start-up capital. Their expectation, however, may well have been that the theater, after several years, would begin to see a profit, or at least to break even.

Faustini, unlike Correr and Duodo, came out ahead on the entire enterprise, since he, in addition to being an equal partner in the company, was renter of the theater and therefore entitled to the annual rents on boxes (as well as profit from the sale of food and drink). More than balancing his expenses of 2,159 ducats (1,319 toward the production and 840 to rent the theater) was an income from the rental of boxes of at least 2,500 ducats (annual rents of 25 ducats on most of the

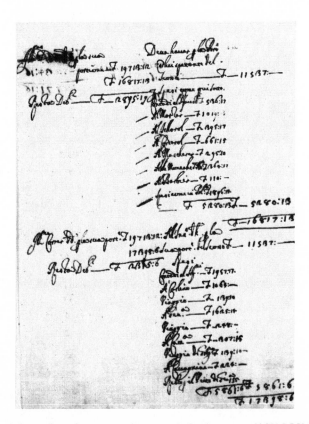

FIGURE 3.2.   Balance sheet for 1657/58 Season at S. Cassiano, pt. 2 (ASV, SGSM, b. 101)

more than 100 boxes in the pepian and first three orders, plus whatever he could earn on nightly rentals of those in the fourth order), leaving him a net profit of 300 ducats or more.

The balance sheet bears no date, but on 16 September 1658 Correr and Duodo signed a declaration of their satisfaction regarding Faustini's management, much as Pasinetto had in 1655.[75] Clearly such satisfaction was not dependent upon the company making a profit: they stated that Faustini had fulfilled his obligations both in terms of capital investment and in his contributions toward the company's losses, with the exception that the singer Silvia Manni remained a creditor for 100 ducats, to be paid to her by Faustini by the end of upcoming carnival.

Faustini at S. Cassiano, 1658–1660

For the 1658/59 season the company produced Francesco Cavalli's *Antioco*, the first of a three-opera commission (although only two would be realized). The figures for this season survive in an account book, discussed by Bianconi and Walker in their magisterial article on opera production.[76] Although Cavalli's three-year contract was signed on 24 July 1658, a number of entries in the book suggest a later start to the preparations than was usual for Faustini, and in November Duodo wrote a letter to Faustini complaining of problems regarding singers, roles, and costumes.[77] Although expenses for the theater proved to be much lower that second year, as demands for new construction had already been addressed, the men still lost a good deal of money, £9,231, that is about 496 ducats per partner. Ironically, the company's successful hiring of Cavalli away from the Grimani theater affected the bottom line in a negative rather than in a positive way: the ticket sales brought in £3,438 less for Cavalli's opera than for Ziani's in the previous season.[78] However, because the expenses for the production were considerably lower, the loss for the 1658/59 carnival was reduced from almost 4,000 ducats to 1,488.

In this second season at S. Cassiano another member of Faustini's circle, Giovanni Antonio Leffio (who lived in Duodo's parish of S. Maria del Giglio), carried out some activities for the company, and became friendly with a number of Faustini's musicians.[79] Although Leffio's family owned considerably more property

---

75 ASV, SGSM, b. 118, receipt book, f. 34.

76 Bianconi and Walker, "Production, Consumption," 221–27.

77 Duodo's letter of 5 Nov. 1658 (ASV, SGSM, b. 188, ff. 19–20) is cited in Bianconi and Walker, "Production, Consumption," 224.

78 For more on the reception of these two operas, see chapter 11. For the 1658/59 figures, see Bianconi and Walker, "Production, Consumption," 226.

79 As previously mentioned, Marc'Antonio Correr sent his greetings to Leffio in his letter to Faustini cited above. Leffio traveled to Ferrara to meet "Giulio da Ferrara," a singer in the upcoming *Antioco*, and he paid the singer Orsetta Parmine 10 doble on 14 Feb. 1659. Faustini paid Leffio 2 doppie on 8 Jan. 1659 to cover his trip to Ferrara (ASV, SGSM, b. 194, account book 1658/59, f. 18); for Leffio's payment of Parmine, see ibid., f. 17. Carlo Andrea Coradini, the lutenist who performed in *L'incostanza trionfante*, wrote in Jan. 1660 that he had received word from Leffio in Rome about the success—or the lack thereof—of Cavalli's *Elena* in 1659/60 (ASV, SGSM, b. 101, f. n., letter of Carlo Andrea Coradini to Faustini, 24 Jan. 1660).

than Faustini's, and he may have had sufficient assets to invest in Faustini's companies, nothing suggests that he did so.[80]

Some time after the conclusion of the 1658/59 season, a change came about in the company. Even though Correr and Duodo had committed to a five-year term of support, they apparently decided to end it after only two years (and Faustini must have accepted that decision). On 25 June 1659 the two noblemen declared themselves satisfied with Faustini's administration, as they had in September 1658. This declaration, written in formal "business" language, reads like an official document, but it takes a different turn after approving Faustini's administration: "Thus, with the present receipt, we make a final and perpetual settlement in the broadest and most valued form, declaring also that we have withdrawn from the company, in witness thereof we have made the present declaration, by which it is also declared that all the debts of the past year remain our responsibility, he [Faustini] having entirely satisfied all [of his], as in the other declaration of 16 September 1658."[81] The noblemen's withdrawal may be borne out by a comparison of the contracts for two singers drawn up in consecutive years, Elena Passarelli's of 9 October 1658, and Lucietta Vidman's of 18 July 1659.[82] While the first contract lists Faustini, Correr, and Duodo as the "interessati," and bears the signatures of all three, the second contract, signed about a month after the noblemen's declaration, lists only Faustini. Another, more telling, indication lies in the letters that Faustini wrote to the Bentivoglio family in Ferrara in July 1659 seeking information about the availability of the singer "Paino."[83] In previous years it was Correr who had written to the Bentivoglios; not only was Faustini lacking his support in the summer of 1659, but he had not found another nobleman to write in Correr's place. Several months later, in November, a correspondent from Naples wrote to Faustini, remarking that he had suggested two sopranos to the nobleman, but had received no reply.[84] Whether the correspondent had written to Correr because he had served as a channel for recruiting in the past, or for some other reason, is uncertain, but Correr's failure to reply almost certainly confirms his absence from recruiting matters. For the 1659/60 season, then, Faustini operated without the fi-

---

80 The Faustini and Leffio families eventually became united in marriage when Leffio's sister Cecilia wed Bortolo Faustini, the son of Marco's relative Giovanni Antonio Faustini, in June 1665. Indeed, it was Faustini who drew up the marriage contract between the two parties, on 9 Apr. 1665 (ASV, AN, Atti, b. 13920, ff. 70–74). We have not been able to pinpoint the exact familial relationship between Giovanni Antonio and Marco Faustini. It would seem, however, that aside from his cousin Elena Bottoni, Marco maintained his closest ties with Giovanni Antonio and Bortolo Faustini. Leffio would remain close to the impresario until his death; Faustini named him the executor of his will. See ASV, SGSM, b. 13, f. 205 and ASV, AN, Testamenti, b. 767, f. 214.

81 "Onde con il presente ricevere li facciamo fine et perpetua quietatione in ogni più ampla et valida forma; dichiarando anco come si siamo cavati dalla compagnia, in fede di che habiamo fato la presente dichiaratione, con che resta anco formato che tutti li debiti dell'anno passato restano sopra di noi, havendo egli sodisfatto tutti intieramete come nell'altra dichiaratione 1658 16 settembre." ASV, SGSM, b. 118, receipt book, f. 39, 25 June 1659.

82 ASV, SGSM, b.194, f. 12 and f. 11, respectively.

83 ASFe, AB, b. 330, f. 211, 231, 5 and 19 July 1659. See Monaldini, *Orto dell'Esperidi*, 137–38.

84 Letter of 4 Nov. 1659 from Naples, sender's name illegible (ASV, SGSM, b. 101, unnumbered).

nancial support of his previous partners; he must have found others to help him fund the production for the 1660 carnival, but no such names have as yet surfaced.

A NEW FINANCIAL AND MANAGERIAL MODEL: FAUSTINI AT SS. GIOVANNI E PAOLO, 1660-1668

After three years at S. Cassiano, Marco Faustini transferred his services to the venerable Teatro SS. Giovanni e Paolo, owned by the patrician Giovanni Grimani (for operas produced there by Faustini, see table 3.3C). No direct evidence explains Faustini's departure from S. Cassiano (other than, perhaps, Francesco Cavalli's unavailability—owing to his departure to France—to complete the third opera specified in his contract), but the answer may in part lie in the political misfortunes of Abbot Vettor Grimani Calergi, a relative of the theater owner.[85] Grimani Calergi, who had been involved with the SS. Giovanni e Paolo production during the 1658/59 season, was banished from Venice soon after. Giovanni Grimani may have sought someone of Faustini's caliber to operate his theater, for Francesco Piva, who signed librettos for the 1657/58 and 1659/60 seasons, ran into financial difficulties during his tenure there.[86] Faustini's move to SS. Giovanni e Paolo was not taken without financial risk, however, for the impresario continued to pay the rather steep rent at S. Cassiano through the end of his lease.[87] Whatever the financial circumstances, Faustini, as well as his old associates Duodo and Correr, had made their last impresarial move.

The transfer to the Grimani theater may well have been considered prestigious, both by Faustini and by his friends and associates. In some ways, however, it provided new challenges and conditions: for the first time the impresario took over a theater with a long history of opera production, and one where the owner took a keen interest in the activities of the company. Faustini acquired control over artisans already in Grimani's employ, and he continued to use some of the singers who had performed previously in the theater. Also, unlike the situation at S. Aponal and S. Cassiano, Faustini could fall back on the Grimani tradition and, presumably, could have relied on Giovanni Grimani to see to some of the recruiting matters, something that Duodo and Correr had done in the past.[88] We do not know if Faustini's desires and preferences ever came to clash with those of the theater owner (as they apparently would later with Grimani's nephews; see below).

Although they had earlier withdrawn from the S. Cassiano company, at SS. Giovanni e Paolo, Correr and Duodo continued to help Faustini, perhaps in some areas where Grimani had previously participated more actively: Duodo facilitated

85 Grimani Calergi's operatic activities will be discussed in a forthcoming article.

86 A legal dispute between Piva and the costumer Horatio Franchi in Feb. 1657 may indicate that Piva was active in opera production, perhaps even at SS. Giovanni e Paolo, the season before the first libretto he signed. See ASV, GP, Dimande, b. 67, f. 154, 19 Feb. 1656 m.v.

87 It is not known if Faustini sublet that theater to a third party for the presentation of commedia dell'arte, or if he allowed it to remain dark.

88 In 1662/63, when his cousin Vettor Grimani Calergi was at S. Luca, Giovanni Grimani did use his typical channels in Ferrara and Florence in order to foil Grimani Calergi's plans to hire desirable singers, thus aiding Faustini's cause.

the painter Ippolito Mazzarini's contract with Faustini in May 1660, and the fore-word of the libretto hints that it was Correr who, among others, convinced the au-thor Beregan to complete his *Annibale in Capua* for that season.[89] For the 1662/63 season, Duodo was particularly concerned with the size and scope of the role for Sebastiano Cioni, a singer he had taken under his protection, but also with general matters of recruiting.[90] Beyond this particular managerial and recruiting assistance, we have little knowledge of the financial underpinnings of the company, nor of the nature of Faustini's arrangement with Giovanni Grimani during the early 1660s.

It has long been assumed that Faustini managed the Grimani theater for nearly eight seasons, that is, from 1660/61 until 15 December 1667. Faustini's receipt regis-ter, the book where composers, singers, dancers and artisans signed for their fees, however, shows a two-year gap during the 1663/64 and 1664/65 seasons. Additional evidence suggests that Faustini relinquished his responsibilities for those two years, beginning shortly after the death of Giovanni Grimani on 14 May 1663; a number of sources point to Vettor Grimani Calergi's involvement during these two years, while none make reference to Faustini. The first term of Faustini's contract almost cer-tainly expired after three years (that is, following the 1662/63 season), and Grimani Calergi, active at the rival Teatro S. Luca in 1662/63 (having returned from his ban-ishment), could have taken advantage of this circumstance in order to seize control over SS. Giovanni e Paolo (the young nephews of Giovanni Grimani, Giovanni Carlo and Vicenzo Grimani, were now the legal owners of the theater).[91] Faustini and Grimani Calergi may have felt they could not work together.[92]

The End of Faustini's Impresarial Career:
The Final Years at SS. Giovanni e Paolo

By the end of the 1664/65 season, the owners of SS. Giovanni e Paolo sought a change or, more accurately, a return to the management of the beginning of the decade. While the particulars of Faustini's first contract with the Grimanis are un-known, his second contract does survive, and its contents are unlike any other pre-vious Venetian contract extant for an opera theater. Faustini did not rent the the-ater, as was the usual custom; instead, the Grimanis paid him to run it. They advanced Faustini 900 ducats, and assigned to him the income from the boxes in the top level (the less expensive soffitto) and the receipts from ticket sales and rental of the scagni.[93] The contract specified an initial three-year term, with

---

89 For Mazzarini's contract, see ASV, SGSM, b. 94, f. 5, 6 June 1660. On Correr, see Beregan, *Anni-bale in Capua*, 7. Correr lived in the same parish as Beregan, and was godfather to his daughter baptized on 24 Feb. 1661 m.v. (ASPV, Parrocchia di S. Angelo, Battesimi, 1639–62).

90 Duodo refers to Cioni's part in ASV, SGSM, b. 188, ff. 2, 3, 21, and b. 101, unnumbered, letter of 1 Nov. 1662.

91 In May 1663 Giovanni Carlo Grimani and Vicenzo Grimani were 14 and 11 years old, respectively.

92 Several letters written by Emperor Leopold of Austria suggest that Grimani Calergi, although only recently returned from his banishment, might have been active at the Grimani theater for the 1660/61 season; see Kalista, *Korespondence císaře Leopolda*, 50.

93 For the contract between Faustini and the Grimanis, see ASV, SGSM, b. 194, f. 134.

the possibility of a renewal for another three years. Without the income from all of the box rentals, which he had been able to rely upon at the other theaters, it is not clear how Faustini expected to break even; while he could count on a total income of about 6,000 ducats (900 from Grimani and the rest from ticket and scagni sales), the expenses for the opera, greater than ever before because of the steady increase in salaries to the prima donna, came to between 8,000 and 9,000 ducats. Unless new documentation about his company comes to light, we cannot know whether Faustini planned to rely upon investors, perhaps including one or more of his old partners, or the theater owners, to make up the gap.[94]

Although the composition of Faustini's company is uncertain, we know that during this period two other acquaintances assisted him with certain aspects of his impresarial duties. The more important was Antonio Ugieri, who held an office at the Provveditori alle biave (grain office). The Ugieri family had lived in the parish of S. Vidal for a number of decades, so that the impresario may have known him as a young man. Ugieri witnessed Horatio Franchi's contract in 1665, wrote out a number of others, and also made some disbursements for the company.[95] A relative of Carlo Pallavicino, he signed for the composer's earnings for *Il tiranno humiliato d'Amore overo il Meraspe* in 1668.[96] Another person living in Venice who may not have been involved in the day-to-day affairs of the company, but who certainly aided in the recruiting of singers, was a man of the church named Erasmo Secreti.[97] In 1665 Secreti, also a resident of Faustini's parish of S. Vidal, received a number of letters from Carlo Mazzini that dealt with the hiring of singers from Rome (see chap. 7).

One of Faustini's primary reasons for resuming his impresarial activities was to perpetuate the name and glory of his late brother by presenting settings of librettos

---

94 Four letters written by Duodo in the summer and autumn of 1665 make reference to monies he laid out: ASV, SGSM, b. 188, f. 372 (8 Aug.); b. 194, f. 148 (7 Nov.); b. 194, f. 150 (14 Nov.); and b. 188, f. 386 (undated). In the second of those letters, Duodo refers also to the other partners from the S. Cassiano years, Correr and Zancarli.

95 ASV, SGSM, b. 118, receipt book, f. 90ᵛ, 13 May 1669. Ugieri also signed Faustini's book in Mar. 1667 (ibid., f. 81ᵛ).

96 ASV, SGSM, b. 194, f. 23, 6 Jan. 1667 m.v. Pallavicino's and Ugieri's fathers both came from Salò. Pallavicino's name appears with those of Ugieri and his brother in a number of Venetian notarial documents. Ugieri may have begun his association with the theater by 1664, as a sheet listing the nightly expenses for Andrea Mattioli's *Ciro*, one of the operas mounted in Faustini's absence, appears to be in his hand; he maintained an interest in opera for some years to come, that is, after Faustini's withdrawal. In 1674 Ugieri was involved in a dispute concerning the fees of the singer Orsola Balsami at SS. Giovanni e Paolo (ASV, AN, Atti, b. 6796, f. 88ᵛ, 5 May 1674). He served, along with Zuane Armano, as the pieggio for Gasparo Mauro, Horatio Franchi, and Hippolito Mazzarini in their capacity as the impresarios at the Grimani theater for the 1674 and 1675 seasons (ASV, AN, Atti, b. 6110, f. 61ᵛ, 22 Aug. 1677; see also ASV, AN, Atti, b. 6108, f. 2, 2 Mar. 1675). In 1679 Ugieri bore some responsibility for the payment of the singer Bianca Grebosi at S. Luca (ASV, AN, Atti, b. 6801, f. 191, 14 Dec. 1679). That same year he was owed 500 ducats for scagni, most likely at one of the Grimani theaters, presumably connected to a theatrical loan (ASV, AN, Atti, b. 6113, f. 110).

97 Secreti, originally from Fermo (ASV, AN, Atti, b. 5510, f. 4ᵛ, and elsewhere) but resident in Venice, held the title of Abbot and of Archpriest of a rural church in the diocese of Padua (ASV, AN, Atti, b. 3485, f. 223ᵛ), and was the Venetian agent of Cardinal Flavio Chigi (ASV, AN, Atti, b. 3514, f. 1126ᵛ, and elsewhere).

that Giovanni had completed, or at least drafted, before he died, but that had never been performed.[98] The staging of Giovanni's librettos did not go according to plan: a new setting of *Doriclea* failed to reach the stage in 1665/66, and two other works, *Alciade* and *Il tiranno humiliato d'Amore overo il Meraspe*, were each performed a season later than anticipated.[99] Instead, two revivals of operas by Antonio Cesti appeared in substitution: *Orontea* in 1665/66, and *Dori* in 1666/67, along with a new work by Cesti.

Faustini's thirteenth and, it turned out, last, season as an opera impresario was 1667/68. He planned to offer Pallavicino's *Il tiranno humiliato d'Amore overo il Meraspe*, the last of Giovanni Faustini's unfinished librettos, originally scheduled for the year before, and an opera by Cavalli, a setting of *Eliogabalo* (to Aureli's revision of another's text). On 15 December 1667, however, about two months short of the end of his three-year commitment at SS. Giovanni e Paolo, and just a day or so after the opening of the season, Faustini ceded control of the theater to Giovanni Carlo and Vicenzo Grimani, and absolved himself (or was absolved) from any profits or losses that would be incurred during the upcoming carnival.[100] The agreement with the Grimani brothers specifies a series of terms, principally involving financial matters and responsibilities, but also mentioning the repertory (at this point, in mid-December, Cavalli's *Eliogabalo* was still scheduled).[101]

The reasons for Faustini's resignation are not clear, nor do we know whether the move was forced by the Grimani brothers or occurred at his own instigation. Several scholars have implied that the owners were dissatisfied with Faustini's choice of operas (especially with his brother's old fashioned librettos), or with his

---

98 See Rosand, *Opera*, 191–95. The preface to Giovanni Faustini's *Alciade*, signed by the printer Nicolini, but almost certainly written by Marco Faustini, is a paean of praise to his beloved brother, in which he cites all the published librettos as well as those still to be mounted, and alludes to his premature death.

99 *Alciade* was planned for the 1665/66 season only when Cesti intimated that he could not finish *Tito* on schedule; when Cesti found he could complete the work, *Alciade* was shelved until the next season. On this series of mishaps, see chapters 5 and 6.

100 ASV, SGSM, b. 188, ff. 199–200, 15 Dec. 1667. The libretto of *Il tiranno humiliato d'Amore overo il Meraspe* bears the dedication date 12 Dec., and the opening would probably have been the following day. Since performances at this point in the season were not usually every night (see chap. 11), it is likely that the agreement was signed after only one had taken place.

101 The terms, briefly summarized, are the following: (1) Faustini cedes his rights to the theater to the Grimani brothers; (2) they may continue to present Pallavicino's opera as many times as they wish, without interference from Faustini; (3) they may present *Eliogabalo* or any other opera they wish; (4) all the income from bollettini and scagni, except for that from the first night, already in Faustini's hands, belongs to the Grimani brothers; (5) the Grimani brothers accept the responsibility for paying the salaries of all the singers and of Pallavicino and Cavalli, and to reimburse Gasparo Mauro for his advance on the scagni, with the income from sales of bollettini and scagni; (6) if the income from bollettini and scagni is not sufficient, they will reimburse Faustini for the difference and will also repay the remainder of Mauro's advance; (7) Faustini will continue to receive the income from those palchi assigned to him in the original agreement; (8) Faustini will be reimbursed for the rent he paid for the granary used as a storeroom; and (9) the nightly employees hired by Faustini, that is doormen, stagehands, and instrumentalists, will retain their jobs for the remainder of the season. The original text of this agreement is published nearly complete in Mancini, Muraro, and Povoledo, *Teatri di Venezia*, 1:309–10.

performance as impresario;[102] given that by this time Faustini had mounted (or attempted to mount) productions of all of his brother's librettos, however, he would, perforce, have moved on to more modern material had he continued to operate the theater. The two young Grimani brothers, one of whom had recently come of age, might have been eager to try their hands at the exciting business of opera without the assistance of a seasoned professional, and Faustini, perhaps tired of the constant difficulties of putting on an opera season (exacerbated by interference from the owners), may have willingly yielded to their desires. What seems to have precipitated the decision, in any case, was the reception of Pallavicino's opera, since the agreement was signed almost immediately following its first performance, and makes it clear that the Grimani brothers, and not Faustini, would decide how long it would run before the second opera would be presented. Although Cavalli did compose *Eliogabalo*, it was not presented. The opera actually performed at SS. Giovanni e Paolo was an entirely different work with the same title by a different composer (Giovanni Antonio Boretti) and on a different libretto, this time written entirely by Aureli.[103] As Mauro Calcagno has shown, it is likely that the two Grimani brothers imposed the switch.[104]

It should be noted that Faustini continued to pay performers and others throughout the remainder of the season.[105] Indeed, one sentence in the agreement of 15 December implies that that would be the case: if, after carnival, the income from the tickets and seats had not been sufficient to pay the musicians, the Grimani brothers were to turn over to Faustini those funds necessary to meet all the obligations.[106] Whatever the circumstances, after no fewer than seventeen years, Marco Faustini's involvement in the production of opera had finished.

FAUSTINI'S SELF-IMAGE AS IMPRESARIO AND THE SUCCESS OF THE COMPANY

Even though Marco Faustini formed only part of an impresarial system that included the noblemen Marc'Antonio Correr and Alvise Duodo and, later, members of the Grimani family, he saw his role as superior to those of the other participants. Regarding the negotiations for the hiring of Giulia Masotti in 1666 he wrote (our emphasis), "*I am the only master,* and to me alone goes the responsibility of being in command, particularly in such an important enterprise where I will have an in-

---

102 See Rosand, *Opera,* 195–96, and Glover, *Cavalli,* 29.

103 Discussions of both versions of *Eliogabalo,* with speculation concerning the reasons behind the cancellation of Cavalli's opera, can be found in Calcagno, "Staging Musical Discourses" and id., "Libretto and Its Discontents."

104 One possible sequence of events is that the brothers, who wished to become more involved in running the theater, made the arrangement with Faustini for him to withdraw while still planning to present Cavalli's *Eliogabalo.* Perhaps only when they took over did they examine the libretto and/or score carefully, and realize that they wanted to make the substitution.

105 ASV, SGSM, b. 118, ff. 86–90ᵛ.

106 ASV, SGSM, b. 188. f. 199, 15 Dec. 1667.

vestment of 3,000 ducats of our money."[107] Faustini used similar language in a complaint against one of his singers, Sebastiano Cioni, in August 1667: "Nor is it fitting that those who operate in my service, and who are paid lavishly by me with a punctuality that is known to all, should profess enmity to me, while they, in regard to the operas, must depend on me for all things, they must be with me daily to receive from me the necessary orders, and they must obey me regarding the business of the operas [for all things] that are entrusted to me *as their sole master*."[108] Faustini controlled the financial strings of the company and he shouldered the main responsibility for the hiring and the payment of the singers and the artisans, as well as for the running of the theater. He also enjoyed some freedom in the selection of the opera to be performed, given the preference shown to the librettos of his brother. We may wonder, then, how he reacted when, in 1665, he received these words from Pietro Andrea Ziani concerning a commission:

> I thank Your Most Esteemed Lordship for the courteous invitation you have made to me for the upcoming carnival; I know from what you have shared with me that you have newly taken the Grimani theater, with the conditions, etc. You should know, however, that Signor Procurator Duodo wrote to me of this upcoming dispatch (that is, the invitation of me together with Forni), saying that you should assist us as his most dear comrade, etc. And he tells me that he did this even without your knowledge, and he presses me to respond immediately.[109]

In acting in advance of Faustini in this important commission, Duodo may have overreached or upset the balance that had developed among the partners, but if the impresario harbored any ill feelings toward him, they did not prevent the operation of the company for another three years. In Correr and Duodo, Faustini had found associates who were well matched in temperament and in their enthusiasm for the business of opera. Starting at the humblest of opera theaters, their passion for opera took them to the most prestigious stage of the time; their longevity as an opera company was unprecedented, and unequaled for the era.

107 "Io sono il solo padrone, et a me solo anco tocca il comandare, particolarmente in un negotio importante dove haverò una interesse di D 3/mila della nostra moneta." ASV, SGSM, b. 188, f. 294^v, undated draft.

108 "Nè essendo convenevole, che quelli, che devono operare in mio servitio et che sono profusamente da me pagati con quella pontualità ch'è notoria, habbino à professar mecco inimictia; mentre essi per occasione dell'opere musicali devino in tutto da me dipendere, dovendo giornalmente esser mecco per ricevere da me gl'ordini neccessarij; et obedirmi nel negotio delle opere, in tutto quello, che da me, come [added: solo] padrone di esse li viene commesso." ASV, AN, Atti, b. 1094, f. 200, 4 Aug. 1667.

109 "Ringrazio infinitamente Vostra Signoria Colendissima del cortese invito che mi fa per il futuro carnovale, so come della participazione che mi da di haver di novo preso il Teatro Grimano con le condizioni, etc. Deve perciò sapere che il futturo dispaccio mi scrisse in questo particolare (apunto con invitarmi assieme col Forni) il Signor Procurator Duodo; dicendo che lei deve assisterli come suo carissimo compare, etc., e mi dice haver ciò fatto ancora senza sua saputa e mi strinse a subita risposta." ASV, SGSM, b. 188, f. 104, 22 Mar. 1665. We would like to thank Mauro Calcagno for his assistance with this passage.

POSTLUDE: MARCO FAUSTINI'S LATER LIFE

During the years he served as an impresario, Faustini's non-theatrical activities continued unabated. The mainstay of his legal business remained the Salt Office, and, in particular, the work brought to him by the holders of its regional franchises. By the mid-1660s, his income from these retainers alone reached over 400 ducats annually. Such an income by itself would have made Faustini quite comfortable, if not wealthy. These stable salaries were augmented by fees from a steady stream of individual cases, both civil and criminal, conducted before a wide variety of courts, ranging from the most important bodies in the Republic, such as the Council of Ten, the Collegio, the Avogaria di comun, and the three Quarantie, to such lower-level courts as the Giudici di petizion and Giudici del proprio, and many ordinary magistracies, including the Rason nove and the Magistrato alle beccarie (see the Glossary). One further aspect of Faustini's legal business that grew in importance during the 1650s and 1660s was the administration of estates and guardianships.

Faustini also provided legal services to several people connected to opera. The first of these was Zanetta Diamante, part-owner of the Teatro S. Aponal: Faustini helped her with some difficulties concerning her co-owner and cousin, Francesco Ceroni.[110] Faustini also aided the composer Francesco Cavalli in a property dispute against one Maddalena Busca.[111] Lastly, he assisted the singer Giovanni Antonio Cavagna with some legal problems during the 1660s, and then later in the decade and into the 1670s regarding an investment he had entered into with the government secretary Allemante Angelo Donini.[112]

Another constant in Marco's life was the Scuola Grande di S. Marco. He rose in the ranks, eventually winning election to the second highest post, vicario, but was never elected to the highest, guardian grande, despite being nominated nine times over the two decades.[113] Although he was respected, he was not considered a prime candidate for these most lofty offices, perhaps because his financial status was not high enough. Nonetheless, he remained among the leaders of the scuola, and was, therefore, among the elite of the cittadino class.

On 7 January 1676, at the age of 69, following two years of declining health, Marco Faustini died.[114] He left no descendants, nor were there any other close relatives to inherit his estate. He made a number of specific bequests, but the residual beneficiary of the remainder of Faustini's estate was the Scuola Grande di S. Marco. The scuola conducted an inventory of the estate, and cataloged the pa-

---

110 ASV, SGSM, b. 110.

111 ASV, Monastero di San Lorenzo, b. 23, no. 22. On f. 2, a list of expenses includes a payment authorized by Faustini. Most of Cavalli's legal needs, however, were handled by the lawyer and librettist Nicolò Minato. See Glover, *Cavalli*, 24 and 36.

112 Letters concerning Cavagna's business investments, which later required Faustini's help, are found in ASV, SGSM, bb. 101, 109, and 188. The notarial documents by which Cavagna gave Faustini power of attorney include ASV, AN, Atti, b. 10866, f. 125ᵛ, 19 Jan. 1662 m.v.

113 The nominations came in 1658, 1659, 1662, 1663, 1664, 1666, 1667, 1670, and 1673 (ASV, SGSM, reg. 27). For more on the scuola see J. Glixon, *Honoring God*, esp. chapter 1.

114 ASPV, Parrochia di S. Vidal, Morti, 1665–1727, f. 17.

pers found in a wardrobe: these now comprise the thirty *buste* of Faustini papers that still remain in the archive of the scuola (most notably, for our purposes, the "bundle of papers concerning the operas performed in 1665, 1666, and 1667," that is, buste 188 and 194 of the scuola's papers).[115] Of no monetary value, the papers were not, like the rest of Faustini's possessions, sold to carry out his testamentary bequests. They were instead brought to the scuola for safekeeping, in the event they needed to be consulted in the future in any legal disputes concerning Faustini's estate. Fortunately, although Faustini's utility to the scuola had ceased, his papers were preserved, providing modern scholars a window through which to glimpse the world of a seventeenth-century opera impresario.

---

115 "filza de scritture concernenti l'opere fatte 1665, 66, 67." Two copies of the inventory are extant: ASV, AN, Atti, b. 10871, f. 162 and ASV, GP, Inventari, b. 379, no. 83.

CHAPTER FOUR

CASE STUDIES: COMPANIES AND
OPERA PRODUCTION AT FOUR
VENETIAN THEATERS

In this chapter we examine the operation of four Venetian theaters—S. Cassiano, the Novissimo, S. Aponal, and S. Luca—over a span of about thirty years. Each theater provides a different window into the challenges of opera production. The early companies at S. Cassiano, a theater built and owned by the patrician Tron family, were pathbreaking, for they helped to establish opera as an entertainment worthy of support and patronage in a city such as Venice. There we see the progression from a self-contained company of artists to one headed by a "professional" impresario, Marco Faustini, and his three partners, with none of them contributing artistically to the company. During the 1640s the Novissimo, built on the grounds of a monastery, strove for new heights of excellence, especially in terms of visual spendor, in an effort to outdo the three older theaters, S. Cassiano, S. Moisè, and SS. Giovanni e Paolo. In recent decades scholars have linked this theater with Venice's Accademia degli Incogniti regarding both its artistic offerings and, possibly, its operation. We look carefully into the economic backing of the theater and, more specifically, at its impresario, Girolamo Lappoli, in order to understand the financial and managerial structure of the theater, which incurred substantial debts that were not settled until after it had ceased operation. In 1650, ten years after the founding of the Novissimo, the small S. Aponal, owned by cittadini, held its own against its more noble competition; here we show how, under the management of Giovanni and Marco Faustini, it provided an advantageously priced venue for opera, but one fraught with difficulties brought on by one of its owners. S. Luca became the last Venetian comedy theater during this period to join the world of opera production, entering the fray only in 1660, more than two decades after S. Cassiano had first presented opera. Our examination of this theater brings into focus both the financial obstacles that plagued opera companies, and the variety of sponsors willing to take part in an operatic enterprise. Throughout the chapter we meet again with the owners and partners introduced in the previous three chapters, but in each case with a new focus.

66

S. CASSIANO

The first three decades of activity of the Teatro S. Cassiano, long famous in the annals of music history as the first public opera theater, demonstrate vividly the difficulties inherent in mounting this expensive entertainment.[1] Indeed, the story of S. Cassiano speaks eloquently to the fragility of any opera theater. A successful operation required sustained commitment at a number of levels; at S. Cassiano, under the ownership of the Tron family, that commitment was lacking, and after almost fifteen years of activity as an opera theater, it temporarily closed at a time when the Grimani theater was presenting operas on a regular basis. Indeed, the succession of at least five different management teams at S. Cassiano from 1637 to 1660 gives some indication of the instability of the enterprise (see the chronology in table 4.1).

The First Company

Because S. Cassiano was the first theater to present opera in Venice, both its proprietors and its artists entered *terra incognita* in late 1636. As various members of the Tron family followed this new path, they fell back on the comedic theatrical traditions of Venice for models of rental practice, but their experience with performers of comedy had not prepared them adequately for the difficulties that lay ahead.

The little documentation that survives from the inaugural season suggests that while the Trons may have dedicated their theater to opera, it was the company of performers themselves that bore the financial burdens of the enterprise. The operation resembled, in its exterior trappings, the workings of a commedia dell'arte troupe. The nearly self-sufficient company that performed Benedetto Ferrari and Francesco Manelli's *Andromeda* comprised, in addition to the composer and librettist, six singers.[2] On 22 December 1636, shortly before the opening of the opera, the company was in need of capital, and found one modest source from within its own ranks. The singer Giovanni Battista Bisucci loaned 100 ducats to the rest of the company; the sum was to be reimbursed from the first monies collected from the performances.[3] The next day, four members of the company signed a contract with the Venetian dancer and choreographer Giovanni Battista Balbi, commissioning him to present three ballets at each performance of the opera.[4] No contracts regarding scenery, costumes, or instrumental performers have come to light. As both extant documents concern expenses generated from within the company,

---

1 On the early history of S. Cassiano, see Johnson, "Short, Lascivious Lives."

2 Several members of the company (Medici, Maddalena Manelli, and Marconi) had performed in Giovanni Felice Sances's *Ermiona* in Padua several months earlier, and that production has been viewed as the catalyst for the beginnings of public opera in Venice. See Petrobelli, "'L'Ermiona'," 125–41, and Rosand, *Opera*, 67–70.

3 ASV, AN, Atti, b. 5973, f. 221, 22 Dec. 1636. For some reason Anselmo Marconi's name is lacking in the agreement.

4 The musicians mentioned in the agreement include Ferrari, Bisucci, Medici, and Angeletti. ASV, AN, Atti, b. 5973, f. 225, 23 Dec. 1636. For more on the dances specified in the contract, see chapter 8.

TABLE 4.1.   Chronology of the Teatro S. Cassiano

Date	Event
1581	Constructed by Tron family to present comedies; closed after one season
Early 17th century	Reopened for comedy perhaps as early as 1612, certainly by 1626
1629	Destroyed by fire
Ca. 1633	Reopened for comedy; 20 December 1633, destroyed by fire
1636/37–1637/38	First two operatic seasons; company (for at least the first season) of Benedetto Ferrari (composer), Francesco Manelli (librettist), and six singers (Giovanni Battista Bisucci, Girolamo Medici, Maddalena Manelli, Annibale Grasselli, Francesco Angeletti, and Anselmo Marconi)
By September 1638	Rented to new company of Francesco Cavalli (composer), Oratio Persiani (librettist), Giovanni Battista Balbi (ballet master) and two singers (Giovanni Battista Bisucci and Felicita Uga)
1639–44	Company directed by Cavalli, with (at least through 1640/41) Balbi
4 June 1644	Cavalli transfers management of theater to company of three noblemen: Ettor Tron (the owner of the theater), Polo Boldù, and Luca Francesco Barbaro; they assume Cavalli's debts. The company operates only one season.
1645/46 and 1646/47	Theater probably closed for War of Candia
April 1648, 1648/49, 1649/50, 1650/51 seasons	Rented to company of Rocco Maestri and Bortolo Castoreo; they operate it for three seasons, after which the theater presents no opera for six seasons. Comedies may have been performed in 1656/57
5 May 1657, 1657/58, 1658/59, 1659/60 seasons	Rented to Marco Faustini for term of five years, renewable for another five. Faustini presents operas there for only three years, after which it ceases to present opera (Faustini pays rent for the remaining two years of the contract)
5 October 1665, 1665/66 season	Galeazzo Passarelli rents theater; after one season, no operas presented until 1678/79

they make no reference to the conditions agreed upon between the musicians and the owners of the theater in such matters as rent and the destination of the ticket and palchi income.

The costs incurred by the company for the first opera are not known, but in a foreword to the libretto for the second season, *La maga fulminata*, the publisher Antonio Bariletti claimed that the latter work had been mounted for no more than

3,000 ducats.[5] Bariletti commented that such an expense was far less than that typically spent for "royal presentations," but it still represented a significant sum, quite large for such a small company.[6] The most likely source for the means to recoup those 3,000 ducats would have been the box rentals. One hundred palchi—approximately the number existing in the theater—rented at 25 ducats each would have brought in 2,500 ducats, and the scagni and the entrance tickets would have provided additional income. The company must have operated on a tight budget, but it may have made a modest profit, especially because there were no highly paid performers to satisfy.

Cavalli's Company of 1638

As opera became more popular in Venice, new theaters entered the market. For some reason—most likely the offer of more advantageous conditions—Manelli and Ferrari, the core of the original artistic team at S. Cassiano, migrated to newer venues. A second company had formed at the theater by April 1638; although its incorporation document did not name a site for the performances, at some unspecified date the members came to an agreement with the Tron family, enabling the noblemen to continue their theater's emphasis on opera.[7] Once again the group comprised a variety of talents: a composer (Cavalli, in his first efforts in the genre), a librettist (Oratio Persiani, who promised to supply two librettos), and two singers. The company agreed to limit its members to four who would contribute equally and share the profits; despite these restrictions, the dancer Giovanni Battista Balbi had joined the group by September 1638.[8] Thus three of the five members overlapped with the previous company, as Bisucci, Uga, and Balbi had participated in earlier productions at S. Cassiano (Uga had sung during the second season). Presumably the limitation to four partners had been designed to increase the profit share, although it would also have necessitated the hiring of extra singers to round out the cast. The contract specified that all in the company must be ready to perform by the feast of S. Martino, that is by 11 November, signifying that an autumn season had been anticipated.[9]

The fate of Cavalli's original company of 1638/39 is far from clear; it is possible that the company had intended to stay together only for one season. Certainly Per-

---

5 The libretto specifies 2,000 scudi. Ferrari, *La maga fulminata* (Venice, 1638). The foreword is transcribed in Rosand, *Opera*, 407.

6 Bianconi and Walker calculate the costs for four performances of *Chi soffre speri* at the Barberini palace in Rome in 1639 at about 33,000 Venetian lire, or 5,322 ducats. See "Production, Consumption," 234.

7 On the formation of this company, see Morelli and Walker, "Tre controversie," 98, 107. They state that the company was to reside at S. Cassiano ("Atto costitutivo di una Accademia di musica e virtuosi, Accademia da intendersi come Impresa teatrale per spettacoli in musica con sede al San Cassiano"; p. 107), but the body of the incorporation document refers to no specific theater where the company would operate.

8 ASV, AN, Atti, b. 647, f. 327, 16 Sept. 1638.

9 ASV, Monastero di Santa Maria dell'Orazion a Malamocco, b. 3. Despite the agreement, only one libretto for S. Cassiano was published that season: *Le nozze di Teti e di Peleo*, dedicated 24 Jan. 1639.

siani provided no new librettos for S. Cassiano after that first year, so that Cavalli found a new collaborator in Giovanni Francesco Busenello. Nonetheless, some degree of stability was maintained, with Cavalli remaining at the head of the company and the dancer Balbi still associated with it in 1640/41 (and entitled to share in the profits).[10] The composer, however, may well have begun gradually to operate the company in a more autocratic fashion, for when he relinquished control of the theater in 1644, only his name, and not those of his associates from earlier years, appeared in the settlement.[11]

The Management of Tron, Boldù, and Barbaro

In the years he presided over the operatic company at S. Cassiano, 1638/39 through 1643/44, Cavalli achieved some degree of success—at least artistically—and formed a new creative partnership with the young Giovanni Faustini beginning with the 1641/42 season. Financially, however, he was less fortunate; as a result, on 4 June 1644 he transferred the operation of the theater to a group of three noblemen (including the owner of the theater, Ettor Tron), who promised to assume his debts, up to a sum of 800 ducats.[12] Cavalli, for his part, was required to supply one or more operas, and to assist in their preparation. Although he transferred all of the physical materials belonging to the theater to the noblemen, it is clear that he, as composer and artistic director, represented one of the greatest assets at S. Cassiano. Certainly, it was in the best interests of the noblemen for him to remain at the theater, for by now he was among the most experienced composers of Venetian opera. With this arrangement the noblemen secured his talents, and must have hoped that through Cavalli's efforts they could maintain a strong presence against two other competing theaters, SS. Giovanni e Paolo and the Novissimo. It should be noted that this agreement would seem to have had validity only for the 1644/45 season.

The partners learned first hand, as had Cavalli, of the financial hazards of opera production. They too must have run into difficulties, for part of the loan made by another nobleman to the trio on 27 April 1645—presumably for opera expenses—still remained unpaid four years later, and the partners did not follow through on their promise to reimburse Cavalli for all of his debts (see below).[13] The operation of the theater is uncertain for the 1646 and 1647 seasons, owing to the political and financial effects of the war in Crete. Although John Whenham has recently shown that some operas were presented in Venice during that time, activity at S. Cassiano has not been securely charted.[14] In any case, by April 1648, just twelve years after

---

10 ASV, AN, Atti, b. 3761, 26 Jan. 1640 m.v.

11 The document is discussed in Morelli and Walker, "Tre controversie," 98, 110.

12 On Cavalli's debts, especially with the wood supplier Pellizzarol, see Morelli and Walker, "Tre controversie," 98–99, 118–20.

13 The loan was made by Massimo Contarini. For the first reference to the outstanding debt, see ASV, AN, Atti, b. 6049, f. 133ᵛ, 28 Aug. 1646. In November 1649 Boldù stated that he had paid for his share of the expenses, while other partners had not (ASV, AN, Atti, b. 1120, f. 115ᵛ, 18 Nov. 1649).

14 Whenham, "Perspectives."

the premiere of *Andromeda*, the theater passed to its fourth management team: Bortolo Castoreo and Rocco Maestri.[15]

The Company of Castoreo and Maestri

The new company bore some similarities to the first two, for Rocco Maestri, the son of a lawyer, was an artisan, in this case a painter.[16] It is likely, then, that Maestri oversaw the scene painting at the theater during his tenancy. S. Cassiano's other impresario was Bortolo Castoreo, a civil servant in the Venetian bureaucracy. He, too, may have entered into the company with the expectation of becoming a creative partner, for he eventually supplied a libretto, *Armidoro*, in the third year of its operation.[17]

The company's agreement with Francesco Tron (Ettor's brother) was unusual in a number of ways. One item required that Tron approve the opera, i.e. the libretto, that was to be presented (see chap. 5). We do not know what sort of problems he sought to forestall, for editorial approval was not typically required in agreements such as these; still, Tron must have seen or read other librettos that had led to his concern. Also atypical were the conditions for the payment of the annual rent. While most contracts specified two annual installments, this one called for the company to pay the sum of about 25 ducats at the time of each performance.[18] Such a system would have been advantageous for the renters because even a successful run of eighteen performances—as was the case for the opera presented, Cavalli's *Giasone*—would have resulted in a total payment of under 500 ducats (rather than a more usual rent of 800 ducats). Certain protections for Tron were built into the contract, however. Should the company fail to mount an opera owing to internal problems, it would be liable for the full 800 ducats, while if an opera were to receive only one or two performances—i.e., if through some problem the opera came to be cancelled—the amount due dropped to 600 ducats. Tron's strategy was undoubtedly tied to income from the box rentals: limited or no performances would have discouraged box payments or would have made them moot altogether, thus necessitating a larger payment from Maestri and Castoreo. Indeed, the contract specifies that the company itself be granted only five boxes, those previously belonging to Cavalli. Therefore, one of the largest possible sources of income, something over 2,000 ducats, would have gone to the theater owner, leaving the renters with only the ticket and bench receipts, yet with all of the financial obligations for the opera. The company lost even further ground some days

---

15 ASV, AN, Atti, b. 667, f. 82, 9 Apr. 1648. The theater was rented also in the names of Andrea Carobbi and Vicenzo Panigai. Panigai withdrew from the enterprise on 16 Apr. 1648, claiming he had never given the authorization for his inclusion in the company (ibid., f. 83ᵛ), while Carobbi's name does not appear in later documentation about the theater.

16 Although Maestri's name appears in none of the usual histories or guides to Venice, his talents were sufficient to gain him a commission to execute a series of paintings for the church of the convent of Corpus Domini in 1653 (ASV, AN, Atti, b. 12449, f. 23, 13 May 1653). The contract was formalized, therefore, after Maestri's involvement at S. Cassiano.

17 Castoreo's brother Giacomo was a more frequent author of plays and librettos presented at S. Aponal and I Saloni.

18 The figure cited is 20 reali (at £8 per reale) (ASV, AN, Atti, b. 667, 9 Apr. 1648).

later when Castoreo and Maestri signed a contract with Cavalli to compose and direct the opera for that season. Cavalli may very well have resisted signing an agreement, for, as mentioned above, Tron and his associates from 1644 had failed to pay all the funds owed to the composer at the time; as a result, Cavalli's contract with the Castoreo and Maestri specified that they had to turn over to the composer each evening about 13 ducats towards the sum previously owed to him.[19] The company did successfully mount *Giasone*, but only with the help of loans from a nobleman amounting to 410 ducats.[20] The loans solved what the company saw as a short-term cash-flow problem, and the monies were to be paid back from income from the performances themselves. The success of the opera encouraged the company to revive the production the following spring, which would have brought in additional income with, presumably, none of the original expenses for scenery and costumes.[21]

After that first season, Cavalli's relations with the new company became less than harmonious. Giovanni Morelli and Thomas Walker have shown how Cavalli disputed the payments previously made to him by the company's fattor, and how the composer's dissatisfaction finally found expression in his disinclination to provide the following season's score, *Orimonte*, in a timely manner.[22] By the next season (1650/51) Cavalli had severed his ties with the theater altogether, moving over to Giovanni Faustini's S. Aponal. This last season of Castoreo and Maestri's tenure was marked by the performance of Castoreo's own *Armidoro*, probably set to music by Gasparo Sartorio.[23]

Faustini's Company of 1657/58

Whether by choice or by default, S. Cassiano presented no opera for six years after the expiration of the Castoreo and Maestri contract, that is, until the arrival of Marco Faustini and his company.[24] Perhaps the Trons had not found suitable in-

19 The figure specified is 10 reali; Cavalli had been owed 246 ducats. It is, of course, possible that Tron could have reduced the nightly rental fees at that point in order to compensate for the company's additional payments to Cavalli.

20 The funds were loaned by Pietro Corner (ASV, AN, Atti, b. 2950, f. 428, 27 Nov. 1648; ibid, b. 2950, f. 429, 18 Jan. 1648 m.v.). They had not been fully paid back on 27 July 1649 (ASV, GM, Sentenze a legge, reg. 330, f. 18). See also chapter 1.

21 On 22 Apr. 1649 the company obtained a loan of 100 ducats from Girolamo Zane for a second mounting of *Giasone* during Ascension (May 13); Zane was to be paid back after the first three performances (ASV, AN, Atti, b. 2951, f. 83ᵛ, 22 Apr. 1649). The encore performances were not commemorated by a libretto that specifically mentioned an Ascension season, so we cannot be sure that they took place. On Ascension performances, see Whenham, "Perspectives."

22 Morelli and Walker, "Tre controversie," 117. On the fattor Fassetta, see also chapter 2.

23 A notice regarding the truancy of a singer at S. Cassiano (Angela Lazaroni) was sent out by Castoreo and Matteo di Grandi, with no mention of Rocco Maestri (ASV, AN, Atti, b. 6681, f. 80, 18 Feb. 1650 m.v.). Di Grandi was a tailor who had manufactured some of the costumes for the 1650/51 season (ASV, GP, Dimande, b. 34, fasc. 57, no. 45, 1 Mar. 1651). In the absence of further documentation we cannot say if he had taken Maestri's place in the company.

24 The only evidence that the theater was used at all during this period is a single reference to production there of comedies in 1656/57 (ASV, GP, Scritture e risposte, b. 184, fasc. 66, no. 23, 14 Mar. 1657).

vestors and impresarios, or the family had tired of the enterprise, thinking that with regular competition from S. Aponal and SS. Giovanni e Paolo, the demand for yet another venue was limited. Whatever the situation had been during those intervening years, by the spring of 1657 the impresarial politics in Venice had changed once again. As is so often the case, none of the documentation completely explains the motivations behind Faustini's move from S. Aponal to S. Cassiano (see also chap. 3 and below, "S. Aponal"). Certainly, relations with Francesco Ceroni, part owner of S. Aponal, had been strained for some time; indeed, he had ordered Faustini to vacate the theater. While this circumstance may explain the exodus from S. Aponal, it does not necessarily account for the move to S. Cassiano. Any rental, naturally, represents an agreement reached by two parties: presumably the Trons wanted to present opera again, and with Faustini at their theater, they knew they had a good chance of competing head on with the Grimanis. On their side, Faustini and his partners also must have wanted to continue their interest in opera production (and in a larger theater), for they could just as easily have left S. Aponal and retired from the business altogether.

One indication of high expectations on both sides can be seen in the duration of the rental: five years, with the possibility of a second five-year term (the same as Faustini had signed with Zanetta Diamante at S. Aponal in 1655).[25] Faustini's arrangement with Carlo Andrea, Ettor, and Pietro Tron (the sons of Francesco), drawn up on 5 May 1657, worked much more in his favor than had the agreement with the previous tenants. Although responsible for a rental fee of 840 ducats, he would receive the income from the palchi, except for six boxes that the Trons retained for their own use. This distribution alone represented a near total reversal of that in the 1648 rental. Most importantly, however, Faustini did not inherit a history of debts as had Castoreo and Maestri. On the negative side, the theater required extensive work following the years it had not been used as an opera theater. The boxes were completely rebuilt, decreasing their number, and other construction materials became an enormous expense for the refurbished theater's first season; indeed, the partners may have settled on a five-year term in the hopes that they would see their investment recouped within that time period. Regarding artistic matters, the contract did not require that the proprietors approve the libretto; Faustini may have refused to cede control in this area, with the intent, perhaps, of producing a posthumous work of his brother.

The visions of success that Faustini and the Trons held for the new company at S. Cassiano eventually went unrealized, although the enterprise began well enough. That first year controversies regarding the text of *L'incostanza trionfante* came to be aired publicly in successive printings of the libretto, but attendance figures remained strong throughout the season, perhaps fueled by the curiosity regarding the libretto (see chap. 5). Presented on twenty-five occasions, at least 7,316 tickets, for boxes and parterre seats combined, were sold for the production. The company must have thought that their prospects would improve the next year with the enticement of Cavalli back to S. Cassiano in 1658 (see chap. 6) for the

---

25 For the S. Cassiano rental, see ASV, SGSM, b. 194, ff. 24–25. On the 1655 agreement with Diamante, see below.

next three seasons after his recent service at SS. Giovanni e Paolo. Cavalli's return represented quite a coup for the company, and for the Tron family as well: the leading composer of Venetian opera had returned to the city's oldest theater, and to the site of his earliest successes. Attendance for *Antioco*, however, did not match that for *L'incostanza*; no specific records survive for the next opera, *Elena*, but a contemporary letter alludes to low ticket sales.[26] At any rate, Faustini's departure after three years of his contract—possibly related to Cavalli's travels to France during the spring of 1660—demonstrates the fragility of these agreements.

Despite ceasing to present operas at S. Cassiano, Faustini fulfilled his contractual responsibilities to Carlo Andrea Tron by making regular payments to the nobleman for the remaining two years of his five-year rental.[27] This time no other company formed to take the place of Faustini's, and during the 1660s only one further attempt to present opera came to fruition, in the unsuccessful enterprise of Galeazzo Passarelli for the 1665/66 season.[28] Although S. Cassiano would reemerge as an opera theater in the decades to come, during the mid-seventeenth century it was unable to compete year to year with newer theaters such as SS. Giovanni e Paolo and S. Luca.

THE NOVISSIMO

The Teatro Novissimo has attracted scholarly attention in recent years—most particularly in the work of Lorenzo Bianconi, Thomas Walker, and Ellen Rosand—by virtue of its unusual origins, as well as for the quality and nature of its artistic creations.[29] As mentioned at the outset of this chapter, the Novissimo differed from the other theaters in Venice in that it was not owned by a specific family, whether noble or cittadino. The theater was newly built by adapting a large shed on property of the friars of SS. Giovanni e Paolo that adjoined the monastery, and the rental payments went directly to the coffers of the religious house. The brief history of the Novissimo—it operated for only five years—gives rise to a number of questions central to the study of opera production. The various types of documentary evidence that have survived, however, while certainly providing a framework from which we can begin an investigation, provide few clear answers.

Origins of the Theater

The most significant issue is why the theater was built at all. For the season of 1639/40—that prior to the construction of the Novissimo—three opera theaters

---

26 Letter of Carlo Andrea Coradini, 24 Jan. 1660. ASV, SGSM, b. 101, unnumbered. For the attendance for *Antioco* and *L'incostanza trionfante*, see chapter 11.

27 ASV, SGSM, b. 118, receipt book, ff. 49, 58, and 61.

28 Passarelli's rental of the theater is mentioned in a document of 5 Oct. 1665. ASV, AN, Atti, b. 12055, f. 208ᵛ. Passarelli was the husband of the singer Elena Passarelli.

29 See Bianconi and Walker, "Dalla *finta pazza* alla *Veremonda*," 410–24; and Rosand, *Opera*, esp. 88–109. See also the chapters on the theater in Mangini, *Teatri di Venezia*, 62–66, and Mancini, Muraro, and Povoledo, *Teatri di Venezia* 1:323–60. For references to the scenery at the Novissimo, see chapter 9.

were in operation in Venice: S. Cassiano, S. Moisè, and the newly renovated SS. Giovanni e Paolo. Scholars such as Rosand, in looking for a raison d'être for the construction of the theater, have sought an answer in Venice's famed Accademia degli Incogniti, founded by Giovanni Francesco Loredano in 1630.[30] Indeed, Rosand claimed—albeit with several reservations—that the men who initiated and agreed to manage the theater, and who insured its success, "were members of the Accademia degli Incogniti, whose involvement with the enterprise determined the entire course of the Novissimo's brilliant though brief career."[31] The documents that survive concerning this theater, often ambiguous in nature, offer at least a partial answer as to who provided the support—both financial and managerial—to sustain this unusual operation. One of the most intriguing questions remains that of the direct participation of several members of the Incogniti, and whether it was incidental (given their general presence in the literary and operatic culture of Venice), or of fundamental importance to the theater's operation and financing.

The first production at the Novissimo was, indeed, a musical setting of a work by an eminent Incognito, Giulio Strozzi. It should be noted, however, that Strozzi's first Venetian libretto had been performed at the inauguration of the Grimani theater, SS. Giovanni e Paolo, and that his subsequent librettos would appear there, too. Strozzi, then, had no inherent need for a new outlet for his talents, and he certainly did not view his connection with the Novissimo as exclusive. Other "Incogniti librettists" such as Giovanni Francesco Busenello and Giacomo Badoaro also favored the Grimani theater, and even the small Teatro S. Moisè served as the venue for *L'Amore innamorato* (1641/42), a work by Incogniti members Giovanni Battista Fusconi and Pietro Michiel. Some academicians' works did premiere at the Novissimo toward the end of the theater's activity: Scipione Herrico's *Deidamia* (1643/44) appeared there in the fourth year of its operation, followed by Maiolino Bisaccioni's *Ercole in Lidia* (1645), mounted during the last season.[32] It is noteworthy, however, that none of the documents concerning the construction of the theater or the first four years of its management reveal a direct connection with the Incogniti, although covert support could have been possible. Certainly the conspicuous promotion of the Republic of Venice in a number of librettos—especially in the prologue of *Bellerofonte* (1641/42), the product of the foreigner Vincenzo Nolfi, a resident of Fano—reveals an ideological agenda for the theater; the source of this agenda, however, is far from clear.[33] Whether the initial impetus for the construction of the theater—and its ideological trappings—came from noble pro-

30 Rosand, *Opera*, esp. 37–40. On the Incogniti and opera in Venice, see also Walker and Bianconi, "Dalla Finta pazza"; Heller, *Emblems of Eloquence*, chapter 2; ead., "Tacitus incognito"; ead., "O delle donne"; and Calcagno, "Signifying Nothing." On the Incogniti in general, see Miato, *Accademia degli Incogniti*. See also Cannizzaro, "Studies on Guido Casoni."

31 Rosand, *Opera*, 89.

32 The productions at the Novissimo after the first season include: 1641/42 *Alcate* (M. A. Tirabosco/F. Manelli) and *Bellerofonte* (V. Nolfi /F. Sacrati); 1642/43 *Venere gelosa* (N. Bartolini/F. Sacrati); 1643/44 *Deidamia* (S. Herrico/?); 1645 *Ercole in Lidia* (M. Bisaccioni/G. Rovetta). Vincenzo Nolfi was a relative of Torelli's from Fano (see Milesi, *Giacomo Torelli*, 415).

33 For a discussion of the ideological issues and political propaganda present in many Venetian librettos, see Rosand, *Opera*, 125–53, and the items cited above in n. 30.

tectors or from one of the creative agents such as Strozzi, the theater certainly served as a showcase during its first three seasons for the music of the Parmesan composer Francesco Sacrati, and, especially, for the talents of the architect and scenographer Giacomo Torelli of Fano, both artists new to Venice for the 1640/41 season (see also chap. 9); indeed, perhaps Torelli acted as one of the motivators, searching for a new venue, built to his technical specifications, in which to test his scenographic innovations.[34]

Unfortunately, the origins of this theatrical enterprise do not emerge clearly from the extant documents; while yielding a number of names, they fail to provide a complete picture (see the chronology in table 4.2). The first reference to the conversion of the property, in a register of the chapter of the monastery of SS. Giovanni e Paolo, specifies a date of 30 May 1640: "given in rent to some gentlemen a shed on the grounds to be converted to a theater for the presentation of opera in music with the conditions registered in the said council."[35] Later documents, however, cite only a formal agreement of 1 July 1640 between the friars of SS. Giovanni e Paolo and the *muschier* (a seller of gloves and musk) Giacomo Somariva;[36] Somariva, however, would not have been the person who had set the project in motion, and his participation in the theater is not clearly documented beyond this rental, although as late as 3 October 1643 he owed the impresario Girolamo Lappoli £438 "to settle their accounts."[37] Either Somariva had stood in for other interested parties when the agreement first came to fruition, or he made way for others at some point after his initial involvement. Somariva's guarantor or pieggio for the rent was a tailor from Ancona, Giovanni Penachin; it is quite possible that Penachin was one of the artisans in the operatic company (perhaps he designed or provided the costumes; on his work for S. Aponal, see chap. 10). The most fundamental question, then, is the identity of the people behind Somariva's and Penachin's activity. The opera chronicler Cristoforo Ivanovich claimed, in his theater chronology published in 1681, that the theater had been built "under the protection of Luigi Michele and diverse cavaliers."[38] Sources discovered by Bianconi and Walker provided the names of three noblemen (none of them Incogniti) who interceded in October 1640 when the enterprise seemed likely to falter during the construction phase: Girolamo Lando, Giacomo da Mosto, and Giacomo Marcello. The initial date of the involvement of Alvise Michiel, however, the only nobleman singled out by Ivanovich (who used the Italian, not Venetian, form of his name), is

34 On Torelli and his participation at the Novissimo, see Milesi, *Giacomo Torelli*. A number of other works discuss the importance of Torelli; one of the earliest is Bjurström, *Giacomo Torelli*. See also Guarino, "Torelli a Venezia." Torelli had responsibilities in the company beyond those of scenery and architecture. It is he who arranged the rental of the *scagni* (bench seats) for the theater with Donato Fiorini (ASV, AN, Atti, b. 3055, 10 Mar. 1642).

35 "Havendo li padri per un loro conseglio fatto sotto li 30 del mese di maggio del presente anno datto in affitto ad alcuni gentilhuomeni nel terreno una tezza per ridurla a forma di teatro per rappresentare opere in musica con conditioni registrate in detto conseglio." ASV, SSGP, Y.V.2–4, f. 132.

36 See ASV, AN, Atti, b. 10983, f. 138ᵛ.

37 "per resto, et saldo di conti tra loro." ASV, GM, Sentenze a legge, b. 304, f. 99, 24 Apr. 1645.

38 "sotto la protezione di Luigi Michele, e di diversi Cavalieri." Ivanovich, *Memorie teatrali*, 399.

TABLE 4.2. Chronology of the Teatro Novissimo

Date	Event
30 May/1 July 1640	Friars of SS. Giovanni e Paolo rent shed for one year to Giacomo Somariva to build theater; Girolamo Lappoli's name not mentioned, but he later claims to have built the theater
September 1640	Evidence of involvement by Giacomo Torelli and Francesco Sacrati
2 October 1640	Enterprise assisted by three noblemen: Girolamo Lando, Giacomo da Mosto, and Giacomo Marcello; rental contract extended to two years
1640/41	*La finta pazza*, first production at theater
6 July 1641	Lappoli seeks financial assistance from Pietro Magno
17 March 1642	Friars demand theater be dismantled
22 December 1642	Contract extended by three months to enable 1642/43 carnival season
1642/43	Josef Camis pays some of Lappoli's debts: Angelo Marcello (the dedicatee of Manelli's *Alcate*, D518); the mercer Tomaso "alla Sorte" (for costuming for Maddalena Manelli, D46); the singers Jacopo and Atto Melani in Pistoia (D150); the nobleman Pietro Loredan (on behalf of the singer Francesco Santi, D96); Hippolito Marruffi (D378 for silks and lace), and Girolamo Lando. He also loaned to Lappoli various jewels worth about D210
4 March 1643	Friars demand theater be dismantled; after negotiations, contract renewed for two more years
17 December 1643	Camis serves as guarantor of Anna Renzi's salary
March 1644	Alvise Michiel and Girolamo Lando borrow D1250 for Lappoli (unclear whether regarding theater or another business venture)
9 February 1645	Camis transfers Lappoli's debts (D1800) to Giacomo Badoaro
February/March 1645	Giacomo Torelli (scene designer) and Paulo Morandi (costumer) sue Lappoli for debts; theater sealed
11 May 1645	Lappoli agrees to cede theater to Maiolino Bisaccioni, who agrees to pay Lappoli's debts, as follows: May 1645: D2000 (D500 for Girolamo Lando; D1500 to Bernardino de Josephis and other creditors) Lent 1646 and 1647: D3300 (D1320 for Girolamo Lando, the remainder for other creditors) Agreement apparently not implemented
20 May 1645	Alvise Michiel assists Torelli in calculating money owed to him for scenery
27 May 1645	Paulo Morandi agrees to allow theater to present Ascension season
20 June 1645	Girolamo Lando, Bernardino de Joseffis, Giovanni Battista Gaggini, and Giovanni Piero Baretta claim Lappoli should pay them first (before Morandi and Torelli)
July 1645	Four musicians (Anna Renzi, Filiberto Laurenzi, and Francesco and Maddalena Manelli) sue Lappoli for failure to pay wages
Before October 1645	Alvise Michiel agrees to pay some of Lappoli's debts
1646	Lappoli leaves Venice, with debts unpaid
19 November 1646	Friars again initiate steps to have theater demolished
September/October 1647	Theater demolished; Alvise Michiel still owes some money to friars to redeem scenic materials

far from certain; as we will discuss below, other sources suggest that he probably began his association with the theater only later in its history.

Several letters written in September 1640 by two of the creative artists in the new company concerning the construction of the theater survive, and they do indeed mention two of these three noblemen. The letters are invaluable in documenting the behind-the-scenes activities of the nobles, and how they were called into action (it should be noted that even in these private letters, no reference is made to members of the Incogniti). All three letters, two by Francesco Sacrati and one by Giacomo Torelli, allude to a work stoppage that had occurred, and of continuing difficulties with the friars of SS. Giovanni e Paolo.[39] They were sent to someone temporarily outside of Venice who was viewed as the power behind the project. This nobleman cannot be securely identified. As one of the letters refers to both "Marcello" and "Mosto" as lending their efforts to ease the situation, however, we might conclude that this particular letter, and the other two, were sent to Girolamo Lando; indeed, later sources reveal that Lando had contributed considerable funds to the theater. The letters do not clarify, however, whether these men had any financial or managerial roles, or whether they were acting simply as protectors for the non-noble principals in the enterprise.[40]

None of the three letters make reference to an impresario: the name of Girolamo Lappoli—the businessman from Arezzo who would figure prominently in the theater's operation—is absent.[41] Even though his initial involvement as impresario is undocumented (Lappoli's name is missing from the earliest sources, i.e., those that mention Somariva and Penachin), later evidence connects him with the theater during all the years of its operation; indeed, a document of 1645—albeit one initiated by Lappoli himself—claims that the theater was built by him:

> The Most Illustrious Signor Girolamo Lappoli . . . having rented from the Most Reverend Fathers of San Giovanni e Paolo the large sheds belonging to that venerable monastery on land behind the monastery, which sheds were converted by Signor

39 Torelli's letter (Vmc, PDC 1051, no. 449, 17 Sept. 1640) is published in Mangini, *Teatri di Venezia*, 63. Two letters by Sacrati, not previously cited, are housed in the same location: PDC 1051, no. 448, 9 Sept. 1640 and PDC 1051, no. 332, 24 Sept. 1640.

40 One other name mentioned in Torelli's letter of 17 Sept. is that of "Valerio," presumably Valerio Michiel, as these three letters form part of the correspondence of the Michiel family. A complicating factor in identifying the recipient of the letters has been the puzzle of why the letters—if they had been sent to Girolamo Lando—survive among the correspondence of the Michiel and Dandolo families in the Biblioteca Correr. Valerio Michiel (1592–1661) was the father of Marc'Antonio Michiel (1614–49); many of the letters in the collection surround Marc'Antonio, his sons (Zuane, Polo, and Girolamo), and his wife, Marina Dandolo. Valerio Michiel's wife was Giulia Barbarigo. As Girolamo Lando also had connections with the Barbarigo family (see below), the letters may have found their way into the collection through Giulia Barbarigo. Further research may reveal additional points of contact between the Lando family and the Barbarigos. Another Barbarigo sister, Marina, was married to Francesco Michiel, who later acted as a sort of protector to Anna Renzi and Francesco Sacrati. Valerio Michiel's family is only distantly related to those of Francesco Michiel, Alvise Michiel, and the Incognito author Pietro Michiel.

41 Lappoli may have been a descendant of the artist and musician Giovanni Antonio Lappoli (1492–1552), active in Arezzo and Florence. Both Girolamo Lappoli's grandfather and one of his brothers were named Giovanni Antonio.

Lappoli to a theater for the presentation of opera called the Novissimo, and because, in order to bring it to this state, he has incurred infinite expenses of wood and other things. . . .[42]

Moreover, *La finta pazza*, the opera produced for the theater's premiere, features both Lappoli's and Sacrati's names imbedded in the text, a sure sign that the Tuscan had played a significant role in the theater's early months.[43] Lappoli would become a powerful player on the Venetian theatrical scene, accustomed to generating enormous expenses by employing some of the best singers and artisans to be found in Italy.

Lappoli's entrance into the Venetian theatrical system has not been explained, but his and his family's participation in Venetian business dated back to the early 1630s, so that he must already have made the acquaintance of a number of important Venetian nobles and businessmen before he became involved with the Novissimo.[44] Indeed, such a link can be established between him and Girolamo Lando. In 1637, about three years before the opening of the theater, the noblemen Domenico and Alvise Barbarigo authorized Lappoli, already acting as their agent, to transact some financial matters for them.[45] These brothers were the sons of the late Marc'Antonio Barbarigo and Marina Duodo;[46] Marina Duodo's second husband, however, was none other than Girolamo Lando, the most heavily documented supporter of the theater.[47] Looking beyond Lando's circle, Lappoli may also have been known, if only by reputation, to Giulio Strozzi, the librettist involved with the first production: as a Tuscan, Lappoli would have fraternized with the Florentine expatriates in Venice, who, in their turn, knew Strozzi, himself the descendant of a noted Florentine family.[48] It is certainly feasible that when Lando,

---

42 "Havendo il Molto Illustre Signor Gierolimo Lappoli quondam Signor Erminio preso ad affitto dalli molto Reverendi Padri di San Giovanni e Paolo li tezoni di raggione d'esso Venerando Monasterio posti in terreno dietro di quello, quali tezoni furno da esso Signor Lappoli redoti in un teatro da rappresentarvi opere in musica che si chiama il Novissimo, et perché, per ridurlo a questo stato ha convenuto fare infinite spese de legnami et altro." ASV, AN, Atti, b. 11743, f. 89, 11 May 1645.

43 Bianconi and Walker state that the reconfiguration of the rental contract in Oct. 1640 mentioned Lappoli—rather than Somariva—as the renter (Bianconi and Walker, "Dalla *Finta pazza*," 415). Rosand, using Bianconi and Walker as her source, supplied the same information. Lappoli's name does not appear in that document, however. Benedetti ("Teatro musicale," 200) states that Somariva was the "procuratore" of Lappoli, that is, acting for him; while that very well may have been the case, no precise documentation to that effect has yet been found. Lappoli's name appeared in conjunction with the renewals of 1643. In Aug. 1642 he referred to himself as the "*patrone* of the Teatro Novissimo on the land of the friars of SS. Giovanni, et Paolo" (ASV, GM, Sentenze a legge, reg. 281, f. 144).

44 Lappoli had worked in Venice for the businessman Claudio Piatti from Apr. 1630 (ASV, Avogaria di comun, b. 3896, C 149.6).

45 ASV, AN, Atti, b. 10797, f. 721ᵛ, 16 Dec. 1637. The arrangement was not severed until 9 Sept. 1645.

46 Marina Duodo was the sister of Girolamo Duodo, and thus the aunt of Alvise Duodo, Faustini's partner. She married Barbarigo in 1614 and Lando in 1623.

47 On Lando's prominence in Venetian society, see Mancini, Muraro, and Povoledo, *Teatri di Venezia*, 1:324.

48 On Giulio Strozzi's contacts with the Florentine community in Venice, see B. Glixon, "New Light."

Strozzi, and their associates searched for a man to serve as impresario, Lappoli's name emerged as someone familiar to several of the parties, and who was accustomed to dealing with both Venetian and foreign business. (Alternatively, if Lappoli had been involved at the outset, he may have brought Strozzi into the enterprise.)

Another significant question surrounding the Novissimo concerns the nature of the friars' intentions in sanctioning the building and operation of the theater, and whether they envisioned an arrangement of some permanence. Something of their reticence in embracing this theatrical adventure can be seen in the durations of the rental contracts for the building. As we can see in table 4.2, the initial period specified in July 1640 was one year;[49] only when the agreement underwent further refinements after the intercession of Girolamo Lando in October 1640 did it increase to two years. Thus, we see an initial reluctance on the part of the friars to commit for more than one season, followed by a slight relaxation to allow for a second, still less than the typical Venetian contract of three to five years. It had always been the friars' intention that the theater would be dismantled upon expiration of the contract, and Venetian rentals routinely featured language requiring that property be turned back to the owner in its original, "pristine" condition. On schedule, then, the friars sought to have the theater torn down after the second season, and notified Lappoli to that effect on 17 March 1642.[50] Lappoli and his supporters eventually prevailed, however, and on 22 December he was granted a brief, three-month rental that would allow him to mount the 1642/43 season.[51] Once again, on 4 March 1643, the friars served notice that the rental had expired; ever hopeful, the interested parties prevailed one more time, resulting, two months later, in another extension, this time for two years, thus running through carnival of 1645.[52] These erratic rentals must represent the friars' acknowledgment of the unusual nature of this undertaking; they apparently did not wish to encumber themselves with a long-term arrangement, and must have doubted the management's capacity or willingness to pay the rent. As we shall see, financial problems did arise, and the extensions, paradoxically, may reflect Lappoli's difficulty in paying the rent as well as the friars' and Lappoli's hopes that one more season would result in financial stability. One other indication of the friars' hesitancy regarding the venture is their insistence that the theater present nothing but operas: they wanted to insure that spoken comedy—a less dignified entertainment than opera—would not be performed on the monastery's premises.[53]

The first production, Giulio Strozzi and Francesco Sacrati's *La finta pazza* (1640/41), proved to be one of the most successful operas in the genre's first few years in Venice. Rosand has described the large number of performances, and the impact that the libretto had on future offerings in Venice; Giacomo Torelli's scenery created new standards for the genre, and *La finta pazza* made a star of its

49 ASV, AN, Atti, b. 10983, f. 138ᵛ.
50 Ibid., f. 148ᵛ, 17 Mar. 1642.
51 Ibid., f. 156, 4 Mar. 1643.
52 ASV, SSGP, Y.V.2–4, f. 7, 14 May 1643.
53 Rosand, *Opera*, 89.

leading female artist, Anna Renzi.[54] Once theatrical presentations had begun at the Novissimo, a series of publications—including two by the Incognito Maiolino Bisaccioni—emphasized the magnificence of the productions; eventually, a number of Giacomo Torelli's scenographic designs were reproduced as a splendid record of several productions, something previously untried during the early years of public opera in Venice (and never repeated).[55] Indeed, it is these post-performance celebratory writings that most clearly separate the Novissimo from the other theaters of Venice. Perhaps the interested parties thought it wise to puff up the reputation of the theater given its unusual location: the subliminal message may have been that despite the Novissimo's site on the premises of a Dominican monastery, as well as the absence of a noble owner, the public could expect productions of the highest quality, equaling or surpassing those found in the other, family-owned theaters of Venice. The publications also speak to Torelli's importance to the operation, and of his desires to document more permanently his work. Artistically, the theater was a resounding success, and it continued to mount productions through 1645 (finishing with Bisaccioni and Giovanni Rovetta's *Ercole in Lidia*), but a number of documents indicate that Lappoli had run into financial difficulties as early as the first season.

Lappoli's Need for Financial Assistance

Lappoli soon faced financial problems, and it is the theater's continuing indebtedness that, in the absence of incorporation agreements and other contracts, has opened for us a window into its operation: notarial documents and court records provide glimpses into the levels of support, and even the identity of some of the artisans associated with the Novissimo. By 6 July 1641–just several months after an Ascension reprise of *La finta pazza*–Lappoli sought monetary assistance in the running of the theater from a Venetian nobleman, Pietro Magno.[56] Magno offered Lappoli the option of two different plans by which they might share the operating expenses.[57] The first would have taken the typical form of a *livello*, or loan with interest: Lappoli would "sell" the theater to Magno for a reasonable price and pay the nobleman an annual or semiannual amount of interest, to be supplied from the theater's income. The second plan, on the other hand, stipulated that the "profits" (*utili*) from the theater be divided into thirds, with one third going to Magno, who would also be responsible for a third of the expenses (excluding those of scenery and rent). More precisely, Lappoli would be entitled to one third of the income from the palchi and scagni outright; the remaining two thirds would be divided

54 See ibid., esp. 88–124. For some previously unpublished accounts of the performances of *La finta pazza*, see Michelassi, "La *Finta pazza* a Firenze," 326–27.

55 The *Cannochiale per la finta pazza, dilineato da M. B. C. di G.* (Venice: Surian, 1641) has been credited to Bisaccioni by modern scholars. Bisaccioni was the acknowledged author of *Apparati scenici per lo Teatro Novissimo* (Venice:Vecellio e Leni, 1644). On the Torelli engravings, see chapter 9.

56 Magno acted as the protector of the singer Silvia Gailarti several years later, in 1645. See B. Glixon, "Scenes from the Life."

57 ASV,AN,Atti, b. 658, f. 363ᵛ, 13 Feb.y 1643 m.v.

according to the given formula, with one third going to Magno. For some reason Lappoli had not chosen between these two plans by 13 February 1644, two-and-one-half years later. On that date Magno served Lappoli with a notice, demanding that he make his choice. No record of his decision has yet been found; in any case, the impresario mananged to stay afloat while accumulating ever-larger debts, evidently with some help from Magno, for Lappoli owed the nobleman money in 1645.[58] Magno's willingness to help out with the expenses of the theater speaks to the possible base of support from within the nobility for the running of the theater. We should note, however, that Magno was a new patron, someone outside the sphere of Lando, Marcello, and da Mosto, and, also, the Incogniti.

Another way that Lappoli could have continued to run the theater in a time of tight funds—apart from outright loans or gifts—was through the system of the guarantor or pieggio (described in chap. 1), which functioned as a built-in safety net for businessmen and their clients. We saw earlier how the tailor Giovanni Penachin served for a number of years as guarantor for rental payment, and Giovanni Battista Gaggini and Giovanni Pietro Baretta served that function in 1643.[59] One other person who assisted Lappoli came from a most unusual source: Venice's Jewish community.

Josef Camis was a prominent Jewish physician and scholar who somehow found his way into Venice's theatrical life. As he knew the Lappoli family by October 1640, and probably even earlier, his entry into the operatic business most likely came through Lappoli, rather than through the others active in the company, although he would have had contact with a number of noblemen and cittadini through his medical practice.[60] The first firm evidence regarding Camis's involvement in the company concerns the 1642/43 season. At that time he paid a series of creditors for expenses owed by Lappoli, among them Angelo Marcello (the dedicatee of Manelli's Alcate, 1641/42),[61] the singers Jacopo and Atto Melani in Pistoia,[62] and two cloth merchants (see also table 4.2). Moreover, the doctor made Lappoli a direct loan and satisfied some of his debts to Girolamo Lando, who had helped the theater at its inception. The following year, 1643/44, despite the large sums already

58 ASV, AN, Atti, b. 662, f. 188, 27 Sept. 1645.

59 ASV, SSGPY/V, f. 7.

60 On the connections between the Lappoli and Camis families see ASV, AN, Atti, b. 11003, f. 102, 2 Oct. 1640. On Camis, see Ravid, "From Yellow to Red." Camis, a favorite student of the famed teacher and rabbi Leon Modena, was the author of a number of manuscripts concerning philosophy, religion, and astronomy. On the Jews of Venice, see Davis and Ravid, Jews of Early Modern Venice. According to Don Harrán, Modena consulted Camis (Joseph Hamits) and Moses Zacato—as experts on the kabbala—about issues relating to text repetition in music (Harrán, "Jewish Musical Culture," 223).

61 The document specifying Marcello's credit dates from the winter of 1642/43, but lacks the date of the original disbursement. Angelo Marcello also acted as the "procurator"—representing her in some matters of business—for Giulia Saus Paolelli, who sang in Bellerofonte at the Novissimo (1641/42). On Paolelli, see Rosand, Opera, 101, and Osthoff, "Zur Bologneser Aufführung," 155–60. According to Giulio del Colle, at the time of Bellerofonte, Paolelli had been singing in Venetian theaters for three years (cited in Rosand, Opera, 418.)

62 In one of the copies of the documentation concerning the transaction between Camis and the Melanis, a Venetian scribe, unfamiliar with the name Atto, transcribed Melani's name as "Ant.o" (Antonio). ASV, AN, Atti, b. 660, f. 229.

paid out on Lappoli's behalf, Camis served as the pieggio for Anna Renzi's enormous salary for *Deidamia*; this act alone could have involved risking another 750 ducats.[63] Even though all those who agreed to serve as a guarantor hoped they might escape turning over the stipulated sums of money—or when that became necessary, that they would eventually see their disbursements repaid—Camis must have known that he might well have had to pay Renzi's fees given Lappoli's history of indebtedness.

Lappoli did not soon reimburse the doctor for the bulk of his transactions. Indeed, on 9 February 1645, in the midst of what should have been the Novissimo's fifth season, Josef Camis transferred the credits still owed to him by Lappoli to Giacomo Badoaro, the librettist of Monteverdi's *Il ritorno d'Ulisse* and *Le nozze d'Enea in Lavinia* (1640 and 1641) and Sacrati's *Ulisse errante* (1643/44), all presented at the Grimani theater. The link between Badoaro and Camis (and, consequently, between Badoaro and Lappoli), through its citation in later documents concerning Lappoli's debts, has been offered by several scholars as evidence of the librettist's financial involvement with the Novissimo.[64] Camis's transfer of the credits to Badoaro certainly implies some financial activity between the two men, but whether such activity involved opera or merely other sorts of business remains unknown; in any case, we cannot assume a relationship between the two men before 1644, that is, the latter portion of the theater's history.

Lappoli and the Teatro SS. Giovanni e Paolo

Lappoli's financial difficulties have been discussed by Bianconi and Walker, Benedetti, and Rosand, but none of these authors were aware of another possible explanation for the impresario's problems: by the 1644/45 season he was renting two theaters, the Novissimo and its chief rival, SS. Giovanni e Paolo, where he was responsible during that year's carnival for a payment of 1,200 ducats "for the rent of the theater of the said Grimani."[65] Although no evidence survives for the three preceding seasons, Lappoli's role at the Grimani theater could have begun earlier, and may explain the movement of personnel—librettists, scenographer, composers, and singers—between the two theaters as early as 1642/43. We may well wonder if Giovanni Grimani had enticed the impresario to his theater with the goal of obtaining the Novissimo's resident talents, Anna Renzi, Francesco Sacrati, and Giacomo Torelli, or if Lappoli himself had sought to gain more of a monopoly in the city. Whatever the case, the geographical proximity of the two theaters must have

---

63 On Renzi's contract, see chapter 7. For a fuller discussion, and a complete transcription of the document, see B. Glixon, "Private Lives." One debt for the season that seems not to have been covered under the arrangements with Camis was that to the choreographer Giovanni Battista Balbi. On 18 Feb. 1644 he petitioned to have the scenes and other materials in the theater seized in order to guarantee his payment (ASV, GE, Interdetti, b. 135, f. 89ᵛ, 18 Feb. 1643 m.v.).

64 Rosand, *Opera*, 90, n. 57; Bianconi and Walker, "Dalla *Finta pazza*," 415, and Benedetti, "Teatro musicale," 185–220.

65 "del teatro di ragione del detto Signor Grimani . . ." ASV, AN, Atti, b. 6047, f. 237ᵛ, 14 Dec. 1644. The document specifies a payment of 1,200 ducats, but whether that was the typical annual rental, or a figure that combined previous installments, is not made clear.

facilitated the exchange of efforts for Lappoli, and for some of the creative personnel responsible for scenery and costumes, as both Giacomo Torelli and Paulo Morandi were owed money for materials and services at both theaters during the spring of 1645.[66]

Lappoli, an outsider and an ambitious entrepreneur, had taken on extraordinary financial risks in order to promote opera in two of Venice's largest and influential theaters. His involvement with two theaters almost certainly increased his indebtedness, contributing in some way to the downfall of the Novissimo, although, as we have seen, the friars of SS. Giovanni e Paolo may never have envisioned a long life for the theater in any event.

Plans to Transfer the Theater to Bisaccioni

The Novissimo was in a precarious financial situation during the winter and spring of 1645. As we have seen, Lappoli continued to suffer from mounting debts. Moreover, the outcome of the 1644/45 carnival season is unclear. Recent literature, following Bianconi and Walker, has stated that opera in Venice was suspended as a result of the war in Crete from January 1645 and continuing on through 1647.[67] According to a notice found by John Whenham, the theater management at the Novissimo had planned to mount a production as early as 8 January 1645, and the libretto for *Ercole in Lidia* had been printed by 18 January.[68] Even though opera performances were curtailed for a time owing to the celebration of a Jubilee, Whenham has shown, as mentioned above, that some theaters did resume their activities, although the sources do not mention the Novissimo specifically; thus, we do not know if the company managed to mount an opera during the carnival season. In any case, by February and March a series of creditors began to pursue Lappoli through several Venetian courts regarding debts from his management of both the Novissimo and SS. Giovanni e Paolo. Two of these creditors, Giacomo Torelli and the woodturner/costumer Paulo Morandi, succeeded in having the theater boarded up in an effort to collect the monies owed to them; Torelli alone was owed 1,550 ducats, and Morandi another 300.[69]

By the spring, Lappoli had tired of his responsibilities and his continuing debts, and on 11 May 1645 he attempted to remove himself from them. Lappoli authorized the transfer of the theater to Maiolino Bisaccioni, the librettist of *Ercole in Lidia*, the opera presented there during 1645. We have seen how Bisaccioni had served the theater previously as a sort of publicity agent, with post-performance

66 For Torelli, see ASV, AN, Atti, b. 10858, f. 39ᵛ, 20 Apr. 1645. For Morandi, see ASV, GP, Dimande, b. 31, fasc. 50, no. 1, 20 Mar. 1645. The documents do not provide specific dates for the services provided.

67 Bianconi and Walker, "Dalla *Finta pazza*," 424.

68 ASV, Arti, b. 166, Privileggi de librari e stampatori, f. 41ᵛ, 18 Jan, 1644 m.v. See Whenham, "Perspectives."

69 For Torelli, see ASV, AN, Atti, b. 10858, f. 39ᵛ, 20 Apr. 1645. This document was drawn up before Torelli's departure for Paris; Torelli authorized Morandi to collect the funds owed to him. For Morandi, see ASV, GP, Dimande, b. 31, fasc. 50, no. 1, 20 Mar. 1645.

descriptions of several operas, but the mounting of *Ercole in Lidia*, along with his proposed undertaking of the management of the theater, constitute his first "hard" connection to the Novissimo. The agreement specified that Bisaccioni would have the rights to the structure, that is, to all of the materials that comprised the theater and the palchi.

The transfer of the theater to Bisaccioni was not automatic, however. It hinged on the resolution of certain of Lappoli's debts amounting to 5,300 ducats, much of it to Girolamo Lando, to be paid off by Bisaccioni according to a particular schedule over a period of two years (see table 4.2).[70] The timing of the payments (May 1645 and the two successive periods of Lent) implies the continuing operation of the theater, with admissions and box rentals supplying the necessary funds; on the other hand, the channeling of such large sums of money toward repayment of debts, rather than for the ongoing costs of opera production, would only have perpetuated the budgetary problems that had existed since the beginning of the theater's operation. In any case, in order for the agreement to take force, the theater had to be free of "impediments" by July 1645, and the legal actions of Torelli and Morandi that had closed the theater stood in the way of the sale.

On 27 May 1645, by which time Torelli may have left Venice for France to oversee the scenery for a Parisian performance of *La finta pazza*, Paulo Morandi gave his consent so that the Novissimo could be opened in order to "present several performances, but only during the fair of the current Sensa." He stipulated that an inventory of the contents of the theater be undertaken both before and after the performances.[71] Morandi, then, facilitated the Ascension performance of Bisaccioni and Giovanni Rovetta's *Ercole in Lidia* featuring the singing of the prima donna Anna Renzi that would later be described by John Evelyn in his diary.[72] As might be expected, however, financial problems persisted despite the Ascension performances: in July four of the musicians, including Renzi, went to the courts in an effort to gain monies owed to them.[73]

Did the "sale" of the Novissimo to Bisaccioni ever take place? In June 1645 four long-standing creditors, including Girolamo Lando, protested Torelli's and Morandi's interdict on the theater because it was blocking the sale; moreover, while they acknowledged the artisans' credits with Lappoli, they regarded theirs as having precedence, having been registered with the court on 28 February 1643.[74] The absence of Bisaccioni's name from later documentation concerning the theater suggests that financial complications prevented the consummation of the agree-

---

70 One of the creditors in this dispute was Bernardo Josephis who had, on 24 Dec. 1644, rented a building behind the Teatro Novissimo from which to sell entrance tickets (ASV, Giudici del forestier, Sentenze, reg. 78, f. 107ᵛ, 9 June 1646). Bisaccioni was also involved at this time in a financial dispute with General Anselmo Truxes (ASV, GE, Estraordinari, b. 43, f. 88, 13 Mar. 1645; ASV, GE, Interdetti, b. 138, f. 44, 18 Feb. 1644 m.v.; see also ASV, Avogaria di comun, b. 2157/107, 16 Mar. 1645).

71 "si contenta che il teatro sudetto sij aperto posino esser fatte diverse recite durante la fiera della sensa presente et non più." ASV, GE, Interdetti, b. 138, ff. 195ᵛ–96, 27 May 1645.

72 Evelyn, *Diaries*, 2:449–52.

73 The petition of Renzi and Laurenzi was made on 5 July 1645 (ASV, GP, Dimande, b. 31, fasc. 49, no. 77); Manelli registered his (on behalf also of his wife) on 11 July (no. 87).

74 ASV, GM, Sentenze a legge, b. 314, f. 103ᵛ.

ment, and thus forced many of Lappoli's creditors to seek restitution for years to come. The demise of the theater must not have seemed imminent, however; indeed, before leaving Venice at the end of September 1645, Pietro Magno left instructions for his palco at the Novissimo to be rented out.[75]

Alvise Michiel and His Financial Involvement at the Novissimo and SS. Giovanni e Paolo

We now return to the question of Alvise Michiel's place and function in the history of the theater. Ivanovich cited him as one of the founders, but it is only several years later that his name begins to appear in the documentation concerning the theater. The earliest involvement we have discovered is his collaboration with Girolamo Lando, in March 1644, to borrow funds for Lappoli's use.[76] In May 1645 Giacomo Torelli claimed that Michiel had assisted in calculating the money owed him for machines and other items. Moreover, at some point Michiel had agreed to pay a number of the theater's debts, for on 5 October 1645 Maiolino Bisaccioni was instructed to bring into the Avogaria di comun, one of the city's courts, the original document where Michiel "promises to pay the debts described therein regarding the Theatro Novissimo, so that Girolamo Lando might see it and have a copy made."[77] Several years later, in 1647, Michiel owed the friars of SS. Giovanni e Paolo 100 ducats for "scenery and other materials."[78]

One of the chief issues concerning Michiel's involvement in the theater is the nature of his relationship both to Lappoli and to Bisaccioni. While Bisaccioni may have agreed to undertake the direction of the theater only through the promise of outside assistance, namely that of Michiel, the latter had not undertaken the responsibility of satisfying all of the theater's debts: Bisaccioni's contract to take over the Novissimo from Lappoli specifies funds to be paid to Lando, but it also endows Lando with the right to pursue legal actions concerning Lappoli's debts, specifically against Alvise Michiel. The terms for Lando's reimbursement may have been arranged so that a number of parties shared the burden: Bisaccioni's responsibilities

---

75 ASV, AN, Atti, b. 662, f. 188, 27 Sept. 1645.

76 This loan, from Domenico Gradenigo, is referred to in ASV, GP, Dimande, b. 29, filza 38, 13 July 1645. One difficulty in ascertaining Michiel's precise relationship with the Novissimo is common to almost all documentation from the Venetian courts: the extant materials represent only summaries of actions. In most cases, although the names of the parties are reported, and usually the amounts in question, the other elements of the disagreements are not. In this case, for example, the document speaks of the loan being made on behalf of Lappoli, but does not mention the theater. In some later documents, however, this loan is linked with other matters clearly for the Novissimo.

77 "la scrittura originale . . . sottoscritta dal N.H. signor Alvise Michiel, et da testimonij, nella qual esso N.H. Alvise promette pagare li debbiti in quella descritti, che si trovano sopra il Theatro Novissimo, affine che il N.H. signor Gierolimo Lando Cavalier possi quella vedere e haverne coppia." ASV, Avogaria di comun, b. 2159/109, 5 Oct. 1645.

78 ASV, GP, Dimande, b. 31 [49], no. 39, 20 May 1645. The friars sent notice in June 1648 that Michiel had neither collected nor paid for the material, which they were apparently holding as security for the debt (ASV, AN, Atti, b. 10983, 5 June 1648).

were specified in the theater transfer, while Michiel's must have been drawn up in a separate document which so far has not come to light.[79]

Our understanding of Michiel's theatrical activities in Venice is complicated by the fact that he, like Lappoli, had ties to two theaters. In May 1645 he was cited in regard to "interests common to [Michiel] and Lappoli at the Grimani theater"; his involvement at SS. Giovanni e Paolo, however, was not merely linked to Lappoli's, for several years later, in 1648 (after Lappoli's departure), he authorized the hiring of singers in Rome for that theater.[80] We do not know just how and when Michiel made his entry into the opera business, but in 1645 we first see him in the role of protector to Anna Renzi, the prima donna who had appeared at both theaters.[81] Michiel could have been drawn into the financing of opera as a result of connections with Lappoli, Renzi, the Grimanis, or even some other party.

The Twilight of the Novissimo

By 1646 Lappoli had left town with a number of debts still outstanding. His former benefactors such as Pietro Magno,[82] Girolamo Lando, and Giacomo Badoaro continued their attempts to claim their credits through the courts, and Badoaro even pursued Lappoli in his native Tuscany by commissioning the Venetian diplomatic officer in Florence, Zuane Zon, to collect the funds owed to him.[83] In November 1646 the friars of SS. Giovanni e Paolo began a series of attempts to have the theater torn down, each time with protests by Lando, who sought representation so that he could make use of the raw materials as repayment of his credits; the task was accomplished, finally, in 1647. The space that had been the theater then came to be used as the "cavallerizza," or riding academy for young patricians.[84]

Conclusions

As we have seen, the sources regarding the Novissimo tell only a partial story regarding the patronage and support offered to Venice's premiere theater of the early 1640s. No documentary evidence suggests that the Accademia degli Incogniti provided the impetus for the construction of the theater; Sacrati and Torelli, on the other hand, seem to have been involved from the start, and the impresario Girolamo Lappoli later claimed to have built the theater himself. The theater's original

79 On 28 Sept. 1645 Alvise Michiel protested Lando's demands for payment (ASV, GP, Scritture e risposte, b. 178, fasc. 49, no. 137). Matters between the two men had not been completely settled as late as 1651. Michiel may have acted as pieggio for Lappoli (he is characterized as guarantor in Mancini, Muraro, and Povoledo, *Teatri di Venezia*, 1:346–47), but he is not mentioned as such in any of the surviving documentation.

80 ASV, AN, Atti, b. 6051, f. 176, 24 Oct. 1648.

81 Michiel drew up the marriage agreement between Renzi and Ruberto Sabbatini in June 1645, and witnessed in 1649 her contract with Giovanni Battista Balbi to appear in an opera in Florence; he was also named as one of the executors of her will in 1652. See B. Glixon, "Private Lives," 515, 518.

82 ASV, AN, Atti, b. 662, f. 188, 27 Sept. 1645.

83 ASV, AN, Atti, b. 665, f. 281, 29 May 1647.

84 The riding academy is described in Sansovino, *Venetia città nobilissima et singolare*, 396.

financial base most likely lay in loans to Lappoli from the Venetian nobleman Girolamo Lando, who must have contributed several thousand ducats of support at unspecified dates. Soon after, another nobleman, Pietro Magno, entered the picture,
followed by the Jewish doctor Josef Camis. None of these men were partners or
investors in the true sense of the word; unlike Alvise Duodo and Marc'Antonio
Correr in Faustini's company, they all expected at least some reimbursement. Alvise
Michiel, who agreed to take on some of the theater's debts, probably came into the
picture only later in the Novissimo's history, while Bisaccioni's intention is unclear.
He undoubtedly lacked the financial resources to sustain the theater, and would
have relied on others to pay most of the theater's debts. It is likely that Lando,
Magno, and other creditors, such as Badoaro and the guarantors Gaggini and
Baretta, sacrificed at least part of their credits with Lappoli, much against their will,
but nevertheless to the benefit of Venice's theatrical system.

S. APONAL

The case studies presented so far have concerned a theater owned by a noble
family (the typical situation in Venice), and one built on the property of a
monastery. Each of these situations offered particular challenges and benefits to the
property owners. Certainly, the Tron family had a special interest in promoting
successful theatrical enterprises, both for reasons of prestige and economic benefit.
The friars of SS. Giovanni e Paolo, on the other hand, would not have seen the
Novissimo as an opportunity for increasing the prestige of their community. They
must have sought rental income, and their concern would have been for propriety,
that is, to foster or, more accurately, to allow to operate an entertainment that was
appropriate in proximity to a monastery. In this next study we look at a different
type of theatrical enterprise, where the building that housed the theater was
owned by cittadini: Francesco Ceroni (along with his brother, Giovanni Battista)
and his cousin, Zanetta Diamante.[85] Problems of personality and of civic use arose,
thwarting the development of this building as a theatrical site. Here we focus
specifically on the value of the theater to the owners, rather than on the operation
of the theater per se.

Warehouse and Theater: Origins and the Faustini
Years

The small Teatro S. Aponal is most famous as the site of the operatic enterprise run
by Giovanni and Marco Faustini and their partners (see chap. 3), but it had operated as a comedy theater even earlier (see the chronology in table 4.3): the building

---

85 The theater is discussed more fully in Glixon and Glixon, "Oil and Opera." See also Glover,
"Teatro Sant'Apollinare." Glover's research was largely based on the librettos and extant scores of the
operas performed at S. Aponal, as well as the documents in ASV, SGSM, bb. 188 and 194. Other histories
of the theater appear in Mangini, *Teatri di Venezia* and Mancini, Muraro, and Povoledo, *Teatri di Venezia*.
See also Rosand, *Opera*, 170–76, 181–84.

TABLE 4.3.   Chronology of the Teatro S. Aponal

Date	Event
Before 1635	Opened as comedy theater
19 May 1650, 1650/51 and 1651/52 seasons	Building rented by Francesco Ceroni and Zanetta Diamante to Giovanni Faustini for five years, to be used as a theater; on Faustini's death, it passes to his brother Marco, who acts as impresario
1652/53 and 1653/54 seasons	Faustini sublets theater to Bortolo Castoreo, Annibale Basso, and Paulo Morandi
1654/55, 1655/56, and 1656/57 seasons	Marco Faustini returns as impresario for three seasons
25 October 1655	Zanetta Diamante rents her half interest in the theater to Marco Faustini for two five-year periods
4 May 1656	Francesco Ceroni, owner of half-interest in the theater, attempts to evict Faustini
16 March 1657	Faustini agrees to terminate his agreement with Ceroni, but that with Diamante is still in effect, and he continues to have rights to the theater, paying her rent through 1662
1657/58 and 1658/59 seasons	Faustini sublets the theater to the Accademia degli Imperturbabili, after which it ceases operation
23 July 1665	Ceroni and Diamante rent theater for three years to Sebastiano Enno and Camillo Nebbia; reconstruction halted because of risk of fire; building never again used as theater

was styled as "the place where they performed comedy" in a document of 1635.[86] The building's history, naturally, went back much further. The property, located in the Corte de Ca' Petrian (also known as the Corte del Botter) off the Grand Canal on the side opposite S. Marco just south of the Rialto Bridge, apparently had belonged to the stonemasons' guild[87] and then became the property of the Belaviti family; eventually it passed to a descendant, Francesco Ceroni, and his cousin, Zanetta Diamante, who shared the property, each receiving half of the income it accrued.[88]

One circumstance that governed the feasibility of this space for theatrical enter-

86 "il luoco ove si recitava la comedia." ASV, AN, Atti, b. 2863, f. 132, 17 Sept. 1635.

87 ASV, DS, b. 387, no. 690. In the absence of more precise documentation, the story of the early years of this property has been inferred primarily from two later documents that discuss, sometimes ambiguously, previous episodes: ASV, AN, b. 11175, f. 19, 18 Aug. 1666 (a declaration from Bortolo Grigis to Francesco Ceroni concerning a legal action by Zanetta Diamante) and ASV, DS, b. 387, no. 690 (Francesco Ceroni's property tax declaration).

88 ASV, AN, Atti, b. 11175, f. 19, 18 Aug. 1666. Details concerning the ownership of the theater by the Belaviti family are discussed in Glixon and Glixon, "Oil and Opera."

tainment was the use of the lower floor as a storeroom, something quite traditional in Venice. By the early seventeenth century, the building was most likely structured as a warehouse with two rooms on the ground floor; above this, with a separate entrance, was another room several stories in height, but unencumbered by permanent floors.[89] In 1622 the ground floor of the property came into the possession of one Santo Grigis, and he, and then his son, Bortolo, used the space as an oil warehouse for decades to come.[90] Eventually the oil stored there came to be seen as a liability, and in the 1660s the operation of the upper floor as a theater was challenged (theaters, with their special needs for lighting, always presented a fire hazard even in the best of situations).[91] But a more basic question concerns the owners' goals in permitting a theater to operate on their property, and how Giovanni Faustini came to choose it in 1650. We do not know if Faustini had sought it out specifically, approaching the owners with an offer, or if Ceroni and Diamante, already having decided to embrace the possible benefits that opera production might hold for their property, approached Faustini after he had ceased to present operas at S. Moisè.[92]

As we have seen, the principal benefit to any owner of a building put to theatrical use was, traditionally, the rental income. Indeed, barring a different arrangement specified by contract, the owner's sole monetary gain was this rent: the profits, as well as the losses, accrued to the theatrical company. Given this arrangement, then, Ceroni and Diamante would have gained little indeed from their agreement with Faustini. The rental for the upper floor of the building as a warehouse usually amounted to 40 ducats, split evenly between Ceroni and Diamante.[93] Giovanni Faustini's contract of 1650, on the other hand, specified an annual payment of 60 ducats, or an increase of only 20 ducats. Since the owners individually did not take in much money from the enterprise, perhaps they derived some satisfaction in knowing that their property added to the entertainment and prestige of the city.

The theater's operation under the Faustini brothers (1650–57)[94] should have been advantageous for the impresarios: at a rent of only 60 ducats per year, as each successive year passed, the overall profit, under most circumstances, would have greatly exceeded the losses initially entailed by the reconstruction needed to turn the warehouse into a theater. The low rent must surely have compensated for the

---

89 There were also one or more small storerooms under the stairway that led to the upper floor. ASV, DS, b. 387, no. 690.

90 ASV, AN, Atti, b. 11175, f. 19, 18 Aug. 1666.

91 See Glixon and Glixon, "Oil and Opera," 139, 141–43.

92 Francesco Ceroni's father, Pietro, had died by 17 June 1641 (see ASV, AN, Atti, b. 996, f. 85); the comedy theater had probably operated earlier under his authority. The building's first use as a theater may not have occurred much before 1635, since it is not mentioned in Girolamo Priuli's listing of theaters presenting comedies in the first part of the century. Priuli's diary is dated 1607, but according to Mangini, the description of the theaters of S. Cassiano, S. Moisè, and S. Luca date from 1626, when Priuli made a number of additions. See Mangini, *Teatri di Venezia*, 34.

93 ASV, DS, b. 387, no. 690.

94 As mentioned earlier, for the 1652/53 and 1653/54 seasons Faustini sublet the theater to the company of Bortolo Castoreo, Annibale Basso, and Paulo Morandi; see Glixon and Glixon, "Oil and Opera," 135–36.

small income generated by only forty-eight palchi, but other factors led Faustini and his partners to abandon S. Aponal in 1657 (for S. Cassiano) before the expiration of their contract.

Francesco Ceroni and Zanetta Diamante: Owners in Conflict

If the operation of S. Aponal as an opera theater in the 1650s was made possible through the agency of Francesco Ceroni and Zanetta Diamante, it was also Ceroni who led to its demise. Ceroni was a lawyer in Venice, and, like Marco Faustini, would have had many demands on his time. Indeed, rather than occupy himself with matters concerning the rental of the theater in 1650, he authorized his cousin to make the arrangements in both their names.[95]

Ceroni and his cousin did not enjoy an easy relationship. To pick one example, on 25 October 1655 she agreed to rent "her half of the theater" to Faustini, effective 21 June 1656.[96] That is, peace had broken down not only between Ceroni and Faustini, but between Ceroni and Diamante. Diamante rented her half-interest to Faustini for a period of ten years, divided into two five-year periods. Faustini's fee for half of the theater remained constant at 30 ducats, and he maintained the right to sublet the theater to others. Diamante's benefits went beyond those 30 ducats, however, for she was to have Faustini's legal services at no charge.[97] Relations between Ceroni and Faustini must have worsened over the next few months. On 4 May 1656, just two months after the success of Cavalli's *Erismena*, Ceroni wanted Faustini out of the theater, and ordered him to pay 500 ducats in rent should he wish to stay.[98] Ceroni's motivations are not entirely clear, but he may have judged the 60-ducat rent too small for a moderately successful theater. Since he already had a signed contract with Diamante, however, Faustini was able to continue operations in the theater as before. Difficulties between the two lawyers continued, and on 16 March 1657, Faustini agreed to give back to Ceroni his interest in the theater, once again, without having to yield the right to present operas.[99]

---

95 ASV, AN, Atti, b. 6053, f. 64ᵛ, 4 May 1650. After the rental of the theater, problems developed regarding the destination of the annual fees. Ceroni, like many Venetians, had a number of debts, so that Faustini's payments eventually went directly to one of Ceroni's creditors, Sebastian Mocenigo. Later, in a sort of domino effect, Marco Faustini directly paid Mocenigo's creditors, Francesco Grimani and Ottavio Bon. The issue of who would ultimately receive Ceroni's rental fees did not interfere with Faustini's operation of the theater.

96 As the relatives each owned a half interest in the theater, Diamante chose to formally rent out her half, in accordance with the previous agreement, even if Ceroni had misgivings about renting his.

97 ASV, SGSM, b. 194, f. 168.

98 ASV, SGSM, b. 194, f. 163.

99 ASV, SGSM, b. 194, f. 169. The conflicts between Ceroni and Diamante concerning their property surfaced in other areas, and ultimately found expression in Diamante's wills. The first that survives is dated 8 June 1656, just a month after Ceroni had ordered Faustini out of the theater (ASV, AN, Testamenti, Testamenti chiusi, bb. 176–85, n. 305, 8 June 1656). Diamante's testament makes clear that the primary bonds of her affection lay not with the Ceronis, but with other elderly relatives, and with a number of close friends. In this particular will she generously forgave Ceroni, along with his brother

As discussed above, Faustini and his partners Correr and Duodo moved on to S. Cassiano in 1657, but Diamante's agreement of 1655 had granted the impresario the use of the theater for ten years. Unable to maintain the theater as a venue for commercial opera by virtue of the incorporation agreement with his partners for S. Cassiano, he turned it over to an academy, the Imperturbabili, whose members presented comedies "with music."[100] Here Faustini proved to be a clever tenant, for he rented the space out for 120 ducats, thereby achieving a profit of 60 ducats for himself, the same income that Ceroni and Diamante had enjoyed for seven years. The space continued to be used as a theater for two years in this fashion, with the stipulation that it not compete with Faustini's operations. Faustini continued to pay Diamante regular installments, ending in March 1662.[101]

1665: The Attempt to Resurrect the Theater

S. Aponal may have fallen into disuse following the activity of the Imperturbabili, but hopes for the theater did not die completely. In July 1665 Ceroni and Diamante signed a three-year rental contract (designating the building this time as "the place where they do comedy, that is, the theater") with Don Sebastiano Enno and one Camillo Nebbia, at the usual rate of 60 ducats per year.[102] Enno, a canon at the Cathedral of S. Pietro di Castello, had considerable experience with singers and opera. He was an active singing teacher, and had himself performed at least once on the Venetian stage, in Francesco Lucio and Giacinto Andrea Cicognini's *Gl'amori di Alessandro magno, e di Rossane*, at Teatro SS. Apostoli in 1650/51.[103] Enno and Nebbia's contract permitted them to build palchi from scratch, as those from the Faustini years were no longer in place. Ceroni and Diamante had hopes that the theater would continue to present operas even after the three years of the

---

Giovanni Battista, the debt owed to her regarding their shared properties, which she deemed "a great sum," but she failed to grant them any other benefits. On the other hand, in her next will, drawn up in 1662, she left them effects worth several hundred ducats, once again forgiving the debts they owed her regarding their shared properties, i.e., the buildings in the parish of S. Aponal. Diamante drew up two more wills toward the end of her life, in 1688 and 1689. The first of these finds Francesco Ceroni as one of her heirs; only a year later, however, Diamante chose, instead, Ceroni's son, Pietro, whom she forbade to share the inheritance with his father (ASV, AN, Testamenti, b. 773, no. 150, 17 Apr. 1688; and no. 151, 12 Sept. 1689). Diamante died on 20 Aug. 1690 at the age of 90 (VAP, S. Nicola da Tolentino, S. Croce, Registri Morti, b. III, Reg. 12, 1685–1774, f. 109).

100 See chapter 3. For more on the rental to the Imperturbabili see Glixon and Glixon, "Oil and Opera." The contract between Faustini and the Imperturbabili is transcribed in Mancini, Muraro, and Povoledo, *Teatri di Venezia*, 1:372. The renewal of that contract in the name of Emmanuel Calafati, one of the members, is dated 26 Jan. 1658 m.v. (ASV, SGSM, b. 118, mazzo A).

101 For the payments to Diamante, see ASV, SGSM, b. 118, f. 61, 7 Mar. 1662. Faustini also made several payments to Ottavian Bon, that is, the creditor of Francesco Ceroni, the last one on 10 July 1662; they appear in the same source, on ff. 20ᵛ, 34, and 64.

102 "il luoco della comedia sive teatro ..." ASV, AN, Atti, b. 12671, f. 83 [145], 23 July 1665.

103 On this production, see B. Glixon, "Music for the Gods?"

rental, as they agreed to reimburse Enno and Nebbia for the value of the palchi, as determined by an outside evaluator, at the termination of the contract.

On 23 August, Enno and Nebbia reached a formal agreement between themselves regarding the income and expenditures of the theater, a necessity given that they had both begun to prepare for the season, during which they planned to present a new version of *Gl'amori di Alessandro magno.*[104] Perhaps unbeknownst to Enno and Nebbia, however, obstacles had already been thrown in their path. Nearly two weeks earlier, on 11 August, the nobleman Francesco Corner complained to the Capi of the Council of Ten, the body responsible, among other things, for public safety; Corner, who had management of one of the ground-floor warehouses, had been able to prevent the use of the space as a dance hall several years earlier.[105] The nobleman cited the danger of fire, which, he said, had already occurred at two theaters, S. Cassiano and S. Luca, and which would be exceptionally dangerous in the area around this theater.[106] He testified that a theater would threaten not only the oil in his warehouse, but the entire district, one, Corner affirmed, "of narrow streets, rotten buildings, and near a bakery, that is to say, ready to burn, because of the canes and wood found there."[107] Corner asked that construction of the theater (that is, conversion of the warehouse) be prohibited. Someone, perhaps even Enno or Nebbia, testified against the prohibition, citing the funds already expended by "a company of virtuosi," and emphasizing the potential financial benefits. In an attempt to address Corner's concerns, the impresarios even reached a compromise with Bortolo Grigis—still the owner of one of the oil warehouses—in which he would reduce the amount of oil stored there for the carnival season in exchange for an unspecified payment, one the impresarios were willing to make even though it would have eroded their profits substantially. Corner's cause was upheld, however, and S. Aponal failed to reopen as an opera theater.[108]

Perhaps Ceroni's and Diamante's building at S. Aponal had never possessed the characteristics that would have enabled its continuing operation as a theater. Still, under the Faustini regime success had been achieved. As we shall see in chapter 11, the operatic offerings of Cavalli and Ziani, along with the support of the nobility in the persons of Alvise Duodo and Marc'Antonio Correr, drew Venetians and visitors alike to visit this humble theater.

104 ASV, AN, Atti, b. 1165, f. 98, 23 Aug. 1665. The name of the projected opera is mentioned in testimony in ASV, Monastero di SS. Giovanni e Paolo, b. XXV.

105 See Glixon and Glixon, "Oil and Opera," 140–41. Corner had gained control of the space through the dowry of his wife Isabetta, the niece of Bortolo Grigis (see above).

106 The Teatro S. Cassiano had burned down in 1629, and S. Luca in 1652. See Mangini, *Teatri di Venezia*, 36, 51.

107 "di calle ristrette, con stabili marcissimi, vicinanza del fornaro, che vol dire esca all'incendio, per le cane, et altre legne, che ivi si atrovano." ASV, Monastero di SS. Giovanni e Paolo, b. XXV. See Glixon and Glixon, "Oil and Opera," 143.

108 We have not yet located a governmental decree banning the operation of the theater, but it is clear the performances never took place. Moreover, Enno produced the intended opera the subsequent year, at S. Moisè.

S. LUCA AS AN OPERA THEATER IN THE 1660S

The Teatro S. Luca (also called S. Salvatore[109] or Vendramin) offers yet another opportunity to view an opera house in its infancy, and to study the strategies its managers developed in order to lead it toward viability. The goal of this enterprise was ambitious: to compete head to head with the successful SS. Giovanni e Paolo, which had been in operation since 1639. That goal was achieved, but only with great difficulties along the way. The success of the venture is significant as it marks the first time since the establishment of SS. Giovanni e Paolo that a new opera theater found stability in the Venetian market: all other contenders had managed only sporadic success during the previous decades.

The Change from Comedy to Opera

If S. Luca's transformation from comedy to opera in 1660 mirrored, at the most basic level, that of S. Cassiano in 1637, it differed in other ways, for opera and its place in Venetian society and culture had changed from what it had been several decades earlier. The business had become more complicated, and the transformation of a theater's repertory could no longer be accomplished by the simple acquisition of a troupe of talented musicians such as Manelli's. In studying the emergence of S. Luca, then, we begin to understand something of the elements necessary to create a successful new theater, of the tremendous debts that could occur, and of the different types of people who might show a willingness to help out with those debts.

It is easy to surmise why Andrea Vendramin, the owner of one of Venice's oldest comedy theaters, changed the sort of entertainment he offered at S. Luca. During the summer of 1660 he would have become aware of an unusual situation: for the first time in several decades, only one theater in Venice remained dedicated to mounting operas.[110] With S. Moisè, S. Aponal, and S. Cassiano closed—and Faustini now at the Grimani theater—all competition in the market had vanished. The move from comedy to opera—whether initiated by Vendramin himself or suggested to him by others—represented a complete change in direction. Unlike the rival comedy theater, S. Moisè, which had presented operas from time to time during the 1640s and 1650s, S. Luca had always specialized in comedy. Although Vendramin had still planned to hire a troupe of comedians as late as 31 August 1660,[111]

---

109 The theater was in the parish of S. Luca, but near the important Augustinian church of S. Salvatore.

110 In 1660 Vendramin brought the previous renters, Caterina Zane and Cristoforo Boldù, before civic authorities for non-payment of rent (Mancini, Muraro, and Povoledo, *Teatri di Venezia*, 1:212). Vendramin's difficulties with Zane and Boldù, however, may have contributed only in a small way to the change in the theater's direction. Had he wished the theater to continue to present comedy, he could have rented it to the new tenant specifically with that intent.

111 ASV, AN, Atti, b. 2983, f. 875ᵛ, 31 Aug. 1660. On that date Vendramin authorized his "cubicularius" (head of household) Ottavio Gelais to make arrangements to hire the troupe of comedians of the Duke of Modena.

by October he had set his new plans in motion.[112] Then, on 13 November (see the chronology in table 4.4), he formally rented the theater for a period of four years to the nobleman Antonio Boldù for the purpose of presenting opera.[113] The contract acknowledged that the time remaining before carnival might be insufficient to present an opera that first season; moreover, it allowed for an initial reduction in the rent, reflecting some of the costs that Boldù would incur in order to adapt the structure of the theater to the necessities of opera production.

Vendramin had always kept a vigilant watch on the renters of his theater, ready to act when he perceived a problem that might interfere with his income. He may have risked little in this late conversion, however, as the rental fees had been backed by a guarantor. During the 1660s Vendramin—unlike the Grimanis—maintained a certain distance from the production aspects of the company, insulating himself both from profits and losses, and from issues regarding artisans and singers.

Antonio Boldù and the Teatro S. Luca

Vendramin found, in his new renter, Antonio Boldù, someone whose familiarity with the Venetian theatrical system came from two close family members who had earlier served as impresarios (see figure 4.1). Indeed, Boldù's family had more impresarial experience in Venice than any other. He did not enter into the enterprise alone, however, and it seems likely—given the outcome of the initial years of operation—that he was not even the most interested party.

The 1660 rental contract provides us with several names other than Boldù's. One member of the company was Carlo Morandi,[114] who was named cashier, that is, in charge of the income from palchi, scagni, and bollettini. The carpenter Pietro Fassetta, who had previously been the fattor at the theater, continued in that capacity. The pharmacist Girolamo Barbieri acted as one of the guarantors for the rent, and the agreement was formalized in his shop.[115] Barbieri also had previous ties to this theater, having helped out with disputes regarding palchi during the 1650s, at the request of one of the tenants at that time, Cristoforo Boldù.[116] As we shall see, Barbieri must have entered into the new company as more than a casual outsider, for he became an active participant in the theater's activities as the decade progressed.

Preparations for the season went better than expected, and about two months

---

112 Giovanni Grimani mentioned in a letter of 16 Oct. 1660 that Vendramin had cancelled his plans to hire a certain company of comedians (ASFe, AB, b. 332, f. 267; see Monaldini, *Orto dell'Esperidi*, 151–52).

113 "per far recitar opere in musica . . ." ASV, AN, Atti, b. 2983, ff. 1110ᵛ–1115. For a partial transcription of the document, see Mancini, Muraro, and Povoledo, *Teatri di Venezia*, 1:263–64.

114 Carlo Morandi was apparently not a relative of Paulo Morandi, who had been involved in several other theaters. On Paulo Morandi, see chapters 3 and 10.

115 The other guarantor was the merchant Pietro Pedozzi.

116 ASV, AN, b. 1083, f. 149ᵛ, 29 Jan. 1653 m.v. Antonio Boldù was Cristoforo's nephew.

TABLE 4.4.   Chronology of the Teatro S. Luca

Date	Event
1622	S. Luca built by Vendramin family as a comedy theater
1652	Theater burns and is rebuilt
13 November 1660, 1660/61 season	Andrea Vendramin rents theater for four years to Antonio Boldù to present opera at a rent of D500 the first year and D1000 in subsequent years; company includes Carlo Morandi (cashier), Pietro Fassetta (fattor), and Girolamo Barbieri (pieggio)
19 July 1661, 1661/62 season	Antonio Boldù withdraws from company and transfers rental (while still being owed over D2500 by the company) to Girolamo Lovato Machiavelli, who transfers his interest to Barbieri; company for second season includes Morandi, Barbieri, and Daniele da Castrovillari (composer)
1662/63 season	Company of Barbieri, Morandi, Don Pietro Moretti, and, as impresario, Abbate Vettor Grimani Calergi
1663/64 season	Company of Barbieri and Marc'Antonio Montalbano (briefly taking over Morandi's share)
1664/65 season	Company of Barbieri (controlling 5/6 of the company), Tomaso Corner (as protector), Nicolò Minato (librettist and partner, holding Morandi's former 1/6 share), Marco Mozzoni (cashier), and the Bolognese Pietro Antonio Cerva (partner and scene painter)
1665/66 season, 1666/67 season	Company of Barbieri (3/6 share), Mozzoni (2/6 share), and Minato (1/6 share); Corner still protector; Mozzoni dies 5 January 1667, Barbieri later in the year
1667/68 season, 1668/69 season	Theater rented to Don Pietro Moretti for six years (rent of D700 first year, D1100 subsequently); company of Montalbano (2/3 share) and Minato (1/3 share); Minato leaves for Vienna after 1668/69 season; Corner still protector
8 December 1669, 1669/70 season	Theater rented to Aurelio Aureli (librettist)

after the registration of the rental contract the company was, remarkably, able to mount a production: *Pasife*, by Giuseppe Artale and Daniele da Castrovillari (who had, the previous year, composed an opera for the Grimani theater), which reached the stage for the 1660/61 carnival. Although many of the singers hired were experienced performers, the theater's operatic debut did not go smoothly.[117] Indeed, one could say that the results of the first opera were disastrous. According to one contemporary, Giovanni da Mosto, members of the audience, unable to further

117 Several members of the cast had sung for Faustini during the previous decade in Venice: Stefano Costa, Francesco Maria Rascarini, Silvia Manni, and Filippo Manin.

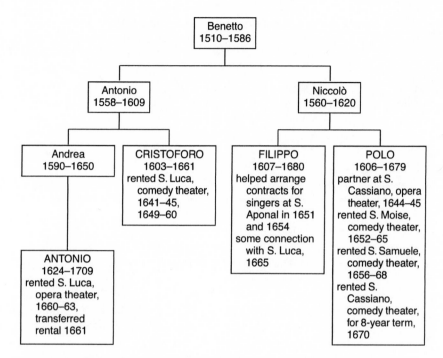

FIGURE 4.1. Theatrical activities of the Boldù Family. Included here are only those family members with theatrical connections and those others necessary to show familial relationships

tolerate the performance, erupted, throwing objects and burning copies of the libretto, so that the opera apparently closed after the first night.[118] The company managed to mount a second opera, a revival of Giovanni Faustini and Francesco Cavalli's *Eritrea*, almost certainly chosen only after the failure of *Pasife*.

A box-office failure could wreak havoc on a new company, and such was the case at S. Luca. Daniele da Castrovillari later claimed that his opera had been performed thirteen times, but this may refer to the combined offerings of *Pasife* and *Eritrea*.[119] The small number of performances that season reduced the company's income, making difficult the payments to performers, artists, and tradesmen alike, and perhaps also the collection of box rentals from disgruntled noblemen. Moreover, on 19 July 1661 Antonio Boldù formally cut his ties to the theater. Although technically it remained in his name, he transferred the rental to Girolamo Lovato Machiavelli, the uncle of Giacomo Dall'Angelo, the lawyer and occasional opera librettist.[120]

118 Mangini, *Teatri di Venezia*, 52–53; Rosand, *Opera*, 185.

119 ASV, GP, Dimande. b. 46, fasc. 86, no. 583 (82), 20 Apr. 1663.

120 Could it be purely coincidental that Dall'Angelo penned the libretto for the next opera to be presented at the theater, *Cleopatra*? On Dall'Angelo, see chapter 5.

Boldù's abrupt departure raises questions concerning his role in the original company, and whether he had been an active participant in the theater's operation, or had been the renter in name only. He was apparently involved in the hiring of one singer, Cecilia Siri.[121] One letter written by Boldù after the season's end, however, shows another side to the story. In March 1661 he thanked the Marquis Bentivoglio in Ferrara for the loan of his singer, Stefano Costa. Boldù remarked that the singer had been requested "under my name, but without my knowledge."[122] The original letter requesting Costa's services, then, had been drafted by Morandi or Barbieri, but signed by the nobleman or one of his representatives; Boldù's family name would have been used to add weight and more "respectability" to the request for Costa's services.

Whether or not he had been concerned with the hiring of singers, Boldù had injected his own money into the enterprise; indeed, he appears to have been one of the major financers of the operation. At the time of the sublease he claimed a substantial credit, and elsewhere he is called the prime investor ("primo interessato") of the company.[123] The transfer makes clear that Boldù intended that he should be reimbursed for his generous outlay, and that if his partners wanted to take over the operation, they would need to repay him fully.[124] Even Boldù's large expenditure of funds had not been sufficient to cover all of the bills, however. Among expenses still outstanding at the time of the sublease were the fees of five singers; Boldù, unwilling to incur further debt, assigned to the new tenant the responsibility of satisfying these musicians.[125] Boldù, then, left the theater when it was still in the red. Faustini's records from S. Aponal and S. Cassiano show that this situation would certainly have been expected for a theater's first year of operation, even if the initial productions had been successful; any opera production was an expensive affair, but expenses multiplied rapidly when a theater had to be partially rebuilt.

Boldù's participation at S. Luca, then, resembled that of some of the noblemen such as Girolamo Lando who had helped to fund the Novissimo during the 1640s. As in that earlier instance (and unlike Faustini's companies), others involved in the enterprise bore the responsibility of paying off the debts, in this case Carlo Morandi, Girolamo Barbieri (Boldù's guarantor from the original rental[126]), and, apparently, the composer for the first two seasons of the theater's activity, Daniele da Castrovillari.

---

121 ASV, GE, Esami e testamenti rilevati per breviario, b. 105, no. 271.

122 "le sia stato richiesto sotto mio nome, senza mia saputa . . ." ASFe, AB, b. 333, f. 333, 16 Mar. 1661. See Monaldini, *Orto dell'Esperidi*, 156.

123 ASV, Avogaria di comun, b. 2187/137, 15 May 1663.

124 Among the sources of funds chosen for the repayment of the loan were the rents from fifty-five palchi, amounting to 1,375 ducats (ASV, AN, Atti, b. 1132, f. 135ᵛ).

125 The singers who had not been paid were Felippo da Padova (Filippo Manin of S. Antonio in Padua), Pellegrino Canner, Silvia Manni, Francesco Maria Rascarini, and "Signor Bastiano," who may have been Sebastiano Chierici (from Ferrara), or the castrato Sebastiano Cioni.

126 On 2 June 1662 Filippo Manin claimed to have been paid only 30 ducats out of his total fee of 150 ducats, and he sued Girolamo Barbieri for the rest of his salary (see ASV, GP, Dimande, b. 45, fasc, 85, no. 185).

The Company of Morandi, Barbieri,
and Castrovillari

Morandi, Barbieri, and Castrovillari continued their interest in the theater in its second season, mounting Castrovillari's *Cleopatra*, to a libretto by Giacomo Dall'Angelo.[127] Dall'Angelo's uncle, however, the sub-renter Girolamo Lovato Machiavelli, had no intention of involving himself in things theatrical: he immediately transferred his sublease to Barbieri, who remained active at the theater until his death in 1667.[128] Still lacking, however, is the name of any nobleman who may have replaced Antonio Boldù, if not as a source of capital, then as a locus of prestige.

Girolamo Barbieri is himself a figure of some interest. As mentioned earlier, he had aided the renters of the theater during the 1650s when problems had developed concerning palco funds, but his interest in opera may have been sparked by a family connection: his son Bortolo had married Francesco Cavalli's stepdaughter, Claudia Giustinian, in 1643.[129] Given the close association between the composer and his wife's family, Barbieri must have known Cavalli during the 1640s, those years when the composer was active at S. Cassiano; eventually—nearly twenty years after that marriage—Barbieri and Cavalli would come together as colleagues in the S. Luca company.[130]

The 1662/63 Season: The Participation
of Vettor Grimani Calergi

For the 1662/63 season Barbieri and Morandi were still at the theater, and Don Pietro Moretti, a priest at the church of S. Marina, also became a partner, satisfying a variety of expenses during the spring of 1663.[131] Moretti would maintain a connection with the theater for a number of years, perhaps an unusual pastime for a parish priest apparently otherwise unconnected to Venice's musical world. The most significant change for that season, however, was the sudden appearance of the Venetian nobleman Abbot Vettor Grimani Calergi, someone with a long history of experience with opera production gained through years of exposure—and various levels of involvement—at the Grimani theater.[132]

---

127 While it is certainly possible that Dall'Angelo had played some part in arranging the sublease to his uncle, his name does not appear in any documentation for the theater.

128 ASV, AN, Atti, b. 1132, ff. 134^v–137^v, 19 July 1661.

129 After the death of her father, Claudia had lived for a number of years in the house of Girolamo Mocenigo, a noted patron of music, especially that of Claudio Monteverdi. We have no knowledge of how this marriage between Claudia and Bortolo Barbieri came to be arranged, but Mocenigo's house (now the Danieli Hotel) and Barbieri's business and home were all located in the parish of S. Giovanni Novo. On Cavalli's stepdaughter and her marriage, see Vio, "Ancora su Francesco Cavalli." Vio discusses the Mocenigo family, but does not mention its patronage of Monteverdi. On Mocenigo, see Monteverdi, *Letters*, ed. Stevens, 275–76 and 279–80; and Fabbri, *Monteverdi*, 202–2, 221–23.

130 Claudia's marriage to Barbieri was short-lived, as she died in 1645. See Vio, "Ancora su Francesco Cavalli," and Glover, *Cavalli*, 16, 20–21.

131 According to Castrovillari, Moretti had made some payments, with some still outstanding (ASV, AN, Atti, b.12674, f. 168, 4 Apr. 1663).

132 Grimani Calergi's activities in opera will be discussed in a future article.

Just the previous year Grimani Calergi had told the Duke of Mantua's diplomatic representative in Venice that he was building his own, new theater.[133] When this plan failed to achieve fruition, he sought another outlet for his passion for opera. If, as seems likely, Giovanni Grimani had prevented his relative's participation that year at the Grimani theater (see chap. 3), S. Luca would have represented the only remaining possibility. Grimani Calergi's participation at S. Luca offered two obvious advantages to the company there: the strong presence of a Venetian nobleman—something lacking since the departure of Boldù—and the wealth of political and artistic connections that Grimani Calergi enjoyed. The nobleman's role differed fundamentally from that of Antonio Boldù's just two years earlier, however. He had no formal agreement of any kind with the theater's owner (the previous arrangement with Boldù was still in place), and bore no responsibility for rental payments. Moreover, even though Grimani Calergi was new to the company, his standing and authority far exceeded that of Barbieri and Morandi: in a word, he brought to the task greater experience, connections in high places, and more sheer social power than any of the original partners.

Grimani Calergi's involvement permeated all aspects of the production for the upcoming season. Indeed, he was undoubtedly responsible for the presentation of *Dori*, composed by his former protégé, Antonio Cesti, whose operas had not been heard in Venice during the previous decade.[134] Grimani Calergi also recruited the singers, dancers, and engineers by corresponding with his friends at the courts of Ferrara and Florence, and he sent Carlo Morandi on a recruiting trip to Ferrara, Florence, and Lucca.[135] Grimani Calergi's activity extended to financial matters, as he was prepared to foot the initial bill for the artists; but, like Boldù before him, he expected to be repaid. A notarial act stipulated that Barbieri reimburse him from the nightly earnings, to be held securely in a locked box kept by Morandi (see chap. 1).[136]

Grimani Calergi had managed to carry out another coup for the young company: he persuaded Francesco Cavalli to compose a second opera for the theater during this brief carnival season, although the work never reached the stage.[137] It

133 ASMa, AG, b. 1572, 30 July 1661. Letter from Abbot Tinti, agent in Venice of the Duke of Mantua.

134 Grimani Calergi referred to Cesti in a letter to the Bentivoglio family dated 19 Oct. 1652 as "il mio musico" (ASFe, AB, b. 312, f. 629; see Monaldini, *Orto dell'Esperidi*, 60). In 1650 the composer was living in Grimani Calergi's house (see Michelassi, "Teatro del Cocomero," 179). During the previous summer the composer Castrovillari had come to a disagreement with Barbieri and Morandi, and had withdrawn from the company. Castrovillari's operatic career in Venice will be examined in a future study.

135 Letters from Grimani Calergi survive in the Medici and the Bentivoglio correspondence. Regarding the travels of Morandi, for Ferrara, see letter of 22 Sept. 1662 to Hippolito Bentivoglio (ASFe, AB, b. 336, f. 346; Monaldini, *Orto dell'Esperidi*, 175). For Morandi's travels to Tuscany, see ASF, MP, filza 5487, f. 777 (22 Sept. 1662) and f. 564 (11 Nov. 1662).

136 ASV, AN, Atti, b. 2989, f. 828ᵛ, 2 Jan. 1662 m.v. This issue eventually came before the courts: Grimani Calergi had the theater sealed to force Minato and Barbieri to repay him (see ASV, GE, Interdetti, b. 167, 16 Oct. 1663, and ASV, GE, Sentenze, b. 64, f. 20, 17 Oct. 1663).

137 ASMa, AG, b. 1573, notes of the Mantuan Resident Abbot Tinti, 25 Dec. 1662.

is likely that Cavalli's collaborator for the opera was his old partner, Nicolò Minato, who had not written librettos for the Venetian stage during Cavalli's two-year residence in France.[138] Even without Cavalli's opera, however, the season was a success, in large part owing to the stunning debut of a new Roman prima donna, Vincenza Giulia Masotti.[139] This third season, then, augured well for the future.

Grimani Calergi had been prepared to stay at S. Luca another year, but when Giovanni Grimani died during the spring of 1663, the Abbot quickly insinuated himself back into the fabric of his family's theater, where he, along with Giovanni Grimani's young nephew Giovanni Carlo, ran the theater for two seasons.[140] Moreover, Grimani Calergi convinced Carlo Morandi to join him at SS. Giovanni e Paolo, creating a vacuum at S. Luca.

S. Luca in the Mid-1660s: The Search for New Partners

With the departure of both Grimani Calergi and Morandi, the company badly needed new members with capital to invest. In search of a nobleman to help deal with a variety of negotiations and other matters, Barbieri gained the reluctant assistance of Marc'Antonio Montalbano, a man of Bolognese descent who had lived for many years in Venice.[141] The grandson of the librettist Maiolino Bisaccioni and a member of a notable family of authors and scientists, Montalbano may well have had access to many important personages. He took over Morandi's share of the company, and had, presumably, made a commitment to shoulder some of the expenses of the production. Tensions arose between him and Barbieri, however, and on 7 January 1664 Barbieri cancelled any agreements they had reached regarding the theater, accusing him of having behaved in a "despotic and abusive" manner, jeopardizing some of the preparations for the production.[142] Barbieri's complaints speak to the myriad of small, delicate interactions necessary to bring a production to fruition.

The opera for the 1663/64 season, *Achille in Sciro*, was an import, having premiered a year earlier in Ferrara, the home of its librettist, Marquis Hippolito Bentivoglio, as well as of its composer, Giovanni Legrenzi. As mentioned above, Ben-

---

138 In his *scrittura* of Jan. 1664 Marc'Antonio Montalbano (see below) referred to Minato as one of the "interessati," so that he must have been involved in the theater, at least for a time, before the production of his *Mutio Scevola* in 1664/65 (ASV, AN, Atti, b. 703, f. 154^v, 9 Jan. 1663 m.v.).

139 For more on Cavalli in 1662, and his availability that season, see chapter 6. On Masotti, see chapter 7.

140 Faustini was absent during those two years. See chapter 3.

141 Montalbano was the son of Lugretia Bisaccioni and the Bolognese Giovanni Battista Montalbano; he may have been born in Venice. Marc'Antonio's uncle Bartolomeo was a composer (see Ficola and Collisani, "Bartolomeo Montalbano"), while his father wrote a number of mathematical works. Another uncle, Ovidio Montalbano—a member of the Accademia degli Incogniti, as well as the Gelati of Bologna—wrote on a number of subjects, including biology, mathematics, and art history. Marc'Antonio Montalbano himself wrote works on mineralogy. He died at the age of 60 in Bologna on 30 Apr. 1695. See Fantuzzi, *Notizie degli scrittori bolognesi*, 6:56.

142 "troppo dispoticamente anzi abusivamente ..." ASV, AN, Atti, b. 703, f. 154, 7 Jan. 1663 m.v.

tivoglio had had previous contacts with the theater, lending his singer Stefano Costa in 1661. It is likely that the company at S. Luca had encountered difficulties finding a composer, and Bentivoglio was able both to provide a ready-made solution, and to facilitate Legrenzi's entrée into the Venetian market, something the composer had attempted earlier without success (see chap. 6). As in the previous year, the company presented only one opera, which opened toward the end of January, several weeks later than the first offering of the Grimanis.[143]

The Participation of Tomaso Corner, Nicolò Minato, and Marco Mozzoni

The next season, 1664/65, was pivotal in several ways. Barbieri had finally found a nobleman to participate actively at S. Luca. Tomaso Corner had joined the company by January 1664 as a sort of protector rather than an investor.[144] Corner helped in recruiting as well as other areas, and he would maintain connections with the company for the rest of the decade. In addition to continuing the theater's previous ties with the Marquis Bentivoglio,[145] he also cultivated a relationship with the Medici court, beginning in the summer of 1664 his annual requests for the popular Medici singer "Vincenzino," at times competing for him against the Grimanis (see chap. 7). The precise nature of Corner's financial assistance is uncertain; as we shall see below, he did not hold shares in the company in 1665.

The company gained another important partner in the lawyer and librettist Nicolò Minato, previously active at S. Cassiano and SS. Giovanni e Paolo; for the 1664/65 season Minato contributed the first of his four librettos that would debut at S. Luca, *Mutio Scevola*, to a score by Francesco Cavalli. The company found further financial support in the person of Marco Mozzoni, who, by the end of the season, had taken on the responsibilities of cashier (see below). One other man, the Bolognese artist Pietro Antonio Cerva, also formed part of the company during the 1664/65 season.[146]

---

143 *Rosilena* (Aureli/Volpe) bears the dedication date 4 Jan. 1664.

144 Corner is most likely the "Signor Cornaro" referred to by Legrenzi as having approached a nobleman with the hopes of obtaining a singer for the Marquis Bentivoglio (ASFe, AB, b. 338, f. 72, 26 Jan. 1664; published in Monaldini, *Orto dell'Esperidi*, 185). As Barbieri acted as guarantor for one of Corner's non-operatic financial transactions the same month as their S. Luca agreement (ASV, AN, Atti, b. 1090, f. 156, 30 Jan. 1663 m.v.), the two of them must already have established some degree of cooperation and trust in monetary affairs.

145 Corner wrote to Bentivoglio on 1 July, 2 Aug., and 14 Sept. 1664 concerning the singers Pastarini and Stefano Costa (ASFe, AB, b. 338, f. 534; b. 339, ff. 16 and 346; see Monaldini, *Orto dell'Esperidi*, 193, 196, and 208).

146 On Cerva's artistic career, see Pigozzi, "Pietro Antonio Cerva." According to his own account, Cerva signed an agreement on 14 Aug. that required that the financial reckoning for the season be completely settled by the end of carnival, failing which Minato and Barbieri would owe him £10 for each day he had to remain in Venice; other details of his participation are not recorded (ASV, AN, Atti, b. 708, f. 254ᵛ, 8 Mar. 1665). Cerva's operatic connections began at least ten years earlier in Bologna, where he signed the dedications of the librettos for *Alessandro vincitor di se stesso* (1655) and *L'Oristeo travestito* (1656).

Except for the anomaly of the first season, S. Luca had presented only one opera per carnival at a time when SS. Giovanni e Paolo unfailingly offered two. As we have seen, Vettor Grimani Calergi had hoped to provide a second opera by Cavalli in 1662/63, but without success. The company once again considered mounting two operas for the 1664/65 season, and approached Giovanni Legrenzi with a commission. During the summer of 1664 the composer wrote to his employer concerning its outcome:

> Before leaving Venice I released myself completely from the aforementioned men regarding the invitation that they made to me also for this year. Because Signor Minato had taken the share in the theater that Morandi had, now as one of the padroni [he has] chosen the second slot for his drama, which Signor Cavalli will compose. Moreover, he has declared that for the first piece he wants an "operetta." Because of this I thought it best to tell [him], with all modesty, that they will not lack for composers who will covet this opportunity to be heard, and that for this year they should excuse me.[147]

Legrenzi's term "operetta" is ambiguous, but implies a work of lesser weight, thus in Legrenzi's eyes, not worthy of his efforts; perhaps it would have been of briefer duration than an "opera," or only partially set to music. We can only speculate, as no printed libretto or any other reports have survived that would suggest the performance of such a work in early January of 1665.

We mentioned above the appearance of Marco Mozzoni, a young man who earned his living supervising postal operations for Ferrara, Modena, and Bologna.[148] He had loaned money for the production expenses for the 1664/65 season, and Barbieri, on 5 March 1665, had authorized that some of the palco monies should be paid directly to him in compensation.[149] By the summer, however, the company still owed Mozzoni 500 ducats; this outstanding debt led him to become part of the company in order to reap his just share of the profits (or at least to keep a closer eye on the operations). The document drawn up for the occasion conveniently provides us with the composition of the company both before and after Mozzoni's entry.[150] Previously, Barbieri had held five-sixths of the shares, with the last portion (originally Morandi's) belonging to Minato. Mozzoni took over one-third of the operation, that is two shares, leaving Barbieri still with half of the *carati*, and Minato still with the remaining sixth. It is notable that despite Mi-

147 "Io prima del mio partire da Venetia mi licentai del tutto con li sudetti signori per l'invito che mi hanno fatto anco per quest'anno, perché havendo il signor Minato preso il caratto, ch'haveva nel theatro il Morandi, et come adesso uno de' patroni elettosi il secondo luocho per il suo drama, che dovrà pore in musica il signor Cavalli, ed in oltre dichiaratosi in primo luocho volere un'operetta, ho stimato bene con ogni modestia dirgli, che a loro non mancheranno compositori ch'ambiscano quest'occasione, di farsi sentire, et che per quest'anno mi dovessero compatire." ASFe, AB, b. 338, f. 631, 30 July 1664; see Monaldini, *Orto dell'Esperidi*, 196.

148 In a letter written several days after Mozzoni's death, on 5 Jan. 1667, the Modenese agent pre Prospero Bonamino mentioned Mozzoni's responsibilities for the post (ASMo, CAV, b. 121, 1667–1670, f. 143 (111/58)).

149 ASV, AN, Atti, b. 1136, f. 3, 5 Mar. 1665.

150 ASV, Inquisitori di stato, b. 914. Published in Giazotto, "Guerra dei palchi," 470.

nato's importance to the company artistically, his potential financial risks and gains fell below those of Barbieri and Mozzoni; moreover, as he received income from the dedication and sale of librettos—a source of income unavailable to the other partners—he may well have welcomed the lesser risk associated with the minimum carat.

Mozzoni's intention was to enjoy one-third of whatever profits were to be had regarding the operation, that is, the box rentals and the sale of costumes, and so he further immersed himself in the company. Tomaso Corner authorized him to make disbursements,[151] and when Pietro Andrea Ziani mentioned the company during the spring of 1666, he referred to it as "Mozzoni's."[152] Mozzoni's desperation was palpable when, on 28 September 1666, he complained to Barbieri and Minato: "For the resolution of a credit that I, Marco Mozzoni, held with you, D. Gieronimo Barbieri, I (to my disastrous misfortune) agreed to receive in payment one-third of the costumes or goods, and other things found at the Teatro di S. Salvatore, having also committed myself for a third part of the production."[153] He rued his decision, spoke of the theater's enormous debt of more than 6,000 ducats, of which he personally had satisfied 5,000, and demanded that his partners reimburse him. The unfortunate Mozzoni died several months later, still owed thousands of ducats, leaving behind his wife, Margarita, and a one-year-old son.[154]

Minato's Final Years at S. Luca, 1667–1669

Starting with the 1664/65 season, Nicolò Minato began consistently to furnish librettos for S. Luca, and his interest in the theater, both financially and as a librettist, continued until his departure for Vienna in 1669. After the deaths of both Mozzoni and Barbieri in 1667, he shared responsibilities, according to a contract of December of that year, with Marc'Antonio Montalbano, the nobleman who had participated in the 1663/64 season; officially, however, the theater had been rented to Don Pietro Moretti, also a participant in previous years.[155] Toward the end of the decade, Minato's debts at the theater continued to mount, and he sought loans. On 23 February 1668 he borrowed 1,210 ducats from the nobleman Sebastian Malipiero; in return, Minato agreed to turn over the income equal to that amount from

---

151 Vcg, Archivio Vendramin, 42/F 6/1–6, Processo no. 20, f. 81.

152 ASV, SGSM, b. 184, f. 268.

153 "Per la consecutione d'un credito ch'io Marco Mozzoni tenevo con voi D. Gieronimo Barbieri, per mia fatal sventura mi contentai ricever in pagamento la terza parte degli habbiti, seu utensilij, et altro, che si attrovava nel Teatro di S. Salvatore, essendo anco entrato per una terza parte, et interessatomi per la medema nella recita." ASV, AN, Atti, b. 1166, f. 160r–v.

154 VAP, S. Silvestro, Morti, 1649–75, 5 Jan. 1666 m.v. Mozzoni died after thirty days of illness, at the age of 32. Afterwards, Margarita Mozzoni and her brother began their prolonged attempts to gain the funds owed to Mozzoni's estate, and to cushion themselves from other debts incurred by the company during his participation. Mozzoni's widow was eventually absolved from expenses connected to rebuilding the house adjacent to the theater. See Vcg, Archivio Vendramin, 42 F 12/2, f. 56, 1 Dec. 1667.

155 The agreement between Minato and Montalbano is in Vcg, Archivio Vendramin, 42 F 6/2, f. 48. The rental to Moretti is in ASV, AN, b. 3004, f. 1159v, Feb. 1667 m.v. (another copy in Vcg, Archivio Vendramin, 42 F 12/2, f. 56).

the palchi within the next year.[156] On 27 April 1668 Minato borrowed another 1,750 ducats, bringing the total amount to almost 3,000 ducats; by the end of the 1669 carnival, the debt was 4,000 ducats. Tomaso Corner, the protector of S. Luca, was pieggio for this latter sum (these loans were not in cash, but in the form of furniture, clothing, and jewelry). On the eve of his departure for Vienna in 1669 to become Imperial court poet, Minato not only had not repaid his loans, but also owed money to musicians and others from recent operatic seasons.[157] With Minato's departure, Corner was left to pick up the pieces, and was still trying to settle the debts to Malipiero as late as 1675.[158] Minato's skills as a lawyer, and his income from a number of librettos, had not been sufficient to stave off the debts that often occurred in the running of a theater. He may have found the invitation to serve the court of Vienna a welcome release from those pressures, but the debts he had built up plagued him for some years after his departure.

Although theater owners, impresarios, and wealthy Venetians constantly searched for ways to manage opera theaters, one thing remained constant amid all the variety: opera as a business seems to have been doomed to financial failure. Only the theater owners, through rental of the theater or income from the boxes, seemed to end up regularly with their accounts in the black. Inevitably, either the impresario, his partners, their backers, or their guarantors always satisfied the debts from their own pockets. Fortunately, a seemingly limitless supply of hopeful managers and generous (whether willingly or by default) investors kept at least some of the theaters open year after year. The shortcomings of the systems so evident in opera production during the first three decades of its operation in Venice eventually led, especially by the 1680s, to the adoption of a wider base of investors, the caratadori, that served to spread out both the financial strain and the civic pride in having sponsored the city's famous entertainment.

---

156 ASV, AN, Atti, b. 3004, ff. 1187–89.

157 On the loans to Malipiero see ASV, AN, Atti, b. 3004, f. 1192ᵛ. Copies of the petitions by musicians and others are in Vcg, Archivio Vendramin, 42F 6/2.

158 ASV, AN, Atti, b. 6797, f. 173, 8 June 1675.

PART II

THE MUSICAL PRODUCTION

CHAPTER FIVE

THE LIBRETTO

Opera production had its foundation in the libretto. The librettist, through the structure and content of his play, generated not only the verses themselves, but the scenery, costumes, dances, and, naturally, the music.[1] The impresario, if he were to present new operas each season (as was the usual practice in the mid-seventeenth century), was forced to search actively for new texts. Very little documentation survives concerning the procurement of librettos during this period, and even less for actual agreements between librettist and impresario. We must draw our conclusions, then, for the most part, from the librettos actually produced, and from statements made by the librettists themselves in their published works.[2]

In this chapter we discuss the opera libretto not as an artistic work per se, but as a commodity, and as a starting point for the production of opera. First we look at the men who wrote librettos, at their social class and the professions they exercised (their "day jobs"). We then look at the questions impresarios would have faced as they decided what type of libretto to produce, and what might have influenced the decision to create a new work or a revival of one previously performed. An examination of the revisions in the printed librettos and frequent multiple editions reveals the complications that often arose between the writing of the text and opening night (or even later). Finally, we discuss the business side of the libretto: the cost of production and the selling price. The data are then contrasted with statements found in the writings of Cristoforo Ivanovich, the cleric and librettist who, during the early 1680s, generally described the procedures behind libretto production. It will be shown that contrary to Ivanovich's descriptions, in the mid-seventeenth century the librettist himself took little financial risk in the printing of the libretto; rather, the printer often accepted the initial expenses, later turning over monies to the author.

---

1 The librettist was, at least in some cases, responsible for supplying the scenographers and costumers with a *scenario* and a *vestiario* that would serve for their labors. See ASV, AN, Atti, b. 6113, f. 201, 1 Feb. 1684 m.v.; this document concerns a libretto completed by Antonio Franceschi, but not performed in the appointed season. Some impresarios, however, chose scenery even before they knew which opera would be presented. See Holmes, *Opera Observed*, 80–81.

2 See Rosand, "In Defense."

THE PROFESSION OF LIBRETTIST IN
MID-SEVENTEENTH-CENTURY VENICE

Musicologists have, logically, called the authors of opera librettos "librettists," yet that term may give us a false sense of the lives of many of the men who produced these works. Some men wrote only one or two librettos, while others produced a stream of works. The libretto for the first opera performed in Venice was conceived by Benedetto Ferrari, who, in addition to his skills as a poet, enjoyed even greater fame as an instrumentalist (he was a famous theorbist) and a composer. Most later librettists, however, were noblemen (Venetian or otherwise), or members of the professional classes. A number of these early authors were dilettantes, anxious to try their hand in the new operatic market, but others were prolific authors of fiction, nonfiction, and poetry, particularly such men as Giulio Strozzi and Giovanni Francesco Busenello, members of the influential Accademia degli Incogniti, that group of intellectuals founded by Giovanni Francesco Loredano in 1630.[3]

Among the most prominent of the noble Venetian librettists was Giacomo Badoaro (author of *Il ritorno d'Ulisse in Patria* and three other works), who, after several terms as a member of the Collegio, the chief advisory body to the Doge, rose as high as the Council of Ten, where he served as one of the even more powerful Capi of the Council.[4] Two other "new" Venetian patricians, Pietro Angelo Zaguri and Nicola Beregan, also wrote librettos; of the two, Beregan was more in the public eye, and had a reputation as a famous lawyer and orator.[5] Ellen Rosand has suggested that the authorship of a libretto was, perhaps, viewed as a dubious accomplishment, and these two men preferred that their work remain anonymous, while others, although allowing their names to appear on their works, minimized their efforts and talents.[6] Also represented in the ranks of librettists were a number of non-Venetian nobles such as Maiolino Bisaccioni of Iesi (*Ercole in Lidia* and *Semiramide in India*) and Pietro Paolo Bissari of Vicenza (*Torilda, Bradamante*, and *Orithia*), both either resident or partially resident in Venice. Giulio Strozzi (*Delia,*

---

3 The literary nature of the libretto, and its academic foundations, is exhaustively treated in Rosand, *Opera*, chapter 2; she also explores the relationship between librettist, composer, and impresario. For a new approach to some of these issues, see Calcagno, "Staging Musical Discourses." On the librettist, see Della Seta, "The Librettist," in Pestelli and Bianconi, esp. 232–40, and Fabbri, *Secolo cantante*.

4 The information on Badoaro is taken from Barbaro, "Albori de' patritii veneti," copy in the ASV. On these governmental bodies, see the Glossary.

5 *DBI*, s.v. "Beregan, Nicolò," by Giorgio E. Ferrari. Both Zaguri (who wrote *Gli avvenimenti d'Orinda* for the 1660 season) and Beregan (author of *Annibale in Capua* and *Tito*, among others) were from families of wealthy non-patricians who had bought their nobility in the years following 1646, when the Republic was desperately searching for funds to fight the war in Crete. On the new nobility, see Alex Cowan, "New Families."

6 See Rosand, "In Defense." Beregan's name did not appear on his librettos; on the other hand, he was mentioned as the author of *Annibale in Capua* in Sansovino's *Venetia città nobilissima* (the 1663 edition), 7. Also listed there among "huomeni letterati" is Pietro Angelo Zaguri, with his three dramatic works (p. 8). Vassilis Vavoulis suggests that the reason for anonymity might be rather for fear of embarrassment should the opera be a failure. See Vavoulis, "Antonio Sartorio," 34. On the issue of noble poets and anonymity in the sixteenth century see Feldman, "Authors and Anonyms."

La finta pazza, and others), a native of Venice, came from an illegitimate branch of a Florentine aristocratic family.[7]

Apart from Benedetto Ferrari, mentioned above, all of the non-noble librettists were members of the professional classes. Giovanni Francesco Busenello, one of the most gifted among them—famous today as the author of Claudio Monteverdi's *L'incoronatione di Poppea*—was not a patrician, as were many of his fellow members of the Incogniti, but of the highest level of the cittadino class, a *cittadino originario* (see app. 2);[8] he was a noted lawyer as well as an academician, and a prolific poet. The profession of lawyer, in fact, was perhaps the most common for a librettist in this period. Besides Busenello and Beregan, other practicing lawyers who managed to find the time to become more or less regular masters of the craft were Nicolò Minato, Aurelio Aureli, and Giacomo Dall'Angelo (or "Angeli," as his name often appears in Venetian documents). Minato drew attention to his "day job" in the foreword to his first libretto, *Orimonte*: "You should know that I am not a poet by profession. My attentions lie in the courts; to serve who may command me, I have robbed myself of some hours of sleep to give you this drama."[9] Minato eventually became a professional librettist, filling the post of court poet for Emperor Leopold I in Vienna.[10] Aureli, too, served a foreign court, that of Parma, from 1689 to 1693, late in his career,[11] but earlier he had held other posts in Venice in addition to his legal practice that, from time to time, occupied his working hours. From 1655 to 1659 he was an administrator at the Scuola Grande di S. Maria della Carità,[12] and from 1665 to 1667 he was chancellor (*cancelliere*) of Murano.[13] Dall'Angelo, although less prolific than either Aureli or Minato, produced four works beginning in the 1650s.[14]

Other librettists pursued a variety of professions. Polo Vendramin (the author of *Adone*), descended from a noble family although not himself a patrician, served as a secretary in the Senate, and as resident (a position similar to, but lower than an ambassador) in Naples in the early 1650s.[15] Three other men—Bortolo and Giacomo Castoreo, and Matteo Noris—were civil servants, occupying such posts as notary or secretary for a government office.[16] The noted dramatist Giacinto Andrea

7 On Giulio Strozzi's ancestry and his career in Venice, see Rosand, "Barbara Strozzi."

8 On Busenello's life, see *DBI*, s.v. "Busenello, Gian Francesco," by Gino Benzoni. See also Livingston, *Vita veneziana*.

9 "Sappi, ch'io non fò del Poeta. Le mie applicationi sono nel Foro: per servire a chi puote comandarmi hò rubbate alcune hore al sonno per darle a questo Drama . . ." Minato, *Orimonte* (1650).

10 On Minato's career in Vienna, see Pirrotta, "Note su Minato."

11 See *DBI*, s.v. "Aureli, Aurelio," by Claudio Mutini.

12 ASV, Scuola Grande di S. Maria della Carità, b. 263, ff. 59, 249.

13 Aureli competed for the post unsuccessfully in later years (ASV, Podestà di Murano, b. 201).

14 Dall'Angelo's four librettos are: *Euridamante* (1654), *Cleopatra* (1662), *Demetrio* (1666), and *Aureliano* (1666).

15 ASV, Collegio IV, Lettere, filza 186, 14 Jan. 1649 m.v.

16 The Castoreo brothers held positions at the police bureau, the Signori di Notte al Criminal (as was traditional among the members of their family); see ASV, AN, Atti, b. 2817, f. 14, 14 Apr. 1674. Matteo Noris, for a time, held the post of "scontro" (comptroller) at the Rason nove (ASV, AN, Atti, b. 1332, f. 933ᵛ, 15 Jan. 1674 m.v.).

Cicognini (a transplanted Florentine who wrote two of the most famous librettos of the 1640s, *Giasone* and *Orontea*) was employed as a secretary to Francesco Boldieri, the chief administrator of the local branch of the Knights of Malta,[17] and Dario Varotari, author of *Cesare amante* (1652), was a Venetian physician and painter.[18] The Neapolitan Giuseppe Artale (*Pasife*), an occasional visitor to Venice, had a career in the military.[19] Several librettists were churchmen. Cristoforo Ivanovich, a native of Budva in southern Dalmatia, occupied the position of canon at S. Marco.[20] Giovanni Battista Fusconi, author of *Amore innamorato* (1642) and *Argiope* (1649), and Giacomo Francesco Bussani, most famous today as the author of *Giulio Cesare in Egitto* (1677), were Regular Canons of the Lateran congregation.[21] One man, however, stands apart from his contemporaries: as we saw in chapter 3, Giovanni Faustini, although a cittadino, did not, to our knowledge, exercise a profession. Relying on the financial support of his brother Marco, he was able to produce a long series of works, even creating a backlog of librettos and sketches for upcoming seasons.

One thing that many of these men shared, noble or citizen, Venetian or not, was membership in one or more of the Venetian academies. Many of the older generation, including Badoaro, Busenello, Strozzi, and Bisaccioni, belonged to the Accademia degli Incogniti.[22] The lawyer-librettists of the 1650s (Busenello, Dall'Angelo, Minato, and Aureli) had connections with the Accademia degli Imperfetti, whose publication of 1651 glorified a Venetian victory in the War of Crete.[23] Cristoforo Ivanovich included in his history of opera in Venice a long list of librettists who were members of the Accademia Delfica.[24] The workings of the Delfica are largely unknown, as they did not sponsor publications in the manner of some other academies.

Another commonality among some librettists was the young age at which they

---

17 Walker, '"Ubi Lucius," cxxxv.

18 Varotari came from a family of noted painters: his father was the famous Alessandro Varotari, called il Padovanino. A number of Dario's paintings are listed in an inventory of his late brother's estate in 1677 (ASV, AN, Atti, b. 13845, f. 405, 5 Jan. 1676 m.v.).

19 See *DBI*, s.v. "Artale, Giuseppe," by Franco Croce.

20 Documents in Venetian notaries from the 1650s regarding Ivanovich refer to him as "reverendo." In 1676 he was elected subcanon at S. Marco. On Ivanovich see Norbert Dubowy's introduction to Ivanovich, *Memorie teatrali*, xxxv–lx. Ivanovich's libretto include *La costanza trionfante* (1673) and *Lisimaco* (1674). *Circe*, originally written by Ivanovich for Vienna and set by Pietro Andrea Ziani in 1665, was performed in Venice with a new musical setting by Giovanni Domenico Freschi in 1679.

21 On Fusconi, whose religious name was Don Agostin, see ASV, AN, Atti, b. 10805, f. 618ᵛ, 8 Nov. 1641). Bussani was associated with S. Maria della Carità in Venice; see *NG II*, s.v. "Bussani, Giacomo Francesco," by Harris Saunders. See also Vavoulis, "Antonio Sartorio."

22 The bibliography on the Incogniti and opera is large; see above, chapter 4, n. 30.

23 *Glorie dell'Armi Venete.*

24 In the list of librettists in *Memorie teatrali* (449–50) Ivanovich identifies the following as members of the Accademia Delfica: Aurelio Aureli, Camillo Badoer, Dario Varotari, Francesco Melosi, Francesco Sbarra, Giacinto Andrea Cicognini, Giacomo Castoreo, Giovanni Faustini, Giovanni Francesco Busenello, Girolamo Castelli, Giuseppe Artale, Nicola Beregan, Nicolò Enea Bartolini, Nicolò Minato, Polo Vendramin, Pietro Angelo Zaguri, Scipione Errico, Vincenzo Nolfi, and the author himself. It should be noted that not all of these librettists lived at the same time, and not all were resident in Venice. On the Delfici and their intellectual environment, see Calcagno, "Staging Musical Discourses," 14–18.

commenced their careers. Giacomo Dall'Angelo was around the age of 21 during the production of *Euridamante* (1654);[25] Nicolò Minato was even younger, possibly only 19 or 20 at the time of his first work, *Orimonte* (1649/50).[26] Marco Faustini insisted on emphasizing the youth of his brother (Giovanni Faustini published his first work, *La virtù de' strali d'Amore*, at the age of 26), even subtracting four years from his age when he wrote of his brother's early death.[27]

It should be noted that several librettists in addition to Giovanni Faustini allowed their interest in opera to expand into an interest in opera production, demonstrating a desire to earn profits, or at least to exercise greater control over their creative work than would have been otherwise possible. As we saw in chapter 4, Minato was a member of the company at S. Luca for a number of years (as was Aureli, for at least one), and Giacomo Dall'Angelo mounted his *Demetrio* and *Aureliano* when he was one of the partners at S. Moisè during the mid-1660s.

The authors of librettos, then, were a diverse group, men active in the political, economic, and cultural worlds of Venice. For most of them, writing librettos was secondary to their main careers, a way to occupy their spare hours and to show off their poetic skills and erudition. Many of them wrote only a small number of works, occasionally just one. Fortunately, this pastime helped supply impresarios with new works, and allowed a variety of men to participate in one of their city's celebrated spectacles.

THE RELATIONSHIP BETWEEN IMPRESARIO AND LIBRETTIST

Several possible kinds of relationships could exist between impresario and librettist. The two roles could, of course, be held by the same person. Alternatively, the impresario could establish a long-term agreement with a librettist, or take someone on for a single opera or season. He could also ask a librettist to revise an existing work. (The easiest option of all, perhaps, but outside the scope of this chapter— and rarely exercised during this time—was the revival of an old libretto with its original musical setting.)

The impresario's simplest solution (besides being himself the librettist) was to have a house librettist, that is, someone who, by contract or agreement, provided librettos exclusively (or as often as needed) to one theater, perhaps even acting as a partner in the enterprise. This was the method employed by the company that produced the first two operas in Venice, when Benedetto Ferrari wrote *Andromeda* and *La maga fulminata* for the Teatro S. Cassiano (1637 and 1638). Although this system made the impresario's job easier, such arrangements were not necessarily

25 Dall'Angelo died in 1705 at the age of 72 (ASPV, Parrocchia di S. Maria del Giglio, Morti, 1680–1705, f. 115, 14 Jan. 1705).

26 Minato's year of birth is generally cited as ca. 1630 (see *NG II*, s.v. "Minato, Nicolò," by Ellen Rosand and Herbert Seifert). This date is confirmed in testimony Minato gave in Venice in 1667, when he stated he was 37 years old (ASPV, EM, b. 100, f. 190ᵛ, 22 July 1667).

27 Not 32, as Marco claimed; see chapter 3, n. 19.

permanent. Oratio Persiani, who formed part of the company of Felicita Uga and Francesco Cavalli at S. Cassiano in 1638, promised to provide two texts, but produced only one for that theater (*Le nozze di Teti*).[28] As a result, Cavalli's next two operas (*Gli amori di Apollo e di Dafne* and *Didone*) were set to librettos by a new author, the lawyer Giovanni Francesco Busenello. Giacinto Andrea Cicognini provided two librettos within three years for SS. Apostoli (*Orontea* for 1648/49 and *Gl'amori di Alessandro magno, e di Rossane* for 1650/51), but his arrangement there was not exclusive, as his *Giasone* (1648/49) played in a different theater.

Over the course of time, an impresario would probably use several of the practices described above, as the situation required. When Marco Faustini returned to S. Aponal in 1654, he first drew on his deceased brother's backlog of librettos, producing *Eupatra* for 1654/55 (that is, an extension of the system of the impresario as librettist). The next year, however, rather than drawing further from Giovanni's works, he turned to Aurelio Aureli, who supplied a libretto for that season as well as for the next (*Erismena* and *Le fortune di Rodope e Damira*). While from our vantage point Aureli may seem to have been poised to become house librettist, substituting for the deceased Giovanni Faustini, he instead moved on to the competition, the Grimani theater, where such a relationship seems to have been established; indeed, Aureli's librettos were produced there for ten out of twelve years, beginning in 1658 (his absence during the 1665/66 and 1666/67 seasons stems in part from the insistence of Marco Faustini—by then at SS. Giovanni e Paolo—on producing the librettos of his brother, rather than new ones).[29] Similarly, the other major opera theater in the 1660s, S. Luca, was able to rely on a single author for much of the second half of the decade: Nicolò Minato formed part of the management there during that time (as mentioned earlier), and also wrote most of the works produced at that theater.

Given the mobility of the most active librettists, and fluctuations in their productivity, an impresario could easily find himself in need of a libretto, so that a single work by a new talent might appear. Francesco Piccoli (otherwise unknown to us except for his poetry for a song by Barbara Strozzi) provided a libretto, or at least started one, *L'incostanza trionfante*, for the rededication of S. Cassiano as an opera theater (1657/58), and then disappeared from the scene altogether.[30] The next year his place was to have been taken by another newcomer, Giovanni Battista Pellicani (see below). For the 1659/60 season at SS. Giovanni e Paolo, Pietro Angelo Zaguri wrote his only opera libretto for Venice, *Gli avvenimenti d'Orinda*.[31] Two other authors, Nicola Beregan and Cristoforo Ivanovich, produced their first works for Faustini in the early 1660s (*Annibale in Capua* and *Amor guerriero*, respec-

28 On Cavalli's company at the Teatro S. Cassiano, see Morelli and Walker, "Tre controversie." The contract is in ASV, Monastero di S. Maria dell'Orazion a Malamocco, b. 3 (document B1 in Morelli and Walker).

29 On the end of the Grimani's relationship with Aureli, see Calcagno, "Fonti, ricezione."

30 Piccoli was the author of "Per un bacio, che rubai dalle labra del mio bene" in Strozzi's *Diporti di Euterpe* (Venice, 1659). For more on *L'incostanza trionfante*, see below.

31 Zaguri had previously written two dramatic works presented privately: *Messalina*, opera scenica, 1656; and *Le gelosie politiche, & amorose*, opera scenica, 1657. On *Messalina* see Heller, *Emblems of Eloquence*, chapter 7.

tively) but, unlike Piccoli, Pellicani, and Zaguri, they went on to complete several other librettos over the next decade and a half.[32]

THE PREDOMINANCE OF VENETIAN AUTHORS

Nearly all of the librettists used by Marco Faustini during his impresarial activity were, if not Venetians, at least resident in the city. Faustini may have tried to keep opera in Venice as "Venetian" as possible (perhaps in memory of his brother), or he may merely have sought to avoid the unnecessary complications that could result from working with an author residing elsewhere who might be unfamiliar with the customs and necessities of the Venetian stage, and also unavailable to make late changes in the work. Other impresarios in Venice during the same period, however, were somewhat more open to outsiders.[33] The physical proximity of librettists and impresarios, as well as the lack of formal contracts for the commissioning of librettos, has left us with almost no written records regarding the selection process for either librettists or librettos.

Despite Faustini's apparent preference for local authors, his reliance on foreign recruiters and vocal scouts produced occasional offers of texts from other cities, none of which the impresario produced. In 1659, someone writing from Naples offered a work, possibly from that city: "What I can certainly [offer] you now is an opera, in all perfection, composed by a poet friend of mine; I hope that in a month at most I will be able to send it to you finished. It is certainly true that the poet wishes that as soon as it is set to music [you] should send it back to him with the music."[34] On 3 April 1666 Pietro Andrea Ziani, writing from Vienna, offered to send Faustini a work of Abbate Domenico Federici, who served as a poet at the Viennese court during this period.[35] Several months later, on 27 June 1666, Antonio Cesti told Faustini that one of his countrymen in Vienna could supply the impresario with a new libretto if he so desired.[36] Offers such as these would be made to the managers or those with connections to Venetian theaters for some time to come.[37]

---

32 Beregan's other librettos were *Tito* (1666), *Genserico* (1669), and *Heraclio* (1671).

33 This is especially the case at S. Luca in the early 1660s, where three of the five operas produced before Minato's involvement were settings of librettos by non-Venetians: *Pasife* (1660/61, by Artale), *Dori* (1662/63 by Apolloni), and *Achille in Sciro* (1663/64, by Bentivoglio); the two works by Venetians were a revival of Faustini's *Eritrea* (1660/61) and Dall'Angelo's *Cleopatra* (1661/62).

34 "quello di che posso io assicurarla ora si è d'un'opera di tutta perfettione composta da un poeta mio amico, e spero fra un mese al più mandargliela finita; è ben vero che il poeta desidera che subito che sarà in musica Vostra Signoria Illustrissima gliela rimandi con le note." ASV, SGSM, b. 101, unnumbered, 4 Nov. 1659. The signature on the letter is illegible.

35 ASV, SGSM, b.188, f. 256, 3 Apr. 1666. In this case, Ziani could offer not only the text, but also his musical setting: he set Federici's *L'onore trionfante* for the emperor's birthday in 1666.

36 ASV, SGSM, b. 188, f. 275, 27 June 1666.

37 In 1677, Giovanni Battista San Giovanni Toffetti wrote from Genoa that a young acquaintance of his had already finished a work entitled *Arianna in Delo*, which the correspondent thought would be suitable for presentation at a Venetian theater (Vmc, MS PDC 1064, f. 218, 26 June 1677). Settimio Olgiati, a friend of Polo Michiel's, facilitated correspondence between Michiel and Giovanni Francesco Saliti, a Tuscan poet, who wrote a libretto that he hoped to have performed in Venice anonymously in 1678 (fully

On one occasion, however, Faustini apparently had accepted the work of a non-Venetian. On 22 July 1658 the Bolognese Giovanni Battista Pellicani signed a contract with the most prolific printers and booksellers associated with opera librettos of this period, Giacomo Batti and Andrea Zulian.[38] The contract, which was registered in the acts of a Venetian notary, is unique for its time; evidently the majority of contracts between librettists (or other authors) and printers during this period were arranged privately. Indeed, the document may owe its existence to the fact that Pellicani lived in Bologna. The purpose of his visit to Venice (other than signing the contract) is unknown, but further evidence of his presence in the city may be the inclusion of a setting of one of his poems in a book of music by Barbara Strozzi.[39] The contract between Pellicani on the one hand and Batti and Zulian on the other specified that Pellicani's libretto was to be performed at S. Cassiano, that is, at Faustini's theater, for the 1658/59 season (although no formal agreement between librettist and impresario survives in Faustini's papers). Extant librettos, however, show that no such work by Pellicani ever reached the Venetian presses nor its stages.[40] In the absence of the expected work by the Bolognese author, Nicolò Minato made a late effort to write *Antioco* (set by Francesco Cavalli), as he explained in the preface to the libretto: "The thought of boring you [with a libretto] was very far from me, when, thus compelled by my masters, and by friends, I wrote *Antioco* in just a few days last October."[41] It may have been some reluctance on Minato's part that had led Faustini or someone else in the company to consider Pellicani as a possible source in the first place.

The absence of the author from Venice sometimes necessitated the involvement of a specialist to proofread the completed text, since the author himself would not be available. Along with the manuscript of his 1678 libretto for *Il fantasma dittatore*, the Florentine poet Giovanni Francesco Saliti forwarded instructions that because he had ventured "some novelties in the style, taking licenses with the words, sentences, and uncommon metaphors," it would be necessary to assign a very knowledgeable person to check the printing;[42] he recommended the librettist Nicola Beregan for the job. Saliti also suggested that an especially large number of copies be printed, to avoid having to repeat the proofreading labor for a second edition.[43]

---

aware that changes would have to be made to suit the Venetian taste) with music by Stradella. Saliti's project, known from the Dandolo/Michiel letters in the Biblioteca del Museo Correr in Venice, is discussed in Gianturco, *Alessandro Stradella*, 36, 41–42, 47. See below for more on this libretto.

38 ASV, AN, Atti, b. 12667, f. 67ʳ⁻ᵛ.

39 He is the author of "Basta così, v'ho inteso" in Strozzi, *Diporti di Euterpe* (Venice, 1659).

40 Two theatrical works by Pellicani were performed in Bologna in 1658 and 1659: *Le gare de' fiumi* (Bologna, 1658) and *Il ritorno vittorioso d'Alessandro* (Bologna, 1659). Pellicani was also the author of some texts for the madrigals of Maurizio Cazzati published in 1661, 1666, and 1667. He composed several secular pieces found in RISM 1670³ and 1685¹. On Pellicani, see *NG II*, s.v. "Sanuti Pellicani, Giovanni Battista," by John Whenham. A biography of Pellicani appeared in Capponi and Zani, *Memorie imprese*, 203–4.

41 "Ero lontanissimo dal pensiero d'annoiarti, quando, così sforzato da' Padroni, e da Amici in pochi giorni del trascorso Ottobre ho composto l'Antioco." *Antioco*, in the foreword (no pagination).

42 "essendosi . . . tentata qualche novità nello stile per le licenze pigliati per i vocaboli, per le frase, e per le metafore non comunemente usate." Vmc, PDC 1064, f. 277. In the correspondence concerning this work, it is referred to by the title *Il fantasma consigliero*.

43 Vmc, PDC 1064, f. 299, 25 Sept. 1677.

NEW LIBRETTO OR OLD?

Almost all of the productions on the Venetian stage between 1637 and 1677 represented new settings of new librettos (or of older librettos never before set to music); there were remarkably few imported operas, revivals, or new settings of previously performed librettos. This practice began to change toward the end of the period, and then even more so in the succeeding decades; it is difficult to assess whether this came about because of a lack of librettos or of composers, or for some other reason. For the 1666 season at SS. Giovanni e Paolo, Marco Faustini uncharacteristically planned to offer Ziani's new setting of Giovanni Faustini's *Doriclea* (originally performed in 1645 with music by Cavalli). Instead, as we shall see, *Doriclea* was replaced with the impresario's first presentation of an old musical setting, Cesti's *Orontea*; the next year's *Dori* was also a revival. For some revivals, the alterations deemed necessary to present the work on the Venetian stage were extensive enough to warrant an acknowledged second authorship. In 1670/71, for example, Aureli refashioned Giovanni Andrea Moniglia's *Ercole in Tebe*, and both authors' names appeared on the title page. In other cases, such as the revision that same season by Matteo Noris of another of Moniglia's librettos, *Semiramis* (retitled *Semiramide*), the changes were presented without specifying the second poet.[44]

CHOOSING THE SUBJECT OF THE LIBRETTO

Besides the selection of the librettist, the other major consideration was the subject of the work to be produced. The artistic autonomy of the librettist is uncertain for this period. We do not know whether the impresario (perhaps in consultation with the owner of the theater) requested a text based on a specific story, or one employing specific characters, or if he even indicated whether he wanted it to be historical, or mythological, or newly invented. Perhaps these matters were left largely up to the author, although, as Ellen Rosand has shown, specific elements, like mad scenes, could be (and were) imposed on other librettists by unnamed "important persons."[45] The rental contract of 1648 for the Teatro S. Cassiano between the theater owner Francesco Tron and the company of Rocco Maestri and Bortolo Castoreo provides a rare exception, for it specifies that Tron should have the opportunity to approve the work beforehand: "That the renters shall be obligated to produce each year at least one opera, all at their own expense with capable musicians; and the operas will first be seen by the most Illustrious Signor Tron . . ."[46]

---

44 On these two revivals of the 1670s, and the significance of the transformation of their librettos, see Bianconi, "Ercole in Rialto"; and Heller, "The Queen as King." On the subject of the revival of Venetian operas outside of Venice, see Brown, "'Con nuove arie aggiunte'." Sometimes, of course, the original poet would be available to make the changes. In the case of Giulia Masotti's suggested substitution of *Argia* in 1666/67, it was understood that the original librettist, Apolloni, would add and remove scenes as needed (ASV, SGSM, b. 188, f. 292, 2 Oct. 1666).

45 Rosand, *Opera*, 123.

46 "Che li detti signori condutori siano tenuti et obligati far recitar ogn'anno al meno un'opera in musica à tutte sue spese con musici suficienti, et con opere prima vedute da esso Illustrissimo Tron." ASV, AN, Atti, b. 667, f. 82, 9 Apr. 1648.

Presumably, this stipulation refers to the libretto rather than to the music; it is hard to imagine that the proprietor would have felt it necessary to comment on the musical score, while he might have been concerned with different aspects of the plot and the general tone of the work. The works of individual librettists differ in their range of topics. Giovanni Faustini's librettos, until *Calisto*, were all written around fictional characters, perhaps indicating a personal preference and the absence of pressure from an outside agent for him to produce a different sort of work (historical, for example). Aurelio Aureli's librettos, on the other hand, varied from fictional to mythological to historical; he apparently enjoyed adapting his dramatic ideas and formulas to a wide range of topics (or he provided librettos to impresarios who liked such variety).[47]

While the librettist may often have been free to choose his own subject, he would have had to invent or suggest scenic elements according to the purse strings of the company. During Giovanni Faustini's second season as impresario at the Teatro S. Aponal, he must have decided to write a libretto, *Calisto*, that would incorporate a wide range of scenes and machines.[48] Similarly, Marco Faustini's inaugural work at SS. Giovanni e Paolo, *Gl'amori infrutuosi di Pirro*, includes a variety of scenic diversions owing to the presence of a sorcerer. We can only speculate whether Marco Faustini—or Giovanni Grimani—specified the theme for his inaugural work at SS. Giovanni e Paolo, or if one of them merely suggested that the libretto should emphasize the scenic splendor of the production.

COMPOSITION AND PRE-PUBLICATION
REVISION OF THE LIBRETTO

Once the impresario had found a willing librettist, and the subject had been decided upon, the librettist would then draft and write the work. Giovanni Faustini's posthumous works attest both to his assiduousness and to his working method: according to the prefaces in a number of his posthumous librettos, he must have worked on several librettos simultaneously, not just on the next one to be performed. At his death he left works finished, nearly finished, and in draft form; some of these latter may have been merely scenarios, others in an intermediate state of completion.[49] Unlike Faustini, however, most librettists must have worked on only one or two librettos at a time, and may have completed them only shortly before the onset of the season. Certainly, the pressure of the deadline for an upcoming carnival might demand a concentrated effort. On 27 September 1659 Minato withdrew from Venice altogether to finish *Elena* in the seclusion of a country villa.[50] Even though Nicola Beregan had begun his *Tito* five years earlier,[51] the

47 On Aureli's dramatic formulas see Rosand, "L'Ovidio trasformato," ix–lvii.

48 On scenes and machines in *Calisto* see chapter 9 and Glixon and Glixon, "Marco Faustini," 54–58.

49 Rosand, *Opera*, 174, 184, 189–95.

50 ASV, SGSM, b. 101, f. n., letter from Minato to Faustini, 27 Sept. 1659.

51 *Il Tito* (1666), [5].

verses were not ready to supply to the composer until shortly before the start of the 1666 season; Beregan sent Cesti the poetry in groups of scenes or act by act as they were finished, rather than as a whole.[52] This practice of turning over to the composer one act of the libretto at a time may even have been standard: Francesco Cavalli's 1648 contract with the impresarios Rocco Maestri and Bortolo Castoreo specifies that he would be paid at the time he received each act of the libretto.[53]

Unfinished and Foreign Librettos

In certain situations, the libretto needed additional work by another author before it could be brought to the stage; this was certainly the case with Giovanni Faustini's posthumous works. When Marco Faustini sought to produce them (even those Giovanni had completed) they needed to be modernized or completed. New arias had to be added to meet the aesthetics of the late 1650s and 1660s, and new characters or plot lines might also be appropriate: another poet had to take over this work (or perhaps, if only arias had to be added, they could have been lifted from other works). For the 1659/60 season, Minato admitted to having touched up Giovanni Faustini's *Elena*; he mentioned in his foreword that the plot had been devised by Giovanni Faustini "of famous memory, and whose talent amazed the theaters of this city, as well as those of the most remote lands."[54] In 1666/67, on the other hand, the foreword to Giovanni Faustini's *Alciade* did not specify a reviser, citing only that the additions had been made by a "virtuoso soggetto" (talented individual).[55] Finally, it was Nicola Beregan who revised the first act of *Il tiranno humiliato d'Amore overo il Meraspe*, the last Faustini work to appear on the stage.[56] Similarly, librettos originally written for other cities had to be adapted to Venetian tastes.

Printers sometimes indicated revisions of these sorts in the libretto. The Venetian alterations for the 1654 production of the Neapolitan libretto *Ciro* were marked in the libretto by double commas, known as *virgole* or *virgolette*, as were the verses added for the Venetian performance of *Arsinoe* (1678). The verses of *L'incostanza trionfante* (1657) that Piccoli managed to write before leaving Venice were provided with *virgole* to differentiate them from those by the poets brought in to complete the libretto. On the other hand, these signs marked Corradi's revisions to Moniglia's *La schiava fortunata* for the 1674 production to "protect" the original author's reputation. The printer Nicolini took particular care with the 1676

---

52 Rosand, *Opera*, 212.

53 ASV, AN, Atti, b. 6673, f. 15ᵛ, 25 Apr. 1648.

54 "Il Soggetto di questo dramma uscì dal Felicissimo ingegno del già Sign. Giovanni Faustini di famosa memoria e della cui Virtù stupirono i Teatri non solo di questa Città, ma quelli ancora de' più remoti Paesi." *Elena* (1659), "Lettore."

55 *Alciade* (1667) , 7.

56 ASV, SGSM, b. 188, 294–95. See Rosand, *Opera*, 193–94. Beregan's reputation for "touching up" librettos was known outside of Venice in the 1670s. In 1677, as we saw earlier, Giovanni Francesco Saliti proposed that Beregan be asked to make any changes to the libretto he was writing (Vmc, PDC 1064, f. 277).

libretto of Minato's *Leonida in Tegea*, marking added verses with virgolette facing one direction, and altered ones with them facing the other.

PUBLISHING THE LIBRETTO

Ivanovich writes that the librettist, not the impresario, was responsible for the printing of the libretto "at his own expense."[57] There is no reason to doubt this statement as the norm for the period of Ivanovich's activity, that is from the 1660s through the 1680s, and it was probably true for the 1650s as well. One of the tasks of the librettist (or, in his absence, the impresario or some other member of the production team), therefore, was to find an appropriate printer, and to reach an agreement that would bring profit to both parties.

Production and Financing of the Printed Libretto

Unlike many books, librettos, since they had a fixed deadline—the opening night of the season—had to be prepared and printed quickly (as we will discuss below, alterations were often made as late as the final rehearsals).[58] The skills and organization needed to accomplish this smoothly and efficiently may have been among the factors that led certain printers to achieve extraordinary levels of domination of the business; indeed, an examination of the librettos issued between 1637 and 1677 shows that at any given time, the majority were the work of only one or two shops.[59] The 1640s saw the most competition, with nine different printers responsible for thirty-five works.[60] In the 1650s, Giuliani (in the Venetian form, Zulian) dominated, issuing eleven of the twenty-eight printed. It is of some note that the second most prolific printer of opera librettos in that decade was Giovanni Pietro Pinelli, also the official printer of the government, who would have been used to a quick turnaround, as he habitually needed to issue government decrees, although they did not involve the additional challenge of setting verses of poetry, along with frequent changes between roman and italic type; on the other hand, Pinelli was also well known for the publication of commemorative volumes, of both prose and poetry, that shared many of the same problems as librettos, as they also had to be issued quickly. In the 1660s, nearly

---

57 "stampati a sue spese." Ivanovich, *Memorie teatrali*, 414. The rest of this passage will be dicussed below.

58 Rosand (*Opera*, 207) cites a letter in the Hannover archive indicating that the printer for the libretto of *Massenzio* (1672) did not complete his work until the evening before opening night (she writes that it was 3 a.m., but the phrase "alle tre di questa notte" actually means three hours after sunset, or about 7:30 p.m. on 27 Jan.; see Talbot, "*Ore italiane*").

59 While seventeen printers were responsible for at least one libretto each in the years between 1637 and 1677, many issued just one or two.

60 Surian printed eight and Milocco six; four printers issued four librettos each: Bariletti, Valvasense, Giuliani, and the company of Leni and Vecellio; Sales and Pinelli printed two each, and Sarzina one (as well as one in 1639). Sarzina was one of the major publishers of works of the Incogniti, but the two librettos published by the shop were not the work of known Incognito authors (Persiani's *Le nozze di Teti, e di Peleo* and Vendramin's *Adone*). On Sarzina and the Incogniti, see Infelise, "*Ex ignoto notus?*"

half of the librettos, eighteen of thirty-nine, came from the presses of Nicolini, who would dominate even more between 1670 and 1677, printing thirty-three of the thirty-seven librettos under his name alone, and two others in partnership with Steffano Curti. Even for these specialized printers, however, producing an accurate libretto in the last-minute rush before opening night was a daunting task. Giuliani, in the second edition of *L'incostanza trionfante* (1658), writes of the first printing that "because of the very short time given to me, it came out filled with errors, in particular of transposed or omitted words, of two verses printed as one, and so forth."[61]

The paucity of extant contracts between librettists and printers makes it difficult to know precisely how the system worked, but several documents, including a dispute between Marco Faustini and the printer Curti (see below), indicate that it was, in fact, the printer who usually took the initial risk, producing the librettos at his own expense. Most likely, the income from the sales (after subtracting whatever commission would be charged by the actual seller) would go first to the printer, until his costs and some agreed-upon fee were covered.[62] After that point, all income, again subtracting the seller's commission, would probably have gone to the librettist. Such a system would have been possible because of the relatively small size of the libretto (and its consequently low cost), and also because of the certainty of at least some sales even in the event of an unsuccessful opera (assuming, that is, that the opera was not cancelled before the season began). It should be noted that the situation could be quite different when a large book was involved, in which case the author might well have to finance such a project on his own.[63]

Papers concerning Marco Faustini and the printer Steffano Curti furnish specific data concerning the cost of libretto production. In late 1665, Curti began work on the first opera of the season, Giovanni Faustini's *Doriclea*, to be revived with music by Pietro Andrea Ziani. As mentioned above, that production was eventually cancelled in favor of Cesti's *Orontea*, but not before Curti had printed 2,000 copies of two and a half sheets, or forty pages, that is, about half of the text.[64]

---

61 "per il brevissimo tempo assignatomi uscì pieno di molti errori particolarmente di parole trasportate, ò tralasciate, di due versi posti in uno, e simili." *L'incostanza trionfante*, second edition (1658). For more on this libretto, see below, and Glixon and Glixon, "Triumph of Inconstancy."

62 According to Infelise (*Editoria veneziana*, 214) the costs, during this period, normally represented about one-quarter of the selling price.

63 Evidence from later in the century shows how Giustinian Martinioni planned to finance a new edition of Francesco Sansovino's *Venetia città nobilissima*. Martinioni formed a "compagnia" with the pharmacist Iseppo Lazaroni for the express purpose of printing the book. Lazaroni promised to provide up to 300 ducats, or whatever would be necessary in order to cover the cost of paper and the printing, for the printing of 1,100 copies, or something less than £2 per copy. The pharmacist was to have been repaid for his expenditures from the sales of the book, and further profits would be divided between Martinioni and Lazaroni (ASV, AN, Atti, b. 2820, f. 207, 21 Oct. 1677). On the other hand, Marco Boschini paid the printer Andrea Baba for both the paper and the type for the publication of his *Carta del navigare pitoresco*; his arrangement with the printer entitled him to 350 copies of the book (ASV, Avogaria di comun, b. 2183/133, 22 Oct. 1660).

64 Papers concerning the dispute between Faustini and Curti are found in ASV, SGSM, b. 194 (ff. 78–81) and b. 117 (folder A, ff. 10–11). The records of the printers' guild include privileges for both *Orontea* and *Tito* (ASV, Arti, b. 166, ff. 78v and 79), but not for *Doriclea*.

This work had been undertaken at Curti's own expense, and Faustini promptly reimbursed him 32 ducats for his labor and materials.[65] Under this arrangement, evidently, Curti would have first printed the entire libretto, then turned over to Faustini as profit all income beyond the agreed-upon printer's fee. Extrapolating from Curti's figures, an average libretto of five folios (eighty pages) would have cost 64 ducats for 2,000 copies, or about 4 soldi per copy, with another small charge for binding.[66] The cost of a libretto to the purchaser is uncertain, though it appears to have been around 1 lira (20 soldi; see below).

The selling price of librettos was probably relatively stable, but the cost of production could vary depending on their appearance. For example, some boasted magnificent engravings for the *antiporta* or frontispiece (in some cases these were by important, or soon-to-be important artists such as Antonio Zanchi[67]), while others included simpler ones, and some had none at all. Variations in typefaces and the presence of decorative borders and initials added to the visual effect of the libretto. Engravings and decorative elements must certainly have added to printing costs, which may very well have been a factor in determining the level of opulence of the printed libretto. On the other hand, the particularly short lead time between the submission of the text and the opening performances of the opera might often have necessitated a simpler layout, or, at the least a standardized one that could be, to some extent, prepared in advance. The uneven type that characterizes many librettos probably results from the exigencies of their production (it is also possible that the printer, if he expected little profit in a particular instance, might have devoted less time and effort to the project). In any event, it is uncertain whether in some cases a printer chose a fancier format in hopes of increasing sales, or in others whether the librettist might have opted for increased prestige in exchange for somewhat lower profits (although, on the other hand, a more visually elaborate libretto could have resulted in a larger dedication gift; see below).

The little documentary evidence that survives concerning printers and librettists suggests a wider variety of financial solutions than Ivanovich suggests. The contract mentioned above between the Bolognese Giovanni Battista Pellicani and the printer Andrea Giuliani and bookseller Giacomo Batti was not based on future sales: Pellicani was to receive a *caparra* (down payment) of 6 doble (about 27 ducats), and then a bulk payment of 100 ducats when the manuscript was handed over to the printer; in addition, he would receive fifty bound copies.[68] In this arrangement, although Pellicani was guaranteed a specific sum, insulating him

---

65 ASV, SGSM, b. 194, f. 78.

66 Bianconi and Walker provide some monetary figures for sales of the libretto of *Il talamo preservato dalla fedeltà di Eudossa* in Reggia Emilia in 1683. Copies sold for 1 Milanese lira apiece, and the resulting profit was 388 Milanese lire, even though 412 of the 1,100 copies printed remained unsold (Bianconi and Walker, "Production, Consumption," 232).

67 On Zanchi, see Aikema, *Pietro della Vecchia*, 84–85. Examples by Zanchi in the 1650s include *Statira, Gli amori di Apollo e Dafne* (in its 1656 reprint), *Medoro, Artemisia,* and *Elena.* On the visual and textual significance of the antiporta in Venetian librettos, see Calcagno, "Staging Musical Discourses," 137–51.

68 ASV, AN, Atti, b. 12667, f. 67r–v, 22 July 1658.

from poor sales, he was denied a windfall if the work proved unusually popular. As discussed above, this arrangement may have been worked out because the author would probably have been absent from Venice during the opera season; the compromise between the two parties must have been viewed as preferable to the difficulty of reconciling accounts over long distances. In the end, though, Pellicani gained nothing: the contract stated that if the work was not performed (and it was not), the author would not be paid and would be obliged to return any monies already advanced to him by the printer.

This same type of arrangment erupted into a legal dispute between the printer Camillo Bortoli and the librettist Matteo Noris concerning *Zenobia*, produced at S. Moisè in the 1665/66 season.[69] According to Bortoli's declaration, he and Noris had reached an agreement in which, in exchange for receiving all the income from sales, the printer would pay the librettist 160 ducats, in two installments, 100 ducats at the signing of the contract and 60 after the first performance, with the initial payment to be returned if the opera was not performed. Bortoli agreed to these terms based on Noris's assertion that "he would print and sell an infinity of copies" and would earn "a great fortune."[70] Because he was short of cash, Bortoli turned over to Noris the equivalent in jewelry, and proceeded with the printing. The opening night (for which Bortoli sold 300 copies of the libretto) was a fiasco: because of the "grumbling and invective"[71] of the audience, the curtain was brought down early and the run ended without even one complete performance. Bortoli tried to get the jewels back (he had borrowed them from someone else), since, as he claimed, the sale of the few librettos from that abortive first night barely covered his labor costs, much less all his other expenses.[72]

Licenses and Privileges

According to Venetian law, before any book could be printed its publishers had to obtain a license that served to guarantee the moral and political suitability of the work.[73] The procedure in effect in the first half of the century was lengthy and complex.[74] Each book was examined first by the Inquisitori di stato and the ducal secretary, who then, if it were deemed politically acceptable, issued a *testamur*, and forwarded it to the Riformatori dello Studio di Padova, where a scholar examined the text for ideological and religious acceptability, granting a license. The official *imprimatur* was then issued by the Capi of the Council of Ten. This process resulted

---

69 ASV, GP, Dimande, b. 44, fasc. 84, no. 44, 3 Sept. 1666.

70 "mi haverebbe fatto stampare et vendere infinità di libri . . . gran fortuna . . ." ASV, GP, Dimande, b. 44, fasc. 84, no. 44, 3 Sept. 1666.

71 "il susurro, et invettive . . ."; ibid.

72 Unfortunately, no further documents for the case have come to light, so the resolution remains unknown.

73 For a discussion of printing licenses and privileges, with emphasis on music publishing, see Agee, "Privilege and Venetian Music Printing," esp. 8–14.

74 See Pesenti, "Stampatori e letterati," esp. 115–18. Over time, the procedures changed, usually by being streamlined, but occasionally with new complications added.

in the statement on the title page (appearing on all but three librettos for the entire period) "con licenza de' superiori." Another requirement for most books printed in Venice, but which appears not to have been in effect for librettos, perhaps because of the restricted time element, was that they be examined for printing accuracy by two bodies, the Sovraintendenze alle stampe and the Pubblici correttori, whose certification would appear at the end of the finished work. This complex system was simplified later in the century, with the issuing of a *testamur* or *fede* from the Inquisitori, certifying acceptability, and one from the Revisore pubblica, attesting to accuracy, following which the license would be issued automatically by the Riformatori. Unfortunately, no records of this process from any of the bodies except the Riformatori survive, so that we are not sure whether the procedures were strictly followed in the case of librettos, nor precisely how long it took for them to be approved. Even the extant records of the Riformatori, which begin only in 1673, are incomplete, and include very few of the librettos actually issued.

The vast majority of the librettos also bear a notice of copyright, the *privilegio* (usually announced along with the license in the formula "Con licenza de' superiori, e privilegio"). The privilege was issued by the printers' guild following payment of a small fee of ½ ducat (£3 s.2), and with the declaration that the book was new, and had not previously been published in Venice. This granted, at least in principle, certain basic rights to the publisher. The request for a privilege often anticipated the performance by only a few days. The application for *Calisto*, for example, was filed on 21 or 22 November, and the first performance followed about a week later, on 28 November 1651.[75] For *Eupatra* the entry, dated 16 December 1654, reads: "Signor Ginammi intends to print the libretto entitled *L'Eupatra*, which [is] a new book and never before printed."[76] According to Faustini's records, the first performance occurred on 19 December, only three days later. For some reason, however, title page of the libretto does not indicate that a *privilegio* had been applied for and granted.

Unfortunately, the register of the printers' guild offers only partial confirmation of the procedures concerning the printing of opera librettos, for it includes applications for only sixteen librettos throughout this entire period, even though the vast majority of librettos printed between 1637 and 1677 included a statement of privilege on the title page.[77] Conversely, two of those for which an application is present, Faustini's *Eupatra* (1654, mentioned above) and Minato's *La prosperità d'Elio Seiano* (1667), were printed without that annotation; in fact, the application for Minato's libretto states that the book had already been printed. Finally, in two other cases, however—*Argia* (1669) and Ivanovich's *La costanza trionfante* (1673)—

75 ASV, Arti, b. 166, f. 53ᵛ.

76 "Il messer signore Ginammi da in nota di stampar il libro intitolato l'Eupatra del signor Giovanni Faustini che per esser libro novo e non più stampato conseguisce privilegio giusto le leggi . . ." ASV, Arti, b. 166, f. 58.

77 ASV, Arti, b. 166. Between 1637 and 1659, only twelve of the fifty-nine librettos were printed without the privilege, and only two between 1667 and 1677. For some reason in the years 1660–66, however, eleven of the twenty-seven lacked one, including all those in the 1662 and 1664 seasons. Perhaps an administrative problem of some sort had arisen in the guild in those years.

although the libretto was issued before the application had been formally registered, the statement does appear.[78]

Revisions to the Libretto Made before Opening Night

The text of a libretto was still subject to change even after the author had turned it over to the composer and, later, to the printer. Quite often, it became necessary during the composition of the score, or during rehearsals, to cut out sections of text, especially portions intended to be set as recitative.[79] If time permitted (and the author consented) the printed libretto might represent the revised version (that is, no evidence of the original state would survive), but in many cases one or both of these conditions did not apply. In one early libretto, the anonymous message alerted the audience that some printed verses would not be performed. Fusconi's *Amore innamorato* offered the following pronouncement: "I must alert you, that in the music some verses that are printed here have been omitted, so as not to excessively tire the listeners, and to satisfy the impatience of some who, having barely heard the beginning of a scene, without any respect, desire for it to end."[80]

A better solution, however, was for the audience to have a libretto that matched the music; when time permitted, printers began to employ, starting in the 1640s, *virgolette* (sometimes called *virgole*), or double commas, alongside the eliminated verses, that is, the same method mentioned above that served to indicate revisions.[81] This technique appears for the first time, without explanation, in the libretto for the 1640 revival of Monteverdi's *Arianna*, which was performed without most of the Mantuan choruses. It does not appear again for several years, next being used in one scene (act 1, scene 2) of the *Semiramide in India* (1648), and then in the prologue of *Giasone* (1649). When the printer Valvasense wished to indicate omissions in two librettos of 1650, *Bradamante* and *Orimonte*, he employed dots rather than *virgolette*, perhaps because just two years earlier, for *Torilda*, he had used *virgolette* to mark the differences between a longer spoken version of the drama and the abbreviated text for an operatic one.[82] With *La guerriera spartana* (1654), the

---

78 Perhaps the printer assumed that the privilege would be granted, or the phrase was added while the press run was already in progress, and it appears in the surviving copies.

79 On the problems faced by writers of librettos, see Rosand, "In Defense" and Rosand, *Opera*, 204–9.

80 "Debbo bene avvertirsi, che si sono tralasciati nella Musica alcuni versi, che qui si ritrovano, e per non stancare soverchiamente gli ascoltanti, e per appargare l'impatienza d'alcuni, che appena udito il principio d'una Scena senza alcun riguardo ne bramano il fine." Fusconi, *Amore innamorato* (1642), 7. This note also indicates that some *canzonette* have been added.

81 On *virgole* and other changes to the libretto, see also Rosand, *Opera*, 18, 207–9. The observations in the following discussions of the libretto are based on an examination of two of the complete sets of librettos: the Zeno collection in Vnm, and the collection in the library of the University of California, Los Angeles.

82 This was a clear improvement over the situation in *La finta savia*, where the libretto simply warned that many of the verses printed in the lengthy text and intended for a spoken performance would be skipped in the musical setting (Strozzi, *La finta savia* [1643], 9).

soon-to-be standard use for virgolette is explained for the first time:"Many verses, which are not sung for reasons of brevity, are indicated in the margin of the book with two commas."[83] For the next several years, most of those librettos employing virgolette for this purpose still carried an explanation, but by 1660 the by-now accepted practice required none. A rare indication that librettists sometimes were content to simply eliminate their verses without resorting to the use of virgolette (and also how close to opening night these changes might be made) can be found in the 1659 libretto of Aureli's *La costanza di Rosmonda*. In a note printed at the end of the libretto, the author writes that "So as not to bore you because of the length of the drama, I removed during the final rehearsals everything that I considered superfluous."[84] Acts 2 and 3 of the printed libretto reflected the final form (there are no virgolette), but, as Aureli writes, "the first act had already been printed, so I beg you to excuse me, and to make up for it with the speed of your glance, where I could not manage in time, with my slow pen, to mark for you with signs those verses that are not sung."[85]

While the placement of some virgolette was probably determined before the printer began to set the type, they could also be inserted after the type was set but before printing, or even, after the press run had begun, as stop-press changes. (Since, however, printers apparently completed the work on one of the three or four gatherings that ususally comprised a libretto before beginning the next, this might mean that two versions of the same libretto would be sold simultaneously, so that this solution would probably have been avoided, if at all possible.) Additions to the libretto, however, or text substitutions, could not be so easily made. When such changes were decided upon after the type was set, or even if printing had begun (except for the final gathering), they could be inserted at the end of the libretto if blank space were available, in the same manner as tables of errors (although, once again, these could have been done part of the way through the run as stop-press changes).[86] In some cases, the printer indicated that the additions had been made (as in *Doriclea*) "to delight the listeners and to please the performers," although most are simply listed without comment.[87] In at least one instance, the change was for even more practical reasons: "Because of the distance of the Fortress of Calpe, Zelmina and Zaida could not be understood, so they will be made to come out to

---

83 "Molti versi, che non cantano per brevità, nella stampa saranno segnati al margine con due virgole." Castoreo, *La guerriera spartana* (1654), 8.

84 "Per non fastidirti con la lunghezza del Drama, hò levato nell'ultime prove tutto quello, che hò stimato superfluo . . ." Aureli, *La costanza di Rosmonda* (1659), 91.

85 "ma perché il primo Atto era già passato sotto il torchio della Stampa, ti prego à scusarmi, & a supplire con la velocità dello sguardo, dove non è potuto giunger à tempo la tardità della penna à segnarti con i punti quei versi, che non si cantano." Aureli, *La costanza di Rosmonda* (1659), 91.

86 Such lists of errors and corrections appear at the end of eight librettos before 1675, beginning with the very first: *Andromeda* (1637), *La finta savia* (1643), *Egisto* (1643), *Veremonda* (1653), *Pasife* (1661), *Ermengarda* (1670), *Domitiano* (1673), and *La costanza trionfante* (1673). The case of the *Orontea* (1649) is unusual: rather than at the end of the libretto, the list of errors is printed at the end of the prefatory material, on page 7, indicating that, in at least some cases, the opening gathering was the last to be printed.

87 "per dilettare gli uditori, & per aggradire a' rappresentanti . . ." Faustini, *Doriclea* (1645), after 89.

sing, and then . . . return inside . . . Therefore, it is necessary to change and add these verses . . ."[88] Most such additions consisted entirely of one or more arias, or even entire scenes, for existing characters;[89] occasionally, however, they signaled the introduction of entirely new characters: a "Hinnada" and an Oread in *Doriclea*, a "plowman [*bifolco*] of Erminone" in *Calisto*,[90] and Cibele in *Pasife*.

Post-publication Revisions to the Libretto

In the not uncommon event that corrections, alterations, or additions to a libretto needed to be made after the entire work had been printed, either before or after performances had begun, the solutions discussed above were no longer possible. Instead, in nearly twenty cases between 1637 and 1675, the printer was forced to issue a separately printed addendum, sometimes more than once for the same libretto.[91] The most common format for these supplements was a single bifolium, but there are a few examples, between 1637 and 1675, of a binion (*Statira* and *Medoro*[92]) or ternion (*Pericle effeminato*, *La guerriera spartana*, *L'incostanza trionfante*, and *Elena*[93]), and even one sexternion, for *Eupatra*.[94] Such a supplement most often supplied the text for added arias or short scenes, usually for characters already present in the drama. The bifolium added to *Achille in Sciro*, for example, includes three arias each for Deidamia and Alcesta, two for Rosalba, and one for Licomede.[95] There are several examples of new prologues—often with different characters—that usually replaced those printed with the full libretto: for *Erismena*, *Le fortune di Rodope*, *Elena*, and *Argia* (which did not have a prologue in the original libretto).[96] Intermedi were also regularly altered (again with new chararcters): for *Erismena* (in an added bifolium different from that with the new prologue, also containing arias and other scenes), *Le fortune di Rodope* (also a different bifolium than that with the added prologue), and *Eupatra*.

The sexternion added to *Eupatra* represents by far the most extensive set of

---

88 "Perche per la lontanza della Fortezza di Calpe, Zelmina, e Zaida, non potevono esser intese, si fanno uscir' fuori a parlare, e poi . . . ritornar dentro . . . Però si devono mutare, & aggiungere questi Versi . . ." Strozzi/Cicognini, *Veremonda* (1653), 93.

89 Arias were added in this manner to *Elena*, *Antigona delusa*, *Gl'amori infrutuosi di Pirro*, *Dori*, and *Genserico*; scenes to *Pericle effeminato*, *Iphide greca*, and *Caligula delirante*.

90 In *Calisto*, the new scenes are added at the end of act 3, on pp. 76–82, but, as with *Orontea* (see n. 87), a warning appears at the end of the prefatory material.

91 It is difficult to be sure that all such supplements have been identified, since they were very likely to have been misplaced and not preserved with the libretto. For example, nine of the additions found attached to librettos in the Zeno collection in Vnm (which seems to have been compiled in a particularly careful manner), are missing from the corresponding copies in the UCLA set.

92 Vnm, Dramm. 3461.2 and 3464.1 (UCLA 87).

93 Vnm, Dramm. 3460.1, 3460.3, 3464.3, and 3465.1 (UCLA 104).

94 Vnm, Dramm. 3461.1 (UCLA 87).

95 Vnm, Dramm. 3468.6 (UCLA 128).

96 Vnm, Dramm. 3461.3, 3463.3, 3465.1 (UCLA 104), and 3473.2 (UCLA 162). The prologue for *Erismena* is actually the third for this opera, although one, which repeated that for *Ciro* of the previous year, appeared only in a scenario, and may never have been performed with *Erismena*.

changes. The nineteen numbered alterations include, as mentioned, two new inter-medi, added arias and scenes, and even an altered sequence of scenery changes. Per-haps the most notable result is the elimination of four singing characters (Neptune, Amphitrite, Juno, and Amor Leteo) and four groups of extras or dancers (marine gods, sirens, silent winds, and furies), counterbalanced by the addition of three comic characters (Dismena, Irbino, and Lisetta) and two sets of dancers (pages and *vil-lanelle*). The insert for *La finta savia* is particularly interesting: beyond a varied aria in act 1, there are replacement intermedi for the ends of both the first and second acts, to be used if the opera is done without dance. This bifolium names the composers of the three new pieces (necessary because the opera is a pasticcio), and even indicates where in the libretto the folded sheet should be inserted. In a few cases, the supple-ment adds no new material, but consists, rather, of a letter or announcement to the reader apologizing for errors in the printing, alerting the reader (without providing details) to cuts, or even adding a portrait of the dedicatee (*Scipione affricano*).

Later Printings of the Libretto

A particularly successful opera, especially during a long carnival season, might re-quire the printer to return to the presses for a second edition, usually indicated on the title page or on an additional sheet added at the beginning of the book. In some cases, this second printing is practically identical to the first, although in nearly every case the type was entirely reset. Even more often, however, the printer and librettist took advantage of the opportunity, and subsequent editions were in some way revised from the original, offering a better solution than the supplemen-tal sheets for those operas successful enough to warrant the added effort. The most basic of these revisions, such as those in *Egisto* and *Ciro* (the version of 1653/54), featured second printings that simply corrected errors in the first, but more often they reflected the same sorts of additions and alterations discussed above, ranging from the simple addition of arias, or the replacement of a prologue, to large-scale replacement of scenes and even characters. The second printing of *La finta pazza*, for example, includes an addendum at the end with changed arias and scenes; a third printing incorporates these into the body of the text in the appropriate loca-tions. Similarly, when *Annibale in Capua* was reprinted, the dedication, which had been supplied for the first printing as a separate bifolium, was now integral. Some-times, the pre-opening night and post-opening night versions are clearly delin-eated. The first printing of *Deidamia*, for example, bears the notation on the title page "da rappresentarsi" (to be performed). The second printing, with some sig-nificant changes, indicates first of all that this work was "rappresentata" (that is, had already been performed), and clarifies the situation with the phrase "In this second printing, corrected and enlarged with scenes and arias by the author."[97]

---

[97] "In questa Seconda Impressione corretta, ed accresciuta di Scene, e Canzonette dall'Autore." Herrico, *Deidamia* (1644). When the opera was revived in 1647, the initial printing for that year was, for some reason, labeled the third. Other second printings with added or changed arias and scenes include *Ercole in Tebe, Caligula delirante, Claudio Cesare, Domitiano, La schiava fortunata, Galieno, Germanico sul Reno, Giocasta, Helena rapita da Paride, Nicomede in Bitinia*, and *Vespasiano*.

The successive reprintings of Cicognini and Cavalli's *Giasone* (1648/49) demonstrate the wide range of possibilities available to the printer. The pre-opening night libretto bore the indication "da rappresentarsi" and included two dedicatory poems; apparently the intermedio at the end of act 2 had not yet been decided upon, and was labelled "Ballo de . . ." [*sic*]. As had been the case with *Deidamia*, a second printing, labelled "rappresentata," included quite a few changes. A note from the printer reads simply "Having run out of copies of *Giasone*, and the requests for it having increased, it was necessary to reprint it";[98] an annotation on the title page, however, explains better what was done: "In this second printing corrected, and with the addition of the new arias."[99] In fact, the changes were quite extensive: the printer replaced the two dedicatory poems with a new sonnet, removed the list of scenery, and included changed and added arias and recitative. In addition, the act 2 intermedio now bore the label "Ballo de' Marinari." A third printing was identical to the second. Exceptionally (this appears to be the only example for this period), the printer Giuliani (whose name did not appear on the printings discussed so far) issued a fourth printing, noting that it included the arias added in the second printing. While the first three printings bore the date 1649, this one was labeled 1650, perhaps indicating that it was printed the next year for the benefit of collectors, a possibility made more likely by the appearance four years later, in 1654, a year with no performances of this opera, of a fifth printing, this time issued by Batti, the bookseller named for the first four.

Changes of the sorts described above all speak to the aim of satisfying the public, of injecting new life into a work, which, in turn, created additional labor for the printers who attempted to keep up with the alterations. In at least one case, however, *L'incostanza trionfante* of 1658, the printing of later editions was brought about by rather more complicated reasons. Problems began with the departure of the original librettist, Francesco Piccoli, and the subsequent completion of the drama by other poets, which apparently resulted in a botched first edition made worse by some apparently unorthodox poetry and word usages that generated criticism. The decision was made to reprint the libretto, with corrections and an explanatory letter. Subsequently—in an attempt to sabotage the integrity of the libretto—someone claiming to represent the management of the theater sent a letter to the printer specifying that the explanatory letter should be removed, and that other changes should be made. After this had been accomplished, the beseiged printer received a message from those actually in charge (unnamed, but presumably Marco Faustini), telling him to ignore the fraudulent instructions. At this point, the printer was either unable or unwilling to reprint the entire libretto again, but did attach another explanatory letter indicating corrections to the text. These problems, then, resulted in at least three distinct editions: a first edition, a second not marked as such, and another second edition so indicated. All of these

---

98 "L'essermi mancate le copie del Giasone, & essendomi cresciute le richieste di esso, mi hà necessitato à ristamparlo." Cicognini, *Giasone*, seconda impressione, "Al lettore."

99 "In questa seconda impressione corretto; con l'aggiunta delle nuove Canzonette." Cicognini, *Giasone*, seconda impressione, title page.

also appear in several variants, as the printer apparently kept already printed materials from each version, and assembled them in various combinations as this affair continued.[100]

THE LIBRETTO AS SOURCE OF INCOME

While most of the men writing librettos (as discussed earlier) were not "professional" librettists, they did expect some financial recognition for their efforts, at least, that is, after the earliest years of opera in Venice. Ellen Rosand has charted the evolution in Venice from the *scenario* (for use during the season, to be followed by a libretto printed after the season had ended, usually labelled "rappresentata") to the libretto printed before the season began (bearing the indication on the title page "da rappresentarsi"); the success of opera made routine the steady flow of printed librettos available to the public shortly before an opera's premiere.[101] We owe our basic understanding of the financial aspect of libretto production to Ivanovich's *Memorie teatrali*; he knew the system well, having supplied three librettos for Venetian theaters, starting in 1663 (see above). He described how, in Venetian practice, librettos eventually came to be written for profit, in contrast to those produced in the earliest years: "For this purpose, the practice was introduced of leaving to the author of the drama, as payment for his efforts, everything that was taken in from the sale of the librettos, printed at his own expense, and from the dedication, which he made of his own free will; this income [from the sales] depends on the success of the drama."[102] The Faustini papers verify Ivanovich's claims that during this period the impresario did not directly pay the librettist for his work: neither the extant account books for Faustini's company nor his receipt book show payments. A decade earlier, however, Francesco Melosio published a poem in which he requested payment from Francesco Cavalli, in his role as impresario of S. Moisè, for his libretto (either *Orione*—planned for performance at that theater in 1642— or *Sidonio e Dorisbe*, which replaced it).[103] Seventeenth-century practice differed from that in the eighteenth century, when librettists were at least sometimes paid by the impresario: the company at the Teatro S. Giovanni Grisostomo for the year 1729/30 paid a sum of about 532 ducats to the librettist Metastasio for a new work, and in 1707 Apostolo Zeno wrote to an impresario in Milan concerning funds owed to Pietro Pariati for a libretto.[104] In the mid-seventeenth century, however,

100 This incident will be examined in more detail in Glixon and Glixon, "Triumph of Inconstancy."

101 See Rosand, "Opera Scenario," and Rosand, *Opera*, 81–88. See also Whenham, "Perspectives."

102 "A questa causa fu introdotto l'uso, che tuttavia si pratica di lasciar all'Autore del Drama per premio delle sue fatiche tutto quello si cava dalla vendita de' libretti stampati a sue spese, e dalla Dedicatoria, che si fa a sua libera disposizione, e quest'utile dipende dalla riuscita del Drama." Ivanovich, *Memorie teatrali*, 414.

103 On Melosio and Cavalli, see Pirrotta, "Lame Horse."

104 The entry for the payment to Metastasio appears in Vnm, Cod. It. xi 426, 8 (12142, 8). See Mangini, *Teatri di Venezia*, 124, 143; and Talbot, *Tomaso Albinoni*, 194–201. For Zeno's letter to an impresario in Milan, see Fabrizio Della Seta, "The Librettist," 243; and Fabbri, *Secolo cantante*, 75–76.

as Ivanovich stated, all of the income derived from sale of the printed book (for printer and librettist) and from the dedication (for the librettist).

The Dedication of the Libretto

The vast majority of librettos (133 of 145) published in Venice between 1637 and 1677[105] included a dedication, usually to a distinguished and wealthy personage. As in other books, the individual's name and titles appeared on the title page, followed by a dedicatory letter, and only then by the other front matter and the actual text. This was not done, of course, simply as a gesture of respect or devotion on the part of the librettist; the author expected something of value, cash or otherwise, in return (see chap. 11 on the dedication as a form of patronage).

A diplomatic report in 1666 mentions one such gift, from Maria Mancini Colonna to the unnamed Nicolò Minato, for *Pompeo magno*: "the new opera performed last night at S. Salvatore is dedicated to the Contessa Stabile Colonna, who has generously given to the author a necklace worth 60 doppie [270 ducats]."[106] These years must have been costly for Colonna, her husband (the Gran Contestabile del Regno di Napoli, Lorenzo Onofrio Colonna), and her brother, Filippo Mancini Mazzarini (the Duke of Nivers), for many librettos around this time were dedicated to them: in the three seasons from 1664 through 1666, nine of the fourteen librettos staged in Venice bore one or more of their names. In 1689 a letter from a correspondent of the Duke of Modena named 100 ducats as the typical fee paid for a dedication; the necklace mentioned above from Colonna, therefore, was a particularly generous gift.[107] Even for a wealthy family like the Colonnas, 1,000 ducats (the minimum those seasons would have cost them) would have represented a considerable sum of money; they must have felt that the increased visibility afforded by the dedications justified the expense.

DEDICATEES: VENETIANS AND FOREIGNERS   Most of the dedicatees of librettos during this period were from the highest levels of society. Not surprisingly, almost half, spread evenly throughout the period, were Venetian patricians, occasionally including the owners or protectors of the theaters, some of whom may have been honored, not in expectation of the standard gift (although that might also have been provided), but in recognition of their contributions, financial or otherwise, to the company or to the librettist. The dedications of five librettos at S. Aponal (out of seven issued during the Faustini years) to Alvise Duodo and Marc'Antonio Correr, speak, perhaps, to a desire, either on their part or on the part of the Faustinis, to link their names to a theater that otherwise lacked noble associ-

---

105 That is, stopping with the opening of the Teatro S. Giovanni Grisostomo. The figures that follow include also data from printed *scenari*, as well as the small number of spoken dramas with musical interludes.

106 "La nuova opera recitata hieri sera a San Salvatore è stata dedicata alla Signora Contessa Stabile Colonna che ha regolato generosamente d'una collana di 60 doppie quello che glie l'ha dedicata." ASF, MP, b. 3033, f. 867, 26 Feb. 1666.

107 ASMo, CAV, b.124, 156.II/8. Quoted in Saunders, "Repertoire of a Venetian Opera House," 58.

ations.[108] Among theater owners to receive dedications were the brothers Giovanni Carlo and Vicenzo Grimani of SS. Giovanni e Paolo and Andrea Vendramin of S. Luca.[109]

Not all of the Venetians honored by dedications were noblemen; one non-patrician was the famous lawyer Marin Dall'Angelo, the father of Giacomo Dall'Angelo, one of the lawyer-librettists mentioned above.[110] Giovanni Faustini dedicated one work (Doriclea) to the physician Mauritio Tirelli, who had been a neighbor in S. Vidal.[111] As we saw in chapter 1, Guglielmo Van Kessel, a Flemish businessman resident in Venice, played a role like those of some of the patricians mentioned above: he helped to finance the mounting of Cicognini's Gl'amori di Alessandro magno, e di Rossane through loans to the impresario, Giovanni Burnacini; in this case, the librettist had already died so that Burnacini was able to honor his benefactor directly.[112]

Dedications to foreigners became much more common in the later decades (reflecting both the increased international prestige of Venetian opera and the recurring presence of certain foreign dignitaries in the city at Carnival); while only four of twenty-five in the 1640s were to non-Venetians, they represented well over half of those in the 1660s (twenty-five of forty). The most frequently represented were the Colonna/Mazzarini family (as mentioned above) and the family of the Dukes of Brunswick, with eleven dedications each. Other rulers, including the King of Poland, the Duke of Parma, and the Marquis Bentivoglio of Ferrara, received dedications, as did several ambassadors to Venice and a few non-ruling nobles. A clear anomaly was the dedication of Fusconi's Argiope (1649) to the prima donna Anna Renzi (who might not have paid the author for his compliment).

The 1670s continued much in the same vein as earlier, with a mix of noble dedicatees, both Venetian and foreign, but this period also marked the earliest appearances, for Venetian librettos, of a more general sort of dedication, not designed to generate any specific reward. In 1670, Pietro Dolfin's Ermengarda, for SS. Giovanni e Paolo, was dedicated simply "to the kind reader" ("al benigno lettore"), while the librettos of both operas performed at S. Luca in 1675 also bore such general addresses: Giulio Cesare Corradi's La divisione del mondo was dedicated to "la Nobiltà Veneta,"

---

108 Calisto and Eritrea were dedicated to Marc'Antonio Correr; and Oristeo and Eupatra were dedicated to Alvise Duodo, while Le fortune di Rodope e Damira was dedicated to both men. Rosinda bore no dedication, and Erismena was dedicated to Giacomo Cavalli. Other dedications honoring "protectors" are Dall'Angelo's 1666 libretto Demetrio to Matteo da Lezze, Matteo Pisani, and Giovanni da Mula, identified as the protectors of Teatro S. Moisè (although any indication of financial assistance from them is lacking), and the same year's revival of Giasone at S. Cassiano to Benetto Zorzi, Giacomo Celsi, and Carlo Andrea Tron, protectors of that theater (Tron was also the proprietor of the theater).

109 The Grimanis were honored in one libretto in each of the 1667–69 seasons: Faustini's Alciade, and two by Aureli, Eliogabalo and Artaxerse; Tiridate of 1668 (Minato's revision of Bentivoglio's Zenobia e Radamisto) is dedicated to Vendramin.

110 It was Aurelio Aureli, a young lawyer himself, who dedicated his first libretto, Erginda, to Dall'Angelo. Although the Dall'Angelo family was among the nobility of the city of Rovigo, as residents of Venice they belonged to the cittadino class.

111 Tirelli lived in S. Vidal in 1641 (ASPV, Parrocchia di S. Vidal, Battesimi, 1641, f. 48).

112 On Van Kessel, see B. Glixon, "Music for the Gods?" and chapter 1.

and Tebaldo Fattorini's *Eteocle e Polinice* to "Le Dame di Venezia." Perhaps those authors had been unsuccessful in securing a dedicatee, or some particular financial arrangement had made the extra contribution unnecessary.

THE AUTHOR OF THE DEDICATION   While the librettist usually both wrote and signed the dedication as well as any message to the reader (this situation obtained in ninety-two of the 133 dedications; see table 5.1), sometimes the librettist did not wish his identity to be known (or, at least, advertised). In other cases he was either deceased or not involved in the publication process (in the case of a revival, for example, or if he were not in Venice), leaving the dedication to be penned by either the printer or the impresario. Some librettos, however, bear dedications signed by a printer or impresario even when the author lived in Venice. Eight of these works were written by patricians who perhaps wanted to avoid whatever negative associations they feared might arise from public authorship of a libretto (or from its possible failure), as mentioned above.[113] The others, however, were products of active librettists who sometimes did sign their dedications, notably Aurelio Aureli, Cristoforo Ivanovich, and Nicolò Minato. Perhaps in these more unusual instances the financial arrangements for the printing of the libretto varied from the standard, with the librettist receiving a fixed fee in exchange for allowing someone else to write the dedication and receive the expected gift.

Two impresarios contemporary with Marco Faustini—and who preceded his

TABLE 5.1   The Authors of Libretto Dedications

Signer of dedication	Number of librettos, 1637–77	Totals
Librettist		92
Someone other than librettist		
Author deceased or not in Venice	19	
Author in Venice, patrician	8	
Author in Venice, non-patrician	10	
Author's status unknown	4	
Total	41	41
No dedication		
Author deceased	1	
Author present in Venice	11	
Total	12	12
Total		145

113 These authors included Giacomo Badoaro, Pietro Angelo Zaguri, Nicola Beregan, and Pietro Dolfin. On anonymity see above, n. 6.

service at SS. Giovanni e Paolo—made the decision to sign dedications; their stations in life were rather dissimilar, a fact that would probably have been known by the purchasers of the librettos. The first, Giovanni Battista Balbi, was a famous Venetian dancer who had helped to introduce Venetian-style opera throughout Italy; his name on a libretto would have been a welcome selling point.[114] The second, however, is generally unknown in the literature concerning theatrical or, indeed, any other activities in seventeenth-century Venice: Francesco Piva (mentioned above in chaps. 1 and 3) was a gilder (indorador) who lived in S. Marina, the parish in which the theater was located.[115] His name appears on a dedication for Pietro Angelo Zaguri's Gl'avvenimenti d'Orinda (1660) and, more unusually, on two works of Aurelio Aureli, Medoro (1658) and Antigona delusa da Alceste (1660). Marco Faustini, on the other hand, chose a different path, and avoided such self-aggrandizement; although he undoubtedly wrote a number of the messages to the readers of the librettos, especially those that concern his late brother, he preferred to remain, at least to the book-buying public, anonymous, leaving the printer (Ginammi, Nicolini, or Bruni) or bookseller (Batti) to sign such dedications.[116]

Twelve librettos published during this period, nearly all the work of librettists alive and resident in the city, bore no dedications.[117] Four of Giovanni Faustini's librettos printed while he was still alive fall into this category; given Faustini's direct reference to debts, especially during the 1650/51 season (see chap. 3), and the lack of other, more stable income, the occasional absence of dedications is certainly curious.[118] Faustini may been unable to find a patron willing to attach his or her name to the work of a novice, or he may have decided to issue those librettos in a less obviously commercial manner, as works created not for obvious profit, but for purer, more literary reasons.[119]

An unusual situation arose with the libretto of Il fantasma dittatore (1677), by the Florentine Saliti (referred to above). The author communicated his intention to forgo both the income from sales and the right to dedicate the work, listing a series of conditions:

---

114 On Balbi, see NG II, s.v. "Balbi, Giovanni Battista," by Irene Alm. On Balbi as an impresario, see Bianconi and Walker, "Dalla Finta pazza." See also chapter 8.

115 In Le fatiche d'Ercole per Deianira (1662) Aureli referred to an earlier dedication written by the "late" Francesco Piva. Piva died in the parish of S. Marina on 29 Aug. 1660 (ASPV, Parrocchia di S. Marina, Libro de' morti 7, 1656–69, f. 32).

116 Portions of a draft of a letter Faustini wrote in preparation for the 1666/67 season are nearly identical to the introductory letter in Alciade, as well as phrases in the forewords to other librettos by Giovanni Faustini. See Rosand, Opera, 193–94.

117 Of these twelve librettos, only one was written by an author not present in Venice at the time of publication (the posthumous 1661 revival of Giovanni Faustini's Eritrea).

118 Librettos of Giovanni Faustini printed during his lifetime without dedications include Egisto (S. Cassiano, 1643), Ersilla and Euripo (S. Moisè, 1648, 1649 respectively), and Rosinda (S. Aponal, 1650/51).

119 One indication that Faustini might have wished to showcase the literary, and therefore noncommercial, value of his librettos can be found in the typography: most of those issued during his lifetime are printed more elegantly than those of other authors, using refined typefaces not used (or rarely so) elsewhere, and bearing attractive borders.

First, the author resolves to make a gift of the libretto to Polo Michiel, who is welcome to have it printed simply as a gift to himself.

Second, since it is the custom in similar cases to do the dedication oneself, Signor Polo is free to dedicate it to whomever it pleases him.

Third, since Signor Polo has no obligation nor intention to dedicate it to anyone, he may have it published under the name of the printer, dedicated to himself by that person, as something that came to him by fortune.[120]

In the end, the printed libretto bore a dedication signed by the printer Nicolini to Abbot Marco Ottoboni, with the note that "this work is a most welcome gift made by the author to the Most Illustrious and Most Excellent Signor Polo Michiel."[121]

Selling and Buying of Librettos

Like the composer, the librettist probably received the bulk of his earnings only after the season was underway; unlike the composer, however, who received a pre-determined salary for his composition regardless of the success or failure of the opera, the sales, and hence the income from the librettist's creative work—other than fees from the dedication—would be based entirely on the whim of the buying public, and geared primarily to the overall success of the production as reflected in the number of performances (that is, barring a different arrangement such as that between Pellicani and Batti already discussed). The printer, of course, risked even more, as he had already expended time and materials in producing the completed work.

The printed libretto was available to the public at several venues. It could, predictably, be purchased at the theater, presumably from the printer or his agent (where this selling point was located, whether inside the theater or outside the front door, is unknown). The operagoer could also purchase the book at the shop of the printer before attending the opera, or, in some cases, through a bookseller whose name was printed on the title page. The most important bookseller for librettos during Faustini's time was Giacomo Batti, whose shop was in the Frezzaria, near Piazza S. Marco. The first reference to Batti appears on the title pages of *Giasone* and *Orontea* (1649), and the practice of listing the bookseller becomes quite regular in the 1650s, especially for librettos printed by Giuliani (active 1641–65) or, later, Nicolini (first libretto issued in 1658). Nicolini, whose printing shop was in the nearby Spadaria, indicated that librettos could be purchased there as well, sometimes with the indication "Si vende in Spadaria e Frezzaria," indicating that

---

120 "Primo pensa l'autore di farne un regalo al signor Pavolo Michiele, il quale si compiaccia di farla stampare come dono fatto semplicemente a sè. Secondo, che essendo l'uso in simile espositione farsi sempre le dedicatorie, rimane con ciò libero il campo al detto signor Pavolo di dedicarla a chi più gli piace. Terzo, che non havendo il signor Pavolo nè obbligo, nè intentione di offerirla a veruno può farla publicare sotto nome dello stampatore con prenderne la dedicatoria a sè da quello diretta, come cosa capitatagli alle mani per fortuna." Vmc, PDC 1064, f. 277.

121 "quest'opera è un gratissimo dono fatto da l'Autore all'Illustrissimo & Eccellentissimo Signor Polo Michiele." *Il fantasma dittatore* (Venice, 1677).

they were available from either himself or Batti, even though names are not mentioned. The latest reference to Batti by name as a bookseller comes in 1660 (he died in 1663), although the phrase "Si vende in Frezzaria" appears through 1666 (one libretto published by Francesco Batti, perhaps Giacomo's son or nephew, was for sale in Piazza S. Marco).[122] Finally, four librettos printed by Nicolini in 1668 and 1669 indicate that they were for sale in the Spadaria, that is at Nicolini's own shop, but such references then disappear, at least through 1677: with the emergence of Nicolini as the nearly exclusive printer of librettos, it was no longer necessary to specify a point of sale; everyone knew where they could be purchased.

As mentioned above, the cost of the libretto to the purchaser is not entirely clear. A manuscript annotation in a copy of Giovanni Faustini's *Doriclea* (1645) indicates that Stefano van Axel purchased it at the theater for 26 soldi (1 lira 6 soldi).[123] A loose sheet of accounts in the Faustini papers for the season 1667/68 (probably for Giovanni Faustini's *Il tiranno humiliato d'Amore overo il Meraspe*) features an entry for the income from the sale of fifteen librettos ("opere") amounting to £17 s.5, or 1 lira, 3 soldi each.[124] Perhaps the 3-lira difference between the two figures represents the fee taken in by the seller (26 soldi for the *Doriclea* libretto and 23 for *Il tiranno humiliato d'Amore*).

Not all of the librettos sold ended up in the hands of ticket holders. In addition to those obvious customers responsible for the great majority of purchases, there was a continuing, if variable, market for librettos for use as gifts or by collectors. Some recipients were Venetians temporarily living outside the city. During the 1660/61 season, Giovanni Da Mosto sent to Ottavio Labia three opera librettos, including that for one of the biggest flops in the history of Venetian opera (Artale's *Pasife*) as well as for one of the most successful (Beregan's *Annibale in Capua*).[125] Polo Michiel, while living in Rome in December 1674, asked his brother Girolamo to send him the latest librettos in order to give them to acquaintances,[126] and in February 1683 his mother Marina Dandolo sent him new volumes along with a letter in which she judged the librettos to be "less than exquisite."[127] Other copies were sent to foreign enthusiasts: in 1670 the Venetian nobleman and librettist Pietro Dolfin supplied librettos of current operas to Johann Friedrich, the Duke of Brunswick.[128]

---

122 Batti died on 2 Nov. 1663 at the age of 47 (ASPV, Parrocchia di S. Giminiano, Morti, 1648–1670, f. 110). Francesco Batti published *Il tiranno humiliato d'Amore overo il Meraspe* in 1668.

123 The copy is housed in Apostolo Zeno's collection of librettos in Vnm. See Laini, *Raccolta zeniana*, 13. Laini's transcription cites the price as 26 "b."

124 ASV, SGSM, b. 188, ff. 197–98.

125 Da Mosto, "Uomine e cose," 117–22.

126 Vmc, MS PDC 1060, no. 17, 8 Dec. 1674. Michiel was the brother-in-law of the theater owner Giovanni Carlo Grimani.

127 "La poesia però per sè stessa non è troppo squisita . . ." Vmc, MS PDC 1068, no. 611, Venice, 25 Feb. 1682 m.v.

128 See letters written by Dolfin to the Duke printed in Rosand, *Opera*, 440, document 2 (26 Dec. 1669) and document 4 (19 Dec. 1670). Similarly, Gasparo Brisighella, who normally informed the Marquis Hippolito Bentivoglio about business matters, wrote in 1678 that he was sending the libretto of the opera performed the previous night at the Teatro S. Luca (ASFe, AB, b. 326, f. 812, 10 Dec. 1678; Monaldini, *Orto dell'Esperidi*, 351).

The librettos themselves, then, and the images of an opera that they might conjure up, held interest for a number of people of various ranks living outside of Venice, including princes and dukes. Expatriate Venetians also welcomed them as reminders of their city's most notable carnival pastime. The owners of librettos (whether or not they had attended the performances) often incorporated these works into their libraries. In November 1677 the library of the doctor Girolamo Rota (who, perhaps not coincidentally, knew the prima donna Caterina Porri quite well) contained seventy-three librettos.[129] In any event, such collections must have been common enough that in the 1740s, Antonio Groppo was able to advertise, in his printed catalogue of Venetian librettos, that he could offer for sale complete sets, which he undoubtedly assembled for the purpose, covering the entire period from 1637 to the date of purchase.[130] At least two of the collections in modern libraries appear to be the result of such an operation: that belonging originally to Apostolo Zeno, now in the Biblioteca marciana, and the one in the library of the University of California, Los Angeles.[131] Librettos, then, differed from a more typical book purchase. They might first serve as aids to the appreciation of an opera, and then as mementos for members of the audience; they also had a value for opera aficionados who had been unable to attend the performances, and for book collectors.

The extant copies often tell the story of whether they were purchased for use in the theater or in the home. Some of those read in the theater show the telltale signs of the candles employed for illumination: one can imagine the operagoer in a semidark theater bringing the libretto close to a candle to be able to follow what was going on, or holding a candle right above the libretto; in either case, the resulting wax drippings are clearly visible. Manuscript notes in some extant copies also that indicate the reader was attending the opera; a number also feature scribblings of various types, often of sums. One spectator even composed poetry describing the various singers and the scenery, which he later inserted into his copy of Giulio Cesare Corradi and Giovanni Legrenzi's *La divisione del mondo* (1675)![132] Other surviving copies are pristine, and might have gone directly onto a collector's bookshelf.

Destination and Use of the Income from Sales

At a price of something over 1 lira for each copy, the income from libretto sales, combined with a dedication gift, could have amounted to a considerable sum. If a printer managed to sell all 2,000 copies (the number mentioned by Curti for the initial printing of *Doriclea* in 1665/66) at a price of 26 soldi, the gross income would have been over 400 ducats. If one quarter of that were the actual cost of the printing, and the same again the combined fees of printer and seller, the librettist might have made, from sales alone of a successful opera, 200 ducats.

129 ASV, AN, Atti, b. 3919, f. 288ᵛ.

130 Groppo, *Catalogo di tutti i drammi*, index, 31.

131 On the collection in Vnm, see Laini, *Raccolta zeniana*; on the UCLA collection see Alm, *Catalog of Venetian Librettos*.

132 See Fabbri, "Recensione 'in rima'."

An incident from 1679 confirms not only the procedure of the printer taking the initial financial risk for printing the libretto (see above), but also shows what could happen when sales were not as high as expected. On 25 May 1679 the printer and bookseller Francesco Nicolini described how Camillo Badoer's first libretto, *Sesto Tarquinio*—performed at the Teatro S. Luca the previous season—had produced about 183 ducats in gross sales (that is, without deducting Nicolini's expenses for paper, binding, etc.).[133] Rather than turning the money over to Badoer directly, Nicolini, under the librettist's instructions, used the money to pay off some of Badoer's debts, specifically for clothing, shoes, a hat, a sword, and silver buttons. These deductions amounted to £1,090 s.12, or 47 lire short of the total sales. As these remaining 47 lire were not enough to cover the printing expenses, Nicolini subtracted those costs from the income generated by the dedication (by Badoer to Ferdinando Carlo, the Duke of Mantua, the patron of the composer of the opera, Giovanni Battista Tomasi), which apparently was also in his hands. If the cost of a libretto to the purchaser were £1 s.6, Nicolini's figure of £1,137 s.12. would have accounted for the sale of 910 librettos (it is unclear if additional income had been collected from sales at the theater and other sale points in the city). In this case, even if libretto sales may have fallen below the author's expectations, they helped to provide him with a new wardrobe, which he may have worn to view his first creation for the stage.

DESTINATION OF THE INCOME WHEN THE LIBRETTIST IS NOT INVOLVED   The procedures regarding income varied from the norm when a preexisting libretto was revised for a new production. Only one contract survives concerning compensation to a librettist for a revision. In October 1667 Aurelio Aureli made some changes to a version of *Eliogabalo* then being set by Cavalli. As a reward for that help, Faustini would share the printing profits with him, and arranged it so that Aureli would reap the benefits of the dedication.[134] This document may result from an unusual situation, or merely the fact that the agreement had been drawn up by two lawyers, although no such contracts survive between Faustini and the lawyer Beregan for revisions to Giovanni Faustini's librettos.

Some opera productions, however, lacked the direct participation of librettist or reviser (principally, if the librettist was deceased or had left the city, or if the production were a revival or a new setting of an old libretto); in this case, the responsibilities for printing the libretto necessarily fell to others, most often, probably, the impresario. This being the case, he or his company would have profited from the sale of such librettos. By mounting his brother's works (or attempting to do so) rather than newly minted ones, Marco Faustini could both honor his memory and ease his own operating expenses. As a result of Faustini's productions that featured missing or deceased librettists—Giovanni Faustini as well as several others—a few costs associated with the production of librettos found their way into his papers.

---

133 ASV, AN, Atti, b. 1184, f. 85ᵛ, 2 Dec. 1679. This production was a notable failure; a letter from Giovanni Legrenzi reports that the poetry and music did not please the audience, and that at times no more than thirty or forty tickets were sold (see Monaldini, *Orto dell'Esperidi*, 351).

134 For the agreement between Aureli and Faustini, see ASV, SGSM, b. 194, f. 31, 10 Oct. 1667.

One sheet of accounts with expenses for the 1667/68 season includes a payment of 4 ducats for the manufacture of the copper plate for the engraving of the frontispiece, a fee that probably included the payment to the artist as well.[135] That same sheet includes a fee for binding some of the librettos in velvet; these special copies would probably have been presented to important personages, and kept by the partners themselves.[136]

For the production of *L'incostanza trionfante* (1657/58) Faustini arranged for a different sort of relationship between his company and a printer, Salvadori, resembling in some respects the one that Pellicani drew up with Batti and Zulian the next year (see above). As we saw in chapter 3, the printer Salvadori[137] agreed to pay Faustini's company 200 ducats in advance, print the libretto at his own expense, and provide one hundred bound copies (as in the case above, probably to be presented to important guests and boxholders, as well the members of the company and their friends).[138] The genesis and printing of this libretto, as mentioned above, was one of the most complicated of the mid-seventeenth century. The foreword states that Francesco Piccoli did not complete the libretto, as he was called out of town; the agreement with Salvadori, then, probably indicates that Piccoli had left by November, and that his hope of a share of the profits had vanished with him.

The libretto, then, served a variety of functions. In its initial stages it generated the scenery, the costumes, and the musical underpinnings of the opera. Its end product, a published book, served as a source of income for the printer and librettist, as a means of glorifying a patron or important personage, and as a collector's item and memento of an evening's entertainment.

135 ASV, SGSM, b. 188, f. 197. In 1651 the company paid £2 s. 10 for a "rame da intagliar," that is for the unengraved plate (ASV, SGSM, b. 112). The artist's fee for the *rame* for the 1668 libretto, therefore, would have been just under 4 ducats. It is unclear whether this expense and the following one were for *Eliogabalo* or *Il tiranno humiliato*.

136 ASV, SGSM, b. 188, f. 197.

137 On Salvadori, see chapter 3, n. 71.

138 ASV, SGSM, b. 112, account book 1657/58, f. 10ᵛ. Six years earlier, during the 1651/52 season (when both librettos had been written by Giovanni Faustini), Faustini also received money from a bookseller: seven payments (a total of £509, or nearly 83 ducats) with no dates specified; they probably represent the profits from the two librettos of that season, in this case again, going back to the company itself (ASV, SGSM, b. 112, account book 1651/52, f. 44).

CHAPTER SIX

THE COMPOSITION AND THE
PRODUCTION OF THE OPERA SCORE

One of the impresario's first tasks for any upcoming season was the hiring of the composer.[1] His considerations were several: whether to recruit a composer with abundant experience or fame (who might demand a large fee), or, instead, hire a novice to the craft; whether to choose a local composer or a foreigner; whether the composer would supply both operas for a "two-bill" season, or only one; and whether the agreement would encompass more than one season. Unlike the librettist, who, as we saw in chapter 5, received his monetary compensation from the sales of the libretto and the fee for the dedication, the composer was paid by the impresario. The contract eventually agreed upon between impresario and composer, therefore, included provisions regarding the fee for composition, the schedule of payments (sometimes a matter of dispute), and whether the composer would be present for rehearsals and performances. The compositional process itself could not begin until the librettist supplied the poetry, and the composer often needed to consider the individual singers who would be performing.

SELECTION OF THE COMPOSER
BY THE IMPRESARIO

When opera production first began in Venice, only one composer long active there—Claudio Monteverdi—had experience in the genre. Monteverdi, however, maintained his silence during the first years of Venetian operatic activity; as others have written, it is likely that the maestro di cappella of S. Marco consciously chose to absent himself from the fray, whether for reasons of propriety (he held one of the most renowned and coveted musical positions in Italy) or of health.[2] As is well known, the impetus for the operatic enterprise came from outside the Venetian sphere, at first in the persons of Francesco Manelli and Benedetto Ferrari, who

---

1 As we saw in chapter 5, only rarely during the mid-seventeenth century did an impresario bypass all of these complications and opt to present a revival.

2 On Monteverdi's entrance into the field of Venetian opera, see Rosand, "Bow of Ulysses," and Carter, *Monteverdi's Musical Theatre*, 237–38.

composed the operas for the initial two seasons.[3] As the business of opera became more established and successful in Venice, other foreigners traveled there: in particular the Parmesan Francesco Sacrati came with the express purpose of mounting a new opera, La finta pazza, and he composed at least three others in subsequent years. Indeed, for most of the first decade of opera in Venice, only three local composers participated: Monteverdi (whose first new work for the Venetian stage appeared in 1640), Francesco Cavalli, and Giovanni Rovetta.[4]

For the earliest opera companies in Venice, selection of a composer was not an issue, as they each included one or two: Manelli and Ferrari at S. Cassiano, and then Cavalli at the same theater (for more on these companies, see chaps. 1 and 4). A later variation of this sort of arrangement obtained at S. Luca beginning in 1660/61, for Daniele da Castrovillari, who composed the operas for the first two seasons.[5] As the business of opera grew (and financial aspects became more complicated) the self-contained company was no longer the norm, so that the impresario had to find someone outside the company willing to take on the task for a fee.

One solution was for the impresario to come to a contractual agreement with a single composer (who would therefore become the "house composer") to provide the music for all the operas presented in the theater; that is, the composer would remain a stable fixture, while the singers, and possibly the librettist, might change from year to year. Marco Faustini and his partners enjoyed this arrangement at S. Cassiano in 1658, when Cavalli signed a three-year contract (see below). In other cases, either the agreement may have been informal, or records of it have not survived. In the first two seasons at S. Aponal, for instance, Cavalli supplied the music for Giovanni Faustini's librettos, and his operas may even have appeared exclusively at that theater, although no formal contract is extant; Cavalli evidently had found it in his interest to continue the collaboration with his librettist that had brought him considerable success in other theaters.

As the popularity of opera grew in Venice, the availability of composers became even more of an issue. During the mid-seventeenth century, very few impresarios enjoyed the luxury of a house composer hired to serve out a lengthy contract. Rather, most theaters featured a number of different composers; this practice, whether planned or not, may have allowed for greater stylistic variety and novelty. For example, during the early 1640s, the Teatro SS. Giovanni e Paolo presented operas by an impressively diverse, even cosmopolitan, group, the largest of any among the active theaters: in addition to Francesco Manelli, Claudio Monteverdi, and

3 The composers' exact whereabouts before 1637 are unclear. Ferrari had worked in Parma (and probably Modena), and Manelli had been active for a time in Rome. On Ferrari, see NG II, s.v. "Ferrari, Benedetto," by John Whenham. On Manelli, see NG II, s.v. "Manelli, Francesco," by John Whenham.

4 Rovetta composed only one opera, Ercole in Lidia, presented at the Teatro Novissimo in 1645.

5 When Castrovillari complained to the other partners that he had not received his full compensation for his labors (ASV, AN, Atti, b. 12674, f. 167v, 4 Apr. 1663), they responded that he still had not compensated them for his portion of the loss (f. 164v, 13 Apr. 1663). The formal agreement for this company has not yet been located. The S. Luca company differed from the first two at S. Cassiano, however, as they also included a choreographer and a librettist.

Benedetto Ferrari (discussed above), it included Marco Marazzoli, Filippo Vitali, and Filiberto Laurenzi, all of whom had worked most recently in Rome; during these same years S. Moisè featured Monteverdi, Ferrari, and Cavalli.[6] These lists—and they represent only two of the four active theaters—point up the activity of some composers at more than one theater. This circumstance resulted, in part, from the sheer multiplicity of theaters in the early 1640s, some of them producing more than one opera per season: the shortage of composers, or at least of those available or attractive to the employers, led both to their mobility, and to a lack of exclusivity between theater and composer.[7]

Impresarios ran into difficulties in part because the lives and careers of the composers were constantly in flux: as with any other population of skilled artisans—and perhaps more so—these men changed jobs, often moving from city to city; they suffered illnesses; and, of course, they died. By necessity, the impresario was forced to compensate for these ongoing changes. In this regard, the 1650s must have proved especially difficult: by that decade, nearly all of the composers responsible for operas during the earliest years of activity had either moved on to other locales or had died. The obvious exception was Francesco Cavalli, who became the most important figure among those working in Venice, but the growing genre certainly demanded more than a single composer, no matter how prolific. Cavalli was joined by younger men with considerably less experience: the Venetians Giovanni Battista Volpe (known as Rovettino), Pietro Andrea Ziani, and Gasparo Sartorio; Francesco Lucio from the nearby town of Conegliano; and two foreigners, the Tuscan Antonio Cesti and the Franciscan from southern Italy, Castrovillari.[8] The end of the decade and the beginning of the next brought changes once again: as will be discussed below, three of the active composers, Lucio, Ziani, and Cavalli, would leave the scene either temporarily or permanently. The procurement of scores, then, remained a challenge as the genre became a fixture of Venetian life.

On occasion, factors entirely beyond the control of a composer might precipitate a change in his employment, resulting in an alteration in impresarial politics. Such was the case for Cavalli at the conclusion of the 1651/52 season. Up until the time of Giovanni Faustini's death in December 1651, and sometimes also acting in the capacity of an impresario, Cavalli had composed most of his operas either for S. Cassiano, S. Moisè, or S. Aponal with Faustini as librettist. Once Giovanni Faustini died, however, and Marco Faustini had ceded control of S. Aponal to others

---

6 The list of composers who contributed to the pastiche *La finta savia* (SS. Giovanni e Paolo, 1642/43) was especially large, comprising—according to the libretto—Filiberto Laurenzi, Tarquinio Merula, Arcangelo Crivelli, Benedetto Ferrari, Alessandro Leardini, and Vincenzo Tozzi. The major part of the opera, however, was composed by Laurenzi.

7 Documentary confirmation concerning Benedetto Ferrari's involvement in the impresarial teams of both S. Moisè and SS. Giovanni e Paolo appears in ASV, AN, Atti, b. 2918, f. 263, 28 Feb. 1641 m.v. Cavalli wrote operas for S. Moisè as well as S. Cassiano, and the impresario Girolamo Lappoli's involvement at two different theaters probably led to the sharing of composers and other personnel. On Lappoli, see chapter 4.

8 The birth years for the composers active during the 1650s are: Cavalli, 1602; Ziani, 1616; Castrovillari, ca. 1617; Volpe, ca. 1620; Cesti, ca. 1623; G. Sartorio, ca. 1625 or 1626; Lucio, ca. 1628.

(see chap. 3), Cavalli was free to move to a different theater (his agreement had apparently been with Giovanni Faustini as impresario, not with the theater itself), so that he began a regular association with SS. Giovanni e Paolo. The death of Giovanni Faustini, then, apart from robbing Cavalli of his artistic collaborator, affected his operatic career in another immediate way: it would greatly complicate his loyalties to various impresarios and theaters in Venice. During the mid-1650s, Cavalli's regular commitment now lay with Giovanni Grimani, although he managed to supply an opera for Marco Faustini at S. Aponal in 1655/56. When Cavalli eventually decided to return to S. Cassiano (under Faustini's direction), his contract was exclusive: it prohibited any performances of his operas in another theater in Venice (see below for details).

Because of Cavalli's new contract (signed in July 1658), it was Grimani who had to search once again for willing composers. The nobleman's choice (or his impresario's) for the 1658/59 season—we do not know if it had been made before or after Francesco Lucio's death in August—was Giovanni Battista Volpe. The selection of Daniele da Castrovillari as the composer for the first opera of the 1659/60 season at SS. Giovanni e Paolo should probably be viewed as an indication of the paucity of available composers, or that some with more experience had declined a commission. Castrovillari had only come to Venice sometime the previous year and, to our knowledge, he had never before composed an opera.[9] Indeed, he may have been the most inexperienced opera composer ever to appear at the Grimani theater, or, at least, the one with the smallest reputation. When Cavalli's career took a new turn with his commission for an opera in France, however, Giovanni Grimani soon found a way to ameliorate his and Faustini's difficulties in finding a new composer: he brought the impresario to SS. Giovanni e Paolo, thus eliminating his operatic competition in Venice, if only temporarily.

OPERA COMPOSERS IN
MID-SEVENTEENTH-CENTURY VENICE

As we saw in the previous chapter, most librettists active in mid-seventeenth-century Venice were dilettantes—usually nobles or cittadini—who pursued other activities during much of their waking hours. In contrast, the composers of operas were professional musicians,[10] but, like librettists, during this era they did not apply themselves exclusively to that task: a composer of opera was, for want of a better term, a "generalist." Just as the burgeoning opera business created a need for more and more librettos and opera singers, it also, increasingly, forced composers of sacred and secular music to consider whether they, too, should try their hand at the young art form.

---

9 In August of 1669, Castrovillari testified that he had lived in Venice about eleven years, i.e., arriving around 1658. ASPV, EM, b. 84 (1669–70), f. 2548. Giovanni Battista Volpe had composed an opera for Grimani the previous year, but evidently was unavailable or chose not to accept another commission at the theater, or was simply not asked to return. It was Ziani who composed the second opera that year at SS. Giovanni e Paolo, his first at the theater.

10 In the eighteenth century, one "amateur" or dilettante would gain prominence as a composer for the Venetian stage: Tomaso Albinoni.

In order to understand what considerations a composer would have taken into account before accepting an opera commission, we must first appreciate what it meant to be a composer in the seventeenth century. The distinction between performing musician and composer during this time—at least toward the beginning of one's career—might well be blurred. The fundamentals of music theory—that is, the basics that one needed to know in order to practice the craft of composition—were taught to all musicians, whether their instruction came in the home, the church, the convent, or the monastery. Many composers of the Renaissance and the Baroque periods typically earned their regular salaries by singing or playing, often composing on the side, or in addition to their usual duties.

The most logical places for a male musician and composer to seek employment (for most composers were male) were the secular courts or the religious institutions of Italy and elsewhere in Europe. Except for those fortunate few in the most prestigious and high-paying posts, however, most professional musicians could not live satisfactorily on the wages from their court or church job. They earned a significant portion of their annual income by taking advantage of the numerous opportunities available in other venues, most notably providing music for the festivities of convents and confraternities, or teaching and performing in the homes of the wealthy.[11] Opera provided another opportunity, one that for composers (as with the lead singers) could be the most rewarding of all, as well as the most demanding.

Francesco Lucio, Pietro Andrea Ziani, and Francesco Cavalli: Opera as Supplementary Income

A look at the careers of three opera composers active in mid-seventeenth-century Venice—Francesco Lucio, Don Pietro Andrea Ziani, and Francesco Cavalli—provides some idea of how the benefits and burdens of opera composing might affect the life of a composer, and suggests the different motivations that might spur a composer to accept these sometimes difficult and disruptive commissions.

Francesco Lucio, the youngest of our group (born ca. 1628), came to Venice from Conegliano (about 65 to the northeast) some time during the 1640s. During parts of the 1640s and 1650s he was the organist at the parish church of S. Martino, a post that paid him 20 ducats annually;[12] by 1650 Lucio had succeeded his mentor, Giovanni Antonio Rigatti, as a teacher at one of the orphanages in Venice, the Ospedale degl'Incurabili.[13] He also served as a freelance musician at several feast-day celebrations at convents in Venice—each of which could have earned him several ducats for a day's work—and it is likely that that sort of occupation was more

---

11 The many money-earning possibilities for musicians in Venice were highlighted by the musician Jacopo Razzi, who wrote to Giacomo Carissimi after Monteverdi's death to encourage him to seek the vacant maestro di cappella position; see Culley, *Jesuits and Music*, 185–87 and 332–33. Monteverdi, writing from Venice in 1620 to Alessandro Striggio in Mantua, had commented similarly on the variety of opportunities available to a composer (see Monteverdi, *Letters*, ed. Stevens, 191).

12 ASPV, Parrocchia di S. Martino, b. 5–10, Cassa di fabrica dal 1636–1652.

13 Walker, "'Ubi Lucius,'" cxxxi.

or less commonplace for him.[14] Indeed, according to his will, Lucio owed money to "musicians" at the time of his death, probably as a result of directing such a performance.[15] One other source of income for Lucio would have been the small profits from the sales of his religious and secular vocal publications.[16] For this composer, then, the fees associated with the commission of an opera—probably from 100 to 150 ducats in his case—would have added greatly to his standard of living. In fact, given his ranking in the musical world of Venice, he may have earned as much from composing one opera as he did in all his other work combined. He started composing opera as a relatively young man, and had death not intervened in 1658, he most likely would have become a regular contributor to the genre.

Of the three composers under consideration, only Pietro Andrea Ziani was a native Venetian, apparently the son of a tailor.[17] During the 1640s (and possibly later) he was an organist at the convent of S. Salvatore (a house of Regular Canons of St. Augustine, the order to which he belonged), with a salary probably in the range of 30 to 40 ducats.[18] In 1640 he published two volumes of music, one secular and the other religious, and in 1650 he was accepted as a tenor in the famed Cappella di S. Marco, at 70 ducats per year.[19] Details regarding his work as a freelance musician are lacking. Ziani's first opera, *La guerriera spartana*, premiered in 1654; by 1657, after the performance of his *Le fortune di Rodope e Damira*, he had been awarded the important post of maestro di cappella at S. Maria Maggiore in Bergamo, with a salary of 225 ducats per year.[20] During this early part of his ca-

14 His service is documented at Santa Giustina, Santa Croce, and the Spirito Santo in 1645 (ASPV, EM, b. 46, f. 596, 24 Mar.; b. 45, f. 14ᵛ, 2 May and f. 68, 3 June); Sant'Anna in 1652 (ASMo, CAV, Venezia, b. 108, 128-VII/27, 2 Aug. 1652), and S. Martino di Burano in 1658 (ASV, Provveditori sopra Monasteri, b. 261, Riferte dei Capitani e Denuncie, 1631–85, 7 Mar. 1658). See J. Glixon, *Music for the Nuns of Venice*.

15 For Lucio's will, see Walker, "'Ubi Lucius,'" cxxxiii.

16 Lucio published two books of motets (*Motetti concertati*, Op. 1, Venice, 1649 and *Motetti concertati*, Op. 2, Venice, 1650), and one volume of secular vocal music (*Arie*, Venice, 1655). See Walker, "'Ubi Lucius,'" cxxxi.

17 According to a notarial document, Ziani's father, named Giovanni Battista, died in 1631, and in 1638 the family was living in the parish of S. Mattio (ASV, AN, Atti, b. 11011, f. 28, 24 Mar. 1638). One "M. Battista Ciani sartor," age 50, died in the same parish on 5 Aug. 1631 (VAP, S. Silvestro, S. Mattio, Morti, 1615–36).

18 No record of Ziani's salary has been located, but that for an organist at S. Salvatore in the mid-sixteenth century was 30 ducats (ASV, Monastero di S. Salvatore, b. 44, T. 93, f. 2). At the large Dominican house of SS. Giovanni e Paolo, the seventeenth-century organists Cavalli, Carlo Filago, and Massimiliano Neri were all paid 40 ducats per year (ASV, Monastero di S. Anna, b. 45, a misfiled book of receipts for SS. Giovanni e Paolo).

19 Ziani, *Partitura delli [24] motetti . . . libro primo, op. 2* (Venice, 1640). A book of secular works, *Fiori musicali raccolti . . . nel giardino de madrigali*, was also published that year. For his hire at S. Marco, see ASV, Procuratori de Supra, Atti, b. 145 (olim b. 75), 12 Apr. 1650. We would like to thank Rebecca Edwards for her diligence in tracking down the reclassified volume.

20 Ziani occupied the post of maestro di cappella at S. Maria Maggiore in Bergamo from 15 May 1657 until 21 June 1659. Colzani, "La cappella musicale," esp. 32–33. His salary was paid as 200 scudi, valued at £7 each, rather than the £9 6s. customary in Venice (the ducat remained during this period at £6 s.4).

reer, Ziani's typical fees were 150 ducats per opera; while the salary from his primary occupation was higher than Lucio's, the money earned from composing an opera would, nonetheless, have added substantially to his annual income. Although Ziani was a man of the church, and as a bachelor could have lived comfortably on his salary and freelance work, he makes clear in his letters (and this is supported by other evidence) that he played an active role in supporting various members of his large extended family, so that the financial rewards of opera composition may well have been an enticement.[21] His rise in stature during his years as maestro di cappella for the Dowager Empress Eleonora in Vienna (a post he accepted in 1662[22]), however, was such that in 1665 he remarked that he no longer needed to accept opera commissions for financial reasons.[23]

Francesco Cavalli's career in Venice bore similarities to both Lucio's and Ziani's. Like Lucio, he came to Venice from another part of the Venetian Republic, in his case from Crema, its most distant mainland outpost, some 27 miles southeast of Milan.[24] He entered the Cappella di S. Marco as a singer in 1616 at the age of 14 with a salary of 80 ducats; by 1635, now a tenor, his fees had risen to 100 ducats, the maximum at the cappella for a singer. He was for a time the organist at the large Dominican monastery of SS. Giovanni e Paolo (at a salary of 30 ducats), and his notable skills on that instrument earned him the position of second organist at S. Marco in 1639, with the substantial salary of 140 ducats. From 1653 through 1668 he earned the highest possible annual salary for an organist of the cappella, 200 ducats; in 1668 Cavalli became maestro di cappella. In addition to the added prestige of that position, his annual income from S. Marco rose to 400 ducats.

Perhaps owing to the importance of his posts at S. Marco, or merely because of the quality of his talents, Cavalli's services were often in demand outside that institution. Like Lucio (and perhaps Ziani), he was active as a freelance musician; in Venice his name appears connected with festival music for the leading confraternities, and for the wealthiest convents.[25] Cavalli also devoted a portion of his time to teaching. He taught at least two women who went on to become composers (Barbara Strozzi and Antonia Bembo), as well as a number of other students, both male

---

21 Ziani had at least seven siblings, and a number of them ran into financial difficulties of various types over several decades of the seventeenth century. Ziani's family will be explored in a future article.

22 See *NG II*, s.v. "Ziani, Pietro Andrea," by Theophil Antonicek, Harris S. Saunders, and Jennifer Williams Brown.

23 ASV, SGSM, b. 188, f. 82, 25 July 1665.

24 For a biography of Cavalli see *DBI*, s.v. "Caletti (Caletti-Bruni), Pietro Francesco," by Lorenzo Bianconi; additional details can be found in Glover, *Cavalli*, chapter 1, and Vio, "Ancora su Francesco Cavalli."

25 See *NG II*, s.v., "Cavalli, Francesco," by Thomas Walker and Irene Alm. Cavalli's freelance activities at confraternities include the Scuola Grande di S. Rocco in 1627, the Scuola di S. Domenico di Suriano in 1636, the Scuola (and convent) of the Spirito Santo in 1637 (see Glixon, *Honoring God and the City*, 287, 212, and 215, respectively). In addition to the Spirito Santo, he also served at the convent of S. Caterina in 1645 (ASPV, Curia Patriarcale, Sezione Antica, Monialium, Atti particulari riguardanti le monache, reg. 6, 1644–46, f. 43; see J. Glixon, "Images of paradise," 439).

and female.[26] Moreover, Cavalli's reputation earned him work outside of Venice; for example, he carried out several commissions for the Medici family during the 1650s, and composed an opera for Naples (*Veremonda*, 1652) and one for Milan (*Orione*, 1653).[27] Cavalli's situation also differed from Lucio's and Ziani's as a result of his marriage, in 1630, to Maria Loredana, the widow of Alvise Schiavina. After his wife's death in 1652 Cavalli possessed and managed a fair amount of property; he was, then, of the three men discussed, the one with the greatest income and financial stability and did not, perhaps, feel the same pressure to earn additional income as did some of his contemporaries.[28] Nonetheless, it was Cavalli who would become the most active composer of opera in mid-seventeenth-century Venice; he would also become—far and away—the most highly paid. This fame also took him away from Venice for several years in the early 1660s, during his sojourn in France.

A musician's life, then, comprised many commitments of time: salaried positions, regular freelance performances at religious festivals, teaching, and, finally, private performances. Musicians who directed the celebrations at convents and other venues were usually expected to provide newly written works for the occasion. Indeed, a popular and successful musician and composer in Venice was most probably a very busy one, too. The commission of a lengthy opera—usually taken on in addition to these other duties—demanded a great effort on the part of the composer. Although Ziani on occasion boasted of turning out a score in a matter of days, the more usual period seems to have been, instead, several months. When one considers that some composers produced two scores for a season (as did Cavalli and Ziani at times), as well as occasional scores for theaters outside of Venice, we can begin to appreciate the burden that could be placed on these sought-after men.

Foreign Composers and the Venetian Stage during the 1660s

The changing market not only provided opportunities for local composers to enter the opera business, but stimulated the aspirations of foreigners as well. Because operas in Venice were attended by visitors from many parts of Italy as well as from elsewhere in Europe, it might be expected that composers from outside Venice would wish to enter the arena to further their careers. One such hopeful entrant was Giovanni Legrenzi, a northern Italian with some knowledge of the

---

26 On Strozzi, see Rosand, "Barbara Strozzi," 257. On Bembo's early life, see Laini, "Musica di Antonia Bembo," and Fontijn, *Desperate Measures*. Cavalli also is recorded in 1645 as the organ teacher of a young daughter of the Grimani family while she was living at the convent of S. Maria delle Grazie (ASV, Provveditori sopra monasteri, reg. 104, Licenze, 1643–51, f. 15; see J. Glixon, "Images of Paradise," 432).

27 Glover, *Cavalli*, 24. Cavalli had written *Hipermestra* as well as a number of sacred works for the Medici. The composer's *Musiche sacre* (Venice, 1656) was dedicated to Giovanni Carlo de' Medici. *Orione* (1653) was performed in Milan in honor of celebrations for the election of Ferdinand IV, King of the Romans.

28 On Cavalli's marriage and family situation, see Glover, *Cavalli*, 15–16; and Vio, "Ancora su Francesco Cavalli."

Venetian music industry, having published his works there beginning in the 1650s.[29] In 1661 while in Venice, he sought to contact Giovanni Grimani regarding the possibility of an opera commission. Because the theater owner was out of town, Legrenzi eventually wrote to Hippolito Bentivoglio of Ferrara, his patron and employer, in an attempt to further pursue his goal: "I beg you to write to him, recommending my person, in case there would be a place in the next Carnival to compose one of the two operas they intend to mount in his theater."[30] The composer's efforts centered around Grimani rather than Faustini, Duodo, or Correr, quite likely because he already knew either Grimani or one of his associates. Indeed, it was Giovanni Grimani himself who, several years earlier, had sent (on behalf of a relative) a letter to Ferrara recommending that Legrenzi be hired for the post at the Accademia dello Spirito Santo in Ferrara,[31] and the Bentivoglios and the Grimanis were on friendly terms. Nonetheless, Legrenzi's initial attempt to break into the Venetian scene was unsuccessful, as shown by the operas eventually performed that year (both by P.A. Ziani). He would, however, achieve his goal of having an opera presented in Venice before too long, although not in the Grimani theater: two years later, in the 1663/64 season (as discussed in chap. 4), his *Achille in Sciro* was mounted at S. Luca.[32]

Offers to impresarios sometimes came from much farther afield, however. An impresario's system for the recruiting of singers could also furnish information regarding composers. As a number of singers traveled from Rome to Venice, they, or their contacts, came to know of composers in Rome eager to have their works performed in the opera industry's leading venue. In 1665 one of Faustini's Roman agents, the lutenist Arcangelo Lori, urged the impresario to consider that city as a source for scores: "You indicate that you have on hand beautiful librettos; I would exhort you to have them composed in Rome if Cavalli cannot set them to music; I know that the city [Venice] would appreciate them more, being able to hear a variety of styles . . ."[33] Curiously, no opera from Rome made its way to Venice during the 1650s and 1660s, even though precedents for such a practice can be seen during the early 1640s. In 1641 Filippo Vitali composed *Narciso et Ecco immortalati*—on a libretto sent to him from Venice—while still in Rome, where he was able to recruit local singers for his work.[34] Marco Faustini preferred, however, to hire local (or northern Italian)

29 By 1661 Legrenzi had published six books of music in Venice, four sacred and two instrumental collections: *Concerti musicali per uso di chiesa* (1654), *Harmonia d'affetti devoti* (1655), *Salmi* (1657), *Sentimenti devoti* (1660), *Sonate, libro primo* (1655), and *Sonate da chiesa e da camera, libro secondo* (1656).

30 "La supplicarei volergli con sua raccomandare la mia persona se vi fosse luocho per il venturo carnevale di fare una delle due opere che si devono rappresentare nel suo teatro." ASFe, AB, b. 334, f. 143, Clusone, 20 July 1661, Legrenzi to Ippolito Bentivoglio; see Monaldini, *Orto dell'Esperidi*, 164–65.

31 ASFe, AB, b. 324, f. 163, letter from Giovanni Grimani to Cornelio Bentivoglio, 23 Sept. 1656. See Monaldini, *Orto dell'Esperidi*, 115.

32 For more on Legrenzi and S. Luca in the early 1660s, see chapter 4.

33 "Mi accena anco, d'haver per le mani opere bellissime, l'esortarei, quando il Cavalli non le volessi metter in musica, far le comporre in Roma, che sò la città le agradirebbe più, per sentire la varietà delli stili . . ." ASV, SGSM, b.188, f. 112, 28 Feb. 1665. On Lori, see chapter 7.

34 Much of our knowledge of the commission comes from letters written by Marco Marazzoli, who eventually collaborated on the project. See Fabris, *Mecenati e musici*, 482–83 and 486–88.

talent when at all possible. Indeed, the list of composers hired by Faustini—Cavalli, Ziani, Volpe, Antonio Sartorio, Cesti, and Carlo Pallavicino—is remarkably short and nearly uniformly local: of these composers, only Cesti was not a native or long-term resident of Venice or the Veneto.[35]

Composers' Considerations: Matters of Time and Health

Not surprisingly, composers found it difficult to maintain a balance among their various commitments. In 1665 Antonio Cesti's duties in Austria delayed significantly the composition of *Tito*.[36] In preparation for the 1655/56 season, Cavalli put his opera commissions ahead of his regular duties: according to a report of November 1655, at the encouragement of some "gentlemen" (possibly Giovanni Grimani and Giovanni Francesco Busenello) Cavalli left Venice altogether for the tranquility of the countryside in order to compose one of his two offerings for the upcoming season, this during a time when he most likely should have been playing the organ at S. Marco.[37] Pietro Andrea Ziani claimed to have composed portions of some operas while traveling ("in viaggio") in order to meet deadlines.[38]

Some composers had to obtain special permission from their regular employers before accepting a commission in Venice. The composer Carlo Pallavicino did this in 1666; just beginning to make his name on the Venetian stage, he wished to participate actively in the carnival season in Venice, and sought a leave of absence from his job as an organist at the Basilica of S. Antonio in Padua. The sequence of events is not entirely clear, but Pallavicino may have come to Venice in November or December to help prepare the first opera, *Demetrio*, returning to Padua for the Christmas festivities. He was back in Venice by 3 January when, immediately following the opening of the season, he wrote to the directors of S. Antonio asking for permission (for himself, as well as for two singers and a violinist) to be absent from the Basilica.[39] He and the others apparently felt confident permission would be forthcoming, and remained in Venice even though the license was not officially granted until the meeting of the S. Antonio directors on 30 January. With this finally in hand, he was free to remain in Venice for the conclusion of the run of the first

---

35 One other possible exception is Giovanni Antonio Boretti, the Roman who composed *Eliogabalo* for the 1667/68 season; he was not paid by Faustini, and may have been taken on by the Grimani brothers (the change in the opera came about after Faustini had agreed to leave the theater); see chapter 3. Boretti had earlier (1659–61) served in Padua, but his employment history from 1662, the year he apparently arrived in Venice, to his death in 1672 is unclear except for an evidently brief stay in Turin in 1663. See Bouquet, *Musique et musiciens à Turin*, 210, and *NG II*, s.v. "Boretti, Giovanni," by Ellen Rosand and Beth Glixon.

36 For a thorough accounting of Cesti's travails during the composition of *Tito*, see Schmidt, "An Episode."

37 From a letter of Paolo del Sera to Grand Duke Ferdinando II of Tuscany, Venice, 20 Nov. 1655. See Kirkendale, *Court Musicians in Florence*, 392, n. 140. The two operas were *Erismena* and *Statira*.

38 ASV, SGSM, b. 188, f. 226, 3 Nov. 1665, letter of Ziani to Marco Faustini.

39 Billio D'Arpa, "Documenti inediti," 138.

opera, which came on 12 February, go back to Padua for the important feast of the Holy Tongue of S. Antonio on 15 February (as he promised he would in his request for the license), and then return once again to Venice to complete the composition and rehearsals of the second opera, *Aureliano*, which was scheduled to open near the end of that month.

One further consideration for some composers was the negative effect that such concentrated work as opera required might have on their health. Indeed, this was one of the arguments Cavalli used when describing to Abbot Buti his reasons for declining a commission in France (which he eventually accepted): "I have a very weak constitution by nature, aggravated by age and by the preparation done [before composing, and] afterwards by the work itself. I compose only when the fantasy takes me, and I am so little resistant to labor, that if I work an hour more than I am accustomed to, I immediately fall ill."[40]

In deciding to accept a commission, the financial rewards would probably have been foremost in a composer's mind. One hundred or more ducats was a sizable sum in the seventeenth century, and this amount could well pay for modest lodging and food for a year. Moreover, the composer would collect even more income (depending on the conditions of the contract) if he led the performances, usually the case if he were resident in Venice. The question of reputation also may have entered into the decision: even though the scores were not published, and librettos quite often failed to mention the composer's name, most of the audience would have been well aware of who had written the music; perhaps some composers hoped that success in the world of opera might lead to enhanced job opportunities (whether operatic or not) in the future.

COMPOSERS' CONTRACTS

Once impresario and composer had reached an agreement in principle, they negotiated a formal contract. In most cases this was in the form of a private agreement (*scrittura privata*): that is, it was drafted and finalized without the benefit (or cost) of a notary, although, as nearly always specified in the text, it was to hold the same legal weight as if it had been officially registered.

As in negotiations for any type of financial contract, each party would have had issues to settle. On the side of the impresario, the most important would presumably have been the date by which the opera should be completed in order to allow adequate rehearsal time for the singers; curiously, however, none of Cavalli's contracts specify such a date. Regarding the fee for the opera, the impresario naturally would have wanted to pay as little as he could but still insure a good product. From

---

40 "Io ho una complessione debolissima per natura, aggravata dall'età e dallo studio fatto, indi dallo esercitio. Compongo solo all'hora che me ne prende la fantasia, e sono sì poco resistente alla fatica, che, se un hora di più del mio uso m'affatico, sono subito amalato." Paris, Archives du Ministère des Affaires Etrangères, Correspondance diplomatique, Rome, 137, f. 263, 22 Aug. 1659; published in Prunières, *Opéra en France*, 393–94, and Glover, *Cavalli*, 168–69. Ziani, too, complained about his health, and its effect on his energies for composition (for example, in a letter to Faustini of 2 Aug. 1665, ASV, SGSM, b. 188, f. 75).

the composer's point of view, the fee certainly would have been the most significant factor, but also important was the scheduling of payments. Additional concerns were copying charges and whether or not the composer was expected to
direct the rehearsals and/or performances. Details of employment would have inevitably varied according to the stature of the composer: a newcomer could hardly
expect to earn as much as a veteran, nor to be granted the same advantages. In addition, certain aspects of the composer's duties depended on whether he was in
Venice or working in some distant city. Naturally, if the composer were present he
would have been available to make changes to the score as the need arose; this may
have resulted in higher fees overall.

Since the composer depended on the impresario for his fee, he had to trust in
the latter's honesty and business skills. Ordinarily, the payments would start only
after the performances had begun, and by that time the impresario would typically
have had many other bills to pay; the composer would have wanted payment as
soon as possible, certainly before the impresario's debts might overwhelm him,
while the impresario might wish to extend the schedule as much as possible. The
extant contracts typically specify a precise schedule that must represent negotiations between composer and impresario.

During Faustini's years at S. Aponal, a composer who conducted his own work
generated earnings in two different ways. Like the singers, he contracted for a
lump sum for his score that did not take into consideration the eventual popularity
of the work: ten performances would yield as much income as thirty. Like the instrumentalists, however, the composer in his capacity as musical director was paid
by the night: more performances meant more pay. During the 1650s Cavalli and
Ziani were able to add significant sums to their income by leading the orchestra
from the harpsichord, as some of the operas ran for thirty or more performances.
Cavalli's later contracts, however, rest on the principle of a lump sum payment for
composition and performing combined, thereby negating or equalizing the effects
either of a successful or unsuccessful opera.[41]

Cavalli's Contracts with Marco Faustini

Cavalli's three-year contract for S. Cassiano (dated 24 July 1658; see app. 3, doc. 1
for the complete text) was drawn up privately (in contrast to his previous two at
that theater). It specifies four obligations for the composer to meet:

1. That he compose the music, supplying the copies and originals at his
   own expense.
2. That he attend all of the rehearsals, adjusting the music as necessary.
3. That during these three years he will not perform a new opera in
   another Venetian theater, whether public or private. (Operas by Cavalli
   could be performed in other cities, however.)

---

41 For Cavalli's relationships and contracts with several impresarios, and a comparison with his
contemporaries, see B. Glixon, "'Poner in musica." For more on the relative success of some of the operas at S. Aponal and S. Cassiano, see chapter 11.

4. That he play the first keyboard instrument for every performance with no further compensation; should he be absent because of illness or another impediment, he must substitute someone appropriate at his own expense.[42]

The obligations of Faustini's company were straightforward. They were to pay Cavalli 400 ducats, with the following schedule: 150 ducats after the first perform-ance, and thereafter 50 ducats after every five performances. Under this agreement, then, the composer would have been "satisfied" after twenty-six performances.

Undoubtedly the contract was beneficial to both sides: Cavalli was guaranteed to receive 400 ducats (twice his annual salary as organist at S. Marco), for which he had to compose only one opera, rather than two. Faustini's company was guaranteed the exclusive services of the most famous opera composer in Venice, forcing the other active theater, as we saw above, to rely on less prestigious talents. One item missing from the contract is any requirement of a date by which the score had to be deliv-ered, so that the company evidently had no protection in this regard.

We can gain some appreciation of the contract's benefit to Cavalli if we look at the accounts for the 1658/59 season, the first covered by the agreement. In that year, Cavalli's *Antioco* was performed twenty-four times; the performances did not begin until the end of January, but then occurred almost nightly, finishing on 24 February, the day before Carnival ended. Cavalli was paid on 26 January, 3 Febru-ary, 11 February, 16 February, and 22 February.[43] During the 1651/52 season, oper-ating under a different arrangement, Cavalli had been paid 150 ducats per opera, plus £40 per night for conducting. Under that older system, the twenty-four per-formances of *Antioco* in 1659 would have netted him about 155 ducats, which, added to the composition fee of 150 ducats—the payment he had received for *Cal-isto*, *Eritrea*, and *Erismena*—would have brought the total to 305 ducats.[44] Certainly, in 1658/59 season the contract worked to Cavalli's advantage, increasing his in-come by about 30 percent.

While Cavalli's 1658 contract may be viewed as straightforward and rather un-exceptional, his next one with Faustini, drawn up nine years later, raises more questions.[45] It came in the impresario's last year at SS. Giovanni e Paolo, 1667/68, and the terms were even more to the composer's advantage, not surprising given his prominence in the field: he was to earn 450 ducats, 50 more than in his earlier

---

42 The contract is also published in Becker, *Quellentexte*, 72–73, and is discussed in Glover, *Cavalli*, 23 and Rosand, *Opera*, 210, with excerpts of the contract on 435–36. The references here and elsewhere to first, second, and third instruments (probably harpsichords or possibly theorbo) are never clearly ex-plained. See chapter 8, n. 24.

43 Cavalli should have been paid 50 ducats on 21 Feb. according to the schedule specified in the contract; by that time, however, Faustini knew that the twenty-six performances needed to meet the payment schedule could not take place by the end of Carnival. Instead, he paid him 100 ducats on 22 Feb., two days before the last performance.

44 We do not know if Cavalli, by 1658, might have been paid more than 150 ducats for the compo-sition of *Antioco*.

45 ASV, SGSM, b. 194, f. 50, 29 June 1667.

contract with Faustini. For some reason the clause prohibiting the composer's works in competing theaters in Venice did not appear; perhaps Faustini already knew that there was little likelihood of that happening, perhaps for reasons of health.[46] More problematic is the absence of any reference to the composer's duties at the performances: only Cavalli's presence at rehearsals is specified. Faustini's omission suggests that Cavalli might not have felt able to perform (thus increasing the value of the commission even further). In the end, Cavalli's participation was not needed, as his opera, *Eliogabalo*, never saw the stage, for it was substituted some time during the winter of 1667/68 with Boretti's opera of the same name (see chaps. 5 and 11). The fate of Cavalli's *Eliogabalo* brings home the advantage of this type of contract to the composer: even when performances of an opera were curtailed or canceled—whether by ruling of government, illness of singers, or some other calamity, or by disfavor with the public—the composer nonetheless gained his full reward. Having supplied the requisite commodity, Cavalli received his 450 ducats.

Cavalli's Other Contracts at S. Cassiano

Cavalli had signed two previous contracts at S. Cassiano, in 1644 and 1648, both of them registered in the acts of Venetian notaries.[47] They contain a number of fascinating details, but are more difficult to assess than the agreements discussed above, as they are not "pure": they represent the attempts of two separate managements at S. Cassiano to hold on to Cavalli's services after the composer had ceased to operate the company, and so contain financial details pertaining to old debts (see chap. 4). Two elements of the 1648 contract are of particular interest. First is the extraordinary manner of payment for Cavalli's composing fees (150 ducats) for one opera, which was, in the event, his very popular *Giasone*:[48]

> The said Signor Cavalli must compose the music for the said opera, and the said Signori Maestri and Castoreo, in compensation for that composition, will pay in cash to the same Signor Francesco, 100 silver scudi [i.e., 150 ducats], to be paid in this manner: that is, when the said Signori Maestri and Castoreo give to Signor Francesco the first act of the opera, they will immediately pay him 40 scudi; with the consignment of the second act, 30 scudi; and with the consignment of the third act, the remaining 30 scudi, without opposition.[49]

---

46 That season S. Luca was unable to find a composer for a new score, and presented two revivals, Sartorio's *Seleuco* and Legrenzi's *Tiridate* (a revision of *Zenobia e Radamisto*, first presented in Ferrara in 1665).

47 See Morelli and Walker, "Tre controversie," 98–100.

48 Ibid., 114 (Doc. B 21, 25 Apr. 1648).

49 "primo: Detto Signor Cavalli doverà componer la musica a detta opera, et detti Signori Maestri, et Castoreo per intiera sodisfatione di detta compositione sborsaranno in contanti allo stesso Signor Francesco scudi cento d'argento, quali doveranno esser pagati in questo modo, cioè, quando detti Signori Maestri et Castoreo consigneranno a detto Signor Francesco il primo atto dell'opera sborsaranno immediate prontamente scudi quaranta, nella consegna del secondo atto scudi trenta, et nella consegna del terzo atto li restanti scudi trenta senza alcuna contraditione." ASV, AN, Atti, b. 6673, f. 15ᵛ, 25 Apr. 1648.

If we can believe the wording of the contract, Cavalli was to be paid upon receipt of the libretto, that is, even before the composition of each act had begun. Why would the impresarios—a civil servant and a painter—have consented to pay Cavalli so early in the process, at a time when their income would have been limited? Perhaps Cavalli mistrusted the impresarios, who were neither experienced nor, presumably, wealthy, and had initially been unwilling to compose an opera for S. Cassiano. His plan may even have been to work exclusively with Giovanni Faustini at S. Moisè rather than lend his services to S. Cassiano. It is certainly possible that only with this unusual form of payment were Castoreo and Maestri able to obtain his services. Here, then, we may begin to see evidence of Cavalli's expertise in dealing with impresarios, and how he must have sought to use the system to his greatest advantage.[50]

A second provision in the contract pertained to Cavalli's nightly conducting wages, which were to be combined with those for the singer Amato Riminuzzi, a young castrato (and perhaps Cavalli's student) who sang at the Cappella di S. Marco, where Cavalli was also employed: "Whenever the opera is performed, Signor Cavalli must attend personally to play [the harpsichord] and direct the opera, and also Signor Amato da Rimini must sing, for which service the said Signori Maestri and Castoreo will pay Signor Francesco 9 silver scudi in total for the two of them each evening that they perform."[51]

Problems with Communication: Two Unsuccessful Negotiations between Faustini and Cavalli

The documentation surrounding Venetian opera of this period is such that, for the most part, we are aware only of successful outcomes concerning the hiring of opera composers: each completed opera score represents a contract that achieved fruition. Indeed, Cavalli's extant contracts provide us with nearly all we know about how an influential composer could enter into an agreement that suited his needs and inclinations. These finished documents, however, cannot offer a full picture of how the various terms were reached, and in most cases—unlike the situation regarding the recruitment of some singers—we are unaware of problems arising during the negotiations, or of dashed hopes on both sides. Two separate

---

50 On a few occasions, even Faustini, for reasons we cannot determine, paid some of the composers' fees in advance: in Apr. 1661, more than six months before the score would be needed, Ziani was apparently paid 100 ducats for *Medea placata* (ASV, SGSM, b. 118, f. 55); Pallavicino received half of his 200-ducat fee for the 1667/68 *Il tiranno humiliato d'Amore overo il Meraspe* in June 1667 (ASV, SGSM, b. 194, f. 47); and Cavalli was paid a 25-ducat advance in July of that same year (for the never-to-be-performed *Eliogabalo*; ASV, SGSM, b. 194, f. 51).

51 "Doverà il signor Cavalli quando si reciterà l'opera assistervi personalmente esso a suonare, et regolar l'opera, et anco il Signor Amato da Rimini a cantare, per intiera ricognition de' quali doveranno detti signori Maestri, et Castoreo pagare a detto Signor Francesco nove scudi d'argento per ogni sera, che si reciterà in tutto fra tutti due . . ." ASV, AN, Atti, b. 6673, ff. 15ᵛ–16, 25 Apr. 1648. Cavalli was also assigned, as a gift, a palco in the theater, free of charge. The 9 scudi awarded each night to Cavalli and Amato would have equalled 13? ducats per night.

episodes between Cavalli and Faustini's company, however, reveal instances of how communication could and did break down; in both cases the differences were irreconcilable, for Faustini went on to produce operas in those years by other composers.

CAVALLI'S COMMISSION FOR 1654/55 AT S. APONAL   In July of 1654 Cavalli wrote Faustini a letter in which he spelled out his grievances concerning an upcoming commission (see app. 3, doc. 2):

Most Learned and Most Excellent Sir, and Most Honored Patron,
So that your Most Excellent Lordship should see the affection that I have always held for you and your theater, and the reverence [I hold] for you, together with your Most Illustrious partners, I am informing you that recently I met with the Most Illustrious Duodo, and among the things we agreed upon to put into the contract were:
That there should be no mention of playing the third instrument, it being enough for me to explain things orally;[52]
That once the first performance is done, I should be given 100 silver scudi;
That every four performances I should be given 50 ducats until the complete payment of the 400 ducats.
These things were most courteously promised to me by the said gentleman, but not then followed in the contract, in which, instead of placing (as agreed) the 100 scudi the first evening, he has put them after the third evening. The 50 ducats instead of [after every] four [performances] he has put after [every] six, so that seeing that those things that were promised to me orally were not maintained in writing, I adjusted the contract, and since the Most Illustrious Duodo had sent it to me, I sent it back to him corrected in that way, and signed it, and those negotiations were completed this Lent. I see, however, from the length of these negotiations, and from the delays in concluding them, the small regard in which my person is held, so that, a month ago, I informed the Most Illustrious Duodo (with a letter I wrote) that I was quitting; but to string me along even more, he did not want to accept [my resignation]. Now, to reach a conclusion, I write this letter to you, which will serve for the entire company, and for your information, that if by the end of the day tomorrow, which will be the twenty-fourth of this month, you have not resolved this for me by signing the [corrected] contract I sent, I declare myself free from the agreement we have had up until now.
Your Most Excellent Lordship will not have occasion to complain about me, since it is up to Your Lordships to secure me, and I declare myself ready to serve you, as long as the said contract is signed; [my request] is not extravagant, but conforms with the previous agreement, nor does it vary in anything (regarding the form of payment) except for two evenings, more or less, for the payment of the 100 scudi, and for one evening less for that of the 50 ducats, something that I cannot believe would

---

52 But if Cavalli were to lead the opera, why would he play the "terzo instrumento" (rather than the first, or even the second)? Perhaps playing the first instrument, and directing, was understood, and this dispute referred to extra duties. It may be that the player of the third instrument was expected to prepare the orchestra or accompany the dances, and thus would need to attend extra rehearsals (chap. 8, n. 24). This matter remains cloudy.

be an occasion to not make me happy with a concession of such little importance. This serves, however, as I have said, as a warning, that if I do not receive the signature by the end of Wednesday, as above, I intend to be entirely removed from any obligation with your Lordships. I kiss your hand. Gambarare, 23 July 1654

The most devoted servant
Of Your Most Learned and Most Excellent Lordship
Francesco Cavalli[53]

Since Lent—that is, the conclusion of the previous carnival season—Cavalli had been negotiating a new contract for S. Aponal with Faustini's partner, Alvise Duodo. Although we will never be certain of how this impasse had been reached, several points stand out. First, Cavalli's compensation of 400 ducats represents the beginnings of the new system featured in the 1658 contract discussed above: it is the first documented instance in which the composer's fee for musical direction and that for composition were to be combined into a single sum. In addition, this quite possibly also represents a higher fee for the composition itself, going beyond the 150 ducats that were typical for the time. It is probable that the new arrangement bore some similarities to what Cavalli had received in the intervening two years at SS. Giovanni e Paolo; moreover, the details of the contract imply that he would be leading the performances at S. Aponal.

The most important issues to be considered are why Duodo, after having agreed to the major financial issues, would have substituted a different schedule and, more importantly, why these new terms become a stumbling block. Cavalli apparently felt his honor and reputation had been stained, and he gave Faustini an ultimatum.[54] Also significant here is the way Cavalli vented his grievance. The composer drafted his letter in the language of an "extragiudiziale," the sort of notice typically served by a public official on behalf of a complainant and registered in the acts of a notary. The accusatory tone of the letter would have been more than familiar to Faustini and his partners, but the mere fact that Cavalli chose to send a letter rather than an actual extragiudiziale may very well have showed the respect he felt towards Faustini, which he alluded to in the beginning of the letter. On Faustini's side—which is eloquent in its silence (partially, perhaps, owing to the loss of additional documentation)—we must wonder if the whole enterprise broke down simply because of an unspoken desire for it to do so, and if the payment schedule had been changed in the hopes that Cavalli would withdraw from a commission that was financially disadvantageous to Faustini and his company.

Perhaps in this case we should assume that neither party truly desired this contract to succeed. Indeed, it is quite likely that sometime after Lent pressure had been put on Cavalli by the Grimani theater to present an opera there. Directing the performances at S. Aponal would, perforce, have meant not doing so at

53 ASV, SGSM, b. 188, f. 14, 23 July 1654. See appendix 5, doc. 2. This letter is transcribed (with some misreadings) in Glover, *Cavalli*, 66 and Rosand, *Opera*, 435.

54 It should be noted that Cavalli, in his letter, states that he must have an answer from Faustini by the next day, which he calls "mercordi" (Wednesday), while the letter itself is dated 23 July, which fell on a Thursday. The composer most likely had drafted his letter earlier in the week and then forgot to change "Wednesday" to "Friday."

SS. Giovanni e Paolo. If Faustini and his partners had made a move during February 1654 to regain Cavalli as the jewel in their crown, the Grimanis, in competition, must have exerted greater pressure on their part in the succeeding months. We do not know if the aborted S. Aponal contract of 1654 represented an equivalency to or an improvement over that which Cavalli had enjoyed previously at SS. Giovanni e Paolo. We can only be certain of the dissolution of the agreement, and of Cavalli's continued presence at the Grimani theater (with his *Xerse*).[55] Any bad feelings between Cavalli and the management at S. Aponal were not long-lived, for he composed *Erismena* for the next season. The details of that contract, however, must have been quite different, for Cavalli was paid his fee of earlier years, 150 ducats; as he did not direct the performances, he must have been occupied in that capacity at SS. Giovanni e Paolo for his *Statira*.

CAVALLI'S COMMISSION FOR 1662/63 AT SS. GIOVANNI E PAOLO
On a later occasion Faustini and Cavalli once again struggled to reach an agreement, but this time the issues were even more basic: how many operas Cavalli would compose for the season. He had completed only two of the three operas specified in his 1658 contract, for his travels to France had prevented the fulfillment of the third, but we do not know if Faustini's attempts to rehire Cavalli related specifically to that contract, as by now the impresario was at SS. Giovanni e Paolo rather than at S. Cassiano. Two letters to Faustini survive concerning this affair, one from Cavalli, and the other from Nicolò Minato, Cavalli's librettist and lawyer.[56] Cavalli told Faustini that, having returned from France, he had resolved to write no more operas. Owing to the history of their past collaborations, however, he was willing to supply Faustini with one new work; he felt that since the carnival season was short, Faustini should recognize that one opera would be sufficient. Because Faustini desired two works, the composer proposed his opera that had been performed in France, *Ercole amante*, in addition to a new one. Both Cavalli's and Minato's letters make it clear that Faustini—perhaps unreasonably—still wanted two new operas by the master.

This incident demonstrates the kind of activity (usually invisible) that could take place during negotiations. Minato's letter describes how Cavalli had gone to see Giovanni Grimani himself, and had talked to various noblemen as well: according to the librettist, all of these men—Faustini's superiors—supported Cavalli's point of view.[57] In this affair both Faustini and Cavalli remained obstinate, for the published librettos show that the impresario indeed produced two operas during

---

55 Cavalli was also composing another opera during the fall of 1654: *Hipermestra*, this a commission for the Medici court. Act 2 of the opera bears the date "2 September" and two letters of Atto Melani point to the opera having been composed and rehearsed during this time. See Jeffery, "Autograph Manuscripts," 197–99.

56 For Cavalli's letter, dated 8 Aug. 1662, see ASV, SGSM, b. 188, f. 380 (Glover, *Cavalli*, 168–69); Minato's letter to Faustini regarding the commission for Cavalli appears in ASV, SGSM, b.194, f. 49. Although lacking both a date and a signature, Minato's letter can be placed in context by virtue of its subject matter: it repeats several points made previously in Cavalli's letter.

57 ASV, SGSM, b. 194, f. 49, undated.

1662/63, neither of them by Cavalli. We do not know what pressure Cavalli's supporters might have used in order to try to change Faustini's mind. We read in libretto forewords, from time to time, how a librettist was convinced to produce a new work by those in positions of power.[58] In this case, however, these two men who had known each other for several decades could not negotiate a settlement: neither man would flinch.[59]

If Cavalli's and Faustini's difficulties of 1654 and 1662 speak to a complete failure to achieve an agreement, in at least one instance with a different composer, Faustini was able to resolve a difficulty. Earlier sections in this chapter have argued in favor of the concept of a progression—whether smooth or not—from an offer, to negotiation, to a contract, and then on to composition. A letter sent from Pietro Andrea Ziani in Vienna, however, suggests that this might not always be the case. On 22 March 1665, the composer thanked Faustini for his offer of an opera commission; he did not decline the commission, but explained that he needed permission from his employer, both for his services and for those of the singer Giovanni Antonio Forni. Ziani's next surviving letter is dated nearly four months later, and the news it contains comes as a surprise: here he says that Faustini, without waiting to hear whether the composer had accepted the commission, and without settling on his compensation for the score, has already sent him portions of the libretto.[60] Clearly, Ziani's first letter had been couched in terms vague enough that allowed Faustini to believe that an agreement had tacitly been reached. In any event, Ziani, for whatever reason, decided to go ahead with the commission, whether or not that had been his original plan.

Salaries

In the previous section we saw, through a look at several contracts, how Francesco Cavalli's earnings rose from 150 ducats during the early 1650s to 450 in 1667. Even though these figures are not entirely comparable, owing to matters regarding fees for musical direction and the like, it is clear that as Cavalli's reputation rose, so did his compensation. As the Faustini papers supply data for seasons from 1652 through 1668, albeit with several gaps, they, along with scattered other documents, yield important information regarding whether there was a basic fee for composing an opera that remained more or less constant, or if other composers' earnings also rose over time. (See table 6.1.)

The fees for Ziani's operas serve as an indicator of trends; not only was he employed by Faustini over a long period, but he was ever ready to complain about his compensation, comparing it to that of Cavalli, Cesti, and even the singers. Ziani's first opera for Faustini's company was *Eupatra*. The impresario's records for that

58 Aureli, for example, in *Le fatiche d'Ercole per Deianira* (1662) says that he writes "to obey the one who commands me" ("per obbedire à chi me lo commanda").

59 Cavalli, having failed to reach an agreement with Faustini, eventually offered his services to Vettor Grimani Calergi at S. Luca, although, in the end, that theater did not present one of his works (ASMa, AG, b. 1573, 25 Dec. 1662). See chapter 4.

60 ASV, SGSM, b. 188, f. 82, 25 July 1665.

year lack any reference to Ziani's compensation for the opera, as he was paid by one of the other members of the company, but his fees for musical direction, £37 a night, came close to Cavalli's £40. Ziani's next two operas each brought him 150 ducats, that is, the same as Cavalli's at that time. In those years, then, Ziani may have felt quite content knowing that his services were valued equally to Cavalli's, even though the older man had over ten years' more experience in the field. As a comparison, during these years we find the young Francesco Lucio earning 100 ducats for the composition of *Gl'amori di Alessandro Magno, e di Rossane* (SS. Apostoli, 1651).[61]

Ziani's fees remained at 150 ducats until he traveled to Vienna in 1662 to begin his new position as maestro di cappella to the Dowager Empress (his service as maestro at Bergamo in the late 1650s had not resulted in increased fees). They then rose to 200 ducats, peaking at 250 for both *Doriclea* and *Alciade* in 1666. That same year, however, Cesti earned 350 ducats for composing *Tito* (directing fees did not enter into the figure, and Cesti was reimbursed for the copying of the score). The letters of both Cesti and Ziani show that they were aware—at least in general terms—of the fees paid to various composers. As a Venetian native, Ziani had many friends and associates who could supply him with juicy details, and Cesti's correspondence with both Nicola Beregan and the singer Giacinto Zucchi undoubtedly kept him, too, abreast of the situation in Venice. This tendency toward gossip regarding financial affairs led to an element of discontent among the composers, and must have made matters difficult for an impresario trying to maintain good relationships with them.

The Faustini figures are helpful not only in gauging the salaries of the most experienced composers, but also those of two composers at or near the beginning stages of their operatic careers. Antonio Sartorio's fees for *Gl'amori infrutuosi di Pirro* (1660/61), at just over 100 ducats—a figure that also includes some compensation for performing—show that a true novice certainly earned less for his efforts; indeed, the sum would seem to be nearly identical to that earned by Lucio ten years earlier. Pallavicino's *Il tiranno humiliato d'Amore overo il Meraspe* (1667/68), on the other hand, was his third opera, and by this time he had traveled northwards to take a post at Dresden; these factors, perhaps, enabled him to earn 200 ducats for his only commission for Faustini.[62]

By the late 1670s the usual fee for composing an opera had risen to 300 ducats, thus still well below Cavalli's during the 1660s. In the fall of 1680 Abbot Vicenzo Grimani wrote to Marquis Hippolito Bentivoglio considering the hiring of Petronio Franceschini: "When, however, Petronio should wish to come to Venice for the fees that have served for Negrenzi [Legrenzi], Sartorio, Ziani, and that we used last year with Pier Simone [Agostini], then I will most happily have him in SS. Giovanni e Paolo, and this is a fee of 300 ducats."[63] Indeed, Grimani's letter takes care

61 See B. Glixon, "Music for the Gods?"

62 ASV, SGSM, b. 194, ff. 47 and 21.

63 "Quando però Petronio voglia venirsene a Venetia col regalo che si prattica con Negrenzi, Sartorio, Ziani, che s'usò l'anno scorso con Pier Simone, io me ne valerò volontieri in S. Giovanni e Pavolo, e questo è di ducati trecento." ASFe, AB, b. 368, f. 378ᵛ, letter from Vicenzo Grimani to Hippolito Bentivoglio, 9 Oct. 1680; see Monaldini, *Orto dell'Esperidi*, 443.

TABLE 6.1. Opera Composers' Fees in Venice, 1650–1668

Composer	Opera	Theater	Year	Fees (in ducats)[a]
Francesco Cavalli	Giasone	S. Cassiano	1648/49	150 + musical direction
Francesco Lucio	Gl'amori di Alessandro magno, e di Rossane	SS. Apostoli	1650/51	100 + musical direction?[b]
Cavalli	Calisto	S. Aponal	1651/52	150 + musical direction
Cavalli	Eritrea	S. Aponal	1651/52	150 + musical direction
Pietro Andrea Ziani	Eupatra	S. Aponal	1654/55	unknown + musical direction
Cavalli	Erismena	S. Aponal	1655/56	150[c]
Ziani	Le fortune di Rodope e Damira	S. Aponal	1656/57	150 [+ musical direction]
Ziani	L'incostanza trionfante	S. Cassiano	1657/58	150 + musical direction
Cavalli	Antioco	S. Cassiano	1658/59	400 including musical direction, copying
Cavalli	Elena	S. Cassiano	1659/60	400 including musical direction, copying
Daniele da Castrovillari	Gl'avvenimenti d'Orinda	SS. Giovanni e Paolo	1659/60	200 + musical direction, copying
Antonio Sartorio	Gl'amori infruttuosi di Pirro	SS. Giovanni e Paolo	1660/61	102 including at least some payment for musical direction
Ziani	Annibale in Capua	SS. Giovanni e Paolo	1660/61	150 + musical direction
Castrovillari	Pasife	S. Luca	1660/61	150 + musical direction
Ziani	[Medea placata]?[d]	SS. Giovanni e Paolo	1661/62	150?[e]
Ziani	Gli scherzi di fortuna	SS. Giovanni e Paolo	1661/62	200 [+ musical direction]
Ziani	Le fatiche d'Ercole per Deianira	SS. Giovanni e Paolo	1661/62	200 [+ musical direction]
Castrovillari	Cleopatra	S. Luca	1661/62	150 + musical direction
Ziani	Amor guerriero	SS. Giovanni e Paolo	1662/63	200
Giovanni Battista Volpe (Rovettino)	Gli amori d'Apollo, e di Leucotoe	SS. Giovanni e Paolo	1662/63	200 [+ musical direction]

Ziani	Doriclea	SS. Giovanni e Paolo	Composed 1665/66, not performed	250
Ziani	Alciade	SS. Giovanni e Paolo	Composed 1665/66, performed 1666/67	250
Cavalli	Pompeo Magno	S. Luca	1665/66	450 including musical direction?[f]
Antonio Cesti	Tito	SS. Giovanni e Paolo	1665/66	350
Carlo Pallavicino	Il tiranno humiliato d'Amore overo il Meraspe	SS. Giovanni e Paolo	1667/68	200
Cavalli	Eliogabalo	SS. Giovanni e Paolo	1667/68	450[g]

Sources for the data include ASV, SGSM, bb. 112, 113, and 118 (receipt book), and a variety of documents from ASV, GP. On Lucio's compensation for Gl' Amori di Alessandro magno, e di Rossane, see B. Glixon, "Music for the Gods?"

[a] The indication "+ musical direction" means that payment for musical direction was in addition to the fee for the composition of the opera. The phrase [+ musical direction] enclosed in brackets indicates that documentation for separate fees for musical direction is not extant, but such earnings are likely to have occurred, given the presence of the composer in Venice and the other documentation. Unless noted, the absence of any indication regarding musical direction means that the composer was not in Venice during the performances.

[b] Although Lucio was required by his contract to direct the performances, he apparently did not do so every night because of a labor dispute; it is unclear whether he would be paid separately for this service. See B. Glixon, "Music for the Gods."

[c] Although Cavalli was in Venice during the performances of Erismena, he was engaged at SS. Giovanni e Paolo with his Statira. Giovanni Battista Volpe (Rovettino) conducted Erismena.

[d] Il Rimino indicates that an opera by this title went into rehearsal, but was dropped before opening night.

[e] Receipts survive for payments to Ziani by Faustini in this amount, without any indication of the opera; these probably represent the fee for the cancelled Medea placata.

[f] It is likely that Cavalli led the performances, especially given the size of the fee, but no confirming documentation survives.

[g] Although the fee is so large that one would expect it to include musical direction, the extant contract makes no reference to this service. The contract does require that Cavalli leave the original score with Faustini.

to emphasize the point that, by and large, all composers would earn the same fees at his theater.[64]

THE COMPOSING OF THE OPERA
AND THE PRODUCTION OF THE SCORE

Once the composer and impresario had agreed upon the fees and other conditions, and had the libretto in hand, the drafting and composition of the opera could begin. There are a number of questions that we might ask about the process. Did the composer set the libretto as given to him, or did he suggest changes, or even alter the poetry according to his own needs? How much did he need to know about the singers? How long did it take the composer to set the libretto? How were the various scores and parts produced, and who retained the score? Some of these questions are easily answered, others less so, owing to a lack of primary materials and documentary evidence.

Relationship between Composer and Librettist

One intriguing question, only in part suggested above, is the whole notion of collaboration between the librettist and composer at various stages of the project. As we saw in the previous chapter, the libretto was often assembled only a few months before the opera season was to begin, and then given or sent to the composer, sometimes act by act. It is unclear whether a composer would have had some influence on the subject matter and other elements of the libretto, that is, whether the librettist thought of his work as purely his own (subject, of course, to the approval of the impresario), or if he would have been open to suggestions from the composer (or others) as to plot elements and character motivations. Perhaps a seasoned composer such as Cavalli might encourage one of his librettists to write a particular kind of plot, or to emphasize a particular dramatic situation.

These issues are appropriate to consider particularly in the case of Cavalli, who maintained a close association with two of his librettists, Giovanni Faustini and Nicolò Minato. In 1641/42, Cavalli provided the 26-year-old Giovanni Faustini with the opportunity to launch a career as a librettist (see chap. 3). The two both lived in the parish of S. Vidal, and most likely had known each other for some time before beginning their artistic collaboration.[65] Nicolò Minato (only 20 years old at the time of his first opera) and Cavalli worked together, albeit with several gaps, from 1649/50 through 1666, and Minato often provided legal services for the

---

64 Salaries outside of Venice, however, were not always as high. Legrenzi received 200 ducats when composing an opera for the Medici theater at Pratolino during the 1680s (although the comparison is not necessarily an exact one, since in this case musical direction was probably not included). See Holmes, "Operatic Commissions," 162.

65 See appendix 2 on the role of parishes in Venetian social relationships.

composer.[66] In other words, Cavalli's relationship with his two partners may have been personally closer than the norm. It is possible, then (but entirely undocumented), that Cavalli, through his particular associations with Faustini and Minato, might have had some influence regarding the subject or even the structure of the libretto, a situation that might not have obtained with more occasional collaborators. Ellen Rosand has explored Cavalli's influence in the genesis of Aurelio Aureli's libretto Erismena, and how in the team's first collaboration the composer must have encouraged the librettist's borrowing from Giovanni Faustini's Ormindo (with the resulting reuse of some of the original music).[67] On the other hand, the structure and plot of Minato's first libretto, Orimonte (1650), would seem to indicate that Cavalli allowed the librettist free rein; it shows a certain amount of awkwardness, and Minato later declined to include it in his list of works: in this case, more intervention from the composer might have been helpful to the new librettist.[68] Certainly, the years of close contact between librettist and composer must have contributed to a streamlined product, that is, one more immediately suitable to the needs of the composer, and thus more quickly rendered into a finished work (in comparison to an operatic score where librettist and composer knew each other little or not at all).

Naturally a variety of relationships between composer and librettist were possible, ranging from close-knit to that of complete strangers. Unfortunately, we simply do not know how often composer and librettist (whether or not they were friends) met, or—if resident in different cities—corresponded during the process of creating the score. Indeed, perhaps this is one of the most intriguing questions of the time: did the composer and librettist collaborate in the true sense of the word (as in later centuries), or was their work accomplished, for the most part, quite separately? When it came to setting the text, did the composer, on his own initiative, substitute words or phrases more to his liking, and more appropriate to his musical conception?

Indeed, extant scores indicate that there might be various levels of changes between score and libretto during the compositional process. Peter Jeffery has shown through an examination of Cavalli's autograph scores how the composer altered his settings in different ways. While many changes were strictly musical, altering the shape of the vocal line, or shifting the balance between recitative and arioso, others concerned the text: certain verses might be excised and others added as the opera evolved. Still further corrections demonstrate that Cavalli's conception of the text/music relationship, and thus the text and music themselves, evolved during the period of composition.[69] We do not know, however, how often textual changes would have been made by Cavalli himself rather than by the librettist. In

---

66 See Glover, Cavalli, 24, 36.

67 See Rosand, "'Ormindo travestito'," 280–81 and Rosand, Opera, 202.

68 It was during the composition of Orimonte that Cavalli stopped work because of financial difficulties with the company. See Morelli and Walker, "Tre controversie." Had these problems not ensued, might Cavalli have worked harder with Minato to achieve a more polished libretto?

69 Jeffery, "Autograph Manuscripts," especially 178, 227–31. See also Rosand, Opera, esp. 201–2, 209–11.

some cases, the librettist, perhaps intentionally, wrote more poetry than practical to set to music.[70]

Letters written by Ziani and Cesti in preparation for the 1665/66 season provide different kinds of evidence on the issue of collaboration. Cesti's letters to the librettist Nicola Beregan regarding *Tito* discuss a wide array of topics, especially the availability of certain singers, but contain little about the composition of the score;[71] it is important to remember, however, that these letters were turned over to Marco Faustini precisely because they contained information important to the impresario, so that others concentrating more specifically on text-setting problems probably remained in the possession of the librettist. Ziani's situation was quite different from Cesti's, as he had the responsibility of setting first one, and then two librettos by the deceased Giovanni Faustini (*Doriclea* and *Alciade*).[72] Unable to write to the librettist himself, he was forced to correspond, instead, with Marco Faustini, who clarified questions regarding the text, as well as more general questions regarding the setting of (and corrections to) the poetry.[73]

In some cases—especially later in the century—the composer and librettist could be entirely unknown to each other, brought together through the impresario. Such was the case in 1673, when Cristoforo Ivanovich wrote to Giovanni Maria Pagliardi, who was to set his *Lisimaco*. The letter serves as an introduction, but also provides a general guide to working procedures. Ivanovich expresses his willingness to cooperate with the composer on a variety of issues: "with the honor of your most humane [letters], I await your frank judgments regarding the drama, in order to gain motivation for some improvements." He continues, "The distance between us would displease me, if your proven intelligence did not hold promise of that fruit that would ripen a personal communication, since you are able to distinguish meanings, understand affects, and express their force."[74]

The Composer and the Singer: Vocal Specifications

After resolving any difficulties regarding the libretto, the composer's next area of concern was the singers. The score was not composed in the abstract, but for a spe-

---

70　As Rosand has discussed, the librettos, through the use of *virgole*, indicate the omitted verses. The same markings, however, could also serve to indicate sections that had been set to music, but were cut before or during the run of performances, either because they were not successful, or because the opera was simply too long. For more on this issue, see chapter 5.

71　These letters are discussed in Schmidt, "An Episode."

72　See Rosand, *Opera*, 194.

73　On one occasion Ziani revealed that he was not sure of the meaning of a passage of the libretto. ASV, SGSM, b. 188, f. 226, 3 Nov. 1665. See also ASV, SGSM, b. 188, f. 354, 28 Nov. 1665, where Ziani mentions having received Faustini's corrections for the third act.

74　"Con l'onore delle sue umanissime attendo pure i suoi liberi sensi intorno al Drama per ricavare motivi di qualche perfezione . . . Mi spiacerebbe la sua lontananza, se la sua esperimentata Intelligenza non mi promettesse quel frutto, che maturarebbe una personale comunicazione; mentre saprà distinguer i sensi, comprender gli affetti, ed esprimere la loro forza." Ivanovich, *Poesie* (Venice, 1675), 372–74 (published in Becker, *Quellentexte*, 63–64).

cific theater and season, so that the composer needed to know the ranges as well as other particulars about the various singers. Ivanovich mentioned this in his letter to Pagliardi: "I suppose that you will receive the list of the singers, so that you can suit the music to the skill of their voices, that being the issue of greatest importance."[75] Nicola Coresi sent specific instructions for Francesco Cavalli in 1667 so that the composer might be more aware of the nature of his wife Antonia's voice.[76] This suiting of the part to the voice was important for all of the roles, not only those of the leading, star singers. A composer's familiarity with the corps of singers, then, could be of great assistance in the drafting of the opera. Indeed, Ziani took the liberty of assigning some of the opera's smaller roles himself—tracking the frequency of the on-stage presence of the various minor figures—in order to complete his task more quickly, i.e., without waiting to receive further instructions from Faustini via the post:

> I must tell you that you did not assign a singer to the role of Lerilda's boatman in the first scene of the third act, so, in order not to lose time, I wrote it as a bass part for Don Giacinto, who seems to me suitable (even more so because he has very little to sing), and that of Lerilda I have written for a soprano, since I see you have an abundance of them. All that remains is for Your Lordship to advise me (if you can do so in time) about [the casting of] the role in the third act for the old lady Elibea, which I do not see listed in the assignment of the other parts; I am thinking meanwhile, so as not to lose time, to write it for Signor Antonin da Muran, who sings the role of Idiotea, who, I note, does not appear on stage for quite some time before.[77]

Production and Revision of the Score

The composition of a score might take a number of months, as in the case of Cesti's *Tito*, or just a number of days, as in Ziani's *Annibale in Capua* and Antonio Sartorio's *Massenzio*.[78] The music was often transmitted to the impresario in single

---

75 "Suppongo, che riceverà la lista de' musici, per adattare all'abilità delle loro voci la musica, in ciò consistendo la maggior importanza." Becker, *Quellentexte*, 64.

76 ASV, SGSM, b. 188 , f. 164, 18 June 1667.

77 "Devo dirle che la parte del nocchiero di Lerilda nella prima scena del terzo atto non è stata da Vostra Signoria assignata per chi la dovrà recitare, che per ciò io per non perder tempo hò messa la parte del nocchiero in basso per Don Giacinto che mi pare propria (tanto più che ha pocchissima parte), e quella di Lerilda l'ho posta per un soprano che vedo ne ha d'abondanza. Resta solo che anco Vostra Signoria mi avisi (se pure sarà in tempo) la parte nel terzo atto per la vecchia Elibea, che non la vedo notata nella destinatione delle altre parti, che io penso in tanto (per non perder tempo) di farla per il Signor Antonin da Murano che fa la parte di Idiotea, che osservo non comparisce in scena un tempo fa." ASV, SGSM, b. 188, f. 354, 28 Nov. 1665. See Rosand, *Opera*, 214–15. Tim Carter has analyzed the roles of Monteverdi's operas in order to compute the number of singers necessary for the casts, reaching the conclusion that assigning one singer to multiple roles was the usual practice. See Carter, "Singing Orfeo" and Carter, *Monteverdi's Musical Theatre*, 96–108.

78 Cesti declared his intention to compose one act per month in a letter of 16 Aug. 1665. For Ziani, see ASV, SGSM, b.188, f. 279, 9 May 1666, where he claims he wrote *Annibale* in five days, or f. 82, 25 July 1665, where he remembers it as six days. A letter written to the Duke of Brunswick claimed that Sartorio's *Massenzio* had been written in thirteen days; see Rosand, *Opera*, 212–13.

acts, or even in smaller portions, and sent to the singers in the same manner. Nicola Coresi wrote to Faustini in September 1666 that he had, the week before, received his role for one act of *Alciade*, and then, on that very day, the remainder, commenting that he had had to work hard to put the two together.[79]

The score transmitted by the composer—as in musical theater today—was subject to changes, in this case cuts in recitative, substitutions or addition of arias, and even entirely new scenes and characters. A number of scores and printed librettos of the 1650s, especially those produced at S. Aponal, bear the signs of these sorts of transformations. Some of the changes in the music of *Calisto* and *Eritrea* undoubtedly stem from the premature death of the lead singer Bonifacio Ceretti.[80] As discussed in chapter 5, however, other changes, traceable through the librettos, were probably made as improvements, to satisfy either the audience or the singers; librettos such as *Eupatra*, *Erismena*, and *Le fortune di Rodope e Damira* feature the addition of comic scenes, and in many other cases, new arias were added.[81] Comments in letters of singers also suggest that other adjustments were made routinely, for we see complaints that the parts did not suit their voices, i.e., were written out of their ranges, or were too short. Nicola Coresi, for example, suggested that his music would have to be improved: "I do not see much there [in the part], but when I am [in Venice] we will try to make it more beautiful, if that will be possible."[82] This request would not have been viewed as unexpected, however; Cavalli's 1658 contract includes a clause to cover the composer's responsibility in such cases: "That the said Signor Cavalli is required and obliged to attend all the rehearsals that will be necessary, and also to change the parts, [and to] alter, remove, and add whatever will be necessary in the music for the service of the opera, as called for by the occurrences and emergencies that arise in such situations."[83] When composers were not present in Venice, other arrangements had to be made. Both Cesti

79 ASV, SGSM, b. 188, f. 218, 22 Sept. 1666. See also, Rosand, *Opera*, 213.

80 On Ceretti, see Glixon and Glixon, "Marco Faustini." See also chapter 5. On the changes in the scores, see Mossey, "Human after all," 567–74.

81 On the addition of arias in various editions of librettos, see Brown, "'Con nuove arie aggiunte.'"

82 "e non ci vedo gran' cosa, ma quando sarò costà cercheremo di abbellirla se sarà possibile." ASV, SGSM, b. 188, f. 281, 22 Sept. 1666. Later he wrote that his role in the prologue of *Alciade* was not in his range, and would have to be rewritten (ASV, SGSM, b. 188, f. 34, 24 Nov. 1666).

83 "Che detto Signor Cavalli sia tenuto et obligato assister personalmente a tutte le prove che seranno necessarie come anco mutar parte, alterar sminuir et aggionger quello fosse neccessario nella musica per servitio dell'opera secondo l'occorenze e emergenze che succedono in simili occasioni." See above, n. 43. A similar clause appears in Cavalli's 1667 contract for *Eliogabalo* (ASV, SGSM, b. 194, f. 50, 29 June 1667). In at least one case, however, revisions were necessitated by the demands of an impresario. For the 1662/63 season Vettor Grimani Calergi, according to the Duke of Mantua's agent, forced Cavalli to accommodate his music to his own taste: "The other opera will be composed by Cavalli, but the Abbot wants music according to his manner; thus, he does not allow free rein to the composer, who, in order to avoid difficulties, does everything as he orders it." ("L'altra opera sarà composta dal Cavalli, ma il Signor Abbate vuol musica a suo modo, et così non lascia in libertà il compositore, che per non haver intrighi gli fa tutto quello che gl'ordina.") ASMa, AG, b. 1573, Tinti minuti, 25 Dec. 1662. Cavalli's opera was not presented that season, however.

and Ziani made reference to this eventuality, and named Giovanni Battista Volpe as the composer they preferred to entrust with their scores. Cesti, for example, wrote to Faustini in December 1665, before the opening of a season that would include his *Tito*: "Should it be necessary to delete, add, change, or do anything else with the music, I pray that Your Most Illustrious Lordship will entrust the task to Signor Rovettino."[84]

Replacements and Revivals

Occasionally, despite long months of planning and work, an impresario was forced, for one reason or another, to make a last-minute change, and replace a scheduled opera. There were several options available to him in such a situation, as can be seen by examining briefly a few cases from the Teatro SS. Giovanni e Paolo.

One possibility for a replacement would be a successful older work, sometimes one associated with a lead singer already contracted for the season:

> *1665/66.* Marco Faustini had slotted Giovanni Faustini and Ziani's *Doriclea* as the first opera of the season. At the last minute, however, it was replaced by Cesti's *Orontea*, which had already been performed in Austria (perhaps by some of the singers already engaged by Faustini for the season, who might even have brought the score with them[85]) and other venues in Italy, but not in Venice. We do not know if it could have been the Grimani brothers who "suggested" that Faustini mount, instead of Ziani's *Doriclea*, this popular opera, resulting in an all-Cesti bill for the season. Ziani complained bitterly that unnamed "enemies" were behind the change.

> *1666/67.* Once again, Faustini planned to open the season with a new setting of one of his brother's librettos, this time *Il tiranno humiliato d'Amore overo il Meraspe*. He offered a revision of the libretto first to Cesti, who declined, and then, at some point (the chronology is not clear), to Pallavicino. In any case, its performance was postponed until the beginning of the following season.[86] Another old opera, Cesti's *Dori*, replaced it, perhaps at the urging of the season's prima donna, Giulia Masotti, who was known for her portrayal of the title role.

---

84 "Occorendo poi di levare, aggiungere, mutar, e qualsivoglia altra cosa nella musica, io prego Vostra Signoria Illustrissima a far supplire al Signor Rovettino." (ASV, SGSM, b. 194, f. 145, 6 Dec. 1665). Ziani's similar request, dated one week later (ASV, SGSM, b. 194, f. 116, 13 Dec. 1665), must have arrived in Venice at just about the time that his *Doriclea* was canceled (in order to mount Cesti's *Orontea*), but well before *Alciade* was also removed from the bill.

85 Brown, "'Innsbruck, ich muss dich lassen,'" 210–11.

86 It is possible that Pallavicino was not the second choice for the composer, that is, someone else could have started the composition for the 1666/67 season after Cesti refused the commission. Pallavicino was paid for his composition in two installments, on 27 June 1667 (in person), and on 6 Jan. 1667 m.v. (signed for by Antonio Ugieri). Had the opera been finished the previous season, Pallavicino almost certainly would have received his payment at that time (ASV, SGSM, b. 194, ff. 23, 47). See Rosand, *Opera*, 193–95.

*1670/71.*The season opened with Ziani's setting of *Semiramide*, composed to Matteo Noris's reworking of a libretto by Moniglia.[87] According to observers, this opera was not a success, and it closed in less than two weeks. The second opera of the season, Ziani's *Heraclio*, could apparently not be moved up, so the theater quickly replaced *Semiramide* with a revival, Cesti's *Dori*—once again, the prima donna for the season was Masotti, and she may have had much to do with the choice.[88]

Another option, if the first of two operas for the year needed to be replaced, was to move forward the premiere of the second, providing a little more time to find and prepare a new work to close the season:

1661/62. Marco Faustini had planned a setting of his brother's *Medea placata* as the first opera (probably with music by Ziani). However, as *Il Rimino* reports on 14 January, "having done the rehearsals, and finding it of little liking to the audience, the company thought it best to put it aside."[89] Rather than use an older work, Faustini, despite the press of time, still preferred to present two entirely new operas. To open the season he presented *Gli scherzi di fortuna*, a sequel to a work of the previous year, which had probably been destined as the second opera for the season; *Le fatiche d'Ercole per Deianira*, which Ziani later claimed to have written in a hurry, closed out the season at SS. Giovanni e Paolo.

In one case, the replacement, although newly composed, bore the same title as the one originally planned:

1667/68. For the third year in a row, Faustini ran into problems with a planned opera, this time *Eliogabalo*, a new setting by Cavalli of an anonymous libretto revised by Aureli. Mauro Calcagno has shown that some of the political aspects of the libretto apparently caused problems for the Grimani brothers, the owners of the theater (although it is also possible that the music by the now quite old Cavalli no longer seemed sure to bring success), and in a rather unclear series of events, both Cavalli's opera and Faustini himself were replaced.[90] The eventual second opera was a setting by Boretti of a different Aureli libretto on the same subject, and with the same title as the one set by Cavalli, but without the same political overtones.[91]

87 Moniglia's *Semirami* was originally set by Cesti, and first performed in Vienna in 1667. On the reworking of this opera for Venice, see Heller, "The Queen as King" and *Emblems of Eloquence*, chap. 6.

88 The failure of *Semiramide* is reported both by a Florentine agent (ASF, MP, filza 3037, f. 409ᵛ, 27 Dec. 1670) and by the agent of the Duke of Hannover (HVsa, AK, Cal. Br. 22, vol. 4, no. 627, f. 224, 26 Dec. 1670; excerpt in Rosand, *Opera*, 441).

89 "ma fattene le prove, e trovatasi di puoco godimento gli Uditori hanno havuto per bene gli interessati di lasciarla da parte." *Il Rimino*, 14 Jan. 1662. See Rosand, *Opera*, 191.

90 For more on Faustini's departure, see chapter 3.

91 On the two *Eliogabalo* operas, see Calcagno, "Staging Musical Discourses," id., "Fonti, ricezione e ruolo," and id., "Libretto and Its Discontents."

While it might seem logical that the sudden need for a score would demand the mounting of a revival, it is clear from these examples that this was not always the case. In Venice, rather, new operas were the norm, and revivals of operas previously performed in Venice, or the import of works premiered elsewhere but not yet offered in Venice, were quite rare (see tables 6.2 and 6.3). Faustini in particular was quite reluctant to stage revivals. In fact, the only times he did so are listed above, when the choice was, in one way or another, taken out of his hands. As tables 6.2 and 6.3 show, other impresarios were not much more predisposed to presenting old works than Faustini. Only sixteen times through the 1670s did a theater present to the public a work that had been heard anywhere else previously, and only eight of those times was the work one that had already appeared on a Venetian stage. Even new settings of old librettos (a practice extraordinarily common in the eighteenth century) were rare, with only three examples, all of them in the 1660s (see table 6.4).

Nonetheless, impresarios did occasionally offer a previously performed opera, and faced different challenges than the ones associated with commissioning a new work. The key to presenting any revival, naturally, was the acquistion of the score, a task that might sometimes prove difficult, as in the case of the 1666/67 revival of Cesti's *Dori*, when the delay forced the performances to be prepared in only eight days.[92] One likely source for a score might be the composer himself, if he were still alive. As Cornelio Bentivoglio was informed in 1655, however, when he tried to find a copy of Cavalli's *Xerse*, locating the score might be the start of a difficult process. Giovanni Grimani wrote that "only the original can be found, in the possession of Signor Cavalli, [but] it is all so worked over, and so filled with annotations that it could not be understood; rather if it were necessary to have it copied, the assistance of the same Cavalli would be necessary."[93] A patron or impresario who had earlier presented the work might be able to provide a score: when Cesti's *Dori* was to be performed in Venice in 1662/63, his patron, the Archduke of Austria, sent a score to Vettor Grimani Calergi.[94] Individual performers might be of assistance in locating scores: in 1666 Giulia Masotti had suggested the substitution of Cesti's *Argia* for one of Faustini's planned operas, and undoubtedly would have facilitated the procurement of the music.[95] Jennifer Williams Brown has suggested that in the case of *Orontea* in 1665/66, one of Cesti's singers could have transported the score when he came to Venice to perform in that season's Carnival.[96] It is reasonable to assume that a singer might even travel with a personal copy of a favorite score, in the hopes of persuading an impresario to offer it. In some cases, however, the impresario kept a copy of a score—Cavalli's 1667 contract for *Eliogabalo*, for

92 *Dori* (Venice, 1667), "Lettore."

93 "solo l'originale si trova appresso il signor Cavalli strapazzato, e pieno di postille in modo che non sarebbe inteso; anzi che dovendosi copiare vi sarà necessaria l'assistenza del medesimo Cavalli." ASFe, Ab, b. 319, f. 211, 11 Sept. 1655, Giovanni Grimani to Cornelio Bentivoglio; see Monaldini, *Orto dell'Esperidi*, 100.

94 ASMa, AG, b. 1573, Tinti minuti, 25 Dec. 1662.

95 ASV, SGSM, b. 188, f. 292, 2 Oct. 1666.

96 Brown, "'Innsbruck, ich muss dich lassen,'" 210.

TABLE 6.2. Revivals of Operas Previously Performed in Venice

Year	Theater	Opera	Composer	Librettist	Previous Venetian performances
1641	SS. Giovanni e Paolo?	Il ritorno d'Ulisse in Patria	Monteverdi	Badoaro	SS. Giovanni e Paolo, 1640
1646	SS. Giovanni e Paolo	L'incoronazione di Poppea	Monteverdi	Busenello	SS. Giovanni e Paolo, 1643[a]
1647	SS. Giovanni e Paolo[b]	Deidamia	?	Herrico	Novissimo, 1644
1661	S. Luca	Eritrea	Cavalli	Faustini	S. Aponal, 1652 (and elsewhere in Italy)
1665	SS. Giovanni e Paolo	Ciro	Provenzale, revised Cavalli, revised Mattioli	Sorrentino, revised Aureli	SS. Giovanni e Paolo, 1654
1666	S. Cassiano	Giasone	Cavalli	Cicognini	S. Cassiano, 1649
1667	SS. Giovanni e Paolo	Dori	Cesti	Apolloni	S. Luca, 1663
1668	S. Luca	Seleuco	A. Sartorio	Minato	S. Luca, 1666
1670	S. Luca	Erismena	Cavalli	Aureli	S. Aponal, 1656
1671	SS. Giovanni e Paolo	Dori	Cesti	Apolloni	S. Luca, 1663 SS. Giovanni e Paolo, 1667

[a]See Whenham, "New Perspectives"; Ivanovich, Memorie teatrali, 434; and Rosand, Monteverdi's Last Operas.

[b]Ivanovich, Memorie teatrali, 434, lists a revival of Gl'amori di Apollo e di Dafne for 1647, for which there is no other evidence, but does not list Deidamia, for which a libretto is extant.

TABLE 6.3. Imports of Operas First Performed Outside of Venice

Year	Theater	Opera	Composer	Librettist	First performance
1640	S. Moisè	*Arianna*	Monteverdi	Rinuccini	Mantua, 1608
1653	SS. Giovanni e Paolo	*Veremonda*	Cavalli	Strozzi	Naples, 1652
1654	SS. Giovanni e Paolo	*Ciro*	Provenzale, revised by Cavalli	Sorrentino, revised?	Naples, 1653
1663	S. Luca	*Dori*	Cesti	Apolloni	Innsbruck, 1657
1664	S. Luca	*Achille in Sciro*	Legrenzi	Bentivoglio	Ferrara, 1663
1666	SS. Giovanni e Paolo	*Orontea*	Cesti	Cicognini	Innsbruck, 1656
1668	S. Luca	*Tiridate*	Legrenzi	Bentivoglio, revised by Minato	Ferrara, 1665, with the title *Zenobia e Radamisto*
1669	S. Luca	*Argia*	Cesti	Apolloni	Innsbruck, 1655

Note: some of these were performed outside their cities of origins before arriving in Venice.

TABLE 6.4. Re-settings of Librettos Previously Performed in Venice

Year	Theater	Opera	Composer	Librettist	First version
1666	SS. Giovanni e Paolo (not performed)	*Doriclea*	Ziani	Faustini	S. Cassiano, 1645, music by Cavalli
1666	SS. Giovanni e Paolo	*Orontea*	Cesti	Cicognini	SS. Apostoli, 1649, music by Lucio
1667	S. Moisè	*Alessandro amante*	Boretti	Cicognini	SS. Apostoli, 1651, music by Lucio with the title *Gl'amori di Alessandro Magno, e di Rossane*

example, specified that the original would be left with Faustini—presumably to be available should he want to perform the opera in the future, or to use certain arias at another time.[97] Other scores also ended up in the hands of individual collectors (such as, most famously, Marco Contarini, whose collection, now in the Biblioteca Nazionale Marciana in Venice, preserves the vast majority of seventeenth-century Venetian scores available today).[98]

Once acquired, the score (and libretto) would inevitably undergo a transformation, with transpositions tailored to the specific cast members, new arias or scenes, and cuts in recitative, most of these changes requiring the assistance of a local poet and composer.[99] Presentation of a revival, when not done under pressure, might have been viewed primarily as an impresarial frugality. Even when new arias were added, these would probably have been obtained more cheaply than a new score.

97   ASV, SGSM, b. 194, f. 50, 29 June 1667. A copy of this score, apparently from Cavalli's workshop (Brown, "L'opera è labile"), is in the Contarini collection in the Biblioteca Nazionale Marciana. Whether this is the one that was supposed to have been left with Faustini is uncertain.

98   The majority of scores in this collection are fair copies either made or purchased specifically for Contarini's library (see Walker, "'Ubi Lucius,'" cxlv–cxlvi). The scores of the works by Cavalli, on the other hand, appear to come from the composer's own collection, and represent several stages from composing score to fair copy with autograph emendations (see Walker, ibid.; Jeffery, "Autograph Manuscripts"; and Glover, Cavalli, 65–72).

99   On revisions to the libretto, see chapter 5. There is little direct evidence for the employment of a composer to revise these scores, but payment of 200 ducats to Legrenzi in the accounts for the 1668/69 production of Cesti's Argia may be for such a task, perhaps combined with musical direction (Vcg, Archivio Vendramin, b. 42 F6/1–6, n. 20; reproduced in Rosand, Opera, 197). In several of the cases referred to above, the necessary changes, in particular the transpositions, made it difficult to prepare the performances in time for opening night. Writing of the preparations for the 1662/63 production of Cesti's Dori, the Duke of Mantua's agent wrote that "it is necessary to transpose the parts, and they are worried that it will not succeed" ("ha bisogna di trasportar le Parti, et dubitano che non riesca"). ASMa, AG, b. 1573, Tinti minuti, 25 Dec. 1662.

CHAPTER SEVEN

SINGERS

In this chapter we enter the realm of the singers, in particular their recruitment and their contractual agreements with the theaters. The search for singers often placed an enormous burden on the impresario, who frequently had to replenish his roster; for their part, singers of both sexes found their work for the stage lucrative, with even the more modest talents significantly augmenting their annual incomes.

INTRODUCTION

The recruiting of singers was almost always difficult for the impresario, and for a variety of reasons.[1] As with composers, singers changed employment, became ill, and died; unlike composers, however, their talents might suddenly decline, rendering them unsuitable to a critical public. In addition, new theaters began to proliferate throughout Italy during the second part of the seventeenth century, increasing the competition for the available pool of singers. The letters of the castrato Giovanni Antonio Cavagna suggest that recruiting pressures could be relentless and full of intrigue: he went so far as to advise that Faustini write to him under an assumed name, Fedrigo Fedrigotti, so that agents working for the rival Teatro S. Luca would not intercept his letters.[2] The impresario often had to deal with yet another person, the singer's "protector"; this individual, usually a nobleman, acted as a buffer. He assisted the singer in moving between the creative and the mercenary worlds, and as an advisor and intermediary, by helping to secure advantageous working conditions; he also arranged legal recourse when necessary. An impresario needed the skills to communicate with both the singers and the nobles who facilitated their careers. Male and female singers also posed different problems for the impresario.

In Venice, as in other cities, employment opportunities for male singers varied according to the season. Each civic and religious organization had its own days on which celebration was enhanced by music, often performed by the leading

---

1 Rosand treats the subject of the recruiting of singers in her book, referring extensively to the Faustini papers. See Rosand, *Opera*, chapter 8.

2 ASV, SGSM, b. 188, f. 85.

musicians of the city or geographic region. Such opportunities had existed for centuries, although the numbers of musicians employed per establishment varied according to financial and other social pressures. In addition, opportunities for music-making and teaching in the houses of nobles and cittadini abounded, although these are often less well documented.[3] When opera began to flourish in Venice, new avenues of employment surfaced. This seasonal work, often quite well paid, substantially changed the lives of many male singers, both with respect to their finances and their professional commitments. For those residing in Venice, opera provided yet another means by which they pieced together a musical life, but singers based in other cities throughout Italy and the courts of Europe would soon become a staple on the Venetian stage.

The recruiting of women singers proved difficult for a variety of reasons. Some of the issues concerning the employment of women singers stemmed from cultural perceptions and practices. While many women learned music as part of their education, most would probably not have thought it appropriate to pursue a career as a professional singer. Those who did found their options limited: other than the stage, employment in a princely home was their only choice. Although women had a tradition of performing publicly as the *prime* and *seconde donne* of the commedia dell'arte, opera singing was perhaps even less socially acceptable; women on the stage could easily acquire a dubious reputation, regardless of their behavior.[4] Church doctrine, particularly as expressed in the seventeenth-century publications of the Jesuit Giovan Domenico Ottonelli, saw women performers as endangering both their own morality and that of their male spectators.[5] Rome was particularly extreme in this respect, and a papal ban preventing women from appearing on the stages of Rome continued until 1798, although exceptions to the rule occurred from time to time;[6] this circumstance served to increase the number of Roman female singers available to sing on the stages of Venice. Indeed, during this time the best female singers—if we judge by the women hired in Venice—were thought to

---

3 For freelance work in Venice in the previous century, see J. Glixon, "Musicians' Union" and Ongaro, "All Work and No Play?" For a sense of the interactions between musicians and a variety of nobles and cittadini see Miller, "Composers of San Marco."

4 Episodes in the lives of the singers Silvia Manni and Caterina Porri well illustrate this point. See B. Glixon, "Scenes from the Life"; ead., "Sirena antica dell'Adriatico."

5 See Giacobello, "Giovan Domenico Ottonelli." On Ottonelli and his discussions of opera, see Bianconi and Walker, "Dalla *Finta pazza*," esp. 406–10.

6 Some operas at the Teatro Tordinona featured women singers during the 1670s, but performances later in the century did not. For the all-male casts at the Tordinona and the Capranica in 1696, see Franchi, *Drammaturgia romana*, 700–2. Operas mounted in other parts of Europe such as Dresden and Munich also routinely excluded women from their casts. During the first years of production in Venice female roles were sometimes the province of castrati, that is, the casts were more reminiscent of those in other parts of Italy. In *Andromeda* (1637), for example, the goddess Giunone was played by Francesco Angeletti, Astrea by Girolamo Medici, and Venus by Anselmo Marconi, all of them castrati. The casting of *Andromeda* surely reflected in part the paucity of women in the self-contained company that presented the opera: Maddalena Manelli seems to have been the only female on stage that year. Several years later at the Teatro Novissimo, castrati portrayed the characters Diana and Melistea in *Bellerofonte* (1641/42). On the cast of *Andromeda*, see Rosand, *Opera*, 71; for Giulio del Colle's description of the singers in *Bellerofonte*, see ibid., 418.

come from or to have been trained in Rome; a number of the earliest prima donnas appearing in Venice (Maddalena Manelli, Felicita Uga, and Giulia Saus Paolelli)
were Roman, and this trend continued for decades to come. During the mid-
seventeenth century these women—if they wanted to sing on the public stage—
had to travel outside their native land.

Public opera in Venice put this new class of women singers in the spotlight, for
better or for worse. Wendy Heller has explored the portrayal of women on the
Venetian stage, and has shown how many of the characters were well known to the
audience through a long history of novels, polemical tracts, and the visual arts.[7]
These famous women—both virtuous and corrupt—such as Dido, Poppea, Ottavia, and Messalina, came to life, their stories now enriched through the powers of
music. Heller proposes that opera played a central role in expressing ideas about
female power in Venice, reflecting the contemporary debates regarding the nature
of women, and even the ambivalent nature of the Venetian Republic's self-image.
The role of women singers themselves, therefore, was particularly critical: it was
through their voices (rather than those of the castrati) that many notions about
gender and sexuality were disseminated to Venetian audiences. Opera also changed
the lives of the women who chose to perform it, perhaps even more than for male
singers of this time: a select few, through their special appeal to the public, earned
enormous sums and achieved the status of "diva."

CASTING

Understandably, hiring singers constituted one of the impresario's greatest concerns,
but it involved much more than just selecting appropriate voices for the upcoming
season. In the matter of the leading roles, he had to balance the often conflicting issues of star-power versus economy; that is, he had to decide whether to rely as much
as possible on local talent—saving time and money on correspondence and travel—
or, instead, to obtain the best singers available on the international market, often at a
great expense. His decision had clear consequences for his budget: the travel costs
from Rome could exceed 150 ducats in each direction (although the amount was
often less; see below); this sum alone exceeded the entire salaries of the more "ordinary" singers. Yet another issue was that of the multi-year contract. Faustini employed a number of singers in consecutive years during the 1650s, and several multi-
year contracts survive from his last triennium. Many singers, however—such as Silvia
Manni, Caterina Porri, Giulia Masotti, and Filippo Manin—switched theaters from
time to time, whether voluntarily or involuntarily.[8] The documents surrounding the

---

7 Heller, *Emblems of Eloquence.*

8 Manni had sung for Faustini at S. Cassiano for two consecutive seasons (1657/58, 1658/59), for
example, but was at S. Luca in its inaugural season (1660/61). Performing with her at S. Luca were
Filippo Manin and Francesco Maria Rascarini, who also had sung previously for Faustini. Caterina
Porri (see n. 4, above) sang at SS. Giovanni e Paolo during the 1650s and early in the 1660s, but she
seems to have been firmly entrenched at S. Luca during the middle and end of the decade. Finally, the
prima donna Vincenza Giulia Masotti sang at S. Luca in *Dori* (1662/63) and *Argia* (1668/69), but at
SS. Giovanni e Paolo on other occasions (see below).

administrations of Faustini and his Venetian contemporaries provide evidence of the yearly struggles endured in order to please the Venetian audiences.

Types of Singers Needed

To a great extent, the categories of singers required by the impresario grew out of the libretto, governed by its dramatic conventions, that is, by the types of characters featured. The typical libretto provided a variety of roles: kings, princes, and princesses; comic nurses as well as male and female servants and confidantes; country bumpkins; young ingenues; military and other governmental advisors; and, on occasion, more exotic characters such as witches or sorcerers. Each opera presented in Venice featured a mixed cast of male and female characters comprising all of the vocal ranges from soprano to bass.

A mid-seventeenth-century opera generally required either two or three women, although additional servant or confidante roles might augment that number on occasion. By this time, the female characters on the Venetian stage—if we exclude the comic nurse—were played by women.[9] Most of the leading male roles, as well as those of some of the servants, went to castrati rather than to tenors or basses, voice parts reserved more often for generals and counselors.[10] The "old nurse" (vecchia), on the other hand, could be played by a contralto or by a tenor (the tenor Giovanni Giacomo Biancucci played such roles[11]). Certain singers, whether tenor, bass, or castrato, specialized in comic roles that helped to facilitate a long career, as stage antics and comic timing mattered more than flawless vocal technique.[12]

RECRUITING SINGERS FROM OUTSIDE VENICE

Because Venice was perceived both by Venetians and by foreigners as the center of the Italian operatic world, impresarios were expected to present the best and most famous singers. They could not, therefore, rely merely on local performers, but had to seek out men and women from throughout the peninsula (as well as Italians serving in Germany and Austria). This meant not only discovering singers who

9 See n. 3 for earlier exceptions to the rule. A castrato must have played a female role during the 1662/63 season at SS. Giovanni e Paolo, when the two operas each called for three women, but only two appear to have been hired. In this case the availability of a prized castrato—coupled perhaps with the lack of a suitable woman—must have led to this anomaly; had an extra castrato not been available, one of the parts, presumably, could have been cut from the score. Conversely, in 1675 the role of Apollo in Giovanni Legrenzi's *La divisione del mondo* was played by Caterina Forti. See Fabbri, "Una recensione 'in rima.'"

10 For a new interpretation of the development of castrati as the male lead, and how they embodied the "ideal lover," see Freitas, "Eroticism of Emasculation." On the rise of the castrato singer, see Rosselli, "Castrati as a Professional Group."

11 ASMa, AG, b. 2804, letter of Count Romoaldo Vialardi, 23 Mar. 1669. Biancucci also played the part of Dema in Cesti's *Argia* (1655). See Seifert, "Antonio Cesti."

12 Tomaso Bovi performed for many years in the Grimani theaters. For Bovi's roles at S. Giovanni Grisostomo between 1678 and 1700, see Saunders, "Repertoire of a Venetian Opera House," 448–59.

would best suit their needs, but also negotiating a complex political and social maze to bring them to their theaters.

Information Gathering: The Search for Talent

Although the impresario could sometimes rely on singers already known to him, he constantly had to find new talents who would appeal to an increasingly sophisticated audience. He, or someone close to him, would send out queries in search of new singers; in the case of Marco Faustini, such correspondence could begin well in advance, even before the end of the previous carnival, though much of it was conducted in spring and early summer.[13] The recipients of those letters, as we shall see, included musicians, noblemen, and others.[14] Musicians were especially helpful in suggesting singers, as they continually formed new networks, moving from city to city as they practiced their art. The letters to Faustini from Carlo Righenzi are particularly rich in this regard, for they recommend singers from various regions of Italy.[15] An impresario might also ask one of the singers he had already hired to supply him with the names of musicians eager to perform: Sebastiano Cioni, for example, wrote a number of letters on Faustini's behalf.[16] Conversely, singers or their representatives could initiate the process by approaching an impresario or others with contacts to a theater.

An impresario, however, needed knowledge beyond a singer's availability and willingness to travel; he required expert advice on his or her suitability for the operatic stage. As Pietro Andrea Ziani remarked, in reference to certain Venetian women and their lack of success in one of Faustini's productions, the chamber and the theater were very different environments, and a reputation in one area did not

13 Appendix 4 shows the sequence of events, including contacts with singers, Faustini followed for two seasons in the 1650s.

14 In 1659 Marco Faustini approached the Milanese Carlo Francesco Ceva, a man involved in the salt trade (Faustini's area of legal expertise), regarding the availability of singers in Milan. Ceva's daughter Maria Domitilla was one of the most famous singers at S. Radegonda, a Milanese convent; Maurizio Cazzati's *Cantate morali e spirituali* (Bologna, 1659) is dedicated to her. Carlo Francesco, however, also had ties to the world of music, for Michelangelo Grancini's seventh book of *Concerti ecclesiastici* (Milan, 1650) is dedicated to him. (See Kendrick, *Celestial Sirens,* 179.) Only one letter survives from Ceva to Faustini, but he must have been considered a useful contact; perhaps Faustini, Duodo, and Correr did not have high-ranking acquaintances who could perform a similar function in that geographical area. Letters went out that same year to at least two correspondents in Naples. Faustini received one dated 4 March 1659, from Girolamo Bon (a Venetian); the other, dated 4 November 1659, bears an illegible signature. The writer of the latter mentions that he had recommended two sopranos to Marc'Antonio Correr (ASV, SGSM, b. 101, ff. nn.). We can assume that many other letters were written to Faustini and his contemporaries, who must have cast a rather large net in their search for talent; unfortunately, traces of most of these contacts have not survived.

15 ASV, SGSM, b. 188, f. 58, 23 Sept. 1665 and ff. 53–54, 7 Oct. 1665; Righenzi mentions the Neapolitan Domenico Sciarra (temporarily in Genoa), Domenico Broglia (in Milan), Vincenzino, and unspecified singers in Cremona, Ferrara, Florence, and Genoa.

16 In the fall of 1665, Cioni exchanged letters regarding employment for the upcoming season with Carlo Righenzi and Giovanni Battista Pizzala; he also met Righenzi in person in Verona. See ASV, SGSM, b. 188, ff. 129 (letter of Cioni), 201 (letter of Righenzi, who says he looked at music Cioni gave him), 374 and 375 (letters of Pizzala); b. 101, unnumbered (letter of Cioni).

guarantee success in the other.[17] Witnesses of some kind had to be found who could assess a singer's suitability; they might be audience members who had attended a performance outside of Venice (as Marc'Antonio Correr did in Verona in 1665), or, more likely, singers and musicians of various locales with contacts in courts, churches, and with local teachers.

Faustini's Roman correspondent Arcangelo Lori (see below) provided critical comments concerning a number of singers. About one of them (whom he identified only by her nickname) he wrote: "With every confidence I tell you that La Guardarobba is a most singular virtuosa, but her voice is very small, and for your theater, she doesn't seem suitable to me."[18] Of another singer he commented:

> She is large, and has a beautiful presence, the voice good rather than bad, she sings very competently, but is not the equal of Giulia [Masotti] and Nina [Tomei], as I believe would be required to succeed on the stage; . . . if you think you might want her to perform, because she is not of the quality I would desire for your service, I would like you to write to some of your friends in Rome so that they could hear her, and then report to Your Lordship regarding her quality.[19]

In at least one case a teacher, Gioseffo Maria Genari from Montagnana, hoped to bring his protégé to Venice (a trip of some 40 miles), to be heard by Ziani. Faustini had already sent the young singer a sample scene, but Genari wanted him to be heard and judged in the proper setting:

> It makes a great difference to hear the boy close up and in a narrow space (as he was heard in Venice), compared to hearing him in a spacious one. It gives a different result, and Your Excellency will be rewarded when you hear him from afar, and especially in a theater. It is true that up close he seems a bit unrefined because he has a head voice; from a distance and in church [however] it stands out, and he will certainly be heard throughout the theater.[20]

In most cases, however, Faustini and his contemporaries had to rely on such reports without the possibility of hearing a singer locally.

Licenses

Once appropriate singers were identified, the impresario had to make contact with them (either directly via the post, or through an intermediary), and, of course,

---

17 ASV, SGSM, b. 188, f. 354, 28 Nov. 1665.

18 "Con ogni sorte di confidenza gli dico che la Guardarobba è una virtuosa singularissima, ma la voce è poco assai e per il suo teatro non me pare approposito." ASV, SGSM, b. 188, f. 92, 8 Aug. 1665.

19 "È grande e di bella presenza, la voce piutosto bona che cattiva, canta assai competentemente bene, ma non è da metter al pari delle signore Giulia e Nina, crederei fosse per far riuscita in scena. . . . ma quando lei havesse tal pensiero, per non esser questa donna della qualità che io desiderei per suo servitio, vorrei che scrivere a qualche suo amico in Roma, acciò la venisse a sentire, e poi riferisse a Vostra Signoria la qualità del soggetto." ASV, SGSM, b. 188, f. 92, 18 July 1665.

20 "È gran differenza a sentir il putello vicino, et in loco angusto come fece sentirsi a Venetia, et sentirlo in loco spatioso, che fa altra riuscita, et Vostra Signoria Eccellentissima resterà paga' quando lo sentirà lontano, et massime in un teatro, è vero, che vicino pare, che sij un poco crudo perché è voce di testa, che campeggia alla lontana, et in chiesa, et si farà sentire certo per tutto il teatro." ASV, SGSM, b. 188, f. 57, 8 Oct. 1665.

reach agreements with them. As mentioned above, however, the typical male singer held some sort of regular post, so that a license had to be obtained if he were to travel to and live in Venice for a number of months. There seem to have been several reasons why patrons and employers would be willing to part with their top singers. Sara Mamone argues, using the Medici princes as models (see below), that reciprocity was expected: that a patron lending out a singer on one occasion would be able to obtain someone he desired for another.[21] While this certainly applied in contacts between princes, Venetian dealings often require other explanations, since the impresarios and theater owners rarely employed musicians they could trade (although they could encourage those they had hired to accept an offer). The benefits to the princes for allowing their singers to travel to Venice for carnival were twofold. On the one hand, a successful season in a Venetian theater might be seen as adding to the prestige of the singer (and, therefore, his or her patron). On the other, the singer's income could be greatly enhanced, making him more content at little or no cost to the patron. Permission to travel to Venice ultimately had to be granted through official channels, with the process initiated either by the musician himself or by some other contact of the impresario at the court.

In 1658 Giovanni Grimani wrote directly to the singer Giovanni Paolo Bonelli, employed at the imperial court in Vienna:

> Because I am in the process of preparing those things necessary to mount a production this year in my theater with extraordinary magnificence, and among the principal things [I need] must be highly regarded singers, I urge you, who rank among the first of these, and are also desired by this entire city, as I know very well, to resolve to come and favor me with your presence, being certain that you will recognize from the reward how much I value your talent . . . [22]

Grimani continued, "If you wish to come, advise me whether you yourself can obtain a license from the appropriate person, or what path one has to follow to obtain it, since I do not wish to miss any opportunity to see you in my theater."[23] Grimani must have known Bonelli well in order to have approached him directly.[24] Several years later Pietro Andrea Ziani, the maestro di cappella for the Dowager Empress Eleonora Gonzaga, offered to smooth the way when Marco Faustini hoped to hire Giovanni Antonio Forni:

21 Mamone, "Most Serene Brothers–Princes–Impresarios."

22 "Perché vado disponendo le cose necessario per fare rappresentare quest'anno nel mio teatro l'opera con magnificenza straordinaria, e tra le principali dovranno essere i virtuosi di gran stima, Vostra Signoria, che tra questi è de primi, et è anco desiderato da tutta questa città, conforme io lo so benissimo, viene eccitata da me à risolversi di venire a favorirmi con la sua persona, sicura, che dagli effetti riconoscerà quanto stimi la sua virtù . . ." ASV, SGSM, b. 101, unnumbered, 8 July 1658. It is unclear how this letter, sent to Bonelli in Vienna, fell into the hands of Faustini; in 1658 the impresario was active at S. Cassiano, the theater of the Tron family.

23 "Volendo venire, mi avviserà, se da sè potrà haverne la licenza da chi si deve, ò pure qual strada dovrà praticarsi per conseguirla, non volendo io mancare à cosa alcuna per vederla in questo mio teatro." ASV, SGSM, b. 101, unnumbered, 8 July 1658.

24 Bonelli's wife had performed at the Grimani theater in 1650. See Bianconi and Walker, "Dalla finta pazza," 403.

As I have said, I will be content to receive your invitation [to compose an opera], and I will procure Forni for you from Her Majesty, but with the express agreement that you should not speak of it [to anyone], that is, so that I alone seek from Her Majesty the license; that will be easier for me than to try to get it through other means . . . because Her Majesty, through her goodness, will not deny me these reasonable favors that I might hope for . . . [25]

Licenses, of course, were not always granted when requested. While the Dowager Empress may have been willing to lend some of her singers, her stepson, Emperor Leopold, had tired of this practice. He wrote on 8 October 1662 to his ambassador in Venice regarding the same singer Grimani had recruited in 1658:

You have done very well in dissuading and denying Abbot Grimani regarding his request to have my singer Giovanni Paolo Bonelli for the next carnival's operas, for I could never allow it, this being something never practiced in this court. Even if other courts do it, I will not, all the more because it would do little for my reputation for my singers to run around the world to perform in public operas mounted purely for profit. Besides, you remember very well that two years ago when I heard that Stefano Boni, also my musician, had performed in similar operas, I ordered a very good and solemn reprimand with the warning that if he did it again I would not keep him in my service. Moreover, during carnival I myself have need of my people and servants, and cannot lend them to others. [26]

Although female singers usually did not hold the sort of position that would require obtaining a formal license before they could come to Venice, they were often under the patronage of a ruler or important nobleman, and would only make such a commitment with his or her consent. Willing patrons and employers, then, were one of the ingredients required to maintain a top-notch, internationally based cast on the stages of Venice.

The Recruiting of Singers: The Evidence from Ferrara, Florence, Turin, and Rome

The art of recruiting as practiced in mid-seventeenth-century Italy required accommodation to the practices and policies of the courts and cities where singers

25 "come ho fatto che io sarò contento di ricever l'invito, e lo procurerò per il Forni da Sua Maestà, ma con patto espresso che non se ne parli acciò possi io solo impetrar da Sua Maestà la licenza, che mi sarà più facile che tentarla per altra banda . . . perché Sua Maestà per sua bontà non mi negarà quelle grazie ragionevoli che posso sperare . . ." ASV, SGSM, b. 188, f. 104, 22 Mar. 1665.

26 "Havete fatto molto bene in disuadere il Abbate Grimani dela domanda di haver il Giovanni Paolo Bonelli, mio musico, per le opere del prossimo carnevale et in negargliela, perchè io non potrei mai farlo, essendo questo una cosa in questa corte mai praticata, se ben altre corti lo fanno, però io non lo farò, tanto più, che sarebbe poca riputatione mia, che li miei musici corressero pel mondo a recitare in opere publiche, fatte solo per guadagno, oltre che vi ricordate molto bene, che havendo sentito avanti 2 anni, che Stefano Boni, pur mio musico, havesse recitato in simili opere, io vi ho comandato una bonissima et solenne reprimenda con minaccie, che se lo farebbe più, non lo havrei più tenuto in mio servitio; di più in quell tempo di carnevale io ho di bisogno istesso di mia gente e servitori senza poterli imprestare ad altri." Letter of 8 Oct. 1662. Published in Kalista, *Korespondence císaře Leopolda I*, 141–42.

resided and were employed, and to the interests and personalities of patrons. The various components of the search for and hiring of singers could combine in many different ways. Some idea of the flexibility of the system and the complexity of the impresario's task emerges from a brief examination of the way singers were recruited for Venetian opera houses from or through four important Italian cities.

FERRARA AND FLORENCE: THE IMPORTANCE OF PERSONAL RELATIONSHIPS   The Bentivoglios, the ruling family of Ferrara in this period, became known for their patronage of singers, and for the depth of their expertise and contacts regarding musicians.[27] They acted frequently as intermediaries between musicians and impresarios, not only for opera in Venice, but also for musical activities in Florence, Bologna, and other locales. Their correspondence provides one of the best pictures of musical culture and the patronage of musicians in seventeenth-century Italy.[28]

The Marquis Bentivoglio typically employed a number of singers in his household, so that some of the correspondence between him and various figures in Venice concerns requests for the use of his singers for the carnival season. The singer most frequently mentioned is Stefano Costa, a long-time employee who had performed in *La finta savia* in 1642/43, but who continued to be recruited through the mid-1660s. During the 1650s another singer in Bentivoglio's service, Raffaele Caccialupi, appeared at Faustini's S. Aponal at the request of Marc'Antonio Correr, and Faustini would write directly to the Marquis in 1659 regarding another singer, Giuseppe Paino (see chap. 3). Bentivoglio maintained especially close ties with Giovanni Grimani, and helped to facilitate the hiring of a number of singers at SS. Giovanni e Paolo over a period of several decades; the family's reliance on the Bentivoglios continued after Giovanni Grimani's death in 1663.[29]

Faustini's records confirm that Boni performed in Venice for the 1660/61 season. Some singers, such as the Tuscan Leonora Falbetti Ballerini, shared Leopold's views of commercial theaters, preferring to perform in more private "ducal" theaters.

27 During Faustini's time the title of Marquis (Marchese) was held by Cornelio Bentivoglio (1606–63) and Hippolito Bentivoglio (d. 1685).

28 The correspondence of the Bentivoglio family relating to the patronage of music has been published recently in two volumes: Fabris, *Mecenati e musici* (for the period 1585 to 1645) and Monaldini, *Orto dell'Esperidi* (covering 1646–85).

29 In 1656 Giovanni Grimani requested that Marquis Cornelio Bentivoglio contact the composer Marco Marazzoli, who would in turn deal with several singers personally (ASFe, AB, b. 322, f. 448, 11 Mar. 1656; see Monaldini, *Orto dell'Esperidi*, 113). Bentivoglio visited Grimani's house during his stays in Venice: two notarial documents concerning him were drawn up in the Grimani palace, on 8 June 1658 (ASV, AN, Atti, b. 692, f. 127ᵛ) and on 4 Feb. 1658 m.v. (ASV, AN, Atti, b. 6061, f. 175ᵛ). In Dec. 1664, after Giovanni Grimani's death, both Giovanni Carlo Grimani and Andrea Mattioli, composer of the upcoming opera (and an employee of the Bentivoglios in the 1650s) wrote to the Marquis in the hopes that he could facilitate the license of Carlo Portio, a singer in the cathedral (ASFe, AB, b. 339, f. 826, 3 Dec. 1664, letter of Andrea Mattioli, Monaldini, *Orto dell'Esperidi*, 214; f. 838, 3 Dec. 1664, letter of Giovanni Carlo Grimani, ibid., 215). Grimani and Mattioli wanted Portio for the roles of Neptune and "a ghost of Atlas," characters in Mattioli's *Perseo*. The composer's letter states that he had already written to Portio, who had informed him of the need to obtain permission from the bishop.

Maintaining contacts throughout Italy, but especially with Rome, Florence, Bologna, and Venice, the Bentivoglio family supported a variety of musical activities in Ferrara, presenting opera from time to time, but also sponsoring the annual musical festivities at the Accademia dello Spirito Santo. They always sought the best musicians, so that a number of singers from Venice often made the trip to perform there after they had fulfilled their duties in the carnival season: eventual reciprocity may have been presumed, then, in some of the letters that passed between Venice and Ferrara.[30]

The ruling family of Tuscany, the Medici, were a far greater power on the political scene than the Bentivoglios. Already known since the fifteenth century as patrons of the arts, the Medici maintained a vibrant musical establishment.[31] During the mid-seventeenth century not only the Grand Duke Ferdinando, but also his brothers the Princes Mattias (governor of Siena), Leopoldo (named cardinal in 1667), and Cardinal Giovanni Carlo took an active interest in music; moreover, each of them employed and maintained close contact with a number of singers, and together they functioned as impresarios in Florence and elsewhere in Tuscany.[32] In part because of the presence of reciprocal government representatives in Florence and Venice, communication flowed freely and frequently between the two states.[33]

The papers housed in the Medici archives comprise a valuable source for the study of opera recruiting. Venetian theater owners and impresarios wrote to the Medici in search of star singers who would fill the leading roles, as well as those who would play supporting parts. Bianconi and Walker drew attention to the Medici role in the recruiting and hiring of the prima donna Anna Maria Sardelli and various members of the Melani family for the Grimani theater, but the Medici brothers facilitated the hiring of a number of other singers, some less well known today.[34] During the 1650s and 1660s Prince Mattias corresponded regularly with various members of the Grimani family. Although the Grimanis, particularly Vettor Grimani Calergi and Giovanni Grimani, wrote concerning a variety of topics, a number of letters center around singers. It is significant that during Marco Faustini's tenure at the Grimani theater very few letters of this type survive from the Grimanis to the Medici; perhaps the impresario preferred for the most part to find singers according to his own methods and contacts.[35]

---

30 On the accademia, see Mele, *Accademia dello Spirito Santo.*

31 For discussions of seventeenth-century patronage of secular music in Florence, see Kirkendale, *Court Musicians in Florence,* and Harness, "Amazzoni di Dio."

32 See Mamone, "Most Serene Brothers–Princes–Impresarios," and Mamone, "Accademie e opera." On Atto Melani, and his relationship with Prince Mattias, see Freitas, "*Atto d'ingegno.*"

33 On opera at the Medici court, and relations between Florence and Venice, see Maretti, "Dal Teatro del principe," Michelassi, "*Finta pazza* a Firenze," Michelassi, "Teatro del Cocomero," 149–84, and Mamone, "Most Serene Brothers–Princes–Impresarios."

34 Bianconi and Walker, "Dalla *Finta pazza,*" 441–44. Other singers requested included Giuseppe Ghini, Cosimo Orlandi, Antonio Rivani, and Vincenzo Olivicciani (Vincenzino). The Sardelli affair is treated in detail in Mamone, "Most Serene Brothers–Princes–Impresarios."

35 We have found three letters from Giovanni Grimani to Prince Mattias concerning opera during Faustini's tenure: 29 Oct. 1660 (ASF, MP, filza 5474, f. 606); 4 Mar. 1662 (ASF, MP, filza 5476, f. 720); and 2 Dec. 1662 (ASF, MP, filza 5487, f. 511).

Like the Marquis Bentivoglio, the Medici might also serve to aid in the hiring of a singer who was not under their direct control. In some cases, one of the princes would act merely as an intermediary: when Vettor Grimani Calergi desired the services of the tenor Francesco Guerra, for example, he would write to Mattias even though the singer was in the employ of the Duke of Massa, under the influence of the Tuscan dukes. As we will discuss below, during the mid-1660s the Grimanis wrote letters to the Medici concerning Giulia Masotti, who was protected by the Medici agent in Rome, the Tuscan Torquato Montauto.

If the Grimanis were on particularly intimate terms with some of the Medici princes, other Venetians concerned with opera were not, and their efforts would have been directed instead toward one of the Medici secretaries, or to the Florentine Resident, the government representative in Venice. Giovanni Poggi Cellesi, who arrived in Venice to serve the Grand Duke of Tuscany as Resident late in 1662,[36] relayed requests from representatives of several theaters for Tuscan singers to various people at the Medici court. A number of letters sent from him to Florence concern the recruiting of the castrato Vincenzo Olivicciani.[37] Vincenzino, as he was known, was especially sought after by the Venetian nobleman Tomaso Corner, who (along with his brother, Marco) requested the singer for several years on behalf of the Teatro S. Luca. Working on Corner's behalf was a rather unusual "agent," Camilla Duodo, a Venetian nun (and later the abbess) at the monastery of SS. Cosma e Damiano, and a distant relative of Alvise Duodo.[38] She had some special connection to the Medici, and she wrote several letters to them on behalf of the Corner brothers when they attempted to hire Vincenzino during the mid-1660s.[39] It may be her participation in the recruiting process that led Faustini's partner, Alvise Duodo, to write a letter to the Florentine court in May 1665 in which he admitted his embarassment and surprise that the management at S. Luca claimed to have hired Vincenzino:

> We, then, are in competition with [the impresarios of] the Teatro di S. Luca, who, with disdain, say that they have Vincenzino for the performances of the upcoming year, something that I will never believe if I do not see it for myself. Because the protection of the Most Serene Prince Mattias allows me to hope for the grace of the Most Serene Grand Duke [Ferdinando II], I then beseech you to make new entreaties, because now we are dealing with a matter of reputation. If you should have occasion to meet with the Grand Prince [Cosimo], and put to him a similar entreaty,

---

36 Poggi Cellesi made his first appearance at the Collegio in his capacity as Florentine Resident on 15 Dec. 1662 (ASV, Collegio, Esposizioni principi, reg. 71, f. 181ᵛ).

37 On Olivicciani, see Kirkendale, *Court Musicians in Florence*, 409–11. Kirkendale's account of the singer at the Medici court begins in 1664, but does not make reference to the remarkable Venetian interest in the singer during the period in question.

38 Camilla Duodo was the daughter of Zuane Duodo, whose family resided in the parish of S. Martial, whereas Alvise Duodo's branch of the family were long-time residents of S. Maria del Giglio. Duodo became the abbess of the convent in 1686, and died in 1692. See Cornelio, *Ecclesiae venetae*, 9:54.

39 The Resident Cellesi wrote that Camilla Duodo was known to "the Most Serene Prince" (Mattias, or, perhaps, Leopoldo). Regarding Duodo, see ASF, MP, filza 3033, f. 592, 4 July 1665; ASF, MP, filza 1572, f. 857, 6 Mar. 1666; ASF, MP, filza 1572, f. 982, 23 Oct. 1666.

I assure you that it would serve my interests well; as I have said, they oppress me, because people are speaking ill of me with little respect.[40]

In the end, it appears that Vincenzino served none of the Venetians who had desired his services that year.[41]

In 1667 the Florentine Resident Giovanni Poggi Cellesi was of particular assistance in recruiting the Florentine Caterina Angiola Botteghi, a young singer protected by Prince Leopoldo. Letters from Poggi Cellesi to Faustini in June and July show the progress of the negotiations; by August, Botteghi herself had written to Faustini, expressing her gratitude at having been offered the part of Erope (the seconda donna) in *Il tiranno humiliato d'Amore overo il Meraspe*.[42]

Tuscans other than the Resident might also provide assistance to Venetian impresarios, however. As a center of trade, Venice attracted businessmen from all over Europe, and many of them remained there for decades at a time. Because they became fixtures in the community, while maintaining strong ties to their home markets and governments, they, too, were well placed to help in matters of recruiting and other concerns regarding singers from their native lands. The Florentine merchant Paolo del Sera, a noted patron of the arts, and an agent to Prince Leopoldo, provided assistance regarding the singers Vincenzino and Giuseppe Ghini, the latter under the prince's protection.[43] Alessandro Guasconi, another Florentine merchant and long-term resident of Venice, served a similar function, and visited the singer Botteghi at Faustini's house, thus assuring the prince of the suitability of her living situation in Venice.[44]

TURIN: THE DIFFICULTY OF OBTAINING LICENSES   Whereas the tradition of borrowing opera singers from the Medici dated back to the early 1640s, and remained a constant for decades, exchanges between Turin and Venice occurred much less frequently during the mid-seventeenth century. The situation most likely resulted from a previous lack of diplomatic relations between the two governments, as well as far fewer personal contacts between individual nobles of

40 "Siamo poi in picca, con cotesto Teatro di San Lucca mentre con sprezzo dicono di havere per la recita dell'anno venturo Vicenzino, ciò non crederò mai se non lo vedo, mentre la prottetione del Serenissimo Prencipe Mattias mi fa sperare la gratia dal Serenissimo Gran Duca, la supplico dunque d'incolorir di novo l'instanze, mentre al presente si tratta di riputatione. Se havesse anco occasioni d'abbocarsi con il Gran Prencipe, e gli porgesse simile instanza m'assicurò, che molto gioverebbe a miei interessi, che come ho detto mi premono, perché sparlano con poco rispetto . . ." ASF, MP, filza 5481, f. 512, 12 May 1665. Although the first letter that mentions Camilla Duodo's involvement dates from July 1665, she may have been concerned in the matter earlier, as Tomaso Corner wrote that Vincenzino had been promised to S. Luca as early as the previous January (ASF, MP, filza 3033, f. 591, 2 July 1665).

41 The series of letters that traveled between Venice and Florence show that the repeated requests for Vincenzino had resulted in some confusion: apparently he had been been promised to the Grimani theater by the Grand Duchess, and to S. Luca by the Grand Duke (ASF, MP, filza 3033, f. 591, 2 July 1665).

42 For letters from Poggi Cellesi to Faustini, see ASV, SGSM, b. 188, f. 178, 4 June 1667; f. 177, 7 July 1667; f. 176, 22 July 1667. For letters from Botteghi to Faustini, see ASV, SGSM, b. 188, ff. 170, 171.

43 On del Sera and the Medici see Goldberg, *Late Medici Art Patronage*, 54–78, 272–89.

44 ASF, MP, filza 5574, no. 378, 26 Nov. 1667. Guasconi served as an important intermediary for Legrenzi's operatic commission for Prince Ferdinando. See Holmes, "Operatic Commissions."

the two cities (the correspondence between the Grimani family and the Savoy court seems to have begun only in 1662).[45] Although Faustini used a singer with Turin connections as early as 1656/57,[46] all of his letters concerning the recruitment of singers from Turin date from the years 1665–68 and concern two of the leading chamber singers there, Giovanni Antonio Cavagna and Francesco Maria Rascarini. The Turin correspondence particularly points up the difficulties that might arise for the impresario when an employer was hesitant to issue licenses releasing singers from their regular employment.

Both Rascarini and Cavagna had sung in Venice in the 1650s before their engagement at Turin; perhaps this explains their continued presence in the theater there during the 1660s.[47] While Cavagna served Faustini intermittently from 1657, we do not know of the negotiations that had been necessary to hire him—by all accounts one of the top singers of the time—during his first years in the service of the Duke of Savoy;[48] "Cavagnino" continued his association with Faustini at the Grimani theater in 1662/63.[49] Beginning no later than 1665, Faustini had a contact in Turin who had expert knowledge of Venice, of the Grimani family, and of the diplomatic and bureaucratic workings of Turin: Abbot Vincenzo Dini.

Dini hailed from Modena, and provided the Duke of Modena with dispatches from Venice during the 1650s and 1660s. During the early 1660s he negotiated (in Venice) a treaty between Venice and the Duchy of Savoy, after which the two governments established full diplomatic reciprocity.[50] Dini then went on to serve the Duke of Savoy as a minister in Turin (and later in Madrid). He spent fourteen years in Venice during the 1650s and 1660s, during which time he came to know Giovanni Grimani and other influential nobles.[51] He was a witness to a number of notarial documents drawn up in Grimani's palace, and probably also knew well the charms of Venetian opera.[52] In other words, he had most likely seen the

45 Viale Ferrero, "Repliche a Torino," 148.

46 Anna Maria Volea, who created the role of Rodope (1656/57), was the daughter of Giacomo Volea, a musician at Turin (see ASV, SGSM, b. 118, receipt book, f. 22). Giacomo is listed as a "musico di camera" for 1650 in Bouquet, *Musique et musiciens*, 157.

47 Cavagna's first appearance probably came in Cavalli's *Statira* at SS. Giovanni e Paolo in 1655/56; he sang for Faustini at S. Cassiano in 1657/58 and 1658/59, that latter year, it would seem, along with Rascarini. Cavagna was hired at Turin in 1658, and, according to his letters, was responsible for Rascarini's employment at the court in 1662 (although Rascarini had performed there in 1660). See ASV, SGSM, b. 188, f. 99, addition to the letter on f. 98, 3 Apr. 1665. Cavagna left Turin by the end of the 1660s, while Rascarini remained there until his death in 1706. See Bouquet, *Musique et musiciens*, 44, 215.

48 Several letters written to the Bentivoglio family in Ferrara during the mid-1650s concern Cavagna, and the possibility of his serving there. See Monaldini, *Orto dell'Esperidi*, 97–99, 112.

49 By that time Faustini had begun to represent him in legal matters; the two would remain close until the time of the impresario's death in 1675; see chapter 3.

50 Claretta, *Storia del regno*, 1:355–58, 2:742.

51 One Savoy diplomat wrote of Dini in 1664: "and the same Signor Abbot, who knows all of Venice" (E lo stesso signor Abbate, che conosce tutta Venetia). AST, LMV, b. 9bis, fasc. 5 (Conte Bigliore), no. 8, 7 June 1664. Dini spoke of his fourteen years in Venice in a report (*memoriale*) to the Collegio (ASV, Collegio, Esposizioni principi, reg. 73, f. 66, 9 July 1664).

52 See, for example, ASV, AN, Atti, b. 6060, f. 22, 23 Mar. 1657.

performances both of Cavagna and Rascarini who, as native of Reggio, was his countryman.

A year after Dini's diplomatic duties had ended in Venice he began to aid Faustini and his partners by helping to secure the licenses of Cavagna and Rascarini. The letters from Dini, along with those from Cavagna, show that the Duke was reluctant to lend his singers for extended periods of time. Cavagna alluded to the difficulties he foresaw on 27 March 1665: "Knowing Your Excellency's [wish] that I should serve you in your operas, I am resolved to advise you that it will be necessary to find me service at another court, as I have already implored you several times, so that I will be at liberty to serve you with a calm spirit."[53] Indeed, the 1665/66 season proved especially problematic because Carnival extended well into March; the Duke gave his approval only around 17 October 1665, and then insisted that the singers return to Turin for the last days of Carnival.[54] Cavagna relayed to Faustini that Dini predicted that once the singers were in Venice, the Duke would allow them to stay,[55] and he was eventually proved right: on 22 January 1666, with over a month of the carnival season remaining, the Duke agreed to grant the singers leave for the entire season, as requested by Giovanni Carlo Grimani.[56] The Duke's generosity that season, however, was repaid with his insistence in the next that the singers return before the end of Carnival in order to appear in the ballet *Il falso Amor bandito, l'humano ammesso, et il celeste esaltato*. Faustini and Giovanni Carlo Grimani were, naturally, unwilling to see Cavagna and Rascarini leave before the end of the carnival season; eventually, after many impasses, the Capi of the Council of Ten released the singers from their contracts, and they left for Turin in accordance with the Duke's request.[57] Faustini's and Grimani's eventual surrender to the Duke's demands undoubtedly enabled Cavagna's return to Venice the subsequent season.

ROME: RECRUITING THROUGH INFORMAL NETWORKS   Our view of the recruitment of singers in Rome during the mid-seventeenth century derives, in large part, from letters written to Marco Faustini, as well as others sent from the courts of Florence and Rome.[58] Faustini's correspondence provides some small indication of the behind-the-scenes activities necessary for the recruiting of singers from the papal city. Unlike the situation in Florence and Turin, where government

---

53 "Sapendo la volontà che tiene Vostra Signoria Eccellentissima ch'io la servi nelle sue opere, mi risolvo avisarla che sarà necessario il procurarmi un altro servitio appresso alltra corte come già più volte l'ho suplicato che così sarò in libertà di servirla con animo quieto." ASV, SGSM, b. 188, f. 102, 27 Mar. 1665.

54 ASV, SGSM, b. 188, f. 218, 19 Oct. 1665.

55 Ibid., f. 209, 24 Oct. 1665.

56 AST, LMV, mazzo 9, f. 227, Nizza, 22 Jan. 1666.

57 See Viale Ferrero, "Repliche a Torino," 148, 159–64. Viale Ferrero provides a series of letters detailing the negotiations regarding the singers' return to Turin. The Capi, normally concerned with matters of state security, probably became involved because of the diplomatic issues involved in this case.

58 Further examination of letters of the leading Roman families will probably yield more information regarding Roman singers and their service in Venice. The letters of the composer Marco Marazzoli provide invaluable information on the recruiting of Roman singers during the early 1640s. See Fabris, *Mecenati e Musici*.

officials carried out many of the arrangements, much of the work in Rome was accomplished through unofficial channels, using a network of musicians, clerics, and nobles.

During Faustini's time male opera singers on the Venetian stage rarely came from the ranks of the famous papal choirs, perhaps because the granting of licenses would have proved difficult. On the other hand, Rome abounded in musical establishments and activities, from the numerous churches and confraternities to the households of noble families and cardinals. Giovanni Agostino Poncelli and Giovanni Capello came to Venice after having performed at S. Apollinare, the church of the Jesuit German College,[59] and, as we have seen, many of the prima donnas came from Rome as well.

As discussed above, singers could be recruited through letters, or sometimes by private visit. In some cases a member of an opera company himself embarked on a recruiting trip. In 1664, for example, Carlo Morandi, acting for Vettor Grimani Calergi, went to Rome in search of singers for the Grimani theater. We know that he expended some effort trying to recruit Giulia Masotti, but he undoubtedly heard and hired other singers as well.[60] Similarly, on 30 June 1665 two of the partners at S. Moisè (Giacomo Dall'Angelo and Camillo Coveglia) authorized the third partner, Cristoforo Raimondi, to hire singers "in whatever city or place, whether in the dominion or outside of it."[61] In other cases, an impresario might choose to delegate authority rather than undertake a lengthy trip. In 1648, for example, the nobleman Alvise Michiel gave a man in Rome, Francesco Martorelli, the authority to hire singers for the Grimani theater.[62]

Faustini relied on both musicians and non-musicians in Rome in his efforts to secure singers for his productions. Just as Venetian opera impresarios counted on Tuscan and Mantuan officials residing in Venice to communicate and negotiate on their behalf, so they could make use of their own government's representatives in Rome and other cities. During the 1657/58 season for example, Faustini's company was helped by the Venetian ambassador in Rome; as we saw in chapter 3, this assistance was more readily available to the impresario and his partners because the ambassador was none other than Angelo Correr, Marc'Antonio Correr's first cousin. The full extent of the ambassador's dealings with the singers is unknown, but money was sent to Rome in his care, and then distributed to two singers, Silvia Manni and Giovanni Agostino Poncelli.[63] Moreover, on at least one occasion the ambassador himself was asked to help in the recruiting process. One of Alvise

<hr />

59 Culley, *Jesuits and Music*, 221, 241–44.

60 ASF, MP, filza 5480, f. 796, 2 Dec. 1664. Carlo Morandi is mentioned in a letter of Torquato Montauto.

61 "qualunque città, e loco tanto nel dominio, quanto fuori . . ." ASV, AN, Atti, b. 6762, f. 12, 30 June 1665.

62 ASV, AN, Atti, b. 6051, f. 176, 24 Oct. 1648. Several weeks later the singer Anna Renzi authorized Martorelli to conduct business affairs for her in Rome (ASV, AN, Atti, b. 1014, f. 120, 14 Nov. 1648). On Michiel's connections to the singer Anna Renzi, see B. Glixon, "Private Lives," and chapter 4. On Michiel and the Teatro Novissimo, see chapter 4.

63 ASV, SGSM, b. 112, account book 1657/58, ff. 39 and 40, 13 Dec. 1657.

Duodo's in-laws, Gregorio Barbarigo, included an anecdote concerning the ambassador in a letter to his brother, Antonio Barbarigo:

> He added that he had two commissions from Signor Marcantonio Correr: the first to listen to a singer and report whether she will succeed; the other, to facilitate her path to Venice. Regarding the first, he told me to tell him [Correr] that he could listen to her, but in regards to how she might succeed, that he, who understood nothing about those things, could not do that. But he would take with him two witnesses.[64]

One of Faustini's contacts referred to the participation of the ambassador in the hiring process during the 1659/60 season: "and you should, with your prudence, make things right with him [Giovanni Cappello] as best as you can; as for me, I promised him 80 doble, as appears on the receipt with the merchant, and as I also discussed with the Signor Ambassador."[65]

Letters written to Faustini and his partners give us an idea of the variety of people who might help out in the recruiting process. In 1658 Abbot Giuseppe Zanchi, a Venetian cleric temporarily in Rome, kept Alvise Duodo informed about problems regarding the recruiting of the singer Girolama, and he also drew up the contract.[66] In some cases Faustini was able to rely on musicians who had performed for him in the past. The lutenist Carlo Andrea Coradini (who performed in *L'incostanza trionfante*, 1657/58) helped recruit the castrato Giovanni Cappello in 1659; similarly, Carlo Vittorio Rotari, a member of the company for *Elena* (1659/60), aided the impresario in Rome during the 1660s by searching for appropriate women singers.[67]

One of Faustini's most intriguing contacts in Rome in 1665 was Arcangelo Lori, an important theorbist, lutenist, and organist; indeed, he seems to have been the leading freelance theorbist active in Rome during the mid-century, appearing

---

64 "Soggiunse haver due commissioni dal Signor Marcantonio Correr: l'una di udir una cantatrice e riferir se riuscirà; l'altra di mostrarle la strada di andar a Venetia facilmente. Per la prima mi disse rispondergli che poteva udirla, ma riferir come possa riuscir, egli, che non se ne intendeva, non poteva farlo. Che però haverebbe condotto due testimoni." Gios, *Itinerario biografico*, 400, letter from Rome, 20 July 1657. On the Barbarigos, and their relationship with the Correr and Duodo families, see chapter 3.

65 "è rimedij lei con la sua prudenza meglio che gli pare in quanto à me gli ò promesso ottanta doble come appariscie per polisa con il mercante è come o trattato anco con il Signor Ambasciatore." ASV, SGSM, b. 101, unnumbered, 24 Jan. 1660, letter of Carlo Andrea Coradini to Marco Faustini.

66 Abbot Giuseppe Zanchi was the son of Bortolo Zanchi, a Venetian wool merchant. Duodo sent Zanchi's report on to Faustini along with his own letter, written 5 Nov. 1658 (ASV, SGSM, b. 188, f. 19). There is no evidence as to whether this Girolama is the same as the Girolama Rossi who was planning to come to Venice to sing in 1641 (see Fabris, *Mecenati e musici*, 485).

67 Coradini was a correspondent of the Bentivoglio family, writing letters in 1655 and 1658 (see Monaldini, *Orto dell'Esperidi*, 83–84). In Faustini's records he is probably the "Carlo" listed among the instrumentalists; a criminal case involving the castrato Giovanni Antonio Cavagna mentions that the two musicians were in close contact daily (ASV, CD, Comuni, filza 598, 25 Aug. 1658). This case will be explored in a future article. Rotari's name appears in the cast list in the libretto for *L'incostanza trionfante*, but no payment records survive for him.

at festivities of a number of Roman churches and confraternities.[68] As the musician's letters reveal a familiarity with Faustini and his friend Giovanni Antonio Leffio (see chap. 3), as well as their environment in Venice, it is possible that he had traveled to Venice in 1661/62 with the singer Caterina Tomei.[69] In any event, Lori's letters to Faustini and Leffio make apparent his activites as a vocal coach and recruiter, and they convey a sense of the friendly discourse that took place between the Roman musician and his Venetian correspondents.[70] Lori writes primarily of the availability of Nina (Caterina Tomei), Giulia Masotti, the elusive "Guardarobba," and the Cimini sisters,[71] but also makes sure that Faustini is aware of new singers he is training that will be available in the future. Certainly the breadth of Lori's musical activities in Rome made him an ideal contact and ally.

Faustini enlarged his network by calling on friends and acquaintances who could use their own contacts to foster negotiations with singers. One such person was the Most Reverend Erasmo Secreti, a native of the ecclesiastical territory of Fermo, but resident in Venice during much of the mid-seventeenth century in Faustini's parish of S. Vidal. While in Venice, Secreti acted for Cardinal Flavio Chigi in some ecclesiastical matters, so it is likely that he knew a number of influential people in Rome. In 1665, while Faustini and Leffio corresponded with Lori, Secreti wrote to Carlo Mazzini regarding Masotti, Tomei, and the Cimini sisters. Mazzini may have corresponded with Secreti exclusively: none of his letters were addressed to Faustini or his partners.[72]

RECRUITING SINGERS FROM VENICE
AND ITS TERRITORY

While most of the lead singers, male and female, were brought to Venice from elsewhere for the opera season, a few prime donne and primi uomini, as well as many of those who sang the smaller roles, were available to impresarios much closer to home, either in Venice itself, or nearby. The task of recruiting these local musicians was quite different than for foreigners.

---

68 See *NG II*, s.v. "Lori, Arcangelo," by Helene Wessely. Jean Lionnet generously provided us with details concerning Lori's biography. Lori's letters in the Faustini papers, all written in 1665, are dated 28 Feb. (ASV, SGSM, b. 188, f. 112), 7 Mar. (f. 113), 21 Mar. (f. 108), 28 Mar. (f. 106), 4 Apr. (f. 101), 20 June (f. 118), 11 July (f. 120), 18 July (f. 91), 8 Aug. (f. 91), and 5 Dec. (ASV, SGSM, b. 194, f. 146).

69 A report that appears to describe Tomei's employment in Venice in 1662 mentions that she had traveled to Venice with a musician (ASF, MP, filza 3029, f. 1529ᵛ; see also Matteini, *"Rimino,"* 92).

70 Lori's involvement with training singers and recruiting is not revealed by sources currently known in Rome. In earlier references to Lori's letters (for example, Schmidt, "An Episode," 449) his name has been transcribed as "Cori," so that this Venetian connection has been missed. Regarding their level of familiarity, Lori often takes care to send the regards of his nephew, Loreto; according to Faustini's own account, he was in Rome in 1664, and thus may have come to know Lori's nephew at that time.

71 The two sisters, Anna Maria and Lucia Olimpia, are usually referred to in the Faustini correspondence with the surname "Fiorare" (or, perhaps, "Fiorane").

72 All of the Mazzini letters are addressed "Molt'Illustre e Molto Reverendo Signore e Padrone Osservissimo," that is, to a man of the cloth. Only the letter in ASV, SGSM, b.101 bears the name of the recipient: Erasmo Segreti (Secreti).

Sources for Local Male Singers:
The Cappella di S. Marco and Beyond

When searching for singers already active in Venice, the impresario's most logical source was the famed Cappella di S. Marco.[73] When few theaters competed against each other, the Cappella might well have provided much of the cast. Indeed, of the male singers in the original company at S. Cassiano in 1637, only Francesco Manelli was not yet a member of the Cappella.[74] This tradition of the sharing of singers between church and stage would continue in Venice into the eighteenth century.

On occasion opera singers recruited from other locales, having suitably impressed the members of the public, were subsequently hired to serve in the cappella.[75] The Paduan tenor Antonio Fabris joined just several months after appearing as "Gorgoglione" in Cesti's *Cesare amante* at the Grimani theater in the 1651/52 season.[76] Cavalli's protégé Giovanni Caliari gained employment in the Cappella shortly after his appearance in Cavalli's *Erismena* in 1656, and Giovanni Agostino Poncelli, another of Faustini's singers, became a member after the 1658 season.[77] Certainly, the Procuratori, the men in charge of the Cappella, wanted to employ outstanding singers, and the importation of new talent to Venice for the carnival season provided them with the opportunity to hear and judge these voices. Faustini's reliance on singers from the Cappella varied from year to year, but some members, like Antonio Formenti and Giacinto Zucchi, often formed part of his company.

Still another possible source of male singers for opera, also in relatively close proximity, was the choir of S. Antonio in Padua (some 30 miles to the west), which boasted one of the leading musical establishments in Italy.[78] Three singers from "il Santo," Pietro Cefalo, Filippo Manin, and Pietro Paolo Benigni, performed in Faustini's productions, while a number of others, such as Carlo Pallavicino and the young Agostino Steffani, appeared at other Venetian theaters.[79] The employment

73 For a look at the Cappella di S. Marco during the seventeenth century, see Moore, *Vespers at St. Mark's*.

74 Rosand, *Opera*, 71.

75 This phenomenon has been followed for the last quarter of the seventeenth century by Olga Termini. See Termini, "Singers at San Marco." See also Emans, "Cappella ducale."

76 A dispatch (17 Aug. 1652) sent to the court at Modena identified Fabris, calling him "Antonio padovano," as the singer who had performed the role of Gorgoglione. A previous letter (2 Aug. 1652) mentions how Fabris was hired at S. Marco after his opera performances (ASMo, CAV, b. 108, 128–vii / 27, f. 2 and 128–vii/35, f. 2).

77 For the election of Fabris to the Cappella, see ASV, Procuratori di S. Marco de supra, b. 145, 14 Apr. 1652; for Caliari, ASV, Procuratori di S. Marco de supra, reg. 146, 30 Apr. 1656; for Poncelli, ibid., 22 Nov. 1658. Opera singers did not always enter the Cappella on the heels of their operatic performance. Giacinto Zucchi joined only in Oct. 1648, about four and a half years after his 1642/43 appearance in *La finta savia* and, most likely, Monteverdi's *L'incoronazione di Poppea* (ASV, Procuratori di S. Marco de supra, b. 145 [olim 75], 30 Dec. 1648). For Zucchi's participation in operas in Venice in 1642/43, see Fabris, *Mecenati e musici*, 493.

78 The best source for music at S. Antonio for this period is A. Sartori, *Documenti per la storia*.

79 On Steffani and Pallavicino, see Billio, "Contributo sugli inizi di carriera," and Billio D'Arpa, "Documenti inediti." The brothers Giovanni Battista and Pietro Veralli, and Antonio Draghi, former employees of S. Antonio, were hired by Faustini after their years of service in Padua. For a full account of Steffani's life, see Timms, *Polymath of the Baroque*.

of singers from S. Antonio could not always have been viewed as ideal, however, as they were expected to return to Padua for the celebration on 15 February of one of the basilica's major feasts, the Translation of the Holy Tongue of St. Anthony, which, in many years, would have fallen in one of the last weeks of Carnival, a time when performances frequently ran nightly. Indeed, in 1667 an unnamed important personage in Venice prevented the young Steffani from returning to Padua, much to the consternation of the church administrators.[80]

If the singers from S. Marco can be characterized generally as local talent, even though many were originally from elsewhere in Italy, few native male Venetians found their way on to the public stage. Of Faustini's singers, only four seem to have been homegrown: the baritone Antonio Formenti, a member of the Cappella; the bass Pellegrino Canner (who joined the Cappella only in 1673); the castrato Giovanni Antonio Divido (Tonin di Muran), who served the Cappella as well as the courts of Dresden and Munich; and another Muranese, Zulian Zulian, who found his way onto Faustini's roster in the impresario's last year.[81] Male opera singers residing in Venice, then, were, for the most part a cosmopolitan bunch, culled from cities, towns, and courts throughout Italy, and often through that local filter of Italian musical talent, the Cappella di S. Marco.

Five Local Women on the Venetian Stage

We referred above to the influx of Roman women who performed on the Venetian stage. A Venetian impresario wishing to cast his opera with local women might have had difficulty gathering together a cast. In Venice there was no particular institution that could supply singers for the stage, although gifted singers emerged from time to time. Ironically, although Venice was famed for its women singers, those trained in Venice's famous *ospedali* were forbidden by the governing boards of those institutions from singing on the stage.[82] The impresario who hoped to hire local talent, then, had to look for musically gifted women unattached to the charitable institutions. During the mid-century, five such Venetian residents (four of them native Venetians) found varying degrees of success in Venetian theaters.

Little is known of the careers of two sisters—Lugretia and Maddalena Marconi—whom the Faustinis hired in the late 1640s and the 1650s. Giovanni Faustini recruited Maddalena to sing for his aborted 1649/50 season at S. Moisè, while Lugretia sang for Marco in 1654/55.[83] Indeed, without the documents concerning the Faustinis' productions, we would know nothing whatsoever of the sisters' participation in Venetian opera. Lugretia Marconi lived with, and bore the child of, Guglielmo Van Kessel, the Flemish businessman who helped to finance the pro-

---

80 Billio D'Arpa, "Documenti inediti," 145.

81 For these singers, see Emans, "Musiker des Markusdoms." For Divido, see also Frandsen, *Crossing Confessional Boundaries.*

82 Constable, "Venetian *Figlie del coro.*"

83 ASV, AN, Atti, b. 6075, 5 Oct. 1649. "Madalena," probably Marconi, was later recruited to sing in the 1657/58 season with a fee of 150 ducats, but she was eventually replaced (ASV, SGSM, b. 112, account book 1657/58, f. 38ᵛ).

duction of *Gl'amori di Alessandro magno, e di Rossane* at the Teatro SS. Apostoli in 1651 (see chap. 1), so it is possible that she performed in that production, as well as others.[84]

Another Venetian woman, Lucietta Gamba, was known as a singer, although not necessarily for performing on the Venetian stage. Several sources, including a poem by the librettist Giovanni Francesco Busenello, suggest that in Venice her reputation was that of a "singing courtesan" (Busenello styled her as "la putta che canta").[85] Gamba's nickname, "La Vidmana," almost certainly signifies that she had been the mistress of one of the Vidman brothers, a family known for its patronage of the librettist Giulio Strozzi during the 1640s.[86] Still, Gamba's talents were considerable enough to win her one of the leading roles in Cavalli's *Elena*, in 1659/60. Any other evidence of an operatic career is lacking.

Gamba's contemporary on the Venetian stage was Elena Lorenzoni, who married the Riminese captain Galeazzo Passarelli in May 1658, just a few months before she appeared in Cavalli's *Antioco*; during her career she seems to have used her married name exclusively.[87] Passarelli achieved some success in Venice, singing for Faustini in the seasons of 1659, 1660, and 1661. We know of no further performances in Venice, although she certainly may have sung at S. Cassiano in 1665/66, when her husband was involved in the management there (see chap. 4). Passarelli's career extended well beyond Venice, however: she went on to sing in Siena (1669) Florence (1670), and Rome (1672 and 1673).[88]

One other successful Venetian *virtuosa* of these years was Margarita Pia (Pio). She came from a musical family: her father and her uncle—the Romans Francesco and Antonino Pio—performed in Venice during the 1650s and 1660s (including some of Faustini's productions); Margarita, then, would have had easy access to any number of music teachers in Venice. She sang as a young woman of 13 at S. Moisè in Sebastiano Enno's production of Giovanni Antonio Boretti's *Alessandro amante* in 1666/67, and then the next year for Faustini at SS. Giovanni e Paolo.[89] Her

---

84 Marconi's name does not appear in the list of accounts detailing Van Kessel's expenditures for the opera at SS. Apostoli. Testimony appearing in diocesan records refers to Marconi as the widow of Van Kessel (ASPV, EM, b. 65, f. 308^{r-v}), but their daughter's baptismal record (Anna, baptized 4 Jan. 1649) suggests that the couple was not married at the time (ASPV, Parrocchia di S. Maria Formosa, Battesimi, 1629–48). On Van Kessel, see chapter 1, and B. Glixon, "Music for the Gods?" 448–50.

85 On Gamba, see B. Glixon, "Private Lives," 522–24.

86 Another famous Venetian singer, Barbara Strozzi, had a long-term relationship with a member of the Vidman family, Giovanni Paolo Vidman. See B. Glixon, "More on the Life and Death."

87 For Elena Passarelli's 1658 marriage contract, see ASV, AN, Atti, b. 6800, f. 309, 15 Sept. 1678. See also B. Glixon, "Sirena antica."

88 For the Siena performance of *Argia*, see Reardon, "1669 Sienese Production"; see also Reardon, *Holy Concord*, 125–29. Passarelli's other operatic performances are detailed in Bianconi and Walker, "Production, Consumption," 222.

89 Documentation for Pia's performances at S. Moisè was presented by Irene Alm in "Singer Goes to Court."

reputation rose, and she went on to sing in other operas in Venice, Bologna, Mantua, and Rome.[90]

Silvia Gailarti was Roman by birth, but came to Venice with her mother, Dionora Luppi (also a singer) in 1639, at about the age of 10; during the 1640s Gailarti appeared in an opera of Monteverdi (probably *Le nozze d'Enea in Lavinia*) and in one by Cavalli (*Titone*).[91] As a Venetian resident, Gailarti was conveniently available when her talent had progressed enough to allow her to perform on the stage. She left Venice probably in 1645, returning to sing for Faustini (using her married name, Silvia Manni) in the 1657/58 and 1658/59 seasons and at S. Luca in 1660/61. Gailarti had at least two teachers in Venice: one of them, Giovanni Carlo Cavalieri of Melfi, is a relatively obscure figure, but the other was the celebrated opera librettist and composer Benedetto Ferrari.

For the most part we are unaware of the teachers who helped Venetian women reach the stage. As we saw earlier, Francesco Cavalli, the most prolific composer of Venetian opera, taught a number of women in addition to his male students, yet none of these are known to have sung in the theater. Another Venetian composer, however, far less prominent than Cavalli, had a more particular interest in preparing women to sing on the stage. In 1665 Sebastiano Enno (mentioned above in regard to S. Moisè, and in chapter 4 for his activities at S. Aponal), a canon at the Cathedral of S. Pietro, contracted with Faustini to supply two singers under his charge, Caterina Masi and Saretta Sabbatini, and during the 1670s, he prepared another, Margarita de Zorzi Capello, to sing at S. Giovanni Grisostomo.[92] Fra Daniele da Castrovillari, the composer of three operas for Venice, was also active as a voice teacher, but we do not know if any of his students appeared in the theater.[93]

The Transformation of "Foreign" Talent into "Local": Roman Prima Donnas as Residents of Venice

Just as some male singers who came to Venice to perform in opera later joined the Cappella, thus becoming part of a pool of local talent from which the impresario could draw, some women, too, came to Venice and stayed. This circumstance, however, is one that has largely gone unnoticed in the musicological literature. Indeed, we have tended to think of the prima donnas as arriving in Venice shortly before

90 Pia sang in Rome (*Massenzio*, 1674) with Caterina Angiola Botteghi, her partner at SS. Giovanni e Paolo in 1667/68. She was considered for a part in *Eudosia* (Mantua, 1669); see B. Glixon, "Scenes from the Life," 139. On Pia's performances in Venice during the 1670s, see Vavoulis, "Antonio Sartorio," 38–39, 49.

91 On Gailarti's life, see B. Glixon, "Scenes from the Life."

92 Enno composed of two books of songs published during the 1650s. He mentioned the training of Margarita in his will (ASV, AN, Testamenti, b. 991, no. 299). See also *NG II*, s.v. "Enno, Sebastiano," by Beth Glixon.

93 ASPV, EM, b. 84, f. 2548. In 1669 Castrovillari gave testimony that he had been the teacher (in Venice) of the Roman Felice Margarita Raimondo.

the season, and leaving immediately afterwards. Faustini's correspondence for 1665 through 1667, in which he continued to recruit women from outside the city, has contributed much to the view of the peripatetic prima donna during this period.

Other documentation from the 1640s through the 1660s, however, shows that some women chose a different way of life. Anna Renzi came to Venice in 1640, following in the footsteps of Maddalena Manelli, Felicita Uga, and Giulia Saus Paolelli, the three Roman women mentioned earlier.[94] Unlike the others, however, Renzi, arguably the most famous prima donna of the time, made Venice her home, albeit with several periods of absence. Presumably she would have been free to take up residence where she pleased, but something must have kept her there, far from her ties in Rome. Perhaps she preferred to remain near to the operatic center of Europe; she may also have found a social and cultural environment that suited her.

Two other Romans, Virginia Rocchi and Caterina Porri, came to Venice several years later to perform in opera, Rocchi around 1649, and Porri in 1653.[95] Rocchi married the middleman (*sanser*) Vicenzo Camuffi in 1652;[96] she remained in Venice for the rest of her life, singing in operas (under her married name) intermittently through the 1660s.[97] Caterina Porri enjoyed a much more successful career as a prima donna in Venice. She too decided to stay in Venice after her first season at SS. Giovanni e Paolo (1653/54), and married a local businessman, Bortolo Caresana, in 1655.[98] Like Rocchi, Porri maintained a residence in Venice after her husband's death in 1666, appearing in operas there well into the 1670s (always using her maiden name). The presence of Porri in Venice helped to ease the tasks and the pocketbooks of impresarios, who could economize on traveling and living expenses for the cast.[99]

CASE STUDY: TRENDS IN RECRUITING AT MARCO FAUSTINI'S THEATERS DURING THE 1650S; LOCAL VERSUS FOREIGN SINGERS

For the most part we have only limited knowledge of the singers an impresario attempted to hire in any given year during the mid-seventeenth century. Indeed, in the case of theaters for which little correspondence and other corroborating mate-

94 On Renzi, see Sartori, "Prima diva"; Bianconi and Walker, "Dalla *Finta pazza*," 417–18, 442; Rosand, *Opera*, 228–35, 385; and B. Glixon, "Private Lives," 512–19.

95 Rocchi was recruited by Giovanni Faustini for S. Moisè; Porri came to Venice to sing at SS. Giovanni e Paolo.

96 ASPV, EM, b. 55, f. 343ᵛ.

97 Camuffi's last documented appearance was in Boretti's *Alessandro amante*, the focus of Alm's "Singer Goes to Court." Giovanni Faustini may have desired her talents when he was at S. Moisè, but apparently did not continue that support in 1651/52, as she is not one of the singers listed in the account book for that year at S. Aponal, nor did she ever appear in any of Marco Faustini's productions.

98 ASPV, EM, b. 63, f. 214.

99 Two other Romans active in opera during the 1650s—Angelica Felice Curti and Anna Felicita Chiusi—may have stayed in Venice after the height of their singing careers. Chiusi died there on 28 Apr. 1664, after having performed in Bologna, Milan, Turin, and Bergamo in the late 1650s and early 1660s (ASPV, Parrocchia di S. Giminiano, Morti, 1648–70).

rial survive, we are fortunate to know of even several members of the cast, for their names did not typically appear in librettos of the time. While letters in Faustini's papers give us a good idea of the singers he had hoped to hire for the 1666 season, such materials are largely absent for the previous decade. On the other hand, Faustini's three account books, along with the receipt book, provide nearly complete cast lists for a number of seasons, pointing up the different balances achieved between local and foreign singers. Faustini's rosters resemble a kaleidoscope, with familiar singers—both local and foreign—moving in and out of view, joined by others who would come and go in similar fashion, in constantly varying arrangements. The sources reveal, especially for the major roles, a remarkable variety of singers on his pay registers from year to year; even Faustini's reliance on members of the Cappella di S. Marco was inconsistent. Increasingly he would rely on the Cappella to fill the lower slots, with the lead castrato roles going to imported singers.

Faustini's first account book, that for the 1651/52 season, shows a mix of locals and foreigners in the cast.[100] At least two members of the Cappella were hired: the Bolognese Don Giulio Cesare Donati and the castrato Bonifacio Ceretti, who died shortly after the season had begun. Several other singers were available locally: the brothers Andrea and Cristoforo Caresana, and, possibly, "Pellegrino." Many of the other singers would seem to have been imported. The terza donna, "Nina," was hired with the help of "Zan Carlo dall'Arpa," quite possibly Giovanni Carlo Rossi, the famous harpist and composer resident in Rome. Several other singers, Fra Tomaso, Lorenzo (possibly Lorenzo Ferri), and the "tenor di Carrara" (perhaps identifiable as Francesco Guerra) were hired through the exchange of correspondence ("aggiustato per lettere").[101] Regarding the prime donne for 1651/52, Caterina Giani came from Florence, while Margarita da Costa's origins are obscure.[102]

Among the singers hired three years later for the 1654/55 season, more of them were local, and, unusually, they were initially paid by the composer Pietro Andrea Ziani or his brother-in-law, Nicolò Personé, rather than by Faustini: "Lodovico," Filippo Melani and his brother (most likely Bortolo), Francesco Simi, and Giovanni Sigonfredi (Antonio Fabris was hired but did not perform).[103] Other locals

---

100 In the account book the male singers under discussion are identified as follows: D. Giulio Cesare, Signor Bonifacio, Fra Tomaso da Bologna, tenor di Carrara, Pellegrino, and Signor Lorenzo (ASV, SGSM, b. 112, account book 1651/52, ff. 28ᵛ–31).

101 Fra Tomaso da Bologna is, most likely, Tomaso Bovi, the contralto who sang in Francesco Bonini's Bolognese opera *Gli sdegni d'Amore* (1646), and whose name would soon appear on the rolls of S. Petronio in Bologna (1653–56). For S. Petronio, see Gambassi, *Cappella musicale*. For Bovi and opera in Bologna, see Bianconi and Walker, "Dalla *Finta pazza*," 426, n.192. The presence of two (and possibly three) singers of Bolognese descent in the case is intriguing: perhaps Don Giulio Cesare Donati, the Bolognese cappella member mentioned above, recruited Fra Tomaso da Bologna and Lorenzo Ferri.

102 Da Costa is most likely not the more famous Margherita Costa, a singer and also a poet. See *DBI*, s.v. "Costa, Margherita," by Martino Capucci, and "Costa," *NG II*, s.v. "Costa, Margherita," by Tim Carter.

103 The Melanis are referred to only as "D. Filippo, et suo fratello" (ASV, SGSM, b. 113, account book 1654/55, f. 47ᵛ). Filippo Melani joined the Cappella di S. Marco in 1652 (ASV, Procuratia di San

included Giacinto Zucchi, and, perhaps, Antonino Pio, whose brother, the instrumentalist Francesco, had already lived in Venice for several years. Of these musicians, Filippo Melani, Zucchi, and Fabris were already singers in the Cappella, and
Bortolo Melani, Antonino Pio, and Giovanni Sigonfredi would be hired in January
1655, that is, during the opera season.[104] Of the male singers Faustini had originally hired, only the Bolognese Lorenzo Ferri (who did not perform) and Antonio
Draghi would not have been already present in Venice before the preparations for
the season had begun. The hiring of so many local men may have resulted from
Ziani's participation in the production, or it may reflect Faustini's absence from the
opera trade for the preceding two years (and a consequent weakening of his recruiting network). A number of the women may also have been living in Venice. As
mentioned earlier, Lugretia Marconi was a resident, and Anna Renzi, although
hired while performing in Innsbruck, could have planned to be back in Venice by
the time of the performances.[105] Angela Angelotti (called "Palermitana" by Faustini), however, was almost certainly recruited from the south.[106] (Figure 7.1 shows
the receipts signed by some of the singers for their salaries for this season).

For the 1656/57 season we see another sharp contrast, for only three members
of the cast were Venetian residents: Anna Renzi, Giacinto Zucchi, and Antonio
Formenti (only two of the eight male singers came from the Cappella). The lead
castrato, Carlo Mannelli, was an import from Rome who would later gain fame as
a violinist and composer.[107] Other men traveled from Padua (Filippo Manin,
Pietro Cefalo) and Ferrara (Caccialupi and Draghi). Caccialupi and Draghi performed for Faustini over several years, so that they, along with Zucchi and Formenti, contributed some stability to the company, if only in the minor roles.

Faustini's accounts from the mid-1650s and 1660s show how a singer could
enter his company, remain for several years (possibly with a multi-year contract),
and then move on when his situation changed. Antonio Draghi performed in
1655, 1656, and 1657, but was employed in Vienna by 1658.[108] Raffaele Caccialupi
sang with Faustini's company in 1657 and 1658, before joining Draghi the next
year in the cappella of the Dowager Empress in Vienna.[109] While other singers, especially in the 1660s, traveled from Vienna to Venice in order to perform in opera,

Marco de supra, reg. 145 (olim b. 75), 1 Apr. 1652). In the account book the entries for Simi and Pesaro
bear only the designations "basso" and "tenor" (ASV, SGSM, b. 113, account book 1654/55, f. 47ᵛ); they
both acknowledged receiving their wages, however, in Faustini's receipt book (ASV, SGSM, b. 118, receipt book, ff. 8ᵛ [see fig. 7.1], 9ᵛ, and 10ᵛ). On Personé, see chapter 3. Sigonfredi moved to Venice in
1653, according to testimony given by his father (ASPV, EM, b. 97, f. 6, 19 Sept. 1661).

104 ASV, Procuratia di San Marco de supra, b. 145 (olim b. 75), 31 Jan. 1654 m.v.

105 The Roman Angelica Felice Curti may also have been living in Venice in the year before
Eupatra, as her mother, Vittoria Curti, was present in Venice in Mar. 1654 (and authorized Abbot
Giuseppe Zanchi, the pieggio for the singer's salary for the 1654/55 season, to act on her behalf), al-
though she could have left at the end of the 1653/54 season.

106 See Prota-Giurleo, *Francesco Cirillo*, 23, 25; D'Alessandro, "Opera in musica," 420, 547.

107 See *NG II*, s.v. "Mannelli, Carlo," by Helene Wessely.

108 On Draghi, see Sala and Daolmi, *Quel novo Cario*.

109 Seifert, "Die Musiker," 535.

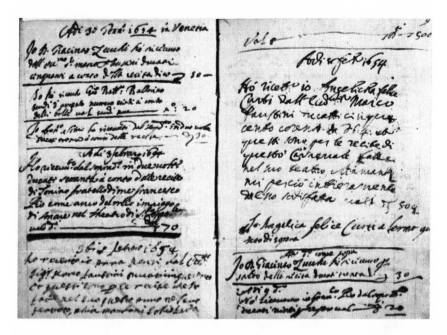

FIGURE 7.1.   Receipts for the 1654/55 Season at S. Aponal, from Faustini's receipt book
(ASV, SGSM, b. 118, ff. 8ᵛ–9)

Draghi and Caccialupi did not. Giovanni Antonio Cavagna's service with Faustini
shows the other side of the coin. Cavagna's employment at Turin remained stable
through the end of the 1660s, but he did not sing for Faustini every year, sitting
out the 1660, 1661, and 1662 seasons. Some local singers such as Cappella member
Antonio Formenti served Faustini often, but certainly not exclusively (1657–59
and 1661–63).

CONTRACTS AND FINANCIAL CONSIDERATIONS

Recruitment represented only the beginning of the process of putting singers on
stage. The impresario had to reach a formal agreement with his selected performers; arrange to bring them to Venice, if they were foreigners, and find them lodging; and, naturally, pay them. For Marco Faustini the signing of contracts usually
began during the summer, and continued for several months (see appendix 4). For
1651/52, for example (see table 7.1), the first contract, with the seconda donna
Margarita da Costa, was signed on 4 August, but the prima donna Caterina Giani
did not sign hers until 16 September, and others were not finalized until mid- to
late October, barely a month before the opening night on 28 November.[110] In

110 ASV, SGSM, b. 112, account book 1651/52. Faustini's four account books from the 1650s provide modest bits of information regarding the hiring and employment of some of the singers under the
category "musici," sometimes specifying the date of agreement (aggiusto) or hire, but sometimes limited
only to the agreed-upon fee.

TABLE 7.1. Contract Dates for Singers in Marco Faustini's Company for the 1651/52 and 1654/55 Seasons

1651/52		1654/55	
Date	Singer	Date	Singer
4 August	Margarita da Costa	12 June	Anna Renzi
8 August	Don Giulio Cesare Donati	13 June	Angelica Felice Curti
19 August	Fra Tomaso (Bovi)	18 August	*Antonio Fabris (Gorgoglione)
21 August	*Amato Riminuzzi	31 August	Antonino Pio
25 August	*Bonifacio Ceretti	1 September	*Lorenzo Ferri
25 August	Andrea and Cristoforo Caresana	12 September	Lugretia Marconi
16 September	Caterina Giani	12? September	Angela Angelotti
22 September	Tenor di Carrara (Francesco Guerra?)	12 September	Giacinto Zucchi
14 October	Pellegrino	12 September	Antonio Draghi
17 October	Nina dal Pavon		
Later	"Putella"; Lorenzo (Ferri?)	Later	Lodovico; Filippo e suo fratello (Filippo and Bortolo Melani?); Francesco Simi; Giovanni Sigonfredi

Sources: ASV, SGSM, b. 112, account book 1651/52; b. 113, account book 1654/55.
* Did not sing.

1654, he began the process somewhat earlier, reaching agreements with the two prime donne, Anna Renzi and Angelica Felice Curti, on 12 and 13 June, respectively.[111] Most of the remaining contracts, however, were not finalized until late August or September. Documentation is fragmentary for the next ten years, but Faustini tried something different when he decided to return to SS. Giovanni e Paolo for the 1665/66 season: he signed at least two contracts immediately after the end of the previous season (Giovanni Giacomo Biancucci on 26 February and Sebastiano Cioni on 7 March[112]), before singers left Venice at the conclusion of Carnival. He did the same the next year with the prima donna Antonia

111 ASV, SGSM, b. 113, account book 1654/55.
112 ASV, SGSM, b. 194, ff. 28, 29. Although Cioni was hired at S. Marco in 1662, he was working outside of Venice by 1665; his letters to Faustini from the spring of that year were written from Turin, and those in the fall from Verona (ASV, SGSM, b. 188).

Coresi (along with her husband Nicola), who signed a contract on 17 February 1666.[113]

Singers' Contracts: An Introduction

Presumably, all opera singers—that is, after the times of the earliest self-contained companies that had operated in Venice—had a contract of some sort with an impresario. Remarkably, however, very few contracts have come to light for the mid-seventeenth century, and only one seems to have been registered in the acts of a Venetian notary at the time of its completion: that of Anna Renzi, the leading prima donna on the Venetian stage, for *Deidamia*.[114] On 17 December 1643 Renzi signed a contract with impresario Girolamo Lappoli to return to the Teatro Novissimo for the 1643/44 season, her third at that theater, after a year's absence (the complete original text is in appendix 3, doc. 3). The principal clauses of the contract stipulated:[115]

> The said Signora Anna is obliged to sing in one or more operas that will be performed this carnival in the Teatro Novissimo, attending each rehearsal of the operas, only, however, [those that take place] in the theater, or at the residence of Signora Anna.[116]
>
> In exchange, the said Signor Geronimo promises to give to the said Signora Anna 500 Venetian silver scudi in this manner: that is, 100 scudi for the current month of December, another 150 at the time of the second performance, another 150 after half of the performances, and, at the penultimate performance, the remaining 100 scudi without any opposition or delay.
>
> In the case of illness (God forbid) of the said Signora Anna (if she has done part of the performances): in this case Signora Anna could only hope to exact one half of the said 500 scudi; but if for any other cause, without exception, Signor Lappoli should be prevented from mounting the production, he would be required to give her the 500 scudi in the above manner.
>
> Moreover, Signor Lappoli is, in any case, obliged to give and consign to her a box[117] for her use for the entire Carnival and, in addition, all the costumes she will need for her performances, all of this at the expense of Signor Lappoli; these costumes will remain the property of Signor Lappoli. For all of the above he pledges his property, both present and future.[118]

---

113 ASV, SGSM, b. 194, f. 139. Coresi had sung the role of the prima donna in *Tito*, and probably expected that she would be the prima donna for the next season. The hiring of Giulia Masotti (see below) meant that Coresi would sing the second role, as Masotti insisted on having the status of prima donna.

114 Parts of contracts, however, were entered afterwards into either notarial registers or records of the courts when singers attempted to obtain unpaid wages.

115 ASV, AN, Atti, b. 658, ff. 163ᵛ–164ᵛ, 17 Dec. 1643. This contract is discussed further in B. Glixon, "Private Lives," 513–14. For a complete English translation, see Strunk and Treitler, *Source Readings*, 569–71.

116 Ivanovich, writing in the 1680s, mentioned that rehearsals were held at the houses of the noble sponsors, of the "interessati," or in the theater.

117 As we saw in chapter 2, the standard annual rate for a palco in a Venetian theatre during the 1650s and 1660s was 20 or 25 ducats.

118 In some early companies, such as S. Cassiano in 1638/39, the performers were expected to supply their own costumes. See chapter 10.

The contract, more detailed than those that survive from the 1650s and 1660s, addresses a number of basic issues: the requirement to attend all rehearsals (apparently some singers failed to accomplish this); the fees to be awarded, in conjunction with a payment schedule; provisions that would apply in the case of illness; and other extras such as the use of an opera box and the furnishing of costumes. A further clause of the contract appointed Josef Camis as guarantor (pieggio) for Renzi's salary; this, at least on paper, would have assured Renzi her fees even if Lappoli himself could or would not pay them.[119]

Renzi's generous compensation for appearing in *Deidamia*, 500 Venetian scudi (or 750 ducats; see below for a discussion of singer's salaries), is an indication of her esteem and popularity at this point in her career; she would earn considerably less in later years (in comparison, the highest paid singers at S. Marco earned 100 ducats as an annual salary). Issues not mentioned in the contract, presumably because Renzi had taken up permanent or semipermanent residence in Venice, were housing and reimbursement for her travel back to Rome. Renzi's high salary—along with the contract's registration with a notary, as well as its late date—may reflect some reluctance on Renzi's part to return to the Novissimo after having sung the previous season at SS. Giovanni e Paolo; she undoubtedly knew of the financial problems the theater had encountered, and may have sought to protect herself from the possibility of financial loss (see chap. 4).

The registration of a singer's contract in the acts of a notary seems, to our modern eyes, the most natural and logical of processes, since contracts of every stripe found their way into the notarial records, but this one is so far unique. Anna Renzi relied on notaries for a variety of services throughout her long sojourn in Venice, so that she may have insisted on the registration of her contract; for some reason, however, this procedure must have been thought unnecessary or perhaps excessive in the majority of cases—even for Renzi—and "private" agreements were the norm.[120]

Contracts in the Faustini Papers: A Sampling

Private, unregistered contracts are, naturally, less likely to survive than those registered with a notary, but several are extant in various collections. The earliest of them, however, for the 1651/52 season at S. Aponal, can hardly be viewed as typical. Indeed, it is a model of brevity, listing only Faustini's promised payment of 300 ducats: "In recognition of the honorable labors of Signora Catterina, daughter of the Florentine Signor Francesco Giani—who is obligated to perform in the Teatro di S. Aponal—I the undersigned promise to pay out D300 comprised of £6 s.4 [per ducat] during the time of the performances, in pledge of which I have made this in my own hand."[121] In this contract we see only the financial particulars re-

119 On Camis, see chapter 4.

120 See B. Glixon, "Private Lives."

121 "Io sottoscritto per recognitione delle virtuose fatiche della Signora Cattarina figlia del Signor Francesco Giani fiorentino, che si è obligata di recitare nel Teatro di S. Apponalle, prometto esborsare ducati trecento dal £6 s4 nel corso delle recite, in fede di che ho fato la presente di mia propria mano." ASV, SGSM, b. 101, unnumbered, 18 Sept. 1651. Massimiliano Neri and Jacopo Maffei, both musicians at

garding Caterina's performances for the operas; another contract, concentrating more specifically on the singer's duties, and on her benefits, must have also been drawn up.[122] It is perhaps worth noting that Giani's compensation for singing in the two operas, 150 ducats for each, was equal to that of Cavalli for their composition. Here, then, we see a sort of parity between prima donna and composer that would soon fade away.

Lucietta Gamba's more complete contract of 18 July 1659 specifies the following conditions (see the complete original text in appendix 3, doc. 4):[123]

1. Gamba must participate in all of the rehearsals and performances.
2. Faustini pledges 150 doble (the equivalent of 677 ducats): 50 after the second performance, 50 halfway through, and the final 50 at the end of the performances.
3. Should Gamba fall ill, she will be paid in proportion to those performances she has completed; the same conditions apply should the performances be canceled by public command.

Gamba's fees fall about 70 ducats short of Renzi's for *Deidamia*, and her protections were also less than those of the famous prima donna, who would have been paid in full if the performances came to be canceled by public command. This agreement was attained through the aid of the nobleman Michiel Morosini, presumably Gamba's protector at this time. Gamba earned nearly twice the amount promised to Elena Passarelli that year, and nearly four times that of the third woman, Anna Caterina Venturi.[124] Gamba's fees are quite large for a local prima donna; indeed, they even surpass those of the Roman Girolama, the leading woman of the previous year (Girolama's contract specified compensation for lodging and food, particulars not addressed in Gamba's case). Her high fees may reflect her reluctance to sing publicly, but we might also wonder if Gamba's compensation was also related in some way to her reputation as a courtesan: her appearance on stage could have been viewed as an exciting curiosity. Or, Faustini may have hired her at the request (and perhaps with the support) of one of her patrons.

As we saw earlier, Faustini employed a number of singers in consecutive years, but no extant multi-year agreements survive until 1665, when he signed three-year contracts with Caterina Masi, Saretta Sabbattini, and Giovanni Antonio Divido.[125]

---

the Cappella di S. Marco, were witnesses to the document. Confirmation of Faustini's payments to Caterina appears on the lower part of the sheet of paper, with each installment acknowledged by her father.

122 Faustini's account book, for example, reveals that he supplied a boat to transport Caterina to the theater, a service he did not provide for any of the other singers; one would expect an "extra" like this to be part of a special agreement.

123 ASV, SGSM, b. 194, f. 11r–v (this contract is published, with some errors, in Brunelli, "Impresario in angustie," 314). A similar contract survives for Elena Passarelli; see ASV, SGSM, b. 194, f. 12, 9 Oct. 1658.

124 Passarelli was paid 361 ducats, Venturi 180 ducats.

125 Faustini arranged to hire Masi and Sabbattini through their teacher Enno, mentioned above (ASV, SGSM, b. 188, f. 64). For Divido, see ASV, SGSM, b. 188, f. 65. Masi and Sabbattini did not complete the terms of their contracts.

Antonia Coresi, who joined the company as a prima donna mid-season for *Tito* (1665/66), signed on for two more years, thus assuring Faustini of a high-caliber lead soprano, this in a year that had brought particular difficulties in recruiting;[126] one of the clauses promised that the soprano would be paid even if she did not sing through some fault or action of Faustini. While some contracts offered particular protections for Faustini, others were more perfunctory, referring only to the fees to be received by the singer.[127]

Salaries: A Singer's Worth

A singer's fees were governed by a variety of factors, including, as we saw in the case of Anna Renzi, the popularity of the artist and the financial reputation and general aspirations of the opera company. Renzi's 750 ducats for *Deidamia* in 1643/44 are a case in point. Although we know of the fees of few other singers of that decade, her fees far exceeded the those of many prima donnas of the 1650s and 1660s (see table 7.2).

Faustini's papers provide us with the most comprehensive view of singers' salaries during the mid-seventeenth century. The fees varied widely, and changed considerably during Faustini's years in opera production.[128] Singers on the bottom of the pay scale earned very little indeed. For *Eupatra* (1654/55), Francesco Simi and Giovanni Sigonfredi each received 40 ducats, well under one-tenth the wages of the prima donna (Simi's signed receipt for his salary can be seen in figure 7.1). On the other hand, Simi earned 50 ducats annually at the time of his hire at S. Marco, and Sigonfredi 60 ducats, so that even at the bottom of the pay scale, their operatic earnings nearly doubled their yearly income.[129]

A number of scholars have commented on the inflation of the fees for prima donnas.[130] Although the Faustini papers provide ample evidence of this trend, they also show that this escalation did not proceed at a steady, gradual rate. Renzi's 750 ducats of 1643/44 at the Novissimo were matched in Faustini's accounts for the first time only eighteen years later, in 1661/62, by another Roman, Caterina Tomei. Tomei's fees represent a spike in a prima donna's earnings at SS. Giovanni e Paolo; the previous year the lead singer Caterina Porri received only 452 ducats; Tomei, as the new import, earned nearly 285 ducats more than her. For the 1662/63 season, Porri regained her status as prima donna, but her fees stayed at

---

126 ASV, SGSM, b. 194, f. 139, 17 Feb. 1665 m.v.

127 Biancucci's contract of 1667 obligated him to "perform those roles that will be necessary to the satisfaction of the said Signor Faustini, being always present at the rehearsals and at the performances, and having to be here in this city by 1 November" ("facendo quelle parti che saranno neccessarie a sodisfatione d'esso Signor Faustini, essendo sempre presente alle prove, et alle recite et dovendo ritrovarsi in questa città per il primo di novembre prossimo venturo"). ASV, SGSM, b. 194, f. 44, 1 May 1667.

128 The wages of some of Faustini's singers are discussed in Bianconi and Walker, "Production, Consumption," 224–25, and Rosand, *Opera*, 222–27.

129 In 1657/58 Abbatoni earned only 30 ducats, but he appears to have performed only in the prologue.

130 See, for example, Rosand, *Opera*, 222–25.

TABLE 7.2.   Salaries for Lead Male and Female Singers in Faustini's Companies

Season	Prima donna	Salary in ducats	Seconda donna	Salary in ducats	Primo uomo	Salary in ducats
1651/52	Caterina Giani	300	Margarita da Costa	300	Bonifacio Ceretti	300
1654/55	Anna Renzi	500	Angelica Felice Curti	500	Lodovico	250
1655/56	Angelica Felice Curti	250	Anna Felicita Chiusi	250	Giacinto Zucchi (bass)	200
					Amato Riminuzzi	200
1656/57	Anna Maria Volea	316	Anna Renzi	300	Carlo Mannelli	300
1657/58	Ginevra Senardi	452	Silvia Manni	375	Giovanni Antonio Cavagna	361
1658/59	Girolama	450	Silvia Manni	345	Giovanni Antonio Cavagna	361
1659/60	Lucietta Gamba	677	Elena Passarelli	362	Giovanni Cappello	361
1660/61	Caterina Porri	452	Elena Passarelli	360	Clemente Antonii	452
1661/62	Caterina Tomei	750	Caterina Porri	452	Giuseppe Romei (baritone)	450
1662/63	Caterina Porri	452	Veronica Mazzochi	300	Giovanni Antonio Cavagna	542
1665/66	Antonia Coresi	750 (1 opera)	Anna Caterina Venturi	452	Giovanni Antonio Cavagna	542
					Giuseppe Donati	500
1666/67	Giulia Masotti	1806	Antonia Coresi	1452	Giovanni Antonio Cavagna	452?
1667/68	Antonia Coresi	1500	Caterina Angiola Botteghi	542	Giovanni Antonio Cavagna	677

Sources: ASV, SGSM, b. 118 (receipt book); ibid., b. 112 (account book for 1651/52 season); ibid., b. 113 (account book for 1654/55 and 1655/56 seasons); ibid., b. 112 (account book for 1657/58 season); and ibid., b. 194 (account book for 1658/59 season).

their previous level rather than rising to Tomei's. Another increase occurred in 1666/67, when Giulia Masotti earned four times more than Porri had in the early 1660s, evidence of Masotti's (and her protectors') skills as a negotiator. Antonia Coresi's earnings during Faustini's last triennium, if not equal to Masotti's, were still substantial, at 1,500 ducats. High fees such as these eventually influenced those of Caterina Porri; for the 1666/67 season at S. Luca she earned 1,500 ducats, over three times what she had in the earlier part of the decade; two years later at the same theater, in Cesti's *Argia*, her fees rose slightly, with 1,550 ducats promised. Giulia Masotti's fees for *Argia* (see below), though, were even higher, at 2,192 ducats (500 doble), the peak for those known during this decade.[131] Clearly, the top women performers of the time operated from a position of power, knowing that their services were viewed—by the impresario and the audience—as indispensable.

Our concept of the prima donna as the single top wage earner in a company did not always apply in Faustini's early years as an impresario: in the 1651/52, 1654/55, and 1655/56 seasons, the two women at the top of the pay scale earned equal fees. This parity, however, soon gave way to a tiered pay scale. In two of Caterina Porri's years at SS. Giovanni e Paolo she earned 452 ducats to Veronica Mazzochi's 300 or 330.[132] By 1668 we see a remarkable range of fees: the three women, Antonia Coresi, Caterina Angiola Botteghi, and the young Margarita Pia earned 1,500, 542, and 100 ducats respectively. It should be noted that for some years, the data in Faustini's records may be misleading. It is unclear, for example, why Angelica Felice Curti and Anna Felicita Chiusi earned 250 ducats each in 1656 when the previous year Curti and Anna Renzi had received double that amount (their receipts can be seen in figure 7.1). It is possible that the lower figure is the amount paid directly by the company, and that their salaries were given a boost by generous noblemen who offered to make up the difference.

One important question is the relative worth of female versus male singers in this time of public opera, and whether the castrati were valued more highly than the tenors and basses (see table 7.2). If we look at the salaries during Faustini's first decade as an impresario, we find certain castrati paid at the level of the prima donnas. Bonifacio Ceretti's fees, for example, would have equaled those of Margarita da Costa and Caterina Giani in 1651/52 for *Calisto* and *Eritrea*. In 1660/61 at SS. Giovanni e Paolo, the famed castrato Clemente Antonii earned fees equal to those of Caterina Porri. The fees of Giovanni Antonio Cavagna show how the value of a top castrato could change according the particular women in the cast. His fees rose steadily between 1657 and 1668, in some years surpassing those of the seconda donna, but only once exceeding those of the prima donna (1662/63). Other castrati, who filled a number of the roles in any opera, earned less. In 1660/61, for example, the fees for the castrati ranged from a high of 452 ducats for

131 Porri appeared in Nicolò Minato and Antonio Sartorio's *La prosperità di Elio Seiano* and *La caduta di Elio Seiano* in 1666/67 (ASV, AN, Atti, b. 1166, f. 277, 4 Jan. 1666 m.v.). For the pay sheet that specifies Porri's fees for *Argia*, see Vcg, Archivio Vendramin, b. 42 F 6/1–6 [49], no. 20, 13 Apr. 1669, reproduced in Rosand, *Opera*, 197.

132 These figures are taken from ASV, SGSM, b. 118, receipt book, ff. 51, 51ᵛ, 67ᵛ, 68.

Clemente Antonii, mentioned above, down to a lowly 73 for Pietro Lucini. At 333 ducats, two other castrati, Cosimo Orlandi and Bartolomeo Fregosi, earned fees substantially below Antonii's, and Orlandi's payment also included his travel expenses. Occasionally, a non-castrato male might also command high fees. The baritone Giuseppe Romei, a Neapolitan dwarf known as Don Peppe, whose appearance on stage would have been viewed as a curiosity, signed for 450 ducats on 24 February 1662, just 10 lire shy of Porri's earnings.[133]

Overall, the impresario's expenditures for singers represented by far the largest portion of the overall budget for a season. In the years, all in the 1650s, for which we have reliably complete figures (see appendix 5), singers claimed between 27 and 42 percent of the total costs. In later years, when, as discussed above, salaries for the lead singers increased dramatically, the percentage was undoubtedly even higher.

Travel and Living Expenses for Foreign Singers

The hiring of singers from outside Venice made their travel and lodging a budgetary issue. As we mentioned earlier, the allowance for the round-trip journey from Rome was usually 150 ducats, but the costs varied according to the singer. Some, particularly the men, traveled alone or with a single servant: in 1659 Giovanni Capello claimed his journey to Venice would amount to 72 ducats each way.[134] Silvia Manni's itemized receipts give us an even better idea of the expenses in 1657: the first leg of the journey, by horse and carriage from Rome to Ancona, came to 27 ducats, and the second, by boat from Ancona to Venice, came to about 23 ducats.[135] Many women, however, arrived with a much larger entourage, and therefore greater expenses. Giulia Masotti apparently preferred to travel with her brother, mother, and a servant, and demanded 200 ducatoni (somewhat more than 400 ducats) for expenses for the round trip, while Caterina Tomei arrived in Venice with her mother, a musician, a servant, and a maid.[136] The cost of travel from a distant city such as Rome, then, as mentioned above, exceeded the entire salaries of some of the more ordinary singers. On the other hand, singers traveling from cities nearby required only a small allowance: the round trip from Ferrara or Montagnana cost only 4 to 6 ducats.[137] In many cases, a singer signed for receipt of his performing fees and travel costs simultaneously, making an accurate determination impossible.

133 The libretto for *Le fatiche d'Ercole per Deianira* reveals that Romei's part had been tailored for him: the character "Pipo" describes himself in act 1, scene 12 as "of small stature": "La natura / Che mie diè / Così picciola statura / Col mio poco / Prende gioco / E sovente si trastulla / Ma s'acaso m'abbasso io resto annulla" ("Nature, who gave me such small stature, makes fun of my littleness, and often amuses herself at my expense. But if by chance I stoop down, I almost disappear").

134 ASV, SGSM, b. 101, unnumbered, letter of 16 Jan. 1660 m.v.

135 That same year, the prima donna Ginevra's receipt for the maritime portion was almost 34 ducats (ASV, SGSM, b. 112, account book 1657/58, ff. 38ᵛ–39).

136 For Giulia Masotti's traveling companions, see ASV, SGSM, b. 188, f. 294. For Masotti's and Tomei's traveling expenses see ASV, SGSM, b. 194, f. 109.

137 For example, Antonio Draghi, traveling from Ferrara for the 1655/56 season, received 6 ducats (ASV, SGSM 118, receipt book, f. 18), and in 1658/59 the unnamed contralto from Montagnana received £28 (about 4 ducats; ASV, SGSM, b. 194, account book 1658/59, f. 16ᵛ).

As might be expected, a singer's rank in large part determined the quality of his or her lodging in Venice. Faustini's contract with Giulia Masotti (see below) mentioned the possibility of her staying in his own house. We do not know to how many prima donnas Faustini extended this offer, but, as mentioned above, Alessandro Guasconi, the expatriate Florentine businessman, visited Caterina Angiola Botteghi there in November 1667, in advance of the upcoming season.[138] We know that Faustini entertained singers in his home, for Arcangelo Lori commented that "Signor Faustini will enjoy having them come to Venice, enjoying in his house their sweet conversation and harmony."[139] Some singers stayed in the palaces of either Venetian or visiting nobles. During the impresario's years at SS. Giovanni e Paolo, one possibility was residence at the palace of the Grimanis, as specified in a draft of Faustini's contract with them.[140] In 1666 Giovanni Antonio Cavagna hoped to lodge either with the Contestabile Lorenzo Onofrio Colonna, or with his brother-in-law, the Duke of Nivers, but as an alternative, he esteemed Faustini's house above all others.[141] Giovanni Capello, the castrato who had traveled from Rome, had wanted to stay either in the house of a certain cardinal, or in that of the "Prince of Brunswick," but followed the demands of Faustini who, for some reason, ordered him to stay elsewhere.[142] Girolamo Barbieri even housed one of his singers at S. Luca in the home of his son-in-law, the lawyer Francesco Butironi.[143] Some singers lived more continuously in the homes of Venetian nobles. As we saw earlier, Bonifacio Ceretti resided at the home of Marc'Antonio Priuli, and housing with Pietro Dolfin was only one of the benefits that Lugretia "Dolfin" enjoyed while she was under the nobleman's protection.[144] The castrato Tomaso Bovi lived at the Grimani palace on a permanent basis.[145] Lodgings such as these normally generated no cost for the impresario. When singers were not provided rooms in a palace, it was necessary to rent rooms for them. During the 1650s basic rental costs varied. Faustini paid 7 ducats per month for Silvia Manni and Ginevra Senardi for the 1657/58 season;[146] the next year the monthly rent for Passarelli's lodgings (which Faustini paid even though she was a resident of the city) came to 10 ducats.[147] These figures, however, represented only a portion of

---

138 ASF, MP, filza 5574, no. 378, Venice, 26 Nov. 1667, Alessandro Guasconi to Leopoldo de' Medici.

139 "e che il signor Faustini goderà d'haverle fatte venire in Venetia, godendo in casa sua la loro dolce conversatione et armonia." ASV, SGSM, b. 194, f. 146, 5 Dec. 1665, Arcangelo Lori to Giovanni Antonio Leffio.

140 ASV, SGSM, b. 194, f. 26.

141 For the request to stay either with the Contestabile or the Duke of Nivers, see ASV, SGSM, b. 188, f. 47, 1 Nov. 1666. Regarding the option of staying in Faustini's house see ASV, SGSM, b. 188, f. 37, 14 Nov. 1666.

142 ASV, SGSM, b. 101, unnumbered.

143 ASV, GP, Dimande, b. 45, fasc. 85, no. 380, 15 Sept. 1662.

144 On Lugretia Dolfin, see Rosand, Opera, 214, 227, 236–37. See also Vavoulis, "Antonio Sartorio," 35. Pietro Dolfin saw to Lugretia's training, and managed her career.

145 In his will Bovi claimed to have lived in the Grimani house for forty-seven years (ASV, AN, Testamenti, b. 1197, no. 291).

146 ASV, SGSM, b. 112, account book, 1657/58, f. 20ᵛ. In some versions of that year's libretto, Ginevra's surname is mistakenly printed as "Fenardi"; see Glixon and Glixon, "Triumph of Inconstancy."

147 ASV, SGSM, b. 118, receipt book, f. 38, 13 Mar. 1659.

the costs. The rooms apparently came unfurnished, and Faustini was paying to house Ginevra with some degree of comfort, so that he disbursed a goodly sum, 27 ducats per month, for furniture for her rooms, as well as £7 per month for a cook and £9 s.6 for a maid.[148] Impresarios were often responsible for board as well as lodging: at S. Luca in 1666, the cost of meals for four singers was £16 per day.[149] Girolama's contract for 1658/59 specified that her lodging would be covered, and that all necessary household goods would be provided; in addition to the 15 ducats for lodging—over double what he had paid for Manni and Ginevra the previous year—Faustini spent over 37 ducats each month for furniture rental and board, but recorded no payments for servants.[150] In any event, the monthly cost for Girolama's room and board came to something between 50 and 55 ducats, meaning, for the entire season, an additional 150 ducats above the agreed-upon salary and travel expenses.

Payment Schedules: Problems and Solutions

From the singers' point of view, perhaps the most important issue concerning their employment was the timeliness of their payments: most were paid intermittently throughout the season, but the schedule varied among the singers, and from year to year.[151] That same issue would have been significant for the impresario as well, although for different reasons: many aspects of the production, including costumes and scenery, were expected to be paid for by opening night, but only at that point did the bulk of the income begin; by delaying payment to the singers the impresario could make better use of the funds available to him in the earlier part of the season. On the other hand, if an impresario became known for his inability to pay musicians on time, recruitment became even more difficult, possibly leading to the demand for increased salaries or more stringent guarantees. As we saw earlier, this may have been the case with Anna Renzi at the Novissimo in 1643/44. Similarly the failure of the S. Aponal company of 1653/54 to pay its singers on time may have forced Faustini, the following year, to offer advance payments: the two top women, Anna Renzi and Angelica Felice Curti, received a total of 450 ducats before the season had begun.[152] More specific evidence of this phenomenon emerges after the 1657/58 season, when Silvia Manni had not been paid in full (see chap. 3; why she was the only singer to be owed money by the company after the end of the season is far from clear). When this became known in Rome, it led to difficulties in the recruitment of Girolama, the intended prima donna for the next

148 ASV, SGSM, b. 112, account book, ff. 20ᵛ–21.

149 ASV, GP, Scritture e risposte, b. 190, fasc. 81, no. 237, 7 Sept. 1669.

150 For Girolama's contract, see ASV, SGSM, b. 188, f. 22. For her miscellaneous expenses, ASV, SGSM, b. 194, account book 1658/59, f. 17.

151 While Faustini's account books list a series of payments, the receipt book on occasion only lists one comprehensive sum, so that it is not always possible to track a precise payment schedule.

152 Renzi received half of her salary in two installments before the opera had begun: one upon her arrival in Venice in September, and the second several days before the first performance. Curti received her first payment on 13 June, a full six months before the opening of the production (ASV, SGSM, b. 113, account book 1654/55, ff. 43 and 44).

season.[153] It must have been difficult to calm the fears of skittish singers, especially ones who had suffered in the past at the hands of other impresarios.

One method of assuring, or hoping to assure payment, was the assigning of a pieggio, or guarantor (see chap. 1). As we saw earlier in the case of theaters and their expenses, the formation of most business companies as well as many financial transactions—including rentals, loans, purchases, and dowries—involved the naming of a pieggio; indeed, the principle was one of the most basic of the financial fabric of the time. The extension of that principle, then, to the hiring of singers was not viewed as unusual. The Renzi/Lappoli contract made provisions for a guarantor, and Faustini himself acted in that same capacity for the singer Amato Riminuzzi for at S. Aponal, probably in 1653/54 when the theater was run by Annibale Basso and Bortolo Castoreo. It was Faustini—in his capacity as pieggio—who paid Riminuzzi in March, shortly after the end of the season.[154] Another singer, Orsetta Parmine, was less fortunate than Riminuzzi, and still had not received her full wages from Annibale Basso years later, in 1657; either Parmine had had no guarantor for her contract, or her (or her protector's) demands for her fees had proved fruitless.[155] This state of affairs concerning the management of singers' payments might, in part, have convinced Faustini to return to the theater in 1654 after his two-year absence.

If Faustini was particularly successful in paying his musicians by the end of the carnival season (as shown by the data in the receipt and account books), some others active in Venetian opera were not. Both S. Luca and S. Moisè had difficulties meeting their obligations to the musicians during the mid-1660s, and a number of them, including Domenico Bordoni and Caterina and Brigida Forti, took their complaints to the Venetian courts.[156] The case of Giuseppe Ghini in particular shows the complex process that could ensue when a singer had to turn to a number of parties in search of his fees.

Ghini, who had sung at S. Moisè, approached one of the Venetian courts, the Giudici di petizion, in April 1666, less than a month after the termination of Carnival, seeking the 90 doppie (about 400 ducats) owed to him; at the same time he wrote to Prince Leopoldo de' Medici describing his frustration.[157] In Spring 1667, he was still seeking satisfaction.[158] A series of letters written by Paolo del Sera, the

---

153 According to Faustini's correspondent, Abbot Giuseppe Zanchi, Girolama wanted a guarantee either from the Venetian Ambassador or from a local merchant (ASV, SGSM, b. 188, f. 409).

154 Faustini paid Riminuzzi 200 ducats "in several installments" (ASV, SGSM, b. 118, receipt book, f. 4ᵛ, 14 Mar. 1654).

155 ASV, AN, Atti, b. 3482, f. 49, 13 Mar. 1657.

156 For Bordoni, see ASV, GM, Sentenze a legge, b. 474, f. 186ᵛ, 14 Aug. 1666. For Caterina and Brigida Forti, ibid., b. 473, f. 27ᵛ, 12 Apr. 1666; for Pietro Lucini, ibid., b. 473, f. 27, 12 May 1666. A number of these cases, all concerning singers at S. Moisè, were pursued in other courts. Many years earlier, Silvia Manni's mother had sued Claudio Monteverdi for part of her fees from the 1640/41 season (see B. Glixon, "Scenes from the Life," 113–16).

157 ASV, GP, b. 48, fasc. 91, f. 13ᵛ, 2 Apr. 1666 (regarding a contract of 12 Sept. 1665). For Ghini's letter to Prince Leopoldo, see ASF, MP, filza 5574, no. 80, 15 Apr. 1666.

158 It is also possible that the lawsuit involved a different failure of payment in the following year, when Sebastiano Enno rented the theater.

businessman active in Venice who served as an agent for Prince Leopoldo, show how pressure could be brought to bear through connections with Venetian noblemen, and with the weight of Leopoldo's name.[159] Del Sera worked at arranging Ghini's payment after the singer had left Venice, presumably to return to Florence. Del Sera's closest contact in the negotiations to obtain Ghini's funds was the Venetian nobleman Francesco Contarini.[160] While del Sera could have written directly to Ghini with news of the negotiations, he, instead, relayed instructions through their joint "employer," Prince Leopoldo; through helping to settle Ghini's problems, del Sera provided further evidence of his utility to the prince.[161]

Funds to be paid to singers long after the season had concluded might be found through a variety of methods. If the theater renters—rather than their guarantors—were to pay the money themselves, one source was incoming palco receipts. Another option that served at least two leading ladies—Anna Felicita Chiusi in 1654 and Virginia Camuffi in 1671—was that of retaining the costumes that they had worn on stage (see chap. 10). Costumes were costly, worth as much as 50 ducats or more, so that the singers may have held on to them in order to pressure the management into settling their accounts.[162] Some singers, on the other hand, whether through their own cleverness or that of their protectors, insisted on immediate payment for their services, and managed to avoid such difficulties. One of them was the Roman Giulia Masotti.

CASE STUDY: THE RECRUITING
OF GIULIA MASOTTI

Episodes early in the career of the Roman Vincenza Giulia Masotti (known as Giulia), who would sing on the Venetian stage through 1673, vividly bring to life the difficulties of recruiting from the points of view of both the impresario and the singer.[163] The first known report regarding Masotti comes from a letter of 25 March 1662, when Carlo Eustachio wrote to Florence about this young student of the noted composer Giacomo Carissimi whom he had heard sing "exquisitely" during the Lenten season.[164] Masotti made her Venetian debut just months after

---

159 ASF, Carteggio d'artisti, busta 6, nos. 489, 490, 492, 494, 495, 503, 504.

160 Contarini's relative Bertuccio Contarini aided Virginia Camuffi in her efforts to gain her wages from S. Moisè for the 1666/67 season; see Alm, "Singer Goes to Court."

161 Occasionally del Sera would enclose a separate letter for Ghini; his letters to the Cardinal, however, imply that he wanted Leopoldo himself to know how much his agent was doing for Ghini. Ultimately Ghini's fees were to come from Giacomo Dall'Angelo, one of the renters of the theater; Dall'Angelo's father, the famous lawyer Marin Dall'Angelo, had acted as the guarantor for the singer's salary.

162 Both Chiusi and Camuffi, however, were ordered by one of the courts of Venice (Avogaria di comun) to return the theaters' property.

163 On Masotti, see Brunelli, "Impresario in angustie," 330–33; Rosselli, "From Princely Service," 11–12; Rosand, Opera, chapter 8; and B. Glixon, "Private Lives," 524–26. Masotti will be the focus of a forthcoming study by Colleen Reardon that incorporates a newly discovered series of letters written by the prima donna.

164 ASF, MP, filza 5340, f. 517, 25 Mar. 1662.

the Medici agent had heard her sing, appearing during the 1662/63 season at the Teatro di S. Luca in Cesti's *Dori*, an opera that would become one of her specialties. Her portrayal of the leading role was so well received that it helped to give the theater its first truly successful season, at the same time taking away some of the glory from the previously reigning diva of the Venetian stage, Caterina Porri, who had been performing at the Grimani theater since the 1650s.[165] Masotti's debut encouraged the protector (and impresario) of S. Luca for that year, Abbot Vettor Grimani Calergi, to make arrangements to hire her for the next season.

As we saw in chapter 4, Grimani Calergi had installed himself at S. Luca in 1662, much to the wrath of his cousin, Giovanni Grimani, owner of the veteran SS. Giovanni e Paolo; Masotti's striking success at the competing theater only added insult to injury, and after the season Grimani revealed his anger and bitterness to Marquis Bentivoglio, as well as his hopes to block Grimani Calergi's access to the singer, with the goal of hiring her himself.[166] The singer could easily have become a pawn in a prolonged family struggle for operatic dominance. Giovanni Grimani was soon overtaken by more urgent concerns, however; already ill during carnival, his condition worsened, and he died on 14 May 1663.

After Giovanni Grimani's death, Grimani Calergi transferred his allegiance back to the Grimani theater, officially under the direction of the 14-year-old Giovanni Carlo Grimani, and one of the priorities for both men was the hiring of Giulia Masotti. Although Masotti had agreed to return to Venice, some confusion had resulted in the singer's mind owing to Grimani Calergi's move to SS. Giovanni e Paolo.[167] Was her commitment to S. Luca or to Grimani Calergi? When Masotti eventually began to voice her reluctance to return to Venice, both Grimani Calergi and Giovanni Carlo Grimani fell back on their alliances with the Medici, writing letters to Prince Mattias that begged his assistance. Mattias had probably aided in recruiting Masotti for Venice in the first place, as she was a protégé of the Medici representative in Rome, Torquato Montauto.[168] In August 1663 Giovanni Carlo Grimani assured the prince that Grimani Calergi had conceded the singer to him, that is to the Grimani theater.[169] A week later, on 1 September, Grimani Calergi wrote to Mattias:

> I, however, beg the kindness of Your Highness to command Count Montauto in good form that likewise for this time only he should wish to assist me with this favor, and for this carnival only, and never again, [and] that he should endure being without the conversation of his adored Signora Giulia, who, I pledge to Your Highness, will be treated, protected, and returned as she came, and returned again.[170]

---

165 ASFe, AB, b. 337, f. 86, Venice, 17 Jan. 1663, letter of Florio Tori; see Monaldini, *Orto dell'Esperidi*, 179.

166 ASFe, AB, b. 337, ff. 294–95, 17 Mar. 1663; see Monaldini, *Orto dell'Esperidi*, 183.

167 ASF, MP, filza 5477, f. 844, 8 Sept. 1663, letter of Torquato Montauto.

168 Mattias, as we saw earlier, had in previous years helped the Grimanis obtain singers for SS. Giovanni e Paolo.

169 ASF, MP, filza 5477, f. 493, 25 Aug. 1663.

170 "Io però supplico la benignità di Vostra Altezza a comandar in buona forma al Signor Conte Montauti, ch'anco per questa volta sola voglia favorirmi di questa grazia, e che per questo solo

Montauto, for his part, passionately recounted to Mattias the actions he had already taken in the service of the prince and the Grimanis. He encouraged Grimani Calergi both to be "gentler" in his urgings, and to promise Masotti that she would not be recruited against her will for the following season.[171] Several years later Masotti referred to Grimani Calergi having "forced me, so to speak, to return to Venice to sing at SS. Giovanni e Paolo . . ."[172] In the end, Masotti honored her commitment, and returned for the 1663/64 season.[173]

Grimani Calergi, on the other hand, despite his assurances, once again sought Masotti for the next carnival. Letters from Montauto to Prince Mattias speak of a series of grueling negotiations lasting three or four hours each conducted by Grimani Calergi's agent.[174] Masotti had to suffer these assaults despite having made frequent declarations to a number of men (Venetian noblemen and others in Rome such as the Contestabile Lorenzo Onofrio Colonna, one of the Princes of Brunswick, and even to Lunardo Loredan, the brother-in-law of Giovanni Grimani Calergi) that she had no intention of traveling to Venice again. Her objections stemmed partly from considerations regarding her health: she had, according to Montauto, suffered after her previous Venetian employment, complaining on her return of illness requiring the administration of large quantities of "stomach oil."

The pressures put on Masotti during these two years by Grimani Calergi, and—through the Venetian's urgings—by Prince Mattias as well, point up the difficulties a popular singer might endure when she did not wish to perform in a particular theater or city. Even though Masotti had an influential protector in Montauto, it was the combination of Montauto's strong ties to the Medici along with Prince Mattias's friendship with Grimani Calergi that prolonged the negotiations regarding the singer; had her protector in Rome been someone outside the Medici orbit, her protestations would most likely have been more easily accepted by Grimani Calergi.[175] Moreover, we can see how complicated the recruiting of singers might become. It is certainly possible that Masotti's contacts in Rome, including the Contestabile Colonna, the Duke of Brunswick, and Lunardo Loredan, may have initiated correspondence in the singer's favor, forcing allies and friends to chose sides.

Masotti remained firm in her resolution not to return to Venice for the 1664/65 season, but the recruiting frenzy soon began again. When Marco Faustini returned to the Grimani theater in February 1665 after a two-year absence, he (and perhaps

carnevale, e poi per mai più altro, si patienti di stare senza la conversatione della sua adorata Signora Giulia, della quale io m'impegno con Vostra Altezza, che sarà trattata, favorita, e ritornata, come è venuta, e ritornata ancora." ASF, MP, filza 5478, f. 103, 1 Sept. 1663.

171 ASF, MP, filza 5477, f. 844, 8 Sept. 1663.

172 "quando il Signor Abbate Grimani mi violentò, così dire, di ritornare à Venetia à recitare in S. Giovanni e Pauolo . . ."; ASV, SGSM, b. 188, f. 301, 9 Oct. 1666.

173 Masotti sang in Volpe's *Rosilena* and Cavalli's *Scipione affricano*.

174 ASF, MP, filza 5480, f. 796, 2 Dec. 1664.

175 It should be noted that while Masotti was pressured to accept employment she did not want, she did have the power to refuse. On the other hand, a male court singer, essentially a highly placed servant, would have no option but to obey a command of his employer.

Giovanni Carlo Grimani as well) was determined to have Masotti at SS. Giovanni e Paolo as the prima donna. The documents pertaining to this campaign come from Faustini's own correspondence, rather than from the archives of the Medici princes, showing that recruiting must have progressed through somewhat different channels. While in the past Masotti had dealt with Vettor Grimani Calergi and his representatives, one of the intermediaries for the 1665/66 recruiting season was, instead, "Bernardo Bolognese," a *muschier* (seller of perfumes, especially musk, and perfumed gloves).[176] Carlo Mazzini, an agent from Rome, informed Faustini during the fall of 1665 that the singer had received letters from Bernardo. Mazzini related, however, that Masotti was offended at receiving an offer from a person of such a low class, and that in the past, she had only gone to Venice at a prince's request.[177] Letters to Faustini from Arcangelo Lori as early as March 1665 should have made it clear to the impresario that Masotti did not wish to return to Venice; nonetheless, Faustini's efforts persisted at least into November 1665. (Alvise Duodo even remarked: "the hope of obtaining Giulia is driving you mad.")[178] Faustini's offer of 200 doble, or just over 900 ducats, about 150 ducats higher than Caterina Tomei's in 1661/62—plus 300 ducats for travel expenses and "a dress made from gold cloth embellished with very fine gold lace"—was a most generous one.[179] For this particular season, however, Masotti held her ground and emerged the victor.

Masotti's resistance affected the recruiting season, and the success of the performances, in a number of ways. Faustini was a tireless fighter unwilling to take Masotti's "no" for an answer until shortly before the season would begin, but, at the same time, he was forced to line up other singers. The impresario hired Caterina Masi (a local woman) and Anna Caterina Venturi, and he was fortunate to obtain the services of the two Roman sisters, Lucia and Anna Cimini, who also had for some time resisted coming to Venice. When Venturi's—and Caterina Masi's—talents proved unequal to the task, Faustini managed to hire (for the second opera) one young Roman singer, Antonia Coresi, who would become a favorite of the Venetian audiences over the next decade.

Undeterred by the failed efforts of 1665/66, Faustini took on the challenge once again the following season: Masotti was still considered one of the top female singers in Italy, and he was determined to have her. She refused to deal directly with Faustini, presumably because he was not a nobleman; the negotiations for the

---

176 "Bernardo" was probably the Bolognese *muschier* Bernardo Mancari, who came to Venice around 1650 (ASPV, EM, b. 98, f. 231).

177 ASV, SGSM, b. 194 f. 147, 28 Nov. 1665. It is unclear how Bernardo came to be involved in the operatic world; invitations to sing at a theater normally emanated either from an impresario or from someone of noble standing. The two items concerning Bernardo in the Faustini papers (ASV, SGSM, b. 188, f. 326; ASV, SGSM, b. 194, f. 30) bear no date, but their content, together with Mazzini's letter (ASV, SGSM, b. 194, f. 147) indicates that they belong to the 1665/66 season rather than to the following one. Mazzini wrote directly to Erasmo Secreti rather than to Faustini (see above).

178 "la speranza di Giulia vi fa delirare . . ."; ASV, SGSM, b. 194, f. 150, 14 Nov. 1665.

179 "Una vesta tessuta d'oro con merli d'oro nobilissima." ASV, SGSM, b. 194, f. 30. As mentioned above, Caterina Porri, from 1661 through 1663, had earned only 452 ducats for her performances.

1666/67 season unfolded in letters written by the Venetian patrician Girolamo Loredan; the Contestabile Lorenzo Onofrio Colonna (the employer of Nicola and Antonia Coresi), who was well connected to the musical worlds of Rome (as a patron) and Venice (as a connoisseur of opera); one Gasparo Origo, a businessman; and Faustini himself. Origo, a Roman, had resided in Venice during the spring of 1665, so that he must have become acquainted with Faustini or one of his associates at that time.[180] Girolamo Loredan, who came from one of the leading Venetian families, was a fitting intermediary, as he had ties to both Masotti and Faustini: he was one of Faustini's neighbors in S. Vidal, while Masotti had known Loredan's brother Lunardo in Rome during the negotiations of 1664/65.[181] As the Loredans' sister Maria was married to Giovanni Grimani Calergi, it is likely that she had come to know the family through Vettor Grimani Calergi.[182]

The communication among these five players (Origo, Faustini, Masotti, Colonna, and Loredan) resembles, at times, a complicated dance occasioned by Masotti's unwillingness to write to Faustini directly. During the prelude to the 1666/67 season, Masotti wrote letters to Colonna, who then sent them on to Loredan. Loredan (in consultation with Faustini, and using drafts supplied by the impresario) wrote both to Colonna and to Masotti;[183] Loredan's departure from Venice to accompany his brother to a new post in Bergamo, however, necessitated a change in the procedures so that Colonna's letters now went to Faustini rather than to Loredan.[184] Origo acted on Faustini's behalf, and wrote directly to him, as well as to some of the others. In contrast to previous years, no letters written by the owners of the theater have as yet come to light; Faustini apparently had his own methods and contacts, and may not have urged his young employer to write letters on his behalf.

Masotti was most grateful to have Colonna act as her protector. She may have reasoned, quite accurately in this case, that he would spend the carnival season in Venice, so that she would have him close at hand should any problem arise. Ironically, she writes that in the past Vettor Grimani Calergi had acted in that regard; indeed, her letters suggest some regret at his loss (he had died in October 1665), and the need to establish new channels of patronage. Except for the one instance mentioned earlier, references to his "menacing" behavior that had caused her such heartache in the past are lacking. Also curious is the inference that Giovanni Carlo Grimani—a young man of about Masotti's age—had not yet replaced Grimani Calergi in this capacity. Masotti emphasizes that she has never dealt with the "interessati" of the theater, only with Grimani Calergi; nor do the letters suggest that

180 ASV, AN, Atti, b. 11043, f. 51ᵛ, 9 May 1665.

181 Girolamo Loredan's family was not closely related to that of Giovanni Francesco Loredano, famous for his role in the Accademia degli Incogniti.

182 Duodo and Loredan were related: Alvise Duodo's grandfather and Girolamo Loredan's great-grandmother, Pisana, were siblings, both children of the famous general Francesco Duodo.

183 Loredan was also in correspondence with Nicola Coresi, the singer in Colonna's employ (ASV, SGSM, b. 188, f. 299, 13 Oct. 1666).

184 On Loredan's posting to Bergamo, see ASV, CD, Comune, reg. 116, f. 68, 17 May 1666. Loredan's travels are mentioned in ASV, SGSM, b. 188, f. 292ʳ⁻ᵛ, 2 Oct. 1666; SGSM, b. 188, f. 293; and SGSM, b. 188, f. 299, 13 Oct. 1666.

she formed any particular alliance with Faustini's partners Duodo and Correr, despite their high social standing in Venetian society.

Finally, after months of correspondence, a contract, dated 23 September 1666, was drawn up for 1,000 scudi romani (equal to about 1,450 ducats, the same amount specified in the contract of Antonia Coresi, the other lead singer), with extra for travel, and a clause that mentioned either "a fine dress" or, instead, the sum of 100 scudi; the salary was then adjusted to 380 doble (1,716 ducats), and the reference to the costume crossed out.[185] A further change, however, saw Masotti earning instead 400 doble, for a total salary of about 1,742 ducats, plus travel, or almost twice the amount offered to her the previous year.[186] Faustini wrote concerning Masotti's exorbitant demands regarding her salary: "[it] is a sum so large that no one has ever seen such a thing; if the Amphions and Orfeos were to return to this world, and if they wanted to sing in a theater, they could not demand a sum this large."[187] Faustini was able to save some funds, however, in regard to Masotti's lodging: the contract specified that she would stay either at his own house, or in that of the Grimanis.[188] Regarding the scheduling of payments, the singer had insisted that she would not agree to perform if her complete salary were not paid to her upon her arrival in Venice, rather than by the typical method that saw singers paid in installments as the season progressed.[189] Masotti, however, signed Faustini's receipt book only on 23 February 1667; it is unclear what proportion of her fees were received before that date.[190]

Masotti's tactics, however difficult for her patrons and onerous for the impresarios, certainly worked in her favor. As we saw in chapter 6, she even managed, at times, to control, or at least influence, the choice of opera, leading to several revivals of Cesti's *Dori*, one of her most successful roles. By 1669, when she sang in a revival of Cesti's *Argia* at S. Luca, her salary had risen even higher, to 500 doble (2,191 ducats, according the exchange rate in 1669), plus 300 ducats for travel, totaling, in all, 2,570 ducats. Masotti continued to drive a hard bargain: the theater managers were short of funds, and of all the singers in that production only she and one male singer received their full salaries at the appropriate time.[191] Masotti had learned to play the operatic system to her best advantage; as a highly desired commodity on the Venetian operatic market, she forced the establishment of new standards for the wages of prima donnas, and had found a way to garner those wages in a timely manner.

185 ASV, SGSM, b. 194, f. 110.

186 These doble were valued at 27 lire each, rather than the more usual 28.

187 "somma così grande, che non è veduta da alcuno; che se ritornassero al mondo gl'Anfioni e gl'Orfei, et che volessero cantare in un theatro, d'avantaggio non potrebbero addimandare una soma così grande." ASV, SGSM, b. 188, f. 294. In 1658/59, Girolama's salary and travel allowance had been half this amount.

188 ASV, SGSM, b. 188, f. 297. Masotti apparently continued to stay with the Grimanis in future years, for a letter from Vicenzo Grimani to the Duke of Savoy (11 Mar. 1673) states that the singer was then in residence (AST, Sezione corte, Lettere ministri, Mazzo 11).

189 Letter from Masotti to Colonna, 2 Oct. 1666, ASV, SGSM, b. 188, f. 286.

190 ASV, SGSM, b. 118, receipt book, f. 81, 23 Feb. 1666, m.v.

191 See Rosand, *Opera*, 224. A reproduction of an account sheet for this opera, with salaries promised to singers versus monies already paid out, appears on p. 197.

CHAPTER EIGHT

DANCERS, EXTRAS,
AND THE ORCHESTRA

While there is no question that the main focus of much of the audience in mid-seventeenth-century Venice was on the singers, the music, the scenery, and the machines, other elements were also essential to the performances. Dance had been an element of opera from its origins, but in Venetian opera its scope was comparatively restricted, often to the intermedi at the ends of the first two acts. The impresario usually hired a choreographer, who supplied the dancers, and provided costumes for two ballets. More variable, depending on the libretto, were groups of extras, similarly costumed and low-paid, but important to the spectacle. No opera could be performed without an orchestra, but its small size and uniform timbre—strings and continuo—meant that the audience would expect instrumental pieces and accompaniments that fell within a certain norm. Both extras and orchestral musicians were paid a nightly wage, like stagehands and technicians, rather than the fixed fee paid to singers and members of the creative team.

DANCE

The most ephemeral component of Venetian opera was dance.[1] In many cases dance music is little evident in the surviving scores; no choreographies have survived for the seventeenth century, and, as Irene Alm has written, the dancers in these operas were professional performers who left no treatises for others who aspired to follow them. Alm has meticulously collected data concerning operatic dance from travelers' reports and, most importantly, from the librettos and scores themselves. Indeed, the vast majority of librettos refer to the many dances performed,[2] and hint at their variety and diversity. The dancers often contributed an exotic element to the operas (bringing to life, in the words of Alm, dances "from the four corners of the earth"), or portrayed elements, such as madness,

---

1 For the first major study of dance in Venetian opera, see Alm, "Theatrical Dance." See also Alm, "Winged Feet." On dance in seventeenth-century opera as expression of aspects of the ancient world, see Heller, "Dancing Desire."

2 Alm lists the number of ballets in "Winged Feet," 273–74.

that were already present in the drama. Some of the characters or themes represented through dance included savages, spirits, dwarfs, soldiers, flowers, and assorted animals.[3]

Choreographers in Mid-Seventeenth-Century Venice: Balbi and His Contemporaries

Until recently we have known very little concerning the dancers who displayed their talents on the the Venetian stage. During the mid-century their names only rarely appeared in the librettos, and for the most part only the choreographer (and, presumably, lead dancer) was mentioned. The most famous of them all was the Venetian Giovanni Battista Balbi, whose choreography merited attention in the libretto of the first opera, *Andromeda*.[4] As we saw in chapter 4, Balbi's contract with the first company at S. Cassiano is one of the few sources to have come to light concerning the first operatic season in Venice:

> Signor Giovanni Battista Balbi, Venetian, son of the late Signor Angelo . . . obligates himself and promises to provide three ballets, one for twelve, another for eight, and another for three [dancers], each time that the musicians mentioned herein will perform their opera at S. Cassiano, as many times as is necessary for the entire course of this carnival. Nor may he provide [the dances] elsewhere during this time, nor give to others the choreography [*inventione*] of these dances. . . . And they [the company] obligate themselves to give and pay to the said Signor Giovanni Battista Balbi 113 ducats in this manner: 20 ducats now, given to him in the presence of me, the notary, and witnesses described herein, and the remaining 93 ducats at the conclusion of the opera . . . mentioned above.[5]

Balbi and his employers sought to create a special impact with the dances in this first opera, as one of them was to feature as many as twelve dancers, and another eight. According to an account in the published libretto, however, the actual dances varied slightly from this prescription, with the middle ballet danced by six (all women), rather than eight; the final dance featured twelve savages. Balbi's offerings for the next season (*La maga fulminata*) included three ballets for, respectively, six dwarfs, eight spirits, and eight cavaliers.

Although Balbi's name would not appear in another libretto until 1651 (in *Alessandro vincitor di se stesso*), he was a member of Cavalli's company at S. Cassiano

---

3 For a discussion of the subjects of dances, see ibid., 237–52.

4 On Balbi, see *NG*, s.v. "Balbi, Giovanni Battista," by Irene Alm, and Bianconi and Walker, "Dalla *finta pazza*."

5 "il signor Giovanni Battista Balbi Venetiano fu del quondam signor Angelo, et se n'obliga, et promette di far tre baletti, uno in dodici, l'altro in otto, et l'altro in tre per ogni volta, che dalli signori musici infrascritti sarà rapresentata a S. Cassano la loro opera musicale quanto volte occorrerà per tutto il corso di questo presente carnevale, nè di far altrove in questo tempo, nè dispensare l'inventione di essi baletti . . . et si obligano di dar, et esborsar al detto Signor Giovanni Battista Balbi ducati cento e tredici in questo modo, cioè, hora ducati vinti esborsatigli alla presentia di me nodaro, et testimonij infrascritti, et li restanti ducati novanta tre fornita, che sia tutta la opera, et fontione soprascritta . . ."; ASV, AN, Atti, b. 5973, f. 225, 23 Dec. 1636. The musicians mentioned in this agreement include Ferrari, Bisucci, Medici, and Angeletti. Balbi's activities in Venice will be highlighted in a future article.

for the 1638/39 season, and continued there beyond that year.[6] On 26 January 1641, during a season that saw operas at four different theaters, Cavalli reminded Balbi in an official notice of his obligations: to "create the ballets for the Teatro di S. Cassiano, and provide your services each time they will be necessary in the opera or operas that would be done by me for the present year."[7] Moreover, Cavalli informed Balbi that he knew of the dancer's commitment to serve in other theaters; he threatened Balbi with severe financial consequences should he fail to fulfill his contract at S. Cassiano. Balbi had most likely offered his services to the Novissimo (and possibly others), which was at that time performing *La finta pazza,* the very opera he would help to introduce to Florence and Paris several years later.[8] Cavalli's notice to Balbi points up both the importance of dance to opera in Venice and an apparent shortage of comparable choreographers.

Balbi went on to produce opera in other cities such as Naples, and also served as choreographer in Brussels, but he still participated in Venetian theatrical life during the 1650s at SS. Giovanni e Paolo. By that time, other dance masters had become established in Venice (see table 8.1). During much of these two decades, Faustini's choreographer was Giovanni Battista Martini, referred to in some documents as "il Sardo."[9] Olivier Vigasio, a native of Verona, did some of Faustini's balli, along with Battista Artusi (see below) in 1656/57 and 1657/58, and on his own for the two operas of the 1662/63 season at SS. Giovanni e Paolo; he was also listed in the libretto for the Murano production of *Le barbarie del caso.*[10] Faustini used a different ballet master for the 1659/60 season: Agostino Ramaccini, a Tuscan who had at that time been resident in Venice for thirteen years.[11]

Battista Artusi, who shared the choreography duties for the 1656/57 and 1657/58 seasons, identified himself as "callegher" or shoemaker. He came from Faustini's own parish of S. Vidal, where his father, Iseppo Artusi Callegher, ran a shoemaker's shop "at the mezza luna" (half-moon). In 1665 Battista, too, listed his

6 ASV, AN, Atti, b. 647, f. 327, 16 Sept. 1638.

7 "vi sette obligato di far nel teatro di S. Cassano li balli, et prestare l'opera vostra ogni volta che farà bisogno nell'opera, ò opere, che fossero da me fatte l'anno presente"; ASV, AN, Atti, b. 3761, 26 Jan. 1640 m.v.

8 Bianconi and Walker, "Dalla *Finta pazza.*" As we saw in chapter 4 (n. 63), Balbi was owed money by the management of the Novissimo in 1643.

9 An entry in one source (ASPV, EM, b. 62, f. 120, 25 Apr. 1657) appears to read "il Sordo" (the deaf one) rather than "il Sardo." It seems unlikely that a dance master would have been deaf, however. No official records attest to Martini's place of birth. He died on 22 June 1683 in Venice, at the age of 70 (VAP, S. Silvestro, Morti 1676–99).

10 Vigasio, from Verona, was probably related to Antonio and Giacomo Vigasio, musicians who served at the court in Graz. See Federhofer, *Musikpflege und Musiker,* 226. Vigasio was a witness in Venice for a document dated 10 Aug. 1670, but we have no evidence of dance activities at that time. See ASV, AN, Atti, b. 3012, f. 646ᵛ.

11 Ramaccini had hoped to go on an extended voyage with the Duke of San Felice to Spain and the Americas in the early 1650s (ASV, AN, Atti, b. 2966, f. 429ᵛ, 7 July 1654). Could the trip have been intended to serve also as inspiration for his choreography? He is identified as a Tuscan dance master (from Pescia) in a document of 1657 (ASV, AN, Atti, b. 3065, f. 388ᵛ, 24 Sept. 1657). In 1665, he attested that he was 32 years old, resided in the parish of S. Cassiano, and had been in Venice about eighteen years, i.e., he came to Venice around 1647, at the age of 14 or 15 (ASPV, EM, b. 79, f. 328ᵛ, 9 Apr. 1665).

TABLE 8.1. Ballet Masters and Dancers Employed by Marco Faustini

Season	Number of operas	Ballet masters and dancers	Payment (in ducats)
1651/52	2	Giovanni Battista Martini (il Sardo) for four balli	105
1654/55	1	Giovanni Battista Martini (il Sardo) two balli, eight dancers each	150 and one pair of silk stockings for each dancer (valued at 5 ducats in all)
1655/56	1	Giovanni Battista Martini (il Sardo)	150
1656/57	1	Battista Artusi Callegher Olivier Vigasio	165 19.5[a] (total: 184.5)
1657/58	1	Olivier Vigasio Battista Artusi Callegher son of Francesco dal Violino	157 30 13 (total: 200)
1658/59	1	Giovanni Battista Martini for two balli, twelve dancers each	200 (also £56 for replacement dancer for 8 nights)
1659/60	1	Agostino Ramaccini	250
1660/61	2	Giovanni Battista Martini	250
1661/62	2	Giovanni Battista Martini	250
1662/63	2	Olivier Vigasio	250
1665/66	2	Giovanni Battista Martini	250
1666/67	2	Giovanni Battista Martini	250
1667/68	2	Giovanni Battista Martini with Lelio Bonetti and Angelo Frezzato	250

[a] This may represent only a partial payment.

profession as "callegher, at the mezza luna"; it would seem, then, that Artusi both danced and made shoes, a happy combination of professions.[12] Lelio Bonetti and Angelo Frezzato, who started to dance with the choreographer Martini around 1645, were, like Artusi, multi-talented. Known as early as the 1650s as painters,[13] in the libretto for *Artaxerse* (SS. Giovanni e Paolo, 1668/69) they are each listed as "ballarino e pittor," which may mean that, in addition to dancing, they assisted the main scene painter, Hippolito Mazzarini, in preparing the sets. Bonetti and Frezzato formed part of the dance corps during Faustini's last season, 1667/68; that

12 ASV, AN, Atti, b. 11182, f. 403ᵛ. At the time of Artusi's involvement with Faustini, he was approximately 26 years old.

13 ASPV, EM, b. 62, f. 120, 25 Apr. 1657. See also Borean and Cecchini, "Microstorie d'affari," 222–31.

they signed for their fees along with Martini indicates some prominence within the dance company.[14] The previous year, however, they had probably danced for another impresario, Sebastiano Enno, in his S. Moisè production of *Alessandro amante*, for the two pursued a legal battle against Enno that began in 1668.[15]

Contracts and Wages for Choreographers and Dancers

As in so many areas, the primary financial documentation for dance in Venetian operas comes from the Faustini papers. Other than the Balbi contract discussed above, no formal contracts for choreographers survive. Faustini did, however, record some of the pertinent details, along with the payments, in his account books. The earliest such notation dates from the 1651/52 season, when he signed a contract with Giovanni Battista Martini (called here simply "il Sardo ballarino") on 1 September. Martini was to provide four dances (that is, create the choreography and pay the dancers) for the two operas for the season, *Calisto* and *Eritrea*, for 105 ducats.[16] Payments began in December, well after the first performances of *Calisto*, and continued through February. For the 1654/55 season, Faustini and Martini signed their contract even earlier, on 19 August. Faustini budgeted a much higher amount this time, as Martini was paid 150 ducats for the eight dancers who would perform in the two ballets for *Eupatra* (one of Martini's signed receipts can be seen in figure 7.1). In addition, Faustini provided Martini and his dancers with a pair of silk stockings each, at a cost of 5 ducats. As before, payments did not begin until after performances were underway, this time on 16 January, with two more to follow in February. From 1655 on the payments for dances all appear in Faustini's receipt book, but that source provides little information beyond the name of the choreographer and the amount paid (see table 8.1).

As mentioned above, for some reason the choreography duties were divided during 1656/57 and 1657/58 seasons. For *Le fortune di Rodope e Damira*, Faustini's final effort at S. Aponal, the impresario paid Battista Artusi 160 ducats, for what the choreographer indicated in his receipts as "half of the dances," but the lone payment to another choreographer, Olivier Vigasio, amounted to less than 20 ducats; this total figure represented an increase of 23 percent over the previous year. Artusi's statement should probably be taken more figuratively, meaning simply that his portion represented the bulk of the dances, as the following year (for *L'incostanza trionfante*) the account book indicates a fee of 157 ducats to be paid to the "ballarino principale," identified in the receipt book as Vigasio, whose name also

14 ASV, SGSM, b. 11, receipt book, ff. 86 and 88. For their earlier connection with Martini, see ASPV, EM, b. 62, f. 120, 25 Apr. 1657.

15 ASPV, Actorum, mandatorum, praeceptorum 1670–74, ff. 1962ᵛ–1985. The case continued into 1673; the documents nowhere refer to the source of the debt, so that the problems may not have been associated with an opera production; also, the debts could have stemmed from the two men's assistance with scenery.

16 ASV, SGSM, b. 113, account book 1654/55, f. 9ᵛ. On the role of dance in *Calisto*, see Heller, "Dancing Desire."

appears on the libretto, with another 30 ducats going to Artusi. The two choreographers, then, traded responsibilities over these two years, each taking the majority of the dances one year and a small portion the other. For *L'incostanza trionfante* Faustini also paid another 13 ducats to the son of Francesco Donadoni (a violinist), who may have performed a solo dance of some sort, bringing the total figure to 200 ducats, or about 15 more than the previous year. Faustini's costs for the personnel for this important visual element had nearly doubled since the 1651/52 season.[17]

The final opera for which we have detailed information is *Antioco* (1658/59). Faustini returned to the choreographer he had used at S. Aponal, Martini, and hired him to choreograph two balli, each using twelve dancers. One of the dancers, named Vettore, apparently needed to be replaced during the season, and Faustini paid the substitute separately (at £7 per night) for the eight times he performed. In general, however, the fee for an individual dancer was fixed, possibly at about 12.5 ducats for the season.[18]

The expenditure for dancing increased again in 1659/60, when Ramaccini was paid 250 ducats for the balli for *Elena*, a salary higher than any previously paid to a dance master; in fact, it equaled that paid to Martini in the succeeding seasons at SS. Giovanni e Paolo, when two operas, rather than one, were performed.[19] While it is possible that this growth reflects an increase in the number of dancers, it seems more likely that this was simply part of the general trend for higher fees in all areas of opera production at this time. Beyond the fees for choreographer and dancers, the impresario had to purchase costumes and some props, payments for which are entered with varying degrees of specificity in Faustini's account books (discussed further in chap. 10).[20]

EXTRAS

Although they did not form part of the musical component of opera, *comparse*, or non-singing (and non-dancing) extras, also lent magnificence to the spectacle. Librettists wove these mute characters, usually in homogeneous groups (soldiers, pages, Turks, etc.) into their plots (they were often included in the lists of charac-

17 The documents do not clarify how much of this increase was due to an expansion of the dance troupe (perhaps to better fill the larger stage of S. Cassiano), and how much to a rise in the fees for individual choreographers and dancers.

18 In 1654/55, Martini charged 150 ducats for two balli with eight dancers each, and in 1658/59 200 ducats for two balli with twelve dancers each. If Martini took 50 ducats for his fee, the increase of 50 percent corresponds precisely with the similar increase in the number of dancers, that is 50 ducats for four dancers, or 12.5 ducats each, regardless of the number of performances. If Martini included himself among the eight or twelve dancers, then the individual payment would have been around 14 ducats. On the other hand, if the choreographer paid dancers for each performance, his own income would be reduced with an increase in the number of performances.

19 The same fees applied the year Vigasio choreographed the dances at SS. Giovanni Paolo in Martini's absence (1662/63).

20 See also Alm, "Theatrical Dance," 281–82.

ters in the librettos, along with dancers), and impresarios such as Faustini were willing to support the costs of their costumes (see chap. 10) and the expense of their nightly appearances. Faustini's four account books each include extras in the listing of nightly expenses (see figure 8.1), with occasional details. The usual fee for an extra amounted to 10 to 15 soldi, or about one quarter of the £2 that was standard for the stagehands.[21] The number of extras, not always indicated, ranged as high as about sixty-four, but was usually about a third less. The accounts for *L'incostanza trionfante* are unusual in that they specify that among the extras were centaurs and monsters. Some additional information can be gleaned from the payments for costumes for the extras (see chap. 10): purchases of sets of costumes for

FIGURE 8.1. Nightly expenses for the 1657/58 season, from Faustini's account book (ASV, SGSM, b. 112, account book 1657/58, ff. 53ᵛ–54)

21 The accounts for *Ciro* indicate the employment of fifteen *comparse* at a total cost of £34 each night, or about 45 soldi each; perhaps the copyist erred, and the number should have been forty-five *comparse*, which would mean a fee of about 15 soldi each, which is more in line with the other documentation. ASV, SGSM, b. 194, f. 268, 5 Feb. 1664 m.v.

Eupatra (1654/55) include thirty-six liveries, twelve of which were for women, and seven for janissaries. The listing of nightly payments for *Antioco* includes, in addition to the regular comparse, also a dwarf (*gobbo*) at 15 soldi per night, and a "lion," at 30.[22] The accounts for *Eupatra* preserve one of the rare indications of the post-opening night changes discussed in chapter 5: listed in addition to the original extras are four cupids at 15 soldi each, beginning with the seventh performance.

THE ORCHESTRA

It is largely thanks to the Faustini papers that we have any specific knowledge of the opera orchestra in Venice during the mid-seventeenth century. Faustini's account books show just how much the size of the orchestra had changed from the sumptuous band Monteverdi had specified for his *Orfeo* in Mantua (1607). Rather than a large ensemble of strings, woodwinds, and brass, with a wide array of continuo instruments, the orchestra of Faustini's time featured a small band of up to five strings with two or three harpsichords and one or two theorbos (see appendix 6).[23] Although many operas at the time featured "trumpet" arias, for the most part strings imitated the typical figurations of the trumpet; only one of Faustini's account books, that for *L'incostanza trionfante*, calls for "trombetti," added at the bottom of the list of the musicians (see figure 8.1).[24]

An impresario had a large pool of instrumentalists on which to draw for his orchestra. Many of the best were employed in the ducal chapel at S. Marco, but their duties were such that they could and did take on other jobs.[25] As with the singers, Venice's instrumentalists had always been adept moonlighters, since no one post provided sufficient income. Fra Pietro Giacomo (see below), for example, had for most of his career as a theorbist at S. Marco earned only 15 ducats per year, standard for members of that ensemble. In 1665 his salary was increased to 30 ducats in honor of his long service, but this was only half of the standard wage for a singer. One long-standing source of additional income, the Venetian confraternities, or scuole, offered wages during the mid-seventeenth century of only about 3 ducats

22 There is no indication, either in Faustini's documents, or in contemporary correspondence, whether this lion was real or an extra in costume.

23 In addition to the data from the account books, one loose sheet specifies the musicians paid for Cavalli's *Ciro*, performed in the 1664/65 season (ASV, SGSM, b. 194, f. 268, 5 Feb. 1664 m.v.), and there is a listing for S. Moisè for the 1666/67 season, discovered by Irene Alm (ASV, Ospedali e luoghi pii, 37, Heredità Virginia Camuffi). The roles of the three harpsichordists are not clear. The first, usually the composer, earned the highest wage, and probably played through all or most of the recitatives and arias, perhaps alternating with the second (whose wages varied considerably, sometimes as low as that of the third) to provide some contrast. The third player earned the least, approximately the same as the string players, and may have played only in instrumental numbers or during the ballets. See chapter 6, n. 52.

24 On the "trumpet" aria, see Rosand, *Opera*, 329–33; on the use of the trumpet in seventeenth-century opera, see Tarr and Walker, "'Bellici carmi.'" Faustini's addition of the trombetti to the list of the musicians, notated beneath his sum of nightly expenses, indicates that they were added later and did not form part of the typical band.

25 Although many of the instrumentalists in the account books are not assigned a full name, some can be identified as members of the cappella.

(having sunk from a high in the late sixteenth-century of about 8), so that operatic wages (along with other short-term jobs, such as playing at the annual festival of a convent or confraternity) could vastly increase a musician's annual income; the twenty-five performances of *L'incostanza trionfante* (1657/58), for example, would have yielded the second violinist just over 48 ducats, and fra Pietro Giacomo, mentioned above, earned 100 ducats for his work ten years later.[26]

On occasion, instrumentalists from outside the confines of Venice performed in the orchestra. In 1661/62, the violinist Cristoforo Storni came from S. Antonio in Padua. Several years earlier, in 1657/58 the orchestra included "Signor Carlo," whose fee, £28 a night, was the highest that year other than for the composer (the nightly payment register is shown in figure 8.1). This Carlo was almost certainly Carlo Andrea Coradini "del Liuto," a Roman who resided during the opera season with the Venetian procurator Alvise Foscarini; his employment could have resulted from a connection with one of the singers.[27] As we saw in chapter 7, the lutenist renewed his connection with Faustini several years later when he acted as a scout for Faustini, helping to secure the services of the castrato Giovanni Cappello.[28]

Typically, wages were paid out to the performers on a nightly basis, at fees ranging from £7 to £24 per performer (other than the director; see below) for each performance. A musician's total remuneration depended both on the instrument he played, with harpsichordists and theorbists earning the most, and also on the success and popularity of the opera. In the documented years, instrumentalists in Faustini's orchestras earned as little as 28 ducats (for the violist in 1657/58— twenty-five performances at £7 each) or as much as 132 ducats (for Martino, probably a theorbist or harpsichordist, in 1651/52—thirty-four performances at £24 each). The instrument tuner, predictably, earned the least: £4 or a bit more per performance. Although these individual amounts are not large, especially in comparison with the salaries of lead singers, the overall expense was considerable, adding up to several hundred ducats per season, representing about 6 percent of the total production cost (see appendix 5). When one or both operas in a season were successful, payments for the numerous performances could raise the orchestra's share of the overall expenditure as high as 12 percent.

For the most part, the instrumentalists did not sign contracts, as did the singers (or at least none have survived), but they were occasionally hired for a predetermined set fee rather than for the more usual payment on a nightly basis. Fra Pietro Giacomo, the theorbist mentioned earlier, signed in Faustini's receipt book for the round sum of 100 ducats. In 1661/62 at SS. Giovanni e Paolo, Cristoforo Storni, the violinist from S. Antonio at Padua, received £200 (about 32 ducats), while an unnamed keyboard player signed for 70 ducats;[29] that same year, the theorbist

26 On music at the scuole, see J. Glixon, *Honoring God*. Fra Pietro Giacomo signed for his fees in Faustini's receipt book, ASV, SGSM, b. 118, receipt book, f. 87.

27 ASV, CD, Criminal, filza 90, 24 Feb. 1657 m.v. Coradini did not remain in Venice, as by August he had transferred to Germany (ASV, CD, Comuni, filza 598, July–Aug. 1658, 25 Aug. 1658).

28 ASV, SGSM, b.101.

29 ASV, SGSM, b. 118, receipt book, f. 59. Storni's performance in opera orchestras can be documented several times later in the century. He requested permission to be absent from Padua for that purpose in 1670 and 1682, and in 1678 he did so without permission. See Sartori, *Il Santo*, 180 and 188.

Nicolò Fadi had to sue the S. Luca impresario Girolamo Barbieri for the full payment of his 70-ducat fee.[30] Considerably earlier Francesco Pio had agreed to serve Faustini as an instrumentalist for 35 ducats at the same time as his brother, Antonino, signed on as a singer in the production.[31]

When possible, the orchestra was led, presumably from the harpsichord, by the composer of the opera, who also earned the highest fee. Thus, Cavalli's name heads the records for the nightly instrumental expenses for 1651/52, and Ziani's for 1654/55 (*Eupatra*) and 1657/58 (*L'incostanza trionfante*). As we saw in chapter 6, Ziani often complained about his salary for composing the operas in comparison with Cavalli's, but the two earned nightly wages for leading the orchestra that were equal, or nearly so.[32] Cavalli's name does not appear on the list for *Antioco* (1658/59), as his overall salary included, according to his contract, compensation for directing and performing (see chap. 6). When someone other than the composer led the band, the nightly wage was lower (£28 for Rovetta, standing in for Cavalli in *Erismena*, and £24 s.16 for "Signor Antonio," who played the first keyboard instrument in *Ciro*.[33] It is not always certain what exactly the composer, or his substitute, did at the performances. While it is clear from his 1658 contract that Cavalli would be playing the first harpsichord, the orchestra listing for 1657/58 includes a "primo clavicembalo" other than Ziani. Perhaps this should simply be taken to mean the first harpsichordist after the director, since it is specified that the tuner would be responsible for three instruments (that is, first, second, and Ziani).

30 ASV, GP, Dimande, b. 45, fasc. 85, no. 239, 30 June 1662.

31 For the Pio brothers, see ASV, SGSM, b. 113, account book 1654/55, f. 44ᵛ.

32 Cavalli's fee for 1651/52 and Ziani's for 1657/58 were the same at £40, and the latter earned £37 s.4 for *Eupatra* in 1654/55, resulting in a range of total income, based on the number of performances, from 161 ducats (Ziani in 1657/58) to 219 ducats (Cavalli in 1651/52).

33 Andrea Mattioli, composer of *Perseo*, the first opera of the season, and reviser of *Ciro*, was present in Venice from December (ASFe, AB, b. 339, f. 826, Venice, 3 Dec. 1664, Andrea Mattioli to Hippolito Bentivoglio; see Monaldini, *Orto dell'Esperidi*, 214), but is not listed as the first keyboard player (the name there is Antonio), the usual place for the composer. There is an Andrea listed for the third keyboard, so it is possible that, for some reason, he participated but did not direct.

PART III

THE PHYSICAL PRODUCTION

CHAPTER NINE

SCENERY AND MACHINES

When the curtain disappeared one saw the stage entirely as the sea, with a distant view so well constructed of water and cliffs that the naturalness of it (even though not real) created doubt in the onlookers whether they were really in a theater or on an actual seashore. The stage was entirely dark, if not for the light provided by some stars, which one after another gradually went out, giving way to the dawn, who came to sing the prologue. She was entirely dressed in silver linen, with a very shiny star on her brow, and she appeared in a most beautiful cloud, which now enlarged, and now diminished (a beautiful marvel), and made its way in an arc across the sky on stage. In that moment one saw the stage become as bright as day. The Prologue was sung divinely by the Roman Signora Maddalena Manelli, after which one heard the most expert musicians play a most sweet symphony, assisted by the composer of the opera on his marvelous theorbo. Then Juno came out on a golden chariot drawn by her peacocks, all dressed in flaming gold cloth, with a wonderful variety of gems on her head and in her crown. To the marvelous delight of the spectators, the chariot turned to the right and then to the left, as it pleased. Mercury appeared in front of her. He was and was not in a machine; that is, he was, because it was not possible that he could fly, but he was not, because no other machine could be seen but his flying body. . . . In an instant one saw the scene change from the sea to a forest, which was so natural, that from moment to moment one's eye moved from that real snowy peak, to that true flowered plain, to that true tangled forest, and to that not-false running water.[1]

Thus begins a published description of the first performance of an opera in a public theater, *Andromeda*, in 1637 in the Teatro S. Cassiano in Venice. To the author (perhaps someone associated with the production), the spectacle, especially the scenery and the machines, was at least as important as the music. Visual display remained, along with virtuoso singers, one of Venetian opera's great attractions throughout the century, as reported by members of the audience. The English trav-

---

1 Ferrari, *Andromeda* (Venice, 1637), 5–7. Translation revised from that in Worsthorne, *Venetian Opera*, 177. The complete original text of this portion of the description can be found in appendix 3, doc. 6.

eler Philip Skippon, recording a 1664 stay in Venice at Carnival time, began his account of *Rosilena* at the Teatro SS. Giovanni e Paolo with a description of the sets and machines:

> The sets were stately, and seemed natural. In the prologue some of the actors hung in the air, and then flew across the stage, and one flew downwards, who represented a fury with two boys holding him by his legs, and then he flew up again . . . The removing of the sets was very neat and artificial; clouds seemed to move, and the walls of a castle to be blown up. There were exactly represented gardens, houses, etc.[2]

The most famous guide to the city, Sansovino's *Venetia città nobilissima*, originally published in the sixteenth century, contained in its 1663 revised edition another description of the wonders of a Venetian opera house: "In the theater of SS. Giovanni e Paolo, during carnival they perform musical operas with marvelous mutations of sets, majestic and most rich costumes, and miraculous flights; one sees on a regular basis resplendent heavens, gods, seas, palaces, forests, and other lovely and delightful images."[3]

One of the first real celebrities of the Venetian opera world was neither a composer nor a librettist, but a set and machine designer, Giacomo Torelli. His designs for productions at the Teatro Novissimo in the 1640s were published and described in lavish books following the runs of several of his operas.[4] While the printed librettos of the earliest operas, including those designed by Torelli, rarely indicate the sets that were employed, such information became standard from about 1644 on, at first within the text of the drama itself. Later, a comprehensive list of sets appeared as part of the usual front matter, with the descriptions repeated at the proper place in the drama. By using this material, even without the survival of actual designs, we can trace with some precision the development of the visual spectacle of Venetian opera.[5]

---

2 Skippon, *Journey*, 506.

3 "In quello di S. Giovanni, e Paolo si recitano il Carnevale Opere Musicali con maravigliose mutationi di Scene, Comparse maestose, e ricchissime, machine, e voli mirabili; vedendosi per ordinario risplendenti Cieli, Deitadi, Mari, Reggie, Palazzi, Boscaglie, Foreste, & altre vaghe, e dilettevoli apparenze." Sansovino, *Venetia città nobilissima*, 397.

4 In 1642 ten engravings of sets from *Bellerofonte* appeared in *IL BELLERO FONTE / Drama Musicale del Sig.r Vicenzo Nolfi da fano / RAPPRESENTATO NEL TEATRO / NOVISSIMO IN VENETIA / DA GIACOMO / Torelli Da Fano Inventore / delli Apparati* . . . (Five of these are reproduced as figures 9.2–9.6.) Two years later a second volume appeared, entitled *APPARATI SCENICI / Per lo Teatro Novissimo di Venetia. / Nell'anno 1644 / d'inventione, e cura / di IACOMO TORELLI DA FANO /* . . . , including engravings (signed by Marco Boschini) of nine sets from *Venere gelosa* (see figures 9.7 and 9.8) and three from *Deidamia*. Reproductions of both sets of engravings appear in Worsthorne, *Venetian Opera*, and Milesi, *Giacomo Torelli*. The extant copies of these books are not all identical (the engravings appear to have been separated, dispersed, and reassembled). For example, a copy with the title page of the 1644 *Apparati scenici* in the library of the University of Michigan includes engravings from all three operas.

5 For an overview of the nature and development of Italian operatic scenery from the beginnings of opera through the mid-twentieth century, see Viale Ferrero, "Stage and Set."

THE MECHANICS OF SCENERY

Unlike Renaissance plays, which relied on either a unitary set (the well-known Roman street) or just a few changes, Venetian opera followed the path blazed by late Renaissance and early Baroque festival productions, and, with few exceptions, featured numerous set changes, usually at least two for each of three acts, plus another for the prologue.[6] The scenery of Venetian opera featured a system that combined physical depth with painted perspective through the use of multiple sets of side wings, or flats, and backdrops. This system, which replaced earlier, less flexible methods, such as the rotating triangular *periaktoi*,[7] first appears in the early seventeenth century, perhaps in Parma, where we find the earliest clear descriptions and illustrations.[8] A set was constructed of three or more pairs of painted flats, positioned parallel to each other, with each successive pair of flats (moving back from the proscenium) smaller and closer together, following the rules of linear perspective. The stage itself was also raked, and the overhead elements hung progressively lower, so that the proportions of the flats remained unchanged as their size decreased. Beyond the last pair a backdrop completed the perspective of the set. Initially the system for changing sets was rather cumbersome. For each of the three or more pairs of flats, the stage was equipped with at least two sets of wooden tracks, within which the flats could slide.[9] For every change in set, many workers were required: some to pull out into the wings the flats from the previous set on one set of tracks, and others to push onto stage the new ones on the second set of tracks. The "backdrops" in this system were also in the form of flats, which, unlike the others, joined in the middle to form a continuous surface. Also spanning the width of the stage were the pieces at the top, one for each pair of flats, that formed the image of the sky for exterior sets or ceilings for interiors; these were dropped down from above on cables. Coordination of the many workers presented a major difficulty, and the noise of the wings sliding in the wooden tracks would very likely have necessitated a complete cessation of the action on stage to avoid the singers being drowned out. Using more than two sets necessitated either additional pairs of tracks or the expenditure of additional effort to replace the flats for one set on the tracks while another was on stage. Despite these difficulties, the capability

6 Exceptions are some of the early pastoral operas, with very limited set changes. Ferrari's 1641 *La ninfa avara* appears to have only a single pastoral set for the entire body of the opera (see Molinari, *Nozze degli dei*, 156).

7 Described in Sabbatini, *Pratica di fabricar scene*, 77–80. This was most likely the technique employed in the late sixteenth-century court festivals, such as those for the Medici in Florence. See Zorzi, "L'immagine della festa medicea," 431–49. Sabbatini also describes a method involving interlocking angled elements that slide forwards and backwards to reveal or cover others (75–76). There is no evidence that this method was ever used in Venice.

8 A drawing and a brief description of a temporary theater erected in a coutyard of the ducal palace in Parma in 1627 are included in a letter by the scenographer Francesco Guitti, and a plan of the theater is in a letter by Francesco Mazzi (both now in the Biblioteca Comunale of Ferrara). The illustrations are reproduced in Ronconi, *Lo spettacolo e la meraviglia*, 136 and 236.

9 Such a system, installed in the nineteenth century, still survives today in a theater in Mnichovo Hradiště (near Prague). See Mohler, "Court Theatre."

of making repeated set changes, while still preserving the sense of illusionary perspective, was the great advantage of this method over its predecessors.

The introduction of mechanical devices to change the scenery made more feasible the multiple settings that became an integral part of Venetian opera. Once again, this innovation seems to have been used first in Parma, with the opening of the Teatro Farnese in 1628 (although the invention itself apparently dates to a decade earlier). The architect of the theater, Giovanni Battista Aleotti, or perhaps the scenographer Guitti, designed a novel method for moving the flats. Rather than sitting on rails set into the stage, with the labor to move them exerted in the wings on both sides of the stage, Aleotti set the flats into slots cut into the stage floor and mounted them onto carriages underneath. These carriages, which rolled directly on the floor of the basement or on tracks, were connected by an elaborate series of ropes and pullies that allowed them to be moved in and out simultaneously, with far less audible disturbance, and by fewer workmen. In 1618, Aleotti wrote to his employer, the Duke of Parma, that he had installed "some of the wings that form the sets, which must go forwards and backwards, and put in its place a cylinder to pull them and push them forwards and backwards."[10] Although the backdrops, which were still constructed as pairs of flats that met in the center of the stage, were probably moved with the same mechanism as the side wings, it is likely that the scenic elements above the stage (for the sky and ceilings) were controlled separately.[11] Aleotti and Guitti also designed extraordinarily complex and ingenious stage machines for productions at the Farnese theater.

No illustrations or descriptions of the mechanisms used at the first Venetian opera houses survive, but it is probable that they resembled those used in Parma in 1628 (but it cannot be ruled out that they were more basic, perhaps even manually operated, like those employed in 1627 at the first Parma theater mentioned above). The dramatic change in technology, and the invention that made the marvels of the Baroque stage famous, was brought about by Giacomo Torelli, a native of Fano, where he got his start in the theater business.[12] Torelli's debut in Venice (he was employed at the Arsenal, the Venetian naval shipyards) was at the newly constructed

10 "furno posti in opera alcuni di quei tellari, che dovranno fare le scene che dovran'andare inanti e indietro"; ASP, Cartella Teatro Farnese, 18 Mar. 1618. Excerpts published in Gandolfi, *Teatro Farnese*, 108. The description in *Corago* (117–18) of scenery in the Parma theater for this production as rising upwards from underneath the stage, rather than sliding in from the wings, seems hard to credit in light of the direct evidence from the scenographer and architect involved. Most likely, the author (or the scribe of the surviving copy of the treatise) was confused by the placement beneath the stage of the machinery to operate the flats, which themselves always remained above.

11 A separate system for the above-stage movements appears to have been retained in Venetian theaters for quite a long time, although the surviving evidence is not clear as to whether the two systems, that below stage for the main flats, and that above for the sky and ceiling, might have been linked by pulleys. The Swedish scenographer Tessin (Bjurström, "Unveröffentlichtes von Nicodemus Tessin," 29) drew the separate mechanism used in the Teatro S. Giovanni Grisostomo, and something similar appears in a drawing of sets from *La divisione del mondo* (Teatro S. Luca, 1675) in the Biblioteca Palatina in Parma (Larson, "Giacomo Torelli," 455, and Mancini, Muraro, and Povoledo, *Teatri di Venezia*, 1:227).

12 The most recent study of Torelli and his works is Milesi, *Giacomo Torelli*. See also Bjurström, *Giacomo Torelli*, Guarini, "Torelli a Venezia," and Larson, "Giacomo Torelli."

Teatro Novissimo, where he was one of the original company members; indeed, the theater was most likely built to his specifications (see chap. 4). A contemporary description of the first production, Giulio Strozzi and Francesco Sacrati's *La finta pazza* of 1641, highlights Torelli's accomplishments (the hyperbole, while certainly deserved, may also be a result of the publication's origins in the circles surrounding the production at the Novissimo):

> And in the twinkling of an eye the maritime set disappeared and it changed into a beautiful and well-proportioned courtyard lined with loggias and bronze statues, in the background of which one saw a triumphal arch, the door of which was covered with a curtain of noble gold brocade. The artifice of this set change was marvelous, because a single boy of 15 years put it in motion, releasing a counterweight that had been held in place by a small iron pin; this weight rotated a cylinder under the stage, by which all the wings, which were sixteen in number, eight on each side, went forward or backward . . . , changing all the parts with a single and very rapid motion, and creating great wonder, as something never before known on stage, and theaters owe thanks to the inventor who made scenery worthy of amazement and delight at the same time; beyond this ingenious artifice, the mind cannot comprehend how so many wings can, all at one moment, in a flash, rather in an instant, move to their proper places to change a set.[13]

The mechanism devised by Torelli was described and illustrated several decades later by the English traveller Skippon, who visited Venice and the Teatro SS. Giovanni e Paolo in 1664 (see figure 9.1):

> Over the top of the stage are many floors; and there is under the stage a long axis [cylinder] AB, which hath fasten' to it the cords d, with iron hooks h, and a long rope E; which being pull'd down by the weight of the stone S, moves over the pully F, and unwinds at CD. This stone, by the help of the cord q, is wound up over the stage, at the turnstile M [the author points out that in the illustration the relative positions of F, S, and M are reversed]; at that being let go, the rope E unwinding from the axis AB, turns the axis from C to D, and winds up the cords d; and the forementioned hooks being put into the nooses of ropes i, etc. pull towards the axis [that is towards the center of the stage] the *anime* or bottoms of frames wherein the painted scenes are, and bring them forward in sight of the spectators; y is a cord that couples two of those anime; and as the hook I is placed in the noose, so the bottoms of the frame or anima move forward and backward; e.g. when xv is drawn forward, then bc is pull'd

---

13 "Et in un batter d'occhi sparì la scena marittima e si cangiò in un bellissimo e ben regolato cortile ripieno di loggie e statue di bronzo, nel cui prospetto vedevasi un'arco ad uso de'Trionfali, la porta del quale era coperta d'una cortina di nobile broccato d'oro. Mirabile era l'artificio di questa mutazione, poiché un solo giovanetto di quindici anni le dava il moto lasciando un contrappeso rattenuto da un picciol ferro: questo peso faceva aggirare un rocchello sotto il palco, per lo quale, secondo il bisogno, andavano or inanzi or indietro li telari tutti, che erano sedici, otto per parte . . . girando tutte le parti ad un solo e velocissimo moto, rendeva grande la meraviglia come di arte non mai più usata in simile occorenza di scene, et i Teatri doveranno la gratitudine all'Inventore, che le ha rese degne di stupore e dilettevoli ad un tratto; et in vero che fuori di questo ingegnoso artificio l'intelletto non s'adegua alla credenza che tanti telari possano tutti in un punto, in un baleno, anzi in un atomo accomodarsi a suoi luoghi per variare una Scena." *Il Cannocchiale per la Finta pazza* (Venice 1641), excerpt published in Mancini, Muraro, and Povoledo, *Teatri di Venezia*, 1:251–52.

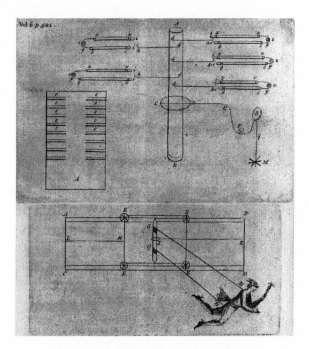

FIGURE 9.1.   Diagram of scenery mechanism in Teatro SS. Giovanni e Paolo, from Skippon, *Journey* (Bancroft Library, University of California, Berkeley)

backward, the cord y moving on the pully z. There is a man always stands ready at M, who, upon a sign given, lets the stone fall, and changes a great number of scenes on a sudden, there being many of these hooks and *anime*. Before another scene appears, the stone must be wound up again. Those scenes which fall downwards as arches etc. [that is backdrops, either open or solid, which have replaced the full-stage-width flats of the Parma system] are let down by a long axis [cylinder] above, just in the same manner. The frames of the scenes move within the slits o made in the floor of the stage A.[14]

Another development in the early seventeenth century, and used in Venetian theaters, but often not clearly understood today, is the physical extension of the depth of the stage. Guitti's and Inigo Jones's theaters had four sets of wings, beyond which, in both cases, was a single backdrop. Larger theaters, such as the Teatro Farnese and those in Venice, expanded to six, seven, or eight sets of main wings, with

14 Skippon, *Journey*, 507–8. A description of the mechanism used at the Teatro S. Giovanni Grisostomo in 1688 is included Tessin's travel journal; see Bjurström, "Unveröffentlichtes von Nicodemus Tessin," 22–23. As mentioned earlier (see n. 11), a drawing of the set-changing mechanism of the Teatro S. Luca from the early 1670s survives in the Biblioteca Palatina in Parma (reproduced in Mancini, Muraro, and Povoledo, *Teatri di Venezia*, 1:226). Mechanisms such as these described still survive in several Baroque theaters, notably those in Krumlov Castle (Czech Republic), Gripsholm, and Drottningholm (both in Sweden).

the possibility of not just a single backdrop at the rear, but also one or more at intermediate points, thus creating the possibility of several versions of the set and of
sets of varying depth. These mid-stage drops were, at least in the mid-seventeenth
century, usually open, in the form of arches or doorways (see figures 9.2, 9.4, 9.5,
9.6, and 9.8).[15] While the descending size of the flats, and the accompanying exag-
gerated perspective, would have made performing from the deeper parts of the
stage unlikely, the illusion of depth was certainly improved (at S. Cassiano, the seventh set of wings was about one-third smaller than the first; the decrease in the
Inigo Jones theater was even more drastic, the fourth and last set being less than
half the height of the first).[16] Some theaters, including those in Venice, went beyond that, installing additional pairs of even smaller wings, referred to as *lontani*, receding into the depths of the stage. These can be discerned in the engravings of

FIGURE 9.2.   Giacomo Torelli, "Cave of the Winds" set for *Bellerofonte* from *Apparati scenici*
(Special Collections Library, University of Michigan)

15 In the plan of the stage of the Teatro S. Luca in the Biblioteca Palatina (Mancini, Muraro, and
Povoledo, *Teatri di Venezia*, 1:224), only one of the five sets of backdrops, the next to last, is shown with
tracks that meet in the middle; the others all are separated by a gap of about 6 feet.

16 A document for S. Cassiano specifies the amount of canvas needed for each of the seven flats:
$9\frac{3}{4}$ braccia for the first, then descending for the remaining six—$9\frac{1}{4}$, $8\frac{3}{4}$, $8\frac{1}{4}$, $7\frac{1}{2}$, 7, $6\frac{3}{4}$ (ASV, SGSM,
b. 194, f. 270). Drawings for Inigo Jones's 1640 production of *Salmacida spolia* in the Masquing House at
Whitehall show five sets of flats descending from 26 feet high at the front through $22\frac{1}{2}$, $18\frac{1}{2}$, and 15 to
14 feet high at the back (Orrell, *Theatres of Inigo Jones*, 153).

Torelli's sets for *Bellerofonte* and other operas (see figures 9.5, 9.6, and 9.8; compare sets with backdrops in figures 9.2 and 9.3). Unlike the main series of flats, however, these lontani were not moved using slots in the floor and understage carriages, but were placed directly on the floor of the stage by stagehands.[17] Although certainly more labor intensive than the normal method of sliding flats, the technique of lon-

FIGURE 9.3.   Giacomo Torelli, "Uninhabited Island" set for *Bellerofonte* from *Apparati scenici* (Special Collections Library, University of Michigan)

17 In the drawing of the stage of the Teatro S. Luca (see n. 11, above), there is a large open area beyond the sixth and final set of main flats. The slightly later plan of Teatro SS. Giovanni e Paolo (figure 2.1) has a similar open area beyond the last backdrop, this time bearing the indication: "Sito per lontani li quali si mose senza anime" ("Place for the lontani, which move without carriages"). Tessin's 1688 journal (Bjurström, "Unveröffentlichtes von Nicodemus Tessin," 27–28) describes precisely this technique, and provides a drawing indicating the flexibility of the system. A pole or peg attached to the back of each frame would be set into a previously placed iron ring in the floor; this served both to keep the otherwise unattached flat upright, and to ensure correct placement. The eighteenth-century set diagrams for the Teatro della Fortuna in Fano (probably representing Bibiena's 1719 decorations; Milesi, *Giacomo Torelli*, 391–405) are even more explicit. Four of the reusable sets employ lontani, and each bears a helpful indication. That for the Garden reads "Lontani del Giardino posti per terra" ("Lontani for the garden placed on the floor," that is, not in tracks). Bibiena does not refer to iron rings, but simply indicates holes in the floor. In order to get the placement of these lontani correct in the four different arrangements, Bibiena devised a simple system, with a distinctive mark for each set: for the Long Gallery by pairs of chisel marks pointing towards the proscenium ("sono segnati con la sgurbia al in giù"), for the Garden with Parterres by brass tacks ("sono segnati con le brocche d'ottone"), and for the Forest by horizontal chisel marks at the outside edges ("sono segnati da fianco con segni di sgurbia").

FIGURE 9.4. Giacomo Torelli, "Temple of Jove" set for *Bellerofonte* from *Apparati scenici* (Special Collections Library, University of Michigan)

FIGURE 9.5. Giacomo Torelli, "Delightful woods in the royal gardens" set for *Bellerofonte* from *Apparati scenici* (Special Collections Library, University of Michigan)

FIGURE 9.6.   Giacomo Torelli, "Throne Room" set for *Bellerofonte* from *Apparati scenici*
(Special Collections Library, University of Michigan)

FIGURE 9.7.   Giacomo Torelli, "City of Naxos" set for *Venere gelosa* from *Apparati scenici*
(Special Collections Library, University of Michigan)

tani allowed the scenographer to design sets of different depths, alternating between sets using the backdrop (the type later known as the *scena corta*) and those using the lontani (the *scena lunga*).

With lontani, the scenographer, not being limited to the placements built into the stage, could also contruct a set that varied from the standard single centrally receding perspective. Torelli's set of the Piazza of Naxos that opened the second act of Bartolini and Sacrati's 1642/43 *La Venere gelosa* at the Teatro Novissimo (see figure 9.7), consists, in the foreground, of a standard classical tragic set, a city street. Toward the back of the stage, however, the street ends at a building (the interior of which is visible through a central door), to the sides of which open two other streets, receding into the distance, angled away from the middle toward the wings. Rather than the usual twelve flats (six pairs), this set required, according to the scenario, forty-eight.[18] Each of the three distant perspectives—the two streets and the

FIGURE 9.8. Giacomo Torelli, "Courtyard" set for *Venere gelosa* from *Apparati scenici* (Special Collections Library, University of Michigan)

18 "Tutta questa macchina di scena era composta da quarantotto telari" (Milesi, *Giacomo Torelli*, 111). Mancini, Muraro, and Povoledo (*Illusione e pratica teatrale*, 57–58, pl. 20) dismiss this as hyperbole. Apparently unaware (in 1975) of the use of lontani, they argue, incorrectly in our view, that this and other sets that did not end with a plain backdrop were constructed using combinations of pierced intermediary backdrops, in the form of arches, a method that finds no documentary support, and seems technically unlikely.

interior of the building—was created by its own set of six pairs of small flats. At the end of each of these perspectives, an even more distant view was suggested, most likely by individual small backdrops. This technique is confirmed by an inventory listing materials for, among other things, a set for the opera *Annibale in Capua*, presented at the Teatro SS. Giovanni e Paolo in 1661 (see below). This piazza is described (like the one in *La Venere gelosa*) as having three perspective views: two of these were probably streets, viewed through triumphal arches, and the central one might have been, as with Torelli's set, a view into a building. The inventory lists first the seven standard pairs of flats, which were employed to depict a central outdoor space, the piazza. It also lists thirty-eight small flats (nineteen pairs of lontani) for the distant views, for a total of fifty-two (quite similar to Torelli's forty-eight). Unless, as in the case of *La Venere gelosa*, such a set opened an act (which allowed the flats to be placed without problem during the interval), it is likely that the delicate work of correctly laying out such a series of distant views was carried out behind the backdrop of the preceding set while the action on stage continued.

Two further innovations occurred during this period. As early as *Bellerofonte*, Venetian scenographers employed what came later to be known as the box set, that is one in which the walls and ceiling are not formed by perspective illusion from separate, parallel flats, as in normal sets, but are actually continuous surfaces, as in a real room (although with the angles distorted to exaggerate the perspective). As described by the Swedish scenographer Nicodemus Tessin, one method for forming such a set consisted of attaching hinged elements to the basic flats, with a mechanism that caused them to swing out perpendicular to the proscenium as they moved into place (whether this was the same technique used in the 1640s cannot be determined). The engraving of the Torelli's final set for *Bellerofonte* shows the box set clearly (see figure 9.6).[19] One last change, which occurred sometime after 1650 (but appears not to have been universally adopted, and was then definitively abandoned in the eighteenth century), was a modification in the alignment of the wings, so that they were angled backwards, rather than parallel to the proscenium (see figure 2.1).[20]

None of the actual scenery from seventeenth-century Venetian theaters survives. As mentioned earlier, however, Torelli issued publications containing engravings of his designs following several of his productions at the Teatro Novissimo, and these provide a good idea of the appearance of the finished works. Two of these books reproduce the sets from Vincenzo Nolfi and Francesco Sacrati's *Bellerofonte* of 1642 (see figures 9.2–9.6) and Nicolò Enea Bartolini and Sacrati's *Venere gelosa* of 1643 (see figures 9.7 and 9.8; the latter along with three sets from *Deidamia*). The surviving engravings and drawings, of course, lack the element of color, but the Museo Civico in

19 See Larson, "New Evidence." Tessin's description of this method can be found in Bjurström, "Unveröffentlichtes von Nicodemus Tessin," 23–24.

20 Skippon (1664) and the ca. 1675 plan of the Teatro S. Luca (as well as the eighteenth-century Fano diagram mentioned in n. 17 and most eighteenth-century illustrations of Venetian theaters) show the flats parallel to the proscenium, while Tessin (1688; Bjurström, "Unveröffentlichtes von Nicodemus Tessin," 25) and the plan of Teatro SS. Giovanni e Paolo (1690s) show them angled.

Fano possesses a set of late seventeenth-century paintings derived from the Torelli engravings for *Venere gelosa* and *Deidamia;* whether they represent the colors of the original scenery, or rather just the imagination of the unknown artist, is not known.[21] That the colors were at least sometimes rather gaudy is clear from the comments of an anonymous critic of the 1675 Venetian production of *La divisione del mondo* preserved in a copy of the libretto in the Biblioteca Comunale Federiciana of Fano.[22] He describes the "transparent palace of Apollo" from act 1 as "a miscellany of columns with a glittering view of green and yellow colors, just like a parrot."[23] The "gallery in Mercury's heaven" (act 2) he saw as follows: "A colonnade of turquoise color which formed in the middle of the stage a small cupola almost the color of lapis lazuli, behind which hung greenish backdrops," to which description he adds the snide comment "And this foolishness in Venice they call an arcade."[24]

THE MECHANISMS FOR THEATRICAL EFFECTS

Much of the machinery that created the spectacular effects for Venetian opera used a complicated system (for a diagram of a simple example, see figure 9.1) of pulleys, levers, wire, and rope to maneuver wooden frames (independent of that used for the scenery) suspended from the area above the stage, to which were attached painted cardboard facades.[25] Some of the same elements served for the flights of characters without visible supports. In addition, some effects, including moving waves and descents into the underworld, involved mechanisms beneath the stage. Many of the techniques for these effects were described by Nicola Sabbatini in his 1638 *Pratica di fabricar scene e machine ne' teatri,*[26] and Skippon, referred to above, provides an illustration of a mechanism for the flight of a single character.[27] Fortunately, a number of drawings of more complicated machinery for specific operas survive as well, in some cases showing them in several positions, and both with and without the painted decorative elements.[28]

---

21 Reproduced in Milesi, *Giacomo Torelli,* 123–33 and 142–46.

22 Fano, Biblioteca Comunale Federiciana, MSS Federici 94. See Fabbri, "Una recensione."

23 "Il palaggio trasparente / é un miscuglio di colonne / con prospetto rilucente / di colori verdi e gialli / giusto come i pa[pa]galli . . ."; Fabbri, "Una recensione," 446.

24 "Un colonato di color turchino / forma in mezo la scena / quasi di lapislazuli / una piccola cupola / a cui dietro pendono / prospetti che verdeggiano. / E questa sciocheria / in Venezia si chiama Galleria." Ibid., 447.

25 While it is possible that canvas-covered frames might have been used, the only evidence refers to the much lighter cardboard (*cartone*): a 1646 summary of materials left in the theater and elsewhere after the season at S. Cassiano refers to "nuole di cartoni," or cardboard clouds (ASV, AN, Atti, b. 667, f. 83ᵛ).

26 Sabbatini, *Pratica di fabricar scene,* esp. book 2.

27 Skippon, *Journey,* 508. See also Larson, "Giacomo Torelli."

28 Most notably, these include drawings of machinery for *Germanico sul Reno* in the Musée de l'Opéra in Paris (see Brugnoni, "Curiose mutanze"), and for *La divisione del mondo* in the Biblioteca Palatina in Parma (see Molinari, "Disegni a Parma," Mohler, "Brief Shining Moment," and Mancini, Muraro, and Povoledo, *Teatri di Venezia,* 1:225–232). Contemporary drawings for machines of Venus and Mars for an unidentified production (not necessarily for Venice, but using the same techiniques) are found in the Archivio di Stato of Parma (see Ault, "Baroque Stage Machines").

Occasionally, the machines failed to achieve the desired effect. One of the spectacular machines in *La divisione del mondo*, at the end of act 2, is described in the libretto as follows: "Here one sees descend an enormous machine, which arrives at the level of the *gloria* from the level of the floor of the stage, forming a majestic stairway of clouds, by which Jove descends, accompanied by a multitude of deities and celestial goddesses."[29] The anonymous critic of the Fano libretto was not impressed, writing, "A stairway of clouds? For shame! / pardon me, architect: / it was a ladder to climb to the roof."[30] At times, the machines specified in the libretto simply were not employed, perhaps for technical or financial reasons. In the last act of *La divisione del mondo*, the libretto calls for Jove to descend with Mercury from the heavens to the seashore to placate Neptune, and then to ascend. The Fano critic reports that the special effect was omitted: "Poet, here either you are tricking me or it's invisible: / Jove isn't in a machine, but is standing on the ground." When Jove is supposed to ascend, the critic writes: "The machine does not appear, / nor can he return to the heavens: the scene is at sea."[31] Such failures must not have been too common, since spectacular effects continued to be popular.

TYPES AND NUMBERS OF SETS AND MACHINES

Most operas through the mid-1650s called for seven or eight different sets, with ten then becoming more usual, although even in the 1650s some included only six or eight, and others had as many as thirteen (and one, *Dario in Babilonia* of 1671, had fifteen) (see table 9.1). In the 1630s and 1640s, however, many productions used only a limited number of different sets, each one of which could appear several times during the opera. The first Venetian public opera, *Andromeda*, introduced two sets in the first act: a maritime set, which opened and closed the act, and a forest in the intervening scenes. Act 2 used only the same two sets, and they returned again in act 3, separated by a new one, a palace. The first two acts of *La maga fulminata* comprised a series of new sets, five in all, but act 3 introduced no new sets (with the exception of a second backdrop to one of those introduced earlier). Instead, visual impact was created by extremely rapid set changes, three in one scene, separated by only a few verses of text, as the sorceress Artusia calls on, in quick succession, spirits of sea, forest, and sky, bringing forth their dwellings with incantations.

Another method for creating variety while using a small number of sets was employed the next year in *Le nozze di Teti e di Peleo* of 1639. The libretto, the first to list the sets in the prefatory matter, a practice that would become the norm in the 1650s, informs the reader that: "The *scena maestra* represents Lepanto, the most

29 "Qui si vede calar grandissima Machina, che arriva da l'altezza della Gloria sino al pavimento della scena formando maestosa scala di nuvole per la quale discende Giove corteggiato da moltitudine di Numi, e Dive Celesti." *La divisione del mondo*, 51. The *gloria* was a circular space, surrounded by rays of light and clouds, at the center of which were one or more gods.

30 "Una scala di nuvole? Oibò / perdonami, architetto: / era una scala da montar sul tetto." Fabbri, "Una recensione," 447.

31 "Poeta, o qui m'inganni o non ci vedi: / non è in machina Giove, è in terra a piedi. / . . . Machina non appare, / né può tornar al ciel: la scena è in mare." Ibid., 448–49.

TABLE 9.1. The Number of Different Sets in Venetian Operas from 1637 to 1677

Number of sets	Operas in the 1630s and 1640s	Operas in the 1650s	Operas in the 1660s	Operas in the 1670s[a]
3	1	0	0	0
4	0	0	0	0
5	4	0	0	0
6	3	8	1	1
7	2	4	1	0
8	5	3	8	2
9	4	5	9	7
10	1	6	11	8
11	2	0	6	7
12	0	0	3	8
13	1	0	0	3
14	0	0	0	1
15	0	0	0	1

Only those operas with libretto or scenari that indicate the sets are included. Most librettos of the 1630s and early 1640s neither list the sets nor do they indicate the changes within the text.
[a] Through 1677 only.

frequented shore of Greece; the others imitate an amphitheater, Hell, the Aegean, the Empyrean, Mt. Peleus, and the Forest of Ida."[32] The meaning of the term "scene maestra" is not clarified by the libretto proper, but is made evident in the scenario published simultaneously. The scena maestra was a set that returned regularly throughout the opera, alternating with a series of others (see table 9.2). In design, construction, and technique, the scena maestra and the sets with which it alternated were all complete, normal sets, whether long or short. The scena maestra would not remain fixed, as has been proposed elsewhere, but would move on and off stage like all other sets, using the standard mechanism.[33] While the recurrence

[32] "La Scena maestra rappresenta Lepanto, Lido più frequentato della Grecia, le altre imitano l'Anfiteatro, l'Inferno, l'Egeo, l'Empireo, il Monte Peleo, il Bosco d'Ida." *Le nozze di Teti e di Peleo* (Venice, 1639).

[33] Elena Povoledo's 1998 attempt to explain this technique ("Controversie monteverdiane," 382) seems to us to be based on a misunderstanding of the concept of deep and shallow sets, the *scena lunga* and *scena corta*. She describes the *scena lunga* as one using a full complement of pairs of flats with a backdrop. The *scena corta* would use only two pairs of flats toward the front of the stage, with a backdrop halfway back. The scena maestra, according to Povoledo, would be a *scena lunga* that remained fixed thoughout the opera, while the other sets would be *scene corte*, whose components would be moved on stage as needed, "covering a part of the scena maestra and changing its appearance." This explanation, accepted in principle by more recent writers such as Tim Carter in his discussions of the late Monteverdi operas, creates some technical problems, both in the mechanism for changing sets and in the re-

TABLE 9.2.   The Scena Maestra: Set Changes in *Le nozze di
Teti, e di Peleo*

Act/Scene	Set
Prologue	Amphitheater
Act 1, scene 1	Hell
Scene 2	*Seashore* [list = Lepanto, scena maestra]
Scene 3	Sea [list = the Aegean]
Scene 5	Heavens [list = the Empyrean]
Scene 6	*Seashore*
Scene 9	Sea
Act 2, scene 1	*Seashore*
Scene 9	Mt. Peleus
Act 3, scene 1	*Seashore*
Scene 6	Forest of Ida
Scene 8	*Seashore*
Scene 12	Hell

According to the scenario; differing descriptions found in the list of sets
at the beginning of the libretto are in brackets; the scena maestra is
indicated in italics.

of one setting was, of course, rooted in the construction of the drama, it also required considerably less physical labor backstage than other methods. The scena
maestra would simply have remained on one set of tracks throughout the opera,
meaning that the stagehands only had to remount flats for the other scenes in the
second set of tracks while the scena maestra was on stage. Without the scena maes-

---

sultant very shallow stage, which would make the operation of machinery for special effects quite difficult. The latter problem is also shared by proposals by Carter and Pirrotta for the occasional employment of backdrops to cover the scena maestra. In part, these suggestions seem to be based on the assumption that only Torelli's Teatro Novissimo had a fully mechanized scene-changing apparatus, and
that the other theaters were much more primitive. Since, however, fully functional mechanisms had
been available for over twenty years, this seems unlikely. It should be remembered that the praises for
Torelli's innovations at the Novissimo refer not to the nature of the scene changes themselves, which
are treated as normal, but to the fact that it took only one person to set them in motion, rather than the
crews needed for other systems. Povoledo's explanation also runs counter to the extant documentary
and iconographical evidence, all of which indicates that all sets in Venetian theaters used the full complement of flats. The distinction between the *scena corta* and the *scena lunga*, as discussed above, regards
not the number of pairs of flats or the use of an intermediate backdrop, but, rather, whether the set ter-
minated with a backdrop or with lontani. This distinction, although without the terms, is clear both in
inventories of scenery in the 1650s and 60s and in contracts for the manufacture of sets. Support for this
use of the terminology can be found explicitly (if a bit later) in the diagrams by Bibiena for the theatre
in Fano: the forest scene, for example, came in two versions, long and short, one with lontani, one without (see Milesi, *Giacomo Torelli*, 399).

tra, with each set being used only once in an opera, every change meant removing one set of flats from the carriages and replacing it with another. Only once in *Le nozze di Teti*, in the middle of act 1, was a more complicated maneuver called for, when two new sets appear between instances of the scene maestra.

The scena maestra idea was, however, only rarely employed in seventeenth-century Venetian operas. The two most famous examples to use it are Monteverdi's late operas, although the term itself is not specified in the original sources.[34] In *Il ritorno d'Ulisse in patria*, it is the palace, or reggia, that acts as the stable element, alternating with a maritime set (which also recurs twice), a forest, a deserted area, and the underworld (the scene employing the last is not extant in the musical sources). For *L'incoronazione di Poppea*, the scena maestra is "the city of Rome," separating Poppea's palace, Seneca's villa, Poppea's garden, and Nero's palace.[35] Contemporaneously, *Bellerofonte*, presented at the Teatro Novissimo with sets by Torelli, demonstrated what would become the standard practice for the following decades: a larger number of different sets, eight in this case, few or none of which were seen

34 See Povoledo, "Controversie monteverdiane," 382–85, and most recently, Carter, *Monteverdi's Musical Theatre*, 81–85.

35 Several solutions to the scenography of these operas have been proposed. It is not our intention to address them here, except in terms of the techniques employed. Pirrotta ("Theater, Sets," 268–69) argues that the basic city set for *L'incoronazione di Poppea* was "probably a backdrop . . . placed on the first or second pair of grooves parallel to the proscenium," behind which "the components of the other sets could be changed without having to rush . . ." Povoledo, on the other hand ("Controversie," 385), employing her concept of the scena maestra (see above, n. 33), argues that the basic street set would be in the background, and that the other sets would be formed in front, using "the rapid movement of a few flats in the foreground (two pairs of side wings and . . . a small backdrop) [which] was sufficient to form the other sets" (our translation). Carter (*Monteverdi's Musical Theatre*, 84) takes yet a third view, which corresponds in part with both of the preceding ones, that the reggia "was somehow created (with flats or a backdrop) in the interior," that is the front, center portion of the stage, and would open, when needed, to display "the maritime and woodland sets [which] alternated in the background." Regarding *L'incoronazione di Poppea*, Carter proposes that a depiction of the city of Rome remained in the background, while the other sets alternated in the foreground. He further suggests that the setting of the prologue, the "scena di tutto cielo" was "presumably a backcloth" in front of which the characters descended in a machine. None of these solutions seems reasonable, given the scenographic techniques used in these theaters. The use of backdrops without corresponding sets of flats is not documented anywhere, nor is there evidence for the use of one set of flats for the front portion of the stage and another for the back. If the front set of flats were to be withdrawn, something would have to replace them, or the offstage wings would be visible to the audience. Partial sets could also lead to the incongruity of walls changing character halfway to the back of the stage. Carter's proposal for the *Poppea* prologue is also problematic—the backdrop could not be at the front of the stage, or there would have been no room for the machine; if it were farther back, the illusion of a heavenly scene would be disrupted, as the painting of clouds would have been surrounded by bare stage on the bottom, and views of the back-stage machinery above and to the sides. The "scena di tutto cielo" was actually a standard and fairly complex set, using the basic system of flats at the sides, with additional elements at the top and bottom. Almost certainly, all of the sets in these two operas (performed at the grand Teatro SS. Giovanni e Paolo, whose patron, Giovanni Grimani, would be unlikely to want to appear so far behind the times as not to have fully operable sets) were normal ones, composed of the usual multiple pairs of flats. All of these scholars seem to have been influenced by their desires to view Monteverdi as a composer who preferred there to be as little visual distraction as possible from the words and music; envisioning his operas as employing the standard mechanisms used in every other opera should not diminish the general picture: his operas still rely less on the visual than those of his contemporaries.

more than once in an opera (in this case, none return, but act 1 does begin with the same setting as the Prologue). From this point on, with only two exceptions, no opera presented in Venice through at least 1677 required more than two returns of a set, and most had none at all.[36] The two exceptions are, however, quite remarkable. The 1653 production of Badoaro's *Helena rapita da Theseo* takes the idea of multiple returns of several sets to an extreme. The opera calls for ten sets altogether (a normal number for that date), six of which occur only once. One other, the forest, returns once, the garden returns three times, and the courtyard and woods return four times each.[37] While a standard opera of the 1650s might require a total of ten set changes (each set, that is, appearing only once), *Helena rapita* required twenty-one (one wonders whether the stagehands were paid more than the regular fee for such extraordinary work). *Bradamante*, produced in 1650 at Teatro SS. Giovanni e Paolo, represents the acme of the scena maestra idea.[38] Seven of the eight sets occur only once in the opera, but one, the countryside, referred to in the libretto as the "scena ordinaria," recurs several times.[39] That this set returns four times is not, in itself, extraordinary (although, as mentioned above, it is unique for this late a date), but what is remarkable—turning on its head the original idea that this method aided simplicity and efficiency—is that with each return the basic set of the countryside was varied by the employment of a new backdrop. Only the frame of the set, therefore, repeated, while the actual setting was different (although all were entirely compatible with the basic idea of the countryside, ranging from sea views to the heavens to mountains).[40]

While opera producers certainly looked for novelty, and individual designs undoubtedly differed, the sets used in Venetian operas fall into a relatively small number of standard types. The most comprehensive attempt to classify these types appeared in a 1681 publication by Claude-François Ménestrier (see table 9.3).[41] While this classification scheme can certainly be applied to the sets of any opera of the period, Venetian set designers did not necessarily conceive of their creations as generic. A glance at the list of sets for Minato and Cavalli's *Elena*, produced at S. Cassiano in 1659/60,[42] makes this clear (see table 9.4). Several pairs of sets that

---

36 Of about 120 operas performed during this period, the librettos of twenty-one call for one set to return, and those of only three call for two returns.

37 Badoaro?, *Helena rapita da Theseo* (Venice, 1653), music possibly by Cavalli.

38 Bissari, *Bradamante* (Venice, 1650).

39 In fact, the terms "scena maestra" and "scena ordinaria" each occur only once in the extant librettos, in the cases discussed here; although the idea was clearly understood by the public, the absence of standard terminology suggests that this technique did not occur very often.

40 The variant of the scena maestra technique employed in *Bradamante* is unlike what has been suggested for *L'incoronazione di Poppea* (see n. 35); for the Monteverdi opera Povoledo and Carter propose that the street set would be altered to show, at times, a room of a palace, which would mean that part of the set would be exterior and part interior. In *Bradamante*, the change was much more subtle and natural— as if one were looking in different directions in the same countryside, to one side the sea, to another a mountain, with the foreground remaining, as it would in nature, essentially the same.

41 Ménestrier, *Des représentations en musique anciennes et modernes* (Paris, 1681), 168–74; the section on set classification published in Becker, *Quellentexte*, 85–88.

42 *Elena* (Venice, 1659).

TABLE 9.3.   Scene Types in Venetian Opera

General type	Examples, as listed by Ménestrier
Celestial	Assemblies of gods; clouds; the several planets; rainbow; heavens; rising or setting of the sun; lightning; tempests
Sacred	Temples (see figure 9.4); altars; sacrifices; sacred grottos; residences of priests, oracles, or vestals
Military	Besieged cities, in which the ramparts, city walls, and outside are lined with soldiers, artillery, and war machines; parade grounds; tents; military encampment; general's headquarters; armories; arsenals; trophies; fields covered with corpses
Rustic or rural	Mountains, valleys, cliffs, fields, deserted places (see figure 9.3), forests, prairies, caves, villages, hamlets, rustic fairs; the countryside during the four sesasons, covered with snow, flowers, greenery, fruit trees, streams, tree-bordered fields, hills, vineyards, river banks
Maritime	The sea, ships, galleys, ports, islands, rocks, tempests, shipwrecks, marine monsters, sea battles
Royal	Palaces (see figures 9.6 and 9.8); thrones; building facades enriched with columns, statues, and other ornaments; balconies; halls; galleries; apartments; cabinets; gardens; fountains; jousting grounds; stables filled with prized horses; guardrooms; treasuries
Civic	City streets; merchants' shops; studios of painters, sculptors, and artisans; a fair; a warehouse; particular houses; prisons; burning houses; buildings under construction; ruins
Historical	Particular cities such as Rome, Athens, Constantinople, Thebes; certain locations in Greece or Thessaly or Europe, where the actions represented take place (see figure 9.7); the Cave of the Sibyl; the cave of Cacus (see figure 9.2)
Poetic	Palace of the Sun, of Thetis, of Eolus, of Fortune, of Curiosity, and the temple of death, honor, fame; places described by Homer, Virgil, Ariosto, and Tasso
Magical	Enchanted palaces and isles; the witches' Sabbath and horrible deserted places populated by demons; Hell; Pluto's court; the Elysian Fields; the rivers Styx, Cocytus, Acheron; caves of magicians, either all black or filled with spirits
Academic	Libraries, cabinets of wise men filled with books and mathematical instruments; cabinet of antiquities; a painting school

Source: Derived from Claude-François Ménestrier, *Des représentations* (1681).

would have been classified identically by Ménestrier, and could have been depicted with one generic set, are clearly intended to be distinct: two seashores (of Laconia and Tegea), two palaces (of Tindaro and Creon, plus the allegorical palace of peace), two courtyards (one in the Palace of Tegea, and the other not specified), and two woods. Similar pairs recur frequently in the set lists of many seventeenth-

TABLE 9.4.   Scenery Called for in the Libretto of *Elena* (Venice, 1659)

Act	Set	Type[a]
Prologue	Palace of Peace (La Reggia della Pace)	Poetic
Act 1	Seashore of Laconia (Lito del Mare di Laconia)	Maritime
	Palace of Tindaro (Reggia di Tindaro)	Royal
	Amphitheater outside the city (Anfiteatro fuori della Città)	Civic
	Forest (Bosco)	Rustic or rural
Act 2	Courtyard of the rooms of the Royal Palace of Tegea (Cortile delle Stanze del Pallaggio Reale di Tegea)	Royal
	Courtyard (Cortile)	Royal
	Seashore of Tegea (Lito del Mare di Tegea)	Maritime
Act 3	Royal Grove (Boschetto Reale)	Royal
	Palace of Creon (Reggia di Creonte)	Royal

[a] Identification of types as in Ménestrier's list; see table 9.3.

century operas. All extant documentation for the period (see below), indicates that in practice such pairs consisted either of two entirely distinct sets or, if saving money were an issue, one set either with two different backdrops, or with a backdrop once and with lontani the second time (that is, once as a scena corta and once as a scena lunga).

Stage machines also fall into a relatively circumscribed set of basic types (although no contemporary writers categorized them in such a way). The most common provide descents and ascents of gods (see figures 9.2, 9.3, 9.5, and 9.7), often in or on clouds (see figure 9.8), which not only moved, but could expand or contract, open up to reveal persons or things inside, or even transform into words or figures. Gods also moved through the air on chariots, frequently drawn by beasts, or in the sea (moving waves being a favored effect), usually in giant shells drawn by sea creatures. Theatrical engineers could imitate a variety of natural phenomena, including storms, the appearance or motion of astronomical bodies, or moving water in various forms. Motion occurred most commonly on or above the stage, but characters could descend below stage as well, or could even fly over the audience, disappearing through the ceiling of the auditorium. Librettists and scenographers made efforts to vary the movements seen by the audience within an opera: a vertical descent might be followed by a diagonal ascent or a horizontal flight.[43] A listing of the main categories of theatrical machines utilized in seventeenth-century Venice, and some of the variations on these types, can be found in table 9.5. Unlike scenery, machines are

43 See Molinari, *Nozze degli dei*, 142.

TABLE 9.5.   Machine Types in Venetian Opera

General type	Subtypes and examples
Water	River, sea (see figure 9.3), spring, fountain
Astronomical bodies	Stars (enlarge and open to reveal Venus), sun (rising, setting), moon (setting), comet, terrestrial globe (divides into four parts)
Natural phenomena	Storms, sea storms, lightning (destroy buildings, split mountains, transform characters), thunder, rainbow, earthquakes (destroy buildings)
Clouds	Colors: Unspecified, silver, gold, of fire Motions: Ascend/descend, move from side to side, emerge from beneath the stage Actions: Carry characters (see figure 9.8), open to reveal characters or celestial buildings inside, expand and contract, separate or come together, disappear, form figures (crowned lion in *La divisione del mondo*), form letters (*Numa Pompilio*), form a staircase (*La divisione del mondo*)
Heavens	Celestial palaces, the Empyrean, Elysian fields
Beasts of the Land	Pull chariot: two centaurs, two lions Carry characters on their backs: elephant Transform into or from humans: lion into girl, tigers into Naiads Arise from beneath stage: dragon Other: serpents emerge from cups and spew fire (*Rosinda*), Penelope emerges from monster
Beasts of the Sea	Pull seashells with characters: two seahorses (Neptune, Cupid), two dolphins (Neptune) Emerge from the sea: dolphin, fish, monster Carry characters on their backs: dolphin Swim in sea: monsters Battle in the sea: monsters Transform into other objects: monster into boat Disgorge characters: whale
Beasts of the Air	Fly above stage (including ascents and descents, balli, and battles: chimeras, dragons, serpents, eagles) Fly and sing above stage: birds Fly over the audience (alone or with characters): swan, eagle Carry characters on their backs: eagle (Jove), Pegasus (Perseus, Bellerophon (see figure 9.3), Prometheus), dragon, monsters Pull chariots: two peacocks (Juno), two dragons, two doves (Venus), two owls (Athena), two dragons, two sphinxes Transform: dragon into soldiers, person into dragon *(La maga fulminata)* Support structures: winged tortoise (*La finta savia*)

(continued)

TABLE 9.5.   Machine Types in Venetian Opera (continued)

General type	Subtypes and examples
Vehicles	Land: triumphal chariot (pulled by beasts, by slaves) Sea: seashell (pulled by beasts), silver seashell, ship, skiff, boat, wheel of fortune (*Zenobia*) Air: clouds (see clouds), chariot (pulled by beasts), golden chariot, ascend or descend, fly across stage, descend below stage, disappear
Characters fly without clouds or vehicles	Gods, spirits, cupids (see figures 9.1, 9.5, and 9.7) Ascend or descend, fly across or around stage, dance in the air, battle in the air, fly over the audience, carry another character, raise the curtain (*Rosinda*); descend from a tower (fall, with parachute: *Scipione affricano*)
Descent or ascent from below stage	Gods, characters, or spirits from or to Hell; emerge from the earth (*Flora*); disappear into the earth (dragons, chariots, beasts, characters, mountains, palaces)
Buildings	Enchanted palaces appear or disappear; destruction of palace, tower, amphitheater, city wall, loggia; heavenly palaces; theaters, including scenery with machines (*Torilda*), or scenery that collapses (*Ciro*)
Transformations	Beasts into people (and vice versa), people into trees, tree into flying dragon
Fires and explosions	Explosions destroy city walls, mines, towers; flames of Hell

Source: Extracted from librettos and scenarios, 1637–77.

listed in the front matter of the librettos only four times between 1637 and 1677.[44] Rather, they are usually described or referred to as they occur during the course of the opera. Lacking such designations, the use of machines can be inferred from such events as the sudden appearance of a god. Although machinery of various sorts might occur at any point in an opera, the great majority of effects, especially the more elaborate ones, are found in one of two places: the prologue (or, in the absence of a prologue, the opening scene), or at the ends of acts 1 or 2, either within the body of the act or as part of an intermezzo; that is they either opened the opera in spectacular fashion or provided a stunning conlusion to an act. Unlike court spectacles elsewhere, Venetian opera did not rely on machines as the principal source of entertainment for the audience, but employed them more as adjuncts to the dramatic or amorous activities of the singing characters.[45] The proverbial deus ex machina who descends from the heavens to resolve the plot at the end of a drama is a rare occurrence in Venetian opera of this period.

44 Machinery lists are printed in *Scipione affricano* (1664), *Mutio Scevola* (1665), *Tiridate* (1668), and *Armida* (libretto dated 1669, but never performed).

45 Molinari, *Nozze degli dei*, 140–42

SCENIC MATERIALS: THE EVIDENCE
OF INVENTORIES

In the absence of surviving sets or detailed contemporary illustrations, one must reconstruct the various components of scenery and machines and how they were used through other means. Among these, the inventories of the contents of theaters can provide some invaluable information.

The Nuts and Bolts of Scenery: The Inventory
of S. Moisè after the 1665/66 Season

In Carnival of 1665/66, after over a decade as a venue exclusively for comedies, the Teatro S. Moisè once again presented operas. A company composed of the lawyer and librettist Giacomo Dall'Angelo and two partners, the businessmen Cristoforo Raimondi and Camillo Coveglia, rented the theater from the Zane family in August of 1665 for a period of four years[46] (though they had clearly reached an informal agreement as early as June, when they began searching for singers[47]). The company presented two operas, both with librettos by Giacomo Dall'Angelo and music by Carlo Pallavicino: *Demetrio* and *Aureliano*. As was so often the case, the season ended with the company in debt, this time amounting to over 550 ducats, primarily to singers (about 280 ducats to Brigida and Caterina Forti) and lumber suppliers (about 170 ducats).[48] On 2 August 1666, Dall'Angelo and Raimondi notified Coveglia that they intended to satisfy as much of the debt as possible by selling off the materials still in the theater,[49] and that they would be sending an expert to inventory and evaluate the property on the fifth of that month (they invited Coveglia to send an expert of his own choosing as well); this practice was standard throughout the Venetian business world when a debt needed to be settled or property transferred. Dall'Angelo and Raimondi hired the scenographer Francesco Santurini to prepare the inventory, which was then sealed. Five years later, at Dall'Angelo's request, the still-sealed inventory was presented to the notary Marco Fratina, and not until eight years later, in July 1679, with the consent of all the original members of the company, was it finally opened, and the contents copied into Fratina's registers.[50] The documents provide no explanation for this extended delay, although it must be assumed that until this point the parties had still disagreed on the settlement of the debts. In any event, the inventory (see doc. 5 in appendix 3 and figures 9.9 and 9.10) offers a snapshot of the backstage materials produced for a single opera season, and provides an overview of the me-

---

46 ASV, AN, Atti, b. 3509, f. 860.

47 ASV, AN, Atti, b. 6762, f. 12.

48 ASV, AN, Atti, b. 8493, 2 Aug. 1666.

49 Perhaps they had already decided to abandon the idea of continuing the company; certainly within a few months, a new company, headed by Sebastiano Enno, was organizing a production for the 1666/67 season.

50 ASV, AN, Atti, b. 6111, f. 74.

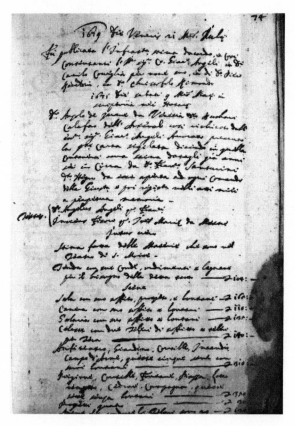

FIGURE 9.9.   Inventory of Teatro S. Moisè, 1666 (copy dated 1679), pt. 1 (ASV, AN, Atti, b. 6111, f. 74)

chanical and visual elements employed in a mid-seventeenth-century Venetian opera theater.[51]

THE CURTAIN   Santurini's inventory begins with what the audience saw first, the curtain:

Curtain, with the ropes, fittings, and wood needed for its use . . . £104

Although Santurini does not provide the details in this case, other inventories list a mechanism for raising and lowering the curtain similar to that for moving the scenery: a cylinder rotated by the falling of a counterweight.

51 We are indebted to Maria Teresa Muraro, whose earlier study of a 1670 inventory for the Teatro S. Luca has provided a model for this case study: Muraro, "Teatro, scena." The 1670 S. Luca inventory is found in Vcg, Archivio Vendramin 42F 16/1, sacchetto 20, proc. 24, f. 23. The other inventories that will be cited below for context and comparison are as follows: S. Cassiano 1646 (ASV, AN, Atti, b. 667, ff. 82–83ᵛ), SS. Giovanni e Paolo 1661 (ASV, SGSM, b. 194, f. 228ʳ⁻ᵛ), and S. Luca 1684 (ASV, AN, Atti, b. 8873, ff. 30ᵛ–34ᵛ).

THE SCENERY   The heart of the inventory, the scenery itself, designed, according to the libretto of *Demetrio*, by Giovanni Battista Lambranci,[52] and valued at over 60 percent of the total, follows next. Unlike some inventories, which simply count the total number of *telleri* (flats) of various sizes, or even just provide a grand total, this document lists the individual sets, in approximate order of complexity and cost. First come those requiring not only side wings and backdrops, but also ceilings (and in one case even elements at the bottom):

Hall with its ceiling, backdrop, and lontani . . .   £165

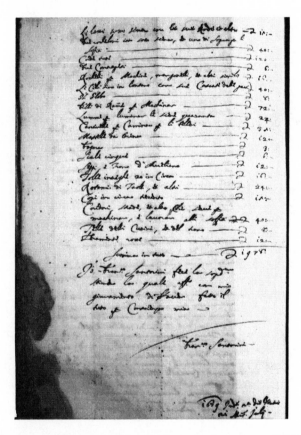

FIGURE 9.10.   Inventory of Teatro S. Moisè, 1666 (copy dated 1679), pt. 2 (ASV, AN, Atti, b. 6111, f. 74^V)

52 Lambranci (also spelled Lambranzi or Lanbranzi) is also credited with scenery for *Artaxerse* (along with Hippolito Mazzarini; SS. Giovanni e Paolo, 1669) and *Eteocle e Polinice* (S. Luca, 1675). He may also be the scenographer identified as Giovanni Battista Lanfranchi who collaborated with Mazzarini for *Gl'amori d'Apollo, e di Leucotoe* (SS. Giovanni e Paolo, 1664).

This set was employed in both the season's operas, as the Sala Reale (act 3, scene 10) in *Demetrio* and the Sala Maestosa (referred in the text of the libretto itself as Sala Reale) in Aurelian's palace in *Aureliano* (act 2, scene 7). It comprises the full range of elements, including the usual side wings (not numbered here, but most likely twelve in all, six on each side), a *prospetto*, or backdrop, and lontani. It may be that one of the two operas used this set with the backdrop and the other with the lontani, to maintain the element of novelty. Given the high cost of this set, it is likely that it was a box set, fully enclosed at the top and sides (see above).

> *Room with its ceiling and lontani* . . . £110

Similar to the hall, but without the backdrop, this set also appears to have been used in both operas, as the apartment of Lamia in *Demetrio* (act 1, scene 17) and the rooms of Zenobia in *Aureliano* (act 3, scene 1).

> *Gallery with its ceiling and lontani* . . . £125

This was the "Gallery of pictures and sculptures" used for the finale of *Aureliano*.

> *Heavens with two telleri for the ceiling and telleri on the floor* . . . £140

The Prologue of *Aureliano* is set in the Celestial Empyrian. Since this type of set must provide the illusion that the performers are in the middle of the heavens, not on the ground, the scenographer provides, as in this example, not only the usual side wings and elements to frame the top of the stage (telleri for the ceiling), but also similar elements, probably depicting clouds, beneath the performers (who sang from machines suspended in mid-air), the "telleri per tera." These latter may have been moved onto stage using the mechanisms usually employed for the prospetti.

The remaining sets are listed by Santurini in two groups, those with lontani, averaging £62 each, and those without, averaging £50 each:

> *Amphitheater, garden, courtyard, fire, battlefield, these five sets with their lontani,*
> £310

The garden set appeared in both operas (garden of the seraglio in *Demetrio* and garden of Aurelian's palace in *Aureliano*). *Demetrio* included two courtyards, the Cortil Reggio of act 1, scene 8, and act 2, scene 18, referred to in the initial listing in the libretto as a loggia that leads to a royal palace, but in the libretto text itself as a courtyard (*cortile*). Which one of these employed lontani and which did not (as in the next entry in the inventory) cannot be determined, nor which one served as the single courtyard in *Aureliano* (act 1, scene 4). The fire and battlefield both appeared in *Demetrio*: the "buildings of the city of Salamina burned by Antioco's army" of act 2, and the concluding "Battlefield with the armies of Antioco and Demetrio facing one another." Neither opera calls for an amphitheater, but *Demetrio's* libretto lists the Campidoglio in Rome, a set not listed in the inventory. Perhaps Santurini, in doing the inventory, was a bit hasty and mistook one for the other (alternatively, the opera could have been revised after the printing of the libretto with one set replacing the other).

Prison, courtyard, fountains, piazza, remote place, cedar grove, countryside, these
    seven sets without lontani . . . £350

The prison ("horrid prisons") and remote place ("remote place filled with ruined buildings") had been used in *Demetrio* (act 2, scene 11 and act 3, scene 1, respectively). The fountains ("isolated place with delightful fountains") and countryside ("countryside near Rome") appeared in *Aureliano* (act 2, scene 1 and act 2, scene 14). Both operas include a cedar grove (in *Demetrio*, however, although included in the initial listing of sets, it does not appear in the text; whether it was added later cannot be determined). The piazza served as the opening set in *Demetrio*, the Piazza of Salamina.

Of the sixteen sets listed in the inventory, then, five were designed to be used in both operas presented in the 1665/66 season, six were intended for *Demetrio* alone, and five for *Aureliano*. The item that follows in the inventory, not described in detail, may represent the elements that distinguished the appearances of the same basic set in the two operas:

Four backdrops [prospetti] . . . £30

Separated from the main set listing is one further element of the visual scenery, the sky that served for all exterior sets:

The sky all the way back to the lontani, with its hangings on the sides . . . £40

While structured basically like the ceilings of the interiors, that is small flats (or perhaps loose cloth hangings without full frames for a softer image) dropped down from above between the side wings and spanning the stage, the sky was also provided with portions that hung down on each side of the stage, probably to soften the junction between the portion of the sky painted on the flats above the images of buildings and the principal portion suspended above the stage. The 1670 S. Luca inventory specifies twelve pieces in all, four in front of the backdrop and eight beyond, above the lontani.[53]

SET-CHANGING EQUIPMENT   Following the main listing of sets are the chief mechanical elements employed in changing from one set to another:

Frames that support the telleri, twenty in number . . . £120

Carriages under the stage with their wheels and other parts . . . £15

Two cylinders, one under the stage, and one above for the ceilings . . . £16

Rope, in all . . . £120

Two counterweights . . . £6

---

53 Muraro's interpretation ("Teatro, scena") of the first part of this entry, "quattro grandi di fori," as referring to portions of the sky displayed through open backdrops, that is with *fori* indicating *prospetti forati*, seems mistaken. Rather, *fori* should be understood as the Venetian form of the Italian word *fuori*, indicating those elements outside of (that is, in front of) the backdrops. The four large elements would hang in the gaps between the six pairs of wings, and the eight smaller ones would begin at the location of the backdrop.

[following several other listings:]

Guides on which the telleri run . . . £35

The painted wings, made of canvas on wooden skeletons, were mounted on frames, or supports, known as *anime*, the bottoms of which, as explained above, extended through the slots in the stage. These lower extensions fitted into the wheeled carriages or chariots (*letti*) on the floor under the stage, which were attached to one another by hooks and ropes, as described in Skippon's account, and rolled in wooden guides, referred to in this inventory as *cantinelle*, and in the S. Luca one as *gargani*. As we saw earlier, these assemblies were set in motion by the turning of a cylinder (*rochellon*) under the stage, which, in turn, was propelled by the falling of a counterweight that had previously been winched upwards into place (the winches, *argane*, are omitted from this inventory). In the system used at S. Moisè (and at other Venetian theaters), there was a second cylinder above the stage, operated by a second counterweight, which moved the ceiling and sky elements into place.[54]

LIGHTING

Forty lamps to illuminate the scenery . . . £24

According to Tessin, Venetian theaters employed at least two different methods to illuminate the scenery. In one, the backs of the frames for the sets were equipped with brackets onto which lamps could be attached, with those on each frame lighting the next wing back, and invisible to the audience. A second method involved free-standing supports, each of which could hold several lamps, which could be placed as needed.[55] The S. Moisè inventory does not indicate which method was employed, but the reference to lamps only, and not supports, makes the first more likely.

MACHINES AND PROPS   Machines rarely show up in theater inventories from the middle of the seventeenth century; perhaps they were cumbersome and tended to be dismantled immediately after the season. In the S. Moisè inventory, the only indications of machines are entries listing parts of the mechanism for putting them into motion:

Cylinders for machines, pulleys, and other similar items . . . £16

Copper wire for machines . . . £72

Only the 1646 inventory for S. Cassiano (see below) lists more: "a large machine" and "a small one." Very likely, these entries represent the basic frameworks upon which the machine builders constructed their marvelous inventions.

---

54 See n. 11, above. Such a double mechanism still survives in the theater at Drottningholm.

55 See Bergman, *Lighting in the Theatre*, 89–98. The eighteenth-century theater at Český Krumlov still has lamps on the backs of the movable flats. Image available at http://www.ckrumlov.cz/uk/atlas/i_semadi.htm (accessed 13 May 2004). The theaters at Drottningholm and Gripsholm, on the other hand, retain the free-standing lighting supports.

Occasionally, as at S. Moisè, inventories also include a few props:

The globe . . . £8

Seats and throne of Aureliano . . . £12

Linen for cushions and for the throne . . . £8

The Prologue of *Aureliano*, set in the Empyrean, begins with Jove on top of "the globe of the earth in the center, sustained by Time, and surrounded by the four parts of the world, Asia, Africa, America, and Europe." The throne and seats, with their cushions, furnished the great hall in Aurelian's palace. Similarly, the 1670 S. Luca inventory lists eight trees and two statues.

OTHER BACKSTAGE EQUIPMENT A theater needed to be equipped with more pedestrian materials for its operation, and these usually show up in the inventories as well. In the case of S. Moisè, these included

Five ladders . . . £6

Corridors, walkways, and the like that are used to work on the machines and in the attic . . . £40

Santurini also notes several items for the comfort of the workers (and also the performers, perhaps):

small barrels for use as urinals . . . £12

a heating kettle . . . £3

The *fogara*, or *foghera*, was a metal container into which hot coals could be placed to provide warmth—clearly a large open fire would not have been desired in a wooden theater, but the workers would have needed some way of warming their hands in the Venetian winter.

MISCELLANEOUS Finally, as in most inventories, Santurini lists miscellaneous scraps and materials, the relationship of which to the operation of the theater is not always clear:

uncut boards, about 20 . . . £16

scraps of boards and the like . . . £24

broken hardware . . . £12

about 300 earthenware tiles £15

Scenery in the Inventories of S. Luca, 1670, and SS. Giovanni e Paolo, 1661

Two other extant inventories provide information that can help us to understand better the S. Moisè sets that Santurini listed in such a concise manner at the beginning of his inventory. The sorts of materials discussed so far are described quite differently in the 1670 inventory for S. Luca, also compiled by Santurini and described by Maria Teresa Muraro.[56] That is, rather than name individual sets (with one exception) Santurini listed more precisely the physical elements that made up the sets. First came the basic groups of side wings for nine sets: "nine changes of scenery with twelve flats each, as far as the backdrop, that is 108 flats in all." Two of those sets were indoor spaces that called for ceilings: "two ceilings of six telleri each, as far as the backdrop, that is twelve telleri in all." The lontani, employed in five sets, are listed separately: "five sets of lontani, including their ceilings, altogether ninety telleri." At S. Luca, a set of lontani comprised six pairs of flats and six ceiling elements. As he did for the S. Moisè inventory, Santurini lists four prospetti (backdrops), further explaining that this comprises "eight telleri in all." That is, each prospetto is made up of two flats, which meet in the center of the stage. The S. Luca inventory, in addition to these brief summaries, includes one set described in detail, apparently because it had been newly constructed: "the hall, newly made, with its ceiling and brackets that come into the set; that is twelve telleri, twelve brackets, and six telleri in the ceiling." This single set cost £300, almost twice the similar one listed in the S. Moisè inventory (both of which were presumably box sets), perhaps because of the considerably greater size of the theater and, therefore, of the sets themselves. The overall value of this portion of the materials at S. Luca was more than 280 ducats, nearly half again as much as the 198 ducats at S. Moisè. In both these cases (and in the 1660/61 inventory for SS. Giovanni e Paolo discussed below), only one season's worth of scenery seems to be present. The situation differs somewhat in a list of the materials at the Teatro S. Cassiano in 1646. Listed in that case were 248 large and medium-sized telleri, ninety small telleri (the lontani, although not labeled as such), and thirteen backdrops.[57] With more than twice the number of telleri, this must represent materials from at least two seasons.[58]

The most precise of the extant mid-seventeenth-century inventories, at least in terms of the sets themselves, is that made after the 1660/61 season at Teatro SS. Giovanni e Paolo.[59] The main part of the inventory comprises descriptions of the materials for sets for the second opera, *Annibale in Capua*, followed by listings of surviving portions, sometimes only fragments, of sets from the opening work of the season, *Gl'amori infrutuosi di Pirro* (see table 9.6). For each of the complete sets, the list includes the number of each type of scenic element: telleri, lontani, and prospetti. It is clear from the descriptions of sets 1, 3, 4, 5, and 7 (and confirmed by

56 See Muraro, "Teatro, scena."

57 ASV, AN, Atti, b. 667, ff. 82–83ᵛ, 9 Aug. 1646.

58 An inventory for the Teatro S. Giovanni Grisostomo from the early eighteenth century (ASV, GP, Inventari, b. 411, f. 22, 22 Aug. 1713) includes a similar number of telleri: 182 for the six main positions, and ninety-three for lontani, as well as numerous prospetti (here called *rompimenti*) both for the back of the stage and between the main flats, several sets of ceilings, and the sky. This lengthy document also lists hundreds of pieces of hardware, both wooden and metal, for sets and machines, lamps (among them twenty-eight for the orchestra pit, 127 for between the flats, and 616 small ones, perhaps for the theater itself), stairways, chairs, ladders, and one relief sculpture, perhaps in plaster or papier mâché, of a "lionfante."

59 ASV, SGSM, b. 194, f. 228ʳ⁻ᵛ.

TABLE 9.6.   Scenery for the 1660/61 Season at SS. Giovanni e Paolo

A. Sets for Gl'amori infrutuosi di Pirro and Annibale in Capua according to the librettos

Sets	Items listed in the post-season inventory (see below)
Gl'amori infrutuosi di Pirro	
Amphitheater	a
Shore of Colco, that on one side shows the Temple of Mars near the sea, and on the other a horrid cavern	4, d, f
Royal loggia	3
Courtyard with a tower . . .	8, g
Garden	5, e
Apartments of Herminia	7, i, j, k?
Piazza of Colco	a
Annibale in Capua[a]	
The Palace of Mars in the Fifth Heaven	—
The Piazza of Capua appears, decorated with trophies and with triumphal arches	1
Battlefield with a company of elephants	2
[Rooms, where Hannibal is resting] [omitted from the list]	3
Countryside surrounded by wild mountains, with a full moon, and magical grottoes	4
Delightful garden with loggias, and waterfalls on the banks of the Volturno River	5
[Reedy] countryside covered with bodies and remains, alongside the River Ausido	6
A backdrop closes off [the back of the set] representing a palace surrounded by groves of laurels with fishponds	6, h?
A wild scene appears with mountainous crags overhanging the sea	4, f
Delightful apartments and loggias of Emilia appear	7
Royal courtyard	8
Throne room lit with torches	9

B. Inventory of sets from Teatro SS. Giovanni e Paolo made after the 1660/61 season
(ASV, SGSM, b. 194, f. 228^{r-v})

1   First set
    Piazza with three perspectives
        With 14 large flats
        And two triumphal arches and 38 small flats
2   Second set
    Company of elephants with 28 flats
3   Third set
    Royal loggias with 14 flats
        And the ceiling, 7 flats
        And its backdrop
        There are also five perspective views, which in all are 27 flats

(continued)

TABLE 9.6.   Scenery for the 1660/61 Season at SS. Giovanni e Paolo (continued)

4   Fourth set
 Magical grottoes with 14 large flats
  And its backdrop
  And 16 flats for the distant perspective

5   Fifth set
 Garden with 14 large flats
  And backdrop
  And the pavillion and 8 small flats for the distant perspective

6   Sixth set
 Field with the dead with 28 flats

7   Seventh set
 Apartments with 14 large flats
  And its backdrop

8   Eighth set
 Royal courtyard with 28 flats
  And its backdrop

9   Ninth set
 Throne room with 28 flats
  And the ceiling all the way to the back, with 16 flats

Obsolete flats

a   Set of the piazza with 12 large flats, some with canvas and some without, and 8 brackets
 and barricades

b   Amphitheater with 8 large flats, and the ranks of seats that form a circle

c   A distant perspective with arches, 8 flats

d   14 columns

e   Distant perspective for a garden, 10 small flats

f   Flats for the sea, 23 in all

g   A tower

h   Two backdrops

i   Covered ceiling, 5 flats

j   [Soletari?] of the ceiling without canvas, 5 flats

k   Two flats left over from the hall

l   10 lamps

m   6 separate small flats

ᵃFrom a list at the beginning of the libretto, with variants in the text of the libretto in brackets.

other documents in the Faustini papers), that this theater had seven pairs of main side wings. The number of lontani, however, is less certain. In the inventory, sets 2, 6, 8, and 9 are listed with no distinction between the main wings and the lontani, probably because the image displayed was of a continuous large space. In these cases, the total number of telleri is twenty-eight, indicating seven sets of lontani. Set 4, the magic grotto, however, separates the two types, and lists sixteen "teleri di lontani," or eight pairs. The garden set, number 5, replaces the forward pairs of lontani (using just the rear four pairs) with a pavillion (*pallazino*). The two indoor sets, the Royal Loggia (set 3), and the Throne Room (set 9), naturally employ ceilings. The ceiling of the former went as far as the backdrop, requiring only seven elements, while the latter was enclosed all the way to the last of the lontani, and required sixteen pieces in all. The backdrop at the rear of the Loggia was apparently pierced in five places, corresponding to five of the interstices between columns in the structure, behind each of which was a separate perspective image (the five *fori di lontananza*). Five of the nine sets employed an individual backdrop (for those without, the last pair of lontani or other structure, or a standard blue sky background completed the rear of the image). The first set in the list, the Piazza, is the most complicated. The main title, "piazza with three lontani," refers to a set somewhat like Torelli's Piazza of Naxos from *Venere gelosa* discussed above. The seven standard pairs of wings depicted a central outdoor space—the piazza—beyond which were three distinct perspective views. Two of these were probably streets, viewed through triumphal arches, and the central one might have been, as with Torelli's set, a view into a building. The thirty-eight small telleri were manually placed lontani (the nineteen pairs could have been divided among the three views in several ways, most likely either six–seven–six or seven–five–seven).

The sets for *Gl'amori infrutuosi di Pirro* are listed separately, under the title "obsolete flats." These include twelve of the fourteen flats for the set of the piazza, some of which are merely frames without the painted canvas (along with eight of the projecting portions of barricades), only eight of the fourteen telleri for the amphitheater (plus the rows of seats, which formed a circle), and fragments of the loggia (some of the lontani and columns), the garden (only ten lontani), and the sea, as well as a tower, miscellaneous prospetti, and some ceiling elements.

THE PRODUCTION OF SETS AND MACHINES: PROCEDURES, COSTS, AND SCHEDULING

The manufacture of such spectacular scenery was, of course, a major task for the impresario, for it required several types of artists and craftsmen and the expenditure of a significant amount of money. The earliest known contract for painted operatic scenery in Venice dates from September 1641, and concerns the upcoming season at S. Cassiano.[60] The two parties were the composer/impresario Francesco Cavalli and Tasio Zancarli, who had painted the scenery from Torelli's designs the previous year for *La finta pazza* at the Novissimo; the opera to be presented, *La virtù de' strali*

---

60 ASV, AN, Atti, b. 1049, f. 94.

d'amore, marked the first collaboration between Cavalli and the librettist Giovanni Faustini. The contract specified the payment for seven distinct sets and three additional backdrops, that is everything that was needed for the production. Zancarli agreed to complete the work by Christmas, by which time, according to Cavalli, the singers would be ready, thus formally allowing about two and a half months for the completion of the task. Zancarli was to be paid 300 ducats in all (for the single opera to be presented), 50 immediately, 25 each in October and November, 50 after the second performance, and another 25 after each successive showing until the total had been paid. That is, 100 ducats were to be paid before the opening of the opera, and the other 200 during the run, when new funds would become available through the sale of tickets and scagni. The 300-ducat fee was intended to pay Zancarli for his labor: Cavalli would provide, at his own expense, the materials needed, including canvas, paper (for the enlargement of the sketches to full scale), and gilding supplies. In addition, the artist was to receive six tickets—worth 24 lire—for each performance, four at S. Cassiano and two at S. Moisè, where Cavalli also bore some responsibilities.

Case Studies: Marco Faustini's Changing Approach to Scenery

The most detailed information on scenery from the point of view of the production company comes from the records of Marco Faustini. Faustini's methods can be deduced from the account books for productions at S. Aponal and S. Cassiano, as well as, to some extent, loose receipts, the receipt book, and contracts that stretch into his years at SS. Giovanni e Paolo. They indicate, as do other segments of production at his company, several changes in procedure from the 1650s to the 1660s, beginning with a very hands-on approach and ending by assigning most of the responsibility to the artisans.

ATTENDING TO DETAILS: THE PREPARATION OF SETS AND MACHINES FOR THE 1651/52 SEASON AT S. APONAL   The scenic elements were labor intensive, and Marco Faustini preferred to allot a generous period of preparation. The contracts for scenery and machines were often among the first signed, and Faustini hoped to have the work completed well in advance of the first performance (see appendix 4). For the 1651/52 season, for which the most detailed records survive, Faustini's earliest formal action (following, naturally, the creation of Giovanni Faustini's libretto) was his contract with Simon Gugliemi, the set painter, on 25 July (more than a week earlier, in fact, than Faustini's purchase of the book in which he recorded the accounts for the season).[61] The contract itself is not extant, but Faustini listed in the account book the specifications of the sets Guglielmi was to paint for *Calisto* and *Eritrea* (corresponding closely to the descriptions eventually published in the librettos), along with their individual costs (see table 9.7 and figure 9.11). The list includes all but one of the sets required for the two operas. It

---

61 ASV, SGSM, b. 112, account book 1651/52, ff. 38ᵛ–39.

TABLE 9.7.   Scenery for Teatro S. Aponal, 1651/52

A. Listing of scenery to be painted by Simon Guglielmi (ASV, SGSM, b.112, account book 1651/52, f. 38ᵛ)

Agreement reached with Ser Simon, painter, for ten scenes

First opera [*Calisto*]

To be paid for the grotto of eternity, with a backdrop	D10
For the arid wilderness with the fountain, with backdrop, and without backdrop	D17
For the peaks of Mt. Liceo, with backdrop and without backdrop	D12
For the plain of Erimanto without backdrop	D18
For the fountains of Ladone with open backdrop	D12

Second opera [*Eritrea*]

For the scene of wild clouds, with backdrop	D17
For the sea cliffs and sea, all the way to the back, and with backdrop	D10
For the rustic courtyard, with open backdrop	D10
For the throne room, with backdrop and without, with a ceiling	D40
For another courtyard, to the back, without backdrop	D24
	D184
[Added:] For the scene of the clouds	D34
	D218

B. Lists of scenery from the librettos

Scenes for Faustini and Cavalli's *Calisto*

Prologue: The Grotto of Eternity

Act 1: Arid Wilderness
            Forest

Act 2: The Peak of Mount Liceo
            The Plain of Erimanto

Act 3: The Fountains of Ladone
            The Empyrean

Scenes for Faustini and Cavalli's *Eritrea*

Prologue: A Scene of Terrifying Clouds

Act 1: The Shores of Sidonia
            The Royal Palace of Sidonia

Act 2: Courtyard of the Palace
            The Atrium of the Palace

Act 3: Throne Room
            The Egyptian Army, with Ruins of the Sacked City

---

should be noted that Faustini requested that all the sets be newly made, even though several of those for the operas of the previous year were of the same topoi: *Oristeo* and *Rosinda* both employed a courtyard, and *Rosinda* had both a seashore and a wood. Faustini indicated for each set that it should be done either "with prospetto" or "without prospetto"; the former included only the main set of flats and a backdrop, while the latter would employ lontani. In each opera, one set employed a *prospetto forato,* that is, a backdrop open in the middle. The throne room,

FIGURE 9.11.　Scenery contract for 1651/52 season at Teatro S. Aponal, from Faustini's account book (ASV, SGSM, b. 112, account book 1651/52, ff. 38^{V}–39)

the most expensive in the original contract, at 40 ducats, also included a ceiling.[62] In three cases, the contract calls for the set to be done both with prospetto and without. Faustini, then, economized by using, in each opera, different versions of the same set to represent two different locales. In *Calisto*, the second set in the list (the arid wilderness) seems to have served, in one of its versions, also for the forest called for in act 1, scene 7. In *Eritrea*, duplication occurred twice: the Sala Regia (fourth on the list) served, probably, not only for the Sala Reale of act 3, scene 1, but also for the Atrium of act 2, scene 5, and the second set on the list opened act 1 with the sea in the distance, using lontani ("mare sino in fondo"), and closed the opera with a prospetto showing the ruins of the city of Sidonia (the contract does not describe what should be painted on the prospetto). At some point after the

---

62　This was probably a box set (as with similar ones discussed above, it is the most expensive of the year's sets) but without further information that cannot be determined.

original contract, Faustini decided to increase the splendor (or complexity) of the opening set of *Eritrea*: to the original fee of 17 ducats for the "set of the horrid clouds," was added 34 ducats for further work, for a total of 51 ducats, making it the most expensive of the season.

Faustini's account book recorded no terms of the contract beyond the total amount Guglielmi would receive for his labors, 184 ducats (increased subsequently to 218). Based on our knowledge of surviving contracts from later years, and on the pattern of payments entered elsewhere in the account book, this fee would have covered primarily Guglielmi's labor: Faustini would provide all the materials needed except for paint. Guglielmi began to collect payments, some of them as small as £18, on 25 July 1651 (when he received his *caparra*, or down payment), with sums received irregularly into early February.

Some of the materials Guglielmi needed were already at the theater (whether this includes previously used items from earlier operas, or raw materials, is unclear). Before purchasing any new canvas, Faustini paid a certain Martino both to prepare the telleri for five sets (before it could be painted, the canvas had to be sized with a hot glue to stiffen it and seal the pores) and to carry them, presumably to Guglielmi's workshop.[63] Among other early purchases were tacks (*brocchi*), used to attach canvas (and possibly also paper) to the frames, and large sheets of heavy paper (*cartoni*). The latter were apparently used in the process of enlarging the perspective drawings to the size needed for the final painting; Faustini purchased them (recording the expenditures in the "extraordinary expenses" section of his account book) regularly beginning in mid-August and continuing through mid-November, shortly before the opening of *Calisto* on 28 November. Similarly, Faustini bought tacks, eventually over 20,000 of them, steadily from mid-September right until opening night.

About a month after the contract with the painter Guglielmi, Faustini signed the second major contract for scenic materials; this was an agreement with the carpenter Anastasio for work valued at 60 ducats.[64] The actual contract does not survive, but (as with the scenery) Faustini listed in the account book the items to be constructed (see table 9.8 and figure 9.12). As with the Guglielmi contract, the detail provided there is greater than for any other season. The fee did not include the necessary materials, the purchases of which Faustini recorded elsewhere in his book. For

63 ASV, SGSM, b. 112, account book 1651/52, ff. 41ᵛ–42. Martino is referred to as a painter in ASV, AN, Atti, b. 10983, f. 365, 26 Feb. 1651 m.v. In a dispute with the members of the Accademia degli Imperturbabili regarding his sets for their 1656/57 production of *Argenide*, the painter Lorenzo Gennari demanded that, in addition to the agreed-upon fees, he be paid 10 ducats "to carry the flats to the theater, for expenditures for wood and charcoal for the fire to make the glue for the sets, for candles, and to put the glue onto the said sets" ("com'in condotte delle telari al teatro, spese in legne, et carbone per il fuoco necessario per le fatture delle colle per le scene, candele, e dar la colla col biso alle dette scene"). ASV, GP, Dimande, b. 40, no. 72, 16 Nov. 1657. No libretto survives for the academy's production of *Argenide*. This dispute will be discussed in more detail in a forthcoming article.

64 ASV, SGSM, b. 112, account book 1651/52, ff. 32ᵛ–34. Although Faustini always calls him simply "Anastasio marangon" (Anastasio the carpenter), he is probably identical to the Anastasio Marchiori who is listed as the machine builder in the libretto of *Le barbarie del caso* (Murano, 1664).

TABLE 9.8.   Machinery to Be Built by Anastasio for Teatro S. Aponal, 1651/52

Agreement reached with Messer Anastasio the carpenter for all of the following
    manufactures, in the amount of 60 ducats   Lire 372

That is:
The serpent of eternity at the second flat with a circuit of the entire scene
Eternity emerging in the middle of the scene
Fountain beyond the backdrop
Descent of Jove and of Mercury, that should also have three different facades; to ascend
    with three persons, and also should serve for the descent of Iris
Open backdrop with a second backdrop for the fountains
Descent of Juno on the chariot
The chariot of Diana, which goes up the mountain, that ascends and descends
The Empyrean, of clouds above and below
The scene of horrid clouds, below
The machine of Boreus
The sea and its slot across the entire stage, in such a way that it serves also for the clouds
Cliffs in the background [only partially legible]
A tree trunk
The ceiling of the room with vaults
Brackets to go entirely around the scene

Source: ASV, SGSM, b. 112, account book 1651/52, f. 32ᵛ.

Calisto, Anastasio was asked to build a number of machines for entrances and exits of
gods: the descent of Jove and Mercury (at the beginning of act 1), which would also,
with a different facing, be used for the ascent of the allegorical characters Nature,
Eternity, and Destiny in the prologue; the descent of Juno on a chariot; and the chariot of Diana, which would ascend and then descend Monte Liceo in act 2. For the
opening set, depicting "The Entrance to Eternity," Faustini asked for a machine for
"the serpent of Eternity," which would circle the entire stage at the depth of the second set of flats ("al secondo teller"), and one for Eternity itself.

Instructions for the opening scene of act 3 of *Calisto* demonstrate how the
work of set painter and machine builder interacted. Guglielmi's contract called for
him to paint the set with a *prospetto forato*. Anastasio's responsibility was to build
the frame for this element (onto which Guglielmi's canvasses would be mounted),
and to manufacture both a second backdrop and the fountain itself, in relief. In the
end, it seems that Faustini opted to install real fountains instead (or perhaps in addition), as a separate listing in the account book records a payment of 15 ducats by
Alvise Duodo for the fountains, and also a payment for the valve to make them
work.[65] The final set of the opera, "The Empyrean," was built entirely by Anastasio; that is, it is not included in Guglielmi's scenery contract, presumably because it
was more machine than traditional set, as it was composed entirely of clouds with,
perhaps, all the action taking place on the machine itself.

65 ASV, SGSM, b. 112, account book 1651/52, f. 58ᵛ.

FIGURE 9.12.   Machinery contract for 1651/52 season at Teatro S. Aponal, from Faustini's account book (ASV, SGSM, b. 112, account book 1651/52, ff. 32ᵛ–33)

The opening scene of *Eritrea*, the horrid clouds of the Prologue, which had become the most expensive portion of Guglielmi's work, also received contributions from Anastasio, who built the machine that produced motion in the clouds at the bottom of the set (using the same mechanism designed for the moving ocean waves in the opening scene of act 2). Also for this set, clearly the most elaborate in the opera, Anastasio built the machine for the entrance and exit of Boreus, the god of the winds. The machine in *Calisto* that carried Jove and Mercury would be reused here (with, most likely, a third facing) for the descent of Iris, the rainbow goddess, also in the Prologue. Anastasio's work in the rest of this second opera was much less extensive than in *Calisto*: he built the sea and cliffs for act 1, the structure for the ceiling of the throne room of act 3, and a tree trunk.

As mentioned above, the fee Anastasio negotiated did not include most materials, as Faustini almost immediately began the purchase of wood and nails, and not long afterwards (beginning in mid-September) of rope and paint.[66] As the season

66 Ibid., ff. 16–18.

approached, he contracted for a few additional elements, most importantly the sky employed for the outdoor sets. Anastasio was to do what was necessary for the frames and Martino was to paint the canvas (the two men also, at the same time, completed work on the auditorium, with Anastasio working on the corridor behind the boxes and installing locks, and Martino painting some cloth to decorate the auditorium). The only indication of the progress of the work on the scenic materials comes in early November, when Faustini paid for the "silvering" of Diana's chariot, which must, therefore, have been essentially complete. By 20 November, the craftsmen began to work at the theater (whether they also continued in their workshops cannot be determined): on that date, and continuing until opening night, Faustini began paying for candles and torches (in this account book their function is not described, but in the later books they are specified as providing light for carpenters and painters or for rehearsals). After the opening night of *Calisto*, on 28 November, through its closing on 31 December, expenditures for sets and machines (except for the regular disbursements to the two artisans, whose fees had not entirely been paid) are reduced drastically, but they resume, not surprisingly, almost immediately afterwards, and continue until the opening of *Eritrea* on 17 January. The final expenditures for scenery, Faustini's last payments to Simon Guglielmi, came on 5 February, just eight days before the closing of the second opera on the thirteenth of the month.

As can be seen from table 9.9, the total cost to Faustini for sets and machines for the season was about 750 ducats, or about twice the amount represented by the two principal contracts, for the painter and carpenter. While it is not possible to ascertain precisely how much of the materials such as wood, canvas, and nails were purchased for other purposes, such as repairing and decorating the auditorium, the scope of the enterprise is clear. Overall, this amount represented about 14 percent of the total cost of the season (see also appendix 5).

REDUCED INVOLVEMENT: FAUSTINI'S PROCEDURES AT S.APONAL AFTER 1652 AND AT S. CASSIANO   In subsequent seasons Faustini tinkered with the system, although not as drastically as he did with costumes (see chap. 10). For the 1654/55 production of Ziani's *Eupatra*, the contract for the set painting, with Simon Guglielmi, was signed on 3 May, more than seven months before the opera would open.[67] The agreement resembled that for 1651/52, although Faustini did not copy the scenic details into the account book. For a price of 200 ducats, Guglielmi would paint ten new sets ("dieci scene nuove"), that is, all that were required, reusing none from previous seasons. As had been the case three years earlier, that fee covered Guglielmi's labor and the cost of paints. Faustini purchased the other materials as needed. The agreement stated that the sets should be completed by the end of October, but Guglielmi accepted some other jobs, creating significant delays. In a notice dated 5 September, and sent to Guglielmi by a public official, Faustini complained to the painter that after four months only two sets had been finished; the impresario, citing the potential damage to his investment, threat-

---

67 ASV, SGSM, b. 113, account book 1654/55, ff. 40ᵛ–41 and 50ᵛ–51.

TABLE 9.9. Cost of Manufacturing Sets and Machines, 1651–1652 at S. Aponal

Item	Cost (in lire)
Nails	310
Extraordinary	
Tacks	64
Cartoni	81
Candles and torches[a]	99
Other	132
Wood[b]	620
Carpenter	700
Painters	1,582
Martino (assisted carpenter and painter)	140
Canvas[c]	930
Total	4,658 (= D751)

Source: Figures from Faustini's totals in ASV, SGSM, b. 112, account book 1651/52, f. 42^v.
[a] Some candles and torches used for rehearsals.
[b] Some of this wood may have been used for work on the theater itself.
[c] Some of the canvas perhaps used for costumes or to decorate the auditorium.

ened to hire as many painters as needed to complete the work on time, all at Guglielmi's expense.[68] The threat apparently was sufficient to get Guglielmi back to work, as Faustini made a substantial payment (20 ducats) to the painter just two weeks later, on 19 September.[69] Since disbursements continued through mid-December, it may be that Faustini's plan to have the scenery ready by the end of October was not realized; the opera finally opened on 30 December, about two weeks after the final payment.

For the machines, Faustini again contracted with Anastasio, but he experimented with a different system. The account book summarizes two agreements with the carpenter, one for 110 ducats, signed on 1 May, and a second, for 125 ducats, dated 15 May (why there were two separate contracts is unclear).[70] The new system is referred to in the second of these (the first indicates only the fee): Faustini indicated that Anastasio would build everything "at his own expense" ("a sue spese"). While Faustini's payments for the three contracts discussed so far were

68 ASV, AN, Atti, b. 10983, 5 Sept. 1654.
69 ASV, SGSM, b. 113, account book 1654/55, ff. 50^v–51.
70 Ibid., f. 40^v.

always in cash, approximately one-third of those to Anastasio in this season were for materials such as nails, tacks, or wood, so that, while the contract is about 50 percent larger than that for machines in the 1651/52 season, the ultimate costs were about the same. The charges for materials that appear in the "extraordinary expenses" section of the account book most likely represent those for the scenery and for repairs and decorations in the auditorium and boxes. Once the work shifted from the workshops to the theater, another change in the system can be seen. In 1651/52, the only new type of expense at this point in the process was for illumination. Similar expenses appear in the 1654 account book, but in addition Faustini began to pay daily wages to carpenters and painters. Whether this represented workmen assembling the sets and machines, or whether Faustini took advantage of the illumination he was already providing to facilitate work on the auditorium, is not known. During this period Faustini also paid for the construction and gilding of eagles, sea horses, and dolphins, and for the purchase of cloth called "sangalo bianco" for a backcloth showing the sea that would be visible beyond the *prospetti forati* of one or more of the maritime sets (act 1, scenes 1 and 11, and act 3, scene 17).

Faustini's outlays for sets and machines increased dramatically with his first season at S. Cassiano with the production of *L'incostanza trionfante* (1657/58), in part because the larger theater required larger (and more numerous) scenic elements, and in part, probably, in order to make a big splash with the new enterprise.[71] Despite nearly doubling the total expenditure (from about 660 ducats in 1654/55 to more than 1,177), Faustini did not substantially alter his methods. The scenery contract, not signed until the very late date of 11 September, required Gasparo Beccari to paint ten "scene tragiche" for the substantial sum of 450 ducats, to cover his labor and, apparently, paints. As usual, Faustini purchased the necessary wood, canvas, and *cartoni* separately (tacks are not listed separately, but were perhaps lumped together with nails; see below). The machinery contract dates from two days later, and, for the first time, clarifies the responsibilities. The fee of 390 ducats would cover everything except "canvas, rope, wood, and large hardware" ("telle, corde, legname, et ferramenta grossa"). Notably absent from that list are nails, and, in fact, Faustini's payment to the carpenters included £94 for a barrel of assorted nails.

For the 1658/59 production of Cavalli's *Antioco*, Faustini simplified his procedures.[72] In the 13 September contract with Gasparo Beccari for ten sets (once again, the full complement needed for the production, even though *L'incostanza trionfante* had also employed a garden, courtyard, and piazza that could have been reused), the impresario specified that the fee of 380 ducats included "paints, tacks, and *cartoni*" ("colori, brocche, et cartoni"), the first such documented instance. The prologue was later changed to represent "a heavenly set with a palace with transparent walls" ("Celeste con palazzo di trasparenti"), and on 8 December Faustini increased the fee by 30 ducats, to include everything but the glass panels (*verri*; for

71 ASV, SGSM, b. 112, account book 1657/58, ff. 37ᵛ–38 and 46ᵛ–47.

72 ASV, SGSM, b. 194, account book 1658/59, ff. 15ᵛ–16 and 20ᵛ–21. See Bianconi and Walker, "Production, Consumption," 225.

which, in a second agreement signed on the same day, Faustini agreed to pay 20 ducats). The 8 October contract with Francesco Santurini for machines was similarly comprehensive: for a fee of 200 ducats, Santurini would do "everything at his expense, that is carpenter's labor, machines, nails, hardware, lumber, rope, tacks, and rope" ("il tutto a sue spese, cioè fature di marangone, macchine, chiodi, feramenti, legname, corde, brocche, et corde [sic]"). Faustini was, therefore, spared the effort, and confusion, of purchasing all the materials for the craftsmen, and could be much more certain of the actual costs.[73]

ALL-INCLUSIVE CONTRACTS: FAUSTINI'S PROCEDURES AT SS. GIO-VANNI E PAOLO   Marco Faustini's contract with Hippolito Mazzarini (6 June 1660) for scenery painted at SS. Giovanni e Paolo represents the earliest document from his tenure there, and is the only extant complete contract between Faustini and a set painter.[74] While providing some new details on Faustini's procedures, it also confirms the basic system that he had established earlier. We should note, once again, the early date of the contract, about six months before opening night. (Faustini required that the scenery should be completed by 15 December). The compensation specified in Mazzarini's contract included monthly payments of 35 ducats for salary and living expenses for the painter and his assistant (totalling 210 ducats for the six months) plus 40 ducats for paints. Materials to be supplied by Faustini included tacks and paper. The contract also specified that the sets should be made to Faustini's satisfaction, and that Mazzarini should take advantage of materials already at the theater in order to reduce expenses: "Signor Ippolito promises to proceed with all possible economy, putting to use those things that will be found in the theater."[75] As in previous contracts, Faustini asked for ten sets.

Faustini's contracts with the machine builder Gasparo Mauro from 1665 and 1666, the latest that survive from his impresarial career, confirm the system that he had established, but also clarify some of the division of labor. The first, and more complete, agreement dates from 8 March 1665 (barely three weeks after the close of the previous season), and obligated Mauro, for a fee of 250 ducats, to completely prepare for production ("poner in scena di tutto punto") the two operas for the following season, Doriclea and Tito.[76] Faustini explains that his responsibility included not only the machines, as would be expected, but also "sets . . . backdrops, lontani, [and] ceilings" ("scene . . . prospetti, lontani, soffitti"). He did not intend that Mauro paint the sets, of course, since that was not his area of expertise (and Faustini paid someone else to do that), but rather to build, rebuild, or repair, as needed, all of the frames on which the painter, Mazzarini, would mount the various elements of his painted scenery. As

73 The relatively small payments in the "extraordinary expenses" section of Faustini's account book for wood, nails, and other items most likely represent either materials for repairs or decorations of the auditorium, or for additional scenic decorations Faustini requested after the original agreements were signed.

74 ASV, SGSM, b. 194, f. 5.

75 "promettendo detto signor Ippolito d'andar con ogni risparmio, ponendo in opera quelle cose che sarano nel teatro." ASV, SGSM, b. 194, f. 5.

76 ASV, SGSM, b. 188, f. 109.

in most earlier years, Faustini would supply, at his own cost beyond the 250 ducats, "wood, canvas, *cartoni*, rope, tacks, nails, and hardware."[77] Faustini maintained a similar system throughout his years at SS. Giovanni e Paolo, paying a fixed fee for labor to both painter and carpenter, and providing materials as needed.[78]

Mazzarini's 9 April 1665 receipt indicates two changes in other aspects of Faustini's procedures: instead of the monthly stipends of the 1660 contract, the signing of the agreement was accompanied by a down payment of 100 ducats.[79] Also, for the first time (as far as we can tell from the extant documentation), Faustini required more than ten new sets: this year Mazzarini was to paint thirteen. In the event, *Doriclea* was not performed, and it is unclear what effect this might have had on Mazzarini's assignment. In the absence of an inventory such as those discussed elsewhere in this chapter, it is impossible to know how many sets might have been designed for multiple use, as in 1660/61, or whether Faustini relied more than he had earlier on sets reused from the previous season.

The manufacture of the scenery and machines, then, transpired over a period of many months; it required a continuous supply of material such as wood and a variety of nails and other joining materials, as well as canvas, glue, tacks, and paper for the painted scenery itself, and, in the final days of work at the theater itself, candles to provide illumination for the workmen. Presumably, set painters such as Guglielmi and Mazzarini created designs that were transferred to large sheets of paper, and then copied onto canvas. The final stage of painting required, of course, considerable skill, especially in adapting the single image of the design to the multiple panels of the wings, but little refinement in the details was needed, since the sets were not to be seen at close range. The English traveller Skippon commented on this, writing: "The pictured sets are very lively at a good distance, and by candle-light; but near hand the work is very great and coarse."[80]

Faustini may have aimed for the completion of the scenic elements by early fall, but difficulties with the dramas themselves sometimes resulted in problems late in the preparatory season. New scenery could be necessitated by a change in the prologue, as in *Erismena* in 1655/56.[81] More urgently, in several other years the operas themselves were changed at the last moment, in which case the scenery from the planned opera was adapted as best as possible to the new work.[82]

---

77 It is unclear how many times the frames could be reused, with or without repairs, or when they would be built anew. There is documentation for the building of a complete new set at least once during Faustini's years at SS. Giovanni e Paolo. Undated accounts from this period detail the canvas (with measurements for each pair of flats) and lumber (with a list of the number and types of boards) needed (ASV, SGSM, b. 194, ff. 270 and 274).

78 Surviving payment records are far from complete, but include, in various years, appropriate amounts of nails, *cartoni*, and wood.

79 ASV, SGSM, b. 194, f. 2.

80 Skippon, *Journey*, 508.

81 The librettos for *Erismena* reveal three different prologues, and the account book contains several entries that refer to new scenery for a prologue.

82 Or, in at least one case, the new work was prepared with the already completed scenery in mind: Aureli claimed to have written the libretto to *Antigona delusa* (SS. Giovanni e Paolo, 1660) to fit the sets painted by Mazzarini for the unsuccessful *Gl'avvenimenti d'Orinda*, which opened the season at the Grimani theater that year.

The Reuse of Scenery and Machines
within a Season

It might seem that with the 1660 contract with Mazzarini, Faustini had shifted procedures, no longer producing entirely new scenery for each season, since he only asked for ten new sets, while the two operas to be performed, Gl'amori infrutuosi di Pirro, by Sartorio, and Annibale in Capua, by Ziani, required together nearly twice as many, seven and twelve, respectively (see table 9.6A). However, a detailed look at one further document, with a careful examination of the particular sets needed, shows that, in fact, audiences at SS. Giovanni e Paolo saw almost exclusively new sets in that season, although they did see some of them more than once.

CASE STUDY: SETS FOR THE 1660/61 SEASON AT SS. GIOVANNI E PAOLO   The inventory drawn up after the conclusion of the 1660/61 season, discussed above, begins with a list of nine sets used in Annibale (see table 9.6B). These are, in fact, all that were needed: the prologue, according to the libretto, was not performed; the third set in act 2 maintained the flats of the second with a prospetto instead of the lontani (the libretto specifies that the backdrop should be put into place, "Si chiude il prospetto," rather than a full change of set), and the final set of that act apparently duplicates the last one in act 1, but now open to the sea in the back (this element also appears in the inventory), instead of to the countryside with grottos.

Following the numbered list of sets for Annibale in the inventory are several incomplete ones listed as "obsolete" ("dismessi," a clear indication that they were not intended to be preserved; see below), which can be linked to the first opera of the season, Gl'amori infrutuosi di Pirro. Five of the seven sets needed for that opera would have been the same ones later used for Annibale, sometimes with slight modifications: the Royal Loggia of act 1 and Apartments of act 3 were used unchanged (that is sets 3 and 7 in the inventory); the courtyard of act 2 would have been set 8 with the addition of the tower also found in the inventory; the garden was set 5, perhaps with the additional set of lontani in the inventory; and the shore with the temple and cavern seems to contain elements used in the final sets of acts 1 and 2 of Annibale (that is, the seashore of act 2 with the grotto of act 1, both with set 4 in the inventory as the basis), with, perhaps, the columns from the inventory serving as the temple (although that is less certain—this might have been one of the incompletely described elements near the end of the document). The opening set of Gl'amori infrutuosi, the amphitheater, would have been the tenth new set painted by Mazzarini. This leaves only the concluding set of the Piazza to be accounted for, the set that opens the second portion of the inventory (the "obsolete flats"). This eleventh set, that is, one more than called for in Mazzarini's contract, might represent one of the rare instances (at this period) of the use of elements carried over from a previous season: act 3 of Antigona delusa, from the 1659/60 season, with sets also by Mazzarini, calls for a piazza, and the painter, having agreed in the contract to use materials that remained in the theater in order to save money, might have resurrected this one, perhaps with a few alterations. All of this seems to imply that sets were left intact until the materials were needed to begin work on the next opera—they were dismantled quickly after the first opera of a two-work season, but might remain untouched from the end of carnival until preparations for the next season got underway.

THE REUSE OF THEATRICAL EFFECTS   The evidence regarding the reuse of machines (as special effects were called in the seventeenth century) from opera to opera is not as clear as it is for scenery, in part because of the sketchier documentation. While most machines appear to be new, there are a few instances of similar effects used in successive years at SS. Giovanni e Paolo, most notably in 1660/61, 1661/62, and 1662/63. *Annibale* of 1660/61 and *Amor guerriero* of 1662/63 both call for flying chariots; *Gl'amori infrutuosi* of 1660/61 and *Le fatiche d'Ercole per Deianira* of 1661/62 call for a character to arrive astride Pegasus (Apollo in the first and Prometheus in the latter); *Gl'amori infrutuosi* and *Amor guerriero* both have storm sets; and in both *Annibale* and *Amor guerriero* a seashell serves as a chariot (carrying Venus and drawn by a pair of tritons in the first opera and drawn by seahorses in the second). Moreover, in most of his years at SS. Giovanni e Paolo, Faustini selected pairs of operas (although coincidence cannot be ruled out) in which one had notable special effects while the other dispensed with them entirely or employed only a few. In 1661/62, for example, *Gli scherzi di Fortuna* called only for a few gods in the prologue, while *Le fatiche d'Ercole* was relatively spectacular. The following season, *Gl'amori d'Apollo* required only several arrivals and departures of the title character, while *Amor guerriero* used elaborate machines in every act. The first operas of the 1665/66 and 1666/67 seasons, *Orontea* and *Alciade*, respectively, required no machines. *Tito*, the second opera of 1665/66, was quite elaborate, but *Dori*, the following season, had only a spectacular prologue.[83] Neither opera planned for Faustini's final season, *Il tiranno humiliato d'Amore overo il Meraspe* and *Eliogabalo*, employed much in the way of effects: the prologue of the first involved gods on several types of machines, but nothing later, and the second required only a triumphal chariot in the first act. The exception to this pattern was Faustini's first year at the theater, 1660/61, when, perhaps to make a good impression, the impresario chose two operas filled with spectacle: *Gl'amori infrutuosi di Pirro* and *Annibale in Capua*.

OPERATING THE SETS AND MACHINES:
PERSONNEL AND COSTS

Once the sets and machines were built and delivered to the theater, additional labor was needed for their operation during the performances, so that an impresario needed to hire a significant number of workmen, although not highly paid ones. Men were needed in the wings to install and replace the flats; above and below stage to operate machines and install and remove ceiling and sky elements; and for the backdrops. The size of the crew, of course, depended in part on the size of the theater and the number of pairs of flats. At S. Aponal, Faustini employed

---

83 Both *Orontea* and *Dori* were substitutes; perhaps their lack of reliance on spectacle, in addition to the presence of singers familiar with these works, influenced their selection.

around twenty-four men in 1651/52 and 1654/55, at wages of £1 s.10 per night each the first year and then rising to what would remain the standard, £2.[84] For 1654/55, Faustini indicated specifically that three men were designated to operate the prospetti. Faustini provided the most detail in his accounts for *Erismena* in 1655/56. Two teams of six men each (with their foremen named) worked in the wings, eleven were stationed "above and below," and others, probably three or four (the fee listed is £7), for the prospetti. The nightly cost at S. Aponal, therefore, ranged from £36 for *Eritrea* in 1651/52 to £54 for *Eupatra* and *Erismena*. For 1657/58, his first season at the larger Teatro S. Cassiano, Faustini lumped together many types of workers, so that the number used for sets and machines cannot be determined, but for *Antioco*, in 1658/59, he indicates forty-two men for these tasks (as well as one to turn the winch to raise the counterweight), for a nightly cost of £84. In addition, for 1654/55 and 1658/59 Faustini paid a fee to the artisans who built the sets and machines to compensate them for their nightly assistance: a small amount, £3 s.6 and £4 respectively for Simon Guglielmi and Anastasio at S. Aponal, and much more, £12 and £14 respectively, for Santurini and Beccari at S. Cassiano. Over the course of the season, the nightly costs for sets and machines, therefore, were considerable, ranging from just over 161 ducats in 1651/52 (about 3 percent of the total cost of the production) to 431 ducats in 1658/59.

AFTER THE SEASON

Although the painted scenery itself was not generally reused after the conclusion of the season (see below), much of the raw material (canvas, wooden frames, and mechanisms) remained for subsequent years. In the event that a company ended its contract in debt, these items could be inventoried and sold (see above). The four extant valuations from this period (see table 9.10) range from just over 300 ducats to more than 600, a significant amount, but not nearly enough to make up for debts that often reached into the thousands of ducats.

DID THEATERS PRESERVE A REPERTORY OF SCENERY?

Some modern writers on seventeenth-century Venetian opera have suggested that each theater had a collection of painted scenery, the *dotazione*, a sort of endowment, that would be reused from year to year, and that this practice explains the recurrence of a restricted number of scenic types. The assertion is made most strongly by Elena Povoledo. She writes of the late 1630s:

> the *dotazione* was born: the sets created for the opening of a theater or its renovation were preserved and recycled. They were often of good quality but reduced in the number of locations and limited, initially, to the five obligatory topoi . . . : a street (or city or tragic set) . . . , a forest, the sea, the underworld, the cloud-filled heavens

---

84 The fees are listed as part of the nightly expenses, in section "S" in each of the account books.

TABLE 9.10.   Valuations of Scenic Materials

Year	Theater	Amount in ducats
1646	S. Cassiano	663[a]
1670	S. Luca	489
1679	S. Moisè	319
1684	S. Luca	600

Source: Vcg, Archivio Vendramin 42F 16/1, sacchetto 20, proc. 24, f. 23.
[a] The notary volume containing the negotiations over the settlement of the company's debts from this season contains two relevant documents: the inventory of materials associated with the carpenter, in the amount of 400 ducats, and a brief statement of the value of materials associated with the painter, at 263 ducats. ASV, AN, Atti, b. 667, ff. 82–84.

. . . The flats were retouched as needed, they were adapted, they were interchanged among themselves. Only if unavoidable would a new setting be added: a courtyard that could become a prison, a garden that could become a place of delights, the walls of a city . . . [85]

The basis for this assertion seems to be the recurrence of standard set types in the librettos. However, the earliest clear evidence on this issue argues against this point of view. The engravings of Torelli's sets for operas at the Teatro Novissimo in the early 1640s[86] show that the repetition of a scenic type did not indicate the reuse of a specific set of flats. For example, *Bellerofonte* (produced 1642), calls for, in act 1, scene 4, a courtyard, as does the opera of the following year, *Venere gelosa*, in act 2, scene 7. The engravings, however, show two clearly distinct sets (see figure 9.8 for the courtyard in *Venere gelosa*; that for *Bellerofonte* is flanked by buildings with Renaissance windows rather than columns, with a backdrop depicting a semicircular, two-story, colonnaded structure[87]). Similarly, although *Venere gelosa* calls for three different wooded sets (the "Deliziosa boschereccia" of the Prologue, a "Prospetto boschereccio" of act 1, scene 2, and the "Boscareccia" of act 3, scene 6), none of them bear any similarity to either of *Bellerofonte*'s similar sets: the "Isola disabitata" of act 2, scene 1 or the "Delizioso e regolato boschetto" of act 3, scene 7 (see figures 9.3 and 9.5). The situation is a bit more complicated for a third opera, *Deidamia*, produced at the

85 "nasce la dotazione: le scene create per l'apertura del teatro o il suo rinnovo vengono conservate e riciclate. Sono spesso di buona qualità ma ridotte nel numero degli ambienti e limitate, inizialmente, ai cinque topoi d'obbligo . . . : una 'strada' (o 'città' or 'scena tragica') . . . , una selva, il mare, l'inferno, il cielo di tutte nuvole. . . . Si ritoccano i telari a disposizione, si adattano, si mescolano fra loro. Soltanto se è indispensabile si aggiunge un ambiente nuovo: un cortile che può diventare una prigione, un giardino che può diventare una delizia, le mura di una città." Povoledo, "Controversie monteverdiane," 380.

86 See n. 4, above.

87 See Milesi, *Giacomo Torelli*, 102 or Worsthorne, *Venetian Opera*, pl. 14.

Novissimo in 1644. Of the ten sets called for in the libretto, engravings of only three were printed, included along with those for *La Venere gelosa*. Since most of those not illustrated are of the same general type as those of the earlier operas, Maria Ida Biggi claims that, "in effect, the Teatro Novissimo, by this date, had already accumulated a real and proper *dotazione*, of splendid manufacture, rich and original in its invention and varied in its settings . . ."[88] The implication is that other than the three sets reproduced, *Deidamia* relied entirely on those from earlier operas; however, nothing in the previous works corresponds with the "Stanza del Fato in aria" of act 2, scene 9, for which no engraving was issued, so that other sets as well, for technical or financial reasons, may also have been omitted from the published book of engravings. Biggi argues further that two of the three sets illustrated, the "Porto di Rodi con il Colosso" of the Prologue, and the "Valle solitaria" of act 1, scene 1, were made up in large part of elements from the earlier sets. However, her statements that the Prologue set includes portions of the seaport from the opening of *Bellerofonte* and that the "Valle" was derived from elements of the sets of both act 2, scene 1 of *Bellerofonte* and act 1, scene 1 of *Venere gelosa*[89] are simply not supported by the evidence of the engravings themselves.

Although some types of evidence may seem to point in the direction of a *dotazione* in mid-seventeenth-century Venice, these are also equivocal (and are counterbalanced by other evidence). Contracts between theater owners and impresarios often included a clause requiring the impresario, when the term of management had ended, or the scene designer, to leave behind all the scenic materials that had been there when he started.[90] Agreements among members of a management company might use similar language. Neither of these, however, especially in light of the evidence presented above, requires a conclusion other than that the materials themselves had some monetary value, or that parts of them (the frames and mechanisms, in particular) were indeed expected to be reused. While most of the inventories of theater materials of the 1650s and 1660s, as discussed above, indicate that only one season's worth of scenery remained at the end of Carnival, two others, one early in the history of Venetian opera, and one in the eighteenth century, also provide apparent evidence in favor of the *dotazione*. The 1646 S. Cassiano inventory referred to above lists 248 flats (representing about twenty-four different sets), rather than the approximately 100 flats used in a normal season, as well as thirteen backdrops and ninety "telleri piccoli" or lontani.[91] Similarly, an inventory of Teatro S. Giovanni Grisostomo of 1713, listing the items turned over from one set designer to his successor, describes materials for at least seventeen sets.[92]

88 "in effetti, il Teatro Novissimo, a questa data, aveva ormai accumulato una vera e propria dotazione, di splendida fattura, ricca e originale nell'invenzione e varia negli ambienti"; in Milesi, *Giacomo Torelli*, 139.

89 Ibid., 138–39.

90 See, for example, ASV, AN, Atti, b. 2991, f. 739ᵛ, 11 Sept. 1663, contract for S. Luca between Andrea Vendramin and Girolamo Barbieri.

91 ASV, AN, Atti, b. 667, f. 83.

92 ASV, GP, Inventari, b. 411, f. 22.

The evidence against the *dotazione* in mid-seventeenth-century Venice, however, is stronger. There is, first, the visual evidence of Torelli's sets, discussed above. Further, every extant contract for the manufacture of scenery demands, usually in explicit terms, that all the sets be new. Finally, inventories of theaters from the 1650s and 1660s, without exception, contain only the scenery employed in the previous season's operas. One of these, for SS. Giovanni e Paolo in 1661, makes it clear that by the end of the season even the sets for the first of the two operas had mostly been dismantled and the pieces used to prepare those for the second work. Given the evidence for the 1650s and 1660s that impresarios during that period nearly always had entirely new scenery painted for each season, these documents might be seen as pointing to some changes in procedures over time. Perhaps in the early years of opera in Venice, some impresarios reused scenery, or at least planned for that eventuality, and therefore accumulated collections. By Faustini's era, if not earlier, this practice was abandoned in favor of continual novelty from season to season (even if, occasionally, a set would be reused in the second opera in a two-opera season). Later on, in the late seventeenth or early eighteenth century, probably for reasons of economy, a *dotazione* became standard.[93] For the period under consideration here, however, Venetian audiences expected to see new images every year, and the impresarios, for the most part, obliged.

---

93 Concrete evidence for this survives in the extant *dotazione* of scenery, consisting of about thirty different settings, at the Drottningholm Theatre in Sweden. See *Enciclopedia dello spettacolo*, s.v. "Drottningholm."

CHAPTER TEN

COSTUMES

As we have seen, visual elements such as scenery and machines received careful attention from the impresario. If the scenery in Venetian theaters was praised for its innovations and splendor, the costumes comprised another important visual layer to be enjoyed by the audience; for the impresario, the costumes demanded judicious consideration, as their production could be costly and complicated.

INTRODUCTION: THE NATURE
OF OPERATIC COSTUMES

Costuming for seventeenth-century opera was not designed with historical accuracy in mind. Rather, the mortal characters, both principals and extras, wore elaborate versions of ancient Roman or contemporary dress with, as necessary, appropriate adornments to indicate royal or military status or exotic, non-European origin.[1] Gods and allegorical characters were more fancifully costumed. No detailed illustrations of specific Venetian operatic costumes from this period are extant, but some of the engravings of Giacomo Torelli's scenery include costumed characters, and they give a general sense of the figures, showing pseudo-Roman dress with seventeenth-century helmets, courtiers with pleated collars, and a number of figures sporting contemporary breeches (see figures 9.2–9.8).[2]

Descriptions in librettos and commemorative volumes for some of the earliest operas in Venice provide clear evidence for the splendor, color, and sometimes fantastic nature of costuming for the singers and extras appearing on the stage. The

---

1 For extended descriptions of costumes in *Bellerofonte*, see Worsthorne, *Venetian Opera*, 177–82. See also *NGO*, s.v. "Costume," by Sidney Jackson Jowers. On early seventeenth-century Italian, but not Venetian, theatrical costuming, see *Corago*, chapter 20, esp. 112–15.

2 The most recent complete reproduction of these engravings can be found in Milesi, *Giacomo Torelli*, 101–7, 115–21, and 140–41. They are also reproduced in Worsthorne, *Venetian Opera*, plates 13–23. The illustration of the set for *Bellerofonte*, act 2, scene 11 (see figure 9.4) provides the best example of the mixture of Roman and modern dress.

printer of *Andromeda* (1637) provided a telling account, bringing to life the characters that had inhabited the stage. The title character, for example, wore a costume "the color of fire, of inestimable value."[3] The sea-god Proteus must have made a singular impression, clothed in silver scales, with a big head of hair, and a beard colored sky-blue.[4] Several years later a volume celebrating *Bellerofonte* (Novissimo, 1641/42) describes the king as wearing "a coat of gold brocade down to his knees, with a superb royal cloak lined with gold and an ermine collar. He carried a jewelled sceptre and, on his head, above a beautiful turban, he wore a golden crown . . ."[5] The same book also brings to life the soldiers and other military figures (see figure 9.4): "The soldiers were armed with cuirasses and helmets with blue plumes. They wore blue stockings, a livery trimmed with great golden roses, skirts of gold lace, sashes of blue and gold crepe from which hung their swords, and gold buskins on their feet. Their captain wore rich armour encrusted with jewels, a blue sash, plume and smart looking half-boots."[6] These costumes may have been quite similar to some of those sketched by Stefano della Bella for the production of Francesco Cavalli's *Hipermestra*, mounted in Florence at the Teatro della Pergola in 1658;[7] the detailed drawings for that production, with their specifications for fabric, color, embroidery, lace, and jewels, attest to the care that went into the design and manufacture of seventeenth-century costumes.

ARTISANS AND DESIGN

It is likely that in the early years the singers supplied their own costumes in the tradition of the commedia dell'arte troupes, as such a practice would have decreased the partners' financial obligations. Indeed, this was the case with Cavalli's company at S. Cassiano for the 1638/39 season, at least for the singers' primary roles. The contract of incorporation (14 April 1638) states: "the performers must provide for themselves the costumes necessary for their main role"; other secondary costumes would be furnished by the company.[8] Soon, however, a different system was in place at the Novissimo. In 1644 the company's star singer, Anna Renzi, bore no responsibility for her costumes, which were provided by and remained the property of the impresario, Girolamo Lappoli.[9] By supplying all of the costumes, rather than relying on those already available to disparate cast mem-

---

3 "di color, di foco, d'inestimabile valuta." *Andromeda* (1637), 7.

4 Ibid., 8.

5 Translation from Worsthorne, *Venetian Opera*, 177–78.

6 Translation ibid., 177.

7 See Massar, "Costume Drawings." The sketches comprise drawings for dancers and dancing characters, as well as singers.

8 "signori recitanti dovranno provvedersi gli abiti necessari alla lor parte essentiale." ASV, Monastero di S. Maria dell'Orazion a Malamocco, b. 3. The document is described in Morelli and Walker, "Tre controversie," 107–8 (doc. B 1 [14 Apr. 1638]).

9 ASV, AN, Atti, b. 658, ff. 163ᵛ–164ᵛ, 17 Dec. 1643. On this contract, see B. Glixon, "Private Lives." The document is also published in Strunk and Treitler, *Source Readings*, 569–71. See also chapter 7.

bers, the impresario could guarantee a stricter and more homogeneous artistic control of the visual elements of the production. This practice remained standard in Venice.

One question surrounding costumes in this repertory, in fact, concerns that of the designer. It has recently been suggested that scenographers such as Giacomo Torelli may have acted in that capacity.[10] Although Stefano della Bella in Florence (mentioned above), Ludovico Burnacini in Vienna, and Jean Berain in Paris combined such talents,[11] in Venice (especially from the 1650s and later) those two areas were the domain of distinct artisans. Horatio Franchi, for example, is referred to several times as the "inventore" (creator) of the costumes (see below), and his contributions were quite separate from those of the scene designer, Hippolito Mazzarini.

While an impresario was sometimes free to choose the suppliers of his costumes, he might also be required to use the designated house tailor. Horatio Franchi worked at the Teatro SS. Giovanni e Paolo beginning in the late 1650s, when he furnished costumes for the impresario Francesco Piva, and he remained there for many years to come, his position remaining stable through a succession of impresarios.[12] When, in 1682, the Grimani brothers rented their theater to a new company, one of the conditions in the contract was that the "house tailors" be employed for the costumes, at a fixed fee.[13]

The costume designer, naturally, did not work in the abstract, but drew his inspiration from the themes and characters depicted in the libretto. Although few anecdotes refer to the collaboration between librettist and designer, in 1685 the father of the dilettante librettist Antonio Franceschi described how his son had provided Horatio Franchi with the list of costumes ("vestiario") that would be needed for his libretto.[14]

10 *NGO*, s.v. "Costume," by Sidney Jackson Jowers.

11 Ibid.

12 This relationship may have begun with the 1656/57 season; see chapter 3, n. 87. Franchi eventually deepened his involvement with the theater, acting as impresario—along with his colleagues Hippolito Mazzarini and Gasparo Mauro, who had also been Faustini's scenery and machinery designers—for a few years in the 1670s (ASV, AN, Atti, b. 6108, f. 2, 2 Mar. 1675).

13 "The shareholders also promise to obtain the costumes for the operas from the house tailors, for which they agree to pay, for each year of rental [of the costumes], 700 ducats, for a total of ten characters, and forty-four extras, and costumes for the dances, and all of them should be finished and in order by 15 November." ("Di più prometono detti signori caratadori prender gl'habiti per vestir l'opere da sartori di casa per i quali sono convenuti pagar per ciaschedun anno di nollo duccati settecento, dovendo esser il numero di diese personagi, et quarantaquatro comparse, et habiti per li balli, e tutte finite cioè all'ordine per li 15 di Novembre.") ASV, AN, Atti, b. 6112, f. 132, 5 June 1682. Despite the phrasing of the contract ("ciaschedun anno di nollo"), the costumes were probably largely made anew, as in Faustini's time; it probably implies, as will be discussed below, that the tailors would retain the costumes at the end of the season. We would like to thank Mauro Calcagno for his assistance with this passage.

14 The father, Gabriel Angelo Franceschi, was one of the Grimanis' agents. Antonio Franceschi's libretto, presumably *Didone delirante*, was not performed that season, but appeared in 1686. ASV, AN, Atti, b. 6113, f. 201, 1 Feb. 1684 m.v.

THE MANUFACTURING AND PURCHASING
OF COSTUMES: MATERIALS AND PERSONNEL

If costumes were valued for their texture, detail, and color, and for the sense of extravagance that they bestowed on the characters portrayed on the stage, the impresario (through his designer and craftspeople) had to find the least expensive path to this opulence. During the mid-seventeenth century an impresario could obtain costuming in a number of ways, usually either contracting for the manufacture of individual costumes or purchasing them from a supplier. During the 1650s Marco Faustini used both of these methods, in a two-tiered system. The first category encompassed individual costumes for the named characters of the cast; they were produced by an artisan (a tailor), and were costly, sometimes reaching a figure of 100 or more ducats for the most magnificent. Additional expenses regarding these costumes included lining and embroidery, the latter accomplished by specialist workers, not by the tailor shop. The impresario sometimes purchased accessories for the costumes, such as shoes or buttons, from specialist craftsmen or suppliers. Helping to keep expenses down is the apparent practice that many characters wore a single costume throughout an opera, perhaps changing accessories as the situation required.

The second category comprised sets of identical costumes for groups of extras and dancers; these more generic costumes could be purchased in bulk, already in finished form, from a supplier of liveries or from a merchant-broker, and came at a much lower price than the specially designed pieces. A typical entry in Faustini's account books might read "costumes for eight men" or "thirty-six liveries";[15] occasionally, however, the impresario made more detailed notations. In 1654, for example, he purchased eighteen complete sets of armor for extras, as well as six uniforms for "janissaries," while the 1658 account book includes payments for costumes for eight moors and eight turbaned pages.[16] It appears that these sets were at times rented rather than purchased for the season. In 1654, Faustini obtained from the tailor Savio costumes for eight pages (not including stockings, boots, or wigs) at a cost of £24 each (less than 4 ducats); four years later, however, when the impresario again turned to Savio for costumes for eight pages—this time, with everything included (even, in this case, turbans)—the cost was much less, only £6 each, probably indicating purchase of the items in 1654, and rental in 1658.[17] By 1678 a sort of costuming warehouse had been established, for the costumer Horatio Franchi indicated that he would not be able to provide the desired set of Turkish costumes for the Bentivoglios in Ferrara since there were so many operas that season that required them that he had no more available.[18]

15 ASV, SGSM, b. 113, account book, 1654/55, ff. 5ᵛ and 7ᵛ.

16 ASV, SGSM, b. 113, account book, 1654/55, ff. 6ᵛ and 5ᵛ; for 1658, ASV, SGSM, b. 194, account book 1658/59, f. 23ᵛ. Unlike the named characters, the extras and dancers who used these sets of costumes would wear different ones at various points in the opera, as the group they represented changed.

17 ASV, SGSM, b. 113, account book 1654/55, f. 5ᵛ; ASV, SGSM, b. 194, account book 1658/59, f. 23ᵛ.

18 Monaldini, Orto dell'Esperidi, 341. In the 1680s, the impresario and costumer Gasparo Torelli rented to Filippo Pallavicino for a production in Genoa of Anagilda overo il Rodrigo the costumes not only for forty-two extras (presumably including dancers), but also for the twelve named characters (Ivaldi, "Spigolature," 44).

The duties of the tailors did not end with the completion of the costumes, however. Faustini's account books from the 1650s reveal one other expense: the employment of one or more tailors at the theater during the run of the opera to adjust and repair them as needed, at a cost of between £8 and £18 per night.[19]

The Supply of Cloth and Other Materials

During the seventeenth century the clothing business was highly developed in Venice, with many fabrics manufactured there in addition to the presence of a large market of dealers, shops, and tailors.[20] An opera impresario (or, indeed, an individual singer who wished to commission a costume) could have dealt with a number of merchants and artisans when assembling an elaborate costume.

After the design of the costume had been executed and approved, the process would begin with the purchase of the cloth, either from a *testor*, who specialized in silk, or a *marzer*, for linen, wool, and cotton. The variety available was remarkable: Faustini's account books show purchases of at least twelve different sorts of cloth, some of them in several different colors. The most prized were several kinds of silk, including *brocado* (brocade, usually the deep red known as *cremesin* or a white called *latesin*, interwoven with silver or gold thread) and *ormesin* (the sort used in the official robes of the Venetian patricians); muslin (*cenda*, usually green, crimson, or white); wool (*rassa* or *rassetto*, in white, yellow, red, or green); and, most varied of all, linen (*tella*), which appears in some twenty colors and qualities or grades.[21]

Made-to-order costumes often required further materials to embellish the cloth, either by the tailor (*sartor*) who was responsible for the assembly of the entire piece, or by specialized workers. Among the most important of such decorations was lace (*merli*) in several varieties, including those made with costly gold or silver thread, but also types such as "Flemish" or "Chioggia" (the latter manufactured in Chioggia, on the southern edge of the Venetian lagoon). Additional materials employed as costume decoration included ribbons (*cordella*), feathers, pearls, and other jewels (probably made of glass paste). Such details as silk or gold thread (*argento falso filado*, *lama d'argento falso*, or *oro cantarin*), were added by embroiderers.[22]

19 For 1651/52, £12 for the first opera and £18 for the second (ASV, SGSM, b.112, account book 1651/52, f. 47ᵛ); for 1654/55, £12 (ASV, SGSM, b. 113, account book 1654/55, f. 71ᵛ); for 1655/56, £8 s.4. (ibid., f. 67ᵛ); for 1657/58, £16 s.8 (ASV, SGSM, b.112, account book 1657/58, f. 53ᵛ); and for 1658/59, £16 (specified as tailors from the shop of Savio; ASV, SGSM, b. 194, account book 1658/59, f. 25ᵛ).

20 See Vitali, *Moda a Venezia*, Romanelli, "Abiti de' veneziani," and Molà, *Silk Industry*.

21 The most commonly used colors included red, yellow, white, *pagera* (straw-colored), and *roan* (a reddish black). Faustini also purchased cambric (*cambrada*), a very fine linen usually used for undergarments; *renso*, another fine linen; *tella sangallo*, a woven cloth that imitated embroidery; and *fustagno*, a blend of linen and cotton. Other qualities or types of fabric, not easily identified today, included *tella della serpa* (the serpent—perhaps a brand name derived from a merchant's shop sign—apparently usually in two colors) and the quaint *tella tre scimmie* (three monkeys, perhaps also a "brand" name).

22 While most of the craftspeople hired by Faustini seem to have been paid a preestablished fee, the embroiderers (*recamadori*), were paid a daily wage. The 1654 account book records payments to embroiderers (the number of workers is not specified) of £9 s.6, or one scudo, per day for twenty-seven days' work (ASV, SGSM, b. 113, account book 1654/55, ff. 1ᵛ–2ᵛ). Faustini also supplied candles when the work continued after dark.

As mentioned above, other parts of costumes, even those for individual characters, were purchased ready-made. These included many items standard in everyday dress, such as shoes and boots (from a *callegher*), stockings (*calze* of silk, wool, or cotton), gloves (from a *muschier*), straw hats, belts, buttons, bracelets, lace sleeves, and breeches (*braghesse*). The plots and settings of the operas, however, often suggested additional items: Faustini purchased a good deal of imitation armor,[23] either in complete sets or for a single individual, including swords and shields, as well as turbans for exotic characters, usually Turkish. Masks—that traditional staple of carnival attire—also found their way onto the operatic stage.

FAUSTINI'S SYSTEMS FOR COSTUME PRODUCTION AT THREE THEATERS, 1650–68

During the nearly two decades Marco Faustini acted as an opera impresario, his approach to costuming the operas he produced changed considerably. As with the scenery, data from the account books of the 1650s allow us to track Faustini's various payments to merchants and artisans, providing a more detailed map of the various expenditures than is possible for other seasons. He started at S. Aponal with a hands-on approach, monitoring every detail and employing directly a wide range of craftsmen and merchants; gradually, in the later 1650s at S. Cassiano, and especially at SS. Giovanni e Paolo in the 1660s, he came to rely more on the skills and expertise of a single specialist.

The amount of money needed to costume an opera was considerable. Faustini's costs varied from a low of 250 ducats for each of two operas in his first three seasons at SS. Giovanni e Paolo in the early 1660s, to a high of 930 ducats for *L'incostanza trionfante,* his first opera at S. Cassiano in 1657 (see table 10.1). The impresario's expenditures—which translated to 16 percent of the overall expenditures for *Calisto* and *Eritrea* in 1651/52, and 14 percent for *L'incostanza trionfante* in 1657/58—appear to have been fairly typical (see appendix 5). As we shall see, the tailor Savio's fee at S. Moisè in 1666/67 was 600 ducats, and the cost at SS. Giovanni e Paolo in 1682 not much more, 700 ducats.

Faustini and Costumes in the 1650s: Evidence from the Account and Receipt Books

Faustini's initial tendency—perhaps following the practice initiated by Giovanni Faustini—was to immerse himself in the details of the costuming. The 1651/52 account book, all in Marco's hand, documents a lengthy process beginning in August 1651, and concluding six months later, a week after the close of the second

---

23 The documents in the Faustini papers do not offer any information on the materials used in this sort of imitation armor, so it is not known whether the pieces were made of thin metal or perhaps of papier mâché painted to resemble metal. A commentary on the 1675 production of Legrenzi's *La divisione del mondo* refers to the character Saturn "with a silver pasteboard halbert" ("Saturno con la falce di cartone d'argento"). See Fabbri, "Recensione 'in rima'," 443.

TABLE 10.1. Marco Faustini's Expenditures for Costumes (in Ducats)

Season	Labor	Complete costumes	Cloth	Other	Costumer	Total
1651/52	252 (30%)	149 (18%)	340 (41%)	97 (12%)	—	838
1654/55 (1 opera)	—	283 (40%)	—	25 (4%)	400[a] (56%)	708
1655/56 (1 opera)	?	250	?	—	—	250[b]
1657/58 (1 opera)	428 (46%)	226 (24%)	279 (30%)	—	—	933
1658/59 (1 opera)	152 (22%)	76 (11%)	420 (60%)	54 (8%)	—	702[c]
1660/61	—	—	—	—	500	500
1661/62	—	—	—	—	500	500
1662/63	—	—	—	—	500	500
1665/66	—	—	—	—	1000	1000
1666/67	—	—	—	—	800	800
1667/68	—	—	—	—	800	800

[a] Faustini paid Nicolò Personé for the cloth and labor for costumes for the named characters.
[b] For this season, the records are incomplete, lacking all payments to tailors or for cloth.
[c] The documents for this season record no payments to a tailor, so these figures cannot be considered complete.

opera (see appendix 5), by which time he had made over 170 separate financial transactions, nearly all listed in a single, continuous section in his account book labeled "expenses for costumes" (*spese per habiti*).[24] By the time the first opera, *Calisto*, opened on 28 November, Faustini had spent about half of the eventual expenditures for the season's costumes; the manufacture of the costumes for the second opera, *Eritrea*, began only after the completion of those for *Calisto*. The company, then, must have worked with a specific allowance in mind for each opera.

The account book does not refer to a contract with a tailor, but lists a series of payments to someone Faustini called "quel dal Can" ("he of the Dog") who can be identified as Paulo Morandi, a wood turner (*tornidor*) whose shop "al cagno-letto" ("the sign of the puppy") was in the parish of S. Lio. We may well wonder how a wood turner came to be involved in the costuming-supply business. By 1651, as we saw in chapters 3 and 4, Morandi had already been involved in the

24 ASV, SGSM, b. 112, account book 1651/52, ff. 2–5.

theatrical world for at least ten years; he provided scagni at several theaters,[25] a service perhaps related to his trade, but he had also become a supplier of costumes, both at the Novissimo and at SS. Giovanni e Paolo during the 1640s.[26] Through his activities in Faustini's companies we see how Morandi had expanded his theatrical interests. He provided Faustini with some accessories and props, but most importantly, he seems to have been his chief supplier for sets of costumes for dancers and extras, that second category of costumes referred to above. Since he was by profession a woodworker, not a tailor, he either acted as a broker or middleman (ordering costumes from appropriate sources when the necessity arose, or keeping a stock of standard costumes on hand), or he had acquired a second area of expertise in the area of theatrical costuming. Morandi continued his interest in opera production at S. Aponal even in Faustini's absence, becoming one of the subrenters of the theater in 1652/53.[27]

COSTUMING ACCOUNTS FOR 1654/55   When Faustini returned to S. Aponal in 1654, after a two-year hiatus, to produce Pietro Andrea Ziani's *Eupatra*, his attention to detail in the costuming was, if anything, even greater than in 1651/52. Although he maintained the two-tier system referred to above, he made some changes in his practices. Faustini apparently contracted for the manufacture of the costumes for individual characters through Ziani's brother-in-law, the cloth dealer Nicolò Personé, for a total cost of 400 ducats.[28] However, rather than simply paying that amount directly to Personé, as he would later do with costumers at SS. Giovanni e Paolo, Faustini himself paid most of the bills for cloth, accessories, and labor as they arose, thereby keeping close track of progress and expenses.[29] The account book does not refer to Personé as the overall contractor; rather, Faustini recorded the expenses for materials and some labor (particularly the embroiderers) in a section simply headed "costumes" (*habiti*), and those for the labor of the unnamed tailor in a separate section.[30] Six months after the season's completion, Personé acknowledged, in signing Faustini's receipt book, that he had been

25 Morandi had also acted as a guarantor for Giacomo Torelli at the Novissimo in 1640/41, and acted as his proxy when he left for Paris in 1645 (ASV, AN, b. 3055, f. 49, 10 Mar. 1642; ASV, AN, Atti, b. 10858, f. 39ᵛ, 20 Apr. 1645). He provided 150 scagni to SS. Apostoli for the 1650/51 season (ASV, AN, Atti, b. 1124, f. 17ᵛ, 17 July 1653).

26 ASV, GP, Dimande, b. 49, no. 1, 20 Mar. 1645. Morandi was still supplying costumes to SS. Giovanni e Paolo for the 1648/49 season; see ASV, GM, Sentenze a legge, b. 328, f. 21, copy of a promissory note dated 24 Jan. 1648 m.v. Morandi's involvement with cloth (as opposed to wood turning, his principal occupation) can be seen also in religious venues, as he arranged for hangings and other fabric decoration for the church of SS. Giovanni e Paolo on behalf of the confraternity of the SS. Nome di Dio for its annual festival (ASV, Avogaria di comun, b. 2158/108, 13 Jan. 1644 m.v.).

27 Glixon and Glixon, "Oil and Opera," 135–36.

28 On Personé, see chapter 3.

29 Faustini's account with Personé was not completely settled until the following fall. See above, p. 47.

30 For materials and some labor, 350 ducats (ASV, SGSM, b. 113, account book 1654/55, ff. 1ᵛ–3ᵛ and 8ᵛ–9); for the tailor's labor, 60 ducats (ibid., f. 5).

paid 400 ducats (including about 40 for the embroiderers) for "the price of all the things of every sort made in my shop . . . destined for the occasion of the opera performed at S. Aponal."[31]

Because of Faustini's day-to-day involvement, the data in the 1654/55 account book are remarkable for their specificity; the records of payments for many of the materials purchased bear indications of how they were to be used. For example, Faustini purchased *tella sangallo* and *tella arzenade* (the latter with some sort of silver coloring) for the three furies, *tella pagera* (straw-colored) for three cupids, silver lace for the costumes of Lugrezia Marconi and for the characters Pompeo and Clisera, and gold lace for those of the title character, Eupatra, and for the singer "la Palermitana" (Angela Angelotti). Unfortunately, the records are not consistent enough for us to determine the entire makeup of any one costume, but they do provide tantalizing hints, and also point to Faustini's knowledge of the detailed work necessary to achive fine costumes.

As in earlier seasons, Faustini handled the costumes for dancers and extras, and a few special items, separately. Beginning in August, he reached agreements, in the form of private contracts, with three different suppliers of costumes: Paulo Morandi, the wood turner mentioned above, the tailor Girolamo Savio, and Francesco Fenestrer.[32] Faustini's notation for Fenestrer's contract mentions that his work should be carried out "according to the designs existing in his possession, signed by me, Marco Faustini, for 60 ducats."[33]

COSTUMING PROCEDURES AT S. CASSIANO   Faustini maintained some aspects of this system when he moved to the Teatro S. Cassiano. In 1657, for example—in preparation for *L'incostanza trionfante*—he bought almost all of the cloth from Cesare Boranga, whose shop he had used frequently in the past, while the costumes for extras (and perhaps the dancers) once again came from Paulo Morandi.[34] For that year Faustini entrusted the bulk of the tailoring to one man,

31 "Del prezo di tutte le robbe di cadauna sorte fate alla mia bottega . . . destinate per ocasione del opera recitata a S. Aponal"; ASV, SGSM, b. 118, receipt book, f. 11ᵛ, 2 Sept. 1655.

32 The contracts themselves are not extant, but are outlined in the account book for 1654/55 (ASV, SGSM, b. 113). The dates of the contracts are as follows: Morandi, 20 Aug. 1654, for thirty-six liveries, later reduced to thirty (f. 7ᵛ); Savio, 26 Oct. 1654 and 10 Nov. 1654, costumes for eight pages and six (later seven) janissaries (f. 5ᵛ); and Francesco Fenestrer, 14 Sept. 1654, for the armor for three male characters, Pompeo, Ariobarzante, and Seleuco, and part of the costume for Irene (f. 6ᵛ). The artisans and brokers were not expected to supply the stockings, shoes, and feathers, which Faustini purchased separately.

33 "giusta i disegni essistenti in sua mano da me Marco Faustini sottoscritta in D60." ASV, SGSM, b. 113, account book 1654/55, f. 6ᵛ. It is unclear whether Francesco or someone else had made the drawings. For the 1655/56 season, the incomplete accounts (ASV, SGSM, b. 113, included in the account book for the previous season) make no mention of costumes, and the only surviving receipts are for payments totaling 250 ducats to Paulo Morandi for all the costumes for dancers and extras (ASV, SGSM, b. 118, receipt book, ff. 15ᵛ–16ᵛ). For Faustini's final season at S. Aponal, 1656/57, the only documentation regarding costumes is a receipt signed by Nicolò Personé for 124 ducats for various expenses (ASV, SGSM, b. 118, receipt book, f. 23).

34 ASV, SGSM, b. 112, account book 1657/58, ff. 1ᵛ–2 (for Boranga) and 33ᵛ (for Morandi).

Horatio Franchi—specifically named in the libretto—who earned a fixed price, 280 ducats, for his labor.[35] Faustini also paid small amounts to several other tailors, including Giovanni Penachin, the stepfather of Pietro Andrea Ziani, the composer of that year's opera.[36] Most elements of the system obtained once again for the production of *Antioco* the next year, although the records are incomplete. As before, Faustini purchased the cloth from Boranga, sometimes clearly specifying the material for particular costumes, such as silk brocade with silver fleurs-de-lis for Tolomeo and Antioco, and he turned to the tailor Savio, rather than Morandi, for the sets of costumes for dancers and extras.[37] In addition, Faustini paid an embroiderer, and purchased costume accessories from Morandi.[38] No reference is made, in either the account book or in the receipt book, to a tailor who would assemble the costumes for the principal characters.

Faustini and Costumes at SS. Giovanni e Paolo during the 1660s

With his move to the Teatro SS. Giovanni e Paolo for the 1660/61 season, Faustini simplified his involvement with costuming. In September 1660, he signed a contract with Horatio Franchi, who would design and provide all of the costumes (i.e., for characters, extras, and dancers) for the two operas to be presented each carnival season for the next three years, that is, for the initial term of Faustini's appointment at the theater.[39] During the 1650s Franchi had served at the court of

35 ASV, SGSM, b. 112, account book 1657/58, f. 31ᵛ. Franchi's is the only name that appears in librettos of the 1650s and 1660s in conjunction with costumes. He was also named in the librettos of *La costanza di Rosmonda* (SS. Giovanni e Paolo, 1659), *Gl'amori di Apollo, e di Leucotoe* (SS. Giovanni e Paolo, 1663), *Amor guerriero* (SS. Giovanni e Paolo, 1663), *Demetrio* (S. Moisè, 1666), *Eliogabalo* (SS. Giovanni e Paolo, 1667), and *Artaxerse* (SS. Giovanni e Paolo, 1669). His name continued to appear for several decades, the last time in 1694 for *La moglie nemica* (S. Luca).

36 ASV, SGSM, b. 112, account book 1657/58, f. 33ᵛ. Penachin, who came to Venice in 1631, married Sulpicia Ziani, the mother of Pietro Andrea Ziani, in 1635 (ASVP, EM, b. 35 (1635 no. 2), f. 94). For Penachin's connection with the Teatro Novissimo, see chapter 4.

37 ASV, SGSM, b. 194, account book 1658/59, ff. 1ᵛ–2, 5ᵛ, for Boranga's materials. Ibid., ff. 23ᵛ–24, for Savio's costumes, which included those for twelve dancers, eight pages with turbans, eight moors, and twelve for the dancers for the second intermedio. As mentioned above, the low cost of these items, from £4 to £8 each (compared with the £24 for those of 1654/55) probably indicates that Faustini was paying for rental, rather than purchase. For the next year's *Elena*, Faustini specified in some cases that he wanted fabrics from Boranga identical to those used for *Antioco*; for the costume of Elena, he requested gold brocade ("brocada d'oro") of the same type used the previous year ("della stessa qualità, che fu fata l'anno passato"; ASV, SGSM. b. 113, loose sheet).

38 ASV, SGSM, b. 194, account book 1658/59, ff. 4ᵛ–5.

39 Franchi's costume business was, of course, not a one-man operation. Several months after the 1658/59 season, when Giovanni Grimani helped arrange for the costumes for an opera production in Mantua, he wrote to Marquis Ottavio Gonzaga that it would be better to have the costumes made in Venice (rather than in Mantua) "because it is the wife [Giovanna Franchi] of the said costume designer who works better" ("sarà meglio eseguito qui, che costà, perché essendo la moglie del detto inventore quella, che lavora meglio," ASMa, AG, b. 1571, 19 Apr. 1659). Giovanna sometimes signed for her husband's fees during Faustini's years at SS. Giovanni e Paolo, especially for the 1666/67 season (ASV, SGSM, b. 118, receipt book, ff. 78ᵛ–79ᵛ and 85ᵛ).

Innsbruck[40] as well as at Faustini's S. Cassiano, but by the 1658/59 season, as mentioned above, he had become the house costumer at SS. Giovanni e Paolo. The general terms of Franchi's 1660/61 contract with Faustini were straightforward:

> We declare that by virtue of the present contract, which will have the same effect as if it had been registered in the acts of a public notary, that Horatio Franchi obligates himself to costume in every particular the two operas to be presented this year by the Most Excellent Signor Marco Faustini in the Teatro di SS. Giovanni, et Paolo, for the characters (both male and female), gods and others who go on the machines, and for all the extras and dancers that will be necessary . . . [41]

Perhaps the phrase that follows reveals Faustini's dissatisfaction with his previous hands-on, time-intensive methods:

> so that Signor Faustini should not have to spend money for anything, but all the expenses for the costumes, [including] shields, cloaks, jewels, embroidery, shoes, silk stockings, boots, gloves, and every other adornment, with nothing excluded, shall be done by the said Horatio, as above, for the women as well as the men, for the extras and the gods, and any other character, named or unnamed, that should be necessary in those two operas.[42]

Faustini, however, had not completely relinquished his involvement with the artistic side of the costumes; indeed, he insisted on his right to approve Franchi's designs before the work could begin.[43] Franchi received a fixed fee of 500 ducats; while this figure is considerably lower than the costume expense for earlier years (only 250 ducats per opera, compared with figures such as 420 to 930 ducats per opera at S. Aponal and S. Cassiano; see table 10.1), Franchi also had the benefit of using any costumes or cloth left over from earlier productions, and would have all the costumes returned to him after the season to do with as he wished (see below for more on the post-season value of costumes). The impresario's separation from the manufacture of the costumes at SS. Giovanni e Paolo led Giovanni Grimani to comment in 1662—somewhat hyperbolically—to the Marquis Bentivoglio, who sought advice on a costume he desired: "About the costume . . . it would be su-

---

40 Payments are listed in Innsbruck to Franchi in 1653 and 1655. See Senn, *Musik und Theater*, 271, 274. Franchi's wife, Giovanna (also referred to as Zanetta) accompanied him to Innsbruck for the production of *Argia* (1655); on this and on his quarantine in Verona upon his return from Innsbruck, see Rigoli, "Virtuoso in gabbia."

41 "Si dechiara per la presente scrittura quale doverà havere rigore, la forza, come se fata fosse negl'atti di publico nodaro, qualmente D. Horatio Franchi s'obliga di vestire di tutto punto le due opere che quest'anno devono farsi rappresentare dall'Eccellentissimo Signor Marco Faustini nel Theatro di SS. Giovanni et Paolo così, di personaggi, huomeni et donne, deità et altri che vanno sopra machine, et di tutte le comparse et ballerini che saranno necessarie . . ."; ASV, SGSM, b. 194, f. 45, 4 Sept. 1660. The document is partially transcribed in Mancini, Muraro, and Povoledo, *Teatri di Venezia*, 1:309–10.

42 "così che detto Signor Faustini non habbia in cosa alcuna benché minima a spendere, ma tutta la spesa di habiti, scudi, manti, girelli, ricami, scarpe, calze di seda, stivaletti, guanti et ogni altro adornamento, niuna cosa esclusa, habbia tutta a farsi da detto D. Horatio, come di sopra, tanto in donne, come in homeni, comparse, et deità, et ogni altra cosa così nominata, come non nominata, che fusse necessario in dette due opere." ASV, SGSM, b. 194, f. 45.

43 Ibid., 4 Sept. 1660.

perfluous to talk about it with Signor Faustini, because he does not give any thought to the costumes, as he pays Horatio a fixed sum so that he may provide all the necessary costumes, and then hold onto them in order to make use of them in the next carnival . . ."[44] Grimani commented, then, both on Faustini's relative detachment from the process, as well as on Franchi's practice of reusing costumes, or, more likely, since the Venetian public demanded constant novelty, recycling the materials from which the costumes were made (see below).

This new system not only saved Faustini money, but also reduced greatly his administrative burden: instead of the nearly 200 separate payments the impresario had made for costumes in the early 1650s, he now made fewer than ten per year.[45] The impresario did, however, make separate payments occasionally; two sheets from 1661 and 1667 list specific articles purchased for the lead women singers.[46]

At the outset of his second triennium at SS. Giovanni e Paolo (1665–68), Faustini drafted a new contract with Franchi (signed 8 April 1665) that included a few new conditions. Franchi was responsible not only for all the usual costumes, but also "if it should be necessary in the said performances, for the dances, [costuming for] some animals or monster, excepting, that is, the manes, tresses, tassels, and silk stockings."[47] The contract specified that the costumes were to be produced to Faustini's satisfaction, and to be made "nobly." Recognizing that the figures in the previous contract had been insufficient, this agreement called for a significantly larger fee, 800 ducats instead of 500. Despite the extraordinary length of the carnival season (ending 9 March 1666), Franchi was still expected to have all of the costumes for the first opera completed by the middle of December, so that at least two performances could be mounted before Christmas.[48] As in the 1660 contract, Franchi was to retain ownership of all costumes at the end of the season.

Even the newly augmented allotment proved insufficient, however, for when the time came to prepare for the second opera, *Tito*, a change in the contract be-

44 "Circa l'habito, che mi ordina, sarebbe superfluo il discorrere con il Signor Faustini, perché egli non ha pensiero d'habito alcuno, mentre da un tanto ad Horatio per tuti gli habiti necessarii, e questo se li ritiene per valersene nel prossimo carnevale." ASFe, AB, b. 335, f. 308ᵛ, Venice, 22 Mar. 1662, letter of Giovanni Grimani to Marquis Bentivoglio; see Monaldini, *Orto dell'Esperidi*, 171. Our reading differs slightly from Monaldini's.

45 According to the contract, two-thirds of the 500 ducats was to be paid to Franchi "from time to time" before the opening of the first opera, and the remaining third no later than the second performance. In practice, Faustini made payments monthly during the summer, with a final settlement at the beginning of the season. In the first year of the contract, however, the last payment was not made until 21 Jan. (ASV, SGSM, b. 118, receipt book, f. 48, 21 Jan. 1660 m.v.).

46 See ASV, SGSM, b. 194, f. 8, for expenses from the 1660/61 season (including lace, cambric, a camisole, and stockings for Caterina Porri). For 1667, expenses including ribbon (*cordella*) for Antonia Coresi, stockings, gloves, and a wig for Caterina Botteghi (ASV, SGSM, b. 188, f. 197). In ASV, SGSM, b. 118 (receipt book), receipts can be found for Giovanni Bellin, bombaser (1661 and 1662), Filippo Fiordiben (a *marzer*, March 1661), and Marc'Antonio Balleli, a supplier of plumes, March 1661.

47 "come anco se occoresse in ditte recite per occasione de balli qualche animale ò mostro. Escluso zazere, capigliature, galani, e calze di setta"; ASV, SGSM, b. 194, f. 42, 8 Apr. 1665.

48 Ibid., f. 42. Faustini was obligated to pay Franchi 500 ducats before the season, 150 ducats at opening night, and the remaining 150 ducats at the time of the mounting of the second opera.

came necessary. In an effort to increase the spectacle, the librettist Beregan decided to replace some of the planned extras with men on horseback. Faustini authorized those improvements, and Franchi agreed to provide the new costumes for five horses and riders for an additional 200 ducats, so that the expenses for the two operas for that season came to 1,000 ducats.[49]

The system that Faustini used for costuming the operas at SS. Giovanni e Paolo—that is, contracting with a single individual for all of the costumes—seems to have been standard for that time. The documents discovered by Irene Alm concerning Sebastiano Enno's production of *Alessandro amante* at S. Moisè in 1666/67 show that Enno hired the tailor Girolamo Savio (whom Faustini had used in some earlier productions) "to make all the costumes at his own expense, that is for the characters, extras, and dancers; for the prologue, and others that appear on machines . . . excluded from this, however, are silk stockings, gloves, and expenses for the barber . . ."[50]

AFTER THE SEASON: COSTUMES AS COMMODITIES

Opera costumes had a second life following the carnival season; they could become the property of a number of people with interest in the theater: the investors, the impresario, the theater owner, the singers, or, as we have seen, the costumer himself. In some cases, the ultimate destination of the costumes was drawn up in an agreement before the start of the season. The partners or others who contributed capital for the production might claim costumes as repayment, since income from ticket sales alone rarely was adequate to recover their investment.

The distribution of costumes within a single company could vary from year to year. For the 1654/55 season at S. Aponal, Bortolo Pasinetto, as the major investor (see chap. 3), was entitled to 70 percent of the costumes, to Faustini's 30 percent.[51] The next year, as the composition of the company changed, so did the distribution of the costumes; the scene painter, Simon Guglielmi, received one quarter of the costumes as part of the return on his investment, and Paulo Morandi another quarter, with Pasinetto and Faustini sharing the remaining half according to a 70/30 percent split.[52] In the event, the company held on to them until it was certain that

49   Ibid., f. 43, 30 Jan. 1665 m.v. Franchi is also credited—in the libretto of Pallavicino's *Demetrio*—as having provided the costumes that same year for S. Moisè.

50   "far tutti li habiti a proprie sue spese così di personaggi, comparse, ballarini, e prologo, et altri in machina, che occoresse . . . eccettuato però le calze di seda, guanti, e spesa di barbiere"; ASV, Ospedali e luoghi pii, no. 37 B. Heredità Virginia Camuffi, f. 4. Savio was to be paid a fee of 600 ducats; payment was arranged somewhat differently than the specifications in Faustini's contracts with Franchi, however: Enno was required to turn over to the tailor 100 ducats at the signing of the contract, and then "pay for such merchandise as will be necessary for the said costumes," for a total of 600 ducats. As with the Faustini–Franchi contracts, the costumes were to remain the property of the tailor.

51   ASV, SGSM, b. 118, receipt book, f. 11.

52   Ibid., ff. 19v–20. On the changing companies at S. Aponal, see chapter 3.

they would not be needed for the next production (*Le fortune di Rodope e Damira*), and they were finally distributed in December 1656.

When Faustini moved to S. Cassiano in May of 1657, the agreement drawn up for the formation of the new company—with Marc'Antonio Correr, Alvise Duodo, and Polifilo Zancarli—specifically addressed the issue of costumes. In this case, they were to become the common property of the company itself: "All the costumes that will be found to belong to the company will be put to the common benefit, including the said Signor Polifilo, with the condition, however, that after the first year has been completed, should he wish to withdraw from the company (which one cannot believe he would wish to do), he must receive the just portion of the costumes . . ."[53]

The value of the costumes came into play at other theaters as well. Andrea Vendramin formally recognized their financial importance, but only a few years after he converted his theater from comedy to opera. In 1663, in advance of the theater's fourth season, the costumes served as a financial guarantee when Girolamo Barbieri rented the theater from Vendramin: they would remain the property of Vendramin until the rental fees had been received (after which, presumably, they would be returned to Barbieri):

> All of the tools, costumes, scenery and every other movable object existing in the said theater should be immediately inventoried and it is intended that they should be given as security to the Most Illustrious Vendramin. They must always remain in the same theater as property of the Most Illustrious Vendramin together with all of the scenery, costumes, and anything else that should be made new in the coming year as pledge, guarantee, and security for his rent from year to year . . . [54]

This clause is in direct contrast with that in the original rental of 1660, when Vendramin had allowed Antonio Boldù to keep outright the costumes that would be produced, along with some other movable items.[55] In some companies, however, such as Faustini's at SS. Giovanni e Paolo, artisan contracts stipulated that the used costumes be returned to the tailor, that is, they could serve neither the investors nor the theater owner as capital. This strategy by the impresario must have served as a means by which he could reduce the amount of cash paid to the artisan up front.

The costumes could be recycled in several ways, regardless of whether they were returned to the tailors or suppliers who provided them for the production,

---

53 "Tutti gli habiti che si attroverano di ragione della compagnia doverano esser posti in opera a benefficio comune, etiam di detto Signor Polifilo, con conditione però fornito il primo anno et volendosi lui cavar dalla compagnia, il che non si può credere, debba ricever la giusta portione de gl'habiti in ragione di saldo"; ASV, SGSM, b. 194, f. 25.

54 "Tutti li utensigli, habiti, scene, et ogni altra cosa mobile essistenti in detto theatro siano di subito inventariati et s'intendino dati loco pignoris ad esso Illustrissimo Vendramin, dovendo sempre restar nel medesimo teatro come cosa de esso Illustrissimo Vendramin, insieme con tutte le scene, habiti, et altro che si facesse da novo l'anno venturo per pegno, cautione, e sicurezza del suo affitto d'anno in anno." ASV, AN, Atti, b. 2991, f. 739ᵛ, 11 Sept. 1663.

55 ASV, AN, Atti, b. 2983, f. 1114ᵛ, 13 Nov. 1660.

were sold to other such professionals, or remained with the impresario or theater owner. It is unlikely that the more costly costumes would have been used intact in future productions in Venice, where novelty was valued so highly, but they might, as mentioned above, have been retained for rental outside of the city. Often, however, they were not preserved intact. In 1655, when Ermes Bentivoglio hoped to obtain costumes from Giovanni Grimani (perhaps as rentals), he was informed that they would probably not be available, because they were "in the hands of tailors to be disassembled and afterwards remade for this carnival's production."[56] A final possibility is that the costumes, especially if the materials had already been recycled several times, might eventually be sold to a *strazzariol*, that is, someone who specialized in the trading of second-hand clothes.[57]

While in many cases costumes helped to settle debts, repay investments, or reduce costs, they could also be used in another way altogether. Because they were sumptuous, expensive creations that could be worn long after the theater had closed for the season, costumes could serve as a sort of an enticement, and form part of a singer's contract. In 1654/55 for *Eupatra*, for example, Anna Renzi received 500 ducats, while the other lead singer, Angelica Felice Curti, was to receive 50 ducats less, plus one of her costumes, or else the same figure in ducats.[58] In the event, Curti chose to take the money rather than keep her dress. Faustini continued to offer magnificent costumes in his efforts to attract top singers. Caterina Tomei's earnings for the 1661/62 season, according to a contemporary account, included a dress of gold brocade; the frequent appearance of costumes of this description perhaps indicate that this was, in effect, the prima donna's "uniform."[59] In 1665 (as discussed in chap. 7), Faustini's original offer to Vincenza Giulia Masotti mentioned a dress made from "gold cloth embellished with very fine gold lace."[60] The next year, negotiations with Masotti for 1666/67 specified either "a fine dress" or, instead, the sum of 100 scudi (150 ducats);[61] that sum would have represented 37.5 percent of the entire costume budget for the opera. Certainly, the dress would have been a spectacular confection, worthy of the prima donna who would have worn it on stage.

The high monetary value of these costumes led some singers to hold onto them as a sort of security when they felt they had not received their just payment. After the 1650/51 season at S. Cassiano, Annetta Miani, one of the singers in *Armidoro*, was sued by the tailor (and partner in the production) Mattio di Grandi, for having refused to return her costumes.[62] Similarly, in 1654, Anna Felicita Chiusi

---

56 "questi sono in mano de sarti per guastarli e poscia accomodarli per la funtione di questo carnevale." ASFe, AB, b. 319, f. 751, 27 Oct. 1655, letter from Ermes Bentivoglio to Cornelio Bentivoglio; see Monaldini, *Orto dell'Esperidi*, 104,

57 On the *strazzariol*, see Romanelli, "Abiti de' veneziani," 23–29. On the second-hand market, especially the need for luxury goods, see Allerston, "Wedding Finery."

58 ASV, SGSM, b. 113, account book 1654/55, f. 43ᵛ, 13 June 1654.

59 Matteini, *"Rimino,"* 92, dispatch of 13 Dec. 1661.

60 "Una vesta tessuta d'oro con merli d'oro nobilissima"; ASV, SGSM, b. 194, f. 30.

61 ASV, SGSM, b. 188, f. 110.

62 ASV, GP, Dimande, b. 34, reg. 57, no. 45, 1 Mar. 1651. Other documents in the case are in ASV, GP, Scritture e risposte, b. 180, fasc. 55 (1651), no. 73 (17 Apr. 1651) and no. 86 (26 Apr. 1651).

kept her dress of gold brocade when a dispute over her services arose between her and the interim impresarios at S. Aponal.[63]

Costumes, then, required a signicant amount of attention and money from the impresario, and occasionally even became the focus of legal disputes. They could also, when successful, bring honor to the production. The libretto for *Amor guerriero* (1662/63) proudly proclaimed: "the costumes are all newly made by Signor Oratio Franchi, who with his most beautiful inventions has provided pomp to the most notable staged works in the courts of Princes."[64]

---

63 On Chiusi and her dispute, see B. Glixon, "Private Lives." Chiusi had fallen ill toward the end of the season; she was unable to complete the performances, so that the impresarios refused to pay her salary in full. Regarding Chiusi's appropriation of the dress, see ASV, Avogaria di comun, b. 2172/122, 13 Mar. 1654.

64 "E gli Habiti tutti fatti di novo del Signor Oratio Franchi; che con le sue leggiadrissime inventioni ha dato pompa a più riguardevoli rappresentationi nelli Corti de i Prencipi." Foreword to *Amor guerriero* (1662).

PART IV

CONSUMERS AND PATRONS

CHAPTER ELEVEN

THE AUDIENCE AND THE QUESTION
OF PATRONAGE

The focus in this final chapter shifts to the audience: its composition, its size, and its effect on the success or failure of individual operas. Once again we look at the boxholders, this time with an eye toward their social status: the majority of boxes were rented by Venetian and foreign nobles, with a select few held by visiting ambassadors and other lesser governmental representatives. An analysis of surviving accounts from several of Faustini's seasons offers the best information on the size of the audience (both the boxholders and those in the parterre) and the relative success or failure of individual operas. We will also look briefly at some of the social aspects of attending the opera, and at the violence and other social problems that could erupt in the theater. We will conclude with an investigation of several questions regarding patronage: do traditional (or even revisionist) concepts of patronage apply? Was Venetian opera "public"? Who, when all was said and done, paid the costs of this expensive and risky venture, and who benefited from it?

THE COMPOSITION OF THE AUDIENCE:
VENETIANS, FOREIGNERS, AND ISSUES OF STATUS

As we saw in chapter 2, most Venetian opera boxes were rented season by season, primarily by Venetian nobles and distinguished foreign visitors, including ambassadors. This process left behind a paper trail that enables us to learn much about the makeup of the audience, and to understand, in part, some of their reasons for attending.[1] The seats in the parterre, on the other hand, were purchased individually for each performance, providing an opportunity for Venetians and foreigners of other classes, as well as some nobles, to attend the opera.

---

[1] Notarial documents are particularly useful for the Teatro S. Luca in the 1660s and 1680s and for the Grimani theaters in the 1670s and 1680s, but are far from complete, dealing, as they do, for the most part, with delinquent patrons. For a discussion of Faustini's palchi at S. Aponal (1653/54–1656/57), see below.

The Boxholders: Seating Strategies and Tendencies

An examination of the extensive documentation regarding the boxes, primarily notarial acts concerned both with the acquisition of boxes and a myriad of problems pertaining to them, reveals several patterns not only in the makeup of the audience, but also of preferences for specific boxes, both in terms of the *ordine*, or row, and position within the row (that is, nearer to the stage or to the center). Some renters would have wanted to sit near the stage to be close to the singers and to be seen better by the rest of the audience, while others might have preferred the most centrally located boxes, for their unsurpassed view of the scenery and its perspective effects, and the aura of importance such a position implied (in other cities, of course, the royal or ducal box would have been in the center of a row; see figure 2.1).[2] Indeed, one could say that patrons viewed their palchi not only as seats for the opera, but also as statements of their social standing and prestige (and perhaps of their character or personality). Many patricians maintained boxes in several theaters, and some of them even paid for more than one box in a single theater; the cumulative cost of the multiple boxes strained the pockets of some of the holders (many of whom were land rich but cash poor), contributing in part to the proliferation of notices regarding late payment. As we saw in chapter 2, a number of nobleman shared boxes, possibly as a means of economizing.

A wide spectrum of the city's patricians, including many of the wealthiest families, occupied most of the boxes, including both young men and distinguished members of the governing elite. This holds true not only at the prestigious S. Luca, SS. Giovanni e Paolo, and S. Giovanni Grisostomo theaters, but also the smaller and humbler S. Aponal. Faustini's list of renters there (see table 11.1) includes, besides more "ordinary" Venetian patricians, several of the highest rank, among them a number of procuratori of S. Marco, one of the most important of all government positions. In addition, some boxes in the first orders were occupied by eminent foreigners such as the Papal Nuncio and the Dukes of Brunswick and Parma. In all theaters the first order (that is, the lowest numbered order, above the parterre-level pepian) was clearly the most prestigious. At S. Luca, for example, in 1687, the occupants of this row included numerous procurators, the Duke of Brunswick, the ambassadors of France, Spain, and the Austrian Empire, and the Florentine Resident.[3] The second rank was somewhat less desirable, only rarely attracting foreign princes, and holding fewer procurators. Indeed, the procurator Nicolò Venier purchased a palco in the second order (a proscenium box) during the first season at the Grimani family's new S. Giovanni Grisostomo with the stipulation that when a suitable box became available in the first order, a substitution would be made.[4]

At the prestigious theaters, non-nobles rarely appeared in the first or second levels; instead, they could be found, predictably, in the pepian, as well as in the third

---

2 On how the relative position of the boxes determined their cost in the late eighteenth century, see Bauman, "Society of La Fenice," 334–36.

3 ASV, AN, Atti, b. 8878, f. 113, 7 Mar. 1687.

4 Vmc, P.D. Venier 124, Tomo 1, f. 384ᵛ.

or fourth orders. Also included in these less desirable regions at S. Luca were some noblemen from the Venetian mainland possessions and various cittadini and merchants.[5] Girolamo Barbieri, one of the impresarios at S. Luca, had a box in the pepian rather than in the upper orders.[6]

The boxholders of S. Aponal (see tables 11.1 and 11.2) offer us a particularly concentrated view of an opera's spectators, as the theater had so few palchi available in comparison with the others in town. Faustini himself was the only non-noble to hold a box in the first order, but several others, including some with connections to the impresario or the opera company, held boxes in the second and third. Giovanni Antonio Curti, one of Faustini's legal clients, held the first box in the second, while Nicolò Personé, who aided the company in 1654/55, occupied a box in the third order, along with "Squadron," either the doctor or the government secretary of that name.[7] Another of Faustini's lists, this one for the top order at SS. Giovanni e Paolo—the only one under his direct control at that theater—confirms some of these trends, while contradicting others (see table 11.3). The non-noble occupants included Faustini and several others with operatic connections (among them Pietro Antonio Ziani's friend Giovanni Maria Savioni, the librettist Aurelio Aureli, and Faustini's former partner, Polifilo Zancarli). Two boxes there were reserved for the Grimani family as owners of the theater, and one for their agent, Gabriel Angelo Franceschi. More surprising in this order are Marc'Antonio Correr, Faustini's noble partner, and a number of other patricians, including two procurators; it is likely, however, that these men held other boxes in the lower orders, keeping these less prestigious ones for friends or additional family members.[8]

In Faustini's accounting of the boxes at S. Aponal, the top order is mostly blank, indicating that even in such a small theater those particular boxes would have been rented out each night on demand. This may have been the case at other theaters as well. Indeed, in September 1665 the company at S. Moisè authorized their caretaker to "rent out the palchi in the attic and the ground level, evening by evening, when they do the performances."[9] In any event, the few annual renters of those less fashionable boxes must have paid their fees more responsibly than the

5 Noblemen from the mainland mentioned in documents of the 1660s include Count Camillo Martinengo Cesaresco of Brescia and Count Gasparo Thiene of Vicenza. A record of 1687 includes members of several Venetian citizen and merchant familes: Astori, Cellini, Negroni, and Manzoni (ASV, AN, Atti, b. 8878, f. 113, 7 Mar. 1687).

6 ASV, Inquisitori di stato, b. 914, 2 July 1665.

7 ASV, SGSM, b. 194, ff. 92–100. On Personé, see chapters 3 and 10.

8 The fifth order would have been the top level (soffitto), the level assigned to Faustini in his contract with the Grimanis. That contract stated that two boxes should be retained for "casa Grimani," and Faustini's accounting of those palchi (ASV, SGSM, b. 194, f. 18) assigns numbers 24 and 25 "per la casa." Faustini had the two boxes nearest the stage (1 and 2), while Polifilo Zancarli had number 15, and Marc'Antonio Correr number 13, i.e., these more centrally located. (See chap. 2, n. 16.)

9 "affitar li palchi in soffitta et a piè pian di sera in sera quando si farano le recite." ASV, AN, Atti, b. 8475, f. 175ᵛ, 24 Sept. 1665. At S. Aponal, four of the sixteen boxes had been claimed for the 1656/57 season. Faustini's list from SS. Giovanni e Paolo, on the other hand, shows twenty-two of twenty-nine boxes already assigned.

TABLE II.I. Boxholders and Occupants in Teatro S. Aponal for the 1654, 1655, 1656, and 1657 Seasons

No.	First order[a]	Second order	Third order[b]
0	For the courtesans ("per le donne")	N.H. Bragadin, Proc.	1 Vacant
1	N.H. Marc'Antonio Corner 1655: vacant 1656–57: Abbot Grimani	Giovanni Antonio Curti 1655: N.H. Marin Barbaro 1656–57: N.H. Marin Barbaro and N.H. Mocenigo	2 Vacant
2	N.H. Alvise Foscarini, Proc.	Given to members of the company 1655–57: Giacinto (1656: occupied by N.H. . . . . 1657: occupied by N.H. Contarini)	3 Vacant
3	N.H. Pietro Dolfino	Vacant 1655: Baron Tassis and Abbot Zanchi 1656–57: N.H. Ferigo Dolfin	4 Vacant
4	N.H. Priuli (1654: occupied by N.H. Lunardo Moresini; 1655: occupied by N.H. Mattio Sanudo)	N.H. Lunardo Moresini 1655: N.H. Lunardo Foscarini 1656–57: vacant	5 Vacant
5	N.H. Lodovico Michiel 1655–57: N.H. Count of Zaffo (Contarini)	N.H. Piero da Canal 1655–57: N.H. Francesco Barbarigo	6 Vacant 1655: Dottor . . .
6	N.H. Marc'Antonio Corraro	N.H. Filippo Capello 1655: N.H. Zaccaria Vendramin and N.H. Zuanne Badoer 1656–57: N.H. Zaccaria Vendramin	7 Vacant 1655: Giovanni Antonio Curti 1657: N.H. Marin Barbaro
7	N.H. Alvise Duodo	Zuanne Vasilico	8 Vacant 1655–57: Mari Fabrizzi

8	Faustini (1654: occupied by N.H. Giovanni Antonio Zen; 1657: occupied by Papal Nunzio)	N.H. Zuanne da Mosto and Lodovico Vidman	9 Vacant
9	N.H. Ambroso Bembo and Aurelio Pianella 1656–57: Aurelio Pianella	Vacant 1655: Faustini	10 Vacant
10	N.H. Alvise da Canal 1656: N.H. Giacomo da Canal	N.H. Zuanne Priuli	11 Vacant 1655–57: Nicolò Personé
11	Abbot Vettor Grimani 1656–57: Duke of Parma	Vacant 1655: English gentleman 1656–57: N.H. Polo Moro	12 Vacant
12	N.H. Vettor Pesaro	N.H. Gherardo Sagredo (1654: occupied by Pietro Onzel) 1656–57: N.H. Antonio Basadona	13 Vacant 1657: N.H. Dolfin
13	N.H. Foscarini, Governor of Padua	given to the members of the company 1655: N.H. Santo Contarini 1656–57: N.H. Corner, Proc.	14 Vacant
14	N.H. Marco Contarini	N.H. Girolamo Contarini 1655: N.H. Filippo Boldù 1656–57: N.H. Pietro Diedo	15 Vacant
15	N.H. Viaro, Proc. 1657: N.H. Viaro and N.H. Antonio Mocenigo	N.H. Pesaro, Proc.	16 Vacant

Source: ASV, SGSM, b. 194, ff. 92–100.

[a] The first name or designation listed for each box indicates the renter for the 1654 season, and for successive seasons unless other holders are indicated. N.H. = Nobil Homo, the standard Venetian indication of a member of the patriciate. Proc. = Procuratore di San Marco, one of the highest offices of the Venetian Republic, held for life. In this table, the spellings in the original document have been preserved unchanged.

[b] While the boxes in the first and second orders were numbered 0–15, those in the third were numbered 1–16.

TABLE 11.2. Social Class of S. Aponal Boxholders by Numbers of Boxes

Order and Season	High-ranking nobles[a]	Nobles with operatic connections[b]	Ordinary nobles	Total boxes occupied by nobles	Foreign dignitaries	Non-nobles	Speciale[c]	Vacant
1 1653/54	5	5	4	14	0	2	2	0
1654/55	5	4	4	13	0	1	2	1
1655/56	6	6	1	12	1	1	3	0
1656/57	6	5	2	13	2	1	2	0
2 1653/54	2	1	7	10	0	2	2	3
1654/55	2	3	5	10	2	2	2	0
1655/56	5	1	7	13	0	1	0	2
1656/57	5	1	7	13	0	1	0	2
3 1653/54	0	0	0	0	0	0	0	16
1654/55	0	0	0	0	0	4	0	12
1655/56	0	0	0	0	0	2	0	14
1656/57	0	0	2	2	0	2	0	12

Source: ASV, SGSM, b. 194, ff. 92–100. If a box is shared by individuals from two classifications, it is listed under both, so the figures may add up to more than the total number of boxes.

[a] This classification includes those holding the rank of Procurator of S. Marco or the title of Cavaliere di S. Marco.

[b] This includes investors in Faustini's company, those who have assisted with recruiting, and others directly connected with opera production.

[c] Boxes assigned to courtesans or members of the company, including performers.

TABLE 11.3   Social Class of Boxholders by Number of Boxes in the Fifth Order at SS. Giovanni e
Paolo for a Season during Faustini's Tenure as Impresario

High-ranking nobles	Nobles with operatic connections	Ordinary nobles	Total boxes occupied by nobles	Foreign dignitaries	Non-nobles	Special	Vacant
2	3	7	12	0	9	2	7

Source: ASV, SGSM, b. 194, f. 18.

patricians in the lower orders as they do not often appear in the lists of those sued
for non-payment.

Reserved Boxes: Owners, Impresarios, "Women," and Ambassadors

Not all boxes were made available to the nobility and other wealthy patrons at
large; rather, some were held back for particular purposes. As might be expected,
the owners of the theaters reserved certain privileges for themselves: they singled
out boxes in the theater rental contracts, keeping them for decades through many
changes of management. When Antonio Boldù rented S. Luca in 1660, for example, Andrea Vendramin cited his rights as owner to "two boxes, number 15 and
numbers 7/8 in the second order. . ."[10] The Tron family kept six palchi in S. Cassiano for their own use, as specified in their 1657 contract with Faustini.[11] The impresarios and their partners would also have had one or more boxes for their own
purposes, further diminishing the number available to the public.[12]

Another population benefiting from special boxes came from a quite different
part of the social spectrum: the famous courtesans of Venice.[13] At S. Aponal, Faustini
styled the first, unnumbered box (that is, the one closest to the proscenium at stage
right) in the first order as "per le donne."[14] A similar designation, with wording that
implies that this was standard practice, forms part of a 1674 agreement concerning
the operation of the Teatro S. Luca: "the Most Excellent Bembo should leave aside

10   "li due palchi numero quindeci, et numero sette e otto, che fa canton nel secondo ordine." ASV,
AN, Atti, b. 2983, ff. 1110ᵛ–1114ᵛ.

11   ASV, SGSM, b. 194, f. 73ᵛ.

12   It is notable that Marc'Antonio Correr, one of Faustini's partners, apparently did not receive his
box at S. Aponal free of charge, but paid just like all ordinary occupants (ibid., f. 9). The situation for
Faustini's other full partner, Alvise Duodo, is less clear (f. 7).

13   On Venetian courtesans, see Barzaghi, *Donne o cortigiane?*, Lawner, *Lives of the Courtesans*, and
Rosenthal, *Honest Courtesan*.

14   Although no documentation specifies the direction of numbering for S. Aponal, all extant
seventeenth- and eighteenth-century documents regarding the other Venetian theaters agree on numbering the boxes counterclockwise, beginning at stage right.

two boxes for the women in the pepian on the side with the stairs next to the stage, as usual."[15] The location of these boxes near the stage would have allowed most of the audience a good view of them; the women's presence was probably considered useful for attracting certain parts of the audience (most likely young patricians). Although it is unlikely that the courtesans actually plied their trade in the theater (which seems to have been the case in the sixteenth-century comedy theaters in which the boxes could be closed to outside view), they could certainly have entertained visitors, and, perhaps, arranged assignations.[16]

AMBASSADORS   Opera boxes were also prized by a small, elite segment of the population: the foreign ambassadors. As one of the great powers of Europe, Venice maintained diplomatic relations with a number of countries and duchies; many of them housed representatives—ambassadors or, for the lesser powers, "residents"—in the city. These men were bound by various restrictions—largely regarding communication with Venetians—designed to protect the security of the Republic. In recompense, they enjoyed a number of benefits, including the right to a box at each of the theaters, if they so desired. The request of the British Resident John Dodington, delivered to the Doge on 26 January 1672, shows that the motivation for obtaining a box might stem from reasons other than the appreciation of opera:

> Most Serene Prince: With all respect I come to ask a favor of Your Serenity, which is, if you please, to grant me two boxes in the theaters of SS. Giovanni e Paolo and S. Salvatore. I do not ask for them for my own satisfaction or taste, seeing, as I declare, that I do not love music. As regards poetry, I do not esteem it, and I do not understand the theater. The only reason I ask for this favor is so that I might keep up appearances: my most recent predecessor had boxes, and all the other residents currently at this court have them.[17]

Once more we turn to chronicler Cristoforo Ivanovich, this time for his description of the methods by which an ambassador procured a box during the last quarter of the century:

> Every rule has its exception. I said in the previous chapter that the boxes, once acquired, are possessed with the right to pass them on to one's heirs, as is widely employed. Yet it can arise that the possessor, by no fault of his own, might come to be

15 "Che siano lasciati dall'Eccellentissimo Bembo due palchi a pepian per le donne della parte della scaletta presso la sena conforme l'ordinario." ASV, AN, Atti, b. 6796, 17 May 1674. The agreement was between Francesco Bembo and Marquis Guido Rangoni.

16 On scandalous behavior in two late sixteenth-century Venetian theaters, see Johnson, "Short, Lascivious Lives," 938, 948–49.

17 "Serenissimo Prencipe: Con ogni ossequio vengo a dimandare una grazia alla Signoria Vostra la qual è, che si compiacia, di concedermi due palchi nelli Theatri di SS. Giovanni et Paolo, et S. Salvatore. Io non li dimando per la propria sodisfattione, ò vero gusto, essendo, che mi dichiaro, che non amo la musica; in quanto alla poesia, non la stimo, et per le scene non l'intendo. La sola raggione, che m'induce a pregarla di questo favore è per il sostenimento del decoro della rappresentanza. Il mio ultimo predecessore l'ha havuto, e tutti gli altri residenti, che sono al presente in questa corte lo godono." ASV, Collegio. Esposizioni principi, reg. 77, f. 91, 26 Jan. 1671 m.v.

deprived of his box, this only on the occasion that ambassadors of the crown make a public petition to be provided with one. Then one usually presents oneself to His Serenity, so that he should order the owner of the theater to provide some number of boxes, which are put into a lottery; the first of these, drawn at random, is given to the ambassador. The one chosen to relinquish his box turns over his key, and he is deprived of his box *for the entire term of the ambassador* [emphasis ours]. After the term has been completed, the box returns to its original owner, and it cannot be included as part of the lottery in similar occasions for a long time.[18]

Problems could easily surface concerning the granting of these boxes, and glimpses of such difficulties occasionally emerged in notarial records as well as in official documents of state. One such example occurred at Faustini's S. Cassiano. In 1658 the French ambassador was awarded palco 9 in the first order, which had already been rented by the nobleman Alvise Dolfin. In recompense, the management offered Dolfin two other choices: number 3 in the third order, or number 8 in the pepian, which the management described as "one of the best palchi in the theater."[19] Dolfin had not made his choice as the season was about to begin; we may well imagine that a palco on one of those two levels would not have met his expectations and social needs. As opening night approached, Dolfin was on the verge of losing the right to one of those "desirable" palchi altogether, as the management threatened to turn both of them over to others, owing to the great demand for the boxes. Even the theater owner Andrea Vendramin risked losing one of his palchi to an ambassador, for he went to the Capi of the Council of Ten shortly before the premiere of the opera for Carnival 1663, asking that the license to open S. Luca not be granted without the assurance that his own boxes would remain outside the pool of those in consideration for the French ambassador. Vendramin received the assurance he sought, and the ambassador was given palco 10 in the first order, chosen by lot according to the usual procedure.[20]

The ambassadors were well aware of the difficulties their rights might cause, and some of them maintained a degree of flexibility and gentility in regard to the boxes selected for them. In 1669 the Spanish ambassador, the Conte della Rocca, declared that one procurator had been greatly inconvenienced by the selection of

---

18 "Ogni regola patisce la sua eccezione. Si disse nel Capitolo antecedente, che i Palchetti acquistati una volta, si possedono sempre con quella ragione di poter passare agli eredi, come diffusamente s'è trattato; e pure nasce un caso, che il Possessore senza demerito può, ma à tempo esser privo del suo Palchetto, e questo solamente in occasione, che gli Ambasciatori delle Corone facciano istanza in publico per esserne proveduti. All'ora suol rimettersi à Sua Serenità, che ordini al Padron del Teatro, che debba presentar qualche numero di Palchetti, de' quali imbossolati col primo, che si cava à sorte, viene proveduto l'Ambasciatore, e a chi tocca di lasciarlo, conviene rinonciare la chiave, e dura per lui la privazione del medemo per tutto quel tempo, che esso Ambasciatore ferma nella carica, qual terminata ritorna il Palchetto al primo Possessore; nè viene imbossolato in altre simili occasioni per lungo tempo." Ivanovich, *Memorie teatrali*, 403–04.

19 "ch'è uno dei miglior palchi di detto theatro" ASV, AN, Atti, b. 691, ff. 478v–479, 17 Jan. 1657 m.v. Two copies of the document appear in the register. The first is the copy made by the notary; Faustini's original appears at the end of the volume.

20 ASV, Capi del Consiglio dei dieci, Notatorio, reg. 43, f. 105, 30 Dec. 1662.

his palco at S. Luca, and asked that the Doge make another choice among those in the center of the row.[21] Another incident involving an earlier Spanish ambassador (Antonio Sebastian de Toledo, Marquis de Mancera) provides a rare look at the process, and demonstrates that the selection of the ambassador's box could be accomplished more informally, and with more behind-the-scenes activity, than the method suggested by Ivanovich. In 1661 the ambassador recounted to the Doge what had occurred following his recent request for a box at the Grimani theater. On the instruction of the Doge, the Spanish envoy had gone to the theater owner to receive one of two palchi under consideration, and he was assigned a box that had earlier been occupied by a predecessor, but was now rented by the dukes of Brunswick, who were not, however, in Venice at the time. Several days later, the ambassador was approached by a representative of the dukes, wishing to reclaim that palco for his employers, who now thought they might come for carnival after all. The ambassador remarked that he himself had not chosen the palco, and would be happy to receive another. The dukes' representative later returned to him, saying that the "Grimanis had made the ambassador padrone of the theater, and that he should choose the palco that would satisfy himself best." In the end, the ambassador told the Doge that as a foreigner he wished to inconvenience no one, and would, in truth, not know how to choose the best box. He asked that the Doge command that he be assigned a different box and that no one "be discontented."[22] The selection of a box for an ambassador, then, could prove a sticky proposition. Compromises might be necessary when the one chosen belonged to an important foreigner, a theater owner, or an influential nobleman; lesser souls had to accept gracefully the temporary loss of their hard-won boxes.

The Audience in the Parterre

If the boxes were for the most part populated by visiting and resident nobles, the composition of the audience in the parterre remains largely speculative. Certainly, many, if not most, of the cittadini in the audience must have sat in the parterre, as their names do not appear in the majority of palchi lists. That part of the auditorium, then, would have been filled with lawyers, other civic officials, and prominent merchants. It is also likely that a number of noblemen sat there, as the boxes would not have been sufficient to accommodate all of that class, and the majority of foreign visitors would have been placed in that area as well. The English traveler Philip Skippon and his friends found accommodation in the parterre in 1664, but some prominent visitors may have been able to occupy a box through the auspices of their local government official or as the guests of Venetian boxholders.[23] As

21 ASV, Collegio, Esposizioni principi, reg. 75 (1667–68), f. 98ᵛ, 12 Jan. 1668 m.v.

22 "dicendomi che i Signori Grimani mi facevano padrone del teatro, et che io eleggessi quello, che fosse di mia maggior sodisfattione . . . che niuno resti scontento." ASV, Collegio, Esposizioni principi, reg. 70 (1660), f. 130, 3 Jan. 1660 m.v.

23 Skippon, Journey, 506. In the latter case, as the government frowned on close contacts between foreigners and patricians, the Venetian might have turned over his box to the distinguished visitor for the night and sat elsewhere, or did not attend at all that night.

Bianconi and Walker have shown, a night at the opera would have been prohibi-
tively expensive for the vast majority of the popolani, as an evening's performance
could have equaled or surpassed a day's wages.[24]

OPENING THE SEASON: PUBLICITY AND PERMITS

As the preparations for an opera production reached their conclusion, the company
took the steps necessary to open the theater. According to Ivanovich, a production
could commence only after an inspection of the theater by architects from the
magistracy of the Provveditori di Comun. Then, after final permission had been obtained from the Capi of the Council of Ten, public notice of the performances,
through the posting of a sign known as the cartello, could take place.[25] Little anecdotal evidence has come down to us concerning this public announcement for the
opera, but several annotations in Faustini's records suggest that it was, in some ways,
a decorative creation (he listed payments for cording, fine silk ribbon, and silk cloth).
We do not know whether the cartello included just the names of librettist and/or
composer with the title and name of the theater, or also named the performers or
designers. Generally, Faustini's account books specify an expense of £1 for the
cartello on the days of performances. The fee, most likely paid to a workman, probably indicates that the cartello was only posted on days there was to be a performance, or that it would be left hanging but would be modified to indicate the next
performance. Usually the documents specify no location for the placement of the
cartello, but Faustini's 1658/59 account book mentions expenses for one at the
Rialto. In the eighteenth century, a cartello was displayed at the Ponte dei Baretieri,
on the busy street between S. Marco and the Rialto.[26] Although the cartello was
clearly intended as publicity for the opera, it could also function as a symbol of the
theater and its management: in 1666 when problems arose with the employment of
one of the singers at S. Moisè, her protectors tore down the cartello in protest. According to one observer, the unrest surrounding the company was brought to the attention of the Capi of the Council of Ten, who would not grant the license for the
theater to open until the matter had been resolved.[27]

TICKETS AND THE SIZE OF THE AUDIENCE

The tickets themselves, called bollettini, were probably printed in a single, undif-
ferentiated batch for each season at each theater; each audience member, whether
seated in a box (including those rented annually) or in the parterre, required a bollettino to enter the theater, although some, as mentioned below, managed to ac-

24 Bianconi and Walker, "Production, Consumption," 227.

25 Ivanovich, Memorie teatrali, 405–6. No documents survive from this period from either of the
two magistracies referred to concerning permits or licenses for the opening of theaters.

26 Vmc, Cod. Gradenigo 67, tomo 3, f. 7ᵛ, 21 Feb. 1754.

27 Vmc, P.D.C. 1055, f. 384ᵛ, 29 Dec. 1665. We have not yet been able to locate the complaint
within the archives of the Council of Ten.

quire one without payment. A surviving example from S. Giovanni Grisostomo
bears only an emblem and a motto—without naming the theater or the date—and
a space in which a number has been added by hand.[28] In 1651/52 Alvise Duodo
had the bollettini printed for Faustini's company at the cost of one ongaro (about
£15); the only other reference to these costs is a payment at S. Moisè of £10 "to
the person who printed the bollettini."[29] The tickets may often have been sold or
collected at a location near but not physically in the theater, rented separately
for the purpose.[30] Faustini's account books always list a nightly expense, either £6
or £10, for "bollettini," almost certainly the wages of the man who sold and/or
collected the tickets. The most detailed description of the ticketing process comes
from Skippon, who wrote in his memoirs regarding his visit to the Teatro SS. Giovanni e Paolo: "In the morning we hired chairs in the cockpit for five, paying
two livres, besides four livres apiece for our bolletini or printed tickets. About
two hours of the night we took our seats, which were marked with one of our
names."[31]

Ivanovich asserts that from the beginnings of opera in Venice, in 1637, "the fair
price was set at the payment of £4 for each ticket, which serves as a passport to the
theater."[32] Faustini's papers and other sources confirm this price (equivalent to 80
soldi) through the middle of the 1670s. Later, in 1674, as Ivanovich goes on to explain, Francesco Santurini, impresario at S. Moisè,[33] having rented the theater and
its contents at a rate lower than usual, decided to gain a competitive advantage by
reducing the ticket price to one quarter of a ducat, or 31 soldi. In short succession,
all the other theaters, with the exception of the new S. Giovanni Grisostomo,
when it opened in 1678, adopted the new price, referred to by some writers simply
as "il trentauno," as the standard. The result, as Ivanovich laments, was, despite the

---

28 See Rosand, *Opera*, 394. It is not clear whether the handwritten number, in this case a "3," indicates the performance, the sequential order of the ticket, or even the number of persons to be admitted
(although the latter seems unlikely, as Skippon, see below, refers to his group having purchased "bollettini," in the plural). The name of the theater, and the price of £4, was added in the lower margin in
what appears to be a later hand.

29 "L'Illustrissimo Duodo fece la stampa delli bollettini per ongaro uno." ASV, SGSM, b.112, account book 1651/52, f. 56. For S. Moisè: "Per contadi a quello che ha stampado li bollettini £10." ASV,
Ospedali e luoghi pii, no. 37 B, Heredità Virginia Camuffi, f. 10ᵛ, 31 Jan. 1666 m.v.

30 Two separate notations—one each for the Novissimo and S. Aponal—refer to rent paid for
places where tickets were either sold or collected. The document concerning the Teatro Novissimo
refers to an area near the theater that was rented by Bernardino de Josephis to "receive the bollettini
from those who were entering to see the opera" (ASV, Giudici del forestier, Sentenze, reg. 78, f. 107ᵛ,
9 June 1646). A notation in Faustini's records also implies that the tickets were sold or collected at a
place outside the confines of the theater, for the company paid a small rent of £12 s.8 for the "place of
the bollettini" (ASV, SGSM, b. 113, account book 1654/55, ff. 9 and 26).

31 Skippon, *Journey*, 506. One attendee wrote his seat number on the scenario of Delia: "terza filla
scagno quinto" (third row, scagno number 5). See Rosand, *Opera*, plate 9.

32 "si limitò come onesta contribuzione il pagamento di lire quattro per bollettino, che serve di
passaporta nel Teatro." Ivanovich, *Memorie teatrali*, 411.

33 This is not the same person as the scenographer (see chap. 9) of the same name. See *NGO*,
s.v. "Santurini, Francesco (i)," by Mercedes Viale Ferrero, and "Santurini, Francesco (ii)," by John
Whenham.

satisfaction of the ticket buyers, that "the income from the gate, which is the principal financial foundation, rather than increasing, is decreasing, with obvious damage, and with the danger of bringing to an end this most noble entertainment."[34]

With the ticket prices stable during the 1650s and 1660s, income, of course, was entirely dependent on the number of tickets sold, a figure that could vary greatly. Successful operas, especially on opening night and the last night of carnival, might well have played to full or nearly full houses,[35] but other less fortunate ones might have a paid attendance as small as thirty or forty.[36]

Case Study: Attendance Figures at S. Aponal and S. Cassiano in the 1650s and S. Luca in 1669

With one exception (the 1669 season at S. Luca), the extant data regarding opera attendance for an entire season in the mid-seventeenth century comes from Faustini's four account books. Tallies of bollettini sold (and scagni, or bench seats, rented) survive, then, for seven operas in all: *Calisto*, *Eritrea*, *Eupatra*, *Erismena*, *L'incostanza trionfante*, *Antioco*, and *Argia* (this information is presented in the form of graphs in appendix 7). Four of the operas took place in the small Teatro S. Aponal, two in the more capacious S. Cassiano, and one in S. Luca, the largest of the three. While the lists provide invaluable data, we must remember that they represent the income from the paid bollettini, that is, not taking into consideration those people admitted without charge. We have no idea of the overall scope of this practice, but scattered notations reveal a number of different classes of attendees so benefiting, perhaps amounting to twenty or so for each performance. Various members of the opera company (including performers and artisans) were provided a number of bollettini gratis (Tasio Zancarli was to be given four for S. Cassiano and two at S. Moisè for each performance "to make use of for his friends, and for his own pleasure").[37] The singers Angela Angelotti and Stefano Costa received bollettini at S. Aponal and S. Cassiano,[38] and the prompters ("quelli che

---

34 "ma l'utile della Porta, ch'è fondamento principale dell'interesse, in vece di crescere si và diminuendo con evidente pregiudizio, e pericolo di tralasciarsi la continuazione di questo nobilissimo trattenimento." Ivanovich, *Memorie teatrali*, 411.

35 Publicity surrounding *La finta pazza* at the Novissimo in 1640/41 suggests that that opera played to full houses throughout the season, but that seems to be an exception: "The public's desire to see it again never ended; and thus, however many times it was repeated, the place was crowded with people, and many were led to curse their own laziness when they arrived and had to leave because they could not find any place to sit." See Rosand, *Opera*, 97.

36 According to Giovanni Legrenzi in a letter of 24 Dec. 1678, an opera at S. Luca had played more than once to houses of "only thirty or forty bollettini at the most, something that you never see here anymore" ("mentre hanno a quest'hora recitato più d'una volta con solo trenta o quaranta bollettini al più, cosa che qui non s'è più veduta"); Monaldini, *Orto dell'Esperidi*, 351. The work was that of the neophytes Camillo Badoer and Giovanni Battista Tomasi. On Badoer, see chap. 5.

37 ASV, AN, Atti, b. 1049, f. 94, 9 Sept. 1641.

38 ASV, SGSM, b. 112, account book 1651/52, f. 30; b. 113, account book 1654/55, f. 46; and b. 112, account book 1657/58, f. 41.

sogeriscano a scena") were given tickets at S. Moisè in the 1666/67 season.[39] It must also have been standard for the members of the management to receive them, as well as the theater owners.[40] Marco Mozzoni's agreement with Girolamo Barbieri (his partner at S. Luca) granted him twenty-four bollettini over the season,[41] while Francesco Piva, the impresario at SS. Giovanni e Paolo, accused his associate Iseppo Zolio of bringing fifteen or twenty people with him free of charge each time *Medoro* (1658/59) was performed.[42]

One curious discrepancy in the documents raises some doubts about the actual attendance at these productions, despite the precision of Faustini's record-keeping. In the account book for the 1657 season, Faustini records ticket sales and scagni rentals totaling £23,965,[43] but the figure for these sales used by the partners to balance the books at the end of the season is considerably higher, £32,161.[44] It is possible that a final tally showed that there had been a consistent undercounting of ticket sales, but the difference is otherwise inexplicable. In the discussion that follows, we use the detailed figures reported in the account books (in the absence of any others). Although they may not represent all those who actually purchased or received tickets, it is reasonable to assume they all probably differ from the real numbers in approximately the same manner, and that the comparisons of night-to-night and year-to-year attendance remain valid.

None of these seven operas, including the most successful ones, played to full houses every night, and operas by more famous composers (such as Cavalli) did not necessarily do better than those by composers with lesser reputations. Even when one can compare figures for different operas performed at a single theater (that is, with the same capacity) however, the numbers must reflect all different sorts of circumstances (both internal and external) that contributed to rising and falling attendance. Performers perceived as inferior might have reduced the crowds, but sometimes factors other than the quality of the work or the fame of its creators and performers could have contributed to audience interest. One case in point is the comparison between Ziani's *L'incostanza trionfante* and Cavalli's *Antioco* in two successive years (see figures 5 and 6 in appendix 7). *L'incostanza* opened to an audience of at least 647 (about half in the boxes and half in the parterre[45]), compared to *Antioco*'s 533, most likely owing to the curiosity surrounding the theater's new dedication to opera.[46] The paid bollettini figures for the second per-

39 "a quelli che sogeriscano a scena"; ASV, Ospedali e luoghi pii, no. 37 B. Heredità Virginia Camuffi, ff. 10–11.

40 For example, at S. Moisè in 1665/66, the owners received two bollettini for each performance (ASV, AN, Atti, b. 3509, f. 860, 17 Oct. 1665).

41 ASV, Inquisitori di stato, b. 914, 2 July 1665. This document was published by Worsthorne, *Venetian Opera*, 8–9, and Giazotto, "Guerra dei palchi," 469–70.

42 ASV, GP, Scritture e risposte, b. 185, fasc. 72, f. 30, 24 July 1660.

43 ASV, SGSM, b. 112, account book 1657/58, f. 56.

44 ASV, SGSM, b. 101, unnumbered. For a discussion of the balance sheet, see chap. 3.

45 The percentage of the paid audience in the parterre appears to have ranged from a high of about 50 percent to a low of around 20 percent, based on Faustini's figures.

46 While it seems unlikely that Silvia Manni's appearance in *L'incostanza trionfante* would have created an undue amount of interest (especially as her presence in Venice between 1645 and 1657 is

formance of *L'incostanza* were still high: the 469 sold exceeded all but the premiere of *Antioco*; this trend continued for most of the run of the two operas. Another curiosity may have contributed to sales of *L'incostanza* once the season was underway. As we saw in chapter 5, a controversy arose concerning the libretto, with accusations of tampering and subterfuge in the printing of the text. In any event, Cavalli's reputation and skill as a composer did not result in improved sales at the box office for *Antioco*.

Four years earlier, operas by Ziani and Cavalli had also played in consecutive years, with far different results. Ziani's *Eupatra* (appendix 7, figure 3) was performed thirty times, with 338 paid bollettini collected on the opening night, and a significant drop-off thereafter. Cavalli's *Erismena* (appendix 7, figure 4) played thirty-two times, to a consistently larger crowd: seven showings of *Erismena* had audiences over 200 paid spectators, compared with three for Ziani's work, and only once were fewer than 100 paid bollettini collected for *Erismena*, as opposed to six times with *Eupatra*. One factor could have been the relative popularity of the competing theater's offering: as we shall see below, rumors circulated about the poor quality of *Statira*, performed at SS. Giovanni e Paolo in the same season as *Erismena*'s run at S. Aponal. We should also note, moreover, that the appearance of Anna Renzi, the most lauded singer of opera during the previous decade, failed to boost sales for *Eupatra* in any extraordinary manner (other than perhaps on the first night).

One final comparison comes from the accounting of the receipts for *Calisto* and *Eritrea*, both performed in the 1651/52 season (appendix 7, figures 1 and 2). The most surprising figures (especially given the modern-day success of *Calisto*), are those of the opening nights. The paid bollettini for the two operas are noted as 232 and 284 respectively, far below the 338 and 326 of *Eupatra* and *Erismena*. Perhaps the absence of the ailing lead alto castrato, Bonifacio Ceretti, who would die just days later, kept audiences away (word of his absence and the possible use of a less-skilled replacement would have spread quickly among the opera-going public of Venice, whether or not officially announced). Alternatively, the operatic audiences could have found the subject matter of the opera—one steeped in issues of female desire—troubling, especially during the Advent season, when most of the performances took place.[47] The opera continued to be poorly received, with paid attendance reaching a low point for the sixth and seventh performances, when barely more than fifty tickets were sold, and it closed after only eleven performances.[48]

Several of Faustini's lists supply dates, permitting an analysis of the spacing between performances. During the early part of the season a day or more of rest often separates the performances, while toward the end of Carnival the opera was

---

undocumented), some may have been curious to see her development as a singer. On Manni's performances as a young girl in Venice, see B. Glixon, "Scenes from the Life."

47 On *Calisto* and the myth of female pleasure, see Heller, *Emblems of Eloquence*, chapter 5.

48 It is not known how the impresario decided how long the first opera in a two-opera season would run. Whatever plans might have been made before the season began, they would need to be flexible, so that the change could happen sooner, in the event of an unsuccessful work like *Calisto*, or later, if the first opera was unusually well received.

mounted continuously, or nearly so (in part because patricians were permitted, during this period, to wear masks outdoors, and thus felt freer to attend public entertainments); the rhythm of the season, then, built to a climax. The patterns in the extant data suggest two possible systems for scheduling performances in the early and middle parts of the season. In one, seen in *L'incostanza trionfante* (appendix 7, figure 5), performances appear simply to have been scheduled for every third night.[49] For most of the other seasons, on the other hand, the scheduling may have been based in part on attendance: when paid attendance dropped, a larger gap between performances usually ensued, and the succeeding performance almost always showed a jump in ticket sales. Perhaps the performers needed the extra time in order to to learn new or changed music that was introduced in hopes of better pleasing the declining audience. Another possibility is that the bollettini were not dated (see above), but were good for the next performance regardless of date, and that the impresario waited until sufficient tickets had been sold before posting the cartello and scheduling a performance.[50] It is also conceivable that the impresario simply delayed performances in the hopes that demand would increase if the market were less flooded.

Faustini's data regarding the continuous performances at the end of carnival are supported by the remarks of the Savoyard ambassador, who mediated a dispute between the Duke of Savoy and the management of SS. Giovanni e Paolo. As we saw earlier, the Duke wanted two of his singers to return to Turin before the end of Carnival, and the ambassador explained how their departure would signal the ruin of the season because of the typical rhythm that the performances followed, described above:

> The usual thing is that in these last weeks of Carnival they perform in the said theater every night, so that closing it because of the absence of these two singers would see the company of partners lose between 7,000 or 8,000 ducats before Lent, at least from what the said two musicians tell me, therefore bringing great damage and total extermination of all of the company . . . and complete ruin of the said partners, who draw in more money as the end of Carnival approaches (given the freedom to wear masks, which is granted from today until Lent) than they did previously, and therefore until now they have only performed three nights maximum per week, and not every evening as they will do from now [5 February] until Ash Wednesday [23 February].[51]

49 An unusual gap of five days occurred in the performances of *L'incostanza trionfante* following a criminal incident involving the lead castrato, Giovanni Antonio Cavagna (between 20 Feb. and 26 Feb. 1658). See chapter 7, n. 67.

50 The bollettino for S. Giovanni Grisostomo reproduced in Rosand, *Opera*, 394, is, in fact, undated. See n. 25.

51 "Essendo il solito (com'è vero) ch'in quest'ultime settimane del carnovale si recita in ditto teatro tutte le sere, onde chiudendosi esso per mancanza di quest due parti verebbe la compagnia de gl'interessati a perdere da sette in otto milla ducati sin'a Quaresima per quello detti due musici dicono, onde essendo un pregiudicio totale ed esterminio di tutta la compagnia . . . total danno di detti interessati, i quali tirano più denari nell'avicinarsi del carnovale al fine, attesa la libertà delle maschere concessa da hoggi sin'a Quaresima, che non tiravano prima, e perciò sin'adesso non hanno mai recitato, che tre volte al più la settimana, e non ogni sera come faranno d'adesso sino al dì delle ceneri." Published in Viale Ferrero, "Repliche a Torino," 161–62. The letter is dated 5 Feb., a little more than two weeks before the end of carnival on 22 Feb. 1667. The opera, however, did continue through the end of Carnival, despite the singers' departure: Camillo Martinengo Cesaresco reports attending a performance on Sunday, 20 Feb. (ASF, MP, filza 1572, f. 373, 26 Feb. 1667).

The other list of ticket receipts that survives for this period comes from the Teatro S. Luca during the 1668/69 season, when the company presented Cesti's *Argia* (appendix 7, figure 7).[52] The records show thirty-five performances, with paid bollettini ranging from a high of 962 (probably near capacity for that theater) for the first performance to a low of 228 on the seventeenth. The numbers flagged during the middle of the run, as nine straight performances (numbers 15 through 23) saw fewer than 300 paid attendees in the audience. Unfortunately, no dates accompany these numbers, so that we do not know how many days separated the consecutive audiences of 229 and 589 for the twenty-third and twenty-fourth nights.

Failure and Success at the Box Office

It is, perhaps, a commonplace that Venetian impresarios strove to satisfy the public. Ellen Rosand has chronicled the musings of a succession of librettists who begged the understanding of "critics" as they made accommodations to the prevailing tastes of the time.[53] We have seen, in particular, how Faustini's company decided against presenting Giovanni Faustini's *Medea placata* when the rehearsals proved unpromising. The body of Venetian librettos shows some signs of attempts to cater to the audience; we mentioned earlier changes to such works as *Eupatra* and *Le fortune di Rodope e Damira*, where comic scenes were added in later printings. Often, however, the librettos tend to form a rather homogeneous mix, offering us little substantive evidence of the reception of the various works. Anecdotal evidence, however, occasionally shows how an opera could be received very badly indeed, and wreak significant damage on a company's resources.

We alluded earlier to problems surrounding three different operas. A letter of Giovanni da Mosto has been often cited regarding the failure of the maiden opera of the Teatro S. Luca, Castrovillari's *Pasife*. Another operatic disaster transpired in 1666 at S. Cassiano, with the performance of Matteo Noris and Giovanni Antonio Boretti's *Zenobia*. As we saw in chapter 5, the opera closed during its first night. Boretti's offering the next year at S. Moisè, *Alessandro amante*, fared somewhat better, but it was not a rousing success. Documents discovered by Irene Alm provide bollettini counts for six nights, with attendees falling from a high of 392 on opening night, to seventy-two, and then to fifty-one. One witness in the case, regarding the payment of the prima donna's wages, stated that for each of the last few performances only twenty to twenty-five tickets were sold.[54] Although S. Moisè was a small theater, these numbers were disappointing, and could hardly sustain the company. Even a composer such as Cavalli could experience a less than enthusiastic audience. As we saw earlier, *Calisto* (1651) was performed only eleven times, with fewer than sixty people in the audience for two of the nights.

Success and failure are, of course, relative. In 1656 Cavalli's *Statira*, according to one correspondent, was playing to audiences smaller than expected:

52 Vcg, Archivio Vendramin, b. 42 F 6/1–6 [49], no. 20, 13 Apr. 1669, reproduced in Rosand, *Opera*, 197.

53 Rosand, "In Defense of the Venetian Libretto."

54 ASV, Ospedali e luoghi pii, no. 37 B, Heredità Virginia Camuffi.

Giovanni Grimani's opera in Venice is going so badly that I don't doubt that it will finish up badly . . . they say it is melancholic. The first evening they took in 832 boletini, the second 362; they have suspended the performances to revive it with some arias. But for me, I doubt that they can do much, because once discredited, the merchandise would struggle to regain approval. Signor Giovanni, still tormented by gout, is enraged about it, and he is right, because if he had been about he would have sensed the opera's problems during the rehearsals.[55]

For Giovanni Grimani then, even an audience of more than 300 was a failure. Five years later, also at SS. Giovanni e Paolo, Aureli and Sartorio's *Gl'amori infrutuosi* did not please the public, yet sales of bollettini were over 400 a night.[56] On the other hand, the second opera that season, with the same company of singers, Beregan and Ziani's *Annibale in Capua*, was a great success: sales were as high as 900 per night, and tickets were in such demand that people were arriving well before curtain time, presumably to be sure they could get in.[57]

The surviving data concerning tickets sold during particular seasons, however, give no indication of the number of *different* spectators, that is, if the audience was made up largely of new people each night or if there were repeat visitors. Certainly, many of the boxholders must have attended numerous times. However, it is likely that the occupants of a box varied somewhat from night to night, with family members, friends, and guests attending with, or in place of, the renter. Several letters of opera enthusiasts do indicate that many people viewed the opera a number of times, a practice that was key to the success of a season. The English merchant Robert Bargrave, in voicing his enthusiasm for Venetian opera, claimed to have seen the same work, probably *Erismena*, sixteen times,[58] and the agent of

---

55 "L'oppera del signor Giovanni Grimani a Venetia riesce così male, che dubito non faccia le male fini, dicono esser melenconica, fecero la prima sera boletini 832, la seconda 362, hano suspeso la recita, per veder di ravivarla con delle ariete, ma per me dubito che farano puoco perche la mercantia, una volta screditata, stenta a rimetersi. Il Signor Giovanni travagliato ancora dalla gotta n'arabia, et ha raggione, perché se lui era in piede, dalle prove n'harebbe conosciuto il diffetto." ASFe, AB, b. 322, f. 214[r-v], letter of 2 Feb. 1656, Maggio d'Italia; see Monaldini, *Orto dell'Esperidi*, 112. The writer's assertion that new ariettas were to be added is substantiated by the survival in at least one copy of the libretto (in the Zeno collection in Vnm) of a supplement containing eight new arias, two duets, and some additions to the second act intermedio.

56 ASFe, AB, b. 331, f. 153, Venice, 29 Jan. 1660 m.v., letter from Carlo Danzetta; see Monaldini, *Orto dell'Esperidi*, 153.

57 Giovanni da Mosto writes that "le persone si vanno accomodare a 23 hore," that is, one hour before sundown. Da Mosto, "Uomini e cose," 117. On another occasion (see below) Skippon says the opera began at two hours after sunset. The issue of the starting and ending times of operas in seventeenth-century Venice is still uncertain; the forthcoming *Calendar of Venetian Opera*, by Selfridge-Field, will address the matter in some detail.

58 Tilmouth ("Music on the Travels," 156) suggests that these sixteen performances were at SS. Giovanni e Paolo (although he misunderstood the more veneto dating and thought the opera was *Artemisia*, performed the year before, rather than *Statira*). However, since *Statira* was apparently somewhat of a failure and may not have been performed that many times (see above) and *Erismena* was a considerable success, Bargrave's enthusiastic remarks make it more likely that it was the latter opera he enjoyed.

the Duke of Brunswick remarked that he and the librettist Pietro Dolfin "go almost every evening to the opera at San Zuane, e Polo."[59] The competition among the theaters even encouraged theater hopping: in 1667 Camillo Martinengo Cesaresco described how one night he went to see one act of *Dori* at SS. Giovanni e Paolo, and then moved over to S. Luca to catch the last scene of *La caduta di Elio Seiano*.[60]

A NIGHT AT THE OPERA: MORE THAN MUSICAL DRAMA

While hearing the music and watching the spectacle must have been one of the primary reasons for attending the opera, the atmosphere was quite different from the silence and respect expected in a modern theater. In 1670 Francesco Maria Massi reminded his employer, Johann Friedrich, Duke of Brunswick, of the typical sights and sounds: "After *Dori* we will have the performance of Signor Nicola's opera [*Heraclio*]. . . Your Serene Highness can picture the usual courtesies, the little gatherings of women here and there; the noise of the keys for the palchi; kowtowing, rivalries, people coming together, [others] drawing apart, and activities of every sort, tender gestures, confusions; pleasurable incidents . . ."[61] Letters such as this make it clear that attending the opera provided entertainment of different sorts, and was a social activity as much as a cultural one. People of various stations might come together, whether in the parterre or in a box. We wrote above of the ambassadors' privileges regarding boxes, which in some part compensated them for the many social restrictions in their lives. One letter, however, suggests that at the opera such restrictions were sometimes ignored. Leonardo Villeré, the representative of the Duke of Parma in Venice, wrote in 1657: "I was invited by [the Patriarch of Aquileia] to go to see the opera; being seated in a box I found myself between Procurator Viaro and one of the Patriarch's brothers. Despite the regulations of the Republic that one should not talk with the Doge's ministers, we talked together throughout the duration of the opera."[62] Such activities must have remained a staple of diplomatic life, as a French ambassador in 1679 explained to a

---

59 "Andiamo quasi ogni sera all'opera di San Zuane, e Polo." HVsa, AK, Cal. Br. 22, Nr. 627 II, 7 Feb. 1670.

60 ASF, MP, filza 1572, f. 373, 26 Feb. 1667.

61 "A questa Dori, succederà la recita del dramma del Signor Nicola. . . . Vostra Altezza Serenissima può figurarsi le solite sollecitudini, di conventicole di dame di qua, conventicole di la; rumori di chiavi de palchi; preminenze, gare, unioni, scarrocciamenti, e pratiche di tutte le sorti, gratie, confusioni; piacevoli accidenti." HVsa, AK, Cal. Br. 22, Nr. 627, f. 224, letter of Francesco Maria Massi, 26 Dec. 1670. We would like to thank Colleen Reardon and Nello Barbieri with their assistance with this colorful passage, in which many of the descriptive terms can be interpreted in a number of ways. Another portion of this letter is published in Rosand, *Opera*, 441.

62 "Fui dal medesimo [Patriarcha eletto d'Aquileia] invitato d'andare a veder l'opera in musica, et essendovi stato in un palchetto, mi trovai fra il Signor Procurator Viaro, et un de' fratelli di esso Patriarcha, e là, nonostante le costituzioni della Repubblica di non parlar con ministri di Prencipe, ragionassimo insieme tanto quanto durò l'opera." ASP, Carteggio farnesiano e borbonico estero: Venezia, Vicenza, Verona, Padova, b. 118, f. 39/4, 13 Jan. 1657.

friend that opera-going facilitated the discovery of secrets that would have been difficult to come by under normal circumstances.[63]

A regular feature of a night at the opera was the presence of sellers of wine and pastries: theater rental contracts often specify the destination of income from the *caneva* (or winecellar) and the *scaleter*, or vendor of *buzoladi*, doughnut-shaped pastries. Few anecdotes from this time, however, comment on eating and drinking. Later edicts from the Magistrato alle pompe (the enforcers of Venetian sumptuary law) prohibited the bringing of picnic dinners to the opera; perhaps the wealthy noblemen were using the occasion to display fancy silver and china, flaunting their wealth in a way disapproved of by that severe magistracy.[64]

Skippon provides us a rare glimpse by an outsider of the dress and demeanor of the audience: "When any thing pleas'd very well, the company cried out, Bien, Bien! The gentlewomen came in masquerade; but when they were in their boxes, they pull'd off their vizards: they wear broad falling lac'd bands. The noblemen were indifferently silent." Besides eating, drinking, and talking during the performance, there was, as Skippon observed, at least one other aspect of audience behavior that would certainly not be acceptable in the twenty-first century. He concluded his remarks about the audience by affirming that "those in the boxes did not spit so often into the pit, as they do at the common plays."[65]

Violence at the Opera

Attending an opera was a social event quite unlike almost anything else in seventeenth-century Venice (except, perhaps, for gambling at the *ridotto*). Large numbers of Venetians, both patricians and non-patricians, along with foreigners, came together at a set time, in a small, enclosed space, and, in general, stayed in fixed and publicly known locations, where they could be more easily found and approached than at almost any other time. Security within the theater was provided, as best we can tell, only by the men at the door and by the fattor (who may have hired assistants), who could probably be relatively easily distracted or bribed to permit access to the corridors behind the boxes, where servants of the boxholders may also have had access. This situation provided opportunities for a variety of violent events, including brawls and attempted murder.

The crowded conditions in a theater could cause a simple argument to grow into a dangerous and threatening event. In 1648, during a performance of Cavalli's *Giasone* at S. Cassiano, according to one report, "twenty-five or thirty Venetian noblemen who were in disagreement drew arms." Fortunately, "the only damage that resulted was that all of the spectators, thrown into disorder, were compelled to flee onto the stage because of the uproar that was going on; after things had quieted

---

63 Worsthorne, *Venetian Opera*, 11 (from Mercure galant, Apr. 1679).

64 Bistort, *Magistrato alle pompe*, 233.

65 Skippon, *Journey*, 507.

down, the opera concluded without other disturbance."[66] According to the same report, at another performance of the same opera an enterprising assassin surreptitiously tried to shoot the Veronese Marquis Canossa through the keyhole of his box at S. Cassiano, wounding him in the shoulder.

The crowds and lack of security made it possible for men to bring firearms into the theater, where they were likely to encounter old enemies, with predictable results. In December 1654, Piero Emo, who had unsuccessfully attacked Zuane Badoer at his home, tracked him down, with the help of some friends, to the Teatro S. Aponal. There, presumably before the victim had taken his seat, and was still masked, they attempted to reveal his face, and then fired several shots and also drew their swords or daggers. They endangered many spectatators, and wounded an innocent bystander.[67] In January 1671, the patrician Zuane Mocenigo, who had a continuing disagreement with two brothers of the Foscarini family, brought two pistols to S. Salvatore, where there was "as usual, a large crowd of the nobility," and fired at both of them, wounding one of them seriously.[68] Acts of violence could result in a theater's closure for several days by order of the Capi of the Council of Ten.

THE PATRONAGE OF VENETIAN OPERA

The discussion of the audience inevitably begs consideration of whether seventeenth-century Venetian opera was, as musicologists have long defined it, "public opera," whether, in light of its financial structures, it might be called "commercial opera," or whether, as some scholars have argued, it was really just a modified form of "court opera."[69] Reaching a conclusion on this issue requires answering several questions that while seemingly simple, are, as the preceding chapters have shown, actually quite complex: Who commissioned the operas? For what audience were they intended? Who paid for them? For the early seventeenth-century court operas, these questions all had essentially the same answer: the ruler in whose court the work was performed. While a courtier or another member of the aristocracy might well have organized the spectacle, it was the ruler who had to authorize it. The performances themselves were attended by a number of people, and

---

66 "fu parimente messo mano all'armi da 25 ò 30 nobili veneziani venuti fra di loro a contesa; senza essere succeduto altro danno, che messo in scompilio tutti li spettatori astretti di fuggire sopra del palco delle scene per il tumulto che si faceva, ed acquietasi si finì poi l'opera senza altro disturbo." ASF, MP, filza 3024, ff. 363ᵛ–364, Venice, 13 Feb. 1648 ab incarnatione (the Florentine year began on 25 Mar., so the year would be 1649 according to modern reckoning).

67 ASV, CD, Criminal, filza 87, 22 Dec. 1654.

68 ASV, CD, Criminal, filza 103, 5 Jan. 1670 m.v.

69 Prominent among those who argue that Venetian opera was a form of court opera are Bianconi and Walker, who write that "through the separation of these two roles [promoter-proprietor and impresario] the feudal relations of production, chased out the door, come back in by the window. Thus at Venice, too, the real addressee and 'owner' of the opera is, as at Rome and at Reggio Emilia, the ruling class." Bianconi and Walker, "Production, Consumption," 241.

it was, of course, desirable that all of them be pleased, but the only audience that really mattered was the ruler himself. Moreover, unless the production were a gift from a family member or friend, it was the ruler who footed the bills. Performances of this type clearly fit into what Claudio Annibaldi has termed aulic or institutional patronage: they were designed to support or enhance the status of the marquis or duke in his role as ruler.[70]

For Venetian opera, none of these questions have such straightforward answers, and, in fact, they must be considered separately for the theaters in which the operas were performed, for the librettos on which they were based, and for the performed musical works themselves. In some respects, because of the developing and changing systems of finance and production, the answers differ in part for nearly every opera.

The Libretto

While in some cases a libretto was requested or commissioned by an impresario (although with no promise of payment), in others it was the poet himself who first created the work ("on spec," as we might say today), and then sought a way for it to be set to music and performed. In the first instance, the patronage relationship is relatively clear (leaving aside for the moment the question of whether the impresario himself was acting on behalf of a patron), whereas in the second instance the term patronage might not even be considered relevant. Complicating the issue for both cases, however, is the factor of the dedication. In his discussion of the music-printing business in the Renaissance and early Baroque eras, Annibaldi argues that the presence of the dedication places the work squarely in the tradition of aulic patronage, in which the composer offers a work that confirms the status of the dedicatee and at the same time places himself under the paternalistic protection of a high-ranking personage.[71] While most Venetian librettos are, in fact, dedicated to people higher in rank than the poet, there are notable exceptions, such as that of Giovanni Faustini's *Doriclea* to his neighbor and friend, the physician Mauritio Tirelli.

According to Annibaldi's principles, the dedicatee of a book is the true audience for that work (those who purchase the book and see the dedication are, in effect, witnesses to both sides of the patronage process, observing that the creator is under the protection of the person whose high status has been affirmed). In the case of an opera libretto, however, the issue of patronage is often clouded: in many cases, the dedicatee has no connection, financial, artistic, political, or even geographical, with the ultimate destination of the libretto, namely the musical performance in a Venetian theater.[72] The author must try, therefore, to satisfy the

---

70 Annibaldi first explained his concept of aulic patronage in his *Musica e il mondo*, 9–42, and refined it in "Towards a Theory" and "Tipologia." See also id., "Uno 'spettacolo.'"

71 Annibaldi, "Tipologia," 68, esp. n. 21.

72 There are, of course, cases where the dedicatee is involved in the production, in one way or another. Notable examples include Vettor Grimani Calergi and Guglielmo Van Kessel (see chap. 1).

needs (whether aesthetic or social) of the dedicatee, while at the same time being sure to produce a work that will provide the basis for a successful opera. Unlike the case of a free-standing literary work, which is sold independently, the number of copies of the libretto distributed is dependent primarily upon the size of the audience at performances, and the number of different people who attended them. It does the dedicatee little good to have a literary work in his name that is a failure at the box office (although libretto collectors outside Venice might be unaware of the work's lack of success in the theater). If the librettist fails to keep the broader public in mind when creating his work, the result might well be that fewer people would see the dedicatee's name in print, and many might associate the literary work with its theatrical failure, perhaps negating the effect of reading his name in large type accompanied by lavish praise.

The Commissioning of the Opera

Who, in the absence of a prince and his court, actually commissioned an opera in seventeenth-century Venice? Someone (or some group of people) had to select the libretto, the composer, the singers, the craftsmen, and even the orchestra and stagehands. In some of the earliest productions, those run by what we have called a self-contained company, there was no outsider at all who commissioned the work: many of the major choices were dictated by the makeup of the company, which might include composer, librettist, scene designer, choreographer, and one or more lead singers. After the first few seasons, this model ceased to be the norm, to be replaced by two others. In one, the librettist or another creator was the impresario (sometimes in partnership with another creator or with one or more investors). In the other, the impresario was an "outsider" (although, such as in the case of Marco Faustini, there might be some connections to the creative team). In these models, the impresario made the decisions, selecting the libretto as a starting point, and hiring the creative and performing team. The principal question here is whether he acted for himself or on behalf of a noble patron, as has been argued by several scholars. Annibaldi, for example, writes that "the role of the impresarios of opera theaters was simply that of managers of theatrical activities intended for and promoted by the local nobility."[73]

It is impossible to answer this question definitively, but the evidence suggests that in most cases the impresario made the choices himself or with his business partners (especially when operating a theater such as the Novissimo or S. Aponal, without a noble owner), although it cannot be denied that he and his partners must have kept in mind the tastes of the theater owner and boxholders, as well as the audience as a whole.[74] In at least one case, the rental contract for the theater

---

73 "Il ruolo degli impresari dei teatri d'opera cittadini fu semplicemente quello di gestori di attività spettacolari destinate al patriziato locale e da esso medesimo promosse." Annibaldi, "Tipologia," 74.

74 While it is certainly conceivable that an impresario may have acted as a figurehead for others who wished to remain out of the limelight, if these secretive persons leave no traces of their activities in the archives, and do not appear as dedicatees of librettos, such a suggestion must remain purely speculative.

expressly gave complete authority to the impresario, guaranteeing that the owner would not interfere.[75] Also difficult to determine is whether the impresario acted on behalf of patrons who remained hidden. This has often been suggested regarding the Novissimo, which Bianconi and Walker and Rosand, followed by others, have considered to have functioned on behalf of the Accademia degli Incogniti (see chap. 4). While it is undeniable that three of the six men who wrote librettos for the theater, Giulio Strozzi (*La finta pazza*), Scipione Herrico (*Deidamia*), and Maiolino Bisaccioni (*Ercole in Lidia*), were Incogniti,[76] and that several of the operas reflect some of the views of the academy, there is absolutely no documentary evidence that either the academy as a body, or any of its members, had any financial ties to the theater before Bisaccioni's attempts to purchase it late in its history (see chap. 4). On the other hand, there is no doubt that for the early years Girolamo Lappoli bore the financial responsibilties and acted as impresario, although he may have done so on behalf of either Strozzi, the librettist of the first production, Francesco Sacrati, the composer, or the scene designer and engineer Giacomo Torelli, for whose spectacular inventions the theater may in fact have been built. It cannot be determined which of the four men (alone or in partnership) made the artistic decisions for the theater.

Certainly, an impresario-librettist like Giovanni Faustini acted on his own behalf when he decided to produce an opera on his own libretto, and it is equally clear that Marco Faustini continued in the role of impresario into the 1660s at SS. Giovanni e Paolo primarily to bring his brother's librettos to the stage. Further, while the elder Faustini employed some of the personnel who had been working at the new theater under other impresarios before his arrival, he also continued to select composers, singers, and craftsmen with whom he was familiar, and had, in many cases, worked with at other theaters. With a few exceptions (such as when Ettor Tron was a partner in the company running his theater in the 1640s), there is little evidence during this period that theater owners had a direct influence on the impresarios running their theaters, and regarding many owners there are few hints that they were really interested in opera as an art form (as opposed to a commercial activity that would guarantee that the rent on their theater was paid and that their name would be kept in the public eye throughout the carnival season[77]). The Grimani family is a notable exception to this pattern: Giovanni Grimani was actively involved in recruiting singers for SS. Giovanni e Paolo, which he owned, and may have even concerned himself with some of the day-to-day management of the theater. That also seems to have often been the case during the reign of his successors as owners, his nephews Giovanni Carlo and Vicenzo.[78] They were involved with the resignation of Marco

75 ASV, AN, Atti, b. 2983, ff. 1110ᵛ–1114ᵛ. The contract was for the rental of S. Luca from Andrea Vendramin by Antonio Boldù in 1660.

76 The others were Marc'Antonio Tirabosco (*Alcate*), Vincenzo Nolfi (*Bellerofonte*), and Niccolò Enea Bartolini (*Venere gelosa*).

77 While keeping the theater open and in the public consciousness might be construed as producing the same result as direct aulic patronage, this is undermined by the fact that the theaters were often referred to by their parish names, without reference to their owners.

78 For the Grimani brothers as impresarios, see Saunders, "Repertoire of a Venetian Opera House."

Faustini as their impresario, and with the changes in repertory for the 1667/68 season, substituting a work by a younger composer, Boretti, for one by the distinguished but much older Cavalli, and, as Mauro Calcagno has shown, insisting on a libretto without some of the troubling political implications of the work planned by Faustini.[79] It is still unclear, however, whether they initiated these changes to satisfy their own desires, or out of concern that a libretto offensive to some sectors of the patrician audience might damage their own status as newly adult noblemen, or because they were concerned that Faustini's choices would not attract a large enough paying audience—that is, whether they were acting, perhaps uniquely for this period of Venetian opera, as princes employing aulic patronage, or whether their interests were, as with most owners, exclusively commercial.

The Audience for the Opera

Many traditional views on patronage have portrayed the artist's goal as satisfying the personal tastes of the patron. In Annibaldi's view, on the other hand, the artist's purpose was to create something that reaffirmed the patron's status, either as ruler or as humanist. In order to understand whether either of these approaches describes the Venetian situation (in which there is no single courtly patron), we must first determine to whom the operas were directed. As with so much else, there is no easy answer. Certainly, the creative team needed to satisfy the impresario who selected them. The impresario, in turn, had a particular audience in mind, and selected the creators who could, in his opinion, produce something that would make money by pleasing large numbers of spectators. Over the long term, the impresario had to guarantee to the boxholders that suitable entertainment would be provided for them, but these patricians and others attended the opera as much for social reasons as anything else. They both rented and renewed their boxes without any knowledge of the works to be performed, or even, necessarily, the name of the impresario. Moreover, in some cases, if they failed to renew their boxes, it was not the impresario who would suffer directly, but the theater owner, to whom the box rental fees were paid. Of course, an impresario who drove away boxholders would probably be forced out by the owner, so that he did have to keep this part of the audience in mind. For the impresario and his company (and his investors), however, the real key to financial success was satisfying the ticket purchasers, daily-ticket buyers and boxholders alike. As we have seen, since box-rental income was essentially stable, the relative financial success of a season (that is, whether the deficit was manageable or not, since profit was not really expected) was determined by nightly ticket sales.

Bianconi and Walker, followed by Annibaldi, as discussed above, argue that Venetian opera is really only an extension of the court opera situation, since the boxholders, whom they view as the principal financial underpinning, were patricians.[80] In Annibaldi's terminology, therefore, this represents aulic patronage, with

79 See above and Calcagno, "Fonti, ricezione" and "Libretto and Its Discontents."

80 Bianconi and Walker, "Production, Consumption," 240–42; Annibaldi, *Musica e il mondo*, 220 (in his introduction to his Italian translation of Bianconi and Walker's article).

opera designed to reinforce the status of the patricians as nobles, worthy of standing alongside the rulers of other states. This is a reasonable conclusion to draw regarding opera performance in general (that is, the fact that operas were regularly presented in Venice placed the Republic alongside, and eventually, perhaps, above, the princely states), but not necessarily for individual operas, nor, even in a broader sense, for the nature of the texts and music of Venetian opera. Although Rosand and Heller have shown that many operas, especially those of the 1640s, contained elements specifically designed to reinforce the myth of Venice—which would tend to confirm the above view—it is important to note that this myth was not the exclusive province of the patricians, but was also strongly held by members of the cittadino and merchant classes.[81]

If we accept the concept that the ticket-buying audience was essential to the financial survival of opera in Venice, then, as with so much discussed in this chapter, we must conclude that the audience for Venetian opera, that is, those whom the performances were designed to satisfy, was multifaceted. The impresario and his creative team had somehow to craft a performed work that satisfied, at one level or another (that is, socially, financially, or artistically), the wealthy theater owners, investors, and boxholders, and also the middle-class ticket buyers in the parterre. If any of these were dissatisfied, an opera, or a season, could fail.

The Financial Support for the Opera

As we discussed in part 1 of this book, the systems for financing opera in seventeenth-century Venice were complex and constantly changing. Since patronage is, in the end, about paying for a work of art, we will reexamine briefly the finances for the best-documented season during this period, 1657/58 at S. Cassiano (see table 11.4). For this season, Marco Faustini was one of three equal partners in the production company, along with the patricians Alvise Duodo and Marc'Antonio Correr.[82] Faustini himself rented the theater from the Tron family, and was sole beneficiary of the bulk of the boxes. The season was a relatively successful one (see above), and the income from the sale of tickets and scagni covered about 50 percent of the costs. Of this total, about one-third came from the audience in the parterre and two-thirds from those in the boxes. Most of the cost of production not met by ticket sales was made up by the three partners. Faustini's share, plus the theater rental, was balanced out by his income from the annual rental of boxes, and he may have made a profit, as well; Duodo and Correr would have paid out of their own pockets. While the basic financial arrangements in this case are quite

81 The strongly patriotic Accademia degli Incogniti included both patricians and cittadini (see chap. 4, n. 30). The scuole grandi, Venice's important confraternities, had among their chief goals the support of the honor of Venice; they were run by cittadini, and their membership was primarily cittadini and men from the working class. On this role of these confraternities, see Glixon, *Honoring God*, chapters 1 and 2.

82 A fourth partner, Polifilo Zancarli, had a more limited role: his investment was limited to 200 ducats.

TABLE 11.4. Financing of the 1657/58 Season at S. Aponal

A. Costs

Item	Cost (in ducats)	Percentage of total
Production	9,540	92%
Theater rental	840	8%
Total	10,380	100%

B. Funding

Source of funds	Allocated to production	Allocated to theater rental	Percent of total financing
Ticket and scagni sales	5,186 (54%)	—	50%
Printer	200 (2%)	—	2%
Polifilo Zancarli (personal funds)	200 (2%)	—	2%
Alvise Duodo (personal funds)	1,318 (14%)	—	13%
Marc'Antonio Correr (personal funds)	1,318 (14%)	—	13%
Marco Faustini (covered by box rental income)[a]	1,318 (14%)	840	20%
Totals	9,540	840	100%

[a] Faustini was solely responsible for paying the rental of the theater, but also received all of the rental from boxes (with the exception of those reserved for the theater owners). In addition to covering the theater rental and his portion of the costs of production, the box rental fees probably provided Faustini a profit of about 300 ducats.

clear, the same cannot be said for the relationship of financial support to the concept of patronage. Although the noble partners certainly held strong views about some of the singers, and they assisted with many negotiations, Faustini apparently made the final decisions regarding selection of the members of the creative and performing teams. Perhaps, having allied themselves with an impresario, they were content, for the most part, to make recommendations and then follow his lead, and to trust that his choices would reflect well on them, providing the same sort of satisfaction as direct patronage.

In some cases (the situation at the Novissimo is a prominent example), the financial support, in the final analysis, had nothing to do with either the usual concept of patronage or Annibaldi's revisionist ideas. The people who ended up paying many of the bills were not involved when the operas were produced, but came into the picture later on, to settle debts; indeed, those who were responsible for running the production (most notably the impresario, Girolamo Lappoli) managed to escape much of the financial responsibility (see chap. 4). At the time of the performances, many of those who had paid for the production, or who would settle the debts later on, were unknown to the audience. They were not patrons in the traditional sense, since the operas were not produced to please them, and they were not patrons in the sense discussed by Annibaldi, since their public status was in no way reinforced. In some cases their involvement can be explained as arising from some unfortunate business decisions and transferred debts. At other times, such people must have thought their actions worthwhile for the preservation of the operatic enterprise, even if it meant personal financial sacrifice with little to show for it.

Opera in Venice, then, had so many different sorts of patrons that perhaps the term "patronage" is not really applicable. The theater owner, the boxholders, the impresario, the investors and lenders, the dedicatee of the libretto, and the ticket-buying audience all mattered. In the traditional theory of patronage, the creators aimed to please the theatrical tastes of all of these groups and individuals, in an effort to maximize income. If we are to apply Annibaldi's theory of aulic patronage, the city of Venice itself perhaps best qualifies as patron: a successful operatic season reinforced the status of the city (and not just its patrician rulers) as the entertainment capital of Europe, equaling or bettering the efforts of the great duchies and kingdoms.[83]

In many ways, the overall financing of seventeenth-century Venetian opera resembles that of a modern opera house. A significant portion of the income derives from season ticket holders, especially those in the more expensive seats, but this is always supplemented, often heavily so, by grants from foundations or government agencies. From season to season, and from theater to theater in Venice, the financing varied, but we can safely say that all of the possible sources of income—annual box rentals, ticket sales, and contributions by wealthy supporters—were required to meet the high costs of this elaborate art form. Is it valid, therefore, to call opera in Venice "public opera"? Without a doubt, in the sense that anyone who could afford to buy a ticket could be admitted; if, however, the designation suggests opera entirely paid for by the ticket-buying audience, then the answer is "no," but such a restrictive definition would probably mean that no fully-staged opera ever has been, or will be, "public." On the other hand, if we define the term as opera designed to satisfy the tastes of the public, and whose financing depends on the sale of a large number of tickets to performances, then the answer is an unequivocal "yes." The poets, composers, artisans, businessmen, lawyers, and noblemen who took on the task of inventing the profession of impresario in mid-seventeenth-century Venice struggled to find ways to organize this complex undertaking and bring to the stage operas that pleased many segments of the Venetian population and the city's curious visitors. Although very few of them probably made much money, either for themselves or for their partners or investors, they can be said, as a group, to have been highly successful, blazing a trail that has enabled their successors to bring opera to the public stages of the world nearly 400 years after the opening of the first opera theaters in the Most Serene Republic of Venice.

---

83 Bianconi and Walker ("Production, Consumption," 241) argued for something similar, but with a narrower scope, when they wrote of the "ruling class (the Venetian aristocracy and merchants)" as proprietors of the theaters.

APPENDICES

A BRIEF CHRONICLE OF OPERA
PRODUCTIONS IN VENICE
FROM 1651 TO 1668

This appendix summarizes the operatic performances in Venice during the nearly two decades of Marco Faustini's activity as impresario. We list all those people whose creative or financial involvement in each production can be documented, including composers, librettists, singers (with their roles indicated in parentheses when these can be identified), artisans, and members of the management team, including impresarios and those who provided financial support.[1] The latter are listed in this chronicle in several different categories, although there is considerable overlap among them: the individual or team who directly managed the production is listed as impresario; partners are those individuals who shared the financial responsibilities and also had some involvement in the management; investors are those who participated financially, either through contributions or loans, but who did not actively participate in the production.

1650/51 (Carnival ends 21 February)

S. Aponal

Oristeo (libretto by Giovanni Faustini, dedicated to Alvise Duodo; music by Francesco Cavalli)
Rosinda (libretto by Giovanni Faustini; music by Francesco Cavalli)
Impresario: Giovanni Faustini (with Marco Faustini?)

SS. Apostoli

Gl'amori di Alessandro magno, e di Rossane (libretto by Giacinto Andrea Cicognini, dedicated to Guglielmo Van Kessel by Giovanni Burnacini, 24 January 1651; music by Francesco Lucio; first performance 25 January 1651?)
Impresario: Giovanni Burnacini
Investors: Guglielmo Van Kessel (by means of a loan)

---

1 Dedicatees' names are listed as they appear in the libretto. Singers for productions at Faustini's theaters are taken from ASV, SGSM, b. 112, account book 1651/52; ASV, SGSM, b. 112, account book 1657/58; ASV, SGSM, b. 113, account book 1654/55, partial entries for 1655/56; ASV, SGSM, b. 194, account book 1658/59; ASV, SGSM, b. 118, receipt book.

Singers: Caterina Maffei, Camillo detto Alcione, Francesco falsetto, Sebastiano Enno[2]
Machines: Giovanni Burnacini

S. Cassiano

Armidoro (libretto by Bortolo Castoreo, dedicated to Giovanni Francesco Zorzi, 20 January
1651; music by Gasparo Sartorio)
Impresario: Company of Bortolo Castoreo, Mattio di Grandi (and Rocco Maestri?)
Singers: Angela Lazaroni, Annetta Miani
Costumes: Mattio di Grandi

SS. Giovanni e Paolo

Alessandro vincitor di se stesso (libretto by Francesco Sbarra, dedicated to Leopoldo
Guglielmo, Arciduca d'Austria, by Giovanni Battista Balbi, 20 January 1651; music by An-
tonio Cesti)
Impresario: Giovanni Battista Balbi
Singers: Anna Maria Sardelli
Dances: Giovanni Battista Balbi
Scenery: Giovanni Battista Balbi[3]
Machines: Giovanni Battista Balbi

1651/1652 (Carnival ends 13 February)

S. Aponal

Calisto (libretto by Giovanni Faustini, dedicated to Marc'Antonio Corraro; music by
Francesco Cavalli; first performance 28 November 1651)
Eritrea (libretto by Giovanni Faustini, dedicated to Marc'Antonio Corraro by Giacomo
Batti [bookseller]; music by Francesco Cavalli; first performance 17 January 1652)
Impresario: Giovanni Faustini and Marco Faustini
Investors: Marc'Antonio Correr and Alvise Duodo
Singers: Margarita da Costa, Caterina Giani, Nina dal Pavon, Bonifacio Ceretti (did not
sing), Giulio Cesare Donati, Tomaso (Bovi), tenor di Carrara (Francesco Guerra?), Andrea
and Cristoforo Caresana, Lorenzo (Ferri?), Pellegrino, putella
Dances: Giovanni Battista Martini
Scenery: Simon Guglielmi
Machines: Anastasio marangon
Costumes: Paulo Morandi and others

SS. Apostoli

Erginda (libretto by Aurelio Aureli, dedicated to Marino Dall'Angelo; music by Gasparo
Sartorio)

---

2 For information regarding these singers, see B. Glixon, "Music for the Gods?"
3 In the libretto Balbi is named as the "inventore degli Apparati di Scene, Machine, e Balli" (creator
of the scenery, the machines, and the dances); no other artists are mentioned.

SS. Giovanni e Paolo

Cesare amante (libretto by Dario Varotari, based on an idea of Maiolino Bisaccioni, dedicatory ode to Giovanni Battista Cornaro dalla Piscopia; music by Antonio Cesti)
Singers: Antonio Fabris (as Gorgoglione)

1652/53 (Carnival ends 25 February)

S. Aponal

Pericle effeminato (libretto by Giacomo Castoreo, dedicated to M. Antonio Cornaro, 7 January 1653; music by Francesco Lucio)
Also the spoken plays *Astrilla* (Pietro Urbano) and, perhaps, *Eurimene* (Giacomo Castoreo)
Sets for *Eurimene* by Domenico Lazari (according to a dedicatory sonnet in the libretto)
Impresario: Company of Bortolo Castoreo, Annibale Basso, and Paulo Morandi

SS. Giovanni e Paolo

Helena rapita da Theseo (libretto by Giacomo Badoaro?; music by [Francesco Cavalli, doubtful])
Veremonda l'amazzone di Aragona ([libretto by Giulio Strozzi based on *Celio*, a libretto by Cicognini], dedicated to Sig. Cav.re di Gremonville by Giovanni Battista Balbi, 28 January 1652 [m.v.?]; music by Francesco Cavalli)
Impresario: Giovanni Battista Balbi
Singers: Jacopo Melani[4]
Dances: Giovanni Battista Balbi
Scenery: Giovanni Battista Balbi

1653/54 (Carnival ends 17 February)

S. Aponal

La guerriera spartana (libretto by Giacomo Castoreo, dedicated to Pietro Foscarini, 6 January 1654; music by Pietro Antonio Ziani)
Impresario: Company of Bortolo Castoreo and Annibale Basso
Singers: Anna Felicita Chiusi (as Chelidonida), Orsetta Parmine, Amato Riminuzzi

SS. Giovanni e Paolo

Ciro (libretto by Giulio Cesare Sorrentino, dedicated to Giorgio Guglielmo and Ernesto Augusto Duchi di Bransvich, e Luneburg by Giovanni Battista Balbi, 30 January 1653; music by Francesco Provenzale and Francesco Cavalli)
Impresario: Giovanni Battista Balbi
Dances: Giovanni Battista Balbi
Scenery: Giovanni Battista Balbi[5]

---

4 ASF, MP, filza 5451, f. 454, letter of 25 Oct. 1652.
5 Balbi is credited on the title page as the "direttore delle Scene, Machine, e Balli" (director of the scenery, machines, and the dances); no other artists are mentioned.

S. Moisè

Euridamante (libretto by Giacomo Dall'Angelo, dedicated to Alvise Mocenigo, 20 January 1654; music by Francesco Lucio)

1654/55 (Carnival ends 9 February)

S. Aponal

Eupatra (libretto by Giovanni Faustini, dedicated to Alvise Duodo by Bartolomeo Ginammi [printer]; music by Pietro Andrea Ziani; first performance 19 December 1654[6])
Impresario: Marco Faustini, with the assistance of Duodo (and Marc'Antonio Correr?)
Investors: Bortolo Pasinetto
Singers: Anna Renzi, Angelica Felice Curti (as Irene), Angela Angelotti, Lugretia Marconi, Filippo (Melani?) and his brother (Bortolo Melani?) Lodovico, Giacinto Zucchi, Antonio Draghi, Antonino Pio, Francesco Simi, Giovanni Sigonfredi da Pesaro; also in contract discussions, but did not perform: Antonio Fabris and Lorenzo Ferri
Dances: Giovanni Battista Martini
Scenery: Simon Guglielmi
Machines: Anastasio marangon
Costumes: Girolamo Savio, Francesco fenestrer, Paulo Morandi (and Nicolò Personé?)

SS. Giovanni e Paolo

Xerse (libretto by Nicolò Minato, dedicated to Marchese Cornelio Bentivoglio, 12 January 1654; music by Francesco Cavalli)
Singers: Pompeo Sabbatini[7]

1655/56 (Carnival ends 29 February)

S. Aponal

Erismena (libretto by Aurelio Aureli, dedicated to Giacomo Cavalli; music by Francesco Cavalli; first performance 30 December 1655)
Impresario: Marco Faustini
Investors or Partners: Simon Guglielmi, Paulo Morandi, and Bortolo Pasinetto
Singers: Angelica Felice Curti, Anna Felicita Chiusi, Orsetta Parmine, Giovanni Battista Veralli, Giacinto Zucchi, Amato Riminuzzi, Antonio Draghi, Girolamo Zorzi (as Vecchia), Stefano Costa, Zanetto Caliari, Pietro Veralli
Dances: Giovanni Battista Martini
Scenery: Simon Guglielmi
Costumes: Paulo Morandi

---

6 Date taken from ASV, SGSM, b. 113, account book 1654/55; only the dates of the first two performances are listed.

7 For part of the season. Monaldini, *Orto dell'Esperidi*, 81.

SS. Giovanni e Paolo

Statira (libretto by Giovanni Francesco Busenello, dedicated to Giovanni Grimani, 18 January 1655; music by Francesco Cavalli; score dated 4 October on first folio)
Singers: Caterina Porri, Giovanni Antonio Cavagna, probably Maddalena Ottonaina[8]

1656/57 (Carnival ends 13 February)

S. Aponal

Le fortune di Rodope e Damira (libretto by Aurelio Aureli, dedicated to Marc'Antonio Corraro and Luigi [Alvise] Duodo; music by Pietro Andrea Ziani)
Impresario: Marco Faustini
Investors or partners: (Marc'Antonio Correr and Alvise Duodo?)
Singers: Anna Maria Volea (as Rodope), Anna Renzi (as Damira), Carlo Mannelli (as Lerino), Giacinto Zucchi (as Creonte), Carlo Macchiati (as Nigrane), Antonio Draghi (as Bato), Pietro Cefalo (as Nerina), Raffaele Caccialupi (as Sicandro), Filippo Manin (as Brenno), Antonio Formenti (as Erpago)
Dances: Battista Artusi callegher
Scenery: Antonio Lech, Antonio Zanchi, and Giovanni Battista Recaldi
Machines: Gasparo Mauro and Francesco Santurini

SS. Giovanni e Paolo

Artemisia (libretto by Nicolò Minato, dedicated to Ferdinando Carlo, Arciduca d'Austria, 10 January 1656 [m.v.]; music by Francesco Cavalli)

1657/58 (Carnival ends 5 March)

S. Cassiano

L'incostanza trionfante overo il Theseo (libretto by Francesco Piccoli and others, dedicated to Prencipi Georgio Guglielmo, Gio. Federico, and Ernesto Augusto Duchi di Branswich, e Luneburgh by Andrea Giuliani [printer], 16 January 1658; music by Pietro Andrea Ziani; first performance 19 January 1658)
Impresario: Marco Faustini
Partners and investors: Marc'Antonio Correr, Alvise Duodo, Polifilo Zancarli
Singers: Ginevra Senardi[9] (as Fedra), Silvia Manni (as Anthiope), Caterina Perini (as Merope), Angelica Felice Curti (as Martesia), Giovanni Antonio Cavagna (as Theseo), Giovanni Agostino Poncelli (as Menesteo), Carlo Vittorio Rotari (as Pithidoro), Giacinto Zucchi (as Amfimedonte, Tifeo), Raffaele Caccialuppi (as Pallante), Antonino Pio (as Sentinella Amazone, la Fama), Antonio Formenti (as Sentinella Atheniese, Plutone, Morfeo), Giovanni Battista Abbatoni (as Egeo), Stefano Costa
Dances: Olivier Vigasio, Battista Artusi callegher, and the son of Francesco Donadoni
Scenery: Gasparo Beccari

---

8 Ibid., 105
9 In many copies of the libretto, the singer's name is misspelled as Fenardi.

Machines: Gasparo Mauro, Francesco Santurini
Costumes: Horatio Franchi, Paulo Morandi

SS. Giovanni e Paolo

Medoro (libretto by Aurelio Aureli, dedicated to Giorgio Guglielmo, et Ernesto Augusto, Duchi
   di Bransvich, e Luneburgh by Francesco Piva, 11 January 1658; music by Francesco Lucio)
Impresario: Francesco Piva, with the participation of Iseppo Zolio

1658/59 (Carnival ends 25 February)

S. Cassiano

Antioco (libretto by Nicolò Minato, dedicated to Marcellino Airoldi, Conte di Lec, 21 Janu-
   ary 1658 [m.v.]; music by Francesco Cavalli; first performance 25 January 1659)
Impresario: Marco Faustini
Investors: Marc'Antonio Correr and Alvise Duodo (with the assistance of Polifilo Zancarli?)
Singers: Girolama, Silvia Manni, Elena Passarelli, Orsetta Parmine, Giovanni Antonio
   Cavagna, contralto di Savelli, Tolomeo, contralto da Montagnana, Giulio da Ferrara, put-
   tello, Antonio Formenti
Dances: Giovanni Battista Martini
Scenery: Gasparo Beccari
Machines: Francesco Santurini
Costumes: Girolamo Savio, Paulo Morandi

SS. Giovanni e Paolo

La costanza di Rosmonda (libretto by Aurelio Aureli, dedicated to Abbate Vittorio Grimani
   Calergi, 15 January 1659; music by Giovanni Battista Volpe)
Impresario: Vettor Grimani Calergi and Giovanni Grimani
Singers: Caterina Porri, Gostanzo Piccardi, Niccolò Milani, Cosimo Orlandi?
Scenery: Alfonso Moscatelli (engineer from Mantua)
Costumes: Horatio Franchi

1659/60 (Carnival ends 10 February)

S. Cassiano

Elena (libretto by Nicolò Minato on a "soggetto" of Giovanni Faustini, dedicated to Angelo
   Morosini, 26 December 1659; music by Francesco Cavalli)
Impresario: Marco Faustini
Singers: Lucietta Gamba, Elena Passarelli, Anna Caterina Venturi, Giovanni Cappello, Nicolò
   Costantino, Domenico Sciarra, Carlo Vittorio Rotari, Giuseppe Ghini, Michel Angelo
   Amadore, Alessandro Collacioppi, Giovanni Battista Maggi, Francesco Galli
Dances: Agostino Ramaccini
Machines: (Francesco Santurini?)[10]

---

10 Santurini's name is mentioned in the receipt of a wood merchant. ASV, SGSM, b. 118, receipt
book, f. 39ᵛ.

SS. Giovanni e Paolo

Gl'avvenimenti d'Orinda (libretto by Pietro Angelo Zaguri, dedicated to the Duchessa di Bronsvich, e Luneburgh by Francesco Piva, 3 January 1659; music by Daniele da Castrovillari)

L'Antigona delusa da Alceste (libretto by Aurelio Aureli, dedicated to Giorgio e Guglielmo, Duchi di Bransvich by Francesco Piva, 15 January 1660; music by Pietro Andrea Ziani)

Impresario: Francesco Piva

Singers: Giovanni Antonio Forni,[11] Gostanzo Picardi, Cosimo Orlandi

Scenery: Hippolito Mazzarini

Machines: Gasparo Mauro

Costumes: Horatio Franchi

1660/61 (Carnival ends 1 March)

SS. Giovanni e Paolo

Gl'amori infrutuosi di Pirro (libretto by Aurelio Aureli, dedicated to Lodovico Vidman, 4 January 1661; music by Antonio Sartorio)

Annibale in Capua (libretto by Nicola Beregan, dedicated to Sofia, Duchessa di Bransvich, by Giacomo Batti [bookseller]; music by Pietro Andrea Ziani)

Impresario: Marco Faustini, with the assistance of Marc'Antonio Correr and Alvise Duodo

Singers: Caterina Porri, Elena Passarelli, Veronica Mazzochi, Clemente Antonii, Cosimo Orlandi, Bartolomeo Fregosi, Stefano Boni, Tomaso Bovi, Giovanni Antonio Forni, Giacinto Zucchi, Pietro Lucini, Antonio Formenti

Dances: Giovanni Battista Martini

Scenery: Hippolito Mazzarini

Machines: Gasparo Mauro

Costumes: Horatio Franchi

S. Luca

La Pasife (libretto by Giuseppe Artale, dedicated to Luigi Foscarini; music by Daniele da Castrovillari)

Eritrea (libretto by Giovanni Faustini, music by Francesco Cavalli, with revisions)

Impresario: Company includes Carlo Morandi, and Daniele da Castrovillari, with Girolamo Barbieri as guarantor for the rent; theater rented by Antonio Boldù, who also provided substantial financial assistance

Singers: Silvia Manni, Francesco Maria Rascarini, Filippo Manin, Stefano Costa, Angelo Maria Lesma, "Bastiano," Pellegrino Canner

1661/62 (Carnival ends 21 February)

SS. Giovanni e Paolo

Medea placata (libretto by Giovanni Faustini, cancelled after rehearsals)

Gli scherzi di fortuna (libretto by Aurelio Aureli, dedicated to Tito Livio Buratini, 12 January 1662; music by Pietro Andrea Ziani; first performance 17 January, according to dispatch[12])

---

11 According to a letter of Giovanni Grimani (28 Apr. 1660) Forni was preparing for a spring revival of *Antigona delusa*. Monaldini, *Orto dell'Esperidi*, 148.

12 ASMo, CAV, b. 120, 18 Jan. 1662, report of Mario Calcagnino.

Le fatiche d'Ercole per Deianira (libretto by Aurelio Aureli, dedicated to Giorgio Guglielmo, Duca di Bransvich, e Luneburgh; music by Pietro Andrea Ziani; to open on 3 February, according to *Il Rimino*[13])

Impresario: Marco Faustini, with the participation of Correr and Duodo

Singers: Caterina Tomei, Caterina Porri, Veronica Mazzochi, Giuseppe Romei, Cosimo Orlandi, Sebastiano Cioni, Gabriel Angelo Battistini, Tomaso Bovi, Giovanni Antonio Forni, Giacinto Zucchi, Antonio Formenti, Francesco Galli, Antonino Pio

Dances: G. B. Martini

Scenery: Hippolito Mazzarini

Machines: (Gasparo Mauro?)

Costumes: Horatio Franchi

S. Luca

Cleopatra (libretto by Giacomo Dall'Angelo, dedicated to Ambrosio Bembo; music by Daniele da Castrovillari; first performance 29 January 1662, according to *Il Rimino*[14])

Impresario: company includes Girolamo Barbieri, Carlo Morandi, and Daniele da Castrovillari; theater rented by Antonio Boldù

1662/63 (Carnival ends 6 February 1663)

SS. Giovanni e Paolo

Amor guerriero (libretto by Cristoforo Ivanovich, dedicated to Ranuccio Farnese, Duca di Parma; music by Pietro Andrea Ziani; performances to begin 16 December, according to account in Collegio[15])

Gl'amori d'Apollo, e di Leucotoe (libretto by Aurelio Aureli, dedicated to Francesco Vidman, 8 January 1663; music by Giovanni Battista Volpe [Rovettino])

Impresario: Marco Faustini, with the participation of Correr and Duodo

Singers: Caterina Porri, Veronica Mazzochi, Giovanni Antonio Cavagna, Giovanni Antonio Forni, Gabriel Angelo Battistini, Sebastiano Cioni, Giovanni Battista Filliberi, Pietro Lucini, Antonio Formenti, Antonio Zuchelli, Tomaso Bovi, Cosimo Orlandi

Dances: Olivier Vigasio

Scenery: Hippolito Mazzarini, Giovanni Battista Lanfranchi (named in libretto for *Gl'amori d'Apollo* = Giovanni Battista Lambranci?)

Machines: Gasparo Mauro

Costumes: Horatio Franchi

S. Luca

Dori (libretto by Apollonio Apolloni, dedicated to Monsignore Pietro de Bonsy [French ambassador to Venice] by A.B. [Antonio Boldù?], 1 January 1663; music by Antonio Cesti)

Impresario: Vettor Grimani Calergi; company includes Girolamo Barbieri and Carlo Morandi; theater rented by Antonio Boldù

---

13 Matteini, *"Rimino,"* 93.
14 Ibid.
15 ASV, Collegio, Esposizioni principi, reg. 71 (1661–62), f. 181, 15 Dec. 1662.

Singers: Vincenza Giulia Masotti, "La Tiepola," Giuseppe Ghini, Lorenzo Ferri, Hippolito Fusai, "putto di Luca," Antonio Pancotti, soprano di Baviera, Hilario Suares, Brunacio?, tenore che fa da Vecchia, un tenor Furlano[16]

1663/64 (Carnival ends 26 February)

SS. Giovanni e Paolo

Rosilena (libretto by Aurelio Aureli, dedicated to Maria Mancini Colonna, Prencipessa Romana, Duchessa di Tagliacozzo, &c., 4 January 1664; music by Giovanni Battista Volpe [Rovettino])

Scipione affricano (libretto by Nicolò Minato, dedicated to Lorenzo Onofrio Colonna, Prencipe Romano. Grande di Spagna . . . Gran Contestabile del Regno di Napoli, &c., 9 February 1664; music by Francesco Cavalli)

Impresarios: Giovanni Carlo Grimani, Vettor Grimani Calergi

Singers: Vincenza Giulia Masotti, Benedetto Trombetta, Cosimo Orlandi, Francesco Guerra, Filippo Melani, Moro[17]

Scenery: (Hippolito Mazzarini)

Costumes: (Horatio Franchi)

S. Luca

Achille in Sciro (libretto by Hippolito Bentivoglio, dedicated to Filippo Giuliano Mazarini Mancini, Duca di Nivers e Donziois by Steffano Curti [printer], 29 January 1664; music by Giovanni Legrenzi)

Impresario: Girolamo Barbieri, with participation of Marc'Antonio Montalbano; theater rented by Girolamo Barbieri

Singers: Cecilia Siri Chigi

1664/65 (Carnival ends 17 February)

SS. Giovanni e Paolo

Perseo (libretto by Aurelio Aureli, dedicated to Filippo Giuliano Mazarini Mancini, Duca di Nivers, e Donziois; music by Andrea Mattioli)

Ciro (libretto by Giuio Cesare Sorrentino, dedicated to Sofia, Duchessa di Bransvich, e Luneburg by Andrea Giuliani [printer], 4 February 1665; music originally by Francesco Provenzale and Cavalli [1653/54], updated by Andrea Mattioli)

Impresarios: Giovanni Carlo Grimani, Vettor Grimani Calergi

Scenery: Hippolito Mazzarini

Costumes: (Horatio Franchi)

---

16 Cast from a dispatch from the Mantuan Resident (ASMa, AG, b. 1573, 25 Dec. 1662). It has not been possible to decipher all the names in this list.

17 ASF, MP, filza 5478, f. 427, letter of Atto Melani, 16 Feb. 1664.

S. Luca

Mutio Scevola (libretto by Nicolò Minato, dedicated to Filippo Giuliano Mazarini Mancini,
Duca di Nivers, e Donziois, 26 January 1665; music by Francesco Cavalli; first perform-
ance to begin 27 January 1665, according to Tuscan correspondent[18])
Impresarios: Company of Girolamo Barbieri, Pietro Antonio Cerva (Bolognese scenogra-
pher), Nicolò Minato; theater protected by Tomaso Corner
Investor: Marco Mozzoni
Scenery: (Pietro Antonio Cerva)

1665/66 (Carnival ends 9 March 1666)[19]

S. Cassiano

Zenobia (libretto by Mattio Noris, dedicated to Filippo Giuliano Mazarini Mancini, Duca di
Nivers e Donziois; music by Giovanni Antonio Boretti); one performance only
Giasone (libretto by Giacinto Andrea Cicognini, dedicated by Camillo Bortoli [printer] to
Benetto Zorzi, Giacomo Celsi, Carlo Andrea Tron, "Protettori di detto Teatro," 23 Febru-
ary 1666; music by Francesco Cavalli and others?)
Impresario: Galeazzo Passarelli
Singers: Anna Caterina and Petromilla Bertino
Costumes: Girolamo Savio
Scenery: Stefano Santurini (machines?)[20]

SS. Giovanni e Paolo

Orontea (libretto by Giacinto Andrea Cicognini, dedicated to Maria Mancini Colonna,
Prencipessa Romana, Duchessa di Tagliacozzo, &c. by Steffano Curti [printer], 10 January
1666; music by Antonio Cesti, with prologue by Pietro Andrea Ziani [from *Doriclea*]). In
substitution for *Doriclea*
Tito (libretto by Nicola Beregan, dedicated to Maria Mancini Colonna, Duchessa di Taglia-
cozzo, &c., Lorenzo Onofrio Colonna, Gran Contestabile del Regno di Napoli, &c. and
Filippo Giuliano Mancini Mazarini, Duca di Nivers, &c. by Steffano Curti [printer], 13
February 1666; music by Antonio Cesti)
Impresario: Marco Faustini, with the assistance of Marc'Antonio Correr and Alvise Duodo
Singers: Anna Caterina Venturi (in *Orontea* only), Caterina Masi (in *Orontea* only?), Anto-
nia Coresi (in *Tito* only, as Marsia), Anna Maria Cimini (in *Orontea* only), Lucia
Olimpia Cimini (as Berenice in *Tito*), Giovanni Antonio Cavagna (as Tito in *Tito*),
Giuseppe Maria Donati (as Domitiano in *Tito*), Sebastiano Cioni (as Celso in *Tito*),
Giovanni Antonio Divido, Francesco Maria Rascarini (as Polemone in *Tito*), Tomaso
Bovi, Giacinto Zucchi, Pellegrin Canner, Zulian Zulian, Giovanni Giacomo Biancucci
(as Agrippa in *Tito*)

---

18 ASF, MP, filza 3033 , f. 374ᵛ, 26 Jan. 1665.

19 Information on roles for this season from ASF, MP, filza 5574, no. 90, letter of Giuseppe Ghini, 13
Mar. 1666. Additional information on the singers at S. Luca from ASV, Provveditori sopra monasteri,
Processi criminali, b. 272, Processo di alcuni musici andati al Monasterio di S. Daniel, 1666.

20 Santurini and Savio are mentioned in ASV, GE, Interdetti, b. 169 , f. 233, 8 Mar. 1666.

Dances: Giovanni Battista Martini
Scenery: Hippolito Mazzarini
Machines: Gasparo Mauro
Costumes: Horatio Franchi

S. Luca

Seleuco (libretto by Nicolò Minato, dedicated to Paulo Spinola, Duca di Sesto, by Francesco
Nicolini [printer], 16 January 1666; music by Antonio Sartorio)
Pompeo Magno (libretto by Nicolò Minato, dedicated to Maria Mancini Colonna, 20 Febru-
ary 1666; music by Francesco Cavalli)
Impresario: Company includes Nicolò Minato, Girolamo Barbieri, Marco Mozzoni
Singers: Caterina Porri, Giovanni Antonio Forni (as Pompeo in *Pompeo Magno*), Giulio
Cesare Donati, Francesco Galli (as Giulio Cesare in *Pompeo Magno*), Antonio Formenti,
Alessandro Moscanera, Antonio da Ferrara, Stefano Costa, Paulo Rivani

S. Moisè

Demetrio (libretto by Giacomo Dall'Angelo, dedicated to Giovanni da Mula, Matteo Pisani,
and Matteo da Legge, 1 January 1666; music by Carlo Pallavicino)
Aureliano (libretto by Giacomo Dall'Angelo, dedicated to Hippolito and Ferrante Ben-
tivoglio, 25 February 1666; music by Carlo Pallavicino)
Impresario: company includes Giacomo Dall'Angelo, Cristoforo Raimondi, and Camillo
Coveglia
Costumes: Girolamo Savio
Singers: Caterina and Brigida Forti, Angelo Maria Lesma (as Aureliano in *Aureliano*), Sebas-
tiano (Chierici?) (as Tetrico in *Aureliano*), Pietro "Pierino" Lucini (as Eresiano in *Aure-
liano*), Giuseppe Ghini (as Tito in *Aureliano*), Agostino Steffani (as Erinda in *Aureliano*),
Domenico Bordoni, Antonio Viviani[21]
Scenery: Giovanni Battista Lambranci
Costumes: Horatio Franchi

1666/67 (Carnival ends carnival 22 February)

SS. Giovanni e Paolo

Alciade (libretto by Giovanni Faustini, dedicated to Giovanni Carlo and Vincenzo Grimani
by Francesco Nicolini [printer]; music by Pietro Andrea Ziani; first performance 19 December 1667[22])
Dori, overo lo schiavo reggio (libretto by Apollonio Apolloni, dedicated to Maria Mancini
Colonna, Prencipessa Romana, Duchessa di Tagliacozzo, &c. by Francesco Nicolini
[printer], 16 January 1667; music by Antonio Cesti). In substitution for *Il tiranno humiliato
d'Amore overo il Meraspe*
Impresario: Marco Faustini, with the assistance of Marc'Antonio Correr and Alvise Duodo

---

21 On Viviani and Steffani, see Billio D'Arpa, "Documenti inediti," 124; and Timms, *Polymath of the
Baroque*, 7.
22 ASF, MP, filza 3033, f. 1256ᵛ, 18 Dec. 1666.

Singers: Vincenza Giulia Masotti, Antonia Coresi, Giovanni Antonio Cavagna, Sebastiano Cioni, Giovanni Antonio Divido, Francesco Maria Rascarini, Giovanni Giacomo Biancucci, Giovanni Francesco Pastarini, Pellegrino Canner, Zulian Zulian
Dances: Giovanni Battista Martini
Scenery: Hippolito Mazzarini
Machines: Gasparo Mauro
Costumes: Horatio Franchi

S. Luca

La prosperità di Elio Seiano (libretto by Nicolò Minato, dedicated to Giovanni Federico, Duca di Bransvich, e Luneburg, 15 January 1666; music by Antonio Sartorio)
La caduta di Elio Seiano (libretto by Nicolò Minato, dedicated to Amalia Regina di Danimarca, e Norveggia . . . nata Prencipessa di Bransvich, Luneburgh, 3 February 1667; music by Antonio Sartorio)
Impresario: Company includes Girolamo Barbieri, Marco Mozzoni, Nicolò Minato
Singers: Caterina Porri

S. Moisè

Alessandro amante (libretto by Giacinto Andrea Cicognini, dedicated to Giovanni Mocenigo by Sebastiano Enno, 28 January 1667; music by Giovanni Antonio Boretti)[23]
Impresarios: Sebastiano Enno and Camillo Nebbia
Costumes: Girolamo Savio
Singers: Virginia Camuffi, Margarita Pia, Felice (castrato), Pietro Paolo Benigni, Giovanni Antonio Boretti
Costumes: Girolamo Savio
Scenery: Francesco Santurini (machines?)

1667/68 (Carnival ends carnival 17 February)

SS. Giovanni e Paolo

Il tiranno humiliato d'Amore overo il Meraspe (libretto draft by Giovanni Faustini, updated by Nicola Beregan and others, dedicated to Gasparo de Teves [Spanish ambassador] by Bortolo Bruni [printer], 12 December 1667; music by Carlo Pallavicino)
Eliogabalo (libretto by Aurelio Aureli, dedicated to Giovanni Carlo and Vicenzo Grimani, 10 January 1667 [m.v.]; music by Giovanni Antonio Boretti)
Impresario: Marco Faustini (with the assistance of Marc'Antonio Correr and Alvise Duodo?) (with responsibilities shifting to Giovanni Carlo and Vicenzo Grimani on 15 December 1667)
Singers: Antonia Coresi, Caterina Angiola Botteghi, Margarita Pia, Giovanni Antonio Cavagna, Giuseppe Maria Donati, Giovanni Giacomo Biancucci, Sebastiano Cioni, Giovanni Antonio Divido, Vincenzo Antonini, Tomaso Bovi, Pietro Paulo Benigni, Pietro Lucini, Zulian Zulian
Dances: Giovanni Battista Martini; Lelio Bonetti and Angelo Frezzato
Scenery: Hippolito Mazzarini
Machines: Gasparo Mauro
Costumes: Horatio Franchi

23 The data regarding the singers and artistic staff come from Alm, "Singer Goes to Court."

S. Luca

Seleuco (libretto by Nicolò Minato, dedicated to Valerio da Riva, 16 January 1668; music by Antonio Sartorio)

Tiridate (libretto by [Hippolito Bentivoglio] and Nicolò Minato, dedicated to Andrea Vendramin by Nicolò Minato, 4 February 1668; music by Giovanni Legrenzi)

Impresario: Nicolò Minato, Marc'Antonio Montalbano; theater rented to Don Pietro Moretti

Singers: Marietta Barbieri,[24] (Cattina Zuliani, Giovanni Carletti)[25]

---

24 See Dubowy, "'L'amor coniugale nel Seicento,'" 206.

25 These singers pursued their fees in the courts following the 1667/68 season, but the records fail to give the dates of their original contracts.

A NOTE ON THE VENETIAN SOCIAL CLASS SYSTEM AND VENETIAN GEOGRAPHY

The Venetian population in the seventeenth century was divided into three classes. At the top, representing less than 10 percent of the population, were the nobles, or patricians. A similar number were *cittadini*, or citizens, and the remainder were commoners, or *popolani*. Nobility in Venice was inherited, but was not, as elsewhere in Europe, based on feudal property holdings. A family was legally a member of the patriciate if its members had sat on the Great Council (Maggior consiglio) in the year 1297, as established by Venetian law.[1] These families, which numbered well over one hundred, and their children were registered in the Golden Book. All adult male members of these families, as many as 2,500 in all, served in the Great Council; only these men could vote or hold offices in the government. The men identified themselves with the initials N.H. (Nobil Huomo), and the women with N.D. (Nobil Donna), and they were entitled to the honorific "Illustrissimo" (some specific government posts entitled them to other honorifics as well). Patricians nearly always married within their class. Children of a patrician man and a woman descended from foreign nobility or the citizen class might preserve their status, but those from other mixed marriages did not.

While the nobility had many privileges, they also were closely monitored by government bodies. They were required to serve in any post to which they were elected, were restricted in showing their wealth in public (by the Provveditori sopra le pompe), and were at times forced to make substantial loans to the government. Originally, the wealth of the patrician families was based on commerce (Venice dominated the spice and silk trade with the East in the Middle Ages), but by the seventeenth century it was increasingly founded on property holdings in the Venetian mainland territories. One consequence was a great disparity in wealth within the patriciate, which included both the richest men in the city and some of the poorest (since they were forbidden to perform manual labor, those at the lowest end of the scale relied on charity and government handouts). When the Republic was in great need of money, it sold nobility to distinguished foreign nobles or Venetian merchants.

Men of the citizen class, the cittadini, served as lawyers, notaries, and secretaries, and were the civil servants of the Republic. Some of these families were old, wealthy, and distinguished, but were excluded from the patrician class because of their absence from the Great Council in 1297. Others were added to the ranks over the years (this process was controlled by the Avogaria di Comun). The ranks of the cittadini were, in fact, constantly enriched by

---

1 On the patricians, see Queller, *Venetian Patriciate.*

the arrival of wealthy, and even noble, families from the Venetian possessions. After residing in the city for a number of years, without having exercised a manual profession (and without having been convicted of a crime), such immigrants, and their Venetian-born children, could qualify for certain degrees of citizenship.[2] The newly created citizens and their sons were eligible for lower-level civil service jobs (those that were not filled by election in one of the patrician councils, but rather through direct appointment) and such professional positions as lawyer or physician. Children of the second generation, assuming the proper training, could become public notaries. The third Venetian-born generation could join the highest rank of citizens, the *cittadini originari*, those eligible for election to the most important levels of the civil service, the *cancellaria ducale* and the notaries and secretaries of such bodies as the Great Council, the Senate, and the Council of Ten (although, in addition, a significant private income, usually from rental properties, was a nearly indispensible asset for those aspiring to such posts). The marriage of a male cittadino of any rank to a foreign woman or to a Venetian popolana in no way affected the citizenship of his descendants. The leadership of the great lay confraternities of Venice, the Scuole grandi, was officially restricted to cittadini originari.

All Venetians not members of the patrician or citizen classes were considered popolani. Members of this vast group ranged from wealthy merchants and guild members, to respectable government workers and laborers, down to lowly fisherman and the destitute.

The city of Venice was divided administratively into six *sestieri*, three on each side of the Grand Canal. On a smaller scale, the city was made up of seventy parishes, or *contrade*. Some of these parishes, especially those on the outskirts of the city, were inhabited mostly by popolani, but most had a mix of residents of all classes, with a higher percentage of patricians in parishes near or along the Grand Canal, and near S. Marco and the Rialto. The focal point of each parish was a public square, or *campo*, with its parish church. On the *campo*, or on streets branching off it, were shops and other local services. Several kinds of activities could bring together adult males of a parish of all classes, most importantly the church and its associated Confraternity of the Blessed Sacrament. Both of these were run by councils comprised of patricians and cittadini, and sometimes guild members, and they served people of all classes.[3] Connections across parish boundaries were formed and maintained through professional and commercial activities (including government service for patricians and cittadini), guilds, and confraternities (especially the Scuole grandi).

2 On the cittadini, see Andrea Zannini, *Burocrazia e burocrati*.
3 On the importance of parishes to the social fabric of Venice, see Romano, *Patricians and Popolani*.

DOCUMENTS

This appendix contains the complete original texts of selected longer documents dis-cussed in the book. In these transcriptions the abbreviations, except for those of mone-tary units, have been expanded silently, and punctuation and capitalization have been modi-fied for clarity. Spelling has been left unaltered, but accents have been added as needed.

Doc. 1. Anna Renzi's contract to sing at the Teatro Novissimo, 17 December 1643 (ASV, AN, Atti, b. 658, ff. 163^V–164^V)

Die iovis, decima septima mensis Decembris 1643, in domo habitationis infrascripte Domine Anne de confinio Sancti Ioannis in Bracora.

Havendo il Molto Illustre Signor Geronimo Lappoli ricercata la Molto Illustre Signora Anna Renzi, che si compiaccia favorire il suo teatro detto il Novissimo appresso SS. Gio-vanni et Paolo con la sua virtù nel recitare le opere, una, ò più, che in detto teatro il venturo carnovale si reciteranno, al che essa, mediante anco l'interpositione de gentil huomini, es-sendo condescesa. Però per vigor del presente instrumento detta Signora Anna da una parte, et il detto Signor Lappoli dall'altra dichiarano et convengono ut infra, cioè:

Che detta Signora Anna sia obligata, si come si obliga, recitare in musica le opere una, ò più che il venturo Carnovale si reciteranno in detto Theatro Novissimo, assistendo ad ogni prova che si facesse, ancora delle opere, solo però nel theatro, overo alla casa dell'habitatione di lei Signora Anna.

All'incontro detto Signor Geronimo promette dare à detta Signora Anna scudi venetiani d'argento effettivi numero cinquecento in questo modo, cioè scudi cento per tutto il corrente mese di decembre, altri cento cinquanta alla seconda recita, altri cento cinquanta alla metà delle recite, et alla penultima recita li restanti scudi cento, senza alcuna contradittione, nè dilatione.

Et in caso di malatia (che Dio non voglia) di detta Signora Anna, doppo fatte parte delle recite, in questo caso detta Signora Anna non possi pretender altro, che la metà delli sudetti scudi cinque-cento, ma se per qual si sia altra causa et occasione, niuna eccettuata, fosse impedito al Signor Lap-poli il far recitare, ad ogni modo sia tenuto darli essi scudi cinquecento nel modo di sopra.

In oltre sia tenuto detto Signor Lappoli in ogni caso darle et consignarle un palco per suo uso per tutto il carnovale, et più tutti li habiti che doveranno servire per le recite per detta Signora Anna a tutte spese di lui Signor Lappoli, quali habiti restino poi al Signor Lap-poli sodetto, per il che tutto detto Signor Geronimo obliga se stesso con suoi beni di qualunque sorte presenti, et futturi.

A maggior cautione della quale Signora Anna, presente alle cose predette, et personalmente costituito l'Eccellente Signor Giosef Camis medico hebreo per se, heredi, et successori suoi si constituisce piezo, fideiussor, et principal pagatore così per li scudi cinquecento, ò per quella parte che si dovesse dare a detta Signora Anna come di sopra, come per ogn'altra obligatione del detto Signor Lappoli nel presente instrumento contenuta, che per ciò obliga se stesso con suoi beni di qualonque sorte presenti, et futturi.

Item, promette detto Signor Geronimo di dare al Molto Illustre Signor Filiberto Laurenzi scudi d'argento numero sessanta perché egli sia obligato sonare così nelle prove, come in tutte le opere che nel soprascritto theatro il carnoval venturo si faranno. Item, al medesimo altri scudi vinticinque per instruire li musici, prologo, et intermedii, si come detto Signor Filiberto qui presente promette essercittarsi in dette funtioni, come si conviene sopra, di che etc.

Testes: Illustrissimus Dominus Franciscus Michael filius quondam Illustrissimi
                Domini Antonii
           Dominus Georgius Georgii quondam Domini Antonii Romanus

---

Doc. 2. Letter from Francesco Cavalli to Marco Faustini concerning negotiations for the 1654/55 season at Teatro S. Aponal, 23 July 1654 (ASV, SGSM, b. 188, f. 14^{r-v})

Clarissimo et Eccellentissmo Signore e Padron Collendissimo:

Perché Vostra Signoria Eccellentissima vegga l'affetto c'ho sempre portato a lei, al suo teatro, e riverenza insieme a gli illustrissimi interressati; le fò sapere, come io ultimamente mi abboccai coll'Illustrissimo Duodo; e fra le cose concertate assieme per porre nella scrittura furno queste: che non si parlasse di far suonare quel terzo stromento, bastando solo la mia esibitione in voce. Che fatta la prima recita mi fosse datto scudi d'argento 100. Che ogni 4 recite mi fossero datti ducati 50 fino all'intiera sodisfattione delli ducati 400. Queste cose mi furno cortesissimamente promesse da detto signore ma non attese poi nella scrittura, ch'invece di porre (come l'appuntato) li scudi 100 la prima sera gli ha posti doppo la terza sera. Li ducati 50 in cambio delle 4 gli ha posti doppo le sei; onde io vedendo che non mi si manteneva in scritto, quel tanto ch'in voce mi s'era promesso, regolai detta scrittura, e si come esso Illustrissimo Duodo mi l'havea mandata a me, Io la rimandai a esso signore coretta in quella forma a ciò fosse sottoscritta, et ultimato questo negotio incominciato fin questa quadragesima. Veggo però dalle longhezze di questo negotio e delle dilationi nel concludere, la poca stima che si fa della mia persona, che perciò, un mese fa mi licentiai (con una mia) dall'Illustrissimo Duodo, ma per portarmela anco più a longo non vuoler accettarla. Onde per venirne a un fine, scrivo questa a lei che servirà per tutta la compagnia, e per informatione, che se per tutto dimani, che sarà li 24 del corrente, non mi haveranno rissolto con la sottoscrittione alla scrittura inviata, io mi dichiaro libero del trattato fin hora havuto insieme. Vostra Signoria Eccellentissima non havrà occasione di dolersi di me, mentre sta a loro signori l'havermi, dichiarandomi pronto a servirli, mentre mi sij sottoscritta la detta scrittura, che non è stravagante, ma è conforme il concerto predetto nè è variata in altro (nella forma del pagamento) che di due sere più ò meno, dell'esborso delli 100 scudi et di una sera di meno, di quello delli ducati 50, cosa che non so credere che vi sij cagione di non mi contentare con una sodisfatione di sì poco momento. Serva però, come ho detto, questo per avviso, che s'io non riceverò questa sottoscrittione per tutto mercordi come sopra, m'indenderò fuori d'ogni obligatione con loro signori. E le bacio la mano.

Gambarare li 23 luglio 1654.

Di Vostra Signoria Clarissima et Eccellentissima,

Devotissimo servitore,

Francesco Cavalli

Doc. 3. Francesco Cavalli's contract for Teatro S. Cassiano, 24 July 1658 (ASV, SGSM, b. 194, ff. 266–67)

1658 24 luglio in Venetia

Gl'Illustrissmi Signori Marc'Antonio Coraro, et Alvise Duodo, et l'Eccellentissimo Signor Marco Faustini da una et il Signor Francesco Cavalli dall'altra, sono convenuti et rimasti d'accordo che detto Signor Cavalli debba per tre anni prossimi poner in musica ogn'anno, un opera da rappresentarsi nel Teatro di S. Cassano, et ciò con li patti, e condittioni infrascritte:

Primo: Che detto Signor Cavalli sia obligato e tenuto poner in musica dette opere con la diligenza et virtù sua propria, facendo a tutte sue spese far tutte le copie et originali che seranno neccessarii, senza che detti signori compagni habbino in ciò a sentir alcuno aggravio così di carta come copista et altro.

Secondo: Che detto signor Cavalli sia tenuto et obligato assister personalmente a tutte le prove che seranno necessarie come anco mutar parte, alterar, sminuir, et aggionger quello fosse neccessario nella musica per servitio dell'opera secondo l'occorenze et emergenze che succedono in simili occasioni.

Terzo: Non possa sotto qual si voglia pretteso niuno eccettuato publicamente ò secretamente nel corso de detti 3 anni poner in musica altre opere che s'havesero a recittare in questa città, così in theatri publici con pagamento come privati, et ciò per patto particolare senza il quale detti Illustrissimi et compagni non sarebbero devenuti alla stipulatione della presente scrittura. Non resti però prohibito ad esso signor Cavalli il poner in musica in detto tempo oppere che fossero per recitarsi fuori della Città.

Quarto: Sij tenuto detto signor Cavalli sonar nell'opera il primo istromento ogni sera che si recitarà senza altra recognitione che del stipendio infrascritto, ed in caso di malattia ò altro impedimento, che Iddio non voglia, sia tenuto sostituire in sua vece un altro che sia idonio senza alcun aggravio della compagnia.

Et all'incontro, per recognitione delle sopradette obligationi, detti Illustrissimi et compagno s'obligano d'esborsar ogni anno al detto signor Francesco Cavalli ducati quatro cento correnti da £6 s.4 per ducato quali doveranno con tutta pontualità esserli esborsati dal cassier della compania nella seguente forma, cioè fatta la prima recita gli sijno contati ducati 150 et per il restante, ogni 5 recite ducati 50 sino all'intiero pagamento, dovendo però li detti ducati 400 esserli pagati senza alcuna contraditione a tutti li modi, ò siano poche ò molte le recite che si faranno dell'oppera, et essendo li detti Illustrissimi Corar e Duodo, et Eccellentissimo Faustini obligati simul et in solidum, all'intiero pagamento predetto.

Per la manutentione di tutte le quali cose le sopradette parti s'obligano vicendevolmente in ogni più ampla et valida forma, et questa vaglia come fatta per mano di publico notaro, dovendo della presente esserne fatte due copie sottoscritte d'ambi le parti.

{
{
{Io Francesco Cavalli affermo a quanto di sopra

Doc. 4. Lucietta Gamba's contract to sing at Teatro S. Cassiano, 18 July 1659 (ASV, SGSM, b. 194, f. 11^{r-v})

1659 adì 18 luglio in Venetia

Si dechiara per la presente scrittura come la signora Lucieta Vidmana si obliga di recitare quest'anno nel Theatro di San Cassano di ragione del Signor Marco Faustini, et esser pronta a tutte le prove et recite con ogni pontualità ad'ogni requisitione di detto signor Faustini senza contraditione alcuna. Qual Signor Faustini si obliga di dare a detta Signora Lucietta per recognitione delle sue virtuose fatiche doble cento cinquanta in questo modo, però: doble cinquanta finita la seconda recita, a meze le recite altre doble cinquanta, et finite le recite altre doble cinquanta, che sono in tutto doble centocinquanta, con espressa dechiaratione, che in caso di malatia di detta Signora Lucieta (che Dio non voglia) resterà sodisfatta in portione delle recite che ci fossero fatte, come anco doverà detta Signora Lucieta rimaner sodisfatta per qual si sia caso che succedesse, eccetto che per publico impedimento, et questo anco a portione del tempo. Che quello succedesse et per conservatione del presente contratto dette parti si obligano vicendevolmente in ogni più ampla, et valida forma. Qual contratto è stato stabilito et concluso dall'Illustrissimo et Eccellentissimo Signor Michiel Morosini fo dell'Illustrissimo et Eccellentissimo Signor Andrea, quale anco ha ricevuto la parola da ambe le parti per la manutentione dell'obligationi predette, e ne sarà fato un'altra simile acciò sottoscritte stiano appresso delle parti.

{Io Lucietta Gamba deta Vidimana prometo quanto di sopra
{Io Marco Faustini affermo quanto di sopra

Doc. 5. Inventory of Teatro S. Moisè, 1666 (ASV, AN, Atti, b. 6111, f. 74)

Stima fatta delle materie che sono nel Teatro di San Moisè:

Tenda con sue corde, ordimenti e legname per il bisogno della detta, tutto	£104
Scene	
Sala con suo soffito, prospeto, e lontani	£165
Camera con suo soffito e lontani	£110
Galaria con suo soffitto e lontani	£125
Celeste con due teleri di soffitto e teleri per tera	£140
Anfiteatro, giardino, cortille, incendio, campo d'arme, queste cinque sene con suoi lontani	£310
Prigione, cortille, fontane, piazza, locco remotto, cedrare, campagna, queste sette senza lontani	£350
Prospetti quatro	£30
Aneme che conduce li telari sono 20	£120
Li letti sotto sena con le sue rode et altro	£15
Due rocheloni, uno sotto scena, et uno di sopra per li soffiti	£40
Corde tutte	£120
Due contrapesi	£6
Rochelli per machine, manganelli, et altri simile	£16
Li cieli sino in lontano con sue cascate delle parti	£40
Il globo	£8
Filli di rame per machinar	£72
Lumme per luminar le scene quaranta	£24
Cantinelle per caminar per li telleri	£35
Mastelle da orina	£12
Fogara	£3
Scale cinque	£6
Seggi, e trono d'Aureliano	£12
Tolle integhe 20 in circa	£16
Rotami di taole, et altri	£24
Copi in circa trecento	£15

Coridori, strade, et altro che serve per machinar, e lavorar alli soffitti   £40
Telle delli cussini, et del trono   £8
Feramente rotte   £12
      Summa in tutto   £1978

Io Francesco Santorini fece la soprascritta stima, la quale affermo con mio giuramento di haver fatto il tutto per conscienza mia.
Francesco Santorini

Doc. 6. Description of the opening scenes of Benedetto Ferrari and Francesco Manelli's *Andromeda* (S. Cassiano, 1637) (*Andromeda*, Venice, 1637, 5–7)

LO STAMPATORE
A' Lettori.

A Gloria de' Signori Musici, ch'al numero di sei (coll'Autore collegati) hanno con gran magnificenza, ed'esquisitezza, à tutte loro spese, e di qualche consideratione, rappresentata l'Andromeda, e per gusto non meno, di chi non l'hà veduta, hò stimato cosa convenevole il farne un breve racconto in questa forma.

Sparita la Tenda si vide la Scena tutta mare; con una lontananza così artifitiosa d'acque, e di scogli, che la naturalezza, di quella (ancor che finta) movea dubbio à Riguardanti, se veramente fossero in un Teatro, ò in una spiaggia di mare effettiva. Era la Scena tutta oscura, se non quanto le davano luce alcune stelle; le quali una dopo l'altra à poco à poco sparendo, dettero luogo all'Aurora, che venne à fare il Prologo. Ella tutta di tela d'argento vestita, con una stella lucidissima in fronte, comparve dentro una bellissima nube, quale hora dilatandosi, hora stringendosi (con bella meraviglia) fece il suo passaggio in arco per lo Ciel della Scena. In questo mentre si vide la Scena luminosa à par del giorno. Dalla Signora Madalena Manelli Romana fù divinamente cantato il Prologo: dopo del quale s'udì de più forbiti Sonatori una soavissima Sinfonia; à questi assistendo l'Autore dell'Opera con la sua miracolosa Tiorba. Uscì dipoi Giunone sovra un carro d'oro tirato da suoi Pavoni, tutta vestita di tocca d'oro fiammante, con una superba varietà, di gemme in testa e nella corona. Con meraviglioso diletto, de Spettatori volgeva a destra, ed à sinistra come più le piaceva, il carro. Le comparve à fronte Mercurio. Era, e non era questo Personaggio in machina; Era, perche l'impossibilità non l'ammetteva volatile; e non era, poiche niun altra machina si vedea, che quella del corpo volante. Comparve guernito de suoi soliti arnesi, con un manto azurro, che le giva suolazzando alle spalle. Fù eccelentemente rappresentata Giunone dal Signor Francesco Angeletti da Assisi; ed'esquisitamente Mercurio dal Signor Don Annibale Graselli da Città di Castello. In un istante si vide la Scena, di maritima Boschereccia; così del naturale, ch'al vivo al vivo ti portava all'occhio quell'effettiva cima nevosa, quel vero pian fiorito, quella reale intrecciatura del Bosco e quel non finto scioglimento d'acque. . . .

THE IMPRESARIO'S YEAR:
A CALENDAR OF MARCO FAUSTINI'S
IMPRESARIAL ACTIVITIES FOR
1651/52 AND 1654/55

Month	Date	1651/52	1654/55
May	1		Faustini's 1st payment to company contract with Anastasio for machinery
	2		Faustini buys account book
	3		Contract with Simon Guglielmi, scene painter
	14		Pasinetto's 1st payment to company
	15		2nd contract with Anastasio for machinery
June	1		Theater rental payment
	12		Contract with Anna Renzi, singer
	13		Contract with Angelica Felice Curti, singer
	25		1st payment for cardboard
July	6		1st purchase of cloth
August	4	Purchase of account book Contracts with Margarita da Costa, singer Contract with Simon Guglielmi, scene painter	
	7	1st purchase of tacks	
	8	Contract with Don Giulio Cesare Donati, singer	
	12	1st costume expenses	
	18	1st payment for cardboard	Contract with Gorgoglione [Antonio Fabris], singer (did not perform)
	19	Contract with fra Tomaso [Bovi], singer	Contract with G. B. Martini for dances

Month	Date	1651/52	1654/55
	20	Contract with Anastasio Marangon, for machines	Contract with Paulo Morandi for liveries for extras
	21	1st purchase of wood Contract with Amato Riminuzzi, singer (did not perform)	
	23	1st purchase of nails	
	25	Contracts with Bonifacio Ceretti, singer (did not perform) and Andrea and Cristoforo Caresana, singers	
	31		Contract with Antonino Pio, singer
September	1	Contract with Giovanni Battista Martini, for dances	Contract with Lorenzo Ferri, singer Contract with Angela Angelotti, singer
	12		Contracts with Lugretia Marconi, Giacinto Zucchi, and Antonio Draghi, singers
	14		Contract with Francesco fenestrer for "armor" and costumes
	?		Contracts with Filippo and his brother [Filippo and Bortolo Melani?], Francesco Simi, Lodovico, and Giovanni Sigonfredi da Pesaro, singers
	16	Contract with Caterina Giani, singer	
	22	Contract with "tenor di Carrara" [Francesco Guerra?], singer	
	24		1st payment to Renzi, singer
October	3	1st purchase of canvas	
	14	Contract with Pellegrino, singer	
	17	Contract with Nina dal Pavon, singer	Frequent cloth purchases begin
	19		Embroiderers begin work
	26		Contract with Savio for ballet costumes
November	9	1st embroidery payment	
	10		Contract with Savio for janissary costumes
	14	Final payment to Anastasio for machinery	
	17		1st candles for work in theater
	19	1st rehearsal[a]	Purchase of "armor"
	20	1st payment for candles	
	28	1st performance of Calisto	Embroiderers finish 1st candles for rehearsals
	29	1st payment to Giani, singer	

Month	Date	1651/52	1654/55
December	2		1st payment to tailor
	4	1st payment to Francesco Cavalli, composer	
	15	1st payment to Caresana brothers, singers	
	18	1st payment to Pellegrino, singer	Final payments for scenes and machines
		Final payment for wood	
	19		1st performance
	22	1st payments to Donati, Nina, and "puttella," singers	1st payments to Zucchi and Lodovico, singers
	23		1st payment to Marconi, singer
	25	1st payment to Martini, for dances	
	29		1st payments to Filippo and his brother [Melani?], singers
	31	last performance of *Calisto*	
January	1		Faustini and Pasinetto make final deposits of capital
	3	1st rehearsal of *Eritrea*b	
	5		1st payments to Simi and Sigonfredi, singers
	6		1st payment to Draghi, singer
	11		Rental payment for theater
	12	Final purchase of canvas	
	13	Final purchase of nails	
	17	1st performance of *Eritrea*	
	18	1st payment to Margarita da Costa, singer	
	20		Final payment to tailor
	31	1st payment to fra Tomaso [Bovi] and "tenor di Carrara" [Guerra?], singers	
February	4	Final payment to Donati	
	5	Final payment to tailor	
		Final payments to Caresana brothers, singers	
		Final payment to Guglielmi, for scenery	
	8		Final payments to Renzi, Curti, Pio, Zucchi, Draghi, Simi, singers
	9		Last day of carnival; final performance
			Final payment to Marconi, singer
	10		Final payment to Martini for ballets
	12	Final payments to Martini, for dances	Final payment to Angelotti, singer

Month	Date	1651/52	1654/55
		Final payments to da Costa and puttella, singers	
	14	Final payments to fra Tomaso [Bovi], Giani, "tenor di Carrara" [Guerra?], Pellegrino, Lorenzo [Ferri?], singers	
	20	Final payment for costumes	
	23	Final performance of *Eritrea*	
March	8		Final payment for cloth
June	7		Final payment to Sigonfredi, singer
August	15		Pasinetto agrees to final accounting for the season

[a] On this date, Faustini provided, for the first time, a boat to bring Caterina Giani to the theater.

[b] On this date, for the first time after the close of *Calisto*, Faustini paid for a boat to bring Giani to the theater.

PRODUCTION EXPENSES FOR THREE
SEASONS IN THE 1650S

Item	1651/52, in ducats (with percentage of total)[a]	1657/58 in ducats (with percentage of total)[b]	1658/59, in ducats (with percentage of total)[c]
Musical expenses			
Singers	1,668 (32%)	2,623 (27%)	2,673 (42%)
Composer	300 (6%)	150 (2%)	400 (6%)
Dances	105 (2%)	200 (2%)	209 (3%)
Subtotal	2,073 (40%)	2,973 (31%)	3,282 (52%)
Physical production expenses			
Costumes	844 (16%)	1,371 (14%)	498 (8%)
Scenery	255 (5%)	450 (5%)	452 (7%)
Machines	113 (2%)	390 (4%)	208 (3%)
Wood, etc.	150 (3%)	535 (6%)	25 (1%)
Canvas	173 (3%)	64 (1%)	144 (2%)
Other	236 (5%)	2,014 (21%)	276 (4%)
Subtotal	1,771 (34%)	4,824 (51%)	1,603 (25%)
Nightly expenses			
Orchestra[d]	638 (12%)	685 (7%)	409 (6%)
Other[e]	738 (14%)	1,057 (11%)	1,037 (16%)
Subtotal	1,376 (26%)	1,742 (18%)	1,446 (23%)
TOTAL	5220 (100%)	9,539 (100%)	6,331 (100%)

[a] ASV, SGSM, b.112, account book 1651/52.

[b] ASV, SGSM, b. 112, account book 1657/58 and ASV, SGSM, b. 101, balance sheet.

[c] ASV, SGSM, b. 194, account book 1658/59.

[d] Note that for the 1658/59 season, the fee for musical direction was included in Cavalli's contract, while for the other two seasons the director was paid nightly.

[e] This includes such expenses as extras (27 lire per night in 1651/52), illumination (38 lire), tailors (18 lire), men to work at the door (ca. 11 lire), stagehands (36 lire), tickets (10 lire), and the *cartello* (1 lira).

VENETIAN OPERA ORCHESTRAS
OF THE 1650S AND 1660S

Presented here are the extant orchestra lists for Venetian operas from the 1650s and 1660s. As the original lists are an inconsistent mix of names and instrument designations, it is not always possible to determine precisely the makeup of the ensemble. The names are given below in the form in which they appear in the documents, with details added where possible. The nightly wages are in lire.

S. Aponal 1651/52

(ASV, SGSM, b. 112, account book 1651/52)

Instrument	Name	Nightly wage
1st keyboard	(Francesco) Cavalli	40
2nd keyboard?	Martino	24
Theorbo	Francesco	10
1st violin	—	16
2nd violin	—	10
Violone	—	12:8
Tuner	—	4
TOTAL		116:8

S. Aponal 1654/55

(ASV, SGSM, b. 113, account book 1654/55)

Instrument	Name	Nightly wage
1st keyboard	(Pietro Andrea) Ziani	37:4
2nd keyboard ("spinet")	—	12
Theorbo	—	10
1st violin	—	15:10
2nd violin	—	14
Viola	—	7
Viola	—	6
Violone	—	15:10
Tuner	—	4:10
TOTAL		124:10

S. Aponal 1655/56

(ASV, SGSM, b. 113, account book 1654/55; this book also includes accounts for the 1655/56 season)

Instrument	Name	Nightly wage
1st keyboard	Rovetta (Giovanni Battista Volpe, detto Rovettino)	28
2nd keyboard	Carlo	9:6
3rd keyboard	Empoli	9:6
Theorbo	—	10
1st violin	—	18:16
2nd violin	—	15:10
Viola	—	5
Violone	—	16:8
Tuner	—	4:10
TOTAL		113:6

S. Cassiano 1657/58

(ASV, SGSM, b. 112, account book 1657/58)

Instrument	Name	Nightly wage
1st keyboard	(Pietro Andrea) Ziani	40
1st (2nd) keyboard	—	12
2nd (3rd) keyboard	—	12
1st theorbo	—	15:10
Theorbo?	Carlo (Andrea Coradini?)	28
1st violin	—	14
2nd violin	—	12
Viola	"Prete dalla viola"	7
Violone	—	15:10
Trumpets	—	9:6
Tuner	—	4:10
TOTAL		169:16

S. Cassiano 1658/59

(ASV, SGSM, b. 194, account book 1658/59)

Instrument	Name	Nightly wage
1st keyboard	[Francesco Cavalli][1]	—
2nd keyboard	Tonin	12

(continued)

[1]Cavalli's name does not appear in the orchestra list in the account book, but he was obligated by his contract not only to compose the opera, but to play the first keyboard (ASV, SGSM, b. 194, ff. 266–67; see appendix 3). Payment for this duty was included in his fee.

Instrument	Name	Nightly wage
1st theorbo	"Tiorba da Padova"	14
2nd theorbo	"Prete della tiorba"	13
1st violin	Don Giovanni Battista	18:12
2nd violin	—	12
Viola	Don Lorenzo	10
Violetta	—	4:13
Violone	—	17
Tuner	—	4:13
TOTAL		105:15

SS. Giovanni e Paolo 1664/65

(ASV, SGSM, b. 194, f. 268)

Instrument	Name	Nightly wage
1st keyboard	Antonio	24:16
2nd keyboard	—	10
3rd keyboard	Andrea	10
1st theorbo	—	4
2nd theorbo	—	11
1st violin	Rimondo	18:12
2nd violin	Domenego	14
Viola	Mattio	12
Violone	Carlo Saion	15
Tuner	—	4:10
TOTAL		123:18

S. Moisé 1666/67

(ASV, Ospedali e luoghi pii, 37, Eredità Virginia Camuffi)

Instrument	Name	Nightly wage
1st keyboard	—	22
2nd keyboard	—	16
3rd keyboard	—	8:10
1st theorbo	—	17
2nd theorbo	—	9:12
1st violin	—	15
2nd violin	—	14
Violetta	—	10
Violone	—	15:10
Tuner	—	12:8
TOTAL		140

PAID ATTENDANCE FOR SIX SEASONS
IN THE 1650S AND 1660S

The graphs that follow summarize paid attendance data for the 1651/52, 1654/55, and 1655/56 seasons at S. Aponal, the 1657/58 and 1658/59 seasons at S. Cassiano, and the 1668/69 season at S. Luca, all those for the period under consideration in this book for which such figures are extant. For the seasons at S. Aponal and S. Cassiano, when Marco Faustini was impresario, the documents preserve two sets of figures: the total number of bollettini sold for each performance and the number of scagni rented for the night. Since it appears that all spectators in the parterre were required to rent scagni, and all spectators in the boxes were also required to purchase bollettini, the difference between the two sets of figures provides the number of spectators in the boxes. For these two theaters we also provide

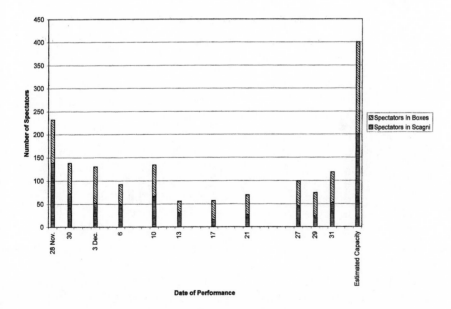

APPENDIX 7, FIGURE I.   Paid attendance for *Calisto* (S. Aponal, 1651/52) (Source: ASV, SGSM, b. 112, account book 1651/52)

an estimate of their capacity, based on the evidence of the number and size of boxes and the maximum paid attendance. For the single season at S. Luca included here, the only figures that survive are for the total number of bollettini sold. As explained in chapter 11, the actual attendance at any performance would have been somewhat larger than the paid attendance, as some people, including the owners of the theater and some of those associated with the production company, were admitted free of charge.

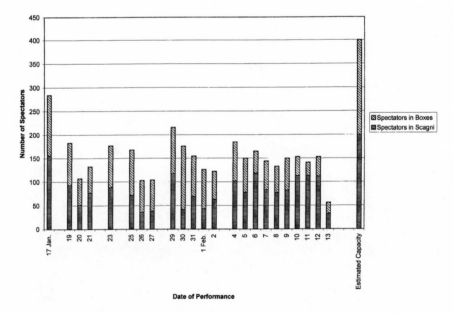

APPENDIX 7, FIGURE 2.   Paid attendance for *Eritrea* (S. Aponal, 1651/52) (Source: ASV, SGSM, b. 112, account book 1651/52)

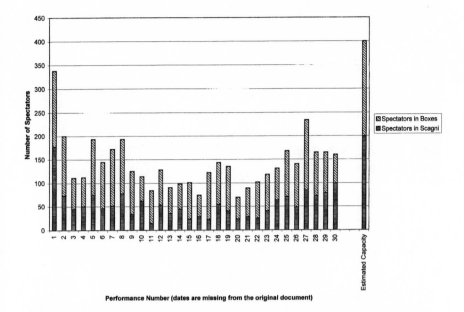

APPENDIX 7, FIGURE 3. Paid attendance for *Eupatra* (S. Aponal, 1654/55) (Source: ASV, SGSM, b. 113, account book 1654/55)

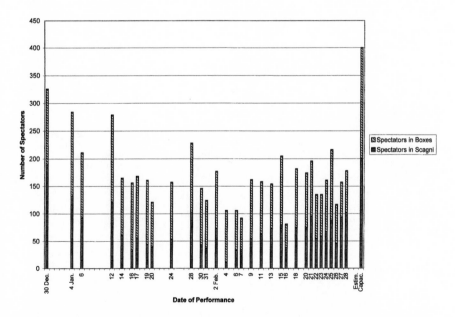

APPENDIX 7, FIGURE 4. Paid attendance for *Erismena* (S. Aponal, 1655/56) (Source: ASV, SGSM, b. 113, account book 1654/55)

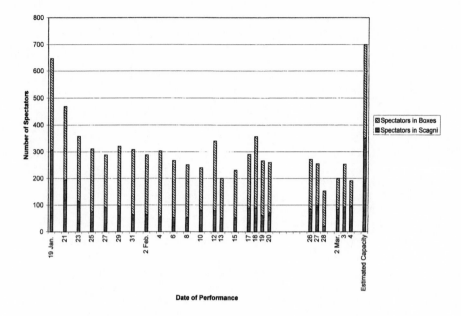

APPENDIX 7, FIGURE 5.   Paid attendance for *L'incostanza trionfante* (S. Cassiano, 1657/58)
(Source: ASV, SGSM, b. 112, account book 1657/58)

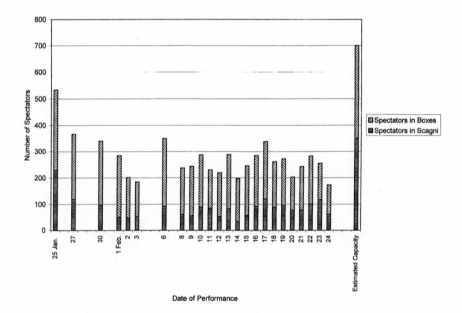

APPENDIX 7, FIGURE 6.   Paid attendance for *Antioco* (S. Cassiano, 1658/59) (Source: ASV,
SGSM, b. 194, account book 1658/59)

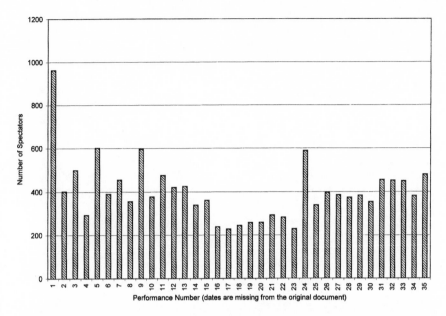

APPENDIX 7, FIGURE 7.   Paid attendance for *Argia* (S. Luca, 1668/69) (Source: Vcg, Archivio Vendramin; see Rosand, *Opera*, 197)

GLOSSARY

Avogaria di comun, Avogadori di comun	state attorneys, also designated the authority to determine membership in the cittadino class
bollettino	entrance ticket for an opera
busta	a folder or box that may contain registri or loose archival documents; also used less formally to indicate any archival unit, such as a registro or filza
Candia, War of	fought 1645–69 between the Venetians (allied with Malta, Tuscany, Naples, and the Pope) and the Turks over possession of Crete and other Venetian colonies
caneva	wine storage or place for distribution of wine
carato, carattadori	a share (often but not always $\frac{1}{24}$) of an enterprise; the holders of such share
carnival	the season preceding Lent; in Venetian practice usually considered to begin the day after Christmas, but the operatic carnival season might begin considerably earlier
cassier	cashier; the person who collected receipts and made payments
cittadino	citizens; the class of professionals and civil servants (see appendix 2)
Collegio	one of the highest bodies of the Venetian government, in charge of foreign affairs
Council of Ten (Consiglio dei dieci);	one of the chief magistracies of Venice,

359

Capi of the Council of Ten	charged with overseeing state security; the Capi were three members of the council, serving in rotation, who could take actions without convening the entire council
Dieci savi sopra le decime in Rialto	magistracy that administered the property tax; each property owner sumitted a declaration listing all income-generating real property
doge	the elected head of state of Venice; served for life
donativo	a one-time fee paid to obtain property rights to an opera box (lit. "gift"); also called *regalo*
ducat, ducato	a Venetian monetary unit; see A Note on the Venetian Monetary System
fattor	agent of a theater owner or impresario, assigned, among other duties, to collect box rental fees
filza	a packet of loose archival documents held together by a string that has been inserted through a hole punched in the middle of each sheet; also used, instead of busta, to refer to any packet of unbound documents
Giudici del forestier	a Venetian court; responsible for adjudicating contract disputes between Venetians and foreigners and disputes between property owners and renters
Giudici dell'esaminador	a Venetian court; responsible for adjudicating certain property disputes and for sealing and auctioning properties to settle debts
Giudici del mobile	a Venetian court; responsible for adjudicating minor property disputes and some contract disputes
Giudici del procurator	a Venetian court; responsible for managing certain inheritances and disputes regarding dowries
Giudici del proprio	a Venetian court; responsible for many issues regarding inheritance
Giudici di petizion	a Venetian court; responsible for, among other things, adjudicating disputes over notarial acts and private contracts, guardianships, and bankruptcies

guardian grande	elected leader of a scuola grande, with a one-year term; always a cittadino
Inquisitori di stato	elected from within the Council of Ten to attend to the most urgent and important criminal and state security matters
lira	a Venetian monetary unit; see A Note on the Venetian Monetary System
livello	a type of loan, in which the owner "sells" his property for cash in the amount of the loan for a set period of years, and then leases it back from the purchaser
Magistrato alle beccarie	officials charged with overseeing butchers and slaughterhouses in Venice
Magistrato del sal, Salt Office	magistracy that administered the government's salt monoply for Venice and its territories
notary	a government-licensed professional who drew up and registered contracts and other agreements (known as *atti*) and wills (*testamenti*)
ordine, order	a level of opera boxes
palco	opera box
partito, partitante	salt monopoly for a designated district of the Venetian empire; the person assigned the franchise for that district
pepian, piè pian	ground floor; boxes at the same level as the parterre
pieggio	guarantor of a loan or contract
Procuratori di S. Marco	high Venetian officials, elected for life; one group of Procuratori (the Procuratori *de supra*), administered the basilica of S. Marco, others administered estates, especially those without an heir
Provveditori alla sanità	health authority; maintained death records for the entire city
Pubblici correttori	official proofreaders, charged with insuring the accuracy of books published in Venice; succeeded by the Revisore pubblica
Quarantie (the Forty)	high criminal and civil courts
Rason nove	magistracy in charge of overseeing certain state expenditures

regalo	a one-time fee paid to obtain property rights to an opera box (lit. "gift"); also called *donativo*
registro	a bound archival volume
Revisore pubblica	official proofreader, charged with insuring the accuracy of books published in Venice; successor to the Pubblici correttori
Riformatori dello Studio di Padova	magistracy with authority over the University of Padua and some matters regarding book publishing
scagno	chair in the parterre, rented for the evening
scaleter	seller of pastries
scrittura privata	a private contract, not registered with a notary
scuola grande	originally, one of the four flagellant confraternities of Venice; later, one of a group of six (ultimately eight) large confraternities whose officers were from the *cittadino* class
soffitto	attic; the highest level of boxes
Sovraintendenze alle stampe	magistracy with authority over some aspects of book publishing
vicario	second highest office in a scuola grande; assistant to the guardian grande

BIBLIOGRAPHY

Archival Sources

Listed below are the principal series of archival documents used for this study, and other individual volumes cited in the text. Not listed are the hundreds of other documents consulted, among them many that provided useful contextual information, corroborating details, or additional data that, for reasons of space and coherence, were not cited in the book. In some fondi, registri and buste are numbered separately, and are so indicated; in others where there is one comprehensive numbering system, no format is listed. Some documents in Florence, Mantua, Modena, and Turin were consulted at the microfilm collection of the Istituto per la storia della società e dello stato veneziano of the Fondazione Cini in Venice.

Venice, Archivio di stato di Venezia (ASV)

Archivio notarile (AN)
Atti: 647, 658, 660, 662, 665, 667, 679, 691–92 (Francesco Beazian e Andrea Bronzini); 700, 703 (Francesco e Bortolamio Beazian e Andrea Bronzini); 708 (Bortolamio Beazian); 732, 736 (Michelarcangelo Bronzini); 996 (Alessandro Basso); 1014 (Pietro Antonio Bozzini); 1049 (Nicolò Bon); 1083, 1090, 1094 (Gregorio Bianconi); 1120, 1124, 1132, 1136 (Lodovico Bruzzoni); 1165–66, 1183, 1184, 1186 (Cristoforo Brombilla); 1330, 1332 (Iseppo Bellan); 2817, 2820 (Girolamo De Capi); 2863, 2892 (Agostino Cavertino); 2918 (Giovanni Battista Coderta); 2950–51, 2966, 2983, 2987, 2989, 2991, 3004, 3012, 3055 (Andrea Calzavara); 3065 (Pietro Centone); 3482, 3485, 3500, 3509, 3514, 3542, 3761 (Claudio Paulini); 3901 (Alvise Centone); 3919 (Martin Corte); 5484 (Battista Ernest); 5510 (Giorgio Emo); 5973 (Giulio Figolin e Teseo Zio); 6047, 6049, 6051, 6053, 6059–61, 6075 (Taddeo Federici); 6102, 6108, 6110–13 (Marco Fratina); 6673, 6681 (Gabriel Gabriel); 6762 (Giovanni Grandis); 6796–97, 6800–01 (Giovanni Antonio Generini); 8461, 8465, 8467, 8475, 8478, 8493 (Alberto Mastaleo); 8504 (Paolo Moretti); 8515 (Paolo Moretti and Simone Porta); 8873, 8878 (Andrea Mastaleo); 10797, 10805 (Giovanni Piccini); 10858, 10864, 10866, 10871 (Alessandro Pariglia); 10983 (Camillo Pincio); 11003, 11011 (Giovanni Battista Profettini); 11043 (Simone Porta); 11175, 11182 (Giulio Pincio); 11743, 11752 (Ottavio Ridolfi); 12042, 12045, 12055, 12145 (Francesco Simbeni); 12445, 12449 (Zorzi Steffani); 12666–67, 12671, 12674 (Camillo Testagrossa); 13845 (Vincenzo Vincenzi); 13920 (Pietro Venier)

Testamenti: 767 (Alessandro Pariglia), 773 (Andrea Porta), 991 (Girolamo Spinelli), 1004 (Niccolò Velano), 1197 (Giovanni Battista Giavarina), 1270 (Agostino Zon)

Testamenti chiusi: 176–85 (Pietro Bracchi)

Archivio Tiepolo, prima consegna 116

Arti 166

Avogaria di comun 2150/100, 2157/107, 2158/108, 2159/109, 2172/122, 2173/123, 2183/133, 2187/137, 2200/150, 3896

Barbaro, Marco, *Albori de' patritii veneti*

Collegio
  Esposizioni principi 63, 70, 71, 73, 75, 77
  Lettere 186

Consiglio de' dieci (CD)
  Comune, registro 116
  Criminal, filze 84, 94

Dieci savi sopra le decime in Rialto (DS), buste 218–20, 223, 387

Giudici del forestier, Sentenze 78

Giudici del mobile (GM), Sentenze a legge 281, 304, 314, 328, 330, 473–74

Giudici del proprio, Parentelle 43–44

Giudici dell'esaminador (GE)
  Esami e testamenti rilevati per breviario 105
  Estraordinari 43
  Interdetti 135, 138

Giudici di petizion (GP)
  Dimande 29, 31, 33, 34, 40, 42, 44–49
  Inventari 379, 411
  Scritture e risposte 178, 180, 184, 190

Inquisitori di stato 914

Monastero di San Lorenzo 23

Monastero di Santa Maria delle Vergini 2 bis

Monastero di Santa Maria dell'Orazion a Malamocco 3

Monastero di Sant'Anna 45 (a misfiled book of receipts for SS. Giovanni e Paolo)

Monastero di Santi Giovanni e Paolo Y–V, XXV

Ospedali e luoghi pii 37 B

Podestà di Murano 201

Procuratia di San Marco de supra, registri 145 (olim busta 75), 146

Provveditori alla sanità 879

Provveditori sopra monasteri 104, 261

Scuola Grande di San Marco (SGSM) 6bis, 13, 27, 101, 109–10, 112–13, 117–18, 184, 188, 194

Scuola Grande di Santa Maria della Carità 263

Venice, Archivio storico del patriarcato di Venezia (ASPV)

Curia patriarcale, sezione antica
  Actorum, mandatorum, praeceptorum 1670–74
  Examinum Matrimoniorum (EM) 35, 43, 45–46, 55, 57, 62, 65, 71, 79, 84, 97, 98, 100

Monialium, Atti particulari riguardanti le monache 6

Archivi parrocchiali
  San Giminiano, morti 1648–70
  San Martino 5-10

San Moisè, morti 1633–58
San Vidal:
  battesimi 1630–78
  morti, registri VI–VII
Sant'Angelo, battesimi 1639–62
Santa Maria del Giglio, morti 1643–80, 1680–1705
Santa Maria Formosa, battesimi, 1629–48
Santa Marina, Libro de' morti 7

Venice, Biblioteca del Museo civico Correr (Vmc)

Codici P.D.C. 1051, 1060–61, 1064, 1068, 2469
Codice P. D. Venier 124, Tomo 1

Venice, Biblioteca nazionale marciana (Vnm)

Cod. It. xi, 426, 8 (12142, 8)

Venice, Biblioteca della Casa Goldoni (Vcg)

Archivio Vendramin 42 F 6/1–6, 42 F 12/2, 42 F 16/1, 42 F 16/4

Venice, Parrocchia di San Salvatore

Battesimi 1647–84
Matrimoni 1647–99

Venice, Parrocchia di San Silvestro

Morti 1649–75
San Mattio, morti 1615–36

Venice, Parrocchia di San Nicola da Tolentino

Santa Croce, Registro morti, busta III, registro 12

Fano, Biblioteca comunale federiciana

MSS Federici 94

Ferrara, Archivio di stato di Ferrara (ASFe)

Archivio Bentivoglio, Lettere sciolte, buste 311, 312, 319, 322, 324, 326, 330, 331, 332, 333, 334, 335, 336, 337, 338, 339, 368

Florence, Archivio di stato di Firenze (ASF)

Carteggio d'artisti, busta 6
Mediceo del principato (MP), filze 1572, 3029, 3033, 3037, 5340, 5474, 5476–78, 5480–81, 5487, 5574

Mantua, Archivio di stato di Mantova (ASMa)

Archivio Gonzaga (AG), buste 1571–73, 2804

Modena, Archivio di stato di Modena (ASMo)

Archivio segreto estense, Cancelleria, Sezione estero, Carteggio ambasciatori, Venezia (CAV), buste 108, 120–21, 124

Padua, Università degli studi di Padova

Archivio antico, b. 152

Turin, Archivio di stato di Torino (AST)

Sezione corte, Lettere ministre, Venezia (LMV), buste 9, 9bis, 11

Hannover, Niedersächsisches Haupstaatsarchiv

Aktes-Korrespondenzen italienischer Kardinäle und anderer Personen, besonders Italiener an Herzog Johann Friedrich (HVsa, AK), Cal. Br. 22, vols. 2, 4 (consulted on microfilm)

Libretto Collections

Los Angeles, University of California at Los Angeles, Music Library, Venetian opera librettos (microfilm, Woodbridge, Conn.: Research Publications, 1993; cataloged in Alm, *Catalog of Venetian Librettos*)
Venice, Biblioteca nazionale marciana, dramm. 3448–83 (the Zeno collection, catalogued in Laini, *La raccolta zeniana*)

Printed Sources

Accademia Nazionale dei Lincei. *Convegno internazionale Cristina di Svezia e la musica, Roma, 5–6 dicembre 1996.* Atti dei convegni Lincei 138. Rome: Accademia Nazionale dei Lincei, 1998.
Ademollo, Alessandro. *La bell'Adriana ed altre virtuose del suo tempo alla corte di Mantova: Contributo di documenti per la storia della musica in Italia nel primo quarto del Seicento.* Città di Castello: S. Lapi, 1888.
———. *I primi fasti della musica italiana a Parigi (1645–1662).* Milan: Ricordi, 1884.
Agee, Richard. "The Privilege and Venetian Music Printing in the Sixteenth Century." Ph.D. diss., Princeton University, 1982.
Aikema, Bernard. *Pietro della Vecchia and the Heritage of the Renaissance in Venice.* Florence: Istituto Universitario Olandese di Storia dell'Arte, 1990.
Allerston, Patricia. "The Market in Second-Hand Clothes and Furnishings in Venice, c. 1500–c. 1650." Ph.D. diss., European University Institute, Florence, 1996.
———. "Wedding Finery in Sixteenth-Century Venice." In *Marriage in Italy, 1300–1650,* ed. Trevor Dean and K. J. P. Lowe, 25–40. Cambridge: Cambridge University Press, 1998.
Alm, Irene. *Catalog of Venetian Librettos at the University of California, Los Angeles.* Berkeley: University of California Press, 1993.
———. "Dances from the 'Four Corners of the Earth': Exoticism in Seventeenth-Century

Venetian Opera." In *Musica Franca: Essays in Honor of Frank A. D'Accone*, ed. Irene Alm, Alyson McLamore, and Colleen Reardon, 233–58. Stuyvesant, NY: Pendragon Press, 1996.

———. "A Singer Goes to Court:Virginia Camuffi and the Disaster of *Alessandro amante* (1667)." Paper delivered at the Annual Meeting of the American Musicological Society, November 1996.

———. "Theatrical Dance in Seventeenth-CenturyVenetian Opera." Ph.D diss., University of California, Los Angeles, 1993.

———. "Winged Feet and Mute Eloquence: Dance in Seventeenth-Century Venetian Opera." Ed. Wendy Heller and Rebecca Harris-Warrick. *Cambridge Opera Journal* 15 (2003): 216–80.

Annibaldi, Claudio. *La musica e il mondo: Mecenatismo e committenza musicale tra Quattro e Settecento*. Bologna: Il Mulino, 1993.

———. "Uno 'spettacolo veramente da principi': Committenza e recezione dell'opera aulica nel primo Seicento." In *Lo stupor dell'invenzione: Firenze e la nascita dell'opera: Atti del convegno internazionale di studi, Firenze, 5–6 ottobre 2000*, ed. Pietro Gargiulo, 31–60. Florence: Leo S. Olschki, 2001.

———. "Tipologia della committenza musicale nella Venezia seicentesca." In *Musica, scienza, e idee nella Serenissima durante il Seicento: Atti del Convegno internazionale di studi, Venezia, Palazzo Giustinian Lolin, 13–15 dicembre 1993*, ed. Francesco Passadore and Franco Rossi, 63–77.Venice: Edizioni Fondazione Levi, 1996.

———. "Towards a Theory of Musical Patronage in the Renaissance and Baroque:The Perspective from Anthropology and Semiotics." *Recercare* 10 (1998): 173–79.

Ault, C.Thomas. "Baroque Stage Machines forVenus and Mars from the Archivio di Stato, Parma." *Theatre Survey* 28 (1987): 27–39.

———. "Tessin's Notes on Baroque Theatre atVilla Contarini, 1688." *Theatre History Studies* 14 (1994): 151–64.

Baggiani, Franco. "I maestri di cappella nella cattedrale di Pistoia." *Bollettino storico pistoiese* 88 (1986): 41–81.

Bann, Stephen. *Under the Sign: John Bargrave as Collector, Traveler, and Witness*. Ann Arbor: University of Michigan Press, 1994.

Barzaghi, Antonio. *Donne o cortigiane? La prostituzione a Venezia: Documenti di costume dal XVI al XVIII secolo*.Verona: Bertani, 1980.

Battaglia, Michele. *Delle accademie veneziane: Dissertazione storica*.Venice: Orlandelli, 1826.

Bauman, Thomas. "The Society of La Fenice and Its First Impresarios." *Journal of the American Musicological Society* 39 (1986): 332–54.

Becker, Heinz, ed. *Quellentexte zur Konzeption der europäischen Oper im 17. Jahrhundert*. Musikwissenschaftliche Arbeiten 27. Kassel: Bärenreiter, 1981.

Bellina, Anna Laura, and Thomas Walker. "Il melodramma: Poesia e musica nell'esperienza teatrale." In *Il Seicento*, 409–32. *Storia della cultura veneta* 4.1.Vicenza: N. Pozza, 1983.

Benedetti, Silvano. "Il teatro musicale a Venezia nel '600: Aspetti organizzativi." *Studi veneziani* 8 (1984): 185–220.

Bergman, Gösta M. *Lighting in the Theatre*.Totowa, NJ: Rowman and Littlefield, 1977.

Besutti, Paola. *La corte musicale di Ferdinando Carlo Gonzaga ultimo duca di Mantova: Musici, cantanti e teatro d'opera tra il 1665 e il 1707*. Mantua: G.Arcari, 1989.

Bianconi, Lorenzo. "L'Ercole in Rialto." In *Venezia e il melodramma nel seicento*, ed. Maria Teresa Muraro, 259–72. Florence: Leo S. Olschki, 1975.

———. "Funktionen des Operntheaters in Neapel bis 1700 und die Rolle Alessandro Scarlattis." In *Colloquium Alessandro Scarlatti Wurzburg 1975*, ed.Wolfgang Osthoff and Jutta Ruile-Dronke, 13–116.Würzburger musikhistorische Beiträge 7.Tützing: Schneider, 1979.

————. *Music in the Seventeenth Century*. Trans. David Bryant. Cambridge: Cambridge University Press, 1987.

Bianconi, Lorenzo, and Giorgio Pestelli, eds. *Opera Production and Its Resources*. Translated by Lydia G. Cochrane. *The History of Italian Opera* 4. Chicago: University of Chicago Press, 1998.

————. *Opera on Stage*. Translated by Kate Singleton. *The History of Italian Opera* 5. Chicago: University of Chicago Press, 2002.

Bianconi, Lorenzo, and Thomas Walker. "Dalla *Finta pazza* alla *Veremonda*: Storie di Febiarmonici." *Rivista italiana di musicologia* 10 (1975): 379–454.

————. "Production, Consumption and Political Function of Seventeenth-Century Opera." *Early Music History* 4 (1984): 211–99.

Billio, Nicoletta. "Contributo sugli inizi di carriera di Agostino Steffani, Antonio Draghi e Carlo Pallavicino, musicisti al Santo di Padova." In *Musica, scienza e idee nella Serenissima durante il Seicento: Atti del Convegno internazionale di studi, Venezia – Palazzo Giustinian Lolin 13–15 dicembre 1993*, ed. Francesco Passadore and Franco Rossi, 55–61. Venice: Edizioni Fondazione Levi, 1996.

Billio D'Arpa, Nicoletta. "Documenti inediti su Agostino Steffani, cantore soprano tra Padova e Venezia (1664–1667)." *Rassegna veneta di studi musicali* 7 (1991): 121–46.

Bistort, Giulio. *Il magistrato alle pompe nella republica di Venezia: Studio storico*. Venice: Tip. Libr. Emiliana, 1912.

Bjurström, Per. *Giacomo Torelli and Baroque Stage Design*. Stockholm: Nationalmuseum, 1961.

————. "Unveröffentliches von Nicodemus Tessin d. J.: Reisenotizen über Barock-Theater in Venedig und Piazzola." *Kleine Schriften der Gesellschaft für Theatergeschichte* 21 (1966): 14–41.

Boccato, Carla. "La mortalità nel ghetto di Venezia durante la peste del 1630." *Archivio Veneto*, 5th ser., 175 (1993): 111–46.

————. "La rilevazione delle cedole testamentarie: Procedura ed esempi in documenti veneziani del secolo XVII." *Archivio Veneto*, 5th ser., 172 (1991): 119–30.

Borean, Linda, and Isabella Cecchini. "Microstorie d'affari e quadri: I Lumaga tra Venezia e Napoli." In *Figure di collezionisti a Venezia tra Cinque e Seicento*, ed. Linda Borean and Stefania Mason, 159–231. Udine: Forum, 2002.

Boscolo, Lucia, and Maddalena Pietribiasi. *La cappella musicale antoniana di Padova nel secolo XVIII: Delibere della Veneranda Arca*. Padua: Associazione Centro Studi Antoniani, 1997.

Bouquet, Marie-Thérèse. *Musique et musiciens à Turin de 1648 à 1775*. Memoria dell'Accademia delle Scienze di Torino, 4th ser., no. 17. Turin: Accademia delle Scienze 1968.

————. *Il Teatro di Corte dalle origini al 1788*. Vol. 1: *Storia del Teatro Regio di Torino*. Turin: Cassa di Risparmio di Torino, 1976.

Brockpähler, Renate. *Handbuch zur Geschichte der Barockoper in Deutschland*. Emsdetten: Lechte, 1964.

Brown, Jennifer Williams. "'Con nuove arie aggiunte': Aria Borrowing in the Venetian Opera Repertory, 1672–1685." Ph.D. diss., Cornell University, 1992.

————. "'Innsbruck, ich muss dich lassen': Cesti, *Orontea*, and the Gelone Problem." *Cambridge Opera Journal* 12 (2001): 179–217.

————. "'*L'opera è labile*': Cavalli and *Scipione Affricano*." Paper delivered at the Annual Meeting of the American Musicological Society, November 2003.

Brugnoni, Tiziana. "'Curiose mutanze, novità, stravaganze': Un esempio di scenografia veneziana del tardo Seicento nei bozzetti per le scene di Germanico sul Reno." *Rivista italiana di musicologia* 27 (1992): 125–44.

Brunelli, Bruno. "L'impresario in angustie." *Rivista italiana del dramma* 3 (1941): 311–41.

Burke, Peter. *The Historical Anthropology of Early Modern Italy*. Cambridge: Cambridge University Press, 1987.

Caffi, Francesco. *Storia della musica sacra nella già cappella ducale di S. Marco in Venezia (dal 1318 al 1797)*. 2 vols. Venice: Antonelli, 1853.

———. *Storia della musica teatrale in Venezia*. 4 vols. MS. I-Vnm It. Cl. IV. Cod. 747–49 (10462–65).

Calcagno, Mauro. "Fonti, ricezione e ruolo della committenza nell'*Eliogabalo* musicato da F. Cavalli, G. A. Boretti e T. Orgiani (1667–1687)." In *La circolazione dell'opera veneziana del '600 nel IV centenario della nascita di Francesco Cavalli*, 77–100. Naples: I Turchini Saggi, 2005.

———. "A Libretto and Its Discontents: Censoring *Eliogabalo* in Seventeenth-Century Venice." *Journal of Interdisciplinary History*, forthcoming.

———. "Signifying Nothing: On the Aesthetics of Pure Voice in Early Venetian Opera." *Journal of Musicology* 20 (2003): 461–97.

———. "Staging Musical Discourses in Seventeenth-Century Venice: Francesco Cavalli's *Eliogabalo* (1667)." Ph.D. diss., Yale University, 2000.

Cametti, Alberto. *Cristina di Svezia, l'arte musicale e gli spettacoli teatrali in Roma*. Rome: Nuova antologia, 1911.

———. *Il teatro di Tordinona poi di Apollo*. Tivoli: Arti Grafiche A. Chicca, 1938.

Cannizzaro, Nina. "Studies on Guido Casoni (1561–1642) and Venetian Academies." Ph. D. diss., Harvard University, 2001.

Capponi, Giovanni Battista, and Valerio Zani. *Memorie imprese, e ritratti de' signori Accademici Gelati di Bologna*. Bologna: Manolessi, 1672.

Carter, Tim. *Monteverdi's Musical Theatre*. New Haven: Yale University Press, 2002.

———. "Singing Orfeo." *Recercare* 11 (1999): 75–118.

Castle Theatre in Česke Krumlov. Online. Available: http://www.ckrumlov.cz/. Accessed June 3, 2004.

Cecchetti, Bartolomeo. "Carte relative ai teatri di S. Cassiano e dei SS. Giovanni e Paolo." *Archivio veneto* 17 (1887): 246.

Claretta, Gaudenzio. *Storia del regno e dei tempi di Carlo Emanuele II, Duca di Savoia*. 3 vols. Genoa: R. Istituto de' sordo-muti, 1877–78.

Colzani, Alberto. "La cappella musicale di Santa Maria Maggiore a Bergamo dopo Legrenzi." In *Giovanni Legrenzi e la cappella ducale di San Marco: Atti dei convegni internazionali di studi, Venezia, 24–26 maggio 1990, Clusone, 14–16 settembre 1990*, ed. Francesco Passadore and Franco Rossi, 29–45. Florence: Leo S. Olschki, 1994.

Constable, M. "The Venetian *Figlie del coro*: Their Environment and Achievement." *Music & Letters* 63 (1982): 181–212.

Il corago: o vero alcune osservazioni per metter bene in scena le composizioni drammatiche. Ed. Paolo Fabbri and Angelo Pompilio. Florence: Leo S. Olschki, 1983.

Cornelio, Flaminio. *Ecclesiae venetae antiquis monumentis*. 13 vols. Venice: Jo. Baptistae Pasquale 1749.

Cowan, Alex. "Love, honour and the *Avogaria di comun* in Early Modern Venice." *Archivio veneto*, no. 126, 5th ser., 144 (1995): 5–19.

———. "New Families in the Venetian Patriciate 1646–1718." *Ateneo veneto* 23 (1985): 55–76.

———. "Rich and Poor among the Patriciate in Early Modern Venice." *Studi veneziani*, n.s., 6 (1982): 147–60.

Crowther, Victor. *The Oratorio in Bologna (1650–1730)*. Oxford: Oxford University Press, 1999.

Culley, Thomas D., S.J. *Jesuits and Music: I. A Study of the Musicians Connected with the German College in Rome during the 17th Century and of their Activities in Northern Europe*. St. Louis: Jesuit Historical Institute, 1970.

D'Alessandro, Domenico Antonio. "L'opera in musica a Napoli dal 1650 al 1670." In *Seicento napoletano*, ed. Roberto Pane, 409–30. Milan: Edizioni di Communità, 1984.

D'Alessandro, Domenico Antonio, and Agostino Ziino, eds. *La musica a Napoli durante il Seicento: Atti del convegno internazionale di studi: Napoli, 11–14 aprile 1985*. Rome: Edizioni Torre d'Orfeo, 1987.

Damerini, Gino. "Cronache del Teatro Vendramin." *Il dramma* 291 (1960): 103–114; 294 (1961): 49–58; 296 (1961): 44–61; 298 (1961): 41–50; 302 (1961): 66–86; 304 (1962): 53–64; 321 (1963): 49–56.

———. "Il trapianto dello spettacolo teatrale veneziano del Seicento nella civiltà barocca europea." In *Barocco europeo e barocco veneziano*, ed. Vittore Branca, 223–39. Florence: Sansoni, 1962.

Da Mosto, Andrea. *I bravi di Venezia*. Milan: Ciarrocca, 1950.

———. "Il teatro a Venezia nel secolo XVII." *Rivista politica e letteraria* 8 (1899): 144–64.

———. "Uomini e cose del '600 veneziano (da un epistolario inedito)." *Rivista di Venezia* 12, no. 3 (1933): 117–22.

Daolmi, Davide. *Le origini dell'opera a Milano (1598–1649)*. Studi sulla storia della musica in Lombardia. Collana di testi musicologici 2. Turnhout: Brepols, 1998.

Davis, Robert C., and Benjamin Ravid, eds. *The Jews of Early Modern Venice*. Baltimore and London: Johns Hopkins University Press, 2001.

Della Seta, Fabrizio, "The Librettist." In *Opera Production and Its Resources*, ed. Lorenzo Bianconi and Giorgio Pestelli, trans. Lydia G. Cochrane, 229–89. *The History of Italian Opera* 4. Chicago: University of Chicago Press, 1998.

Di Luca, Claudia. "Tra 'sperimentazione' e 'professionismo' teatrale: Pio Enea II Obizzi e lo spettacolo nel Seicento." *Teatro e storia* 6 (1991): 257–303

Dubowy, Norbert. " 'L'amor coniugale nel Seicento': Das Leben der Sängerin und Komponistin Marietta Barbieri erzählt von Faustini Barbieri aus Brescia." In *Barocco padano*, ed. Alberto Colzani, Andrea Luppi, and Maurizio Padoan, 1:181–208. Como: A.M.I.S. (Antique Musicae Italicae Studiosi), 2002.

Durante, Sergio. "The Opera Singer." In *Opera Production and Its Resources*, ed. Lorenzo Bianconi and Giorgio Pestelli, trans. Lydia G. Cochrane, 345–417. *The History of Italian Opera* 4. Chicago: University of Chicago Press, 1998.

Einstein, Alfred. "Italienische Musiker am Hofe der Neuberger Wittelsbacher, 1614–1716." *Sammelbände der Internationalen Musik-Gesellschaft* 9 (1907–8): 336–424.

Eitner, Robert. *Biographisch-bibliographisches Quellen-Lexikon der Musiker und Musikgelehrten der christlichen Zeitrechnung bis zur Mitte des neunzehnten Jahrhunderts*. New York: Musurgia, 1947.

Emans, Reinmar. "La cappella ducale di San Marco in Venezia, punto di partenza per la carriera internazionale dei cantanti." In *Barocco padano*, ed. Alberto Colzani, Andrea Luppi, and Maurizio Padoan, 2:247–62. Como: A.M.I.S. (Antique Musicae Italicae Studiosi), 2002.

———. "Die Musiker des Markusdoms." *Kirchenmusikalisches Jahrbuch* 65 (1981): 45–81; 66 (1982): 63–82.

Enciclopedia dello spettacolo. 9 vols. Rome: Le Maschere, 1954–68.

Evelyn, John. *Diaries*. Ed. E. S. de Beer. 6 vols. Oxford: Clarendon Press, 1955.

———. *The Memoires of John Evelyn*. 2 vols. Ed. W. Bray. London: H. Colburn, 1819.

Fabbri, Paolo. *Monteverdi*. Trans. Tim Carter. Cambridge: Cambridge University Press, 1994.

———. "Una recensione 'in rima' della *Divisione del mondo* (1675)." In *Giovanni Legrenzi e la cappella ducale di San Marco: Atti dei convegni internazionali di studi, Venezia, 24–26 maggio 1990, Clusone, 14–16 settembre 1990*, ed. Francesco Passadore and Franco Rossi, 433–56. Florence: Leo S. Olschki, 1994.

————. *Il secolo cantante: Per una storia del libretto d'opera nel Seicento*. Bologna: Mulino, 1990.

Fabris, Dinko. *Mecenati e musici: Documenti sul patronato artistico dei Bentivoglio di Ferrara nell'epoca di Monteverdi (1585–1645)*. Lucca: Libreria Musicale Italiana, 1999.

Fantuzzi, Giovanni. *Notizie degli scrittori bolognesi*. 6 vols. Bologna: Stamperia di S. Tommaso d'Aquino, 1781–94.

Federhofer, Hellmut. *Musikpflege und Musiker am Grazer Habsburgerhof*. Mainz, B. Schott's Söhne, 1967.

Feldman, Martha. "Authors and Anonyms: Recovering the Anonymous Subject in *Cinquecento* Vernacular Objects." In *Music and the Cultures of Print*, ed. Kate van Orden, 163–98. New York: Garland, 2000.

Ficola, Daniele, and Giuseppe Collisani, "Bartolomeo Montalbano da Bologna, musicista francescano." *Studi musicali* 16 (1987): 133–56.

Fileti Mazza, Miriam. *Eredità del Cardinale Leopoldo de' Medici: 1675–1676*. Centro di Ricerche Informatiche per i Beni Culturali, Accademia della Crusca, Strumenti e Testi 4. Pisa: Scuola Normale Superiore, 1997.

Fontijn, Claire. *Desperate Measures: The Life and Music of Antonia Padoani Bembo*. New York: Oxford University Press, forthcoming.

Franchi, Saverio. *Drammaturgia romana: Repertorio bibliografico cronologico dei testi drammatici pubblicati a Roma e nel Lazio*. Rome: Edizioni di Storia e Letteratura, 1988.

Frandsen, Mary. *Crossing Confessional Boundaries: The Patronage of Italian Sacred Music in Seventeenth-Century Dresden*. New York: Oxford University Press, forthcoming.

Freitas, Roger. "*Un Atto d'ingegno*: A Castrato in the Seventeenth Century." Ph.D. diss., Yale University, 1998.

————. "The Eroticism of Emasculation: Confronting the Baroque Body of the Castrato." *Journal of Musicology* 20 (2003): 196–249.

Frick, Carole Collier. *Dressing Renaissance Florence: Families, Fortunes, and Fine Clothing*. Baltimore and London: Johns Hopkins University Press, 2002.

Gambassi, Osvaldo. *La cappella musicale di S. Petronio: Maestri, organisti, cantori e strumentisti dal 1436 al 1920*. Historiae musicae cultores, Biblioteca 44. Florence: Leo S. Olschki, 1987.

Gandolfi, Vittorio. *Il Teatro Farnese di Parma*. Parma: L. Battei, 1980.

Giacobello, Sebastiano. "Giovan Domenico Ottonelli sulle donne cantatrici." *Studi musicali* 26 (1997): 297–311.

Giampaoli, Stefano. *Musica e teatro alla corte di Massa: I Guglielmi*. Massa: Palazzo di S. Elisabetta, 1978.

Gianturco, Carolyn. *Alessandro Stradella 1639–1682: His Life and Music*. Oxford: Clarendon Press, 1994.

Giazotto, Remo. "La guerra dei palchi." *Nuova rivista musicale italiana*, 1 (1967): 245–86, 465–508; 3 (1969): 906–33.

Gios, Pierantonio. *L'itinerario biografico di Gregorio Barbarigo: Dal contesto familiare all'episcopato: Lettere ai familiari (1655–1657)*. San Gregorio Barbarigo, fonti e ricerche 2. Padua: Istituto per la storia ecclesiastica padovana, 1996.

Glixon, Beth L. "More on the Life and Death of Barbara Strozzi." *Musical Quarterly* 83 (1999): 131–41.

————. "Music for the Gods? A Dispute Concerning F. Lucio's *Gl'Amori di Alessandro Magno, e di Rossane* (1651)," *Early Music* 26 (1998), 445–54.

————. "New Light on the Life and Career of Barbara Strozzi." *Musical Quarterly* 81 (1997): 311–35.

————. " 'Poner in musica un'opera': Cavalli and his Impresari in Mid-Seicento Venice." In *La circolazione dell'opera veneziana del '600 nel IV centenario della nascita di Francesco Cavalli*, 59–76. Naples: I Turchini Saggi, 2005.

————. "Private Lives of Public Women: Prima Donnas in Mid-Seventeenth-Century Venice." *Music & Letters*, 76 (1995): 509–531.

————. "Scenes from the Life of Silvia Gailarti Manni, a Seventeenth-Century *Virtuosa.*" *Early Music History* 15 (1996): 97–146.

————. "La sirena antica dell'Adriatico: Caterina Porri, a Seventeenth-Century Roman Prima Donna on the Stages of Venice, Bologna, and Pavia." In *Musical Voices of Early Modern Women: Many-Headed Melodies*, ed. Thomasin LaMay, 211–37. Aldershot: Ashgate, 2005.

Glixon, Beth L., and Jonathan E. Glixon. "Marco Faustini and Venetian Opera Production in the 1650s." *Journal of Musicology* 10 (1992): 48–73.

———— "Oil and Opera Don't Mix: The Biography of S. Aponal, a Seventeenth-Century Venetian Opera Theater." In *Music in the Theater, Church, and Villa: Essays in Honor of Robert Lamar Weaver and Norma Wright Weaver*, ed. Susan Parisi, 131–44. Warren, Mich.: Harmonie Park Press, 2000.

————. "The Triumph of Inconstancy: The Vicissitudes of a Venetian Libretto." Forthcoming.

Glixon, Jonathan E. *Honoring God and the City: A Documentary History of Music at the Venetian Confraternities, 1260–1807*. New York: Oxford University Press, 2003.

————. "Images of Paradise or Worldly Theaters? Towards a Taxonomy of Musical Performances at Venetian Nunneries." In *Essays on Music and Culture in Honor of Herbert Kellman*, ed. Barbara Haggh, 423–51. Paris: Minerve, 2001.

————. *Music for the Nuns of Venice*. Forthcoming.

————. "A Musicians' Union in Sixteenth-Century Venice." *Journal of the American Musicological Society* 36 (1983): 392–421.

Le Glorie dell'Armi venete celebrate nell'Academia de' Signori Imperfetti. Venice: Gio. Pietro Pinelli, 1651.

Glover, Jane. *Cavalli*. New York: St. Martin's Press, 1978.

————. "The Teatro Sant'Apollinare and the Development of Seventeenth-Century Venetian Opera." Ph.D. diss., Oxford University, 1975.

Goldberg, Edward L. *Patterns in Late Medici Art Patronage*. Princeton: Princeton University Press, 1983.

Grendler, Paul F. *Books and Schools in the Italian Renaissance*. Aldershot: Ashgate, 1995.

———— *Schooling in Renaissance Italy: Literacy and Learning, 1300–1600*. Baltimore and London: Johns Hopkins University Press, 1989.

Groppo, Antonio. *Catalogo di tutti i drammi*. Venice, 1745. Repr. Bologna: Forni, 1977.

Guarino, Raimondo. "Torelli a Venezia: L'ingegniere teatrale tra scena e apparato." *Teatro e Storia* 7 (1992): 35–72.

Harrán, Don. "Jewish Musical Culture: Leon Modena." In *The Jews of Early Modern Venice*, ed. Robert C. Davis and Benjamin Ravid, 211–30. Baltimore and London: Johns Hopkins University Press, 2001.

Harness, Kelly. "Amazzoni di Dio: Florentine musical spectacle under Maria Maddalena d'Austria and Cristina di Lorena, 1620–1630." Ph.D diss., University of Illinois, Urbana-Champaign, 1996.

Heller, Wendy. "Chastity, Heroism, and Allure: Women in Opera of Seventeenth-Century Venice." Ph.D. diss., Brandeis University, 1995.

————. "Dancing Desire on the Venetian Stage." *Cambridge Opera Journal* 15 (2003): 281–95.

————. *Emblems of Eloquence: Opera and Women's Voices in Seventeenth-Century Venice*. Berkeley: University of California Press, 2003.

————. " 'O delle donne miserabil sesso': Tarabotti, Ottavia, and *L'incoronazione di Poppea.*" *Il saggiatore musicale* 7 (2000): 5–46.

————. "The Queen as King: Refashioning Semiramide for Seicento Venice." *Cambridge Opera Journal* 5 (1993): 93–114.

————. "Tacitus Incognito: Opera as History in *L'incoronazione di Poppea*." *Journal of the American Musicological Society* 52 (1999): 39–96.

Hill, John. "Le relazioni di Antonio Cesti con la corte e i teatri di Firenze." *Rivista italiana di musicologia* 11 (1976): 27–47.

Holmes, William C. *Opera Observed: Views of a Florentine Impresario in the Early Eighteenth Century*. Chicago: University of Chicago Press, 1993.

————. "Operatic Commissions and Productions at Pratolino: *Ifianassa e Melampo* by Moniglia and Legrenzi." *Journal of Musicology* 17 (1999): 152–167.

————. "The Teatro della Pergola in Florence: Its Administration, its Building, and its Audiences." In *Musica Franca: Essays in Honor of Frank A. D'Accone*, ed. Irene Alm, Alyson McLamore, and Colleen Reardon, 259–82. Stuyvesant, NY: Pendragon Press, 1996.

Infelise, Mario. *L'editoria veneziana nel '700*. Milan: Franco Angeli, 1989.

————. "*Ex ignoto notus*? Note sul tipografo Sarzina e l'accademia degli Incogniti." In *Libri tipografi biblioteche: Ricerche storiche dedicate a Luigi Balsamo*, ed. Istituto di biblioteconomia e paleografia, 207–23. Florence: Leo S. Olschki, 1997.

————. "La crise de la librairie vénitienne 1620–1650." In *Le livre et l'historien: Études offertes en l'honneur du Professeur Henri-Jean Martin*, ed. Frédéric Barbier, Annie Parent-Charon, François Dupuigrenet Desroussilles, Claude Jolly, and Dominique Varry, 343–52. Histoire et civilisation du livre 24. Geneva: Droz, 1997.

Ivaldi, Armando Fabio. "Gli Adorni e l'hostaria-teatro del Falcone di Genova (1600–1680): I." *Rivista italiana di musicologia* 15 (1980): 87–152.

————. "Spigolature del barocco musicale genovese." *La berio: Bollettino d'informazioni bibliografiche* 22 (1982): 16–47.

————. "Teatro e società genovese al tempo di Alessandro Stradella." *Chigiana* 39, II n.s., no. 19 (1982): 447–574.

Ivanovich, Cristoforo. *Memorie teatrali di Venezia*, ed. Norbert Dubowy. Venice, 1688. Repr. Lucca: Libreria musicale italiana, 1993.

Jander, Owen. "The Prologues and Intermezzos of Alessandro Stradella." *Analecta musicologica* 7 (1969): 87–111.

Jeffery, Peter. "The Autograph Manuscripts of Francesco Cavalli." Ph.D. diss., Princeton University, 1980.

Johnson, Eugene J. "Jacopo Sansovino, Giacomo Torelli, and the Theatricality of the Piazzetta in Venice." *Journal of the Society of Architectural Historians* 59 (2000): 436–53.

————. "The Short, Lascivious Lives of Two Venetian Comedy Theaters, 1580–1585." *Renaissance Quarterly* 55 (2002): 936–57.

Kalista, Zdenek. *Korespondence císaře Leopolda I. s Humprechtem Janem Cernimem z Chudenic: I. Duben 1660-zari 1663*. Prague: Nakladem Ceske Akad. ved a Umeni, 1936.

Kendrick, Robert L. *Celestial Sirens: Nuns and Their Music in Early Modern Milan*. Oxford and New York: Clarendon Press, 1996.

Kirkendale, Warren. *The Court Musicians in Florence during the Principate of the Medici with a Reconstruction of the Artistic Establishment*. Historiae musicae cultores, Biblioteca, 61. Florence: Leo S. Olschki, 1993.

Kretzschmar, Hermann. "Die venetianische Oper und die Werke Cavallis und Cestis." *Vierteljahrsschrift für Musikwissenschaft* 8 (1902): 1–76.

Laini, Marinella. "La musica di Antonia Bembo: Un significativo apporto femminile alle relazioni musicali tra Venezia e Parigi." *Studi musicali* 25 (1996): 255–81.

————. *La raccolta zeniana di drammi per musica veneziani della Biblioteca nazionale marciana, 1637–1700*. Ancilla Musicae 6. Lucca: Libreria Musicale Italiana, 1995.

Larson, Orville K. "Giacomo Torelli, Sir Philip Skippon, and Stage Machinery for the Venetian Opera." *Theatre Journal* 32 (1980): 448–59.

————. "New Evidence on the Origins of the Box Set." *Theatre Survey* 21 (1980): 79–91.

Lawner, Lynne. *Lives of the Courtesans: Portraits of the Renaissance*. New York: Rizzoli, 1987.

Liess, Andreas. "Materialen zur römischer Musikgeschichte des Seicento." *Acta musicologica* 29 (1957): 137–71.

Lindgren, Lowell Edwin, and Carl B. Schmidt. "A Collection of 137 Broadsides Concerning Theatre in Late Seventeenth-Century Italy: An Annotated Catalogue." *Harvard Library Bulletin* 28 (1980): 185–233.

Lionnet, Jean. "La musique a Saint-Louis des Français de Rome au XVIIe siècle." *Note d'archivio per la storia musicale*, n.s., supplemento 3 (1985).

Litta, Pompeo. *Famiglie celebri italiane*. 10 vols. Milan: P. E. Giusti, 1819–83.

Livingston, Arthur. *La vita veneziana nelle opere di Gian Francesco Busenello*. Venice: V. Callegari, 1913.

Mabbett, Margaret. "Italian Musicians in Restoration England." *Music & Letters* 67 (1986): 237–43.

Maione, Paologiovanni, "Giulia de Caro 'seu Ciulla' da commediante a cantarina: Osservazioni sulla condizione degli 'armonici' nella seconda metà del Seicento." *Rivista italiana di musicologia* 32 (1997): 61–80.

Mamone, Sara. "Accademie e opera in musica nella vita di Giovan Carlo, Mattias e Leopoldo de' Medici, fratelli del granduca Ferdinando." In *Lo stupor dell'invenzione: Firenze e la nascita dell'opera: Atti del convegno internazionale di studi, Firenze, 5–6 ottobre 2000*, ed. Pietro Gargiulo, 119–38. Florence: Leo S. Olschki, 2001.

————. "Most Serene Brothers–Princes–Impresarios: Theater in Florence under the Management and Protection of Mattias, Giovan Carlo, and Leopoldo de' Medici." *Journal of Seventeenth-Century Music* 9 (2003) Online. Available: http://sscm-jscm.press.uiuc.edu/jscm/v9/no1/Mamone.html. Accessed June 6, 2004.

Mamy, Sylvie. *Les grands castrats napolitains a Venise au XVIIIe siècle*. Liege: Mardaga, 1994.

Mancini, Franco, Maria Teresa Muraro, and Elena Povoledo. *Illusione e pratica teatrale: Proposte per una lettura dello spazio scenico dagli intermedi fiorentini all'opera comica veneziana; catalogo della mostra*. Vicenza: N. Pozza, 1975.

————. *I teatri di Venezia*. 2 vols. I Teatri del Veneto 1–2. Venice: Corbo e Fiore, 1995–96.

Mangini, Nicola. "Alle origini del teatro moderno: Lo spettacolo pubblico nel Veneto tra Cinquecento e Seicento." *Biblioteca Teatrale*, n.s., 5/6 (1987): 87–103.

————. *I teatri di Venezia*. Milan: Mursia, 1974.

Maretti, Alessandra. "Dal Teatro del principe alla scena dei virtuosi: Indicazioni sul mecenatismo di Mattias de' Medici (1629–1666)." *Medioevo e rinascimento* 6/n.s. III (1992): 195–209.

Massar, Phyllis Dearborn. "Costume Drawings by Stefano della Bella for the Florentine Theater." *Master Drawings* 8 (1970): 243–66.

Matteini, Nevio. *Il "Rimino", una delle prime "gazzette" d'Italia: Saggio storico sui primordi della stampa*. Bologna: Cappelli, 1967.

Mayer, Martin. *The Met: One Hundred Years of Grand Opera*. New York: Simon and Schuster, 1983.

Maylender, Michele. *Storia delle accademie d'Italia*. 5 vols. Bologna: L. Cappelli, 1926–30. Repr. Bologna: Forni, 1976.

Megale, Teresa. "Altre novità su Anna Francesca Costa e sull'allestimento dell'*Ergirodo*." *Medioevo e rinascimento* 7 (1993): 137–42.

————. "Il principe e la cantante: Riflessi impresariali di una protezione." *Medioevo e rinascimento* 6 (1992): 211–33.

Mele, Donato. *L'Accademia dello Spirito Santo: Un'istituzione musicale ferrarese del sec. XVII*. Ferrara: Liberty House, 1990.

Miato, Monica. *L'Accademia degli Incogniti di Giovan Francesco Loredan. Venezia (1630–1661)*. Accademia Toscana di scienze e lettere "La Colombaria." Studi, no. 172. Florence: Leo S. Olschki, 1998.

Michelassi, Nicola. "La *Finta pazza* a Firenze: Commedie 'spagnole' e 'veneziane' nel Teatro di Baldracca (1641–1665)." *Studi secenteschi* 41 (2000): 313–53.

———. "Il Teatro del Cocomero di Firenze: Uno stanzone per tre accademie (1651–1665)." *Studi secenteschi* 40 (1999): 149–84.

Milesi, Francesco, ed. *Giacomo Torelli: L'invenzione scenica nell'Europa barocca*. Fano: Fondazione Cassa di Risparmio di Fano, 2000.

Miller, Roark Thurston. "The Composers of San Marco and Santo Stefano and the Development of Venetian Monody (to 1630)." Ph.D. diss., University of Michigan, 1993.

Mirto, Alfonso. "Librai veneziani nel Seicento: Combi-La Noù ed il commercio con l'estero." *Bibliofilia* 91 (1989): 287–305.

Mohler, Frank. "A Brief Shining Moment: An Effect that Disappeared from the Illusionistic Stage." *Theatre Symposium* 4 (1996): 83–90.

———. "The Court Theatre at Mnichovo Hradiste: The Groove System Survives on the Continent." *Theatre Design and Technology*, Winter 2003, 48–58. Also online. Available: http://www1.appstate.edu/orgs/spectacle/mnichovohradiste.html. Accessed June 3, 2004.

Molà, Luca. *The Silk Industry of Renaissance Venice*. Baltimore: Johns Hopkins University Press, 2000.

Molinari, Cesare. "Disegni a Parma per uno spettacolo veneziano." *Critica d'arte* 70 (1965): 47–64.

———. *Le nozze degli dei: Un saggio sul grande spettacolo italiano nel Seicento*. Rome: M. Bulzoni, 1968.

Monaldini, Sergio. "Gli anni ferraresi di Antonio Draghi." In *"Quel novo Cario, quel divin Orfeo": Antonio Draghi da Rimini a Vienna*, ed. Emilio Sala and Davide Daolmi, 15–34. Lucca: Libreria italiana musicale, 2000.

———. *L'orto dell'Esperidi: Musici, attori e artisti nel patrocinio della famiglia Bentivoglio (1646–1685)*. Lucca: Libreria italiana musicale, 2000.

Monteverdi, Claudio. *The Letters of Claudio Monteverdi*. Ed. and trans. Denis Stevens. Revised edition. Oxford: Clarendon Press, 1995.

Moore, James H. "'Venezia favorita da Maria': Music for the Madonna Nicopeia and Santa Maria della Salute." *Journal of the American Musicological Society* 37 (1984): 299–355.

———. *Vespers at St. Mark's: Music of Alessandro Grandi, Giovanni Rovetta, and Francesco Cavalli*. Ann Arbor: UMI Research Press, 1981.

Morelli, Arnaldo. "Legrenzi e i suoi rapporti con Ippolito Bentivoglio e l'ambiente ferrarese. Nuovi documenti." In *Giovanni Legrenzi e la cappella ducale di San Marco: Atti dei convegni internazionali di studi, Venezia, 24–26 maggio 1990, Clusone, 14–16 settembre 1990*, ed. Francesco Passadore and Franco Rossi, 47–86. Florence: Leo S. Olschki, 1994.

Morelli, Giovanni, and Thomas Walker, "Tre controversie intorno al San Cassiano." In *Venezia e il melodramma nel Seicento*, ed. Maria Teresa Muraro, 97–120. Florence: Leo S. Olschki, 1976.

Mossey, Christopher John. "Human after All: Character and Self-understanding in Operas by Giovanni Faustini and Francesco Cavalli, 1644–1652." Ph.D. diss., Brandeis University, 1999.

Muir, Edward. *Civic Ritual in Renaissance Venice*. Princeton: Princeton University Press, 1981.

Muraro, Maria Teresa. "Teatro, scena e messinscena: Lessico degli addetti ai lavori." In *Le parole della musica*. Vol. 2: *Studi sul lessico della letteratura critica del teatro musicale in onore di Gianfranco Folena*, ed. Maria Teresa Muraro, 47–55. Florence: Leo S. Olschki, 1995.

Murata, Margaret. *Operas for the Papal Court, 1631–1668*. Ann Arbor: UMI Research Press, 1981.

——. "Why the First Opera Given in Paris Wasn't Roman." *Cambridge Opera Journal* 7 (1995): 87–105.

Nacamulli, Flavia. "Notizie su alcuni pittori operanti a Venezia nella seconda metà del Seicento." *Arte Veneta* 4 (1987): 184–88.

Ongaro, Giulio Maria. "All Work and No Play? The Organization of Work among Musicians in Late Renaissance Venice." *Journal of Medieval and Renaissance Studies* 25 (1995): 55–72.

O'Regan, Noel. *Institutional Patronage in Post-Tridentine Rome*. Royal Musical Association Monographs 7. London: Royal Musical Association, 1995.

Orrell, John. *The Theatres of Inigo Jones and John Webb*. Cambridge: Cambridge University Press, 1985.

Osthoff, Wolfgang. "Filiberto Laurenzis Musik zu 'La finta Savia' im zusammenhang der Frühvenezianischen Oper." In *Venezia e il melodramma nel Seicento*, ed. Maria Teresa Muraro, 173–97. Florence: Leo S. Olschki, 1976.

——. "Zur Bologneser Aufführung von Monteverdis 'Ritorno di Ulisse' im Jahre 1640." In *Oesterreichische Akademie der Wissenschaften. Anzeiger der phil.-hist. Klasse 1958*. Mitteilungen der Kommission für Musikforschung 11, 155–160. Vienna: R. M. Rohrer, 1958.

Pascucci, Daphne. "European Stage Design in the Age of Monteverdi: Costume in Early Italian Opera and Spectacle." In *Proceedings of the International Congress on Performing Practice in Monteverdi's Music: The Historic-Philological Background*, ed. Raffaello Monterosso, 215–64. Cremona: Fondazione Claudio Monteverdi, 1995.

Passadore, Francesco, and Franco Rossi. *San Marco: Vitalità di una tradizione*. 3 vols. Venice: Edizioni Fondzione Levi, 1996.

Pedani Fabris, Maria Pia. *"Veneta auctoritate notarius": Storia del notariato veneziano (1514–1797)*. Milan: Giuffré, 1996.

Pellicelli, Nestore. "Musicisti in Parma nel secolo xvii." *Note d'archivio* 9 (1932): 217–46; 10 (1933): 32–43, 116–26, 233–48, 314–25.

Pesenti, Tiziana. "Stampatori e letterati nell'industria editoriale a Venezia e in Terraferma." In *Il Seicento*, 93–129. *Storia della cultura veneta* 4.1. Vicenza: N. Pozza, 1983.

Petrobelli, Pierluigi. " 'L'Ermiona' di Pio Enea degli Obizzi ed i primi spettacoli d'opera veneziani." *Quaderni della Rassegna musicale* 3 (1965): 125–41.

——. "La partitura del *Massimo Puppieno* di Carlo Pallavicino (Venezia 1684)." In *Venezia e il melodramma nel Seicento*, ed. Maria Teresa Muraro, 273–97. Florence: Leo S. Olschki, 1976.

Pigozzi, Marinella. "Pietro Antonio Cerva decoratore e scenografo bolognese del '600." *Carrobbio* 13 (1987): 279–89.

Pirrotta, Nino. "The Lame Horse and the Coachman: News of the Operatic Parnassus in 1642." In *Music and Culture in Italy from the Middle Ages to the Baroque: A Collection of Essays*, 325–34. Cambridge, Mass.: Harvard University Press, 1984.

——. "Note su Minato." In *L'opera italiana a Vienna prima di Metastasio*, ed. Maria Teresa Muraro, 127–63. Florence: Leo S. Olschki, 1990.

——. "Theater, Sets, and Music in Monteverdi's Operas." In *Music and Culture in Italy from the Middle Ages to Baroque: A Collection of Essays*, 254–70. Cambridge, Mass.: Harvard University Press, 1984.

Povoledo, Elena. "Controversie monteverdiane: Spazi teatrali e immagini presunte." In *Claudio Monteverdi: Studi e prospettive,* ed. Paola Besutti, Maria Teresa Gialdroni, and Rodolfo Baroncini, 357–89. Florence: Leo S. Olschki, 1998.

————. "Una rappresentazione accademica a Venezia nel 1634." In *Studi sul teatro veneto fra Rinascimento ed età barocca*, ed. Maria Teresa Muraro, 119–69. Florence: Leo S. Olschki, 1971.

Powers, Harold S. "*L'Erismena travestita.*" In *Studies in Music History: Essays for Oliver Strunk*, ed. Harold S. Powers, 259–324. Princeton: Princeton University Press, 1968.

Preto, Paolo. *Peste e società a Venezia 1576.* Vicenza: Neri Pozza, 1978.

Prota-Giurleo, Ulisse. *Francesco Cirillo e l'introduzione del melodramma a Napoli.* Grumo Nevano: a cura del comune, 1952.

————. *Il teatro di corte del Palazzo Reale di Napoli.* Naples: Imp. L'arte tipografica, 1952.

Prunières, Henry. *Cavalli et l'opéra vénitien au xviie siècle.* Paris: Rieder, 1931.

————. *L'Opéra en France avant Lulli.* Paris: H. Champion, 1913.

Pullan, Brian. *Rich and Poor in Renaissance Venice.* Cambridge, Mass.: Harvard University Press, 1971.

Puppi, Lionello. "Il Teatro Fiorentino degli Immobili e la rappresentazione nel 1658 dell'*Ipermestra* del Tacca." In *Studi sul teatro veneto fra Rinascimento ed età barocca*, ed. Maria Teresa Muraro, 171–92. Florence: Leo S. Olschki, 1971.

Queller, Donald E. *Venetian Patriciate: Reality versus Myth.* Urbana: University of Illinois Press, 1986.

Rapp, R. T. *Industry and Economic Decline in Seventeenth-Century Venice.* Cambridge, Mass.: Harvard University Press, 1976.

Ravid, Benjamin. "From Yellow to Red: On the Distinguishing Head-Covering of the Jews of Venice." In *The Frank Talmage Memorial Volume*, 2:179–210. Haifa: Haifa University Press, 1992.

Reardon, Colleen. "The 1669 Sienese Production of Cesti's *L'Argia.*" In *Music Observed: Studies in Memory of William C. Holmes*, ed. Susan Parisi and Colleen Reardon, 417–28. Warren, Mich.: Harmonie Park Press, 2004.

————. *Holy Concord within Sacred Walls.* Oxford: Oxford University Press, 2002.

Ricci, Corrado. *I teatri di Bologna.* Bologna: Successori Monti, 1888.

Riccoboni, Alberto. "Antonio Zanchi e la pittura veneziana del Seicento." *Saggi e Memorie di Storia dell'arte* 5 (1966): 55–135.

Richards, Kenneth, and Richards, Laura. *The Commedia dell'Arte: A Documentary History.* Oxford: Blackwell, 1990.

Rigoli, Paolo. "Teatri per musica a Verona nella seconda metà del xvii secolo." *Atti e memorie della Accademia di agricoltura, scienze e lettere di Verona* 156 (1979/80): 215–37.

————. "Il virtuoso in gabbia: musicisti in quarantena al Lazzaretto di Verona (1655–1740)." In *Musica, scienza e idee nella Serenissima durante il Seicento. Atti del convegno internazionale di studi, Venezia–Palazzo Giustinian Lolin, 13–15 dicembre 1993*, ed. Francesco Passadore and Franco Rossi, 139–50. Venice: Fondazione Ugo e Olga Levi, 1996.

Romanelli, Giandomenico. "Gli abiti de' veneziani: mille mestieri di una città di moda." In *I mestieri della moda a Venezia dal xiii al xviii secolo*, 23–29. Venice: Stamparia di Venezia, 1988.

Romano, Dennis. *Housecraft and Statecraft: Domestic Service in Renaissance Venice, 1400–1600.* Baltimore: Johns Hopkins University Press, 1996.

————. *Patricians and Popolani: The Social Foundations of the Venetian Renaissance State.* Baltimore: Johns Hopkins University Press, 1987.

Ronconi, Luca. *Lo spettacolo e la meraviglia: Il Teatro Farnese di Parma e la festa barocca.* Turin: Nuova Eri, 1992.

Rosand, Ellen. "Barbara Strozzi, *virtuosissima cantatrice*: The Composer's Voice." *Journal of the American Musicological Society*, 31 (1978): 241–81.

————. "The Bow of Ulysses." *Journal of Musicology* 12 (1994): 376–95.

———. "In Defense of the Venetian Libretto." *Studi musicali* 9 (1980): 271–85.

———. *Opera in Seventeenth-Century Venice: The Creation of a Genre.* Berkeley: University of California Press, 1991.

———. "The Opera Scenario, 1638–1655: A Preliminary Survey." In *In Cantu et in Sermone: For Nino Pirrotta on his 80th Birthday*, ed. Fabrizio Della Seta and Franco Piperno, 335–46. Florence: Leo S. Olschki, 1989.

———. " 'Ormindo travestito' in 'Erismena'." *Journal of the American Musicological Society* 28 (1975): 241–81.

———. "L'Ovidio trasformato." In Aurelio Aureli and Antonio Sartorio, *Orfeo*, ed. Ellen Rosand, ix–lvii. Drammaturgia musicale veneta 6. Milan: Ricordi, 1983.

Rosenthal, Margaret. *The Honest Courtesan: Veronica Franco, Citizen and Writer in Sixteenth-Century Venice.* Chicago: University of Chicago Press, 1993.

Rosselli, John. "The Castrati as a Professional Group and a Social Phenomenon, 1550–1850." *Acta musicologica* 60 (1988): 143–79.

———. "From Princely Service to the Open Market: Singers of Italian Opera and Their Patrons." *Cambridge Opera Journal* 1 (1989): 1–32.

———. *The Opera Industry in Italy from Cimarosa to Verdi: The Role of the Impresario.* Cambridge: Cambridge University Press, 1984.

———. *Singers of Italian Opera: The History of a Profession.* Cambridge: Cambridge University Press, 1992.

Rostirolla, Giancarlo. "La musica nelle istituzioni religiose romane al tempo di Stradella." *Chigiana* 39, n.s., no. 19 (1982): 575–831.

Ruderman, David B. *Jewish Thought and Scientific Discovery in Early Modern Europe.* New Haven and London: Yale University Press, 1995.

Rutschman, Edward. "*Orimonte*: Anatomy of a Failure." In *L'opera italiana a Vienna prima di Metastasio*, ed. Maria Teresa Muraro, 31–41. Florence: Leo S. Olschki, 1990.

Sabbatini, Nicolò. *Pratica di fabricar scene e machine ne' teatri.* Edited by Elena Povoledo. Collezione del centro di ricerche teatrali. Rome: Carlo Bestetti, 1955.

Sala, Emilio, and Davide Daolmi, eds. *"Quel novo Cario, quel divin Orfeo"; Antonio Draghi da Rimini a Vienna: Atti del Convegno Internazionale, Rimini, Palazzo Buonadrata, 5–7 ottobre 1998.* Lucca: Libreria italiana musicale, 2000.

Sansovino, Francesco. *Venetia città nobilissima et singolare . . . con aggiunta di tutte le cose notabili . . . da D. Giustiniano Martinioni.* Venice: Curti, 1663. Repr. Farnborough: Gregg, 1968.

Sartori, Antonio. *Documenti per la storia della musica al Santo e nel Veneto.* Fonti e Studi per la storia del Santo a Padova, fonti 4. Verona: Neri Pozza, 1977.

Sartori, Claudio. "La prima diva della lirica italiana: Anna Renzi." *Nuova rivista musicale italiana* 11 (1977): 335–38.

Saunders, Harris Sheridan, Jr. "The Repertoire of a Venetian Opera House (1678–1714): The Teatro Grimani di San Giovanni Grisostomo." Ph.D. diss., Harvard University, 1985.

Schulze, Hendrik. "The 1657 Production of Francesco Cavalli's *Artemisia*." Paper delivered at the Ninth Biennial Baroque Conference, Dublin, 2000.

Schmidt, Carl. "Antonio Cesti's *La Dori*: A Study of Sources, Performance Traditions, and Musical Style." *Rivista italiana di musicologia* 10 (1975): 455–98.

———. " 'La Dori' di Antonio Cesti: Sussidi bibliografici." *Rivista italiana di musicologia* 11 (1976): 197–229.

———. "An Episode in the History of Venetian Opera: The *Tito* Commission (1665–66)." *Journal of the American Musicological Society* 31 (1978): 442–66.

Schwager, Myron. "Public Opera and the Trials of the Teatro San Moisè." *Early Music* 14 (1986): 387–94.

Seifert, Herbert. "Antonio Cesti in Innsbruck und Wien." In *Il teatro musicale italiano nel Sacro Romano Impero nei secoli XVII e XVIII*, ed. Alberto Colzani, Norbert Dubowy, Andrea Luppi, and Maurizio Padoan, 105–20. Como: A.M.I.S. (Antique Musicae Italicae Studiosi), 1999.

———. "Die Musiker der beiden Kaiserinnen Eleonora Gonzaga." In *Festschrift Othmar Wessely zum 60. Geburtstag*, ed. Manfred Angerer, 527–54. Tutzing: Hans Schneider, 1982.

———. *Neues zu Antonio Draghis weltlichen Werken*. Vienna: Verlag der Österreichischen Akademie der Wissenschaften, 1978

———. "La politica culturale degli Asburgo e le relazioni musicali tra Venezia e Vienna." In *L'opera italiana a Vienna prima di Metastasio*, ed. Maria Teresa Muraro, 1–16. Florence: Leo S. Olschki, 1990.

Selfridge-Field, Eleanor. *The Calendar of Venetian Opera*. Palo Alto: Stanford University Press, forthcoming.

———. "Dramaturgical Hours: How Lunar and Solar Cycles Influenced the Length and Character of Venetian Operas." Paper delivered at the Eleventh Biennial Baroque Conference, Manchester, 2004.

———. *Pallade veneta: Writings on Music in Venetian Society, 1650–1750*. Venice: Fondazione Levi, 1985.

———. *Venetian Instrumental Music from Gabrieli to Vivaldi*. New York: Praeger, 1975.

Senn, Walter. *Musik und Theater am Hof zu Innsbruck*. Innsbruck: Österreichische Verlagsanstalt, 1954.

Skippon, Philip. *An Account of a Journey Made thro the Low-Countries, Germany, Italy, and France*. London, 1682. Repr. in Awnsham Churchill. *A Collection of Voyages and Travels*. London, 1752.

Smith, Patrick. *The Tenth Muse: A Historical Study of the Opera Libretto*. New York: Knopf, 1970.

Sperling, Jutta Gisela. *Convents and the Body Politic in Late Renaissance Venice*. Chicago: University of Chicago Press, 1999.

Strunk, W. Oliver, and Leo Treitler, *Source Readings in Music History*. Revised edition. New York: W.W. Norton, 1998.

Talbot, Michael. *Benedetto Vinaccesi: A Musician in Brescia and Venice in the Age of Corelli*. Oxford: Clarendon Press, 1994.

———. "*Ore Italiane*: The Reckoning of the Time of Day in Pre-Napoleonic Italy." *Italian Studies* 40 (1985): 51–62.

———. *Tomaso Albinoni: The Venetian Composer and His World*. Oxford: Clarendon Press, 1990.

———. "A Venetian Operatic Contract of 1714." In *The Business of Music*, ed. Michael Talbot. Liverpool: Liverpool University Press, 2002.

Tamburini, Elena. *Due teatri per il principe: Studi sulla committenza teatrale di Lorenzo Onofrio Colonna (1659–1689)*. Rome: Bulzoni Editore, 1997.

Tarr, Edward, and Thomas Walker. " 'Bellici carmi, festivo fragor': Die Verwendung der Trompete in der italienischen Oper des 17. Jahrhunderts." *Hamburger Jahrbuch für Musikwissenschaft* 3 (1978): 143–203.

Taviani, Ferdinando, and Marotti, Ferruccio. *La commedia dell'arte e la società barocca*. Rome: Bulzoni, 1991.

Termini, Olga. "From God to a Servant: The Bass Voice in Seventeenth-Century Venetian Opera." *Current Musicology* 44 (1990): 38–60.

———. "Singers at San Marco in Venice: The Competition between Church and Theatre (c. 1675–c.1725)." *Royal Musical Association Research Chronicle* 17 (1981): 65–96.

Tessari, Roberto. *La commedia dell'arte nel Seicento: Industria e arte giocosa della civiltà barocca*. Florence: Leo S. Olschki, 1969.

Tilmouth, Michael. "Music and British Travellers Abroad, 1600–1730." In *Source Materials and the Interpretation of Music: A Memorial Volume to Thurston Dart*, ed. Denis Stevens, 357–82. London: Stainer & Bell, 1981.

———. "Music on the Travels of an English Merchant: Robert Bargrave (1628–61)." *Music & Letters* 53 (1972): 143–59.

Timms, Colin. *Polymath of the Baroque: Agostino Steffani and His Music*. New York: Oxford University Press, 2003.

Ulvioni, Paolo. *Il Gran Castigo di Dio. Carestia ed epidemie a Venezia e nella Terraferma 1628–1632*. Milan: F. Angeli, 1989.

———. "Stampa e censura a Venezia nel Seicento." *Archivio veneto* 106 (1975): 45–93.

Van Orden, Kate, ed. *Music and the Cultures of Print*. New York: Garland, 2000.

Vavoulis, Vassilis. "Antonio Sartorio and Giacomo Francesco Bussani: Two Makers of Seventeenth-Century Venetian Opera." Ph.D. diss., University of Oxford, 2001.

———. "A Venetian World in Letters: The Massi Correspondence at the Hauptstaatsarchiv in Hannover." *Music Library Association Notes* 59 (2003): 556–609.

Viale Ferrero, Mercedes. "Repliche a Torino di alcuni melodrammi veneziani e loro caratteristiche." In *Venezia e il melodramma nel Seicento*, ed. Maria Teresa Muraro, 145–70. Florence: Leo S. Olschki, 1976.

———. *La Scenografia dalle origini al 1936*. Vol. 3: *Storia del Teatro Regio di Torino*. Turin: Cassa di Risparmio di Torino, 1980.

———. "Stage and Set." In *Opera on Stage*, ed. Lorenzo Bianconi and Giorgio Pestelli, trans. Kate Singleton, 1–123. *The History of Italian Opera* 5. Chicago: University of Chicago Press, 2002.

———. "La tipologia delle scene per alcune opere musicate da Legrenzi e il catalogo tipologico delle "Décorations" stabilito da C. F. Ménestrier." In *Giovanni Legrenzi e la cappella ducale di San Marco: Atti dei convegni internazionali di studi, Venezia, 24–26 maggio 1990, Clusone, 14–16 settembre 1990*, ed. Francesco Passadore and Franco Rossi, 419–31. Florence: Leo S. Olschki, 1994.

Vio, Gastone. "Ancora su Francesco Cavalli: Casa e famiglia." *Rassegna veneta di studi musicali* 4 (1988), 243–63.

———. "Per una migliore conoscenza di Anna Girò (da documenti d'archivio)." *Informazioni e studi vivaldiani* 9 (1988): 26–45.

———. "Per una migliore conoscenza di Tomaso Albinoni: Documenti d'archivio." *Recercare* 1 (1988): 111–22.

Vitali, Achille. *La moda a Venezia attraverso i secoli: Lessico ragionato*. Venice: Filippi Editore, 1992.

Walker, Jonathan. "Bravi and Venetian Nobles, c. 1550–1650." *Studi veneziani*, n.s., 36 (1998): 85–114.

Walker, Thomas. "'Ubi Lucius': Thoughts on Reading *Medoro*." In Francesco Lucio, *Medoro*, cxxxi–clxiv. Drammaturgia musicale veneta 4. Milan: Ricordi, 1984.

Weaver, Robert Lamar, and Norma Wright Weaver. *A Chronology of Music in the Florentine Theater, 1590–1750*. Detroit: Harmonie Park Press, 1978.

Whenham, John. "Perspectives on the First Decade of Public Opera at Venice." Forthcoming.

Wiel, Taddeo. *I codici musicali contariniani del secolo XVII nella R. Biblioteca di San Marco in Venezia*. Venice, 1888. Repr. Bologna: Forni, 1969.

Wolff, Helmut Christian. *Die venezianische Oper in der zweiten Hälfte des 17. Jahrhunderts*. Berlin, 1937. Repr. Bologna: Forni, 1975.

Worsthorne, Simon Towneley. *Venetian Opera in the Seventeenth Century*. Oxford: Clarendon Press, 1954.

Woyke, Saskia Maria. "Studien zum Opernschaffen von Pietro Andrea Ziani (1616-1684)." Ph.D. diss., University of Hamburg, 2004.

Zannini, Andrea. *Burocrazia e burocrati a Venezia in età moderna: I cittadini originari (sec. xvi–xviii)*. Istituto Veneto di scienze lettere ed arti. Memorie. Classe di scienze morali, lettere ed arti, vol. 47. Venice: Istituto Veneto di scienze, lettere ed arti, 1993.

Zorzi, Lodovico. *Il teatro e la città: Saggi sulla scena italiana*. Turin: Einaudi, 1977.

Zorzi, Elvira Garbero. "L'immagine della festa medicea: la tradizione di un mito." In *Claudio Monteverdi, Studi e Prospettive*, ed. Paola Besutti, Maria Teresa Gialdroni, and Rodolfo Baroncini, 431–49. Florence: Leo S. Olschki, 1998.

INDEX